OXFORD GUIDE TO WORLD ENGLISH

Tom McArthur

OXFORD
UNIVERSITY PRESS

OXFORD
UNIVERSITY PRESS

Great Clarendon Street, Oxford OX2 6DP

Oxford University Press is a department of the University of Oxford.
It furthers the University's objective of excellence in research, scholarship,
and education by publishing worldwide in

Oxford New York

Auckland Bangkok Buenos Aires Cape Town Chennai
Dar es Salaam Delhi Hong Kong Istanbul Karachi Kolkata
Kuala Lumpur Madrid Melbourne Mexico City Mumbai Nairobi
São Paulo Shanghai Singapore Taipei Tokyo Toronto

Oxford is a registered trade mark of Oxford University Press
in the UK and in certain other countries

Published in the United States
by Oxford University Press Inc., New York

British Library Cataloguing in Publication Data
Data available

Library of Congress Cataloging in Publication Data
Data available

ISBN 019–860771–7

2

Typeset in 9/12pt Melior by Graphicraft Ltd., Hong Kong
Printed in Great Britain by Clays Ltd., Bungay, Suffolk

CONTENTS

1·13518

Preface

1982 Since English began to spread around the world in the great age of exploration five hundred years ago, all its varieties have taken on an independent history, some of them much influenced by local circumstances, others responding to changes in the prestige dialects of Great Britain and the United States, and all of them affected by the inexorable trends in language change that affect every community from one generation to the next. By 1975, English was the sole official language of twenty-one nations, and in sixteen more it is the co-official language of government, education, broadcasting, and publication.

– Preface, Richard W. Bailey & Manfred Görlach, editors, *English as a World Language*, Ann Arbor, the University of Michigan Press, vii.

The above comment was made at a point when the sheer scale and diversity of the English language had begun to impress itself worldwide on scholars and lay people alike. When I first opened a copy of Bailey and Görlach's book, at the stall of the University of Michigan Press at a TESOL conference in Hawaii in 1982, the collection of papers which they had brought together seemed very well timed indeed. As the editors also noted in their introduction: 'Only in the last decade has the study of the forms and functions of English around the world begun to take shape as an academic discipline. In earlier scholarship, the most detailed studies were those of the English of Great Britain and the United States.'

Who's 'centric' now?

The turning point was the 1970s, before which the focus was not in fact straightforwardly 'Britocentric' or 'Americocentric'. Rather, it was even more restricted, pre-eminently to the emergence and nature of the higher-level social usage of southeastern England on the one hand and of the north-eastern United States on the other—without much apparatus for, as it were, considering the two together or considering whether there might in some sense be a one-world common-denominator standard language (in actuality or in the making). From each of these 'rival' centres accounts would radiate outward (and at times downward), becoming hazier the farther one moved from the core regions, bringing in the rest of the UK and US, then such neighbours as Ireland and Canada, then in a fairly minimalist way such farther-off territories as New Zealand and the Philippines, India and South Africa, Nigeria and Malaysia. And this was partly because of the worldview of the time and partly because any research done in the farther-flung regions was minimal or unknown to the heartland writers.

Bailey and Görlach's book helped bring that era to a close, and in the year 2000 Oxford University Press in Australia confirmed the closure when it brought out a collection of conference papers with the title *Who's Centric Now?—The Present State of Post-Colonial Englishes*, about English worldwide, edited by Bruce Moore of the Dictionary Centre of the National University of Australia in Canberra.

By the early 1990s, English was manifestly a universalizing medium and acknowledged as such. In fact, the process of universalization had been proceeding—and accelerating—for decades, and English had been polycentric for at least two centuries, a condition most notable where, at the formal level, a dictionary or a style guide emerged elsewhere than in the UK and the US—notably in Australia, Canada, New Zealand, and South Africa, and more recently in the Philippines and Singapore. In addition, it became increasingly clear that an account of any one language today (and especially of *this* language) could no longer limit a discussion of the other languages with which it has interacted in such processes as hybridization and the transfer of material in both directions.

Nor can discussions of language at large, and especially of *this* language, be hygienically marked off locally or globally from such issues as politics, economics, science, and technology, or indeed such facts of life as wealth and poverty, health and disease, and social change, including indeed terrorism and outright war. It is not simply that all such matters impinge one on another and on language: they *saturate* language, and language in turn animates them.

A shared possession

At the same time, the aim of any specialist work is to remain true and close to its subject, resisting the temptation to use it as a vehicle for the discussion of something else. Consequently, the focus in this work is language and languages, and primarily the English language, with the aim of providing a decent balance between discussions of pronunciation, grammar, and vocabulary on the one hand and social, historical, and cultural commentaries on the other. In this, the *Oxford Guide to World English* takes up where its 'mother book', *The Oxford Companion to the English Language*, left off, and very particularly from a statement I made in its Introduction, as published ten years after Bailey and Görlach:

> **1992** In the closing years of the twentieth century, the English
> language has become a global resource. As such, it does not owe
> its existence or the protection of its essence to any nation or
> group. Inasmuch as a particular language belongs to any

> individual or community, English is the possession of every
> individual and every community that in any way uses it,
> regardless of what any other individual or community may think
> or feel about the matter.
>
> – 'The Organization of the *Companion*, p. xvii.

This statement is even more to the point in 2002 than it was a decade ago—and indeed more widely accepted (to such an extent that for some people it may have in the meantime become a truism).

The organization of *The Oxford Guide to World English* (*OGWE*)

The Oxford Companion to the English Language (*OCELang*), with its abridged and concise versions in 1996 and 1998, was alphabetically organized, manifestly covered a wider area of language study and use than the present volume, and rested on the expertise of over 150 editors, contributors, and commentators. *OGWE*, on the other hand, has emerged out of discussions with Oxford over several years, regarding ways in which the national, regional, and international language information in *OCELang* might be foregrounded, updated, and expanded in order to provide as comprehensive and accurate a description as possible of English as a world (or global or international or universal) language today—beauty spots, warts, and all.

To do this, *OGWE* takes a different approach from *OCELang*, being organized not alphabetically but thematically, continent by continent. This approach has given me the freedom to re-work, update, and, where necessary, expand the relevant texts from *OCELang*, discussing the world's many varieties of English in an interconnected way within their more or less self-contained regional blocs, while also noting the ties that bind varieties and regions that happen to be geographically far apart, as with, for example: West African English and African-American English; Scots, Ulster Scots, the Scotch-Irish migrations to Appalachia in the US, and country and western music; and aspects of Australian, New Zealand, South African, and Falklands English as southern-hemisphere varieties). The end-product seeks to indicate and differentiate, as appropriate, sociolinguistic issues which are local, regional, national, continental, and global, within the following eight sections:

❶ Introduction

Discussing English as a language among languages and as the world's 'lingua franca'

❷ Europe

Reviewing the continent's territories and languages, and the varieties and roles of English as a European language, both in traditional offshore terms and on the Continent, where it has recently acquired the new label 'Euro-English'

❸ The Americas

Looking at English as a language of the Americas, primarily in terms of the US, Canada, and the Caribbean, but also covering (among other dimensions) matters relating to Spanish in Latin America and the United States, and French in Canada and Louisiana

❹ American and British

Comparing and contrasting the two standard varieties that together constitute the 'dual standard' that by and large dominates world English, pre-eminently in print and therefore notably in terms of grammar, orthography, and usage

❺ Africa

Focusing primarily on the sub-Saharan region, and discussing the varieties and roles of English as an African language, distributed throughout West, East, and Southern Africa, and alongside indigenous African languages and other Africanized European languages

❻ Asia

Dividing the vast region into West, South, South-East, and East, each with its own marked characteristics vis-à-vis English and Asian languages, English and other European languages in Asia, and English as an Asian language

❼ Australasia, Oceania, and Antarctica

Covering the most vast and varied region in the world, but with the smallest population of speakers, many of whom use 'southern-hemisphere' varieties of the language

❽ Conclusion

Reviewing, among other matters: the nature and power of large languages; such issues as gender and political correctness; the role, status, and nature of broken and/or fractured English; the worldwide English language teaching industry; and the issue of standardness, considered both locally and globally.

Such a continental/regional approach allows one to look more closely at language realities on the ground rather than in terms of the political divisions marked on maps. Thus, within the Americas, political and linguistic boundaries are not always the same thing: although something homogen(e)ous called *American English* rules the linguistic roost worldwide, the actual English of Americans is immensely diverse, is rife with social and cultural distinctions, and is also inclined to leak: northwards into *Canadian English* and Canadian French and southward into *Caribbean English* and Spanish and Portuguese. In addition, many other languages in the western hemisphere, both indigenous and immigrant, leak into American as well as Canadian and Caribbean usage—as well as into one another.

Linguists, models, and the ecology of language

Since the early 20th century, the dominant name for the scholarly or scientific study of language has been *linguistics* (from Latin *linguistica*, 'matters of the tongue'), which largely replaced the more classical term *philology* (from Greek *philología*, 'love of speech'). However, whereas *philologist* was once a fairly clear-cut title for someone academically interested in language, the term *linguist* when used for someone trained in the more recent science of *linguistics* is by no means neat and tidy, clashing as it does with the longer-established and more widely-known sense of 'someone skilled in languages' (especially as an interpreter and/or translator, as for example in the title of the international London-based *Institute of Linguists*).

By no means all students of linguistics are linguists in this older and more widely understood sense, and in any case neither kind of linguist has a monopoly on the study of language(s). Many literary humanists, for example, argue that the compilation of linguistic data, the objective analysis of language structure, and theorizing about the ultimate nature of language do not and cannot replace (and should indeed also take account of) the more traditional and subjective insights of those who engage in and study literature, drama, and the media—and who, in any case, when necessary also adopt objective techniques. *OGWE* consequently takes a 'broad church' view of language studies, and, to cast a wide net and avoid confusion, generally refers to investigators of language as 'language scholars'.

All models are convenient fictions, from the Equator to the Millennium, and often have a bewitching quality. Most models of English often, whether explicitly or implicitly, take the form of—or may be open to interpretation as—a hierarchy or (to put the matter more fiercely) a pecking order. These range downwards from the most prestigious standard varieties of the United States and the United Kingdom through, say, Australian English and South African English (which are middle-range peckers of the varieties 'below' them and of the languages 'around' them), to Indian, Singaporean, and Malaysian English in Asia, Bahamian and Falklands English in the Atlantic.

By and large, the aim here has been to describe all such matters appropriately but also to offer a novel perspective on a language complex that is simultaneously highly diverse in territorial and functional terms and yet 'blessed' with a remarkably coherent world print standard and a bearable range of 'educated' accents. I have also sought to be even-handed with regard to the power, prestige, pressures, and practicality of world English on the one side and the manifest threat that this juggernaut—and other large languages—represents for many smaller, often endangered languages planet-wide: sometimes nowadays tellingly compared with the world's environmental crises; a matter of 'language ecology' parallel to environmental ecology. Depending on circumstance, English can be either a blessing or a curse—or both at the same time. An international requirement over the next decade at least is finding a means through which English can function usefully as the world's first-ever universal language while its users—especially those in positions of influence and authority—also take a committed interest in global linguistic damage control.

Tom McArthur,
Hong Kong, October 2001

Note

OGWE includes a map, a chronology, a select bibliography, and an index. Not all works quoted in the body of the book are listed in the bibliography, but all quotations are appropriately sourced on the spot, whether those sources are in the index (if immediately concerned with English) or not.

Acknowledgements

I wish here to record my abiding debt to all the contributors of material published in the original *Companion to the English Language*. Although *OGWE* is largely a novel enterprise, it rests on the work we undertook between 1986 and publication in 1992, followed by the *Abridged* in 1996 and the *Concise* in 1998. In particular I would like to acknowledge:

- The late Feri McArthur (Fereshteh Mottahedin), A. J. (Jack) Aitken, Frederic G. Cassidy, Paul Christophersen, Sidney Greenbaum, John Platt, Peter Strevens, and Martyn Wakelin.

- The associate editors of, and primary contributors to, the original *Companion*: John Algeo, Robert E. Allen, Richard W. Bailey, Whitney F. Bolton, Raymond Chapman, Sidney Greenbaum, Braj B. Kachru, Suzanne Romaine, Loreto Todd, and Christopher Upward; and Robert F. Ilson for his innovative work in comparing and contrasting American and British English, from which I have greatly benefited.

- The 'varieties' and 'languages' contributors: Jon Amastae, Laurie J. Bauer, John Baugh, David Blair, Eyamba G. Bokamba, Jean Branford, William Branford, Lawrence D. Breitborde, Robert W. Burchfield, Garland Cannon, Lawrence D. Carrington, Isagani R. Cruz, Connie C. Eble, John Edwards, Stanley Ellis, Margery Fee, Jean-Marc Gachelin, Charles Gilman, Andrew Gonzales, Anjum R. Haque, Mohamed Heliel, Yamuna Kachru, Gillian S. Kay, G. Douglas Killam, Francis E. Knowles, Sangsup Lee, Marcia Leveson, Peter H. Lowenberg, J. Derrick McClure, Iseabail C. MacLeod, Rajend Mesthrie, Leslie Monkman, Salikoko S. Mufwene, Cecil L. Nelson, Noel E. Osselton, Rajweshwari Pandaripande, William S. Ramson, Roger Robinson, Paul Sharrad, Larry E. Smith, S. N. Sridhar, James Stanlaw, Sol Steinmetz, Mary Tay, Peter Trudgill, Heidi Weber, Lise S. Winer, Margaret E. Winters.

- I would like also to thank Susie Dent, Alysoun Owen, Helen Cox, Hilary Hodgson, and Mick Belson, for their specific and invaluable help with *OGWE*.

English throughout the World

A numbered list and map of territories for
which English is a significant language

 1 Anguilla
 2 Antigua and Barbuda
 3 Argentina
 4 Ascension
 5 Australia
 6 Bahamas
 7 Bahrain
 8 Bangladesh
 9 Barbados
10 Belize
11 Bermuda
12 Botswana
13 British Indian
    Ocean Territory
14 Brunei
15 Cameroon
16 Canada
17 Cayman Islands
18 Channel Islands
19 China
20 Cook Islands
21 Dominica
22 Egypt
23 England
24 Falkland Islands
25 Fiji
26 Gambia
27 Ghana
28 Gibraltar
29 Grenada
30 Guyana
31 Hawaii
32 Honduras
33 Hong Kong
34 India
35 Indonesia
36 Iraq
37 Irish Republic
38 Isle of Man
39 Israel
40 Jamaica
41 Japan
42 Jordan
43 Kenya
44 Kiribati
45 Korea

46 Kuwait
47 Lesotho
48 Liberia
49 Malawi
50 Malaysia
51 Maldives
52 Malta
53 Maritime Provinces
54 Mauritius
55 Montserrat
56 Namibia
57 Nauru
58 Nepal

59 New England
60 Newfoundland
61 New Zealand
62 Nicaragua
63 Nigeria
64 Northern Ireland
65 Oman
66 Orkney
67 Pakistan
68 Panama
69 Papua New Guine
70 Philippines
71 Puerto Rico

1 Introduction: A Global Lingua Franca

1995 Our infinitely adaptable mother tongue is now the world's lingua franca—and not before time.

– Lead-in, 'The Triumph of English,' *The Times* of London, 25 February

1997a [T]he use of English as a global lingua franca requires intelligibility and the setting and maintaining of standards.

– David Graddol, *The Future of English?: A guide to forecasting the popularity of the English Language in the 21st century* (London: British Council)

1997b [T]he spread of one language across the globe as the one monopolizing tongue, part lingua franca, part 'master' language, and in part the sole language that gives access to the world.

– Michael Toolan, 'Recentering English: New English and Global', in *English Today* 5 (13:4), (Cambridge: Cambridge University Press), October

1997c . . . a stabilized and standardized code leased out on a global scale . . . English the *lingua franca*, the franchise language.

– Henry G. Widdowson, 'EIL, ESL, EFL: global issues and local interests,' *World Englishes*, 16:1, Oxford: Blackwell

2001 Jazz is in the process of becoming the *musica franca*, the one language spoken everywhere, a glue in the global village, the musical common denominator, like English.

– Mike Zwerin, 'Global Jazz: Everything Is Fusing With Everything', *International Herald Tribune* (14 April)

1998 lingua franca . . . **noun** (pl. **lingua francas**) a language that is adopted as a common language between speakers whose native languages are different.

– *The New Oxford Dictionary of English*, Judy Pearsall (ed.), (Oxford: Clarendon Press)

1999 Lingua franca . . . (*plural* **lingua francas** or **linguae francae**...) *n*. **1. LANGUAGE USED FOR CONVENIENCE** a language or mixture of languages used for communication by people who speak different first languages . . .

– *Encarta World English Dictionary*, Kathy Rooney editor-in-chief, Bloomsbury

There are, at the present time, three labels for English as the universalizing language of the human race. The first of these is *world English* (with or without a capital *W*, and perhaps first used in the 1920s), which covers every kind of usage and user. It takes in everything from the most polished diplomatic, academic, and media practice to the broadest of vernaculars and the most fractured of foreignisms. The second is *international English* (with or without a capital *I*), which, depending on context, covers both Standard English (with or without a capital *S*) worldwide and the kind of common-denominator business English (with or without a capital *B*) used by natives with non-natives and non-natives with one another. The third and most recent is *global English* (usually with a small *g*), which runs parallel with economic *globalization*. It has an MBA quality about it: the medium (and part maybe of the message) of a fast-moving deal-making globe-girdling élite.

In tandem, the recent close to clichéd use of *lingua franca* in terms of English is not quite what the dictionaries say 'lingua franca' means. Traditionally, a lingua franca has been a rough-and-ready socially low kind of medium between people who (for the most part) do not have it as a mother tongue. In recent years, however, the sense of the phrase (notably when applied to English) has been extended: a lingua franca can now be a fully formed 'high' language that also serves as a medium for people who do not use it natively. As a result, at the start of the 21st century, we have an avowed worldwide lingua franca that happens also to have a centuries-old literature, a vast array of media and electronic outlets, and over 300 million native speakers, many of whom cannot communicate effectively or at all in any other language. For them, it is not in the least a lingua franca, and a foreigner who uses it like a traditional lingua franca has 'broken' or 'fractured' it.

Because of this unique set of circumstances, commentators have found it useful to extend the phrase *lingua franca* from its traditional meaning to something rather complex, such as: 'a language common to, or shared by, many cultures and communities at any or all social and educational levels, and used as an international tool'. In the two large desk dictionaries quoted above, both Oxford University Press and Bloomsbury/Microsoft seek to cover this 'world English', Encarta using the phrase in its title, introduction, and publicity and Oxford in its introduction and publicity. Yet in their definitions of *lingua franca* neither has quite kept up with the times in relation to the language in which they work and which they have sought to describe in global terms.

This is not surprising. We now have a universalizing language, used by over a billion people, of whom native speakers constitute maybe a quarter: the statistics (as the panel on page 3 demonstrates) are very soft. In addition, when English is used in an airport or hotel (in Amsterdam, Delhi, London, Hong Kong, Johannesburg, New York, Tokyo, Zurich, and the like), native and non-native users are rendered equal by mutual strangeness: Tokyo people in the company of folk from Yorkshire, Puerto Ricans with Nigerians, a Californian college kid and a Singaporean taxi-driver. Except perhaps for places such as an airport check-in counter or the tills in a McDonalds (where formulas predominate), everybody needs to negotiate.

It is this element of bargaining towards comprehension that makes the phrase *lingua franca* appropriate, but even a definition from a third, fuller dictionary, the *New Shorter Oxford English Dictionary* (two volumes, editor Lesley Brown, 1993), does not stretch quite far enough. There, *lingua franca* is 'a system of communication providing mutual understanding'. Yes, of course, in principle, but there is no guarantee. In airports, hotels, restaurants, shopping centres, and bazaars, English

The statistics of world English

Three 1997 estimates of number of users of English worldwide (in millions):

	Native	Second-language	Foreign-language	TOTAL
The British Council English 2000 campaign	350m	350m	100m	800m
David Crystal *English as a Global Language* (Cambridge University Press)	320–380	150–300m	100–1,000m	570–1,680m
David Graddol *The Future of English?* (British Council)	375m	375m	750m	1,500m

Three firmer facts:

1 English is used in over 70 countries as an official or semi-official language and has a significant role in over 20 more: 90 in all.

2 Worldwide over 1,400 million people live in countries where English has traditionally been in use (one billion of them in India).

3 Some 75% of the world's mail and the world's electronically stored information is in English. Of an estimated 40 million users of the Internet in 1997, a majority used English.

offers a basis across cultures only for *negotiating* understanding. Success is not underwritten.

At another level, however—in science, the humanities, higher-level publishing, the global media (notably *The Times* and *TIME*, CNN and BBC World), and in organizations such as the United Nations and the World Bank—an English is used which goes well beyond the phrase *lingua franca* either as traditionally understood or currently extended. At such social altitudes, in its full panoply of grammar, vocabulary, idiom, and nuance, English is *both* the world's key up-to-the-minute operational language *and* a kind of living classical language. Indeed, it draws very fully on the resources of Latin and Greek, the languages that have provided much of the fundamental currency of Western scholarship, science, and education. As a result, the middle classes everywhere, whether or not they have it themselves, want English for their children. At this level, English is the Latin or Sanskrit of our time. Or, to draw on yet another culture, it is the medium of the world's new mandarins, and quality control is strict.

Uniquely human

The original French
La langue est une raison humaine qui a ses raisons, et que l'homme ne connaît pas.

The English translation
Language is a kind of human reason, which has its own internal logic of which man knows nothing.

– Claude Lévi-Strauss, *La Pensée Sauvage*, and its English translation *The Savage Mind*, 1962

For scholars and scientists who have studied language, the faculty of speech is a defining part of being human. Chimpanzees are our nearest relatives: indeed, in terms of their genome they are closer to us than we could ever have imagined. They are intelligent and live on the edge of language, and can be coaxed a little further by dedicated researchers, but their limits appear to be anatomically and neurologically fixed; they cannot go where we go. Among humans, however, languages differ both in how they portray the world and how they portray what English calls 'language'. The above translation of just one line from the work of a major 20th-century French anthropologist indicates this difference, and these two languages have been neighbours for a thousand years.

The preceding paragraph says something, but its Englishness shapes and limits what can be said, just as French shaped and limited what Lévi-Strauss wrote in 1962. A discussion of the nature of communication is not likely to be the same in the various linguistic shapes that our communication takes, despite the fact that they share some universals, such as the use of the tongue. A raw machine translation into English of Lévi-Strauss's elegant and very French sentence might be: 'The tongue is a human reason that has its reasons, and man does not know it.' That would hardly do. Yet his French has a poetic quality which the English translation has not caught, although it has certainly caught the scholarly intention.

In English, the word *language* is used not only to label a uniquely human faculty, but is rhetorically stretched to cover such other more or less related matters as animal cries and movements (*the language of birds*), gesture systems (*sign language*), and mechanical codes (*machine language*), as well as occurring metaphorically in such phrases as *the language of dreams* and *the language of the genes*. Whenever such a word is invoked in speech or writing, all its senses, nuances, and potential come implicitly with it, no matter how carefully it is delineated. The same is true for comparable words in other languages, but the kinds of core meaning and the kinds of stretching will in each case be different.

In etymological terms, *language* is 'what the tongue does'—from Latin *lingua* through French *langue*. In terms however of anatomy, physiology, neurology, sound, expression, and gesture, it is much more. Language is primarily both an individual and a collective physical activity, involving mouth, ears, face, hands, indeed the whole body, and it has gone several stages beyond that: to writing on tablets of clay and treated animal skins, to printing on smoothed-out wood pulp and the like, and to using electricity to inscribe short-lived text on back-lit screens. Broadly speaking, these stages constitute four successive communicative shifts in human history: speech, script, print, and electronic multimedia. And it will probably go further, in ways that we cannot now imagine, just as ancient Romans could never have imagined laptops.

The meaning and use of the word *language* also extends to such registers as *legal language*, *scientific language*, *journalese*, and *slang* (even *slanguage*). The term has also narrowed in social range, as in *bad language*, *foul language*, and *strong language*, and further still in the warnings 'Mind your language!' and simply 'Language!' Even there, the elastic does not break. A writer might urge readers to use their mother tongue better, in a book with the playful title *Mind Your Language*. And even when dealing with the most profound issues of communication, the everyday senses of the word and their subversive implications need to be borne in mind. Whatever the context in which a word performs, and however restricted it is

to one sense and set of associations, it carries with it all its other resonances—
whence the possibilities of wordplay, jokes, and misunderstanding.

'True' or 'full' linguistic communication is multi-modal: on one side, speech,
gesture, stance, and touch, on the other writing, printing, calligraphy, the media,
and electronic usage, all of them inter-operative. Seen from this perspective, the
faculty of language has at least the following ten elements, aspects, or properties:

❶ A primary vocal/auditory channel

Technically *the phonic medium*, in which sequential sounds are produced by vocal
organs and vocal tract, received by the ear, and encoded and decoded by the brain.

❷ Convertibility to additional channels

Extensions or analogues of speech include *the graphic medium* (writing, printing,
and keyboarding, etc.), *the visual medium* (including sign language, notably for
the hearing-impaired), and *the tactile medium* (including Braille, for the visually
impaired). Some kinds of language are also beyond direct communication: in
thinking and in dreams (an inner *neurological medium*, often set aside by language
scholars because it defies easy discussion and examination).

❸ The use of arbitrary symbols

There is no motivated link in most elements of language between spoken and
written (etc.) forms and the meanings they express: that is, the old-time farmer was
wrong when he said, when watching some of his animals feeding: 'Rightly be they
called pigs.'

❹ Double articulation: medium and message

In principle, languages have two modes of expression: on the one side phonic
or graphic symbols, on the other the meanings that invest those symbols. Thus, the
word *cat* is a flow of sound and a set of letters (the medium) that refer to a kind of
animal (the message, which may include extensions of meaning and reference).
Both modes, when operating together, constitute *double articulation* ('the duality of
the linguistic sign').

❺ Interdependence

Language functions as an integrated structure in which the role of every element in
the system is defined and made possible by the roles of the other elements, including a semantic system that maps many of these phonic, graphic, or other elements
on to a wider universe of objects, activities, and relationships.

❻ Open-endedness

Language is marked by a productivity and creativity in principle without limit:
the number of possible communications is indefinitely large, as is the number of
'words' (discrete units with both form and meaning) in any language. The distinctness of words is less obvious in rapid speech and more obvious in those forms of
writing and print that require space between groups of characters. A capacity to
recognize listable 'words' as a category within language could well be a consequence of the development of writing systems.

❼ Displacement

All language allows reference to events that are removed in time and place, including states of affairs which have never existed, do not yet exist, or may never exist,

as in telling lies, creating imaginative stories and writing fiction, formulating hypotheses, and talking about the future.

❽ Continual change

Individual languages are in a state of change, sometimes slower, sometimes more rapid. Although 'movement' in particular 'directions' of form and meaning may be discernible, there is no evidence that either progress or decay inherently emerges from such change, although people may perceive change as (among other things) good or bad. Such perceptions may have a sociocultural impact, and be noted and assessed, as in discussions of style and standardness.

❾ Turn-taking and solo performance

Spoken and some other kinds of language activity (such as conversation, telegraphy, and Internet chat) commonly involve structured exchanges in which people take turns in communicating. However, there are also occasions for solo performance, as in: monologue and lectures; soliloquy (as a special stage performance, to let an audience know what a character in a play is thinking); the authorial 'voice' in a novel (purportedly 'telling' a story); and talking to oneself.

❿ Classification

Scholars can marshal languages variously in terms of what they share, such as a deduced common origin (as with the Indo-European language family, to which English, Persian, Sanskrit, and Spanish all belong) or a range of attributes (as with the contrastive use of tone in Chinese and in certain West African languages, or the syllable-timed 'rat-a-tat-tat' rhythm of French and Japanese, as opposed to the stress-timed 'HUMpty DUMpty SAT on a WALL' rhythm of traditional English).

Language behaviour matures in the first fifteen or so years of life, in that (to use a computer metaphor cautiously) it has been 'programmed' to emerge at stages in one's development (if the nervous system and the environment are in appropriate states). Occasionally, normal development and usage are impaired, some situations being temporary (as with paralysis of the speech mechanisms, induced for example by fear), while others are long term, maybe permanent (as with aphasia and dyslexia). Some language disorders are situational, and unique to the sufferer; others may be inherited. The language faculty is now generally considered to be, in some sense, a matter of genetic predisposition, but currently the nature and extent of any in-born contribution and its triggering mechanisms are uncertain and controversial. Environmental influences are better understood, although much work remains to be done. Considerable attention has also been bestowed in recent decades on how education relates to language development, notably (though not always so stated) in how children at school acquire the standard version of the language they speak.

There have been various attempts to define the sociocultural notion of 'a language'. Political and geographical boundaries do not necessarily coincide with linguistic boundaries, nor do ethnic or national names necessarily coincide with the names of ethnic or national languages. Thus, German is regarded as both the national and the ethnic language of the Germans, but it is also the national language of Austria and one of the national languages of Switzerland, leading to such special names as 'Austrian German' and 'Swiss German' that may prompt, in fun or seriously, such a term as 'German German'. Some Belgians speak French, others Dutch, others German. The Scots, the Irish, and the Welsh all speak English, and some also speak a Celtic language, so that one can talk of 'Scottish Gaelic' and 'Scottish English', as well as 'Irish Gaelic' and 'Irish English'. These lead on contrastively (and inevitably) to 'English English', a term now common among scholars of the English language. Furthermore, varieties of the 'same' language can be mutually incomprehensible: in England, a Cockney from London and a Geordie from Newcastle may or may not always understand one other; in the United States, a Texan may not always grasp what a New Yorker is saying; and in the wider world a Jamaican may not be transparent to someone from New Zealand. Yet all have used 'English' all their lives.

Scholars of language tend to regard the circle of a particular language as defined, by and large, by those who say (without intent to deceive) that they speak it, not by where they live or what other people think (including other people claiming to speak the same language). This point is central to making sense of very large languages, such as Arabic, Chinese, English, Hindi-Urdu, and Spanish. Scholars are well aware that across two or more politically distinct languages there may be considerable understanding—enough, say, to place Danish, Norwegian, and Swedish within the framework of a 'Common Scandinavian'. Or indeed that the range and variety of kinds of American, British, Caribbean, Indian, and Singaporean English can lead to failures of understanding within what is traditionally regarded as a single language.

Language as a phenomenon is one thing, everywhere, but establishing the status of individual languages and their varieties within that single reality is often far from easy. Any such status is not, in the normal way of things, based on linguistic criteria alone, but can be untidy, socially controversial, and often resistant to neat classification. The many non-linguistic factors that often come into play include nationalism, ethnicity, ideology, religion, politics, and culture, often in complex (and sometimes explosive) mixes.

Dialects, varieties, and 'English languages'

The many forms of English around the world are commonly defined as 'English' because, in the first instance and most cases, that is how their speakers identify them, usually for good historical reasons. However, in such a large and diverse complex, awareness of (and the effort to adhere to) an internationally manageable norm may or may not be enough to allow users of different varieties to cross-communicate. Nor is it surprising that, in such a complex, a variety may (on occasion or commonly and routinely) be regarded as a language in its own right, if there is enough of a literary, religious, social, or national tradition behind it. An ancient example is Scots in Scotland and Northern Ireland; other examples, all with centuries behind them, are Patwa in Jamaica, Pidgin in West Africa, Saramaccan in Surinam in South America, and Tok Pisin in Papua New Guinea. All are, in a serious sense, 'English languages', and are being increasingly recognized as such.

Indeed, a 'variety' can be regarded as a 'dialect' for some purposes and a 'language' for others, and casual ambivalence about such matters is common worldwide. Thus, the French of Quebec in Canada can be regarded as both part of world French and a distinct language, as in Léandre Bergeron's *Dictionnaire de la langue Québécoise* ('Dictionary of the Quebec Language'). Comparably, African-American Vernacular English ('Ebonics') has ties with kinds of English in the Caribbean and West Africa, and is regarded as a distinct language by many African Americans, for various reasons. Such a claim is most successfully made for one of its highly distinctive historic forms: Gullah in the Sea Islands of Georgia and South Carolina. Such matters tend to be controversial, people often dividing into opposing (and sometimes hostile) camps, but they and their claims or beliefs cannot simply be dismissed with a wave of the hand.

A geographical subdivision of an established language has been known for centuries in Europe as a *dialect*, as in *the dialects of French* and *German dialects*. This word and its equivalents in other languages are, however, both insufficiently precise and often negative when used on a worldwide basis to contrast everyday vernaculars with one another and, crucially, with a prestigious religious, court, or school variety that is not itself usually classed as a dialect (although it may have arisen out of one, and people will generally agree to that). A potent example is the contrast between the 'high' form or forms of Chinese (known traditionally as Mandarin and in China for national purposes as Putonghua, 'Common Speech') on the one side and a range of regional 'dialects' on the other, many of them so mutually opaque that it is hard not to regard them as distinct languages. Elsewhere in the world such varieties might well qualify as independent languages. A traditionally avowed Chinese dialect that manifestly functions worldwide as a distinct language is Cantonese.

In the West, everyday vernaculars are often contrasted with an elevated level of what is manifestly the same language, to which however the name of the whole language is commonly and unreflectingly applied. Thus, the term *English* routinely (but ambiguously) refers to both a major language with many varieties and that aspect of itself which is regarded as (more or less) above regionalism, either within a country such as England or the United States or throughout the world. This high variety is nowadays usually called *Standard/standard English*, but it has also often been referred to (more judgementally) as *good English* or even *the best English*. Commonly, in a more socially stratified past, in the UK and elsewhere, it was called *the King's/Queen's English* (a term still current, but far less so than in the first half of the 20th century). Similar, though not identical, contrasts and statements have been made about such languages as French, Portuguese, Russian, and Spanish.

Largely to avoid such difficulties and the social judgements that go with them, language scholars have in recent decades used the term *variety* to label a subdivision within a language. Varieties may relate to place or community (as with *Indian English* and two of its subvarieties, *Anglo-Indian English* and *Gujarati English*), to uses (as with *legal English* and *advertising English*), and to combinations of the two (as with *British legal English* and *American advertising English*). It has not been easy, however, to apply the term *variety* directly to vernaculars long associated with the word *dialect*; it is not (or at least not yet), for example, usual to refer to *Yorkshire dialect* as the *Yorkshire variety* (*of English in England*), although the phrase is accurate and appropriate. Even the unusual phrase *Yorkshire English* may make sense, say, when contrasted with *London English*, a range of speech that is manifestly no longer amenable to the term 'dialect' (if indeed it ever was). In the case of Yorkshire, however, affection and respect for the variety is so strong that the usage

Yorkshire dialect tends to escape the long-established negative implications of the term *dialect* in England and elsewhere.

In recent years, *variety* has proved to be a fairly safe term, allowing language scholars to avoid being too specific about kinds of speech and usage on occasions when being specific is not necessary and/or when there is a risk of being charged with discrimination against a group by calling its usage 'a dialect'. The negative baggage that attaches to this term in English is greater than any occasional positive connotations it may have. We can consider here the contrast between the phrases *speakers of dialect* and *speakers of the standard language.* Historically, varieties labelled as dialects have tended to retreat in the face of the standard, or manage to survive as 'working-class' or 'rural' usage with a kind of subversive counter-prestige.

In addition, the terms *dialect* and *accent* are commonly used as rough synonyms, often in ways that arouse apprehension and/or resentment. In social and technical terms, *dialect* has always meant more than a difference of pronunciation; it covers speech, grammar, vocabulary, and idiom, but even when used clinically the term may jar on the ear. To say, for example, that the Queen of England speaks a 'prestige dialect', as some scholars have done, is for many people a contradiction in terms, and for quite a few is a slur on both the monarch and her usage—or even on dialect. All in all, the use of *variety* allows more to be said with fewer risks.

Most importantly, however, the term *dialect* fails when discussing English as a world language. Although it has done sterling service in detailing, for example, regional variations in Old, Middle, and Modern English in Britain, and for regional varieties of English in the United States (notably Northern, Midland, and Southern), it is entirely inadequate in other situations, as for example two of the most vigorous US 'Englishes': African-American English (which has never neatly fitted the traditional dialect criterion of regionality), and the entity not quite covered by the term 'Spanglish': a hybrid of Spanish and English used by Spanish-speaking immigrants from Latin America in many parts of the country. Indeed, not far from the *fons et origo* of English, many people in Ireland, Wales, and the Highlands of Scotland, because of their links (past or on-going) with Celtic languages, have never fitted the native-speaker dialect model. Rather, their communities have nativized a foreign language, usually to the detriment of the indigenous language. Many users of English in the world today are in positions closer to theirs than to traditional speakers of 'dialect'.

Kinds of stability, kinds of change

A majority of cultures has sought to homogenize and standardize their most prestigious languages or varieties of a language, so as to refine and regulate them, and sometimes fix them forever. None, however, has succeeded in doing more than limit the rate of change in times when their community has been stable and enough children have been going to school for enough time. History's most successfully fixed languages have ended up being labelled 'dead', in that they stopped being passed by word of mouth from parent to child, but have instead been kept going by priests and scholars and formally (often rigidly and painfully) taught to novitiates. Latin, Sanskrit, Classical Greek, Classical Arabic, and Mandarin Chinese have all been sustained in such tough-minded (often ascetic and disciplinarian) ways.

It can be argued that the standard varieties of many present-day languages (buttressed by writing, print, radio, television, and now computer systems) are rather similar to the classical languages. They are institutionalized, geared to schools, colleges, and professions, and in many ways are distinct from everyday colloquial usage. Such registers are hardly 'dead', but they are to a great extent artifacts geared to writing, print, and public performance, and are the outcomes of cultural programmes similar to (and sometimes historically associated with) the methods used in transmitting Latin, Classical Greek, Classical Arabic, Sanskrit, and Mandarin to select members of the next generation. Among the upper and middle classes of a society they may be close to the language of the home, but among the majority in many populations they can be far removed from everyday life.

In this sense, the standard stratum in a language like English can be regarded as 'semi-classical'; it is an artifact acquired at school and has within it masses of material absorbed from two fully classical (and therefore 'dead') languages. This process began centuries ago because kinds of lexical, stylistic, rhetorical, and grammatical enrichment from these sources were greatly desired. Such learnèd strata can be found among many languages, such as French (also drawing on Latin and Greek), Hindi (drawing on Sanskrit), Persian (drawing on Arabic), and Urdu (drawing on Persian and Arabic).

In addition to its classical inheritance, English not only continues to take in material from other languages but also serves as a conduit through which such material passes into still further languages. Notable among these are Malay and Japanese. For Malay in both Malaysia and Indonesia there have been planned lexicographical approaches through which English technical terms are systematically Malayanized, In the case of Japanese, there has been a free-and-easy conversion of English words into *gairaigo*, a reservoir of borrowings into everyday Japanese, usually written in the katakana script. Examples from Malaysia are *derebar* ('driver'), *mesin* ('machine'), *sepiar* ('sphere'), and *kalorifik* ('calorific'). Examples from Japanese are *erebeta* ('elevator'), *masukomi* (abbreviated from 'mass communication'), *sekuhara* (a casual abbreviation of 'sexual harassment'), and *wapuro* (adapting 'word-pro', from 'word processor').

Even an apparently dead language does not remain immune to change. Classical Latin, though 'fixed' on paper, came in the Middle Ages to be spoken in many different national and institutional styles, usually aligned with the mother-tongue pronunciation of its ecclesiastical and scholarly users. The Italianate Latin of the Vatican and the High Anglican Latin once common at the universities of Oxford and Cambridge are prime examples of such change. Mutual intelligibility under such circumstances can come only with effort: at that time in international Latin; today in international English.

Change may affect any aspect of a language: pronunciation, orthography, grammar, vocabulary, word-formation, usage, and idiom. It may be massive or slight, abrupt or gradual, on one occasion or incremental. The adoption of new spelling conventions in a publishing house or of a new national orthographic style may happen overnight and become stable quite quickly (despite conservative grumbles) or may change very slowly (to the chagrin of radicals). The competition in England between such spellings as *labour* and *labor* came to an end quite quickly at the turn of the 18th and 19th centuries after the Americans chose *labor*. Over a longer period, however, without pressure to adapt, radical changes in pronunciation can leave spelling far behind, as with *debt* ('det') and *sergeant* ('sarjint'). In writing, *debt* contrasts with *debit* (which has a similar etymology, a related meaning, but a very different pronunciation), and the ancient form *sergeant* contrasts (in the British Army at least) with the soldier's informally abbreviated 'sarge', the officer's clipped 'sarnt', and the routine written abbreviation *Sgt.* (as a title).

Sometimes creative change is rapid, radical, and system-wide, as when pidgins come into existence. These makeshift languages are hybrids formed, by and large, through the blending of elements from two or more existing languages, the vocabulary of one (usually the more powerful) being prominent while the grammar of the other(s) provide(s) a structural base. If the need later arises for an expanded vocabulary, the resources of the new variety (or language) are likely to be flexible enough to provide it. Thus, the English word *cardboard* has not passed into everyday Tok Pisin ('Talk Pidgin') in Papua New Guinea, but the concept is covered by *strongpela pepa* ('strong-fellow paper'). In less vivid cases, however, change spreads so gradually across and within languages that people hardly notice it, as with the slow processes through which whole areas of Greek entered French and English through Latin. The list below highlights some changes in sound, structure, and wording that have affected English:

Pronunciation

1   Many changes in patterns of speech have extended over long periods of time and may or may not have extended to all varieties within a language or language group.

2   A noted series of changes, known as the Great Vowel Shift (*c*.1400–1600) was responsible, among other things, for such universal present-day pronunciations as *house* and *mouse*, where previously the pronunciations were 'hoose' and 'moose'. This change did not however affect Scots, in which such forms as *hoose* and *moose* have continued to this day, allowing such rhymes as 'a moose loose aboot the hoose' and jokes about the difference between a Scots moose and a Canadian moose.

3   Scots usage has as a result been described as more conservative than English usage. A social outcome of this description has been a view, common in both England and Scotland, that English pronunciation is therefore more dynamic and up-to-date. Many Scots have however disagreed and others still have never been able to make up their minds about whether Scots has been successfully traditional or sadly behind the times. In strict linguistic terms, something like a sound shift is neither positive nor negative; it simply takes place or does not take place. But in social terms it may have a variety of repercussions.

Grammar

1   Because of changes in syntax and morphology over centuries, speakers of Modern English cannot understand Old English without serious study— and even if they have studied it would never normally seek to speak it. The structure of Old English (OE) is similar to Latin insofar as words have a range of inflected endings. Thus, the form of the definite article, now only *the*, varies in OE according to case, number, and gender, as in: *se mona* ('the moon': masculine nominative singular); *seo sunne* ('the sun': feminine nominative singular); and *thaet tungol* ('the star': neuter nominative singular).

2   Word order in OE is therefore more flexible than later English, because grammatical relations are indicated by the endings: *Se hund seah thone wifmann* ('The dog saw the woman') could also be expressed as *Thone wifmann seah se hund*, because the inflected forms of the definite article make it clear that *wifmann* is the direct object in both cases. If the woman saw the dog, it would be *Se wifmann seah thone hund.* In Modern English, grammatical relations are indicated largely by word order, so that *The dog saw the woman* and *The woman saw the dog* mean entirely different things. It is difficult to imagine a greater change than this in what has often been thought of as 'the same' language over time, supporting the case for classifying Old English (Anglo-Saxon) and Modern English (English) as distinct languages rather than different temporal states of the same language.

3   Comparably, Modern English has lost its system of classifying nouns into three grammatical genders, as in German. This does not mean that English has ceased to be historically and typologically a Germanic language; it has simply become a rather distinct kind of Germanic language. Scots, on the other hand, has remained markedly more Germanic, notably in pronunciation and vocabulary, and Scottish English reflects this feature to varying degrees.

Vocabulary

1   Change in words comes about through both *internal* and *external* factors.

2   *Internal change* may alter both the meanings and forms of words and phrases, and the history of the adjective *tawdry* is a striking illustration of this. The Anglo-Saxon name of the patron saint of Ely Cathedral in Cambridgeshire (died 679) is *Etheldreda*. The Normans, in the years after 1066, reduced her name to *Audrie*, and an annual fair in Ely came to be known as *Saint Audrie's Fair*, at which was sold a fine silk lace called *St Audrey's lace.* In due course, this came to be known as *tawdry lace*. The quality of the lace declined over time, giving *tawdry* (in this and then in other contexts) the meaning 'showy, but cheap and ill-made'. However, it makes no difference to the present use of *tawdry* that the 't' came from *saint* and the 'awdry' from *Etheldreda.*

3   *External change* includes the adoption of words from other languages, which may be rare (as with the adoption from Persian through Turkish into English of *divan* and *kaftan/caftan*) or overwhelming (as with the flow into English of French, Latin, and Greek words, of which *madam*, *multitude*, and *metamorphosis* are representative in their look, sound, and relative lengths.

Conservatives are often wary (if not downright suspicious) of change, including the novel expressions that delight the young. Most of the world's language changes are safely in the past, and no longer disturb their comfort, but have produced kinds of usage that may seem fusty and even unjust to radicals. Sometimes changes are deliberate, as with adaptations towards gender equalization in English; often they are the outcome of usage that shifts with circumstance. The only guarantee is that as long as a language is 'alive' it will, like the biological organisms that use it, undergo various kinds of shift, large, small, and continual. The remarkable thing is that in such a vast and varied complex as present-day English there is so much that remains stable.

The world's default mode

1949 English is now well on the way to becoming a world-language: and this means many types of English, many pronunciations and vocabulary-groups within the English language. There is, for instance, an Indian—and even a Bengali form of English. . . . Language is a social activity: and whether it is really desirable for English or any other language—real or invented—to become a world-medium, is a question which perhaps concerns the anthropologist and other students of the 'social sciences' rather than the student of the English language.

– C. L. Wrenn, *The English Language* (London: Methuen), 185, 205

1999 In 1500 Henry VII of England had barely 2m subjects. Even 100 years later English-speaking inhabitants of the British Isles were a none too large majority. Yet before long two major English-speaking nations emerged in rapid succession to dominate by turns the 19th and 20th centuries. No less a figure than the first German chancellor, Bismarck, called the English colonisation of North America 'the decisive fact of the modern world'.

– unsigned, 'America and Britain: Water is thicker', *The Economist* (London, 13 March)

There is no agreed figure for the number of languages in the world at the present time. Estimates cluster around 4,000–6,000, and there is a great deal of justified concern about how rapidly many of the small languages are dying out. Some of the reasons for the statistical uncertainty are:

❶ Diversity and similarity

Some parts of the world have not yet been fully explored in linguistic terms, including areas rich in languages, such as Papua New Guinea and Central Africa. Deciding whether a newly encountered community speaks a distinct language or a variation of one already charted often takes considerable time and effort. Normally, people who readily understand each other are said to speak the same language (even if an effort is required and despite major differences, such as between Cockney usage in London and Yat in New Orleans). In some situations, however, variation may be less a matter of typology and comprehension than of culture and/or politics, as with Hindi and Urdu, whose speech forms are close but whose scripts are different, aligned with Hinduism and Islam respectively.

❷ Re-classification

Assumptions about status as a language may change as circumstances change. In the 19th century, Dutch and Flemish were regarded as similar but distinct, while Netherlands Dutch and Cape Dutch ('Afrikaans') were taken to be the same. However, in the early 20th century, Afrikaans established itself as a distinct language and, in the later 20th century, Flemish came to be regarded in both Belgium and the Netherlands as a variety of Dutch.

❸ Cultural, legal, and other pressures

Politics, religion, and other factors can play a part in deciding what is a language and what is a variety of a language. For some people, Scots has for centuries been a language, and the European Bureau of Lesser Used Languages (an agency of the

European Union based in Dublin) takes this view. Others consider Scots a northern dialect of English, and others still consider that it was once a language (with a significant literature), but that this has not been the case for several centuries. Such matters are not simple: in Scandinavia, for example, Danish, Norwegian, and Swedish are widely agreed to be *both* distinct national languages *and* varieties within a common Scandinavian.

❹ Rapid social change

Changes in the perception of the status of a language can occur quite quickly, as in the Balkans at the close of the 20th century, when the disintegration of Yugoslavia disrupted the unity of Serbo-Croat as a national language, re-creating two avowedly distinct South Slav languages (Serbian to the east written in Cyrillic, Croatian to the west written in Roman).

Because situations and definitions vary so much, it is impossible to establish a single canonical total for languages in the world today. It is also not easy to indicate the number of speakers of particular languages. In many territories, people speak several languages and may find it difficult or even impossible to decide which is their first. In addition, in many places, everyday hybridization across languages is common, a fact which may embarrass some people when their attention is drawn to it but which has always been a fact of life in complex societies.

Just such hybridization took place, and on a massive scale, when Middle English emerged as a composite of Anglo-Saxon, Danish, and Norman-French (all of which died out as distinct languages in England). Immense amounts of Greco-Latin poured into this new kind of language throughout the Middles Ages and Renaissance and the flow has continued to this day. The result is Modern English, which in its vocabulary is polysystemic. Its 'word store', 'vocabulary', or 'lexis' falls into three broad areas:

❶ Germanic

'The children came running into the house'; 'Little Bo Peep has lost her sheep/And doesn't know where to find them.'

❷ Latinate

'A series of relevant experiments was recently concluded at the Institute'; 'Let us reflect on the Latinate content of formal composition'.

❸ Greco-Latinate

'Our thesis requires a systematic exegesis of the various ontogenetic and phylo-genetic factors involved'; 'A team of paleontologists worked on the fossiliferous Mesozoic strata'.

This layered aspect of English can be demonstrated in terms of three-part lexical groups such as *bird*, *aviary*, and *ornithology*. All three words in this group relate to creatures that generally have feathers and wings. The first, *bird*, is vernacular Germanic (like *be*, *bad*, *beach*, *bear*, *but*); the second, *aviary*, is 'educated' and Latinate (like *apiary*, *aquarium*, *attraction*, *complexion*, *universe*); and the third, *ornithology*, is from Greek as a source of erudite technical words (like *agnostic*, *anorexic, atheistic, diagram, diaphragm, diagnosis*). *Bird* is typical Germanic, with extended and often slangy usages ('aircraft as bird', 'woman as bird'). An *aviary* is a place where birds are kept in cages or a netted area, and *ornithology* is the scientific study of such creatures. Each word is physically and stylistically distinct, but all three belong conceptually and often contextually together, despite the differences. As a broadcaster on an informal radio programme put it some years ago in the UK: 'Plenty happening tonight, folks. We start off with a visit from an ornith-, an orthinol- —a *birdman*.'

In the early 20th century, the American linguists Edward Sapir and Benjamin Lee Whorf took an interest in the differentness of languages. They argued that each language has its own way of framing reality, a proposition now known as both the Sapir–Whorf Hypothesis and the Whorfian Hypothesis. It has two forms: the *strong form*, which says that the differences among languages cannot ultimately be reconciled (all languages really *are* islands), and the *weak form* (accepted by most language scholars) that there is routinely a lack of fit among languages, which can be an impediment to communication, acquisition, and translation, but even so such things remain necessary, desirable, and—to a considerable extent—possible.

No language has a perfect 'take' on the world we live in, and the fewer the languages in the world, the fewer such takes there will be. It may be argued, however, in defence of linguistic hybridization (which is a commoner phenomenon worldwide than might be supposed), that if anything can reduce the Sapir–Whorfian separateness of mind across languages it could be the flowing together of elements and structures from several languages into one language. If this is so, and if the world must have a single medium available to all, then it could be beneficial if that language is itself traditionally a hybrid and open to further hybridization. Much can be said against some of the social processes through which English and other world languages have reached their current positions. Equally, however, there are things that can be said in their favour; in terms of English, its versatility in drawing on other languages and in turn being drawn into those languages has long been cited as a notable advantage (although purists might disagree).

There are many books in English on language(s) at large, such as the *Encyclopedia of the Languages of Europe*, edited by Glanville Price (Blackwell, 1998/2000), which provides detailed comment on Albanian, Basque, Corsican, Frisian, Gaelic, Latvian, Crimean Tatar, Welsh, and many other languages. In the production of such volumes, we can note two distinctive and fairly novel roles for English, roles that complement and extend its historic versatility:

❶ As a *metalanguage*

According to *The New Oxford Dictionary of English* (above, p. 1), a metalanguage is 'a form of language or set of terms used for the description or analysis of another language'. According to the *Encarta World English Dictionary* (see p. 1), it is 'a language or system of symbols used to describe or analyse another language or system of symbols'. English has, as it were, become a kind of super-metalanguage, a worldwide vehicle for the discussion of language and languages in general.

❷ As a *default language*

Adapting a term from computer programming, English can be described as the option likely to be used in the world's system of communication if one does not or cannot opt for any other. In the same way that many people accept the default mode in a computational system, then use it without further ado, so they may in a more general way accept (or tolerate) English as the world's default medium for information, whatever the technology and circumstances involved.

Many factors have brought a simultaneously hybridizing and standardizing English language to its current position of global pre-eminence. Factors likely to sustain it in that position include historical and institutional momentum and the current investment of effort by hundreds of millions of people. However, in the long run, practicality is the measure, and such a measure is unsentimental. One does not have to love a lingua franca, a metalanguage, or a default mode. One simply has to find it useful.

2 Europe

1997 The English language has not existed in isolation and has always been in close contact with other European languages . . . English pronunciation is largely Anglo-Saxon, but also in part Danish and French. English grammar is basically Germanic, but it has been modified by French and Latin.

– Gerry Knowles, *A Cultural History of the English Language* (London: Arnold)

1996 Worldwide, English spread in the wake of British conquests. It was diffused as the language of the peoples of North America. And in African and Asian colonies it often came into use as the language of communication with the original population, and . . . often as the common vehicle for communication. Yet it is a veritable newcomer on the European Continent.

– Cay Dollerup, 'English in the European Union', in *The English Language in Europe*, ed. Reinhard Hartmann (Oxford: Intellect)

The continent of Europe is, in strict geographical terms, a peninsula jutting west into the Atlantic Ocean. In a strict physical sense it is a subcontinent within Eurasia, much like the Indian subcontinent that juts south into another ocean. There is no common sense in the status of Europe as a continent, only centuries of familiarity: Europeans might intellectually accept that they live in a vast land mass called *Eurasia* only since the 19th century, but that could never make them *Eurasians*, a word that serves very different ends, referring to individuals and communities that came into existence only because Western Europeans found a way to sail east by first sailing south.

The easterly islands of the North Atlantic belong traditionally to Europe, but no logic or planning ever went into making them European: their proximity and people's ignorance of what lay beyond them was enough. What else could they be but European? What else was there to the west besides Europe?; in any case, for centuries being European was hardly important, when people had trouble enough being French or German. It would be no surprise, however, if the Europeanness of the inhabitants of the islands was different from that of such heartland regions as Hungary and Poland, or even from the peoples who lived in western coastal regions, like the Portuguese, the French, the Dutch, and the Danes. Location matters, and its significance is as real for both language and attitudes to language as for anything else.

What Knowles (above) wrote in 1997 accords with earlier histories of English, pointing out as he does how much the present-day language owes to the mainland European tongues. Dollerup's comment, however, identifies a less-discussed matter: that English is a major European language which nonetheless for centuries had little impact on the Continent. Dominant in the home island and prominent overseas, it has been hugely influenced from across the Channel but has done little influencing in return. That is, until the second half of the 20th century, when everything linguistic in mainland Europe began to change.

Britain, the Atlantic, and the West

In Atlantic Europe there emerged the primary elements of a society and a culture now identified worldwide as simply 'the West'. At first this concerned only some coastal and insular peoples, but in the course of half a millennium this West expanded—first to eastern North America, then across to California, then further still to Hawaii and maybe even Guam (where, as it were, West has met East by the back door). For some four decades, the Iron Curtain provided a tidy, if sinister, line between two European power blocs, described as Western and Eastern, in terms of which the ancient concept *Central Europe* disappeared, only however to re-surface quite swiftly in the 1990s. In addition, following the collapse of the Soviet system after 1989, many territories in the European East have expressed the wish 'to join the West', in terms that include the North Atlantic Treaty Organization, the European Union, and the use of English as a lingua franca.

A world away, Australia and New Zealand have long routinely claimed—and been accorded—Western status, despite being in both the southern and eastern hemispheres, and in recent years also seeking (more or less) to be in some sense part of Asia. It is clear, however, that Australasia (ironically, 'Southern Asia' in Latin) is indeed Western in a sense that adds something to everyday geography. Its population is predominantly Atlantic European in origin, lives in much the same way as Western Europeans and North Americans, and operates overwhelmingly in the Atlantic European language English. The majority of Australasians, while celebrating their Antipodean distinctiveness, fully and routinely expect to go on being Western and acknowledged as such, while other territories settle for Westernization.

Broadly, the process of in some sense Westernizing all humanity refers to a cultural, technological, and educational shift in which literal westernness has long been secondary, although migration patterns (legal and illegal) make it clear that for millions location *does* matter. English has become the linguistic icon of the West not only because it was dominant in the erstwhile British Empire, but because of its overwhelming presence in North America, where two other Atlantic European languages are also used: Spanish in Mexico and the United States, and French in Canada and the United States.

English is therefore, inevitably, both the world's lingua franca and the primary communicative vehicle of Westernization, a process widely perceived as desirable (despite reservations and opposition), either as an unexamined whole or in more or less controlled doses that permit other societies to keep their identity more or less intact and still flourish, notably in eastern Asia, as with Japan, South Korea, Taiwan, Singapore, and Hong Kong. In all of this, however, the English language has hardly been alone: Spanish, French, Dutch, Portuguese, German, and Italian have all had worldwide mercantile and colonial associations, all originate in Western Europe, all have been massively disseminated via the Atlantic Ocean, and all have been vehicles for Western perspectives and techniques.

At the heart of this immense complex of shifts in cultures, populations, and languages are the physical nature and social history of Atlantic Europe, in which at least the following fifteen points are worth noting with regard to the English language:

❶ Insularity (etymology: Latin *insula* 'island')

The cultures of the islands of Atlantic Europe—most notably Britain, Ireland, and Iceland—have for centuries been physically and psychologically distinct from mainland Europe.

❷ Isolation (etymology: through French from Italian *isola* 'island' from Latin *insula*)

By AD 1500, when the Americas had been discovered, English had no apparent prospect of becoming a significant language in Europe (and therefore the world). English was however by then the most involved of the insular languages in developments on the Continent.

❸ Linguistic distinctness yet dependence

For speakers of English, their separateness from the European mainstream prompted both pride in being different and concern about being left behind, a condition alleviated to some degree by the centuries-old influence of French and Latin.

❹ Sociopolitical independence

Although the peoples of Britain and Ireland have often strongly disagreed about what constitutes freedom, they have sought it assiduously. Notable instances have been: Magna Carta in England in 1215, the Declaration of Arbroath in Scotland in 1320 (one a declaration of rights, the other of rights and independence), and the drives for Irish self-determination and the survival of Welsh.

❺ Tradition, freedom, and eccentricity

In Britain, jealously guarded civil rights have co-existed with kinds of eccentricity and paradox (especially as judged from the Continent): democracy has co-existed with aristocracy and monarchy, and the assertion and denial of human rights have gone side by side. The phrase 'an Englishman's home is his castle' asserts a right to both freedom and eccentricity.

❻ Ship-based expansion

Once ships became capable of navigating the open Atlantic in relative safety, six rival nations (and their languages) were free to compete for primacy both there and beyond: in rough historical order, Portugal, Spain, the Netherlands, France, England, and Germany.

❼ Literary and religious canons

At the turn of the 16th–17th centuries, English acquired both a dramatist, William Shakespeare, capable of writing on an epic scale, and a people's bible, the Authorized Version of 1611.

❽ Government non-involvement in language

No government, either before or after the Union of England and Scotland in 1707, concerned itself directly with the condition or prestige of the language. No academy was created, and there was no government promotion or vetting of dictionaries, grammars, or orthographic systems. The same hands-off approach followed in both the Empire and the United States.

❾ The Union of Crowns and Parliaments

The reorganization of England, Wales, and Scotland within the United Kingdom of Great Britain reduced then eliminated internal wars and disputes, and encouraged the consolidation of a single language with a standard for writing and print in Britain, Ireland, and overseas territories, notably including the colonies that became the United States.

❿ Educational publishing

The emergence of a publishing industry, especially in London, Oxford, Glasgow, Edinburgh, and New York, catering first to adult then to children's needs, creating a tradition of manuals, textbooks, dictionaries, and other works that strengthened and disseminated the standard printed language.

⓫ University and other studies in and of English

In 1762, the first academic department of English was established at the University of Edinburgh. Over the next 200 years, such departments became common place in English-speaking territories and elsewhere, and participated in a vast and profitable worldwide language-and-literature 'industry'.

⓬ The autonomy of the United States of America

In 1775, thirteen American colonies declared their independence. The new nation adopted English as its key language (like the UK, without making it official) and established a distinctive style, notably in print and orthography.

⓭ The British Empire and American world influence

The 19th-century extension of British power and trade created a large piecemeal empire 'on which the sun never set' (heyday *c.*1880–1920). The effort needed to win two world wars enfeebled this empire at the same time as it enhanced the global position and usage of its ally, the United States (with its own quasi-imperial interests worldwide).

⓮ The industrial-communicative revolutions and 'globalization'

When technology and commerce began to develop in Western Europe, their epicentre was in Britain. Shipping, railways/railroads, telecommunications, television, electronics, and other technological developments became hallmarks of both the Industrial Revolution and globalization, developments that further consolidated the position of English worldwide.

⓯ The global primacy of US usage

A key feature of the present English-language complex is polarity and complementarity between UK and US usage, the US predominating (and including a strong influence on UK usage). All other Englishes (and many other languages) also experience the impact of the US and its usage within a socio-economic web that centres/centers on the media, Hollywood, the Internet, and information technology.

These developments cover some fifteen centuries, during which the major languages of mainland Western Europe also emerged. All such languages belong within an intricate social, cultural, and linguistic tradition that notably includes the five following events, features, and developments:

❶ The fall of Rome

The slow disintegration of the Western Roman Empire in the 4th to 6th centuries AD entailed vast upheavals and migrations, in which the Dutch, English, French, German, Portuguese, and Spanish languages had their rough-and-ready beginnings.

❷ The rise of the Atlantic European empires

When their speakers began to extend their influence beyond Europe, the six major Atlantic European languages experienced various commercial and colonial diasporas. In each empire, Latin was used for centuries in various roles and, when a standardizing form of each language became entrenched, its prestige began to resemble that of Latin. In addition, when such languages spread worldwide, Latin spread with them.

❸ A shared Graeco-Latin inheritance

To strengthen and embellish their prestige varieties (and because they were themselves generally comfortable with the classical languages), educated users of the newer European languages (including the six above) 'borrowed' or 'loan-translated' Latin and Greek words and word elements in large numbers. English was so notably receptive to the inflow of such 'classical' material that its 'hybrid heritage' has often led people to call it both 'a mongrel tongue' and see it as virtually an additional member of the Romance language family.

❹ A liberalization and hybridization of the Graeco-Latin inheritance

This process of classicizing English has never stopped. However, throughout the 19th–20th centuries, the use of classical material became less conservative and more flexible, leading in recent years to such relaxed 'post-classical' forms as *cell phone*, *cyberspace*, *genomics*, and *glocalization* (mixing *global* and *local*). Many are nowadays hybridized with native English forms and often abbreviated, as with: *hifi*, *dot.com*, *hyperlink*, and *Internet* (terms that would have been labelled 'barbarisms' at the beginning of the 20th century).

❺ The concept of 'civil society'

Complex techno-cultural and other developments with linguistic dimensions emerged after the Renaissance and Reformation periods, including: the nation-state; open-sea navigation; regulated schools and public examinations; armed forces with literate officers and sergeants; gunpowder-based weapons; alphabet-based typography; mechanized printing; commercial publishing; industrial mass production; parliamentary-style legislation; and documentation backed by copying and filing systems, contracts, law, and government policy. A currently popular term in English for the type of stable, productive, and relatively safe community served by such a social and technical complex is *civil society*, a condition widely asserted at the present time as a fundamental requirement for all communities on earth.

Drawing on both their Graeco-Latin heritage and vernacular translations of the Hebrew/Greek Bible, the users of Western European standardizing languages possessed a mass of shared knowledge and experience, in terms of which they constitute variations on a common theme. Despite their rivalry, mutual suspicion, and often warfare, all had access to the same pool of institutions, motifs, allusions, and lexical and stylistic resources. The forms through which this shared tradition was expressed grew increasingly diverse and mixed as these countries undertook transcontinental quests for resources, trade, knowledge, and kinds of glory, including the creation of empires that echoed Rome in their senates and monuments.

Their options were in fact limited. The Austro-Hungarian Empire, Russia, and the Islamic world blocked expansion to the east (an exception being the movement of German settlers into eastern Europe) but, after improvements in both navigation and weaponry, and with the discovery of new lands on its far shores, the Atlantic became a liberating medium, allowing passage west to a new world, and south and east to an older one. In the process of exploiting new resources and peoples (and spreading both ideas and disease), the Atlantic nations had the satisfaction of outflanking and disconcerting old rivals in Central and Eastern Europe, North Africa, and West Asia.

English was one among many languages, large (such as French and Spanish) and small (such as Basque and Welsh), which were carried to new regions. At first it had no great prestige. Well into the 18th century, Spanish and French were surer candidates for cultural and linguistic glory, and Spain and France were ahead of England in consolidating their national languages. In the 16th–17th centuries, the founders of European academies for the protection and elevation of the 'polite' and 'pure' forms of their languages considered that the kind of miscegenation typical of English was reprehensible, and some observers in 17/18th-century England agreed with them. But there was no support for an English Academy. When Johnson produced his *Dictionary of the English Language* in 1755, he was widely applauded—and taken to be worth forty 'immortal' French Academicians any day.

Origins: Indo-European and Germanic

Such an overview of the development of Atlantic Europe is necessary, but not sufficient, to set the stage for world English. Another, older dimension needs to be discussed: the shared origins of English and many of the languages with which it has been in contact, from Ireland to India. Language scholars agree that the ultimate roots of English lie in what is now by common agreement called *Proto-Indo-European* (*PIE*), a hypothetical language that was probably spoken some five thousand years ago, perhaps near the Black Sea. For some two hundred years, it has been accepted that small changes over decades and centuries adapted this single original tongue into many very distinct languages. A well-known example of the resultant radiation from one source are such cognate words as Modern English *daughter*, Old English/Anglo-Saxon *dohtor*, Scots, Dutch, and Old Frisian *dochter*, German *Tochter*, Old Norse *dóttir*, Persian *dokhtar*, Armenian *dushtr*, Classical Greek *thugater*, and Sanskrit *duhitrí*—all descended from an ancestral form reconstructed as **dhughater*.

Such radiations from older into newer Indo-European forms continue to occur, even though they may be disguised by institutionalized spellings. Thus, the written form *daughter* contains a fossil *gh* unpronounced for centuries, but still pronounced in its nearest linguistic neighbours Scots, Frisian, Dutch, and German. This archaic spelling accidentally serves to conceal a range of pronunciations that include 'dawtuh' (an informal representation of Received Pronunciation) and 'dahdur' (in informally spelt General American). These variants, in strict phonetic terms, only have initial *d* in common, a condition within a single language that offers proof of language change as convincing as any that can be demonstrated across related languages.

Some IE words have undergone changes so profound that a common origin would be hard to discern if it weren't for the many easier parallels. Thus, English *father*, Old Irish *athair*, French *père*, and Armenian *hayr* do not look or sound as though they could ever have had a shared origin, yet there is adequate evidence that they too share a common ancestor. Indeed, divergence of this kind characterizes much of the sound, structure, and vocabulary of all Indo-European languages. It was a growing awareness of such shared yet diverging patterns that led the 18th-century philologist and Indologist Sir William Jones (whose observations led to the concept of PIE), to make the following much-quoted observation to the Asiatic Society (which he founded):

> **1786** [T]he *Sanscrit* language . . . bear[s to Greek and Latin] a
> stronger affinity, both in the roots of verbs, and in the forms of
> grammar, than could possibly have been produced by accident;
> so strong indeed, that no philologer could examine them all three,
> without believing them to have sprung from some common
> source, which, perhaps, no longer exists.

Currently, scholars agree that PIE was differentiated through population dispersal after *c.*2000 BC. Its increasingly distinctive offspring apparently emerged through a combination of migration, natural language change, and contact with other languages—some of them exhibiting both hybridization and pidginization. One of the intermediate 'daughter' languages of *Proto-Indo-European* is *Proto-Germanic* (*PG*), for whose existence there is also no direct evidence, because there were no writing systems in northern Europe when it emerged. Indeed, as a natural language, without writing or print, it was probably never homogeneous.

PG differed from other earlier descendants of PIE in certain features of pronunciation and grammar, and in a vocabulary that included non-PIE words (that is, there was a degree of hybridization). Early speakers of this original Germanic appear to have moved west from the IE homeland to what is now northern Germany and Scandinavia, from which some moved on, leaving behind a North Germanic that eventually became Norwegian, Swedish, Danish, Icelandic, Faroese, and Norn (formerly in Orkney and Shetland). There was also a Proto-East Germanic out of which emerged the long-extinct Gothic language, and a Proto-West Germanic that became German, Dutch, Frisian, and Letzburgish (Continental West Germanic) and English and Scots (Insular West Germanic). Two West Germanic languages with exceptional histories are Yiddish from German, becoming an international Jewish language, and Afrikaans from Dutch, becoming an autonomous language of southern Africa, and the only Germanic language to come into being outside of Europe.

The Germanic languages of central interest in this discussion are English and Scots, traditionally regarded by many scholars as two forms of the same language (one major, one minor), but regarded for centuries by most Scots as a distinct language ('the guid Scóts tongue'), increasingly accepted as such by contemporary language scholars, and most notably recognized recently by the European Bureau for Lesser-Used Languages (set up by the European Union in 1982) and regarded sympathetically by the devolved Scottish Parliament (set up within the UK in 1999). Whatever view is taken, the common source of English and Scots died out just under a millennium ago, and is known as both *Old English* and *Anglo-Saxon*.

Some cognate Germanic words

English	Scots	Old English	Dutch	German	Swedish
one	ane, yin	an	een	eins	en
two	twa, tway	twa	twee	zwei	tva
three	three	thrie	drie	drei	tre
come	come	cuman	komen	kommen	komma
day	day	daeg	dag	Tag	dag
earth	yird, erd	eorthe	aarde	Erde	jord
hay	hey	heg	hooi	Heu	höouml
live (verb)	leeve	libban	leven	leben	leva
water	watter	waeter	water	Wasser	vatten
young	young	geong	jong	jung	ung

Origins: Old English or Anglo-Saxon

1994 The term 'Old English' itself . . . is not unproblematical. There is no single or uniform corpus of Old English, but rather a collection of texts from about the seventh to the eleventh centuries, representing dialects spread out from the North of England to the West Country and Kent. This collection is extremely heterogeneous, as the range suggests: runic OE of the seventh century is in many ways as different from the 'classical' literary OE of the eleventh as Chaucer's language is from Shakespeare's.

– Roger Lass, *Old English: A Historical Linguistic Companion* (Cambridge University Press), 1

Long before there was an English language, the earliest recorded word associated with Britain appeared in the record of a pioneering voyage west in the 4th century BC, led by a Greek mariner called Pytheas. Although he did not provide a name for the largest island he found off the coast of Atlantic Europe, he called its people *Pretanoi*. The later Latin version of this word was *Britanni*, applied to a people who evidently painted their bodies blue with a dye called *woad* (from the plant *Isatis tinctoria*). The place-name *Britannia* appears therefore to have meant, originally, 'Land of the Painted People'. In parallel, the Latin name for the unconquered north-ernmost inhabitants of the same island in Roman times was *Picti* ('Painted People': *Picts* in English). This name suggests that those Britons beyond the reach of Rome continued to 'wear' woad, much as such North American peoples as the Mohawks and the Hurons later used war paint.

From the 5th century AD, Germanic settlers in a disintegrating Roman Britain called the island *Breten* or *Bretenland*, and some of their leaders used the title *bretwalda* ('Brit-ruler'), probably translating the Latin phrase *dux Britanniarum*: 'leader/duke of the Britains'. Only much later did the bulk of post-colonial south Britain become *Englaland* ('Angleland') then, more compactly, *England* (Latin *Anglia*), whose language was later spelt as *Englisc* (probably pronounced 'Ing-lish', without a hard *g*). The newcomers called the Celtic territory to their west *Wales* ('Land of Foreigners/Slaves') and later a mixed Celtic and Germanic territory to the north came to be known as *Scotia* in Latin and *Scotland* in English, after the *Scoti* or *Scots*, Celtic settlers from Ireland every bit as opportunistic as the Germans.

Traces of the usage of the first Anglo-Saxons survive primarily in place-names (often side by side and mixed with Celtic and Latin), and names formulated later do not help much in assessing what people were called during the first two centuries of settlement and expansion. Such words as 'English', 'German', 'Welsh', and 'Scottish' have very different current implications from both their earlier forms and such Latin equivalents as *Anglicus*, *Germanus*, *Cambrensis*, and *Scotus* as used at the time. In addition, such present-day semi-technical terms as 'language' and 'dialect' also inadequately describe Germanic speech during and after the collapse of the Western Roman Empire.

Until around AD 600, most Germanic peoples appear to have been able to under-stand each other. Thus, when the missionary Augustinus (later St Augustine of Canterbury) and his companions (Latin-using southerners who knew no Germanic) set out to convert 'the English' in 597, they engaged Franks to interpret for them. These intermediaries apparently did well, because the conversion of the English to Christianity followed quite quickly.

There are no eye-witness accounts of the inflow of Germanic settlers into post-Roman Britain. Much later, however, around AD 730, the historian Bede wrote in Latin about three groups of invaders, the *Angli*, *Saxones*, and *Iutae* (routinely translated as 'the Angles, Saxons, and Jutes'). Such settlers probably also included Frisians, Franks, and maybe others, and the various groups could only have become homogeneously 'English' after several generations, when all of them, no doubt along with Romano-Celtic-Germanic offspring, all came to see themselves as *Angelcynn* ('Angle-kin').

Of these, the Angles occupied the Midlands and the east coast from the Thames to the Forth, their two great dialects being *Mercian* (in the Midland kingdom known in Latin as *Mercia*, from the Thames to the Humber) and *Northumbrian* (in the kingdom known in mixed Latin and English as *Northumbria*, from the Humber to the Forth). The Saxons settled around the Thames and in the south-west: *East Saxons* in 'Essex', *Middle Saxons* in 'Middlesex', *South Saxons* in 'Sussex', and *West Saxons* in 'Wessex'. The *West Saxon* speech associated with Wessex became the culturally dominant dialect and the primary (but not the sole) literary medium. The Jutes settled in Kent and along parts of the south coast, and very little is known about them.

The first written form of 'Old English' (or 'Anglo-Saxon', as it has often been called in recent centuries) used runic letters, derived from *runes*, marks cut on wood, bone, and stone that were themselves early adaptations of Romano-Greek letters. Such marks were often accorded magical properties, as in 'the casting of the runes' when telling fortunes. A more conventional Roman alphabet replaced them after 597, when the English were converted to Christianity. The new script retained several runic letters, along with certain letter shapes used by Irish scribes, to represent sounds not present in Latin, such as the distinct *th*-sounds in *this* and *three*—a distinguishing feature lacking in the present-day writing system of English.

However, although Old English had an alphabetic writing system, developed a literature, and was the language of the annals called the *Anglo-Saxon Chronicle*, it was culturally lower than Latin, which continued after the Empire as the high language of the West and of Roman Catholic Christianity. Its script was much less standardized, and varied from dialect to dialect, and it continued for centuries, but within a hundred years of the Norman Conquest (1066) it was defunct. By that time, spoken usage in much of England had been affected by both the settlement of Danes in the east and north and the influence of French and Latin, especially in the south-east.

Old English/Anglo-Saxon can be conceived in at least three ways, either choosing one in absolute terms (as 'the truth') or using all three relativistically:

❶ As the first of several phases in a single on-going language

In this more or less standard approach, English as the language of England passes through three (or four) stages whose boundary points are not clear-cut but tend to be treated as if they were. The stages are *Old*, *Middle*, and *Modern* (the last usually subdivided into *Early Modern* and *Modern*). In this model, Scots is usually treated as part of the Northern dialect and its distinct national history, literature, and dialects are given limited consideration.

❷ As the ancestor of an English within which Scots is a distinct entity

In this more radical approach, *Old English* is the extinct language from which two further more or less distinct languages have evolved in succession, primarily in England: *Middle English* (also extinct), and *Modern English* (generally known simply as *English*). Here, Scots is treated as a part of the language that developed in distinctive ways north of the border, with a literary high point in the late Middle Ages, followed by decline as standard English spread after the Union. In this perspective the terms *Old English* and *Anglo-Saxon* are synonyms.

❸ As the common ancestor of both English and Scots

In this most radical approach, *Old English* is the common ancestor of two closely related national varieties of Insular West Germanic. Its more southern and more northerly branches developed as in effect separate languages in separate nations, as Middle English and Old and Middle Scots (within distinct time periods), each with

its own literature, followed by an internationalizing Modern English and a belea-
guered Modern Scots (in Scotland and Northern Ireland). Its most appropriate
name in this perspective is probably *Anglo-Saxon*, which serves to underline its
distinctiveness.

Old English or Anglo-Saxon, however we regard it and name it, was spoken for
some seven hundred years (5th–12th century). Although its surviving texts are as
unintelligible to present-day users of English as Latin to speakers of French, even
after modest exposure some sense can be made of them, as with the following
sentence, from Bede's *Ecclesiastical History of the English People*:

- **Anglo-Saxon** Breten is gar-secges iegland thaet waes geo geara Albion haten.
- **Gloss** Britain is sea's island that was ago years Albion called.
- **Translation** Britain is an island of the sea that was formerly called Albion.

In the original, word order in the main clause is the same as in present-day English,
but in the subordinate clause is markedly different (with suggestions of German).
Some words are the same as, or close to, Modern English (*is*, *Albion*, *Breten*, *waes*),
some are further removed but easily identified after translation (*iegland* 'island';
geara 'years'), and some are entirely alien (*garsecges* 'of the sea'; *geo* 'formerly', and
haten 'called'). A second set of sentences, taken from the *Anglo-Saxon Chronicle*, is:

- **Original version** On thissum geare com Harold cyng of Eoferwic to
  Westmynstre.
- **Gloss** On this year came Harold king of York to Westminster.
- **Translation** In this year, Harold the king of York came to Westminster.

Although an adequate understanding of Old English requires considerable time,
study, and effort, there is enough in common, even after a modest examination,
for present-day users of English to make some sense of this ancient tongue. This,
however, is only true if the present-day alphabet and its print styles are used. If
Old English is presented in either runic or Old English script, the problem of
understanding becomes insurmountable without prolonged study. Below are
some general points of pronunciation, spelling, and grammar which also indicate
the extent to which the vocabulary of OE differs from present-day English and
resembles such languages as Dutch and German:

Pronunciation and spelling

1 The effects of the first Germanic sound shift, generally known as Grimm's
   Law, can be seen in Old English. Indo-European *p*, as in **peku* ('property',
   Latin *pecus*), becomes *f* in OE *feoh*; IE *t*, as in **trei* ('three'), becomes Latin
   tri- and OE *thri*. The speech patterns of OE are comparable to those of its
   fellow North Sea languages Old Frisian and Old Dutch.

2 In words of more than one syllable, OE stress falls typically on the first
   syllable (marked here with an acute accent), as in present-day English:

mórgen ('morning'); *séttan* ('to set'). However, when the first syllable is a prefix, stress in nouns and adjectives is on the prefix, but not in verbs: *ándswaru* ('an answer') and *ándward* ('a current'), but *forgíefan* ('to forgive', cf. Dutch *vergéven* and German *vergében*), *tobérstan* (also simply *bérstan*, 'to burst': cf. Dutch *bérsten*), and *gethólian* ('to tolerate', whose base *thol* survives in Scots *tae thole* and Yorkshire *to thoil*, with much the same meaning).

3   All the elements of initial consonant clusters are pronounced in all written positions, as in the *gn*, *cn*, *hl*, and *wr* of *gnagan* ('to gnaw'), *cneo* ('knee'), *hlaf* ('loaf'), and *writan* ('to write').

4   Double letters represent 'geminated' sounds, as in Italian, so that *biddan* ('bidden') is said like 'bid den'.

5   Non-initial *h* is pronounced like either German *ich* or *nacht*, or Scots *ach* and *loch*.

6   Written *g* after or between vowels made at the back of the mouth is pronounced as in the German *sagen* (a voiced version of the *ch* in *loch*).

7   There are several distinctive letters: *ash* (æ), the sound of the RP vowel in *that hat* (almost 'thet het'); *eth* (ð), the sound of *th* in *this*; *thorn* (þ), the sound of *th* in *three*; *wynn* (ω), the sound of *w*; and *yogh* (ʒ), a variant of *g* that in written Middle English came to represent the *y* in 'yellow' and 'beyond'.

8   The letters *f* and *s* both have voiced and voiceless values, neither *v* nor *z* being normally used. The spelling *faet* is used for both the words now spelt and pronounced as *fat* and *vat*; each could be pronounced either way, depending on dialect. The *v*-version has survived in the West Country pronunciation of such words as *fat* and *feeling* as 'vat' and 'veelin'.

9   Thorn can represent the *th* sound in both *three* and *these*, much as *th* does now.

10 The letter *c* has the value 'k' before the 'hard' vowels *a*, *o*, *u*, *y*, and any consonant, and the value 'tch' before the 'soft' vowels *e* and *i*, as in *ceaster* ('chester': town) and *cirice* ('church').

11 Comparably, *g* is hard before *a*, *ae*, *o*, *u*, and any consonant, as in *gast* ('spirit') and *grim* ('fierce'), and has the value of *y* as in present-day *yet* before *e* and *I*, as in *geac* ('cuckoo') and *gif* ('if').

12 The letter combinations *sc* and *cg* have the values 'sh' and 'dzh', as in *scip* ('ship') and *bricg* ('bridge'). Although Anglo-Saxon was considerably different from present-day English, such orthographic conventions serve to make it look more alien to it actually was.

Grammar

1   The grammar of OE is more like that of German or Latin than Modern English, having singular and plural number as today but also masculine, feminine, and neuter gender, and nominative, accusative, genitive, dative, and instrumental cases.

2   Verbs, as in ModE, vary according to whether they are strong (rather like *give/gave/given* or *swim/swam/swum*) or weak (rather like *love/loved* and

try/tried). A typical combination of pronouns and verb is *Heo beswac hine* ('She betrayed him').

3 Like other IE languages, OE distinguished three grammatical persons, not only in the plural (as in ModE *we, you, they*) but also in the singular (as in E ModE *I, thou, he/she/it*).

4 OE also distinguished three genders and five cases, categories that extended to the article, adjective, and noun, and no longer exist even as the remnants of a system.

Despite the use of such closely related names, Old English and present-day English are as different one from the other as Classical Latin and present-day French. While the links are manifest, Old English and present-day English are not the same language, just as French is manifestly not Latin. It is as valid a matter to study Old English or Anglo-Saxon as ancestral to contemporary English as it is to study Latin as ancestral to contemporary French, Spanish, and other languages, but such studies are not essential for an understanding of either French or English. In addition, if one studies Old English as an aid to understanding later phases of the historical English-language complex, one cannot study it alone. One also needs to pay attention to Old Danish, because in the 9th–11th centuries Danes settled and consolidated themselves in large numbers in eastern England. Contact between the Anglo-Saxon and Danish communities affected both. Danish eventually died out in England, but not before it had radically changed Old English, including providing it with the definite article *the*.

Origins: Middle into Modern

Retroactive scholarly titles such as *Old*, *Middle*, and *Modern* are both handy and awkward: they affirm both stability and transition, but at the same time impose a view from the wrong direction. The unknown creator of the epic poem *Beowulf* did not know that he was composing it in *Old* English, but *we* know, and judge accordingly. Geoffrey Chaucer had no perception that the hybrid in which he wrote *The Canterbury Tales* would occupy an unkempt middle ground between ancient and modern phases of a language that was once (apparently) neat and tidy and would one day (apparently) again be so, but in a very different way. Chaucer did not know he was in the middle, but *we* do, and this is in a serious sense false, because Chaucer was no more in the middle of anything historical than we are today. It was later commentators who place him between Old and Modern.

'Middle English' can be considered a language in its own right, characterized by low status and the impact of Danish, French, and Latin. It came to an end around 1450, with the emergence of somewhat standardizing government usage and the first European printing press, after which it became elevated enough to become, in retrospect, something else (and implicitly something better): Early Modern English. Traditionally, and crudely, but in a powerfully symbolic way, Old English belonged to the Dark Ages (after the decline and fall of the Western Roman Empire, also often called 'the Early Middle Ages'), Middle English to the (Late) Middle Ages, and

Modern English to something new in the world: an ever-evolving, never-ending modernity with no precise cut-off point. The model does not allow for a transition from Modern into anything else: certainly not into 'Postmodern'.

A tripartite schema of this kind has worked usefully for many languages, especially but not only in Europe (Old, Middle, and Modern French, Old, Middle, and Modern Persian, and the like), and suggests a cycle in which however the earliest and youngest phase is the oldest, because it happened longest ago, and the oldest phase is 'Modern', because it includes us, the labellers. The model also has implications of 'progress' associated with a period of 'enlightenment' in which scholarly and scientific rigour became a touchstone for all things. In addition, by implication, only a 'modern' language can go beyond speech and writing into print and now into electronic modes.

None of this, however, means that the three-ages-of-English model is useless. Quite the contrary: it not only highlights change but also allows scholars to identify and track features over time. Thus, three key features of Middle English manifestly contrast with Old English: grammatical inflections are much reduced; lexical borrowing from other languages has massively increased; and orthography is volatile, in both writing and early print. These changes are clear in the following sentence from Chaucer's translation in the later 14th century of *De consolatione philosophiae*, I:VI ('On the Consolation of Philosophy'), by Boethius:

> **Middle English**
> First woltow suffer me to touche and assaye the estat of thy thought by a fewe demaundes, so that I may understonde what be the manere of thy curacioun?
>
> **Translation 1 (Early Modern)**
> First wilt thou suffer me to touch and try the state of thy thought by a few demands, so that I may understand what the manner of thy curation might be?
>
> **Translation 2 (Present-day)**
> Will you first let me try to assess the state of your thinking with a few questions, so that I can see how you set about curing people?

There is little left here of Old English, and many words in Chaucer's original have the same spelling in Modern English (*first, suffer, me, to, and, the, of, so, that, I, may, what, be*), although meanings may or may not be the same (for example, *first* is the same but *demandes* means 'questions'), while some are alien at first encounter but become less so on translation (as with *woltow*), and some remain strange but manageable (as with *curacioun*, whose modern form would be 'curation'). A notable grammatical element is the loss of subjunctive *be* in *so that I may understonde what be*. Middle English's blending of Germanic and Romance (in sound, spelling, and vocabulary) was often forced (because it was all rather new). It took several centuries for the major sources of English (Anglo-Saxon, Danish, French, Latin, and Greek) to come together so seamlessly that the joins are now barely detectable, especially in speech. In spelling, however, the sources are easier to detect: *voyage* from French; *dictator* from Latin; *photosynthesis* from Greek. These can seldom be mistaken for Germanic material like *begin, set up*, and *takeaway*.

In this internationalizing area, a notable feature of present-day English vocabulary first emerged in Middle English: parallel pairs of Germanic and French-cum-Latin words, such as *freedom/liberty*, *hearty/cordial*, *knight/chevalier*, *(un)lawful/(il)legal*. In each pair there is both closeness and distance: the words are synonymous but have different takes on the world and tend to keep different company. As the vocabulary of English also, in course of time, acquired items from Greek material, the web of relationships grew more complex, as in the set *hearty/cordial/cardiac*.

Throughout its history Middle English, even in London, was lower than French and Latin, but a number of factors combined to increase its status. Although the capital was close to the South-Eastern dialect area, forms of the East Midland dialect began to dominate in the city and disproportionately absorb French and Latin material. Over time, the higher social words and phrases came to serve the needs of the court, government, commerce, and the new printing presses, entirely displacing French and laying the groundwork of a standard written and printed English language. Among the many developments of the time are the five following features of pronunciation and spelling:

1 Orthography

For several lifetimes the written language retained many of the features of pre-Conquest Old English orthography. When both script and style eventually changed under the influence of French, the visual results were radically different, obscuring for later readers any continuity of pronunciation between the two writing systems. Notably, the script lost its distinctive rune-based letters, thorn being the last to go.

2 Spelling

Whereas OE spelling was relatively stable and regular, ME spelling varied greatly from place to place, person to person, and period to period, offering many variants for the same words: thus, OE *lē/af* (ModE *leaf*) had the ME forms *life*, *lieif*, *leif*, *leue*, *leuue*, *leaue*, etc.

3 Sound changes

Some ME sound changes altered vowel values, resulting for example in such present-day sound differences as between singular *child* and *staff* (a large stick) and plural *children* and *staves*.

4 cn- and kn-

The pronunciation of the OE sounds/letters *cn-*, as in *cnawan*, continued for centuries, but with such new spellings as *know* (indicating in this instance the loss of infinitive ending -*an*) the link between the two forms was no longer obvious. Furthermore, when the pronunciation of the *k* at length died out, the present-day language was left with such fossil written forms as *know*, *knee*, *knight*, and *knot*.

5 -gh-

Comparably, pronunciations like that of the *ch* in German *ach* and *Nacht* continued for most of the ME period in England (and continue at the present time for certain purposes in Scotland), but were represented in ME by *gh*, which also survives as a fossil in present-day spelling, either unpronounced, as in such words as *light*, *height*, and *night*, or pronounced as 'f' in such words as *rough*, *tough*, and *laughter*.

The period of Middle English was unstable. It was caught both in speech and writing between two very different language types (Germanic and Romance) and subordinated to French in a time of great and rapid change. In this, its condition was much like that of subordinated languages worldwide at the present time. Many such languages are in the shadow of World Standard English, and they exhibit the same fluidity and tendency to absorb usages of all kinds from more influential languages, again notably English. In some cases, hybridization has been so great that some languages are changing towards English just as Middle English became half-Romance, especially in lexical terms. Some present-day languages have their own ancient literary traditions while for others literacy is still a novelty; for both, however, their status may hover uneasily between a vernacular and a fully institutionalized local, regional, or national language.

It was during the first century or so of the modern British period, around 1603–1707, that English took on a written and printed form which can still be understood without much difficulty. It was also in that period that the language began to take root beyond Britain and Ireland. In a serious sense, therefore, Modern English has been global from its very beginning: that is, it is an inherent feature of the English language since the early 17th century that it has been spoken in a range of widely separated places and therefore in contact with a large number of other languages in a varied range of environments. By and large, when the language began to spread, it was already a British and Irish rather than simply an English entity, and its standardness was insecure, because there was at the time no firm standard of any kind. In addition, in the ships that began to carry the language worldwide and in their ports of call there were all kinds of English and other languages and mixes of languages.

In the early Middle Ages, when England, Scotland, and Wales became distinct entities, the term *Britain* for several centuries had no real political or ethnic significance. A major exception, however, were the epic romances sung, recited, and written about King Arthur and his knights. The origins of these stories were however Celtic, not Germanic, Roman, or French, and their cycle came to be known first as the *Matière de Bretagne* (in French), then the *Matter of Britain* (in English). When the part-Welsh Tudor dynasty gained the throne of England in 1485, uniting Wales with England in 1536, many Welsh people favoured *Britain* as a name for this Anglo-Welsh union, but the English had no interest in such a change and little sense at the time of 'Britishness'. The matter was left unclear until 1603, when James VI of Scots became James I of England. He described himself at the time as in fact re-uniting 'Britain', but again this new use of an old name had little appeal for the English or indeed the Scots. As a result, *Britain* with its Celtic Arthurian echoes did not become part of official nomenclature until just over a century later, with the Union of the Parliaments in 1707.

Mild official efforts were made to replace or complement the old national names and promote harmony after centuries of war and ill will. In some acts of the combined Parliament in London, England (with Wales) was called *South Britain* and Scotland *North Britain*, within the framework of *Great Britain* (a usage that once served to distinguish the island from 'Little Britain' or Brittany, in France). In 1803, when Ireland was brought into the Union, it was re-cast as *West Britain*, and in the 19th century the phrase *Greater Britain* was occasionally used for the Empire. However, apart from *Great Britain* as an official title and *Britain* for general purposes, such usages had little impact. Currently, the full formal title of the country is the *United Kingdom of Great Britain and Northern Ireland.*

For the Scots, Welsh, and Northern Irish, the term *Britain* has been psychologically vital, enabling them to cope within a unitary state dominated by the English. The shared generic has been especially important because, for most purposes, these communities have long used a language massively identified with England both by the English and the rest of the world. A nagging problem nonetheless developed when, from the 18th century onward, the terms *Britain* and *England* came to be widely treated as synonyms (and therefore stylistically interchangeable), again both in England and the world at large, as in:

> **1974** By the late nineteenth century such a thing was regarded as intolerable in Britain. It was not only that many Englishmen now regarded England's prosperity as being bound up with that of India; England's prestige too was now heavily committed.
> – M. E. Chamberlain, *Britain and India.*

Such equations continue, but, by the beginning of the 21st century, as part of an increasing wish for fair representation in such matters as gender and ethnicity, there has been a mild tendency in England towards accuracy rather than synecdoche.

The history of the terms *Britannia* and *Britain* is complex. Romans used *Britannia* for both the island as a whole and the part they controlled. The Emperor Claudius established a province in AD 43, which expanded in stages until it reached the line of the rivers Solway and Tyne. To protect the province of *Britannia Romana* ('Roman Britain'), the Emperor Hadrian built a wall (*c.*128) that is still a feature of the landscape. Much later, the Emperor Severus (d. 211) divided the territory south of the wall into two provinces: *Britannia superior* ('Upper Britain'), so called because closer to Rome, its capital Londinium (London), and *Britannia inferior* ('Lower Britain') to the north, its capital Eboracum (York). Beyond the wall lay *Britannia barbara* ('Barbarian Britain'), made up of a more or less neutral region then Caledonia, the mountainous home of the Picts. Almost two millennia later, much of this nomenclature and some of its implications still survive.

The figure of Britannia with her helmet and shield dates from Roman times, but as a symbol was more or less forgotten until 1665, when Charles II put her on a coin to symbolize the unity of his kingdoms. As word and symbol, this Britannia has connotations linked with the vision of a God-favoured island: Shakespeare's 'sceptr'd isle . . . the envy of less happier lands' (*Richard II*, 1595). In 1735, William Somerville addressed the same thought with: 'Hail, happy Britain! highly favoured isle, and Heaven's peculiar care!' The supreme panegyric, however, was 'Rule Britannia', a song formulated for the United Kingdom by the Scottish poet James Thomson in 1740. Its first stanza runs:

> When Britain first, at heaven's command,
> Arose from out the azure main,
> This was the charter of the land,
> And guardian angels sung the strain:
> 'Rule Britannia, rule the waves;
> Britons never shall be slaves.'

British English, British Empire

The phrase *British English* is not straightforward. In principle, it means 'the English language as used in Britain', but in practice it may not. It contrasts with names for kinds of English used elsewhere, and especially with *American English*, which means 'English as used in America' (where *America* is the United States alone). For many people, especially in England, *British English* is tautological, and in the UK the term is not much used. Thus, the language-teaching company Linguaphone for years distinguished, in advertising its courses, between 'English' on the one hand and 'American English' on the other (in a list along with 'French', 'German', 'Spanish', etc.). The phrase *British English* has, however, a monolithic quality, as if it offers a single clear-cut variety as a fact of life (alongside providing a brand name for language-teaching purposes). It shares, however, all the ambiguities and tensions in the word *British*, and as a result can be used and interpreted in two ways, more broadly or more narrowly, within a range of blurring and ambiguity:

❶ The broader use and interpretation

The English language as used in the entirety of Great Britain (England, Scotland, and Wales) or of the United Kingdom of Great Britain and Northern Ireland, depending on the sense of *British* intended. Here, the term (unless qualified) covers *all* varieties of the language—standard and non-standard, formal and informal, at all times, in all regions, at all social levels. It is unlikely, however, to cover *Lowland* and *Ulster Scots*, which in this context are usually taken, explicitly or implicitly, to be distinct (whether valued or disparaged, whether viewed as a language or a dialect). In this interpretation, British English is a heterogeneous range of accents and dialects which includes standard varieties as used in the educational systems of England and Wales, Scotland, and Northern Ireland.

❷ The narrower use and interpretation

The form of Standard English used in Britain, or in England, or in south-east England: traditionally the medium of the upper and (especially professional) middle class, and by and large of education. The term may be expanded into the more or less synonymous forms *British Standard English* and *Standard British English*. Although not limited to one accent (most notably in recent decades), it has been associated since at least the late 19th century with the accent that, since the 1920s, has been called *Received Pronunciation* (*RP*), and with the phrases *the Queen's English*, *the King's English*, *Oxford English*, and *BBC English*. Most notably, when the term 'British English' refers to a model of English taught to foreigners, it is an idealization based on south-eastern middle-class usage as presented in dictionaries and other materials prepared for foreign learners, notably in editions since 1917 of Daniel Jones's *English Pronouncing Dictionary*.

The naming of the kinds of English used in the UK and in those parts of the English-speaking world influenced by them (mainly in the Commonwealth) has been affected by tensions and controversies that relate to region, class, and accuracy of description, much as follows:

❶ Region

There are different perspectives and preferences in different parts of Britain. These include strong objections on the part of the non-English to being categorized as English. While they object to this on grounds of ethnic reality, they also object to occasions when English people, especially from the south-east, treat the use of English by others as amusing, quaint, or inferior (a tradition that goes back for centuries). The Scots in particular often argue that they experience the worst of both worlds: they are called English when they are not English while their use of English is dismissed as not English and their use of Scots is dismissed as just a dialect, and an uncouth one at that. There are also powerful tensions within England, most notably between North and South, in which *Northern English* is often seen as secondary to *Southern English*, principally because the north has no historical educated spoken standard to weigh against the south's RP.

❷ Class

Issues of class have long been significant in Britain, often mixed with regional, ethnic, and linguistic issues. Many working-class people regard the standard language and RP as beyond their reach, as upper- and middle-class impositions, and/or as not worth adopting anyway. Standard usage of any kind is also often seen as élitist and filled with intimidating 'big words' (lexical material from Latin and Greek). RP and near-RP accents, despite or because of their prestige, are perceived as *posh*, *hoity-toity*, *put on*, or *toffee-nosed* (that is, snobbish and affected).

❸ Precision in description

Issues relating to region and class become linguistic when their clarification depends on the preciseness or looseness of the terms being used to discuss them. The range of scholarly debate includes both defences of and objections to the presentation of the RP-linked variety of English as a unified and universal prestige form when in fact it is the spoken variety of only a small national minority: 2–3% of the population. The English sociolinguist Peter Trudgill has observed:

> **1984** My own preferred label for varieties of English from England is 'English English', by analogy with 'American English', 'Australian English', etc. . . . Note that, whatever label is used, we have been careful in this book to distinguish between the terms 'English English' and 'British English'. The latter is often used . . . , particularly, it seems, by Americans and writers on English as a foreign language, where it is really the former that is intended.
> – Introduction, *Language in the British Isles* (Cambridge University Press)

It is not, however, surprising that the term *English English* is not yet much used. To the English, it seems as tautological, silly, or clumsy as 'German German' (when compared with 'Swiss German') or 'French French' (in contrast with 'Quebec French'), although such repeat-forms occur and can be useful: compare 'Indian Indians', when people want to make it clear that they do not mean 'American Indians'. However, to many Irish, Scots, Welsh people, and indeed English people with similar perspectives (or hang-ups), some such term as 'English English' is necessary so that they can usefully talk about the key varieties of British English. Trudgill's term has gained increasing currency in recent years for this purpose, being more direct than its competitors 'Anglo-English' and 'English in England'. Equally, however, the terms *Scottish English*, *Irish English*, and *Welsh English* can often seem odd to all concerned, because such phrases are in other contexts contradictions in terms. The term *Irish English* can seem especially bizarre, because of the centuries-old connotations of whimsical illogic acquired by the word *Irish*, especially in England (as in *Irish joke*), and the discomfort among many Irish people at anything that links them too closely with England.

Language scholars in the (north-eastern) United States and (south-eastern) England, as members of groups with strong positions in the pecking order, have tended to find 'American English' and 'British English' convenient contrastive labels for their respective varieties and standards, without further qualification, and indeed the contrast often works well. However, in recent years, interest in, and efforts on behalf of, varieties of English overseas have made it difficult for these labels to be used as sweepingly and uncritically as in the past. It has also become increasingly difficult to resist such terms as *English English*, *Scottish English*, *Welsh English*, *Hawaiian English*, *Indian English*, and *Singaporean English* on the grounds that they are tautological, paradoxical, bizarre, or dubious. Since the 1980s, scholars, journalists, and others, through their regular use of such terms, along with the provision of evidence for the reality of what they represent, have made them largely uncontentious—even conventional—in 2002.

Many of the 'new Englishes' (a plural term that also became common in the 1980s) evolved over centuries, in many parts of the British Empire. The term *British Empire* has itself traditionally had two senses: Great Britain and its colonies together and the colonies collectively on their own. Although the Empire is now history, it cast a long social, political, cultural, and linguistic shadow, as indicated by the five following points:

❶ On-going dependencies

The UK continues to administer a number of small, scattered dependencies (no longer called colonies). These include Gibraltar in Europe, Bermuda in the North Atlantic, Anguilla and Montserrat in the Caribbean, and Saint Helena, Ascension Island, Tristan da Cunha, and the Falkland Islands in the South Atlantic. Each has its own distinctive language history.

❷ The monarch as head of state

The British monarch remains head of state in many post-imperial nations, including Australia, Canada, New Zealand, and several Caribbean countries, and is symbolic head of the Commonwealth of Nations, an association of post-imperial states that, with the recent accession of Mozambique (a former Portuguese dependency in Africa), has in principle and practice opened the club doors to other territories.

❸ Quasi-imperial honours

In the UK, honours for distinguished service to the nation are named and bestowed as if the sun never set, as with the *MBE* and *OBE* (*Member* and *Order of the British Empire* respectively).

❹ Separatist movements

Irish nationalists argue that the British 'province' of Northern Ireland is a continuing manifestation of empire, while Scottish and Welsh nationalists hold that the British state has served, and continues to serve, the quasi-imperial ends of England in Scotland and Wales.

❺ Post-imperial implications and consequences

In various parts of the world, consequences and associations of empire continue to work themselves out, as for example the role of the Royal Navy and the British Army alongside (but distinct from) UN peace-keeping forces in protecting lives and helping restore order in 2000–1 in the 'failed state' of Sierra Leone, a former British colony.

Whatever the past and present realities, the Empire was the primary channel through which English came to be used across continents and oceans. Historians have written of a first empire based on commerce, profit, ports, and trading posts in the 17th century, followed by a second empire after the mid-18th, when vast overseas territories were acquired. Together, these phases spanned some four centuries. Whenever, however, and wherever the Empire was acquired, after the Second World War (under pressure from the United States, the United Nations, indigenous nationalism, and centrist and left-wing opinion in the UK itself), its dissolution was swift, from 1947 to 1970. This may well be the greatest and swiftest shedding of territorial control in history, by an imperial power weakened in war and beset with tensions between colonial-commercial practices and liberal-democratic ideals.

The heyday of empire was c.1890–1920, when 'the sun never set on the British Empire', which covered one-fifth of the world's land mass. Much was made of a duty to educate non-white subjects, characterized by the English writer Rudyard Kipling as 'new-caught, sullen peoples,/Half-devil and half-child' (in his poem *The White Man's Burden*, written in support of the Americans taking over the Philippines from the Spanish in 1898). But the key motivations for empire were economic, commercial, industrial, and political, and the gaining of overseas possessions was often haphazard, sometimes almost absent-minded, tinged with evangelism and leavened by humanitarianism, as with the abolition of slavery within the Empire in 1833. Colonialism, capitalism, and paternalism united a missionary zeal, as in Africa, with grim official expediency, as in sending convicts to Australia. Out of that unlikely start a loyal and useful colony was expected to emerge—and it did exactly that.

Within the empire, the British maintained class and regional distinctions among themselves and racial and cultural distinctions in managing other 'races'. Traders and plantation and mine owners dealt in such commodities as tobacco, sugar, minerals, and (before 1833) human beings, much as their rivals did in the other Atlantic European empires. In effect, however, there were at least four gradations in the territories of the empire:

❶ The white settler colonies

Such as Canada and Australia (regardless of any minimal indigenous populations), which always had a considerable freedom within the Empire, and latterly had 'dominion' status.

➋ The non-white colonial territories

Such as India, Jamaica, and Nigeria, which were not colonies in a technical sense but administered areas where the British did not usually settle or constitute a significant part of the population after independence.

➌ The 'mixed' colonies

Such as South Africa and the Rhodesias, territories with large indigenous populations in which the British and other Europeans did settle, where the aim by and large was similar or identical to dominion status.

➍ The protectorates etc.

A diffuse 'sphere of influence' with a range of protectorate treaties, mandates, and other arrangements, as in Egypt, Palestine, the Gulf, southern Iran, and Sarawak.

In all such locations, English was used in at least four ways: as a mother tongue; as a major second or shared language, for various purposes; as a lingua franca (often mixed with one or more other languages); and as a pidgin/creole.

In the meantime, in the British Isles, English had by the beginning of the 19th century largely supplanted the Celtic languages, which came to be regarded (when thought of at all beyond their immediate limits) as part of a geographical and psychological 'Celtic Fringe'. The situation of these languages can be seen as the first of many subsequent shrinkages and shifts prompted by the central position of English, especially in education and employment. The indigenous languages in Canada, the Aboriginal languages in Australia, and Maori in New Zealand all have 'Celtic-Fringe' aspects.

The same casual early mixing of English with Gaelic and Welsh proceeded strongly in other parts of the world, engendering hybrid vernaculars in Africa, the Caribbean, Asia, Australasia, and Oceania. English has been a challenge even to such large languages as Bengali, Hindi, Tamil, and Urdu in the Indian subcontinent, and Swahili, Xhosa, Yoruba, and Zulu in Africa, stirring them variously into a Western-style modernity that involves officialization, standardization, use in formal schooling, the creation of newspapers, and radio and television services. The growth and influence of English can be described in terms of the five following élite groupings that can also be represented as circles within circles:

➊ In the regional British heartland

A prestigious core that emerged in the 18th–19th centuries among royalty and the upper classes of London, Oxford, Cambridge, and the Home Counties, and in the 1920s in the BBC: a core that extended to include such upper imperial levels as royalty and nobility (dukes, rajahs, emirs, and chiefs, etc.), higher-level administrators and civil servants (élite British and other), and from the 1930s the British Council, which in the later decades of the 20th century evolved into a social and cultural organization with a more egalitarian ethos.

➋ In the 'mother country'

Arising at much the same time, a supporting élite of middle-class people holding significant positions in non-Oxbridge, non-Home Counties England, and in Scotland, Ireland, and Wales.

❸ In the 'daughter' territories (the dominions, etc.)

An established circle of prominent people in the 'white dominions' of Australia, Canada, New Zealand, to some extent in South Africa, and for a time Kenya and the Rhodesias, and even the United States, a self-amputated extension of empire never quite disowned, and always a key area for financial investment.

❹ In the non-white colonies

A circle of individuals and groups in the various territories and protectorates, both large (as with India and Nigeria) and small (as with Fiji and Hong Kong) whose personal and family interests were identical or similar to those of the managers of Empire.

❺ On the rim

Individuals in a range of other territories in which Britain has had interests, such as Arab territories in the Gulf, the Palestine Mandate, and the Anglo-Egyptian Sudan, as well as in Persia/Iran, which at one point was divided into unofficial spheres of Russian influence in the north and British influence in the south. All such territories are now autonomous states, each with its own legacy of complex attitudes towards, and links with, the British.

The linguistic situation of such an empire was uncannily previewed in 1599 (especially as regards North America) by the Elizabethan man of letters Samuel Daniel, in a poem quoted by several recent writers interested in the spread of English:

> **1599** And who in time knowes whither we may vent
> The treasure of our tongue, to what strange shores
> This gaine of our best glorie shal be sent.
> T'inrich vnknowing Nations with our stores?
> What worlds in th'yet vnformed Occident
> May come refin'd with th'accents that are ours?
> – in *Musophilus, or a generall defence of learning*

The public schools, RP, and the BBC

The major private residential schools of England, and to a lesser extent Scotland and Ireland, have been known since at least the 16th century as 'public schools', the most prominent of which are Eton, Winchester, Westminster, Harrow, Rugby, Charterhouse, and Shrewsbury ('the Seven Public Schools'). The markedly uniform variety of speech that developed there in the later 19th century has been referred to as a 'public school accent' (often augmented by distinctive 'public school slang', which has tended to vary from school to school).

Originally, a public school was also a 'grammar school', founded or endowed for the use and benefit of the public, and often associated with the Church of England, and to a less extent with the Roman Catholic Church and other denominations. Although this usage once contrasted with the term 'private school' (meaning a school maintained by a proprietor strictly as a business), the term has since the later 19th century been applied especially to old endowed grammar schools that developed into large, fee-paying boarding schools which draw pupils from the UK and abroad. Traditionally, young men were prepared for the universities (pre-eminently in the past Oxford and Cambridge) and public service, including both the civil service and officerhood in the armed forces. Although this is still often the case, in recent years it has become less of a determining feature, and girls in their public schools have a much wider spread of opportunities. The term *public school* in England is quite distinct from its American use, which is equivalent to the general British term *state school*.

Separately, from the early 19th century at least, the term 'received pronunciation' (typically without initial capital letters) was used to mean a form of speech regarded by arbiters of usage as correct or proper, as in 'the theoretically received pronunciation of literary English' (A. J. Ellis, *On Early English Pronunciation*, vol. 1, 1869) and 'Edinburgh and Dublin have their received pronunciations' (Simeon Potter, in *Changing English*, 1969). In the early 20th century, several names were used for the avowed 'best' pronunciation for English, including 'Received Standard English' and 'Received Standard' by Henry Cecil Wyld, who also however used the phrase 'Public School English' for the same thing and notably commended the spoken style of British Army officers. He noted:

> **1914** It is proposed [here] to use the term *Received Standard* for that form which all would probably agree in considering the best, that form which has the widest currency and is heard with practically no variation among speakers of the better class all over the country. This type might be called Public School English. It is proposed to call the vulgar English of the Towns, and the English of the Villager who has abandoned his native Regional Dialect *Modified Standard*. That is, it is Standard English, modified, altered, differentiated, by various influences, regional and social. Modified Standard differs from class to class, and from locality to locality; it has no uniformity, and no single form of it is heard outside a particular class or a particular area.
>
> – *A Short History of English*, Murray,

The phonetician Daniel Jones used the term *Public School Pronunciation* (or *PSP* for short) prior to adopting *Received Pronunciation* (with initial capitals) in the mid-1920s, when he and Wyld served together as language advisers for the newly created British Broadcasting Corporation. Since its initial description as PSP by Jones in his classic *English Pronouncing Dictionary* (*EPD*), published by Dent in 1917, this PSP or RP has probably been the most described and discussed accent on earth, and a target for more learners than in all prior human history.

The terms *Received Pronunciation* and *RP* have never been widely known outside the circle of English-language scholars, teachers of English as a foreign or second language, and their more advanced students. More commonly, it has long been variously known as *the King's/Queen's English*, *BBC English*, *Oxford English*, and *Public School English*. Members of the middle class have often called it a BBC or public school accent, members of the working class formerly commonly described it as 'talking proper' or 'talking posh', and for many people of all classes in the UK in the 20th century the term 'well-spoken' could be applied to anyone for whom it was natural. The form which phoneticians call 'advanced RP' relates to a small royal and upper-class minority, and to many ears it has an artificial or over-done quality. Artificial or over-done RP accents—notably as used by people judged as 'not from the top drawer'—have tended to be labelled *la-di-dah* ('talking very la-di-dah') by the working class, or as 'put on' or, worse still, as *a cut-glass accent*—not real crystal at all.

RP has often been described as—or assumed without discussion to be—simply the best pronunciation for British (or indeed *any*) English. It has therefore been widely regarded and described as 'the gold standard' of English speech, and even if learners never quite managed to strike gold the effort would be salutary. Although North Americans have not usually subscribed to this view, many admire RP as the representative accent of educated or refined Britain, and indeed of 'class' (in the qualitative if not also in the social sense); others however associate it with the theatre and, in men, with effeminacy and homosexuality. Many people in England, Scotland, Wales, and Ireland associate it with snobbery and unearned privilege (while at the same time they may be, or certainly may in past decades have been, rather in awe of it).

The high-water mark for RP was in the period around and including the two world wars. Its possession was, among other things, a criterion for selecting young men as officers during the First World War, and throughout much of the 20th century was the favoured accent for recruits to the Foreign Office and other services representing the United Kingdom, including for many years the British Council. Newcomers to the British social élite have tended to ensure that their children acquired RP by sending them to 'the right schools' or, especially in the past in the case of girls, to elocution lessons. In such schools, the accent has never been overtly taught, but indirectly promoted, including through peer pressure that has included mockery and disapproval of any other style of speech.

RP has been the voice of national announcers and presenters on the BBC since it was founded in the 1920s, but from the 1970s to the time of writing there has been a move towards RP-influenced regional accents among announcers and presenters on all national radio services and TV channels, and towards unadapted regional accents among presenters on local and broadly popular (especially commercial) radio channels. In addition, there has always been a tendency for sports comment-ators, weather forecasters, and commentators on farming and gardens to be more 'down market' in their styles on radio. This tendency was extended to television and currently appears to be moving into most areas of broadcasting.

ELT pronounced elite: The phonemes of Received Pronunciation

Phonemic symbol	Letters	As in:
ɪ	i, y	*kit, bid, hymn, intend, basic*
e	e	*dress, bed*
æ	*a*	*trap, bad*
ɒ	o, a	*lot, odd, wash*
ʌ	u, o	*strut, bud, love*
ʊ	oo, u	*foot, good, put*
iː	ee, ea, i	*fleece, sea, machine*
eɪ	ay, ea, a-e	*day, steak, face*
aɪ	i, igh, i-e, y	*high, price, try*
ɔɪ	oi, oy	choice, boy
uː	oo, u, ue, wo	*too, blue, goose, two*
əʊ	*schwa/u*	goat, show, no
aʊ	au	mouth, now
ɪə	i/schwa	near, here, serious
eə	e/schwa	square, fair, various
ɑː	a (long)	start, father
ɔː	aw	thought, law, north, war
ʊə	oo/schwa	cure, poor, jury
ɜː		nurse, stir
i		happy, radiation, glorious
ə		the first vowel of *about* and the last vowel of *comma*

The description of RP in A. C. Gimson's *An Introduction to the Pronunciation of English* (Edward Arnold, 3rd edn, 1980; 4th edn, 1990, revised after his death by Susan Ramsaran) is widely regarded as standard. His standard set of RP phonemic symbols has often been used as a reference norm for the description of other varieties of English, with very minor presentational differences in the styles of such publishers of English language teaching courses and dictionaries as Oxford and Longman. A comparison between RP and 'GenAm' (General American) is a key element of John C. Wells's *Longman Pronunciation Dictionary* (1990). RP differs little from other accents of English in the pronunciation of its consonants, and is a non-rhotic accent in which the so-called linking or intrusive *r* is present—often widely commented on, usually negatively, in relation to such phrases as *law(r) and order* (often satirized as the name of a young woman, *Laura Norder*). This attribute is not however conventionally taught as part of the RP pronunciation model for ELT students worldwide. The vowels and diphthongs of RP are its most complex aspect.

Although RP continues to be socially pre-eminent in Britain, and especially England, it has in recent years become less pervasive and monolithic, both phonetically and socially. Phoneticians recognize several varieties, including a generation gap. In his introduction to the 14th edition of the *EPD* (1977), Gimson noted of RP that its 'regional base remains valid and it continues to have wide intelligibility throughout Britain . . . [but there] has been a certain dilution of the original concept of RP, a number of local variants formerly excluded by the definition having now to be admitted as of common and acceptable usage. Such an extended scope of usage is difficult to define.' He retained the name, however, because of its 'currency in books on present-day English', but even so the mid-20th-century observations of the British phonetician David Abercrombie still largely apply:

> **1951** This R.P. stands in strong contrast to all the other ways
> of pronouncing Standard English put together. In fact, English
> people [i.e. people in England] are divided, by the way they talk,
> into three groups; first, R.P. speakers of Standard English—those
> [regarded as being] without an accent; second, non-R.P. speakers
> of Standard English—those with an accent; and third, dialect
> speakers. I believe this to be a situation which is not paralleled
> in any other country anywhere.
>
> – 'R.P. and Local Accent', a presentation first given in 1951, and published in *Studies in
> Linguistics and Phonetics* (Oxford University Press, 1965) 12

Because most British teachers of English as a foreign or second language have in the past had an RP accent or an accent (more or less) convincingly modified towards it, untravelled overseas learners have tended to assume that it has in fact been (as so often implied) the majority accent of British English—or at least of *educated* British English. RP retains into the 21st century its position as the preferred (or at least avowed) target for Commonwealth learners, although in countries such as India and Singapore local pronunciations with a degree of prestige have emerged and may have begun to offer models that can operate alongside kinds of RP, or even replace them. In teaching English as a foreign or second language (EFL, ESL), RP increasingly competes with General American (GA). It continues to be strongly buttressed by a decades-old methodological and financial investment in RP by British ELT publishers, especially in the highly profitable area of learners' dictionaries.

RP therefore continues as a matter of course to be selected or offered worldwide as the reference norm for any discussion of spoken British English (and often of other varieties of English), as well as for such activities as automatic speech synthesis. However, since most British people do not speak RP, know RP as a coherent system, or even know what 'RP' means (or, if told, know what the phrase 'Received Pronunciation' signifies), pedagogical statements about British English that are centred on RP can be incomplete—and often misleading. It is not easy, for example, to tell students about the wide use of the glottal stop in relation to the consonants *p*, *t*, and *k* in all kinds of British English at all social levels when the glottal stop has no place in the standard account of RP consonants.

Many British people dislike (yet may be in reluctant awe of) Received Pronunciation. For them, it is a mark of privilege and (especially among the Scots, Northern Irish, Welsh, and at times the Northern English) of domination by the (especially south-eastern) upper- and middle-class English. RP has, however, had a strong gravitational pull throughout the UK and indeed the Irish Republic, with the result that many middle-class people in England and elsewhere speak with accents adapted towards it: accents known nowadays among British phoneticians as both *modified regional accents* and *modified RP*. Comparable adapted accents in Australia, New Zealand, South Africa, and elsewhere are also sometimes referred to, following the British phonetician John Wells, as *near-RP*.

Received Pronunciation has always been a minority class-related accent, unlikely ever to have been spoken by more than 3% of the UK population. Phoneticians and linguists have often described it as 'regionless' (in that it is not possible to tell which part of the UK an RP speaker comes from), but it is never described as 'classless', because it identifies the speaker as (upper) middle class or upper class, and it has its epicentre in the Home Counties. In the most recent edition of Jones's *EPD*, the 15th, edited by Peter Roach and James Hartman and published by Cambridge University Press, the authors state that the long-established name has lost much of its meaning—and in its place they use another of its names that Wyld and Jones would have been unlikely to object to: *BBC English*. In the introduction, they note:

> **1997** For this edition a more broadly-based and accessible model
> accent for British English is represented, and pronunciations for
> one broadly-conceived accent of American English have been
> added. The time has come to abandon the archaic name *Received
> Pronunciation*. The model used for British English is what is
> referred to as *BBC English*: this is the pronunciation of
> professional speakers employed by the BBC as newsreaders on
> BBC1 and BBC2 television, the World Service and BBC Radio 3
> and 4, as well as many commercial broadcasting organisations
> such as ITN. Of course, one finds differences among such
> speakers, but there is still a reasonable consensus on
> pronunciation in this group of professionals, and their speech
> does not carry for most people the connotations of high social
> class and privilege that PSP and RP have done in the past.
> – *English Pronouncing Dictionary*, 15th edn, Cambridge University Press.

Although RP (or BBC English) continues to evolve, and incremental changes occur in the idealized model in its wake, the system offered to foreign learners has yet to take account of significant changes in the last quarter century, such as an increased use of glottal stops among the younger generation in such expressions as *a little bit of luck*. However, although such glottalization is unlikely to be consciously taught to them, learners with a good ear will note it and probably adopt it, to fit in or because it is part of the reality around them.

There is currently no obvious alternative to an up-dating of RP as the model for foreign learners of the British brand of the world's lingua franca. In all likelihood, a model of RP for foreign learners (modified in a sense very different from Wyld's 'Modified Standard' 80 years ago) will continue to evolve, in which the teaching of a rhythm of strong and weak syllables will probably feature more strongly than the achievement of narrowly precise vowel sounds. And students, as by and large they have generally done, will acquire an English that retains in varying degrees the phonological and other features of their own languages.

England

1986 Constitutionally, England does not exist. It is not mentioned in the title of the sovereign who rules 'the United Kingdom of Great Britain and Northern Ireland and other Realms and Territories'. Scotland, Wales, and Northern Ireland have certain governmental institutions of their own, but England . . . needs no special mention. Holding more than four-fifths of the population, . . . England's dominance of the United Kingdom is beyond question.

– 'England', *The Encyclopaedia Britannica*, vol. 4 (Chicago: Micropaedia)

2000 We began this chapter by referring to the role that English has played in killing off other languages with which it has shared these islands. It is ironic to have to end with a discussion of the efforts made to rescue from oblivion the remnants of the dialects of English itself before they too decline to the point of extinction.

– Glanville Price, 'English', in Price (ed.), *Languages in Britain and Ireland* (Oxford: Blackwell), 156

For many older people in England, expressions such as *English English* and even *British English* (as used in contrast with *American English*, *New Zealand English*, and so forth) are at best unnecessary and at worst absurd. For them, the English language in its place of origin and primary development needs no modifiers. It is simply—pre-eminently—the language of their country, just as French is the language of France and German of Germany. For them, just as the French of Quebec or German in Switzerland is peripheral, so all varieties of English elsewhere are peripheral to the mother variety: no matter how many, no matter how powerful. Among younger people in England, however, a more relaxed and eclectic view predominates. They are generally comfortable with English beyond England, and many of them see England's English as simply one among many kinds of English.

Yet the traditionalists have a point. The English of England was manifestly for centuries the trunk of the tree, and the usage of upper-class England was (from at least the 18th until the mid-20th century) the best English, by general acknowledgement (whether enthusiastic, detached, or grudging). As a consequence, there are difficulties in treating the English of England as just another national English. After all, traditionally, if other varieties are different, it is the standard usage of England that they have customarily been assessed as different *from*. In at least a historical sense, therefore—whatever nationhood, democracy, fairness, and even redress may require worldwide—a case can be made that the English of England (warts and worries and all) is 'first among equals'.

Standard, dialect, and compromise

Since the extinction of Anglo-French in the late Middle Ages and the weakening of Latin after the Reformation, English in England has had no competition. There have, however, been some assumptions regarding the time when it was at its best.

Notably, in the 18th century, the leaders of society in the 'Augustan' reign of Queen Anne (1702–14) were considered to have spoken and written the best English. Unlike the Church of England, however, their language was never officially 'established', although the institutions with which 'the best English' has long been informally but firmly associated have all had impeccable Establishment credentials:

1 Monarchy: *the Queen's/King's English*

2 A prestigious university: *Oxford English*

3 Private fee-paying schools favoured by the rich and influential: *Public School English*

4 Drawing rooms and the rites of the Church of England: *Received Pronunciation* ('Is Lady Brackenbank receiving today?'—'receiving the Communion wafer on the tongue')

5 The voice of the nation (England or Britain): *BBC English*, especially when carried abroad by the World Service

This kind of unofficial official status makes the Standard English of England different from the French of France or Spanish-cum-Castilian in Spain, and indeed from English in India or South Africa, in each of which its role is clearly delineated by the state. But it is not different from English at the federal level in the United States, where it also has no constitutional status yet is also the sole language of power.

Despite, or perhaps because of, the unestablished nature of Standard English (in England and the UK at large), several organizations have been concerned with—and about—its welfare in the 20th century. The Simplified Spelling Society was founded in 1908 to seek reforms in orthography, while both the Society for Pure English (1913, defunct by mid-century) and the Queen's English Society (1972–) have taken up arms against a sea of perceived deficiencies, from inadequate language instruction in schools to deplorable media usage. In addition, the semi-commercial and media-savvy Plain English Campaign (PEC: 1974–) is part of a growing international movement for greater simplicity and clarity in language, especially in governmental, commercial, and contractual statements, and in labels for medicines and health-and-safety products. Of these organizations, the 'plain language' movement has been the most popular (in both senses of the word) and effective, as also in Australia, Canada, and the United States.

Considerable confusion exists in England—and elsewhere—regarding the phrases *Standard English* and *Received Pronunciation* (*RP*). Currently, most scholars and teachers worldwide define Standard English largely in terms of grammar and vocabulary. Many people in England, however, and many Anglophiles elsewhere, have assumed for at least a century that Standard English includes—even depends on—the on-going use of RP. For them, spoken Standard English and RP are one and the same; even if many users of something like the standard language do not have RP accents, it would (the traditionalists consider) be better if they did. Historically, however, standardness in England as elsewhere has primarily been identified through (and usually been discussed in terms of) writing and print, although people do not always notice that this is so. Standard English logically either has many accents (because educated people have many accents) or no accent (because no single accent, however broadly defined, covers all the modes of educated speech). But, notoriously, views on language are not always amenable to logic and reality.

Stereotyping and discrimination in terms of accent have a long history. By the 16th century, the London élite had begun to regard regional and lower-class accents as comic, quaint, inadequate, and *vulgar* (initially and etymologically, 'of the people', ultimately simply 'rude and crude'). But such disdained accents were not, then or later, absolute bars to success. The seaman, courtier, and writer Sir Walter Raleigh spoke with a Devon accent, Shakespeare had a Warwickshire accent, and since those days accentual outsiders have often made it to the metropolitan heights, as with Samuel Johnson in the 18th century, with his Staffordshire accent. But the need to list problems indicates that an accentual élite has long been a feature of life in England and territories pervasively influenced by England.

It was not, however, until the 19th century that an upper-class kind of accent was explicitly sought and implicitly offered *en masse* in fee-paying schools to the offspring of out-lying gentry and the *nouveau riche*. In addition, local councils decided late in the same century that the children in their schools should also be rendered as 'well spoken' as possible.

There has also, in the last hundred years or so, been a steady reduction in England of the social distance among accents and dialects (as elsewhere in the traditional English-speaking world). This is largely a consequence of urbanization, universal education, and an expansion of the media, whose writers, news presenters, continuity people, and actors have moved closer to general schooled usage or have in fact never used anything else. As a result, at the beginning of the 21st century, regional ('dialect') pronunciation, grammar, and vocabulary are far less marked and diverse among people younger than 50 and certainly a hundred years ago. The phonetician John C. Wells put it as follows three decades ago:

> **1970** [T]he English of most English (and English-speaking Welsh)
> people is neither RP Standard English nor a rural dialect. The vast
> mass of urban working-class and lower-middle-class speakers use
> a pronunciation nearer to RP, and lexical and grammatical forms
> much nearer to Standard English, than the archaic rural dialects
> recorded by the dialectologists.
> – 'Local accents in England and Wales', *Journal of Linguistics*, 6, 231

Although this is the case, diversity remains, along with a tug between the local and the national as centred in middle-class London. In and around such large cities as London itself, Birmingham, Manchester, and Newcastle speech-forms that once varied over short distances have tended to merge into wider local varieties attracting wider local loyalties, again prompting and being strengthened by local voices on both local and national radio and TV. Pressures from the educational system and the media have also tended to make more widely intelligible some of the highly distinctive localisms at the same time as they have made people aware of, and more accepting towards, diversity (at home and abroad, and notably from non-English speakers of English). This global/local development has been strengthened by the long-term nationwide success of region-based TV drama, notably *Coronation Street* and *East-Enders*, as well as TV series from the United States, Scotland, Ireland, Wales, and Australia.

An English city or town and its hinterland nowadays contains a range of spoken usage determined by geographical, social, educational, and generational factors rather than a stark contrast between the 'refined' usage of land-owners and professionals on the one side and the unrefined 'dialect' of farm and factory workers on the other. In addition, immigration from many parts of the world has brought in new varieties and fostered novel blends, the second generation usually acquiring a local accent while their parents keep the speech style of their homelands (African, Caribbean, Asian, or other), whether it is another language or another English, or both.

Notably, then, many long-established regional vernaculars in England have evolved while retaining and consolidating their distinctive natures and styles. This state of affairs would have surprised the dialectologists of the late 19th and earlier 20th centuries, who worked as fast as possible on their projects because they regarded time as rapidly running out. Regional usages may since then have lost some of their diversity, but (despite compromises) the dream of a uniform England-wide standard speech based on RP is as far off as ever it was.

Down South and Up North

A classic division within England is *North* and *South*, often more emphatically expressed as *Down South* and *Up North*. In terms of the island as a whole, the abiding cleavage is between England 'south of the border' and Scotland 'north of the border', but within England itself is a division, less clearly delineated but just as powerful, between *the North of England* and *the South of England*, to which such other areas as *the Home Counties* (around London), *the Midlands*, *East Anglia*, and *the West Country* are subordinated. However, just where 'the North' begins is by no means clear. The border with Wales, though dramatic, has less psychological force than the border with Scotland, which in an important sense lies to the north of North (whereas for Scots 'down south' simply means England—all of it). The division within England is in its way just as archetypal as with Scotland and Wales: if there have been two Englands in terms of social class there are also two Englands in terms of geography. As a leading contemporary British language scholar has put it:

> **2000** London complicates the polarity of North and South: as the centre of 'power', of government, monarchy and cultural prestige located in the South, it leads to a focus of *austrocentrism*, a discrimination in favour of the South of England and Britain. London acts as the deictic anchorage, the point of reference (the *origo*), by which everything else is judged inferior and insignificant. The Midlands may be the geographical centre of England, but they are not the *perceived* centre of things. Susie Blake on the *Victoria Wood Show* [on television] in the 1980s summed up this austrocentrism, this condescension, in her role as a London television announcer [presumably about to acknowledge a flaw in service]: 'I should like to apologise to viewers in the North. It must be really awful for you.'
> – Katie Wales, 'North and South: An English Linguistic Divide?', in *English Today*, 16:1, January, 4

Scholars traditionally divide the dialects of English that grew up in medieval Britain into four regions:

1 **Northern**
   Spoken both south and north of the English/Scottish border

2 **Midland**
   Extending west to the Welsh border (West Midland) and east to East Anglia and the London area (East Midland)

3 **Southern**
   Extending west to Cornwall

4 **Kentish**
   Confined to the extreme south-east

At the present time, the old Northern, Southern, and West Midland categories still largely hold true, but East Anglia is now generally distinguished from a South East that includes London and the Home Counties (with Kent) and a South West (or West Country) that runs roughly from Dorset to Cornwall. The five regional areas to be discussed here are therefore: the South East (London and the Home Counties); the South West; the Midlands; East Anglia; and Northern.

When William Caxton set up his printing press in London in 1476, a powerful boost was given to the already highly influential manuscript tradition of the capital, although it took several centuries for print style to settle down and for spelling to become more or less standard. As a shared centralized style for script and type began to evolve, the use of manuscript writing associated with non-London speech began to decline, leaving a rather weak tradition of dialect writing and publishing today. However, before the standardization of text became complete, ample evidence was left (in letters, manuscripts, public comment, and representations of dialect in novels) that local speech continued to thrive. It was typical well into the 18th century among members of the aristocracy, gentry, and upper middle classes who lived at a distance from London and the Home Counties. Although matters in due course changed for these groups, local vernaculars have continued to the present day among industrialists, politicians, and public figures from lower middle- and working-class backgrounds: often pugnaciously so, especially among left-wing political activists.

Since the 18th century, novelists have sought to represent local usage in dialogue, most notably Thomas Hardy. Scholarly interest in the forms of non-standard English in England emerged in the early 17th century, when Alexander Gil in his *Polychronicon* (1619) initiated a tradition of comparing local dialect and educated usage. However, although scholars were increasingly aware of historical ties across all forms of English, the term *dialect* became increasingly identified with lower social positions and lack of education, and with the disdain felt by the socially and educationally more elevated, making a dispassionate use of the term virtually impossible from the 19th century onward (although strenuous efforts have been made to keep the term going academically).

The English Dialect Society (1873–96) published commentaries as part of its work for a dictionary compiled by its secretary Joseph Wright at the University of Oxford, and duly published by the University Press in six volumes (1898–1905) as the *English Dialect Dictionary*. This epic project covered the entire British Isles over a period of two centuries, but did not have much impact on social and educational attitudes. Instead, a year later, in 1906, Oxford published *The King's English*, a usage book compiled by the brothers Henry W. and Francis G. Fowler—still in print, unrevised, in 2002, almost a century later: a living testament to an abiding widespread wish for guidance in the use of 'proper' English.

London's languages

> **1995** One of my favourite stories concerns the American woman of means who took a whirlwind tour of 14 European countries in as many days. Her method of survival was to walk into a store where she wished to trade and shout loudly, 'Does anyone here speak English?' This seemed sufficient until one day after attempting her ploy, a clerk sidled up to her discreetly and whispered, 'Madam, this is London!'
>
> – Christopher C. DeSantis, Translation Supervisor, The Church of Jesus Christ of Latter-day Saints, Salt Lake City, Utah, in Letters to the Editor, *Language International* 7.2

In its two thousand years of existence, London has experienced many languages: Celtic; the Latin of the Empire, the Catholic Church, and international scholarship; Old English; Anglo-French; Middle and Modern English; and at the present time languages from every corner of the world, many spoken by established communities of many thousands, as with Arabic, Cantonese, and Hindi-Urdu. Since 1993, the Languages of London Project has been researching the number of languages spoken by London schoolchildren. To date over 275 languages have been listed, enough to suggest that the languages currently used in London represent over 95% of the world's peoples. Work continues on mapping the location of groups, and researchers hope to produce in due course *The Languages of London Handbook*. Tim Connell, a professor at City University, and a prime mover in the project, notes:

> **1999** [This wealth of languages is] a point that has not been lost on organisations such as London First, who report that an increasing number of international firms give as a reason for re-locating to London the fact that they can recruit staff with any range of language skills, an increasing number of whom are bilingual in English and have UK university qualifications.
>
> – 'Language provision in an international environment: a case study of the City of London', a paper presented at the 11th ENCoDE Conference, Barcelona, July

This is the up side to multilingualism in London. The down side is learning difficulties among children in schools whose pupils may have thirty or more languages among them. *The Economist* has noted:

> **2000** Scrubby playing fields and prefabricated huts surround White Hart Lane school, in Haringey, North London. Building a community in a school whose pupils speak 55 different languages has not been easy. Of 1,200 pupils, one out of three come from asylum-seeking or refugee families. . . . At White Hart Lane, refugee children are taught English alongside their work on the national curriculum. The sooner such children are integrated into

mainstream school life, the better they do. At home, Bukurije
Dauti teaches her children to read and write Albanian. Lejla finds
this hard. 'My brothers have difficulty too, because, although we
speak Albanian at home, everything else is in English,' she says.

– unsigned, 'Learning difficulties, in 55 languages', 26 August 2000

London is a vast metropolitan area that for at least five centuries has had its high and
low kinds of English. It is currently home to four well-publicized varieties: *the
Queen's English*, *BBC English*, *Cockney*, and *Estuary English*. The key locations are
the West End, synonymous with RP, prestige, style, and money, and *the East End*,
identified with Cockney, counter-prestige, wry humour, and often poverty. Both the
West End and East End are north of the Thames; the vast reaches of South London
have tended to go under-reported.

Almost nothing is known of London's Romano-Celtic history, and the city had
no serious role in Anglo-Saxon culture until the reign of Edward the Confessor
(1042–66). However, after the Norman Conquest, in the year of Edward's death,
the fortunes of the city rose: its élite became speakers of Norman French, a French-
English hybrid emerged, and the more socially elevated variety of East Midland
usage, laced with French, provided the basis for a future standard language. The
poet Geoffrey Chaucer (1343?–1400), a Londoner, generally used an older and more
southern variety closer to Kentish, but was fully up-to-date in mixing English with
the Anglo-French and Latin of his time. In the following example (in which the
French is underlined) he mentions Southwark, a district on the south bank of the
Thames:

> In Southwerk at the <u>Tabard</u> as I lay
> Ready to wenden on my <u>pilgrimage</u>
> To Caunterbury with ful <u>devout corage</u>,
> At night was come in-to <u>hostelrye</u>
> Well nyne and twenty in a <u>companye</u>,
> Of sundry folk, by <u>aventure</u> y-falle
> In felaweship, and <u>pilgrims</u> were they alle.
>
> – from the prologue of *The Canterbury Tales*

Much later, in 1589, when French had long since ceased to be a living language of
royalty, George Puttenham in *The Arte of English Poesie* commended to his readers
'the vsual speach of the Court, and that of London and the shires lying about London
with lx [sixty] myles, and not much aboue'. At the same time, Shakespeare's use
of accents in his plays shows that Londoners were well aware of other kinds of
English, all of them outlandish. One is the 'stage southern' accent of Edgar in *King
Lear*' (an ancestor of Mummerset, below); others are the wild-and-woolly usages
of the Welsh captain Fluellen and the Scottish captain Jamy in *Henry V*. When
dialogue was written for plays or novels, a distinctive spelling often served to mark
speakers of dialect and low usage, while the established orthography was kept for
educated speakers and for the language of the story, a tradition that survives to the
present day.

In 1721 the hymnographer Isaac Watts, in his *Art of Reading and Writing English*,
dismissed the 'dialect or corrupt speech that obtains in the several counties of

England' and listed words which differed from 'their common and frequent pronunciation in the City of London'. He added however that 'there are some other
corruptions in the pronouncing of several words by many of the citizens themselves', citing *yourn* ('yours'), *squeedge* ('squeeze'), and *yerb* ('herb').

An increasingly common view of uneducated non-metropolitan speech as
corrupt draws for its imagery on discussions of manuscript errors: Latin *errores*
('wanderings' from the right path). Such slips were seen as a sad misrepresentation
of truth in a sinful world, from which even the inhabitants of the *capital* (at the very
'head' of the nation: Latin *caput*) could not escape. Samuel Pegge, in his *Anecdotes
of the English Language* (1803), noted words whose pronunciation 'is a little
deformed by the natives of London', including both the confusion of *v* and *w* (*wery
vell* 'very well') and 'an affected refinement' that pronounced *daughter* like 'daater'
and *sauce* like 'saace'. Below are five points that can usefully be made about London
usage, past and present:

❶ Diversity and hybridization

London usage has been diverse for centuries. It co-exists and hybridizes in many
mixed communities with scores of other varieties and languages, whose speakers
range from fully bilingual to just getting by in English.

❷ The local vernaculars

London's vernacular styles vary socially and geographically, and are not easily
distinguished and described. Although the term *Cockney* identifies a range of
demotic speech recently virtually institutionalized in the long-running and popular
BBC TV soap opera *EastEnders*, it is still primarily a vernacular of the working-
class East End. The term needs to be used with caution: some people are proud to
be Cockneys, some shun the term, and others do not care.

❸ Local diversity and hybridization within English

English-speakers in London who come from other parts of the UK or from the Irish
Republic may or may not be defensive about their usage. They may also think that
born-and-bred Londoners can be superior about language, although in their view
without justification. They will probably however adjust to local usage, unwittingly
assimilating until people back home point out how far they have succumbed.

❹ Global diversity and local hybridization within English

There are communities in London from every English-speaking territory in the
world. They may have lived long enough in an area to assimilate to some degree,
hybridizing between their own English and other kinds around them, and they too
may be sensitive about their usage.

❺ Global diversity and local hybridization across languages

There are established communities in and around London from every major and
many a minor language worldwide: *c.*350 in all. The UK capital is a key city of the
Arabic-speaking world and for the languages of the Indian subcontinent. The languages of all such communities interact in at least four ways: with the Englishes
of London; with Englishes brought to London; with hybrids developed by native
English-speaking incomers in London; and with hybrids among and within non-
native communities variously using English.

Thus, a younger member of the London Greek Cypriot community may speak Cypriot Greek at home and share a mosaic of English with friends 'down the pub', who could include: a native-born Londoner; someone from Manchester who has lived in London for years (and from a Manchester point of view has been Londonized but from a London point of view is a pure Mancunian); two incomers from Glasgow still so alien that some people do not think they speak English at all; a London Jamaican whose parents speak Patwa while he speaks to them in London Jamaican and to everybody else in 'General London'; a Hong Konger whose parents have a Chinese takeaway but who sounds local, and speaks a Cantonese that would worry the folks back in Choi Hung; and a New Zealand *au pair* just off the plane who's tired of being taken for an Australian.

Cockney

The term *cockney* dates from the 14th century, and has since at least 1600 been used (as both noun and adjective, with or without a capital *c*) to refer to working-class East-Enders and their speech. Despite being stigmatized as the usage of the gutter, Cockney has long been a defining feature of life in the capital, and lies at the core of a range of usage among some seven million people in the Greater London area.

In Langland's poem *Piers Plowman* (1362), the term *cokeneyes* refers to eggs that are small and misshapen, as if laid by a cock. Chaucer, in *The Canterbury Tales* (*c*.1386), uses *cokenay* in the sense of a mother's darling, but by the 16th century country people had extended the term to city-bred people ignorant of real life. By the 17th century, however, this disdain had narrowed to one city and widened to people of any age: the 'Bow-bell Cockney' (1600); 'our Cockney of London' (1611); 'A *Cockney* or *Cockny*, applied only to one borne within the sound of Bow-bell, that is, within the City of London' (1617); 'Cockneys (to whom all is Barbary beyond Brainford; and Christendome endeth at Greenwitch)' (Richard Whitlock, *Zootomia, or observations on the present manners of the English*, 1654). However, comments on Cockney usage date only from the 18th century. After setting out the faults in the English of the Irish, Scots, and Welsh, the elocutionist John Walker noted:

> **1791** There are dialects peculiar to Cornwall, Lancashire, Yorkshire, and every distant county in England; but as a consideration of these would lead to a detail too minute for the present occasion, I shall conclude these remarks with a few observations on the peculiarities of my countrymen, the Cockneys; who, as they are the models of pronunciation to the distant provinces, ought to be the more scrupulously correct.
> – from the preface to *A Critical Pronouncing Dictionary of the English Language*.

Walker lists four faults common among these pillars of metropolitan good usage:

❶ Odd plurals

Among people of 'the lowest order', the habit of pronouncing words like *fists* and *posts* as if there were a vowel between the *t* and the *s*: 'fistiz', 'postiz'.

❷ 'Wery vell'

Common to the lowest order, but not confined to it, 'the pronunciation of *v* for *w*, and more frequently of *w* for *v*' (vine and weal for 'wine and veal'): 'a blemish of the first magnitude'.

❸ A *wh*-problem

Failure to pronounce *h* after *w*, so that 'we do not find the least distinction between *while* and *wile*, *whet* and *wet*, *where* and *were*, &c'.

❹ An initial *h*-problem

'Sinking the *h* at the beginning of words where it ought to be sounded, and of sounding it, either where it is not seen, or where it ought to be sunk. Thus we not infrequently hear, especially among children, *heart* pronounced *art*, and *arm*, *harm*.' He also notes that words like *humour* are pronounced as if written '*yewmour*'.

Walker concludes: 'Thus I have endeavoured to correct some of the more glaring errors of my countrymen, who, with all their faults, are still upon the whole the best pronouncers of the English language.' In the 19th century, however, the term *Cockney* was limited to the lower orders, whose usage was disdained and could never serve as a model for anyone. By the time the Irish playwright George Bernard Shaw brought out his play *Pygmalion* in 1913, Cockney was generally regarded as debased ('gutter Cockney'), and Shaw's flower-girl Eliza Doolittle needed far more help from Henry Higgins than Walker thought his 'fellow countrymen' needed just over a century earlier.

Walker's list of faults makes strange reading now. His first two (*fistiz* for 'fists' and *vine and weal*) have entirely vanished, while his third is part of the general usage of England at large, including RP (which has the same *w*-sound in *while/wile*, *whales/Wales*). The omission of initial *h* ('dropping one's aitches') is also close to universal in the speech of the English, and teachers and others are more relaxed about it. RP however is an *h*-pronouncing accent, and the middle class traditionally would never dream of dropping an aitch.

The term *Cockney* today refers to a range of usage still centred on the East End of London, with fringe forms shading out into neighbouring areas that include the counties and towns around the city, notably among the young. The term loosely covers a diffused variety of working-class speech in south-eastern England, of which traditional Cockney is the best known (or most notorious) representative. It is the core of working-class London speech, especially north of the Thames, and is not usually applied to lower-middle or middle-class usage, in which however Cockney-like features can be heard. The parts of London most associated with Cockney are: Aldgate, Bethnal Green, Bow, Hackney, Limehouse, Mile End, Old Ford, Poplar, Shoreditch, Stepney, Wapping, and Whitechapel. Like many language varieties, it is most easily identified through its extreme forms, and like other stigmatized urban dialects, such as Brummie (Birmingham), Scouse (Liverpool), Glasgow, and New York, it is vigorous, influential, and generates its own counter-prestige. Its key features are:

Pronunciation

1 Cockney has an *f*-sound instead of an unvoiced *th*-sound, as in 'fiʔee fahzn' ('thirty thousand': with a glottal stop for the *t*), and a *v*-sound instead of a

voiced *th*-sound in mid-word positions, as in 'bovvah' (*bother*) and 'muvvah' ('mother'). In initial positions, the sound is closer to the norm in such words as *this* and *these*, but pronunciations like 'viss' and 'vese' can be heard. *Everything*, *nothing*, and *something* are 'evreefink', 'nuffink', and 'sumfink' or 'sunnink', and a shibboleth for *f*/*v* usage is the alliterative phrase 'Fi?ee fahzn fevvahs on a frush's froa?' (*Thirty thousand feathers on a thrush's throat*).

2 Like most other regional varieties in England, Cockney has no initial *h* in such words as *house* and *hollow* ('Nowbody lives in them ouses in the ollow'), and may add an *h* for emphasis or as hypercorrection, as in *hevah* for *ever: Did you hevah see the like?*

3 Distinctive diphthongs include a schwa (weak vowel) before the long *ee*-sound in *beet* and *seat*, and an *eye*-like sound in such words as *fate* and *great*. Conversely, the single vowel sound *ah* serves for the more general *ow*-sound in *about* ('abaht') and *thousand* ('fahzn'). Cockney is also known for stretching and multiplying vowel sounds, often shown in print as three or more vowels together, as in Shaw's 'daownt' for *don't* in *Pygmalion*.

4 Glottal stops (brief stopping actions in the glottis, in the upper throat) replace *t*, *k*, and *p* when they occur in middle or final positions in words, as in *but*, *butter*, *hectic*, *technical* (sounding rather like 'tetnical'), *stop*, and a glottalized *ksh*, as in *actually* (sounding like 'atshellee').

5 Like RP, there is no *r* after a vowel in Cockney, unless it starts a new syllable: 'cah' *car*, 'cahd' *card*. Cockney shares the general linking *r* of south-east England, including in RP, as in 'draw/r/ing room' for *drawing room* and 'Shah/r of Persia' for *Shah of Persia*.

6 The *l*-sound in such words as *tell* and *technical* is vocalized as a *w*-sound, so that 'Tell him about the technical college' sounds like 'Tewwim abah? the te?nicaw cowwedge'.

Grammar

1 The grammar of Cockney is more or less 'general non-standard', typically with double negatives (*There aint nuffink like it* 'There is nothing like it') and *done* and *seen* for *did* and *saw* ('I done it yesterday', 'I just seen er').

2 Question tags are widely used to invite agreement or establish one's position, as in *I'm elpin you now, innI?* ('I am helping you now, ain't I?', meaning 'Although I may not have helped you before or wanted in fact to help you at all, I'm doing it now'); *Well, e knew all abaht it, dinnee?* ('Well, he knew all about it, didn't he?', meaning 'Because he knew all about it, it's not surprising that he did what he did').

3 The prepositions *to* and *at* are frequently dropped in relation to places: *I'm goin down the pub* ('I'm going down to the pub'), *He's round is mate's* ('He is round at his friend's house'), *They're over me mum's* ('They're over at my mother's').

Vocabulary and word-play

1 Items from a range of languages have come into the area or were encountered and used elsewhere and brought back home. Such contacts have been demotic, not literary or academic, and so their etymologies have tended to be ignored or

difficult to establish unambiguously. However, key sources include Romany, Yiddish, Arabic, and Hindi:

- Romany (from the usage of gypsies in East London): *chavvy* ('child'); *mush* ('mate, buddy'), and the phrase *put the mockers on* ('to jinx').

- Yiddish (from the usage of European Jews): *gazump/gezumph* ('to swindle': now, throughout England, to beat people to buying a house by offering more than they have done just before the signing of the contract); *schemozzle* ('a disturbance'); *schlemiel* ('a fool'). Cf. New York.

- Arabic and Hindi, through Forces slang in the earlier 20th century: *ackers* ('money': Arabic *fakka* 'small change'); *bint* ('a girl': Arabic); *cushy* ('soft, easy'), as in *a cushy billet* 'an easy job' (from Persian through Hindi *khush* 'pleasure'); *dekko* ('a look', from Hindi *dekho* 'look!'); *shufti* ('a look': Arabic) as in 'Take a shufti at that'; *doolally* ('mad', from *Deolali*, a town in western India where a British Forces mental hospital was once located).

2 Minced oaths and euphemisms, especially relating to God, such as: *Cor/Gor* ('God') and *blimey* ('blind me') either on their own or in combination as (*Oh*) *Cor/Gor blimey*; such phrases as *Cor love a duck*, *Cor stone the crows*, and *Cor strike a light*; *Gordon Bennett*, the name of a 20th-century car-racing promoter, often substituting for *God in heaven*.

3 Slangy truncations of words, especially with -*o* added (cf. Australian slang): *aggro* ('aggravation' = aggression, now widely used) and *rarzo* ('a red nose', from 'raspberry').

4 Back-slang, as in the common example *yob* ('boy'), often in the form *yobbo* (compare the colloquial *boyo*), often defined as 'a backward boy' (applied to young men with no manners).

5 Run-together phrases that sound like (and are often playfully written as) single words, as with: *Gawdelpus* ('God help us'); *Geddoudovit* ('Get out of it': cf. New York *Fuggedaboudit* 'Forget about it'); and *Wotcher/Wotcha* ('What cheer?', a once widespread greeting: 'What good news is there?').

The exchange of *v* and *w* proved to be the most controversial of the Cockney shibboleths listed by John Walker in 1791. Some commentators have even accused the London journalist and novelist Charles Dickens of inventing it. Dickens used it freely in *The Pickwick Papers*, as typical of the speech of Mr Pickwick's servant Samuel Weller, whose father calls him 'Samivel Veller'. An example:

> **1837** 'I had a reg'lar new fit o' clothes that mornin', gen'l'men of the jury,' said Sam, 'and that was a wery partickler and uncommon circumstance vith me in those days. . . . If they wos a pair o' patent double million magnifyin' gas microscopes of hextra power, p'raps I might be able to see through a flight o' stairs and a deal door; but bein' only eyes, you see, my wision's limited.'
> – *The Pickwick Papers*, ch. 34

Walker provides the proof that Sam's usage existed well before Dickens created him. It appears, however, to have been in decline when Dickens turned it into a literary stereotype, and by the 1870s it had virtually disappeared, as noted by George Bernard Shaw in an appendix to *Captain Brassbound's Conversion*:

> **1900** When I came to London in 1876, the Sam Weller dialect had passed away so completely that I should have given it up as a literary fiction if I had not discovered it surviving in a Middlesex village, and heard of it from an Essex one. Some time in the eighties the late Alexander Tuer called attention in the Pall Mall Gazette to several peculiarities of modern cockney, and to the obsolescence of the Dickens dialect that was still being copied from book to book by authors who never dreamt of using their ears, much less of training them to listen.

Since the time of Dickens, Cockney dialogue has often been included in standard texts. A fairly consistent orthography has therefore developed for it, as with *abaht* ('about'), *Gawd* ('God'), *larf* ('laugh'), *muvver* ('mother'), *orful* ('awful'), *orl* ('all'). The apostrophe is used to mark an absent *h* as in *'abit*, and an absent *g* signals the pronunciation of *-ing* as syllabic *n*, as in *cuttin'* and *shoutin'* (with glottalized *t*'s). Writers generally use just enough for flavour, along with typical Londonisms and a cheap and cheerful style, as in:

> **1892** The 'eathen in 'is blindness bows down to wood an' stone;
> 'E don't obey no orders unless they is 'is own;
> 'E keeps 'is side-arms awful: 'e leaves 'em all about,
> An' then comes up the Regiment an' pokes the 'eathen out.
> – Rudyard Kipling, *The 'Eathen*

Although C. S. Forester's mechanic Allnutt, in the heart of colonial Africa, is less orthographically assertive, he remains unequivocally a working-class Londoner:

> **1925** 'Why not?'
> 'Rapids, miss. Rocks an' cataracts an' gorges. You 'aven't been there, miss. I 'ave. There's a nundred miles of rapids down there. Why, the river's got a different nime where it comes out in the Lake to what it's called up 'ere. It's the Bora down there. That just shows you. No one knew they was the same river.'
> – C. S. Forester, *The African Queen*, ch. 2

Literary approaches to Cockney have generally been the work of middle-class non-Cockneys. Their conventions have, however, been both used and queried by Cockneys writing about their own speech:

> **1980** But the short ou of 'out' and 'about' is the chronically misrepresented Cockney vowel. For a hundred years there has been a convention of writing it as 'ah'. Shaw put 'baw ya flahr orf a pore gel' into Eliza Doolittle's mouth: 'rahnd the ahses' is the classic way of conveying East London speech. It is painfully wide of the mark. Whatever a Cockney's 'out' may be thought to sound like, it is not 'art'—which is what 'aht' would make it. The sound is a lengthened short *u*. It might be written 'uht', the *u* as in 'cut'

> but stretched out; more precisely, it is 'uh-ert'. The phonetic
> version of a Cockney's 'buy a flower off a poor girl' would be
> 'bah-eeya fluh-er orf a pore gel'. Practically any Cockney does this
> when he talks, but in a street vendor's chant it would become a
> flourish and almost musical.
>
> – Robert Barltrop and Jim Wolveridge, *The Muvver Tongue* (London & West Nyack, The
> Journeyman Press).

A striking aspect of Cockney, especially when compared with RP, is its effusive range of tone and emotion. On this point, Barltrop and Wolveridge comment:

> The East Londoner likes his utterances to be attention-catching
> whether they are plaintive, indignant, gloomy or humorous. . . .
> Nagging, anecdote, giving opinions and even greeting a friend in
> the street are done with the same mobility of voice, to squeeze the
> utmost meaning out of them, and it is noticeable in ordinary
> conversation.

The devices of vigorous delivery include a wide range of tones, emphatic loudness, strong facial expression, and vigorous body language. There is in particular pitch prominence on content words (nouns, verbs, adjectives, and adverbs) and their vowels are often stretched, as in *You ought to ave SEEEEN it—It was ever so GOOOOD*. In tandem, Cockneys are generally more uninhibited socially (laughing loudly, complaining vigorously) than middle- and upper-class Londoners, a feature which may have been influenced by the presence (among others) in the East End of Gypsies, Jews, and the Irish.

Associated with Cockney, but by no means confined to it, is *rhyming slang*, whose primary values are group solidarity, amusement, and (when necessary) total opacity to outsiders: *Would you Adam n Eve it? E's left is trouble n strife!* ('Would you believe it? He's left his wife!'). The creative principle is twofold: first, coin a two-part phrase that rhymes with a single original word (as with *apples and pears* for 'stairs'), then clip off the second part of the phrase, so that an opaque synonym is created for the word (*'E went up the apples* = 'He went up the stairs'). Several rhymes for a single word may emerge and perhaps compete, as with *Rosy Lea* and *you n me* for 'tea'. The history of rhyming slang is unclear, but it probably began in the thieves' cant of the 19th century, became fashionable in the West End of London in the 1930s, and became widely known through comedy and drama on radio and television. The 1970s TV comedy series *Steptoe and Son* used such expressions as *Brahms and Liszt* ('pissed', drunk), and *berk*, a clipping of *Berkeley/Berkshire Hunt* (based on 'cunt': first *OED* citation, 1936). The word *berk* is now widely used for a stupid person whom the speaker does not like, and many users do not know about the original obscene association.

Clipping off the second part of the rhyme phrase is common, so that *a butcher's hook* ('a look') becomes simply *a butchers*, and many expressions survive only in the shortened form. *Bristol Cities* for 'titties' (pluralizing the name of a soccer team) has become simply *Bristols*, and may originally have been a media-inspired coinage. The more traditional Cockney was either *Manchester Cities* (from another team) or *thrupnee* [*threepenny*] *bits* ('tits': from the name of a pre-decimalization coin). Clipping permits such an in-group male remark as 'Cor, tike a butchers at them bristols!' Rhyming slang has contributed to informal British English usage the expressions: *cobblers* ('rubbish, nonsense'), an expression of scepticism clipped from *cobblers' awls* ('balls, testicles'); *rabbit on* ('to talk all the time'), from *rabbit n pork* ('to talk'); and *raspberry*, for a derisive blowing sound with the lips, apparently from *raspberry tart* ('fart').

Cockney and neighbouring varieties constitute the most widespread and prominent urban dialect cluster in the UK, the next being Glasgow Scots. It is part of a long-established working-class tradition with considerable media and other influence on UK usage at large, notably through the tabloid newspapers, radio, and TV. The stigma is less, but still significant. The authors Barltrop and Wolveridge put the matter as follows twenty years ago:

> **1980** We wanted to write for Cockneys as much as about them. The language is constantly shown as picturesque or comic, and almost invariably as inferior; it is taken for granted as coming from a people who do not know any better. We hope to persuade Cockneys as well as others that it is more than the equal of any other form of speech. . . . The Cockney does not have to define class—it defines him. While East Londoners are defined by the social system as are all other working people, they are resentful of it in a resigned sort of way and strongly conscious of 'Them and Us'. . . . Thus, speaking well—'talking posh'—does not make a great impression; it smacks of being the enemy's language.
> – Robert Barltrop and Jim Wolveridge, *op cit.*

Cockneys share such sentiments with users of other urban working-class varieties closely associated with the Industrial Revolution. Like speakers of Scouse in Liverpool and Brummie in Birmingham, they remain a socially embattled community that often thumbs its linguistic nose at the establishment. Paradoxically, Cockneys have often been regarded as letting London down at the same time as they are affectionately invoked as a key defining element in the life of the city.

Estuary English

The term *Estuary English* was coined in 1984 by the English phonetician David Rosewarne, as the title of an article in the *Times Educational Supplement* of 19 October. He used it as a means of identifying an accent common among younger people in the counties of Essex and Kent that straddle the estuary of the Thames. This accent was not new, but had not been much discussed before this point; in the following decade, however, it became a hot media and linguistic topic, prompting among other things a laid-back pop-linguistic paperback with the title *Do You Speak Estuary? The New Standard English: How to Spot It and Speak It* (Bloomsbury, 1993) by Paul Coggle. The issue remains controversial. For some, the concept is flawed, and no such entity exists; for others, Estuary is an intriguing and positive social and linguistic development; for others still, it is real but deeply to be deplored; and for yet others, whether their own response is positive, negative, or neutral, the development itself has considerable social implications.

Estuary English is generally perceived as a compromise between demotic London usage (most obviously Cockney) and Received Pronunciation. It appears to be most typical of young upwardly mobile working-class South-Easterners trading up in social and linguistic terms and young people educated in public (that is, private) schools trading down from RP, perhaps—as both Rosewarne and Cottle suggest—to increase their 'street cred' (a slang 1980s shortening of *street credibility*, the easy and confident familiarity one might have with fashionable urban and especially youth culture). As David Rosewarne has put it:

> **1994** The heartland of this variety still lies by the banks of the Thames and its estuary, but it seems to be the most influential accent in the south-east of England. In the decade since I started research into it, Estuary English has spread northwards to Norwich and westwards to Cornwall, with the result that it is now spoken south of a line from the Wash to the Avon. It is also to be heard on the front and back benches of the House of Commons and is used by some members of the Lords, whether life or hereditary peers. Ken Livingstone M.P. [in 2001 the Mayor of London] was given in the first article in *The Sunday Times* on 14 March 1993 as an example of an Estuary speaker. Interviewed a couple of days later in *The Daily Mail*, he said he was pleased with the label, adding 'I think it's true that this kind of dialect is emerging.' Tony Banks M.P., interviewed on the B.B.C. radio programme 'Word of Mouth' on 29 June 1993 reported that Estuary English is now spoken by Conservative members of Parliament as well as Labour.
>
> – 'Estuary English: tomorrow's RP?', in *English Today*, 37 (10: 1), January (Cambridge University Press)

The Estuary accent is located more or less midway along a continuum between RP and Cockney, and is particularly noted for four Cockney-like features:

❶ L, r, and w

The use of a *w*-like sound is common where RP has *l* and *r*, especially towards or at the end of words, as in 'aw' for *all*, 'miwk' for *milk*, and 'Spaw's Cathedwaw' for *St Paul's Cathedral*. This pronunciation creates homophones that may lead to misunderstanding, as for example where 'fowty toowz' may be interpreted as either *forty tools* or *faulty tools*.

❷ L-dropping

In some words, the *l* is dropped entirely, as in 'vunnerable' for *vulnerable*. (cf. the traditional loss of an *l*-sound before an *m* in such words as *calm* and *palm*.)

❸ Glottal stops

The use of glottal stops instead of *k*, *p*, and *t* and at the end of syllables and words, as in 'te?nicaw' for *technical*, 'sto?' for *stop*, and 'gwo?aw' for *glottal*.

❹ I-lengthening

The use of 'ee' instead of a short *i*, as in 'lovelee' for *lovely*, and 'reallee' for *really*.

At least the following three factors appear to be at work in propagating Estuary so widely and swiftly:

❶ Demographics

Large numbers of Londoners have migrated since the Second World War into the surrounding counties, including especially such new towns as Basildon, Harlow, Slough, and Milton Keynes, where their big city style has had higher prestige among the young than the traditional dialects.

❷ Radio and television

It is now commonplace to hear a wide range of accents on both the BBC and commercial radio and TV, both locally and nationally, including Estuary.

❸ Accent compromise and accommodation

A move towards greater linguistic comfort and compromise, RP speakers trading down as people with the local accent trade up, resulting in accentual convergence.

Although the Estuary phenomenon has been startling and powerful, its novelty may have been exaggerated. There have long been accent compromises between working- and lower-middle-class London usage (including Cockney, but by no means confined to it) and RP, and indeed the speech of educated Londoners has tended to be varyingly near RP without being part of it as classically understood— although RP has hardly itself been as uniform as the model in Daniel Jones's *English Pronouncing Dictionary* has suggested from 1917 onwards. Indeed, it would be an acute or bold observer who could guarantee to analyse and assign all the features of speech in a random selection of born-and-bred Greater Londoners.

British Black English

The general name for any of several varieties of Caribbean Creole English used in the UK (primarily in London and some other major cities in England) by the children of immigrants from the Commonwealth Caribbean since the 1950s. It is also known as (*London*) *Jamaican*, because of the majority presence of people from Jamaica, and *Patois* or *Patwa*. Its range is wide: while older people of West Indian background often retain the full West Indian speech continuum (from Creole to Standard English), younger locally born speakers use varieties of British English alongside, and sometimes mixed with, Caribbean usage, and the focus of the term is mainly on such younger people.

The use of a distinctive British Black English (BBE) is often associated with 'black' youth culture (both local and international). It includes elements of Rastafarianism and reggae, and has its own in-group counter-prestige to white usage. Although its speakers sometimes call their speech *Jamaican*, it is considerably different from Jamaican Creole. In Jamaica, Patois has, for example, no gender or subject/object distinction in the third-person pronoun: male, female, subject, and object are all *im* ('him'). In London, however, both *i* (unaspirated 'he') and *shi* ('she') are also in use, as imports from conventional English.

Linguists do not agree as to whether a continuum of varieties links conventional kinds of English in England with Creole, as happens with standard and Creole in Jamaica, or whether the systems are largely discrete. Many speakers appear to switch between full English and full Patois with few intermediate forms. Most such speakers of BBE live in London, Birmingham, and Leeds, and their usage is part of a continuum with majority local speech. Some white children in black peer groups also use Patois, and in recent years there has been an increasing range of written and performed works, especially in poetic and rhythmic forms, in black British usage.

The West Country and Mummerset

The terms *the West Country* and *the West of England* have imprecise boundaries, but certainly cover the 'cider counties' of Avon, Devon, Dorset, Gloucestershire, and Somerset. Wiltshire and parts of Hampshire are sometimes included, and Cornwall is a candidate because of its location and despite its ancient Celtic connection. There is also uncertainty about the 'heart' of the West Country: some favour Dorset, others Somerset, and expressions dating from Saxon times have been used until recent centuries where the two counties meet. Thus, the Old English first-person pronoun *ic* (pronounced 'itch': compare German *Ich*) continued in use into the 19th century in what the dialectologist A. J. Ellis called 'the land of utch' (around Montacute in Somerset and into Dorset). In the 1950s, fieldworkers for the Survey of English Dialects recorded there the primordial statement *Udge am gwain* ('I'm going'). The following points cover key features of present-day West Country:

Pronunciation

1 Although the traditional West Country accent cluster is now largely confined to the West and South West, it was once common across all of England south of a line from the Severn to the Thames. The current boundary is from the river Severn round Gloucestershire, including the Forest of Dean on the other side of the river, round the north-east boundary of Wiltshire, and passing through Hampshire to the sea around Portsmouth.

2 The typical West Country burr (a retroflex *r*, the tip of the tongue curled up and back) is widely regarded as a survival of the full Anglo-Saxon *r*. Although it contrasts strongly with non-rhotic RP, it is often remarked on as a pleasing feature, comparable to the Irish *r* and the usage of Canada and the northern United States. The present-day range of usage extends from 'broad' rural and working class through accents modified towards RP in the lower middle class to near-RP and full RP in the middle and upper classes.

3 An *r* after a spoken vowel is widely retained in such cities as Bristol and Exeter, despite the influence of RP. In other cities, such as Plymouth and Bournemouth, the degree of rhoticity varies; indeed, locally variable *r*-pronunciation can be found as close to London as Reading in Berkshire.

4 A second, less frequent local feature is an initial *w* in such words as *old oak*, pronounced 'wold woak'.

5 The name of the main city of the region, *Bristol* (formerly in Somerset but now in the newer county of Avon) exemplifies a distinctive feature of its area: an intrusive final *l* in words that end in a weak vowel, as with *areal* ('area'), *cinemal* ('cinema'), and *the Victorial Centre* ('the Victoria Centre', a shopping

mall). *Bristol* was formerly *Bristow* (and earlier still *Bricgstow*, 'the holy place by the bridge').

Grammar

1 The following grammatical forms are generally regarded as working-class and rural.

2 The use of *thick* or *thicky* and *they* as demonstrative pronouns: *thick man* ('that man'); *they houses* ('those houses').

3 Present and past participles often preceded by *a-*, as in *a-goin* and *a-done* (Where are you a-goin then?', 'What's he a-done?').

4 The frequent use of auxiliary *do*, as in *He do go every week* ('He goes every week'), *They do be ard-workin* ('They really are hard-working').

5 The present tense of the verb *be* regularized and simplified to a single form: *I be, you be, he be, she be, we be, you be, they be*.

6 The negative *baint*: *I baint* ('I am not'), *baint I* ('am I not'), *ye baint* ('you aren't'), *baint ye* ('aren't you'), *they baint* ('they aren't'), *baint they* ('aren't they').

Vocabulary

1 Many items of South West vocabulary are now restricted to parts of individual counties. However, words formerly widely known and used include: *fardel* ('a burden'); *lew* ('dry'); *mazzard* ('a black cherry'); *truss* ('a bale' of hay); *tiddly* ('to do light housework').

2 In *The Grockles' Guide: An Illustrated Miscellany of Words and Phrases of Interest and Use to 'Voreigners' in Somerset* (Jeremy Warburg & Tessa Lorant, Thorn Press, 1985), the following words are listed as current, among many others: *anywhen* ('any time'); *aps* ('a boil'); *backalong* ('homeward'), as in *I'll be doddlin backalong now*; *brize* ('to bring pressure to bear on', as in *to brize down on someone*); *caddle* ('a muddle or difficulty'); *chammer* ('to chew noisily, chatter'); *chatterbag* ('a gossip'), *clumble-fisted* ('awkward with the hands'); *combe* (pronounced 'coom', from Celtic: 'a valley'); *emmet* ('an ant, small fly'); *gert* ('great, large'); *jibber* ('a restless horse'); *leary* ('hungry, tired, thin, empty'); *mugget* (the intestines of a young heifer or sheep); *pissabed* ('dandelion'); *quirk* ('to moan, whine, complain'); *rafty* ('rancid, off, crafty'); *randy* ('a party': *on the randy*, 'out to enjoy oneself'); *rozzum/ruzzum* ('a tall tale'); *scrumpy* ('farmhouse cider'); *somewhen* ('sometime'); *teddy* ('a potato'); *verdic* ('a viewpoint, opinion': compare *verdict*). The term *grockle* for a holiday-maker or tourist is of uncertain origin and apparently recent, its first *OED* citation being 1964.

For many people in Britain, traditional West Country usage has become stereotyped as rustic, two particular shibboleths being associated with country yokels leaning on gates and sucking straws: a strong West Country burr, as in *Arrr, that it be* ('Yes, that's so'), and the use of *v* and *z* for *f* and *s*, as in *The varmer zaw er* ('The farmer saw her'). The stage accent known as *Mummerset* (blending *mummer*, 'someone who mutters, murmurs, or mimes', and *Somerset*) has long exploited these features. Shakespeare was probably the first literary exponent, using a distinctive spelling, as when Edgar in *King Lear* (disguised as the peasant Tom a Bedlam) says *Chill not let go Zir, without vurther 'cagion* ('I'll not let go, sir, without further occasion', where *chill* is a combination of *utch* and 'will'). The Scottish novelist Compton MacKenzie indirectly commented in a novel on the BBC's habit of using RP when authoritative voices were needed and West Country for homelier matters, such as promoting powdered eggs: 'Nowadays you can't be sure if they *are* eggs, even when somebody on television says they are in B.B.C. Mummerset' (*Paper Lives*, 1966).

Mummerset tends to be heavily drawled, emphasizing the local *r*, made by curling the tongue back, *z* rather than *s*, and *v* for *f*, as in 'Arrr, that'll be roit, zurr. We ain't zeen 'im zince last Vroiday'. Comedians have often added pseudo-dialect words to make the brew richer, such as describing how the locals harvest 'crundle-weed'. West Country folk have, however, retaliated by creating *grockle* (above), as an amused, patient, but slightly sharp-edged label for tourists which has proved successful with both locals and grockles.

In the 19th century the usage of the South West was made widely known by two writers of national stature: the novelist and poet Thomas Hardy (1840–1928), in his Wessex novels, and the schoolmaster and philologist William Barnes (1801–86), who wrote poetry in the Dorset dialect and sought to preserve it. Hardy's novels gave regional usages a worldwide readership. Following the example of Walter Scott, Hardy sought to render the speech of ordinary people as accurately as possible, varying dialect according to speaker. Thus, of Tess, the heroine of *Tess of the d'Urbervilles* (1891), he observes: 'The dialect was on her tongue to some extent, despite the village school: the characteristic intonation of that dialect for this district being the voicing approximately rendered by the syllable UR, probably as rich an utterance as any to be found in human speech.' The dairy maids in the book, on the other hand, were uneducated and used such forms as *zid* (past tense of *zee*, 'see'), *hwome* ('home'), and *I be, so be you* ('I am, so are you').

Hardy was born at Higher Bockhampton, Dorset. Trained as an architect, he returned to Dorset from London for reasons of health in 1867 and began to write as a hobby while continuing his career. However, with his second published novel, *Under the Greenwood Tree* (1872), he found his *métier*: describing life in the imaginary world of 'Wessex', based on Dorset and the surrounding counties (in which many of his locations can be identified). He used local dialogue in both tragic and comic episodes and varied its intensity to suggest the status of the characters and the degree of their relationship. He valued and defended the dignity of Dorset usage, which he saw not as a deviation from the standard but as a survival of the ancient speech of Saxon Wessex. His contemporary, William Barnes (1801–86), a prominent philologist and language reformer, wrote poetry in the Dorset dialect in a more specialized non-standard style, as with:

> Then they took en in hwome to his bed,
> An' he rose vrom his pillow no mwore.
> Vor the curls on his sleek little head
> To be blown by the wind out o' door.
> Vor he died while the hay russled grey
> On the staddle so leately begun:
> Lik' the mown-grass a-dried by the day –
> Aye! the zwath-flo'r's a-killed by the zun.

– 'The Child and the Mowers'
[*en* 'him', *staddle* 'the lower part of a stack of corn', *zwath* 'swath, a line of mown crops'.]

The West Midlands and Brummie

In medieval times, the Midland dialects appear to have had fairly well-defined boundaries: north of the rivers Severn and Thames and south of a line from Heysham on the west coast to the mouth of the Humber in the east, the north–south line of the Pennines dividing the West Midland and East Midland areas. Some dialectologists consider that such boundaries are still significant while others argue that post-industrial dialects (Birmingham, Wolverhampton, Leicester, etc.) now exert greater influence than those of the countryside and smaller towns. Apart from a tiny minority of middle-class RP and near-RP speakers, most West Midlanders share features of pronunciation with the North rather than the South of England. They generally have a distinctive short *u*-sound in words such as *but, come, fun, some* (*put* and *putt* being homophones) and a short *a*-sound where RP has a longer rounder sound (the Midland vowel being the same in *bat, bath, last, pat,* and *path*).

Midland speech is not, however, homogeneous. People in the West are more likely to use *ng-g* in words such as *singing* ('sing-ging-g') and *tongue* (*tong-g*), and to use a short tight vowel in such words as *man* and *pan*, as well as to be mildly rhotic in words such as *far* and *farm*. People in the north west of the region are generally likely to say 'uz' for *us*, to have *r* and not *t* in *got a book* ('gorra book'), and to tap the back of the upper teeth for *r* (instead of the more widely used post-alveolar approximant of RP), much as the people of Liverpool do.

Birmingham, the largest city in the West Midlands, is commonly referred to locally as *Brum*, an abbreviation of *Brummagem*, the local working-class version of the city's name. Its inhabitants are consequently known as *Brummies*, and their speech is called *Birmingham, Brummagem,* and *Brummie*. Local accents vary according to such factors as age, education, locality, region of origin, and social aspirations.

Middle-class speech in the city is RP or near-RP, and the following points apply mainly to the majority form, working-class speech, which is non-rhotic, aitchless, and usually has the same short *a* in *bat* and *bath*. The pronunciation of *Edgbaston* (the name of a better-off part of the city) is a class shibboleth, *a* short among the working class (who stress the first syllable: 'EDGE-bistn') and long in 'posh' usage (with stress on the second syllable, which has a full RP vowel: 'Edge-BAHstn'). The vowel *i* tends to sound like 'ee': *it* sounds like *eat* and *did* like *deed*. The vowels in such words as *tie* and *toy* have merged, so that it may be uncertain what is intended by the question *Where's my new t—?* Words and syllables ending in *-ng* tend to close with a *g*, as in 'keeng-g' (*king*) and 'seeng-geeng-g' (*singing*). This feature has been criticized so often that many Birmingham speakers tend to overcompensate in the attempt to avoid it, as a result completely omitting the *g*-sound in such words as *finger* and *linger*.

Birmingham people range from middle-class with a more or less standard grammar and vocabulary and a greater or less affinity to RP, through working-class using non-standard forms also common elsewhere in the UK, to those whose English is influenced by a mother tongue such as Caribbean Creole, Punjabi, or Urdu. Broad Brummie includes the use of *them* as a demonstrative ('them things') and a general non-standard use of verbs ('I seen it', 'I done it', 'It's broke', 'She give it me yesterday', 'We come here last year', and 'We was' for 'We were'). Features especially among older speakers include: *up* instead of *to*, 'He went up the pub half an hour ago'; *her* instead of *she*, 'What's er doing then?'; and use of *as* as a relative pronoun, 'It wasn't im as went'. Although most people use a general vocabulary, older people may use such long-established local words as *brewins* ('an outhouse'), *miskin* ('a dustbin/trashcan'), and *suff* ('a drain').

East Anglia

Although East Anglia traditionally consists of only the counties of Norfolk and Suffolk, it is generally nowadays taken—as in effect 'the East (of England)'—to include Cambridgeshire, Bedfordshire, Northamptonshire, and Essex (although this last is also commonly regarded as part of the South East). The urban areas of Norwich in Norfolk and Ipswich in Suffolk notably tend to influence the speech of the areas around them. Usage is however internally diverse, Essex speech being closer to London than to Norfolk and Suffolk speech, and the so-called 'singing Suffolk' accent having a wider pitch range and a higher rising intonation at the ends of sentences than other accents and intonations. Some features are:

Pronunciation

1 Many local accents are marked by a rhythm that tends to lengthen stressed vowels and reduce or eliminate unstressed short vowels.

2 Traditional East Anglian usage is non-rhotic, and there tends to be no *y*-sound in words such as *dew* and *dune*, making *dew* and *do* homophones (as in the US). The pronunciation 'boo?iful' for *beautiful* (the *t* glottalized) is a regional shibboleth for Norfolk in particular, and for some Norwich speakers *boat* and *soap* sound like *boot* and *soup*.

3 Word-initial *h* tends to occur in Norfolk and Suffolk but not in Cambridgeshire or Essex.

4 Glottal stops in such words as *cat* and *kettle* are common throughout the area.

Grammar

1 In casual speech, the unmarked verb form is often used with all subjects in the present tense: *I go there every day*; *He go there every day*.

2 *That* is often used rather than *it* in such greetings as *That's a cold day!*, *That's nice now*.

3 A formerly widespread feature, now recessive, is the conditional use of *do*, as in: *They don't go there now. Do, they'd have a surprise* ('They don't go there now. If they did, they'd get a surprise').

Vocabulary

Distinctive rural words include: *hodmadod* and *dodman* ('snail'); *fourses* (a light afternoon meal about four o'clock: compare the more general *elevenses* for morning coffee); and *neathouse* (a shed for *neat* 'cattle'). Scandinavian influence was once strong and can still be found, notably in northern Suffolk, where streams continue to be called *becks*.

The pronunciation of East Anglia at the turn of the 15/16th centuries played a significant part in the formulation of the speech of the north-eastern United States, in that many of the emigrants who set sail across the Atlantic in the *Mayflower* from Plymouth in Devon to set up the new 'Plimoth Plantation' in what became the state of Massachusetts hailed from this area. The 'nasal twang' of the Yankees of New England is said to derive from the speech of English Puritans, many of whom were nasal East Anglians.

Northern

Northern English usage is different from all the varieties of southern England, and tends to be more homogeneous. Shibboleths abound for contrastive purposes between Northern and Southern usage (Northern in such situations often being taken to include Midland), such as the Northern *u* as in *cup*, which to Southern ears sounds close to 'coop'. The North/South contrast has been much discussed, and two names are associated with the dialect area:

❶ Northern English
The term has two broad meanings: (more historical and comprehensive) the Northumbrian, Anglian, or Anglic dialect of Old English and its successor dialects in the North of England and Lowland Scotland; (primarily in modern terms) English as used in the North of England, sometimes extending to include Scots and Scottish English, but usually without providing much detail beyond the border. The contrasting term *Southern English* is much less common.

❷ North Country/north country
The term refers either to England beyond the Humber (as in 'a North Country story') or the accent(s) and dialect(s) of the North of England ('"If you borrow you make bad friends"—a flash of honest north country peeped through the trained accent': C. Drummond, *Death at Bar*, 1972); '[The Lancashire singer] Gracie Fields reverts to the characteristic mixture of North Country, standard English and American overtones' (*The Times*, 30 December 1974). There is no matching **South Country*.

The most noted Northern dialects are Yorkshire, Lancashire, Cumbrian, and Geordie, which in many instances have more in common with Scots than with the dialects of the South Midlands, the South East, and the South West, and Geordie sounds to Scottish ears more like Scots than English. There are three distinct traditional South/North language regions in England and Scotland (each with its variations): Southern England, Northern England, and Lowland Scotland. In this model, Midland is an area of transition between the two great English dialect areas. Wales and the Highlands and Western Isles of Scotland sit apart from this continuum because the varieties of English in these areas are in effect the nativized English of speakers of other languages, a situation comparable to Celtic Ireland and indeed to Quebec in Canada (with its French dimension) and Singapore (with its Chinese, Malay, and Tamil associations).

Yorkshire

Historic Yorkshire was the largest county of England, administered from the city of York and divided into three *ridings* (originally *thridings* or 'thirdings': the East, West, and North). These divisions are now counties in their own right: respectively East, West, and North Yorkshire (with some territory assigned to the new county of Humberside). The name *Yorkshire*, however, continues informally for the entire area, and in wider national terms people are hardly conscious of the change. The name also refers to the dialect of the original area, as in 'He speaks broad Yorkshire'.

The Yorkshire dialect(s) derive from Anglian, the northernmost of the Anglo-Saxon dialects, an early text of which is the song of Caedmon, a lay brother at the coastal monastery of Whitby (*c*.670). Scandinavian influence, arising out of invasions and occupations from the 9th century to 1066, was profound. Some Middle English writers can be identified as writing a Northern variety representing Yorkshire speech: notably, Richard Rolle, a hermit who lived near Doncaster, the author of a religious work called *The Ayenbite of Inwit* ('The again-bite of in-wit', usually translated as 'The Prick of Conscience', *c*.1340). A feature of Northern Middle English orthography was the use of *quh-* rather than *wh-*, as in *quhilk* for southern *hwich* (which), which was also the norm in Older Scots. Although Yorkshire usage has often been considered a single dialect, it has in fact many varieties, some of which were traditionally close to mutually unintelligible.

Pronunciation

1 Yorkshire accents are non-rhotic, with the mild exception of East Yorkshire, where an *r* sound after a vowel is occasionally heard in stressed syllables and final unstressed syllables, the word *farmer* therefore having two possible spoken *r*s.

2 The *a*-sound before *s*, *f*, and voiceless *th* is short and tight-lipped, as in *fast*, *staff*, and *path*, and in all positions in *My aunt can't dance* (in total contrast to RP).

3 Some mainly rural speakers in the North and East Ridings have preserved something of the northern vowels of Middle English in an unchanged long vowel giving 'hoose' for *house* and *doon* for *down* (as universally in Scots) and in the distinctive 'ah'-vowel of such words as *know, saw, swan*, and *quarry* ('nah,' 'sah', 'swahn', and 'kwahry').

4 The pronunciation or non-pronunciation of *the* is a well-known Yorkshire shibboleth, varying from absence in the East through a kind of suspended *t* in the central areas (as in *Gie t'book to t'man* 'Give the book to the man'), to *d* in the North before voiced consonants and *t* before voiceless consonants (*d'book, t'packet*), and in the extreme West to *th* before vowels and *t* before consonants (*th'old man, t'book*).

5 Traditional short *u* in Yorkshire and elsewhere in the North has the same sound in such words as *up, come, wool, put*, but words in -*ook* have retained the long vowel: *book, cook, look*.

6 Regional variations often contrast greatly, especially between West on the one hand and North and East on the other; thus, *soon, road, stone* in the West

sound like 'sooin, rooad, stooan', and in the North and East like 'see-en, reead, steean' (with 'sioon' for *soon* in the North West).

Grammar

1 *While* is often used instead of *until*: *I'll stay here while eight* and *Wait while the light is green* (usages that have been known to cause confusion for outsiders).

2 The echoic tag *is that* is common, as in *It's a fine car, is that!* and *That's right nice, is that.*

Vocabulary

1 The words *aye* and *nay* are widely preferred, especially in rural areas, to *yes* and *no*.

2 The once-universal second-person singular pronouns *thou* (pronounced 'thoo' in the East and North, and 'tha' in the West) and *thee* are common, as in *Ah'll gi it thee* ('I'll give it to you').

3 The word *happen* is widely used rather than *perhaps/maybe*, as in *Happen 'e'll come, happen 'e won't* ('Maybe he'll come, maybe he won't').

4 The form *summat* ('somewhat') is common, as opposed to 'something', as in *There's summat up* and *I've summat to tell thee.*

5 The Scandinavian element is strong in rural and especially in agricultural usage in much of the north of England (and now as obsolescent as the objects referred to), as in: *flaycrow* ('scarecrow'); *stoops* ('gateposts'); *stower* ('rung') of a *stee* ('ladder'); *lea* 'scythe'; *flake* ('hurdle'); *pike* ('small stack of hay').

6 Many items still in common use descend from Old Danish/Norse, including: *addle* ('to earn'); *beck* ('stream, brook'); *cleg* ('horse-fly', shared with Scots); *lake* or *laik* ('to play'); *spaining* or *speaning* ('weaning' animals); and *ted* ('to spread hay').

7 The West Yorkshire version of the Northern and Scots verb *thole* ('to permit, endure, tolerate') is *thoil*, which also carries the Old English sense of 'suffer'. It is applied mostly to spending money on something desirable but too expensive, as in: *Nay, Ah couldn't thoil ten pound for that* ('No, I couldn't permit myself to spend ten pounds for that').

8 The Northern and Scots *bairn* ('child') is common, as is the distinctively Northern *childer* as a plural for *child* (also used in Northern Ireland). As part of Northern English generally, *lad* and *lass* (as in *We have a little lass* 'We have a small daughter') are common, as is *love* (pronounced like a tighter, shorter version of 'loov') as a form of address man to woman and woman to man ('Time t'go 'ome now, love').

Although there has been considerable immigration (from Ireland and Eastern Europe in the late-19th/early-20th centuries; from the Caribbean and South Asia since the mid-20th, mainly to Leeds, Bradford, and Huddersfield), such influxes have not modified local speech. The speech of the children of these mainly working-class incomers is usually a variety of Yorkshire with lexical influences from the parents' mother tongues. Despite claims that increasing mobility and the standardization of education are causing dialect to die out, working-class (that is, majority) usage, especially accent, among the young in the cities of Yorkshire fully retains its distinctiveness.

Yorkshire dialect began to be written for literary purposes in the 17th century with the publication of an anonymous poem, possibly from the Northallerton area, entitled 'A Yorkshire Dialogue between an Awd Wife ('Old Woman'), a Lass ('Girl') and a Butcher' (printed at York, 1673). It opens:

> **Awd Wife**
> Pretha now lass, gang into t'hurn
> An' fetch me heame a skeel o' burn.
> Na pretha, barn, mak heeaste an' gang,
> I's mar my deagh, thou stays sae lang.
> ['Prithee now, girl, go into the corner of the field
> And fetch me home a bucket of water.
> Now prithee, child, make haste and go,
> I'll spoil my dough, you stay so long.']
>
> **Lass**
> Why, Gom, I's gea, bud for my pains
> You's gie me a frundel o' your grains.
> ['Why, grandmother, I will go, but for my trouble,
> Give me a handful of your malt-grain.']
>
> **Awd Wife**
> My grains, my barn! Marry! not I,
> My draugh's for t'gilts an' galts i' t'sty.
> Than, pretha, look i' t'garth an' see
> What owsen i' the stand-hecks be.
> ['My malt-grain, my child! Mary! Not I,
> My grain-refuse is for the sows and boars in the sty.
> Then, prithee (please), look in the yard and see
> What oxen there are in the stalls.']

Perhaps the most famous representation of Yorkshire dialect in literature is Emily Brontë's, in her novel *Wuthering Heights*, as in the following excerpt from chapter 9, when the servant Joseph says:

> **1847** Yon lad gets wur an' wur! . . . He's left th'yate ut t'full swing
> and miss's pony has trodden dahn two rigs uh corn, un plottered
> through, raight o'r intuh t'meadow! Hahsomdiver, t'maister ull
> play t'divil to-morn, and he'll do weel. He's patience itsseln wi'
> sich careless, offald craters—patience itsseln he is! Bud he'll not
> be soa allus—yah's see, all on ye! Yah mumn't drive him out of his
> heead for nowt!
>
> ['That boy gets worse and worse. . . . He's left the gate wide open
> and the young lady's pony has pressed down two ridges of corn
> and floundered through right over into the meadow! However, the
> master will play the devil tomorrow, and he will be right. He's
> patience itself with such careless, awful creatures—patience itself
> he is! But he'll not be so always—you'll see, all of you! You
> mustn't drive him off his head for nothing!']

Many 19th-century working men began to represent their vernacular in writing, both prose and poetry. Their works were often published in informal 'Almanacks', annual notes of local events and calendar entries with passages of dialect, and similar prose continues in current Yorkshire newspapers. The poetry tradition also continues.

The first formal group concerned with the dialect came together in 1894 as a Yorkshire Committee of the English Dialect Society, to assist in the preparation of Joseph Wright's *English Dialect Dictionary* (1898–1905). After the disbanding of the *EDS* in 1896, its work being considered complete with the publication of the dictionary, the local committee re-formed in 1897 as the Yorkshire Dialect Society, which combines the scholarly study of local speech with the publication of prose and poetry in various forms of local dialect. It meets at colleges and university premises throughout the three Yorkshires as well as at industrial and folk museums, and promotes joint meetings with other groups. Activities include: the presentation of papers on place-names and local vocabulary; readings and recitations; and the publication of *The Transactions of the Yorkshire Dialect Society*.

Lancashire and Scouse

The name *Lancashire* is used both for a large north-western English county (historically associated with the city and Duchy of Lancaster, whose duke is the reigning sovereign) and the dialect of that county. It shades into the Cumbrian and Geordie dialect areas to the north, the Yorkshire dialect area to the east, and the North Midland dialect area to the south. Although it is particularly associated with the cotton towns in the south-east of the county, such as Burnley, Bolton, and Rochdale, its subvarieties include the usage of the cities of Liverpool and Manchester. The following lists cover some of the key aspects of Lancashire usage:

Pronunciation

1 Traditional local pronunciation is non-rhotic, with the exception of a small and decreasing number of speakers in the towns of Rochdale, Accrington, and Preston.

2 Word-initial *h* tends to be lost ('ouse' for *house*, 'at' for *hat*), while the 'short' *a*-vowel is used for words in such pairs as *gas/grass* and *sam/psalm* (where RP has a long *a* in the second member of each of these pairs).

3 There is usually no distinction between the vowels in such words as *hoot* and *hut*.

4 The long *u* sometimes becomes two vowels in such words as *moon* ('moo-in') and *school* ('skoo-il'), especially to the north of Burnley.

5 There is a tendency to use the long single vowels *e* and *o* in such words as *take* and *soap*, where RP has diphthongs.

6 The *l* in -*ld* clusters is often lost, *old* and *cold* being realized as 'owd' and 'cowd' (rhyming with *loud*).

7 In words ending in -*ng*, a *g*-sound is added, as in 'long-g' for *long* and 'sing-ging-g' for *singing*. Compare West Midland and Brummie.

Grammar

1 Multiple negation is common: *I haven't done nothing* ('I haven't done anything').

2   *Them* is commonly used as a demonstrative adjective: *I don't know them people*.

3   Such non-standard irregular verb forms as *I seen* and *He done* are common.

4   In rural southern Lancashire, *aw* and *(h)oo* continue to be occasionally used for *I* and *she* (as in the verse below), while in the south-east *thou* and *thee* have been traditionally used (as in Yorkshire), especially to mark intimacy and solidarity (although standard *I, she, you* are increasingly common).

5   There is a tendency to drop the *to* in infinitive constructions, especially when the first verb ends in a *t*, as in *What d'you want do?*

6   The definite article is often reduced to *th* before both vowels and consonants (as in the verse below).

7   The negative modal verb *maun't* ('mustn't') is sometimes used in rural areas, but the positive form *maun*, as in Scots, is rare.

8   Again like Scots and Scottish English generally, such forms as *I've not seen it* are more widely used than *I haven't seen it*.

9   *Owt* ('anything') and *nowt* ('nothing') occur frequently: *I didn't say owt and she gave us nowt*.

10   *Right, well,* and more recently *dead* are colloquial intensifiers: *We were right/dead lucky and they were well merry* ('They were pretty drunk').

Vocabulary

1   Lancashire shares dialect words with other northern areas, including: *elder* ('udder'); *freet* ('superstition'); *fuddle* ('drinking bout'); *mither* ('scold'); *oxter* ('armpit').

2   Items that do not occur elsewhere include: *alicker* ('vinegar'); *deggin-can* ('watering can'); *judy* ('girl'); *kay-fisted* ('left-handed'); *maiden* ('clothes-horse'). Most such words are no longer widespread and tend to be used only by old people, comedians, and dialectologists.

The first well-known writer in Lancashire dialect was John Collier (1708–86), a schoolmaster who lived near Rochdale and wrote under the pen name *Tim Bobbin*. The most famous is an admirer of his, Edwin Waugh (pronounced 'Waff'), the son of a shoe-maker who became a journeyman printer and later a full-time writer (1817–90). He wrote, among other things, of the oppression of a work system that forced a father to leave home to gain employment. In the following lines (where apostrophes are heavily used to indicate non-standardness), a woman is 'reporting' to her absent husband:

> When aw put little Sally to bed,
> Hoo cried, 'cose her feyther weren't theer,
> So aw kiss'd th'little thing, an aw said
> Thae'd bring her a ribbin fro' th'fair.
>
> An' aw gav' her her doll, an' some rags,
> An' a nice little white cotton-bo';
> An aw kiss'd her again, but hoo said
> 'At hoo wanted to kiss *thee* an' o.
> [*thae* 'thou/you', *bo* 'ball', *'at* 'that', *o* 'all']

Organized interest in the dialect centres on the Lancashire Dialect Society, founded in 1951 largely through the efforts of the late G. L. Brook, Professor of English Language at the University of Manchester. The Society publishes an annual journal devoted to both the academic study of, and writing in, the dialect. The collection *Songs of the People*, edited by Brian Hollingworth (Manchester University Press, 1977), contains examples of conservative dialect usage.

Scouse is the name for the often stigmatized dialect of the city of Liverpool, on the Mersey. It derives from the 18th-century term *lobscouse* (a sailor's dish of stewed meat, vegetables, and ship's biscuit), and as a result *Lobscouser* was a slang name for a sailor. However, the terms *Scouse* and *Scouser* for someone from Liverpool (and especially its working class) seem to be recent, and linked with the nature of the city as a major port. The *OED* cites the *Southern Daily Echo* (1945), in which 'a scouse' is explained as 'a native of Liverpool where they eat "scouse"'.

The Liverpool accent combines features of Lancashire with varieties of English predominantly from Ireland but also from Wales, brought in through 19th- and 20th-century immigration. Local accents range from broad Scouse through modifications towards RP to RP itself in the middle and upper classes. Among the distinctive expressions in Scouse are *the Pool*, a nickname for Liverpool, and *Liverpudlian* (the facetious but serious name for someone born in Liverpool, substituting 'puddle' for 'pool'). Non-Scousers, especially from north of the city, are sometimes called *woollybacks* (sheep), a nickname suggesting rusticity and lack of wits.

Pronunciation

1 In such pairs as *fur/fair* and *spur/spare*, the second member of each pair sounds the same as the first: 'Don't do that—it isn't fur'; 'I can't spur any more money right now'. *There* sounds similar, as in 'Just put it over thur'.

2 For words ending in -*ng*, there is a syllable-final combination *ng-g*: 'long-g' for *long*; 'sing-ging-g' for *singing*. Compare West Midland and Brummie.

3 Such words as *pin* and *sing* sound close to 'peen' and 'seeng-g'.

4 Liverpool pronunciation is non-rhotic. The *r*-sound is a distinct tap at the beginning of a word (*rabbit*, *run*), after stops and fricatives (*breathe*, *grass*, *three*), and between vowels (*carry*, *ferry*).

5 A *t* between vowels is often replaced by *r*, sometimes shown in print as *rr*, as in 'marra' for *matter* ('What's the marra with you then?'). In a publicity drive for a Liverpool clean-streets campaign, litter was described as 'norra lorra fun'.

6 Some speakers, especially working-class Catholics of Irish background, replace *th* with *t* and *d*, so that *these three fellows* is 'dese tree fellas', while *month* may be pronounced with an added t ('muntth').

7 At the beginning and end of syllables, the sound of *ch* in Scottish *loch* and German *ach* can follow *k*, as in 'kching' for *king* and 'backch' for *back*, and a *z*-sound can follow a *d* as in 'me dzad' for *my dad*, and 'badz' for *bad*.

The voice quality of Scouse has often been described as adenoidal, and phoneticians have speculated about the origins of such a feature. David Abercrombie, for example, noted that children may acquire such a quality of voice from others who have an adenoidal problem:

> **1967** A striking example . . . is afforded by some urban slum communities where adenoids, due doubtless to malnutrition and lack of sunlight, are prevalent, with their consequent effect on voice quality, but where people can be found with adenoidal voice quality who do not have adenoids—they have learnt the quality from the large number who do have them, so that they conform to what, for that community, has become the norm. . . . The accent of Liverpool seems to have had its origin in such circumstances.
>
> – *Elements of General Phonetics*, Edinburgh University Press.

In technical terms, the tongue is brought backwards and upwards in the mouth, there is a tightening of the pharynx, the cavity immediately behind the mouth, and the larynx rises. This process produces an adenoidal effect even though the speaker's nose is in no way blocked.

Cumbrian, Northumberland, and Geordie

The name of the north-western English region of Cumbria is Latinized Celtic (from *Cumbri*, the name of an ancient British people over 1,500 years ago) and cognate with Modern Welsh *Cymru* ('Welsh'). In the earlier Middle Ages, Cumbria also covered present-day south-west Scotland. Its inhabitants were known in Welsh as the *gwyr y gogledd* ('men of the north'), and scholars often refer to them as the Northern Welsh. The name currently applies to a county of north-western England formed in 1974 from the older counties of Cumberland and Westmorland, and part of Lancashire; it includes the Lake District (or Lakeland), the home of the poet William Wordsworth. The region was at one time trilingual: Cumbric spoken until the 11th century, northern Old English (Anglian) from the 7th century, and Norse in the 9–11th centuries. Local place-names reflect all three: Cumbric/Welsh, as in *Culgaith* ('back wood') and *Penrith* ('head of the ford'); Old English, as in *Broomfield* ('broom-covered field') and *Rottington* ('the farmstead of Rotta's people'); Norse, as in *Witherslack* ('wooded valley'), *Haverthwaite* ('the clearing where oats are grown'), and (indicating that the Norwegians had come from Ireland and brought Irish people with them) *Ireby* ('Irishman's Farm').

The traditional dialect is close to Scots and the other dialects of Northern England. Within Cumbria, Westmorland speech has features in common with the north-western Yorkshire Dales, such as 'skyool' for *school* and 'gaa' for *go*, and the dialect around Howden in East Yorkshire has more in common with Cumbria than with Wakefield, only 20 miles away in West Yorkshire. The speech of Lancashire North of the Sands (now part of Cumbria) is closer to Lancashire proper than to Lakeland; and the dialect boundary between North Midland and Northern (running from the Humber to Morecambe Bay) cuts across the area. Dunmail Raise, between Ambleside and Keswick, is said locally to be the linguistic boundary, and people north and south of the pass used to speak doubtfully of those who lived *ower t'Raise* ('over the Raise').

The Lakeland Dialect Society was founded in 1939. It publishes an annual journal whose poetry and prose attempt to display precise local usage with distinctive variants in spelling. The following examples, from a poem in North Westmorland dialect by Evelyn Metcalfe and a tale in North Cumbrian by Harold Forsyth, appeared in the 1990 Society journal:

> I like to hear t'auld sayins
> An teals fwok telt lang sen
> They mun herv lived, these caracters
> Beath women fwok an men.
> [*t'auld teals* 'the old tales', *fwok* 'folk',
> *telt lang sen* 'told long since/ago'
> (cf. Scots *Auld lang syne*)
> *mun herv lived* 'must have lived',
> *beath* 'both']

> Ther' wes yance a teal aboot a gadgie 'at stop't at a fillin' stashin
> ta git fullt up wid petrol. Them wes t'days afoor this self-service
> carry-on, when t'garridge lad wad gie this windscreen a bit wipe
> wi' an axe if ther wes owt else he cud deu fer thee.
> [*yance* ('once'); *gadgie* ('car'); *'at* ('that'); *them wes* ('those were');
> *afoor* ('before'); *wad gie* ('would give'); *axe* ('ask'); *owt*
> ('anything'); *cud deu fer thee* ('could do for you')]

Things are somewhat different on the other side of northernmost England, where the most prominent usage is urban rather than rural, although country people regard the traditional usage of Northumberland and County Durham as the true speech of the North-East, not the usage of Tyneside and the city of Newcastle upon Tyne or Teeside and the city of Middlesbrough. The dialects of the region all derive from Northumbrian, one of the three divisions of Old English. The dialect of Newcastle and Tyneside, generally known as *Geordie*, does however dominate the North-East, and the term *Geordie* is often loosely applied by outsiders to all the people in the North-East of England and to their speech, a state of affairs that can cause offence to non-Tynesiders generally and the people of Wearside and Middlesbrough in particular (although all the North-East belongs within a single dialect continuum).

The word *Geordie* is a diminutive of *George* that dates at least from the 18th century. It has long been favoured in both the North of England and Scotland as an affectionate name, not only for individuals but also for miners and sailors in general and even for coal-boats in and from north-east England, as well as for Scots in Australia and New Zealand. Its use as the name for both someone (especially a man) from Tyneside (widely known as *Geordieland*) and the Tyneside dialect is widely thought to derive from George Stephenson, the Newcastle engineer who built the first successful steam locomotive in 1814 and became manager of the Stockton to Darlington Railway (the world's first public railway line) in 1821. The dialect is essentially the working-class speech of Tyneside, which stands out as strongly in the North-East as Brummie and Scouse do in the Midlands and Lancashire. The following are key features of Geordie:

Pronunciation

1 It is the only urban accent of England in which initial *h* is not dropped.

2 A glottal stop replaces the consonants *p*, *t*, *k* in syllable-final position and often also in mid-word (as in *caper*, *daughter*, *packet*).

3 The uvular *r*, known as the *Durham Burr* or *Northumberland Burr* (made at the back of the mouth identically to the standard *r* of French), was once common in the general north-east but is in decline, probably because it was widely regarded—and treated in schools—as a speech defect.

4 The pronunciation of *r* is now generally dental, alveolar, or post-alveolar, but the burr has left a legacy in 'broad' Geordie, in which certain vowels are pronounced as if still followed by the burr: *cure* (as 'kyooah'), *nurse* as ('no-ahss').

5 Commonly, there is a long *aa* in such words as *all*, *talk*, *walk*, *war*, so that Geordie *walk* sounds to non-Geordies like 'waak', and *work* like 'walk'. A joke recounts how a man went to his doctor because of a painful knee. The doctor bandaged it and asked: 'Do you think you can walk now?' The man replied: '*Work?* I can hardly *walk*!'

6 A long Scots-style *oh*-vowel is usually followed by a weak vowel (schwa) in such words as *told*, *don't*, *know* (sometimes represented as 'toald', 'doan't', 'knoaw'), while the vowel in such words as *down*, *town* ranges from the *u* of Scots *doun*, *toun* ('down', 'town') to its RP value.

7 The closing vowel in words like *bonny* ('pretty') and *happy* is *ee* ('bonnee', 'happee'). In addition, a low rising tone in statements may to non-Geordies seem tentative or questioning.

Grammar

1 The typical Geordie pronoun form usually spelt *Aa*, as in *Aa doan't know* ('I don't know'), is identical to the *Ah* of Scots.

2 Another Scots parallel is the traditional but now sporadic use of negative *-na* rather than *not* or *n't*, as in *Aa canna bide yon chap* ('I can't stand that chap').

3 The form *diven't* is a traditional local alternative to *don't*, as in the double-negative *I diven't do nothin'* ('I don't do anything').

Vocabulary

1 Common forms of address include *bonny lad* (to a man or boy), *bonny lass* (to a woman or girl), *hinny* (honey: to a woman, girl, man, or boy), as in *How there, bonny lass?* ('How are you, dear?').

2 Geordie shares many words with Scots and Scottish English, as with: *bairn* ('child'); *bonny* ('fine, good-looking': used of both women and men); *canny* ('steady and cautious', but with a local nuance of 'good, kind, gentle').

The dialects of Northumberland and County Durham are in many ways closer to Border Scots than to Yorkshire, and many Scots regard the people of the region as much like themselves. A social and historical curiosity is the city of Berwick-upon-Tweed, which has been English since 1482, after having changed hands thirteen times between Scotland and England. Prior to the period of dispute, Berwick was the main Scottish port, and many Scots regard it as by right a Scottish town. To strengthen the anomaly, the county of Berwickshire is in Scotland, and most of its inhabitants speak Border Scots.

In 1996, Oxford University Press published the *Concise Ulster Dictionary*, edited by Caroline Macafee, a Scot. A feature of traditional Ulster usage is influence from Britain, notably from Scotland and the north of England, beginning in the early 17th century. In her introductory essay, Macafee notes that Ulster usage relates closely to Scots, 'the normal language of Lowland Scotland in the sixteenth and seventeenth centuries, regardless of social class'. As she puts it, 'much of the vocabulary of Scots extends south into England to a greater or less extent, and may therefore have reached Ulster from various communities in Scotland and England. A frequent form of words in the etymologies [in this dictionary] is "Scots and Northern English". For our purposes, the old English counties of Northumberland and Cumberland, which border on Scotland, are counted as Scots.' This approach emphasizes links not only between Scots and the usage of Northern England but also with Ulster usage.

Scotland

> **1996** Scotland has not one but two indigenous languages: Gaelic
> and Scots. Both have been largely displaced by English over the
> past 300 years. But displaced certainly does not mean destroyed.
> The languages have survived and produced considerable
> literatures. . . . There are active campaigns to extend the use
> of both languages. Gaelic, with government assistance, has a
> presence on television, and is undeniably a language because
> it is distinctive. Scots, however, has a close relationship to
> English . . . and so is easier to ignore.
>
> – 'Auld acquaintance be forgot: Letter from Edinburgh', *The Economist*, 10 February

Scotland consists of a mainland and three archipelagos. The mainland in turn has three regions: the *Highlands*, *Lowlands*, and *Southern Uplands* (part of a range of hills shared with England). The islands to the north-west are the *Western Isles* or *Hebrides*. The rest are the *Northern Isles*, in two groups: *Orkney* (also, especially formerly, *the Orkneys*) closer to the mainland, and *Shetland* (also, especially formerly, *the Shetlands*) further north. Both Orkney and Shetland belonged in medieval times to Norway, and are not far from *Faeroe* (also, especially formerly, *the Faeroes*), a self-governing Danish archipelago, which in turn is not far from Iceland: a name that means 'island', not 'land of ice'. Scotland's history is as intricate as its geography: in addition to its 18th-century union with England (and Wales), it was once (and for centuries) allied with France against England, and has had a long, close involvement with Ireland, from which came its very name.

Some key matters routinely regarded as Scottish were once Irish—or, like *whisk(e)y* and music, have been shared with Ireland. Over a thousand years ago, *Scotia* was a Latin name for Ireland, in the north of which lived the *Scot(t)i*, speakers of the Celtic language Gaelic. Paradoxically, these Scots of Ireland converted to Christianity under the influence of Patricius (Saint Patrick), a Romanized Briton whose home was probably in what is now southern Scotland. Catholic missionaries from Ireland were active on the early medieval European mainland, where they left behind such monuments as Vienna's *Schottenkirche* ('Scots-church'), which has no connection whatever with Scotland.

The great shift in names and their applications occurred after AD 500, when the Scots established a colony in Argyll in northernmost mainland Britain. In due course, they took over the entire Highland region of *Alba*, and gave their name to a whole new country known in Gaelic as *Alba*, in Latin as *Scotia* and *Caledonia*, and in English and Scots as *Scotland*. Paradoxically, therefore, the Germanic language Scots is named after Irish Celts.

Seven languages

By the time Scotland came together with England (and Wales) in 1707, to form the United Kingdom of Great Britain, seven languages had at various times been used there, four of which were either extinct or no longer in use:

❶ Pictish

A language in the Highlands in Roman times that was slowly displaced after the Scots arrived. Little is known about it, apart from inscriptions on stones and a range of place-names, especially those beginning with *pit* (a piece of land), such as *Pitlochry*, *Pittenweem*, and *Pitcairn* (later also the name of a South Pacific island). Pictish died out in the early Middle Ages.

❷ Cumbric

In Strathclyde, a Celtic language sometimes called *Northern Welsh*. The Cumbric narrative poem *Y Gododdin*, about an ill-fated war party that went south into what is now Yorkshire, to fight the Angles, is the earliest surviving poem of Scotland and also of the Welsh language.

❸ Gaelic

In the Middle Ages, the speech of the majority of Scots, a Celtic language with ancient roots in Ireland and a recently extinct relative on the Isle of Man. Now in what may prove to be terminal decline, with fewer than 100,000 speakers, it has a long and rich poetic and literary tradition.

❹ Inglis

The common name in the 14–15th centuries for an institutionalized national spoken and written variety of Northern English (heavily influenced by Anglo-Danish), known later by such other names as *Scots*, *Lowland Scots*, *Lallans* ('Lowlands'), and *the Doric* (after a comparison with the Doric Greek of Sparta, in contrast with English as the Attic Greek of Athens). The name *Inglis* had fallen out of general use long before parliamentary union with England in 1707.

❺ Norn

A variety of Norse spoken in the Northern and Western Isles, and the adjacent mainland, later restricted to Orkney, Shetland, and Caithness, then replaced by Scots, and now extinct.

❻ French

Norman French spoken among many of the nobility in medieval times as well as the language of an ally against England (in the so-called 'Auld Alliance').

❼ Latin

The longest continuously used language, originating with Roman military camps in the south, later serving as a language of the church, scholarship, literature, law, and written record till the Reformation, and continuing as a language of learning into early modern times.

In 1503 James IV King of Scots married Princess Margaret of England, in the Marriage of the Thistle and the Rose, as a result of which, in 1603, on the death of the childless Queen Elizabeth, James VI King of Scots became James I of England—an event known as the Union of the Crowns. In 1707, a further development took place between the two kingdoms, the Union of the Parliaments, in which the Scots Parliament was dissolved into an expansion of the English Parliament in London, creating a British Parliament. In the Act of Union, each country retained its own legal and educational systems and its national Protestant church. There was massive unease in Scotland at the time of this union, which had been achieved by both hard bargaining and threats and bribery from south of the border.

Although a majority of Scots has subsequently supported the idea of Great Britain, and their country has benefited economically from the Union, waves of nationalist feeling have ebbed and flowed ever since, demands ranging from 'home rule' (an older term replaced in recent years by 'devolution') through federalism to complete separation. The Scottish National Party currently favours independence within the European Union. A confused referendum among Scottish voters in 1979 did not lead to devolution but indicated a groundswell in its favour, but a second referendum in 1997 provided a clear mandate for the establishment of a devolved Scottish parliament in Edinburgh for national affairs while the Westminster parliament continued to oversee the UK as a whole. That parliament came into existence in 2000, and presented itself officially to the Scottish people as bilingual, English and Gaelic (with a sympathy for Scots).

From the 16th century, the standardizing variety of English in England grew increasingly influential in Scotland, and became the *de facto* (but never *de jure*) public language of the United Kingdom after the Union of the Parliaments in 1707. Of the old profusion of tongues only Gaelic and Scots survived, each influenced by and often mixing with 'Scottish English', a paradoxical term in recent decades for what has been the standard public language since the 18th century. During the same period there has been controversy and confusion over the nature, distinctness, worth, use, and viability of Scots, notably as to whether it was ever a language in its own right or had always been a dialect comparable to Yorkshire and Lancashire usage in England. On this point, the Scottish lexicographer A. J. Aitken concluded in his article on Scots in *The Oxford Companion to the English Language*:

> **1992** Scots is the substratum of general English in Scotland:
> most Scots use mixed varieties, and 'full' traditional Scots is
> now spoken only by a few rural people . . . None the less,
> despite stigmatization in school, neglect by officialdom, and
> marginalization in the media, people of all backgrounds have
> since the 16c insisted in regarding *the guid Scots tongue* as their
> national language, and it continues to play an important part in
> the awareness of their national identity.

Shortly before his death, however, he added a much more radical statement, in a report on Scots for the *Encyclopedia of the Languages of Europe*, edited by the Welsh scholar, Glanville Price (who in an earlier work, *The Languages of Britain* (Edward Arnold, 1984), declared that he could not make up his mind about the status of Scots). Aitken wrote:

> **1998 Scots** The Germanic language most closely related to
> English. It is derived partly from the Old English of the Angles of
> early Northumbria and partly from the Scandinavianized Middle
> English of immigrants into Scotland from medieval northern and
> central England. Originally spoken only in Lowland Scotland, it
> was also carried from there in the 17th c. to parts of Northern
> Ireland.
> – Blackwell, 409.

For almost three centuries, Scottish English has shaded into, and compromised with, both Scots on one side and the usage of England and Ireland on the other. Most people range from kinds of urban and rural Scots through mixed usage to kinds of Scottish Standard English. By and large, the rest of the population falls into four groups: a middle class using Scottish Standard English; a small, influential RP-speaking upper class, educated in England or in private schools in Scotland, using select Scotticisms as badges of belonging); a minority of near-RP-speaking professionals and others; and people from elsewhere domiciled in Scotland. In addition, three sources of tension (all with implications for language) have long been a feature of national life:

❶ Between Scotland and England

Many centuries of rivalry and warfare with a more fertile and populous England included a resentment of both its interference and its wealth. Although tensions steadily decreased after the Union in 1707, a relationship of mingled benefits and frustrations has included the issue of what it is to be 'Scottish' and speak a language called 'English'. One creative consequence of the discomfort has been, since the 18th century, the publication of English-language textbooks and dictionaries (many of which have influenced England, North America, and Empire territories and their successor states, such as Canada, Australia, and India. British publishers of Scottish provenance include Chambers, Collins, and Macmillan.

❷ Between Highlands and Lowlands, Scotland and Ireland

There has been a centuries-old suspicion (and formerly often conflict) between Gaelic-speaking Highlanders and Islanders and Scots-speaking Lowlanders, each often disdaining the other as *Teuchters* (the Gaels) and *Sassenachs* ('Saxons', the Lowlanders). The term *Sassenach*, however, is now applied by all Scots to the English, often amiably. In many cases, Highland/Lowland tension has tied in with religious conflict (see next).

❸ Between Protestants and Catholics

Since the Reformation there has often been severe tension between Protestants and Catholics, but this has greatly declined in recent decades. It is comparable to, and has often been linked with, religious and political divisions in Northern Ireland. This tension arose largely for two reasons:

- Scottish Presbyterians settled in Northern Ireland in significant numbers in the 17th century, where a distinctive Ulster Scots community emerged, becoming the source of the 'Scotch-Irish' migrations to the United States and Canada. The Protestant Northern Irish have retained ties with Scotland especially through the Orange Order, a 'loyalist' fraternity with strong anti-Catholic traditions (named after the 17th-century king William of Orange: 'King Billy').
- Irish migration to Scotland (especially Glasgow and the Central Lowlands), from the 19th century onward, massively enhanced the Roman Catholic presence in the West of Scotland and influenced the vernacular of the Glasgow area. Such Irish Catholics often shared both religion and Gaelic with Highland migrants.

From the Middle Ages to the 17th century, power in Scotland steadily became concentrated in the hands of the Lowlanders who, after the Clearances of the late 18th and early 19th centuries (when many Highlanders were forced by their landlords to leave their homes, often as a result emigrating to North America) and the Industrial Revolution (when many Highlanders and others moved to the cities of Scotland and England, or variously emigrated), have constituted the vast majority.

The King's Scots

The Germanic language of Scotland has had many names. The oldest, the Northern Middle English word *Inglis* (pronounced 'inglz', without a hard *g*-sound) derives, like *English*, from the Anglo-Saxon *Englisc*, and has long been defunct. Next came *Scottis/Scottys* (pronounced with a single long *o* as either 'Skótis' or 'Skóts'. For some time, *Inglis* and *Scottis* were used more or less as synonyms. Sometimes, however, to add to the complexity, 16th-century Scottish writers used *Inglis* only for the language of England and kept *Scottis* for their own usage, as in:

> **1513** Lyke as in Latyn beyn Grew termys sum,
> So me behufyt quhilum, or than be dum,
> Sum bastard Latyn, Franch or Inglys oys,
> Quhar scant was Scottys.
> – Gavin Douglas, Prologue to Book I, translation of the *Aeneid*

> ['Just as in Latin there are some Greek terms,
> So it behoved me whiles ('at times'), rather than be dumb,
> Some bastard Latin, French or English to use,
> Where Scots was scant'].

The term *Scottis* was also used in contrast to *Sotheroun/Suddroun/Southron* ('Southern': an entirely unambiguous term for the English of England). Only from the early 18th century was the present-day terminology consistently applied, with *Scots* as the name for the vernacular of the Scottish Lowlands and *English* as the name for both the traditional language of England and the standard national 'British' variety imported from England into Scotland and Scotticized.

The period from 1376 to 1560 was the high noon of classic Scots literature; as a consequence, literary writers have often stated that Scots was manifestly a language in its own right at that time because it had a literature with a wide range of styles and a large, varied, and distinctive vocabulary. The major poets (or *makars* 'makers') were: John Barbour, 14th century (an epic poem *The Brus*, about King Robert the Bruce); King James I, 15th century (*The Kingis Quair* 'Quire'); Robert Henryson, 15th century (*The Morall Fabillis* 'Moral Fables'; *The Testament of Cresseid*); 'Blind Harry', 15th century (an epic poem *The Wallace*, about William Wallace, and the basis for the Hollywood movie *Braveheart*); William Dunbar, 15th–16th centuries (religious, courtly, humorous, satirical poems); Gavin Douglas, 15th–16th centuries (a translation of the *Aeneid*); and Sir David Lyndsay, 16th century (*Ane Satyre of the Thrie Estaitis* 'A Satire of the Three Estates', a play). The following paragraph is from John Bellenden's translation, *c*.1531, of Hector Boece's Latin chronicles of Scotland, 1527:

> **c.1531** The samyn tyme happynnit ane wounderfull thing.
> Quhen Makbeth and Banquho war passand to Fores, quhair
> King Duncan wes for the tyme, thai mett be the gaitt thre weird
> sisteris or wiches, quhilk come to thame with elrege clothing.
> [Translation: 'At that time a wonderful thing happened. When
> Macbeth and Banquo were on their way to Forres, where King
> Duncan was at the time, they met by the roadside three 'sisters of
> fate' or witches, who approached them in unearthly garments.'
> Both of the words *eldritch* and *weird* have close associations with
> Scots.]

Another name for Scots from the 16th century onward has been *Lallans* (less commonly *Lallan*), adapted from *lawland(s)/lawlans* ('lowland/lowlands'), and contrasting with Gaelic, which was the language of the *hielan(d)s* ('highlands'), pronounced 'heelans'. The term *Lallans* tends to be confined nowadays to literary use, having been adopted after the Second World War by the 'Scottish Renaissance' poets. The Standard English term *Lowland Scots* (formerly also *Lowland Scotch*) remains a common name for the vernacular and its literature. Some Gaels claim that users of the Lowland tongue usurped the name *Scots* to differentiate their *Inglis* more clearly from *Southron* (a common early name in Scotland for English in England). The use of *Scottis* rather than Inglis dates from the 16th century, and the 18th-century addition *Lowland* served to remove any ambiguity in relation to Gaelic. Nowadays *Scots* is commonly used without *Lowland*, and the term *Lallans* is growing less common.

The term *Synthetic Scots* was coined in the 1920s for an eclectic literary variety which brought together terms from widely separated dialects and periods. The revivalist and nationalist writer Hugh MacDiarmid pioneered this style, which some critics re-named 'Plastic Scots'. The following excerpt is from 'The Eemis Stane' (in *Sangschaw* ['Songshow'], 1925) and demonstrates his eclecticism. It is laced with apostrophes, a device which present-day writers generally avoid because it concedes orthographic primacy to Standard English.

> I' the how-dumb-deid o' the cauld hairst nicht
> The warl' like an eemis stane

Wags I' the lift;
An' my eerie memories fa'
Like a yowdendrift.

[*how-dumb-deid* (Jamieson, below: 'the middle of the night, when
silence reigns; Ayrshire'); *cauld* (general Scots: 'cold'); *hairst*
(general: 'autumn'); *nicht* (general: 'night'); *warl'* (general:
'world'); *eemis* (Jamieson: 'insecurely balanced, toppling'); *stane*
(general: 'stone'); *lift* (archaic: sky, cf. German *Luft*); *fa'* (general:
'fall'); *yowdendrift* (Jamieson: 'snow driven by the wind'). The
archaic words *how-dumb-deid*, *hairst*, *eemis*, and *yowdendrift*
have all been taken from John Jamieson's *Etymological Dictionary
of the Scottish Language* (1808).

More significant than its name, however, has been the issue of whether Scots as
constituted today can reasonably be described as a distinct language. There are
many viewpoints in this debate, and it is even possible for people to hold several of
the following positions at the same time:

❶ Was formerly a language, but is not now

Argument: In the late Middle Ages and during the Renaissance, *Inglis* or *Scottis* was
a distinct language, notably because of its rich and influential literature and its use
as a formal language of record alongside Latin. When its literature faded, Scots
faded with it.

❷ Has its own dialects and a literature

Argument: Scots cannot simply be a dialect of English because it has distinct
dialects of its own as well as an on-going centuries-old literature, one of whose
features is a variable orthography.

❸ Is an untidy overspill from England

Argument: Scots has always been an indeterminate northern overspill from a
language whose discussion, as its name indicates, properly focuses on England.

❹ Is the English of Scotland

Argument: Scots is straightforwardly the distinctive indigenous English of
Scotland, descended from Anglian, whether regarded as a dialect group within
English at large, or a separate language, or both (depending on one's perspective).

❺ Is a Germanic language in its own right

Argument: Scots is a Germanic language as distinct from its sister 'Insular
Germanic' language English as Swedish is from Danish, and its distinctiveness
would have been recognized long ago if the two countries had remained separate.
Indeed, the Anglian dialects of Northern England are closer to Scots than to usage in
southern England.

❻ Is a matter of opinion, and not important

Argument: The issue is not particularly important and people are free to think whatever they like, including whether it is worth thinking about Scots at all. Standard
English as taught in the schools is the medium that matters.

Despite the controversy, Scots has since the early 18th century been the object of investigation by scholars. Such Scotticists have, as with English and other languages, divided its history into periods: *Old English/Anglo-Saxon* (to 1100); *Older Scots* (1100–1700), divided into *Early Scots* (1100–1450) and *Middle Scots* (1450–1700); and *Modern Scots* (1700 onwards). They divide its current dialects into four groups: *Central Scots*, in the most heavily populated Central Lowlands (including the working-class vernaculars of Edinburgh and Glasgow); *Southern Scots* (also Border Scots), in the Border districts; *Northern Scots*, from Caithness to Aberdeenshire and Angus; and *Orkney and Shetland*, the Scandinavian-tinged usage of the Northern Isles. The major features of the mainland dialects include:

Pronunciation

1 Like the dialects of Northern England, Scots exhibits an early divergence from the Midland and Southern dialects of Middle English: *hame, stane, sair, gae* as against 'home, stone, sore, go'; *hoose, oot, doon, coo* as against 'house, out, down, cow'; *ba, saut* as against *ball, salt*; *gowd, gowf* as against 'gold, golf'; *fu, pu* as against 'full, pull'; *buit, guid, muin, puir* as against *boot, good, moon, poor*.

2 Early Scots long *i* ('ee') split into two distinct vowel sounds typical of both Scots and Scottish English: as in *ay(e)* for 'yes' (*Aye, Ah'll come*) and for *buy, alive, rise, tied*, etc., and a tighter sound in *aye* for 'always' (*Ye're aye welcome here*) and for *life, rice, bite, tide*, etc.

3 The consonant system retains the Anglo-Saxon/Germanic sound in the exclamations *ach* and *och*, and in *dochter* ('daughter') and *nicht* ('night'), together with such adoptions from Gaelic as *loch* ('lake') and *clarsach* (a kind of harp).

4 Particularly distinctive is the Northern dialect use, around Aberdeen since the 15th century, of *f* where other dialects have *wh*, as in a well-known example sentence *Fa fuppit the fyte fulpie?* ('Who whipped the white whelp?').

5 South-Eastern and Southern dialects have *twae, whae, away, whare, waken, waiter* while Western and Northern dialects have *twaw/twaa, whaw/whaa/faa, awa/awaa, whaur/whaar/faar, wauken/waaken, wauter/waater* ('two', 'who', 'away', 'where', 'waken', 'water') on either side of a stretch of country from Musselburgh on the Firth of Forth to Gatehouse-of-Fleet on the Solway Firth.

Spelling

1 By the late 14th century, Older Scots was developing distinctive orthography marked by such features as *quh-* (English *wh-*), *-ch* (English *-gh*), *sch-* (English *sh-*), and the use of *i/y* as in *ai/ay, ei/ey* to identify certain vowels: compare Scots *quheyll, heych, scheip, heid, heyd* with English *wheel, high, sheep, heed, head*.

2 Following the Anglicization of the 16th–17th century, the literary Scots of Allan Ramsay, his contemporaries, and his successors in the 18th century had discarded some forms but retained others, including *ei* as in *heid* ('head'), *ui* or *u-e* as in *guid/gude* ('good'), and *ch* as in *loch* and *thocht* ('loch, thought'). This orthography, however, was in the main an adaptation of English orthography to represent Scots, as can be seen from the free use of apostrophes to this day to mark 'missing' letters.

3   Unlike English, but like Older Scots, present-day Scots is tolerant of spelling variation, and resists such regulation as the *Scots Style Sheet* of the Makars' [Poets'] Club in 1947. The *Concise Scots Dictionary* (Chambers, 1985) records many spelling variants, such as *breid*, *brede*, *bread*, *braid* ('bread'), and *heuk*, *huke*, *hook* ('hook'), and the larger dictionaries record many more.

Grammar

1   The regular past forms of the verb are *-it*, -t, or *(e)d*, according to the preceding consonant or vowel: *hurt/hurtit* ('hurt/hurt'); *mend/mendit* ('mend/mended'); *skelpit* ('smacked'); *ken/kent/kenned* ('know/knew/known'); *tell/tellt/tauld* ('tell/told/told'); *dee/deed* ('die/died').

2   Some verbs have distinctive principal parts: *gae/gaed/gan(e)* ('go/went/gone'); *gie/gied/gien* ('give/gave/given'); *greet/grat/grutten* ('weep/wept/wept').

3   There is a set of irregular noun plurals: *eye/een* ('eye/eyes'); *cauf/caur* ('calf/calves'); *coo/kye* ('cow/cows': compare archaic English *kine*).

4   Nouns of measure and quantity remain unchanged in the plural: *twa mile* ('two miles'); *five pun(d)* ('five pounds').

5   There are two forms for an adjective/adverb specifying distance well away from the speaker: *yon/yonder* and *thon/thonder* (that and those there, at some distance): *D'ye see yon/thon hoose ower yonder/thonder?*

6   Ordinal numbers that end in English with *-th* end in *-t* in Scots: *fourt*, *fift*, *saxt/sixt*, etc.

7   Diminutive suffixes are common and include: those in *-ie/y* (*burnie* 'small *burn*/brook'; *feardie/feartie* 'frightened person, coward'; *gamie* 'gamekeeper'; *kiltie* 'kilted soldier'; *postie* 'postman'; *wifie* 'wife'); those in *-ock* (*bittock* 'little bit'; *sourock* 'sorrel', also a term of endearment for a woman); and those in *-ockie/-ickie* (*hoosickie* 'small house', *wifeockie* 'little/dear wife'). Note the five times diminished or endeared *a little wee bit lassockie*.

8   Double modal verbs: *He'll no can come the day* ('He won't be able to come today'); *Ah micht could dae it the morn* ('I might be able to do it tomorrow/I could maybe do it tomorrow'); *Ah used tae could dae it, but no noo* ('I could do it at one time, but not now').

9   Verbless subordinate clauses that express surprise or indignation are introduced by *and*: *She had tae walk the hale lenth o the road* ('She had to walk the whole length of the road . . .') *an her seeven month pregnant* ('. . . and she was pregnant too'); *He tellt me tae run and me wi ma sair leg tae* ('He told me to run and me with my sore/painful leg too').

10   Negation is either by the adverb *no* (North-East *nae*): *Ah'm no comin* ('I'm not coming'), or by *-na/nae*, (depending on dialect, and equivalent to *-n't*, as in *Ah dinnae ken* ('I don't know'); *They canna come* ('They can't come'); *We couldna hae tellt 'im* ('We couldn't have told him'); *Ah huvnae seen her* ('I haven't seen 'er').

11   Verbs of motion may be dropped before an adverb or adverbial phrase of motion: *Ah'm awa tae ma bed* ('I'm off to my bed'); *That's me awa hame noo* ('I'm off home now').

12   Scots prefers the order *He turnt oot the licht* ('He turned out the light') to
     He turned the light out and *Gie me it* to *Give it (to) me*.

Vocabulary

1   The vocabularies of Scots and English overlap, and Scots has words that are
    unique or shared with Northern English dialects or have passed into
    international English.

2   Germanic words not shared with any dialect of England include: *but and
    ben* ('a two-room cottage': *but* the outer room, *ben* the inner room); *cleuch*
    ('a gorge'); *haffet* ('cheek': facial); *skeich* (of a horse: 'apt to shy or rear');
    swick ('to cheat').

3   Words shared with Northern dialects of England include: *bairn* ('a child');
    bide ('to live in a place'); *dicht* ('to clean': in England *dight*); *dwam* ('a stupor,
    daze'); *hauch* ('a riverside meadow', in England *haugh*); *snell* (of weather:
    'bitter, severe'); *speir* ('to ask'); *thole* ('to endure, tolerate').

4   Words taken into general and literary English include: *bannock, eldritch, fey,
    gloaming, raid, wee, weird, wizened*. Both *weird* and *fey* have the original
    senses 'destiny' and 'fated to die'. The phrase *Tae dree yir ain weird* means
    'to endure what is destined for you'.

5   Words from Scandinavian include: *big* ('to build'); *blae* ('blue', whence
    blaeberry); *blether* ('to chatter, talk nonsense'); *brae* ('slope of a hill'); *cleg*
    ('a gadfly'); *gate* ('road'); *gowk* ('cuckoo'); *graith* ('equip, equipment'); *kirk*
    ('church'); *lass* ('girl'); *lowp* ('to leap'); *lug* ('ear').

6   Words from Gaelic, passed on to English, include: (1) Early borrowings: *bog,
    cairn, capercailzie, clachan* (a hamlet or group of stone houses), *clan, clarsach*
    (the Highland harp), *glen, loch, ptarmigan, slogan* (originally a war cry), *sonsy*
    ('hearty, comely, buxom'); *strath* ('wide valley'); (2) From the 17th century
    onward: *ben* ('mountain'); *brogue* (a Highland shoe for walking in rough
    places); *corrie* (a cirque or circular hollow on a mountainside); *gillie* (a
    hunting attendant); *pibroch* (solo bagpipe music); *sporran* (a purse worn in
    front of a kilt); *whisky*.

7   Words from French include: (1) Once shared with English: *cowp* ('to capsize
    or upset', from *couper* 'to cut, strike'); *douce* (originally of a woman or
    manners: sweet, from *doux/douce*); *houlet* ('owl', from *hulotte*); *leal* ('loyal');
    tass/tassie ('cup', from *tasse*); (2) Primarily or exclusively Scots: *ashet* ('serving
    dish', from *assiette*); *fash* ('to bother, trouble', from *fâcher*); *Hogmanay* (from
    Old French *aguillanneuf* 'a New Year's gift'); *sybow/sybie* ('spring onion',
    from Old French *ciboule*); *vennel* ('an alley', from Old French *venelle*).

8   Words from Dutch include: *howf* ('a favourite haunt/pub', from *hof*
    'courtyard'); *loun* ('lad'); *mutch* ('a kind of woman's cap'); *pinkie* ('little
    finger': passed to American English); *trauchle* ('to overburden, harass').

9   Onomatopoeic words of uncertain origin: *birl* ('to whirl'); *dunt* ('a thump');
    skreich ('to shriek'); *wheech* ('to move in a rush'); *yatter* ('to chatter').

10 Typical reduplicative words: *argybargy* ('a dispute'); *clishclash* and
    clishmaclaver ('idle talk, gossip'); *easy-osy* ('easy-going'); *eeksie-peeksie* ('six
    and half a dozen'); *the hale jingbang* ('the whole caboodle'); *joukerie-pawkerie*
    ('trickery'); *mixter-maxter* ('all mixed up').

11 Distinctive, often fanciful combinations and formations: *bletherskate* ('an incessant talker'); *camshauchle* ('distorted'); *carnaptious* ('quarrelsome'); *carfuffle* ('a commotion, passed on into English); *collieshangie* ('a noisy squabble'); *sculduddery* fornication (whence American *skullduggery*); *tapsalteerie* ('topsy-turvy'); *whigmaleerie* ('a trifle, strange whim').

12 Iteratives, intensives, and others: *donnert* ('dazed', stupid'); *scunner* ('to disgust; someone or something disgusting: from the root of *shun*: also Northern English); *shauchle* ('to shuffle'); *shoogle* ('to joggle, shake'); *shoogly* ('shaky, wobbly').

13 Common words of various derivations, some obscure, some now general beyond Scotland: *bogle* ('ghost': perhaps Celtic: note *tattie-bogle* 'a potato bogle, a scarecrow'); *bonny/bonnie* ('handsome, beautiful': probably from French *bon* 'good'); *braw* ('fine, excellent'); *couthy* ('homely/homey, congenial': from *couth* 'known': compare general *uncouth*); *eerie* ('fearful, ghostly'); *glaikit* ('foolish', from *glaik* 'trick, deceit, flash'); *glamour* ('a spell', and a kind of socially magical quality: etymologically a doublet of *grammar*); *glaur* ('mud'); *gomerel* ('a fool'); *gumption* ('get-up-and-go, guts': now widespread).

14 Recent creations: *fantoosh* ('flashy', probably a play on *fantastic*); *gallus* ('mischievous, ready for anything'); *heidbanger* ('madman'), *high-heid-yin* ('high-head-one': boss, manager); *multy* ('a multi-storey tenement'); *skoosh* ('to gush; a fizzy drink'); *squeegee* ('askew').

In Edinburgh, not far from the new Parliament, the Indian restaurant *Suruchi* has a menu in Scots, with the heading 'Welcome tae Suruchi' and a note that the usage of the menu was 'providit by the Scottish National Dictionary Association'. It states:

> **2001** The word Suruchi means 'Guid Taste' in Sanskrit, an in a wheen modern Indian leids. But Suruchi isnae juist the name o wir restaurant: it tells ye we're committit tae bringin ye the brawest Indian food, music an atmosphere.

To do this, the menu lists and describes what is available, with occasional glosses, as in:

Aloo Gol Morich
Makkit fae a tradeetional Bengali receipt [recipe]. Tatties an green peppers cookit wi fresh green chillies

Assorted kebab
For fowk that's daft aboot kebabs. A braw feast o chicken, mince an lamb.
Aw wir starters is servit wi caller [fresh] chutney an tangy mint sauce for dookin.

Suruchi's chice o rice an breid
Ye'll get sindrie types o rice in Indian cookin. But Suruchi yaises the maist weel-kent (an the brawest)—Basmati. Its name means 'the fragrant yin'.

The existence of Scots in its own right, of a majority continuum between Scots and Scottish English, and of a Scottish English in its own right appears to be the current reality. This reality differs from the past two centuries in that the situation has begun to be re-assessed, especially in education and publishing—and occasionally in surprising settings.

Gutter Scots versus Morningside and Kelvinside

Gutter Scots is a pejorative but common term for urban working-class speech in Scotland, *Scots* often being replaced by a local name, primarily *Glasgow*. The largest city in Scotland and third largest in the UK, Glasgow is at the centre of a sprawling conurbation with a population of around a million in a national population of some five million. Its working-class speech is known variously as *Glasgow English*, *Glasgow Scots*, *Glaswegian*, *Glasgow*, *Glesca*, *Gutter Glasgow*, and (more racily) *The Patter* or *Ra Pa?ur* (with *r* for *th* and a glottalized *t*). It has long been the archetypal stigmatized Scottish speech, commonly described as 'debased', 'hopelessly corrupt', or simply 'the language of the gutter'.

The Industrial Revolution led to a vast influx of immigrants into Glasgow and the Central Lowlands from the Highlands and Ireland, resulting in a large Roman Catholic minority and a Protestant/Catholic sectarian divide similar to that of Belfast in Northern Ireland. However, the decline of heavy industry (iron and steel, engineering, and ship-building) between and after the world wars led to high levels of unemployment and alienation. Though the slums for which the city was once notorious have since 1946 largely been cleared or renovated, the peripheral housing estates into which much of the working-class population was 'decanted' are often physically and socially bleak. Even so, however, Glasgow is a noted artistic and academic centre, and its vernacular is probably the most demographically potent in the UK after London, enjoying a strong counter-prestige much like Cockney in London, Scouse in Liverpool, and Geordie in Newcastle.

The following features relate primarily to 'Gutter Glasgow', but are representative of the urbanized Central Lowlands at large, and some features are shared with major urban areas in England and Ireland.

Pronunciation

1   A key feature is the glottal stop, which realizes *t*, *p*, *k* as glottal plosives after vowels and the consonants *l*, *n*, *r*, so that, for example, *better butter* is rendered *be?ur bu?ur*. The *t*, *p*, or *k* is typically glottalized in such words as *bottle*, *quarter*, *shelter*, *keepin'*, *workin'*.

2   An *h*- often substitutes for *th*-: *Ah hink* ('I think'); *hing* ('thing'); *sumhn* ('something'); *nuhn* ('nothing'); and *hr*- for *thr*-, as in *hree* ('three') and *hred* ('thread').

3   In the Glasgow area, the vowel in *air* commonly rhymes with *err*, so that *rare floor* sounds like 'rerr flerr' and *Mary* and *merry* are homophones.

4   Also in the Glasgow area, many speakers realize voiced *th* as *r*, as in *ra* ('the') in *ra polis* ('the police'), *ramorra* ('tomorrow'), *ma brurra* ('my brother'), *oor murra* ('our mother').

5 In such words as *want*, *water*, *wash* the vowel is 'ah', so that *matter* and *water* ('watter') rhyme. The distinction is sometimes written as *aa*: *Ah waan? wan* ('I want one').

6 The words *away*, *two*, *who*, *whose*, *where* all have an *aw*-sound: 'awaw', 'twaw', 'whaw', 'whause', 'whaur'.

7 An unstressed final *a* appears in such words as: *barra* ('barrow'), *fella* ('fellow'), *Glesca/Glasga* ('Glasgow'), *ra morra* (Glasgow: 'tomorrow'), *awfa/awfy* ('awful'), *yisfa* ('useful').

8 In both Glasgow and Edinburgh, the informal negative equivalent to *-n't* is *-nae*, as in *cannae* ('can't') and *dinnae* ('don't'), whereas other dialects have *-na*: *Ah canna dae it* ('I can't do it'), *He huzna goat it* ('He hasn't got it').

9 Final *d* is generally lost after *l* and *n*, as in *caul* ('cold'), *staun* ('stand'), *roon* ('round': *staunin roon aboo?* 'standing round about'), *grun* ('ground'), *win* ('wind').

10 The form *wan* ('one': as opposed to Scots *ane*), and the adding of a *t* to *wance* as *wanst* (for 'once') and *twice* as 'twyst' probably came over with immigrants from Ireland.

11 Final stressed vowels may be greatly prolonged, as highlighted and caricatured in the poet Tom Leonard's 'Tea Time' (in *Intimate Voices*, Galloping Dog Press, Newcastle, 1984): *ahm thaht depehhhhndint/ hingoanti ma vowwwwulz/ hingoanti ma maaaammi* ('I'm so dependent/I hang on to my vowels/I hang on to my mummy').

12 Where Glasgow has an unstressed word-final weak *-a*, as in *barra* ('barrow'), Edinburgh has a weak *-ie*: *barrie* ('barrow'); *elbie* ('elbow'); *fellie* ('fellow'); *Glesgie/Gleskie* ('Glasgow': compare Glasgow's *Glasga/Glesca*); *awfie* ('awful'); *moothfie* ('mouthful'); *yisfie* ('useful').

Grammar

1 Multiple negation, usually for emphasis: *Ah dinnae waant nane* ('I don't want any'); *Ah'm no gaun ne'er Ah'm no* ('I am not going neither am I not').

2 Double auxiliary *have*: *Ye'da saw im if ye'da came* ('You'd have seen him if you'd come').

3 *An here* and *Here* as exclamations of surprise: *An here, the shoap wis open efter aw!* ('And here, the shop was open after all!'), *Here, what d'ye hink ye're daein?* ('Here, what d'you think you're doing?').

4 Repetition of the reporting use of *say*: *He says tae me e says Ah'm no comin, an Ah says tae him Ah says Jis you shut up well!* ('He said to me he wasn't coming and I told him just to shut up!').

5 Minced oaths as exclamations of surprise: *Jings!* ('Jesus!'), *Crivvens!* ('Christ!'), *Help ma Boab!* ('Help my Bob!' = Help my God!).

6 *See* often used as an emphatic and focusing device: *See me, see ma sister, see ma sister's man, see kippers, e hates them* ('Y'know, my sister's husband *really hates* kippers').

7   Of Northern Irish origin, the plural forms of the second-person pronoun *you* include *youse* (subject of the sentence or for emphasis), *yese*, *yis* (object or unemphatic), and *youse-yins* ('you ones/you people'): *Youse get oot o here!*

8   An emphatic first-person form *Ah'm ur* ('I am are' = 'I really am'): *Aye, Ah'm ur gaun* ('Yes, I *am* going') and the triple negative *Naw, Ah'm urnae* ('No, I am are not' = 'No, I definitely am not').

9   Sentence tags used for reinforcement (probably from Ireland) include the second element in the following: *Ye're drunk, so ye ur; Ah'm fed up, so Ah um/so Ah'm ur; Ah feel terrible, so Ah dae; Ah didnae touch nuhn, ne'er Ah did* ('I didn't touch anything, neither I did').

10 The use of emphatic final *but*, as in: *Ah dinnae waant it but* ('But I don't want it'); *She's no comin but* ('But she's not coming').

11 In the Edinburgh area, the pause-filler *ken* ('y'know') is common and often repetitive, as in *Weel, ken, ye dinny pey, for ti jist watch them, ken* ('Well, y'know, you don't pay, just to watch them, y'know').

12 Also in the Edinburgh area, the routine tag *like* is widely used, as in *Ah thocht Ah heard ye greetin, like* ('I thought I maybe heard you crying') and *Am Ah gettin an invite, like?* ('Am I getting an invitation maybe?').

Vocabulary

1   Long-established usages in the Greater Glasgow area include: *dunny* ('basement'); *ginger* (a soft drink of any kind); *stank* (a grating over a drain); *wallie close* (the tiled entrance hall of a better-class tenement); *tummle yir wulkies* ('to turn somersaults').

2   Slang usages include: *bampot, bamstick* ('idiot'); *boggin, bowfin* ('smelly'); *hairy/herry* and *hingoot* ('hang-out') ('girl', disparaging); *heidbanger/heidcase* ('lunatic'); *lumber* ('a pick-up, a boy/girlfriend, one's date'); *brassie/riddie* (a red face, a cause of shame); *malkie* ('a weapon').

3   Edinburgh usage prefers the traditional Scots word *bairn* ('child') where Glasgow generally has *wean*, short for *wee ane* ('small one'), pronounced *wane* (with a single-vowel *ay*-sound).

Unremarkably, matters have been different among the bourgeoisie. Morningside and Kelvinside are similar middle-class districts in Edinburgh and Glasgow, and the similar names also cover the accents common, especially formerly, among their inhabitants. In effect, they are one accent, originating among well-off people who aspired to southern gentility but did not have easy access to RP as a model. What emerged was an affected, hypercorrect, and not always stable approximation.

The shared variety is closely identified with two shibboleths: one is suggested by the spelling 'ectually' for *actually*, the other by the pronunciation of such words as *five* and *time* as 'fayv' and 'taym' (rhyming with *behave* and *game*, each spoken with a single-vowel *a*). The features come together in 'Eh'm quate well aware of thet fect' (the words of Mrs M'Cotton, in Helen W. Pryde's *McFlannels United*, 1949). As a stigmatized stereotype, Kelvinside is on record since 1901, Morningside since the 1940s, but the style probably originated in 19th-century girls' private schools and was not regionally restricted. Although the stereotype still thrives, the accent itself is in decline.

Norn and the Orkney and Shetland dialects

The term *Norn*, first recorded *c*.1485 in Shetland, is from Old Norse *norroena mál* ('northern language'), as applied to the language of ancient Norway and its colonies. It was therefore a variety of Norse as spoken in and around the Northern Isles, and had two subvarieties: *Orkney Norn* and *Shetland Norn*. The name has also recently been applied to Norse spoken in medieval Caithness on the mainland (*Caithness Norn*). Orkney and Shetland were settled in the 9th century by Norse-speaking farmers mainly from south-western Norway, who imposed their language on the local Picts. These were only part of a series of such settlements in Caithness, the West Highlands, the Western Isles, Ireland, and the east coast of England. But nowhere else in the British Isles did links with Scandinavia endure so long and leave such strong imprints on local usage, place-names, and culture.

Influence from the Scots language began in the family of the earls of Orkney in the 12th century. In 1379, the Sinclair family from Lowland Scotland gained the earldom, and in 1468/9 the King of Norway and Denmark pledged both island groups to the King of Scots, in a marriage dowry, after which the islands were dominated by Scots-speaking rulers, officials, and clerics. From the 16th century, Scots was the high and Norn the low language: 'Scho aundit in bitt, quhilk is ane Nourn terme and to [be] exponit into right longuag is alse mikill as scho did blaw her breath thairin' ['She *aundit in bitt* ("blew into a bucket"), which is a Norn term and expressed in proper language is as much as to say she blew her breath therein']: from *Orkney Witch Trial*, 1633, in *Register of the Privy Council of Scotland*, 2nd series, v. 545.

Norn was apparently superseded by Scots in Caithness in the 15th century and by Gaelic in the West Highlands and Islands in the 16th, but appears to have endured to the later 18th in Orkney and the 19th in Shetland. Garbled fragments—rhymes, proverbs, riddles, and snatches of songs—persisted in Orkney and especially Shetland folklore into the 20th century: until 1958 on the island of Foula. The scanty records reveal a speech related to Faroese, but with a decaying inflectional system, as in this passage from the Lord's Prayer (as recorded by James Wallace in *Account of the Islands of Orkney*, 1700), followed by its equivalent in Old Norse:

1700

Norn

Ga vus da on da dalight brow vora,
firgive vus sinna vora,
sin vee firgive sindara mutha vs.

Old Norse

Gef oss dag um dag dagligt brauð vort,
fyrirgef oss syndir várar,
sem vér fyrirgef syndir i móti oss.

Translation

Give us each day our daily bread,
Forgive us our sins,
As we forgive sins against us.

Local documents in Older Scots (from 1433) contain many administrative and legal terms of Norn origin, and court records from the early 17th century use many Norn words, such as: *galt* ('boar'); *grind* ('gate'); *heavie* ('straw basket'); *row* ('to "roo" or pluck (sheep)'); *spick* ('blubber, fat'); *voe* ('inlet'); *voir* ('springtime'). Most of the 450 or so *noa* (constituting in the main the former 'sea language' of Orkney and Shetland fishermen) are Norn expressions, and many other Norn usages survive in these conservative varieties. Some features are:

Pronunciation

1 Retention of the old front rounded vowel (compare French *sur*), written as *ui*, *u-e* and *ö*, as in *guid*, *gude*, and *göd* ('good') and *scuil*, *scule*, and *scöl* ('school').

2 The unique full preservation of the double opening consonants *kn-*, *gn-*, *wr-* as in *knee*, *gnaw*, and *wrang* ('wrong').

3 Under the influence of the Norn substrate, the pronunciation of *this* and *them* etc., as 'dis' and 'dem' etc., and of *three* and *earth* etc., as 'tree' and 'eart' etc.

4 The pronunciation of *j* as *ch* ('chust' for *just*, 'chump' for *jump*), as in Gaelic English.

5 The tendency in Shetland to pronounce *ch* as *sh* ('sheese' for *cheese*, 'ship' for *chip*).

6 In Shetland usage, as in Icelandic, the merging of 'hw' and 'kw'; in most places, towards 'kw', *white* sounding like *quite*, but in south Mainland towards 'hw', *quite* sounding like *white*), or the sounds are reversed: 'kweel' for *wheel*, 'hween' for *queen*.

Grammar

1 The use of familiar *thou*, *thee*, and *thy* alongside respectful singular *ye*, *you*, and *your*.

2 The use of gender-marked personal pronouns that are probably Norn in origin, notably *he* for weather, time, and other natural phenomena: *He was blaain a gale* ('It was blowing a gale'); *Whin he begood tae flou, sheu set on an teuk brawly* ('When he [the tide] began to flow, she [the fish] set to and took (the bait) splendidly').

3 Commonly, *be* preferred to *have* to mark a completed action: *I'm walked a piece the day* ('I've walked a long way today').

4 A limited use of inversion to form questions, as an alternative to the use of an auxiliary: *Whit tinks du?/Whit does du tink?* ('What do you think?'); *Is du heard aboot yun afore?* ('Have you heard about that before?').

5 Characteristic reflexive usages, especially in commands: *Heest dee!* ('Haste thee!', 'Hurry up!'); *Dip dee a meenit!* ('Sit down for a minute!'); *A'll geng an rest me whin a'm pitten da bairns ta da scöl* ('I'll go and have a rest when I've got the children off to school').

Vocabulary

1 Massive borrowing from Norn, of which over a thousand items survive: *benkle* ('to dent, crumple'); *frush* ('to splutter, froth'); *gaan* ('to gawp'); *glaep* ('to gulp

down, swallow greedily'); *oag* ('to crawl'); *peedie* in Orkney and *peerie* in Shetland ('little, small'); *skoit* ('to peep, take a look'); *smucks* ('carpet slippers'); *spret* ('to rip open, burst'); *tirn* ('angry'); *trivvel* ('to grope, feel one's way').

2   Some words structurally unusual for Scots: *andoo* ('to row a boat slowly against the tide'); *brigdie/brigda* ('basking shark'); *fluckra* ('snow in large flakes'); *glimro* (Orkney: phosphorescence); *hyadens* (Shetland: animal carcasses).

3   Old Norse inflectional endings fossilized in some words:

● the strong masculine -*r* in *ilder* ('fire', in the now-obsolete Shetland sea-language), *shalder* ('oyster-catcher': a bird)

● the weak masculine -*i* in *arvie* ('chickweed'), *galtie* ('pig, boar'), *hegrie* ('heron')

● the weak feminine -*a* in *arvo* ('chickweed'), *shaela* (Shetland: hoar-frost)

● the vocative in the former Birsay terms of address, *gullie* (said to a man), *gullo* (said to a woman)

● the gender distinctions in the Shetland sea-terms *russie* ('stallion'), *russa* ('mare').

4   Some nouns contain the Old Norse suffixed definite article *(i)n*: *croopan* ('the trunk of the body'), *fyandin* (Shetland: 'the devil'), *knorin* (Shetland: 'boat'), and the Shetland sea-terms *birten* ('fire'), *hestin* ('horse'), *monen* ('moon'), and *sulin* ('sun').

5   Unique to Shetland, though now mostly archaic, are words borrowed from Dutch fishermen, who have visited Shetland since the 17th century: blöv ('to die'), *forstaa* ('to understand'), *kracht* ('energy'), *maat* ('friend'), *stör* ('penny').

Dialect writing has been common throughout the varieties of Scots, and includes strong traditions since the 1880s in both Orkney and Shetland. Below are examples from *The Orkney View* (Feb/Mar 1989) and *The New Shetlander* (No. 168, March 1989):

1989: Orkney

So Geordie gleppid the last grain o tea ooto his cup and meed fir the byre. Noo Geordie was bothered sometimes wae a sore back when he waas been sta'an bent ower fir a while. So when he caam tae 'Reed coo', the bonniest and most litesome o aa the kye in Orkney, he glammed a haad o her yurrie waey his great knaves and keeled her ower i' the oddlar so he could milk her waeoot bendan doon too muckle.

– Karen Drever, Westray, *Geordie o Pizzlewusp*, first prize, dialect competition for under-16s, *The Orkney View*, February/March 1989

[*glep* 'swallow', *grain* 'drop', *meed* 'made', *noo* 'now', *wae/wy* 'with', *waas been sta'an* 'had been standing', *coo/kye* 'cow/cows', *glam* 'grab', *haad* 'hold', *yurrie* 'udder', *knave* 'fist', *keeled her ower* 'threw her over', *oddlar* 'drain in a byre', *muckle* 'much'.]

1989: Shetland

Twartree weeks later da story gaed roond at it wis a kist fae da Island a Hascosay, an it wisna a bonny story. Wan night lang fae syne a sailing ship had gone on a skerry in a storm dere an da men managed ta sween ashore an wan o dem trailed his kist wi him and da folk on da Island cam doon ta da shoormel an murdered

> da whole lot an dis man wis sittin on his kist lid whin he wis
> struck doon.
>
> – Joan M. Olsen, short story, 'Da Hascosay Kist', *The New Shetlander* 168, Mar 1989
>
> [*twartree* 'two or three', *gaed* 'went', *at* 'that', *kist* 'chest', *fae* 'from', *wisna* 'was not',
> *lang fae syne* 'long ago', *skerry* 'reef', *sween* 'swim', *shoormel* 'shoreline']

Gaelic and Gaelic English

Gaelic (generally pronounced 'Gallic', but sometimes 'Gaylic', as in Ireland) was the foremost language in Scotland until the 12th century, and it dominated the Highlands and Western Isles until the late 18th century, after which it went into decline. General and official attitudes towards the language at the start of the 21st century have been more positive than previously, encouraging bilingualism and giving it a more valued place in education, but such measures may be too little too late. Gaelic is now an everyday language only in the Western Isles, and the number of competent speakers may be no more than 80,000.

Scottish Gaelic has an ancient literary tradition and paradoxically its literature has flourished in recent decades, with such poets as Sorley MacLean, Derick Thomson, and Iain Crichton Smith (also a novelist in English). The songs of Donnchadh Bàn Mac-an-t-Saoir (Duncan Bàn Macintyre), Alasdair Mac Mhaighstir Alasdair (Alexander MacDonald), and Rob Donn continue to be sung, and recital and composition are encouraged by the *National Mod*, an annual competitive festival of music and poetry organized by *An Comunn Gaidhealach/The Highland Association*, which was founded in 1891 to support the language and its culture. *Comunn na Gàidhlig* (the Gaelic Association) was set up in 1984 with the more specific aim of promoting the language.

There has been a strong two-way traffic in words between Gaelic and Scots/English over the centuries, some words making more than one journey: thus, Gaelic *clann* ('children of a family') became first Scots then English *clan* (a community under a chief, with a common surname, such as *Cameron* or *MacGregor*), which was then taken back into Gaelic in this newer sense. Gaelic has influenced the pronunciation and grammar of English in both present and former Gaelic-speaking areas, and borrowings from English and Scots into Gaelic are numerous and increasing, especially in technical and administrative fields: for example, *teilebhisean* ('television'), *rèdio* ('radio'), and *briogais* ('trousers': from Scots *breeks*, cf. English *breeches*).

The influence of English and Scots on the grammar of Gaelic is considerable, now that virtually all Gaelic-speakers know both. Pronunciation has been less affected, but phonemic changes based on English or Scots are noticeable in the speech of children of Gaelic-speaking city-dwellers. More of these children now speak Gaelic, however, because of a recent increase in Gaelic playgroups and schools. The language is taught in three of the Scottish universities, two of which (Edinburgh and Glasgow) have a chair of Celtic.

English as used in the Highlands and the Hebrides differs from the English/Scots mix in the Lowlands, because of both the influence of Gaelic and traditional classroom instruction, and there are many similarities between Gaelic English in Scotland and Hiberno-English in Ireland. Gaelic influence takes two forms: a direct living impact, as the mother tongue of many, and the on-going effects of former use on the mainland. Since the late 17th century, most people in the Highlands and Western Isles have learned Scottish Standard English by the book, mostly from Gaelic-speaking teachers, some of whom had studied in Inverness or the Lowlands.

Pronunciation

1 A loss of voicing in certain consonants, so that: *just* becomes 'chust', *pleasure* 'pleashure', *whatever* 'whateffer', and *bring* 'pring': all shibboleths of Gaelic-influenced speech.

2 The insertion of an *h* before *k*, *p*, and *t*: 'wee*h*k', 'ha*h*pen' for *happen*, 'abou*h*t'.

3 The same consonants are also aspirated at the start of words: 'p*h*ig' for *pig*, 'thake' for *take*, 'kheep' for *keep*.

4 Many speakers lengthen vowels that are short in general Scottish usage: for example, in *bad*, *father*, *parlour*, *brainy*, *make*, *table*, *equal*, *heat*, *weak*, *boat*.

Grammar

1 Sentences and other constructions in which the order of words and the general structure is changed for purposes of emphasis (technically known as thematic fronting): *Isn't it her that's the smart one?* ('Isn't *she* smart then?'); *It's led astray you are by the keeping of bad company* ('Keeping bad company has led you astray').

2 Simple verb tenses instead of perfect forms: *I'm a widow for ten years now*; *All my life I never went to the mainland.*

3 Progressive constructions: *Don't be learning bad English to the bairn*; *We were having plenty vegetables that year*; *If you can be waiting till the morning, our sale will be starting then.*

4 Distinctive uses of modal verbs, including 'double *would*': *Try and get here before the rain will come*; *If she would know about it, she would be over straight away.*

5 The formula *to be after doing (something)*, replacing the regular perfect or past: *I'm just after taking the bus* ('I have just taken the bus'); *That's me just after cleaning it up* ('I've just this minute cleaned it up').

6 A non-reflexive use of *-self*, notably to specify someone: *It's glad I am to be seeing yourself*; *I'll tell himself you are here*; *Herself will not be too pleased at that.*

7 Sentence-initial *sure*: *Sure, it'll spoil the taste of it if you do that.*

8 Pronouns introducing noun phrases, especially in questions: *Who is he, the man?*; *Did you see him, the minister?*

9 The use of confirming or negating statements rather than (or to supplement) *yes/aye* and *no*: *Did Iain give you the letter?—He did*; *Is Morag coming?—She is not*; *Did you get the job finished?—Aye, we did/Aye, so we did.*

10 The preposition *on* features in a number of idioms: *The minister has a terrible cold on him*; *That beast has a wild look on it*; *They're putting on him that he stole the sheep*; *It's on himself the stairn* ('confidence') *is.*

Vocabulary

1   In general, vocabulary is the same as in Scottish English, and most people use such Scots words as *bairn* ('child'), *brae* ('slope'), *greet* ('weep'), *oot* ('out'), the negatives *no* (as in *He's no in*) and *na/nae* (*Ah canna say*), and *aye* ('yes').

2   Many Gaelic words are freely used, such as: *athair* ('father'); *baile* ('village'); *balach* ('lad'); *bodach* ('old man'); *bothan* ('shebeen'); *caileag* ('young girl'); *cailleach* ('old woman, wife'); *duine bochd* ('poor fellow'); *ropach* ('messy').

3   Gaelic terms of address, vocatives, and salutations are common: *m'eudail*, *mo ghraid* ('my dear'); *A Chaluim* ('Calum', addressing a man called Calum); *A Mhammi* ('Mammy/Mummy'); *beannachd leat/leibh* ('goodbye'); *oidhche mhath* ('good night'); *tapadh leat* ('thank you'); *slàinte, slàinte mhath, slàinte mhór* ('health, good health, big health': all three expressions known and used throughout Scotland as toasts).

A three-way hybridization is common in the Islands, casually mixing English, Scots, and Gaelic, as in: *Geordie m'eudail, come oot till ye see the ronnags* ('Georgie my love, come out and see the stars') and *I have the cadal-eunain* ('pins and needles') *in my fingers*.

Scottish English

According to Augustan ideals of good taste and propriety (shared for decades by socially aspiring people in both England and Scotland), Scots was to be deplored as 'provincial' and 'unrefined'. As a result, aspirants to gentility sought to rid themselves of all traces of their ancient national usage by attending lectures on elocution, notably in Edinburgh from 1748. Indeed, they had since the late 17th century been making great efforts to eradicate 'Scotticisms' from their writing and speech. In tandem, the tongue 'yet used by the Vulgar' was considered by the elite to be 'barbarous', 'corrupt' and deserving 'total extinction' (John Pinkerton, 1786).

However, not all educated Scots accepted such propositions. From early in the century, a new literary Scots, which (unlike literary Middle Scots) was based on up-to-date colloquial speech, burgeoned in the writings of Allan Ramsay (1686–1758) and some contemporaries, and successors such as Robert Burns. A stream of vernacular literature was accompanied early in the 19th century by approving interest among the middle and upper classes, partly inspired by John Jamieson's *Etymological Dictionary of the Scottish Language* (1808). It was now felt necessary to record the old language before it was too late, or to undertake the preservation or even restoration of Scots, which Robert Louis Stevenson referred to in 1887 as Scotland's 'own dying language'.

Modern Scots has however remained a vernacular: widely used, freely hybridized with English, but by and large not quite welcome in the front rooms of the middle class. The trend since even before the Union has been to favour English as the language of power and prestige. Written Scots has as a result tended to be a rather artificial minority activity (more hobby than literature) and has had only a marginal role in the media, comic strips, cartoons, and jokes, notably as in the immensely popular newspaper *The Sunday Post*, and couthy ('cosy') columns in the popular and local press. Even so, there is currently more Scots in the broadcast media, including drama, than in the recent past, and it remains popular in songs and drama, where the emphasis is more on contemporary urban usage than literary tradition. Scots has neither died out nor has English achieved total coverage, and Scots seems to manage best in a hybrid bond with English.

Since at least the 1970s, scholars have argued for a broad and flexible continuum of usage in Scotland, from a Scottish Standard English that is school- and media-friendly through a range of mixes to a vernacular with its own dialects and (perhaps uniquely) a venerable and seemingly disproportionate literature, including the work of the national poet, Robert Burns. Looked at from one point of view, Scots is manifestly part of the complex of world English, while from another it has enough distinctiveness and autonomy to be a language on its own, with a literature, a national poet, and a translation of the New Testament of the Bible. Although there is no neat consensus, scholars agree that Scots and Scottish English are sufficiently distinct for each to have its own linguistic description, while in Scotland at the present time neither goes far without becoming tangled up with the other. A description of Scottish English includes at least the following points (many of them hard to separate off from Scots):

Pronunciation

1   Like Scots, Scottish English is rhotic, all vowels and diphthongs being unchanged before *r*, as in *beard*, *bird*, *laird*, *lard*, *moored*, *word*, *heard/herd*, *cord*, and *hoard*.

2   The Scots are traditionally supposed to rrroll their *rrr*s, and many may do this routinely or on occasion. The majority usage is, however, a single tap of the tongue on the ridge behind the upper teeth, and a small minority has a uvular ('French') *r*. In addition, a retroflex Irish- or American-style *r* is gaining ground in the middle class, notably among younger women.

3   The same vowel as in the pronoun *I* occurs in *rise*, *tie/tied*, *sly*, *why*, etc., while a tighter sound occurs in *rice*, *tide*, *slide*, *while*, etc., as also in such borrowings from Scots as *ay(e)* meaning 'always' (in contrast to *ay(e)* meaning 'yes') and Scots *gey* meaning 'very' (as in *It's gey sair* 'It's very sore/painful').

4   There is no vowel distinction between *Sam* and *psalm*, both having a short *a*, between *cot* and *caught*, both having a short *aw*, and between *full* and *fool*, both having a short *u*. There is also a single vowel each in *steel*, *stale*, *stole*, *stool*. The monophthongs and diphthongs of Scottish English total 14 sounds as opposed to 22 in RP.

5   Scottish English retains from Scots the *ch*-sound in such names as *Brechin* and *MacLachlan*, such Gaelicisms as *loch* and *pibroch*, such Scotticisms as *dreich* and *sough*, and for some speakers such words of Greek origin as *patriarch* and *technical*.

6   The *wh* in such words as *whale*, *what*, *why* is pronounced *hw* and in such pairs as *which/witch* each word is clearly distinct.

7   Phonological options include: *length* and *strength* pronounced with either *n* or *ng*; *fifth* and *sixth* spoken with final *th* or *t*; *raspberry* with an *s* or (less likely) a

z; *December* with a *z* or an *s*; *Wednesday* usually with a *d*; *tortoise* and *porpoise* pronounced as they look and with equal stress on each syllable; verbs ending in *-ise/ize* and *-ate* and some others given their main stress on the final syllable, as with *advertíse, baptíze, realíze, recogníse* and *adjudicáte, haráss, indicáte, reconcíle, survéy.*

Grammar

1 Many speakers do not use *shall* and *may* in informal speech, but use *will* (as in *Will I see you again?*), and *can* for permission (as in *Can I come in?*), and *might* or *will maybe* for possibility (as in *He might come later/He'll maybe come later*).

2 Both *should* and *ought to* express moral obligation or advice (as in *You should/ought to try and see it*), but otherwise *would* is used rather than *should* (as in *I would, if I was you*, not *I should, if I were you*).

3 The passive may be expressed by *get*, as in *I got told off.*

4 In tandem with Scots *no* and *-nae*, *not* is preferred over *-n't*: *He'll not come* (rather than *He won't come*); *You're not needed tonight* (rather than *You aren't needed tonight*); and similarly *Is he not coming? Can you not come? Do you not want it? Did he not come?* (stressing *not*).

5 Verbs of motion elide before adverbs of motion in some contexts: *I'll away home then*; *The cat wants out.*

6 *The* is used as in Scots and American English, as in: *to go to the hospital/the church.*

7 *Anybody, everybody, nobody, somebody* are preferred to *anyone, everyone, no one, someone.*

8 *Amn't I?* is used virtually to the exclusion of *aren't I?*: *I'm expected there too, amn't I?*

Vocabulary and idiom

1 Many words of Scottish provenance have been used in English at large for so long that few people think of them as Scottish: *caddie, collie, cosy, croon, eerie, forebear, glamour, golf, gumption, lilt, (golf) links, pony, raid, rampage, scone, uncanny, weird, wizened, wraith.*

2 Many words are widely used or known and generally perceived to be Scottish: *bannock, cairn, ceilidh, clan, clarsach, corrie, first-foot, glengarry, gloaming, haggis, kilt, pibroch, sporran, Tam o' Shanter, wee, whisky.*

3 Many words have some external currency but are used more in Scotland than elsewhere: *bairn* ('child'); *bonnie* ('beautiful, handsome, fine-looking'); *brae* ('slope of a hill'); *burn* ('stream'); *canny* ('careful, steady, thoughtful'); *Hogmanay* ('New Year's Eve'); *kirk* ('church', especially if Protestant); *peewit* ('lapwing'); *pinkie* (also in American English: 'little finger'); *skirl* (verb and noun: of the sound made by bagpipes).

4 General words that have uses special to Scotland include: *close* (with an *s-*, not a *z*-sound: an entry passage (and stairs) in a tenement building); *stair* (a flight of stairs, or a group of flats served by a single close in a tenement); *stay* ('to reside': *Where d'you stay?*); *uplift* ('to collect' the rent, a parcel, etc.).

5 Scottish technical usages, many of Latin origin, and especially in law, religion, education, and official terminology, include: *advocate* ('courtroom lawyer': in England *barrister*); *convener* (chairman of a committee); *induction* (of an ordained minister of religion to a ministerial charge); *janitor* (caretaker of a school: also in American English); *leet* (list of accepted candidates for a post); *procurator-fiscal* (a law official combining the offices of coroner and public prosecutor); *provost* ('mayor': *Lord Provost*, 'Lord Mayor'); *timeous* (mainly legal and contractual: 'timely').

6 Colloquial words used and understood by all manner of Scots and by the middle class as overt Scotticisms (in most cases drawn from Scots) include: *ach* (a dismissive interjection, quite distinct from English *ah*); *braw* ('fine, good-looking'); *footer about* ('to mess or fuss around'); *gillie* ('hunting attendant'); *girn* ('to whine, moan, complain'); *glaikit* ('stupid'); *haar* (a cold sea-fog: East Coast); *howf* ('a public house'); *och* (an interjection similar to but firmer than conventional English *oh*, which is also used); *pernickety* ('fussy'); *scunnered* ('sickened'; *to take a scunner at* 'to be sickened or thoroughly put off by'); *wabbit* ('tired out'); *wannert* ('wandered': mad, out of one's right mind, temporarily or otherwise).

7 Traditional Scots words are easily introduced into standard English contexts in the media: *bogle* ('a phantom'); *dominie* ('a schoolmaster': retrospective, not now used of teachers); *eident* ('diligent'); *forfochen* ('exhausted'); *furth of* and *outwith* ('outside (of)'); *hochmagandie* ('fornication'); *leid* ('a language'); *makar* ('poet', in Scotland in the Middle Ages); *owerset* ('to translate'); *yestreen* (rather poetic: 'yesterday evening').

A feature of Scottish English in its wider sense is the capacity and willingness of its speakers to move—more or less consciously, and often for the satisfaction it gives—from a more Scots to a more Scottish English way of speaking and back again, employing differences in pronunciation, grammar, vocabulary, and idiom, all of which add nuances to the communication. In addition to their use of overt Scotticisms as a token of solidarity, the middle classes may also use Scots (including Gutter Scots and shibboleths often avoided, and notably when no non-Scots are around) routinely, humorously, even proudly, according to inclination, personal style, and circumstance.

A spectrum of writing

Literature in Scotland has been subordinate to literature in England since the mid-16th century, when the combined influence of English-trained printers and widely disseminated works of theology (most importantly the Geneva Bible) led to a rapid assimilation of Scots usage towards the evolving orthographic, grammatical, and lexical canons of south-east England. John Knox's *History of the Reformatioun within the realme of Scotland* (1587) shows a random mix of Scots and English forms, and the 17th-century poet and historian William Drummond of Hawthornden was the first major writer to adopt a virtually unmixed English for his work.

During the surge of Scottish artistic, scholarly, and scientific activity in the 18th century, when Edinburgh was hailed as 'the Athens of the North', the standardizing English of England became a key prose medium, notably for the works of David Hume on philosophy (1739, 1751), James Hutton (1788, 1795) on geology, and Adam Smith (1776) on economics. Economics and a European language shift were key factors in this: there was a much larger market for such works if written in the standardizing usage of southern England, and Latin was in decline as a general scholarly and print medium.

One of the most influential European literary works of the century was James MacPherson's *Fingal, an Ancient Epic Poem, in Six Books* (1762), based loosely on early Gaelic tales and written in a highly poetic English prose. Purportedly based on the work of the Gaelic poet Ossian, it is now usually called MacPherson's *Ossian*, and was a focus of great controversy. Highly regarded in Britain and on the Continent, it was praised by Goethe and Schiller and was one of Napoleon's favourite works. However, Samuel Johnson and other critics were doubtful about its authenticity and, when asked to show the originals, MacPherson produced fabrications. Whatever the morality of the episode, like his equally devious but more successful Welsh predecessor Geoffrey of Monmouth with the stories of Arthur, Lear, and Cymbeline, the bilingual MacPherson succeeded in adapting and translating Celtic material into English, in the process helping to launch the Romantic Movement.

Scotland's national poet, Robert ('Rabbie') Burns (1759–96), in his earlier poems shifted across social as well as national boundaries, between rural Scots and Augustan English, but the influence of Robert Fergusson finally inclined him towards Scots. Burns was eclectic, drawing on folk song, story-telling, preaching, social banter, daily work, the Bible, and high English verse, with a subtle capacity for modulating between English and Scots, as in:

> But pleasures are like poppies spread;
> You seize the flower, its bloom is shed;
> Or like the snow falls in the river,
> A moment white—then melts for ever;
> Or like the Borealis race,
> That flit ere you can point their place;
> Or like the rainbow's lovely form
> Evanishing amid the storm.
> Nae man can tether time or tide;
> The hour approaches Tam maun ride;
> That hour, o' nicht's black arch the key-stane,
> And sic a nicht he taks the road in,
> As ne'er puir sinner was abroad in.
> – from *Tam o' Shanter*, 1791

Others followed, using an English coloured with the vocabulary and idiom of one or other of Scotland's speech styles: South-West Scots in John Galt's *Annals of the Parish* (1821); North-East Scots in Lewis Grassic Gibbon's *A Scots Quair* (1932–4); Gaelic and Highland English in Fionn Mac Colla's *The Albannach* (1932). Others, however, have opted matter-of-factly for Standard English, as with J. M. Barrie's drama, the fiction of Arthur Conan Doyle, John Buchan, and Eric Linklater, and the children's literature of A. A. Milne.

Sir Walter Scott established in his Waverley novels the norms for written dialect in English at large, notably influencing Thomas Hardy's 'Wessex' novels and the work of the Brontë sisters in England and James Fenimore Cooper and Mark Twain in the United States. Scott and Stevenson both drew on Scottish history and social life, as well as venturing much further afield, while Conan Doyle modelled the deductive techniques of his detective Sherlock Holmes on those of Alexander Bell, an Edinburgh professor of medicine and an uncle of Alexander Graham Bell, the inventor of the telephone.

From the 1960s, writings in and about Glasgow in particular have included caricature by comics on stage and TV and authors of joke and cartoon collections, alongside edgy kinds of poetry, drama, and fiction. Representations of local speech, sometimes using fake phonetic and pseudo-illiterate orthography, have played games with the city's vernacular speech, often seeking a humorously grotesque effect. Two examples:

> **1973** ach sun
> jiss keepyir chin up
> dizny day gonabootlika hawf shut knife
> inaw jiss cozzy a burd.
> – Tom Leonard, 'The Miracle of the Burd and the Fishes', *Poems* (Dublin: O'Brien)

> ['Ah, son.
> Just keep your chin up.
> Doesn't do going about like a half-shut knife.
> And all just because of a bird (girl).']

> **1982** Another interesting word heard in the discotheque is
> *jiwanni*. To a young lady a gentleman will make the request—
> *Jiwanni dance?* Should she find that he is over-anxious to ply
> her with refreshments she will regard him with suspicion and
> inquire—*Jiwanniget mebevvid? Jiwanni* in certain circumstances
> changes to—*Jiwanna*, used generally in conjunction with the
> word *beltoanramooth*.
> – Stanley Baxter, *Parliamo Glasgow*.

> [*Jiwanni* ('Do you want to'), *mebevvid* ('me bevvied' = me drunk:
> from *bevvy*, a clipping of *beverage*), *Jiwanna beltoanramooth*
> ('Do you want a belt (= blow) on the mouth?')]

In more recent years, a range of publications relating to Scots has appeared. The most notable (and successful, including beyond Scotland) have been novels that seek to portray urban realism at its most stark, where the author is using language contrasts to say to the reader: 'We both know this game, don't we?' The first of the quotations below represents Edinburgh, the second Glasgow, and both use the device of an interview between a middle-class health professional and the working-class narrator:

> **1993** [*Note: ay* here means 'of', not 'yes' or 'always']
> Ah've never been incarcerated for junk. However, loads ay cunts
> have had stabs at rehabilitating me. Rehabilitation is shite:
> sometimes ah think ah'd rather be banged up. Rehabilitation
> means the surrender ay the self. . . . Doctor Forbes, the
> psychiatrist, used non-directive counselling techniques. . . .

This involved getting us tae talk aboot ma past life and focus oan unresolved conflicts. . . . A typical exchange:

DR FORBES: You mentioned your brother, the one with the, eh, disability. The one that died. Can we talk about him?

(pause)

ME: Why?

(pause)

DR FORBES: You're reluctant to talk about your brother?

ME: Naw. It's just that ah dinnae see the relevance ay that tae me bein oan smack [heroin].

DR FORBES: It seems that you started using heavily around the time of your brother's death.

ME: A loat happened around that time. Ah'm no really sure how relevant it is tae ma brar's death. Ah went up tae Aberdeen at the time. The Uni. Ah hated it. . . .

DR FORBES: What was it about Aberdeen that you hated?

ME: The University. The staff, the students and aw that.
Ah thought they were aw boring middle-class cunts.

– Irvine Walsh, *Trainspotting* (Vintage, 1999), 181–2 (first published by Secker & Warburg, 1993)

1994   So ye're no saying I'm blind?

It isn't for me to say.

Aye but you're a doctor.

Yes.

So ye can give an opinion?

Anyone can give an opinion.

Aye but to do with medical things.

Mister Samuels, I have people waiting to see me.

Christ sake!

I find your language offensive.

Do ye. Ah well fuck ye then. Fuck ye! Sammy crumpled the prescription and flung it at him: Stick that up yer fucking arse!

Yes good morning.

Ya fucking eedjit! Sammy stood there. He started smiling then stopped it.

Yes, thank you.

Fucking thank you ya bastard. Sammy grasped at the desk; there were papers there and he skited them; he turned and headed to where he thought the door was.

– James Kelman, *How Late It Was, How Late* (Vintage, 1998) (first published by Secker & Warburg, 1994, and winner of the Booker Prize, 1994)

In both works, in addition to the orchestrated contrast of consultant and patient, the non-standard punctuation complements the crazy-paving of speech and class. Although such oppositions and antagonisms can be found in many places, the dichotomy is made particularly sharp by an ancient apartheid of usage.

Scot, Scotch, Scots, Scottish, Scotticism

A distinctive and delicate aspect of the use of English in relation to Scotland is the naming of its people and products. Many of the names of the English-using world are awkward (*English* itself, *American*, and *Indian* are three that come easily to mind), but the nouns and adjectives that refer to Scotland come close to the top of the awkward list. The following glossary provides a contrastive etymological, historical, and social account of five key terms.

Scot

[From Latin *Scotus*] A noun that referred originally to a native of Ireland or a member of a northern Irish tribe, and since the Middle Ages has meant a native of Scotland. The plural has tended to be commoner than the singular (*the Scots*), with the gendered variants *Scotsman* (formerly also *Scotchman*, no longer favoured) and *Scotswoman* (formerly also *Scotchwoman*, no longer favoured). Currently, *Scot* tends to be preferred because it is concise and gender-free.

Scotch

A late 16th-century contraction of *Scottish*, first in Early Modern English then in Older Scots, with uses as both an adjective (*Scotch mist*) and a noun (*a Scotch and soda*). For generations, *Scotch* ousted *Scottish* in England as the prevailing adjective form. In Scotland, the native form *Scots* predominated until, during an Anglicizing vogue in the 18th century, *Scotch* became fashionable. In the early 19th century, however, some writers expressed doubts about it as an innovation and preferred *Scottish* and *Scots*; others, including J. A. H. Murray, the Scottish editor of the *Oxford English Dictionary*, continued to use *Scotch*. By the early 20th century, disapproval of *Scotch* among educated people in Scotland was so great that teachers there discouraged its use, except for such stock phrases as *Scotch broth*, *Scotch mist*, *Scotch terrier*, *Scotch tweed*, and *Scotch whisky* (often elsewhere known simply as *Scotch*). In England and North America, *Scotch* remained the dominant general adjective and collective noun (*the Scotch*, *the Scotch-Irish*) well into the 20th century, but many people in both locations are more aware of Scottish distaste for it (except in terms of whisky, tweed, and the like). The *OED Supplement* (1982) reported that in deference to Scottish sensibilities the English were abandoning *Scotch* in favour of *Scottish* and less frequently *Scots*, and preferred *the Scots* to *the Scotch* as the name of the people. This trend appears to have continued and strengthened since then.

Scots

[Late 16th century: a contraction of Older Scots and Northern English *Scotis/Scottis*, often used in contrast to the modern southern English form *Scottish*] **1** An adjective meaning 'relating to or characteristic of Scotland, its people, languages, cultures, institutions, etc., as in *Scots traditions, Scots usage*'. In certain uses it has always been the preferred form (as in *Scots Law*, *the Scots Greys* (a cavalry regiment), and such now historical terms as *a Scots mile* and *a pound Scots*, but in other uses its popularity declined (because of its un-English sound and look) and tended to be replaced by *Scottish* and *Scotch*—reviving when *Scotch* fell out of middle-class favour in the 19th–20th centuries. **2** A noun which has served to name both the Celtic and Germanic languages of Scotland: now known respectively as Gaelic and Scots. In Scots, the pronunciation of the vowel is long, rhyming with the Scottish pronunciation of *oats*.

Scottish

[From Middle English *Scottisc*, Old English *Scyttisc*]. An adjective meaning 'relating or belonging to Scotland, its people, institutions, etc.' This is the most neutral and inclusive of the adjectives *Scottish, Scots, Scotch.* In the late 16th century, as part of the Anglicizing fashion of the time, *Scottish* began to be used in Scotland as well as England as an alternative to *Scots,* which from the mid-18th century it surpassed in popularity in most, especially formal and official uses, as in *the Scottish Episcopal Church, the Scottish language, the Scottish Office,* and the title *The Scottish Monthly Magazine* (1836–7) as compared with *The Scots Magazine* (1739–). When, by the early 20th century, *Scotch* had fallen out of favour in educated usage in Scotland, *Scottish* and a resuscitated *Scots* superseded it in nearly all adjectival uses: for example, when the *Scotch Educational Department* had its name changed by Act of Parliament (1918) to the *Scottish Education Department.* It was formerly used (since the 17th century) in England and Scotland as a collective noun, 'the Scottish', but in Scotland it is virtually confined to use as an adjective, unlike *Scots* or *Scotch,* as in 'the clannishness of the Scots/Scotch'—never 'the Scottish'.

Scotticism

A feature specific to Scotland and the Scots, in English or any other language: most usually, however, a Scotticism is a word or usage from Scots or that relates to Scotland. The term has often been pejorative, including in Scotland itself, where, from the late 17th well into the 20th century, it has served to mark a usage to be avoided for reasons of refinement at home or ease of communication abroad. As the Anglicization of Scots usage proceeded after the Union of the Crowns in 1603, socially insecure Scots (especially writers) began apologizing for or seeking English help in avoiding Scots expressions.

Collections such as James Beattie's *Scoticisms arranged in Alphabetical Order, designed to correct Improprieties of Speech and Writing* (Edinburgh, 1787, with *c.*500 entries) were published from the 18th to the 20th century. The general response was mixed:

1   Some were eliminated, as with *come/sit into the fire* and the French-derived verb *evite* ('to avoid')

2   Some entered general English, as with *burial* for *funeral, Come here* (where refined 18th-century usage in England preferred *Come hither*), *Close the door,* where *Shut the door* had been preferred; and *liberate,* where *set at liberty* had been preferred.

3   Others have simply continued in present-day Scots and Scottish English, but have become more noticeable as such.

A distinction can be drawn between *covert* and *overt* Scotticisms. The covert forms may well be shared with other varieties, especially in North America, and are used unreflectingly as normal expressions assumed to be universal, such as: *cast up* ('to reproach'); *handless* ('clumsy'); *miss oneself* ('to miss a treat'); *pinkie* ('the little finger'); *get a row* ('to receive a reprimand'); *sort* ('to mend'); *stay* ('to live, reside': *Where do you stay?*); *swither* ('to hesitate between options'). The overt forms make up a repertoire of hundreds of words, sayings, and idioms universally recognizable as Scots, which middle-class speakers of Scottish English sprinkle through their speech and to a less extent their writing, to show membership of the group: *ay(e)* ('yes'); *hame* ('home'); *hoose* ('house'); *braw* ('good-looking, fine'); *the craitur* ('the creature': whisky); *dreich* (dreary: said of the weather, a speech, etc.); *kirk* ('church'); *wabbit* ('exhausted'); *keep a calm sough* ('to stay calm').

The term *Scotticism* was the first of the many *-isms* in English, such as *Australianism*, *Canadianism*, *Indianism*, and *Philippinism*. The term *Americanism* was first used on the analogy of *Scotticism* in a publication in Philadelphia in 1781 by a Scot, the Reverend John Witherspoon, a signatory to the Declaration of Independence.

Wales

> **2001** Memories of the 1970s, when militant Welsh nationalists set fire to English people's Welsh country cottages, flickered this week when an eminent Welshman [John Elfed Jones, a former chairman of the Welsh Language Board] declared that non Welsh-speaking outsiders (ie, the English) were the human equivalent of foot-and-mouth disease.
>
> – 'Dim diolch' [No thank you], *The Economist*, 11 August

The name of Wales derives from an Old English word that has not itself survived: *Wealas*, the plural of *Wealh* or *Walh*, which had four senses that narrowed with the passage of time: 'foreigner', 'slave', 'Briton', and 'someone Welsh'. The (more complimentary) equivalent in Welsh is *Cymru* (pronounced 'Kumry') from Celtic *Cumbroges* ('Compatriots'). Of the two languages in the principality today, English is profoundly dominant, used by virtually 100% of the population, while Welsh is used by *c*.25% and has no official standing, although, since 1982, there has been a *Sianel Pedwar Cymru* (*S4C*: 'Channel 4 Welsh') on TV. Education is predominantly in English, with some state-supported Welsh-medium schools.

The Welsh language acts of 1967 and 1993 have moved the principality towards more adequately accommodating the language, in that forms and official documents are now available in both languages, although English remains the sole language of legal record. The act of 1993 treats the two languages as equal in the conduct of public business, including matters of law, while a previously non-statutory Welsh Language Board now has a duty to advise government on parity for Welsh and complaints from the public, but has no powers to enforce that parity. Although Welsh is a fully functioning modern language and its position has indeed improved in recent decades, it nonetheless remains second-class in its own ancient territory:

> **2000** Of all the languages spoken in Britain today, Welsh has by far the oldest roots. Wales is the only part of Britain in which a version of Brittonic has been spoken uninterruptedly down to the present day, the transition from Brittonic to Welsh having taken place, probably, somewhere between AD 400 and 700.
>
> – Janet Davies, 'Welsh', in *Languages in Britain and Ireland*, ed. Glanville Price (Oxford: Blackwell), 78

In classical times, the region now known as Wales was part of a general Celtic culture over much of Western Europe, and was strongly influenced by Latin during the four centuries in which southern Britain was a province of the Roman Empire. After the expansion of the Anglo-Saxons in Britain (5th–9th centuries AD), Wales was the sole autonomous Celtic territory in the south, and in succeeding centuries its peoples warred both among themselves and with the English, Irish, Norse, and Danes. In the 8th century, to make the Welsh Marches ('borderlands') safer for his people, Offa, king of Mercia, built a wall from the Dee to the Wye, which duly came to be known as *Offa's Dyke* and, in the 9th century, Rhoddri Mawr ('Roderick the Great') finally united the country west of that wall.

Edward I of England invaded Wales in 1282, and in the ensuing fighting the last native Welsh prince, Llewelyn ap Gruffydd, was killed. In 1301, Edward's son Edward was crowned *Prince of Wales*, a title borne to the present day by (most of) the eldest sons of English, later British, monarchs. Wales was in effect England's first colony, and served as a springboard to Ireland. The part-Welsh nobleman Henry Tudor became Henry VII of England in 1485 and Wales was incorporated into England in the Acts of Union of 1535 and 1543, after which English became the sole language of administration, education, and trade. Although there was already a body of Welsh law, the *Cyfraith Hywel* ('Law of Howel'), it was increasingly superseded by English law from the 13th century, and after the Union the law of England was applied throughout the country.

Welsh and Welshness

Like *Wales*, *Welsh* is an English word, and has both a complex history and a generally little-known set of associations. It derives from a group of Old English forms that include *Wilisc*, *Wylisc*, and *Welisc*, which like *Wales* descend from *Weala(s)*, a name equivalent to both German *Wahle* ('Celt, Roman, foreigner') and the Old Norse plural *Valir* ('Gauls, Frenchmen'). The English adjective corresponds to Middle High German *walh-*, *wälhisch*, *walsch*, and German *wälsch*, *welsch* (terms used to describe the Romans, Italians, and French) as well as to Dutch *waalsch* (which corresponds to English *Walloon*, the name for a French-speaking Belgian). In all of these usages the fundamental historical sense has been 'a neighbour who is not Germanic'.

By the 16th century, the major written forms of the word were *Welsh* (as in *Welsh history*) and *Welch* (as in the *Welch Regiment*), supplanting such earlier variants as *Welische*, *Welsc*, *Walsshe*, and *Walsh*. This last survives as a family name, as does the Scottish variant *Wallace*, which comes through Anglo-French *Waleis*, and originally referred to the Cumbric-speaking inhabitants of Strathclyde (the ancient 'Northern Welsh'). *Wallace* is a common surname in Scotland, most famously for the national medieval hero William Wallace, much as the name *Walsh* is common in England.

In addition to being a noun and adjective for the people of Wales, *Welsh* is the English name of the ancient Celtic language known in Welsh as *Cymraeg* ('Cumbric'). Welsh and Breton are the only surviving members of the ancient British or Brythonic subdivision of the Celtic language family. Although a literary language since the 6th century, Welsh has been in decline since Henry Tudor gained the

English throne in 1485. Its current condition is relatively stable with about half a million speakers, and numbers of non-Welsh-speaking Welsh people and others, including immigrants from England, are learning it. It is taught in all schools and is a medium of instruction in some. Notably, in the northern county of Gwynedd it is a language of local government and appears with English on road signs. However, Welsh-language activists continue to press for more.

The spoken language consists of several dialects, has had a significant influence on Welsh English, but little impact on English beyond the principality. In turn, English has had little influence on everyday spoken Welsh in terms of pronunciation and structure, but a massive influence in terms of vocabulary. The most characteristic sounds of Welsh are the voiceless alveolar lateral fricative (spelt *ll* as in *Llandudno*), the alveolar rolled or trilled *r* (spelt *rh* as in *Rhondda*), and the velar fricative (represented, as in Scots and German, by *ch*, as in *Llywarch*). Typically of Celtic, there are grammatical mutations, as in the noun *ci* ('dog'), where the initial sound is affected by the modifier, as in *dy gi* ('your dog'), *fy nghi* ('my dog'), *ei chi* ('her dog'), and *tri chi* ('three dogs').

Although large numbers of emigrants from Wales have settled in North America and Australasia, among other places, the language has generally failed to stay the course with them. As Alan Thomas has put it: 'English became the instrument for advancement for the Welsh in the emerging world outside' ('English in Wales', *The Cambridge History of the English Language*, vol. V, 1994). A singular exception, however, has been a Welsh settlement in Patagonia in Argentina, in the extreme south of South America, whose community is bilingual in Welsh and Spanish.

In 1962, an organization was formed to promote the Welsh language: in Welsh, *Cymdeithas yr Iaith Gymraeg*, in English the *Welsh Language Society*. Although it is a militant element in Welsh nationalism, the Society's primary role is the spread and strengthening of Welsh. Its demands include bilingual road signs and official forms. Its methods have included demonstration, civil disobedience, and selective law-breaking, such as painting out English-only road signs and the non-payment of broadcasting licence fees. Militants have from time to time damaged property, such as television transmitters and the holiday homes in Welsh-speaking areas of non-Welsh people from England. If the perpetrators are caught, the ensuing court appearances are used to raise demands for trials conducted in Welsh. The activities of the society have evoked a mixed response in Wales and almost no attention elsewhere.

There has, however, been some response to the society's demands, with bilingual signs in some areas, bilingual signs being increasingly available, and more Welsh in broadcasting. Where previously Welsh could only be used in courts if a person spoke no other language, the 1967 Welsh Language Act did not give Welsh equality of status with English, but permitted its use of Welsh in court on the basis of preference alone (with translation services as appropriate). In 1993, a second Welsh Language Act established a Welsh Language Board whose function was to promote and facilitate the use of Welsh and advise the Secretary of State for Wales on matters concerning the language. With regard to the current health or otherwise of Welsh, the language scholar Janet Davies has noted:

> **2000** At the end of the twentieth century, the position of the
> Welsh language seems to justify a degree of optimism, though

> there are certainly no grounds for complacency. The steady
> decrease in the numbers of Welsh-speakers appears to have been
> checked and the language has a much higher profile in the fields
> of education, broadcasting and public life. This change is reflected
> in the vitality of the Welsh-language scene. . . . Once restricted
> largely to chapel-based activities, Welsh is now the language of
> licensed clubs. Nor is it any longer excluded from business and
> professional life; there are associations for Welsh-speaking
> doctors and scientists, for public-relations experts and for
> commercial consultants. Business organizations have been
> established to encourage economic development in Welsh-
> speaking areas, and there are housing associations which
> operate through the medium of Welsh.
>
> – 'Welsh' *op cit*, 106

In the 18th century, the Morris brothers (Lewis, Richard, and William) preserved medieval texts and encouraged poets to use the ancient Welsh metres, and the poet Goronwy Owen started a neoclassical school. The *Cymmrodorion Society* was established by the Welsh in London as a centre of literary studies, co-operating with the *Cymreigyddion Society* and *Gwyneddigion Society* in Wales to encourage the revival of *eisteddfodau* or poetic assemblies. As a result, the *National Eisteddfod* was revived in the early 19th century. At this time, lyrical hymns and religious verse were popular, as well as ballads that used *cynghanedd*, a complex traditional blend of accentuation, alliteration, and internal rhyme. The modern period of literature in Welsh began in the late 19th century with the establishment of the University of Wales, a federal institution with campuses throughout the country. Current writing encompasses all the genres of Western literature.

Welsh distinctness survives, mildly reinforced by a devolved Welsh Assembly in 1999, but the closeness of England and the ambiguous status of Wales (united with but distinct from England) inevitably create tensions. In 2001, Alan Pugh, the deputy education minister, told the Assembly that the Welsh language was under threat from the 'linguistic globalization' of English. Other prominent people have complained about English immigrants, including Gwilem ab Ioan, a member of the national executive of Plaid Cymru, who asserted that Wales had become a 'dumping ground for England's oddballs and misfits'. However, the opportunities to use the Welsh language in public life are much greater, although progress in one area can mean alarm in another: many large companies have gone bilingual, but the pressure that usefully persuaded them can worry smaller businesses that cannot afford the cost. As a former Plaid Cymru leader, Dafydd Williams, told the Assembly's culture committee: 'What is reasonable for a privatised utility might not be for a small business in Newport' (The *Economist*, 11 August 2001).

The crunch question remains: whether, to be truly Welsh, one must know Welsh. By and large, unilingual English-speaking Welsh people do not regard knowledge of Welsh as a criterion of Welshness, and tend to resent any assumption that it can or should be. Present-day Wales has in effect an Anglo-Welsh culture, known for song and poetry in both languages, and an enthusiasm for practical and artistic talent in using the human voice. Its dual linguistic and cultural heritage includes:

❶ Choral singing

Notably male-voice choirs that originated in the industrial English-speaking south in the 19th century, performing in both languages.

❷ Eisteddfodau

(plural, 'arts festivals': singular *eisteddfod*) Cultural gatherings where performances are in Welsh.

❸ Nonconformist Protestantism

Popularly called 'the chapel', where public speaking has been highly valued.

❹ A tradition of radical politics

Associated first with liberalism (the charismatic early 20th-century British Liberal prime minister Lloyd George was Welsh) then with socialism (a leader of the British Labour Party, Neil Kinnock, currently a 'Eurocrat' in Brussels, is Welsh), and then with the politics of *Plaid Cymry*, the Welsh nationalist party.

❺ Rugby

A male passion for rugby football that transcends language and politics.

Welsh English

> **1990** 'establishing "Welsh English" or even discussing its possible existence is a political act', invoking 'distinctions such as that between "the state" (and its language—necessarily English), and "the region" (and its subordinate variety of the state language—Welsh English)'.
>
> – G. Williams, quoted in Nikolas Coupland (ed.), *English in Wales: Diversity, Conflict, and Change*, Multilingual Matters, 1990

As the excerpt indicates, the relatively recent term *Welsh English* (apart from sounding like a contradiction in terms) is deeply controversial. English is over-whelmingly the majority language in Wales and, as in many other parts of the English-speaking world, such an oxymoronic term has proved hard to avoid. It is increasingly applied by language scholars to English usage in Wales that has three influences operating on it: the Welsh language; dialects in adjacent counties of England; and the standard language as taught in school and used in the media. The influence of Welsh is strongest in the northern counties, which are sometimes referred to as *Welsh Wales* and in which Welsh/English bilingualism is significant. This influence is weaker in mid-Wales and weakest in South Wales, but even in such southern cities as Cardiff and Swansea the influence of the Welsh language is present and has been increasing.

It is not certain when speakers of English arrived in Wales, but settlers from the Midland Anglo-Saxon kingdom of Mercia were probably in the valley of the river Wye by the 8th century, when Offa built his dyke. In the winter of 1108–9, Henry I established a group of Flemish settlers in Pembrokeshire among whom there were probably English-speakers. English settlements grew up in the 12–13th centuries in the Gower Peninsula, the Usk valley, and the towns of Beaumaris, Caernarfon, and Harlech in the north and Brecon and Carmarthen in the south. Since most trade was in the hands of the English, the earliest regular Welsh users of English were almost certainly traders. Features of Welsh English include:

Pronunciation

1   Commonly perceived, a melodic quality of speech (often called by outsiders a lilt or said to be 'singsong'), largely created by a rise-fall tone at the end of statements (as opposed to a fall), and by equal stress on the syllables of such words as *ticket* ('tick-et') and *connection* ('co-nek-shun').

2   Welsh English is usually non-rhotic, but people who regularly speak Welsh are likely to have a postvocalic *r* in all positions, as in *runner* and *worker*.

3   The accents of South Wales generally have no *h* at the beginning of such words as *hurry* and *Harry* (''Urry up, 'Arry!'); in North Wales, this *h* is retained because it also occurs in Welsh.

4   Single vowels are often more likely than diphthongs in such words as *late* and *hope*.

5   Such words as *dad*, *gas* and *dance*, *glass* tend to have the same short *a*-vowel, as opposed to RP's contrasting 'dad' and 'dahnce'.

6   The weak vowel or schwa is often preferred to an *uh*-sound in such words as *but* and *cut*.

7   Diphthongs are often turned into two syllables: *beer* into 'bee-uh'; *poor* into 'poo-uh'.

8   Three consonants from Welsh are in common use. Attempts by non-Welsh speakers to pronounce the sound represented by *ll* as in *Llangollen* often come out as 'Thlangothlen' or 'Clang-gothlen' (Technically, the Welsh *ll*-sound is a voiceless alveolar lateral fricative.) The rolled *r* ('rrr'), spelt *rh* as in the place-names *Rhondda* and *Rhyl* is similar to traditional Scots. And the *ch*-sound in *Pentyrch* is identical to Scots *loch* and German *machen* (and is technically a voiceless velar fricative).

9   The ending -ing is often realized as '-in': 'dancin' for *dancing*.

10   There is a tendency, especially in the north, to substitute *s* and *sh* for *z* and *zh*, so that *is* becomes 'iss' and *division* is 'di-vi-shon' (a feature shared with traditional speakers of Gaelic English in Scotland).

11   The -*y* ending in words such as *happy* and *lovely* is realized by 'ee': 'appee', 'lovelee'.

Grammar

1   Working-class people in Wales tend to use the following constructions, also found elsewhere in the UK: multiple negation (*I 'aven't done nothin' to nobody, see?*); *them* as a demonstrative adjective (*We don't need them things*); *as* as a relative pronoun (*'E's the one as played for Cardiff, isnee?*); non-standard verb forms (*She catched it*; *The coat was all tore*); *'isself* for 'himself' and *theirselves* for 'themselves'; the adverbial use of an adjective (*We did it willin'*: 'willingly'); the addition of *like* at the end of phrases and sentences (*'E looked real 'appy like*) .

2   Non-standard forms reflecting an influence from Welsh include: *do/did* + verb, to indicate a regularly performed action (*He do go to the rugby all the time*; *He*

did go regular like); foregrounding for emphasis (*Goin' down the mine 'e is*
'He is going down the mine'; *Money they're not short of* 'They aren't short
of money'); *there* and not *how* in exclamations (*There's lovely you are!*);
a generalization of the question tag *isn't it?* (*We're goin' out now, isn't it?*);
too for *either* (*I don't like it.—I don't like it too*).

3 *Look you* ('you see') is widely regarded as a shibboleth of Welsh English, as in:
Tried hard, look you, but earned nothin'. *See* is also common in this role:
We were worried about 'im, see. The non-use of the subject pronoun is also
characteristic of Welsh-influenced English: *Saw 'im, bach; saw 'im yesterday.*

Vocabulary

1 Words drawn from Welsh generally relate to culture and behaviour: *carreg*
('a stone'); *clennig* ('a gift of money'); *eisteddfod* (plural *eisteddfodau*: a
cultural festival); *glaster* ('a drink of milk and water'); *iechyd da* ('yakhy da')
good health (a salutation or toast, from *iechyd* 'health', *da* 'good'); the use of
bach and *del* as terms of affection: *Like a drink, bach?*; *Come near the fire, del.*

2 Words shared by Welsh English and dialects of England include: *askel*
('a newt'); *dap* ('to bounce'); *lumper* ('a young person'); *pilm* ('dust');
sally ('willow'); *steam* ('a bread-bin').

3 General English words with local extensions of meaning include: *delight* ('a
keen interest'), as in *She's getting' a delight in boys*; *lose* ('to miss'), as in *'Urry
or we'll lose the train*; *tidy* ('good, attractive'), as in *Tidy 'ouse you've got, bach.*

4 The form *boyo*, from *boy*, is common as both a term of address and a reference
for men, and may be negative in tone: *Listen, boyo, I've somethin' to say to you*;
That boyo is not to be trusted.

In Wales, little stigma attaches to Welsh English, as compared with Gutter Glasgow
in Scotland or Brummie in Birmingham; rather, speakers of Welsh English are, by
and large, positively viewed. There is, however, considerable tension with regard to
the use of Welsh, especially in schools and the media, and this can affect attitudes
to English. Many people in Wales consider that education should be bilingual,
so that all Welsh people can have access to Welsh as their national language; others,
including some parents from England, feel that bilingualism in schools puts an
unnecessary strain on children, and are not likely to regard Welsh as central to their
lives. This last view fits well with how the Welsh scholar Alan Thomas sees things
developing: more in terms of influence from England than within Wales. He notes:

> **1994** As the use of English expands in all social circumstances
> in Wales, it comes increasingly under the influence of standard
> English for its formal varieties, and of more prestigious 'England-
> based' vernaculars for its non-standard ones, given the role of
> the media in disseminating vernacular English, particularly
> through television and radio situation comedies. Welsh English,
> as a distinct dialect, is a transitional phenomenon which is
> particularly associated with dominantly bilingual communities,
> like those in the south-west and the north. Increasing
> monolingualism, removing productive interference from Welsh,
> reinforces the tendency . . . towards a general erosion of dialect

differences in grammar. Welsh English will increasingly come
to be characterised as a distinct accent, rather than as a dialect,
though its vocabulary and idiomatic usage will no doubt continue
to be significantly distinguished from other varieties of English in
Britain—at least in speech.

– 'English in Wales', in Robert Burchfield (ed.), *The Cambridge History of the English
Language, Volume V: English in Britain and Overseas, Origins and Developments*
(Cambridge: Cambridge University Press)

This prediction fits many South Walians who only speak English, although the
marks of their Welshness in pronunciation, intonation, and expressions are unlikely
to vanish away. The English of Wales, especially in its relationship with the Welsh
language, is much more than an extension of the vernaculars of Liverpool and the
West of England.

Ireland

1910 *Leprechaun*; a sort of fairy, called by several names in
different parts of Ireland: luricaun, cluricaun, lurragadaun,
loghryman, luprachaun. This last is nearest to the Gaelic original,
all the preceding anglicised forms being derived from it.
Luprachaun itself is derived by metathesis from Irish *luchorpán*,
from *lu*, little, and *corpán*, the dim. of *corp*, a body:—'weeny little
body.' . . . It is very hard to catch a leprachaun, and still harder to
hold him.

– P. W. Joyce, *English as we speak it in Ireland*, 1910 (reissued with a foreword by Terence
Dolan, Dublin Wolfhound Press, 1979, 1988)

1993 Irish . . . 1 Of, pertaining to, or native to Ireland, an island
lying west of Great Britain, now divided into the Republic of
Ireland and Northern Ireland. M[iddle] E[nglish]. b. [obsolete] Of,
or belonging to (the Gaelic inhabitants of) the Scottish Highlands,
M[id]16–M[id]18. **2** In, of, or pertaining to the language Irish.
M[id]16. **3** Having a nature or quality (regarded as) characteristic
of Ireland or its people; (of an expression or statement)
paradoxical, (apparently) illogical, self-contradictory.
L[ate]16. . . .

– *The New Shorter Oxford Dictionary on Historical Principles*, ed. Lesley Brown (Oxford:
Clarendon Press)

The nuances of *Irish* range from the geographical and general (*Irish Sea* and *Irish
whiskey* with an *e*) through the political and historical (*Irish Question*, *Irish patriot*)
to the humorous (*Irish bull*, *Irish joke*) and the wry and ironic (*an Irish hurricane*:
flat calm weather with drizzling rain) and *Irish confetti* (stones and bricks to throw
at people). If a remark seems fey or doesn't chime with everyday logic, then someone non-Irish might say: 'That's a bit Irish, isn't it?' The Irish themselves have often
taken part in the sardonic comment, but Brendan Behan (in his play *Richard's Cork
Leg* in 1973) spread the burden wider: 'Other people have a nationality. The Irish
and the Jews have a psychosis.'

The word *Irish* is commonly used for the Gaelic ['Gay-lik'] language of Ireland: 'In Connemara they speak Irish.' Paradoxically, however, the word was sometimes used in the 19th century for English as used in Ireland: 'The *Irish* of the peasants, which is nothing but English Hibernicised' (*The Westminster Review*, 21, 1834). There was also a time when the name *Irish* was applied in Scotland to both people and language: 'We oft finde the Scots called Irishes, like as we [the writer was Scottish] yet term commonly our Highlandmen, in regard they speak the Irish language' (Spottiswoode, *History of the Church of Scotland*, 1655).

The days are long gone however when Scottish Gaelic was called *Irish* (or its variant, *Erse*), but such confusion over names, peoples, and languages is not unusual in Europe's western islands: Scottish Gaelic was once called *Scots* (a name now reserved for the Germanic vernacular of the Lowlands, and the Scots were once an Irish people who colonized Scotland). In Ireland, the indigenous language is known as *Gaelic*, *Irish Gaelic*, and *Irish*, while in Scotland it is *Gaelic* (usually pronounced 'Gallik' by Scots and 'Gay-lik' by others) or *Scottish Gaelic* or *the Gaelic* (a common usage among Gaels themselves when speaking English). The Irish and Scottish forms of Gaelic are mutually intelligible with an effort.

Ireland, England, Wales, Scotland, Britain

The name *Ireland* dates from before the 10th century, and is a hybrid, the *Ire-* an adaptation of *Eire*, the name of the island in Gaelic. Ireland has often been defined as an island of the British Isles: for example, in the *Longman Larousse* encyclopedia (1968) and the *Oxford Advanced Learner's Dictionary: Encyclopedic Edition* (1992), but many Irish people, especially in the Republic, and generally if Catholic in Northern Ireland, consider such a description both inappropriate and offensive. They would prefer the definition in the *Encarta World English Dictionary* (1999): 'island in northwestern Europe, in the North Atlantic Ocean, west of Great Britain.' But many might like to remove the 'Great'; for them, Ireland should in no sense be linked with Britain, great or otherwise. However, in the six counties of Northern Ireland, which is part of the United Kingdom, the island's place in the British Isles is entirely agreeable to the slightly majority Protestant population.

The Romans never invaded the island, which they called *Hibernia* (a name of uncertain origin), and as a result the Irish escaped direct Romanization. Paradoxically, however, after the decline of the Empire, Ireland became a focus of Christian culture and Latin was used for religious and scholarly purposes. Irish cultural, scholarly, and religious influence in Europe, mainly through Latin, was in course of time weakened by two waves of Germanic invaders: the Vikings (9–11th centuries) from Scandinavia, then the Anglo-Normans (12th century onward) from England via Wales. The close, prickly, and unequal relationship between Irish and English is therefore some eight centuries old. In that time, the fortunes of each have fluctuated in a vast mix of conquest, rebellion, religion, ethnicity, migration, politics, and educational policies.

In 1155, the English-born Pope Adrian IV granted the Anglo-Norman King Henry II of England permission to invade Ireland, to bring about religious reform there. Henry declared himself 'Lord of Ireland', and his assault from Wales was successful. By 1175, half of Ireland was under Anglo-Norman control, and by 1250 almost three-quarters of the island had been divided into English-style shires. The polyglot expeditionary force of English, French, Welsh, and Flemish invaders found a local language with strong and distinctive traditions, and medieval Anglo-Irish statutes demonstrate both the strength of Irish and even the need to protect English from it.

In 1285, a letter sponsored by the Bishop of Kildare and sent to the king in England recommended not promoting Irish-speaking clerics in areas controlled by England, because they sought to maintain their language. In 1366, the Statutes of Kilkenny (written, ironically, in French) enjoined speakers of English in Ireland not to take up Irish names, customs, and language. Irish, however, flourished even at the highest levels controlled by England: thus, in the same century, the Earls of Ormond and Desmond (who owed fealty to the English crown) spoke Irish by choice, and Desmond, who was Lord Chief Justice, wrote poetry in it. The fortunes of the invaders were in fact uncertain for a long time. They felt secure only in the pacified country around Dublin, known (14th–16th century) as 'the Pale'; the natives 'beyond the Pale' were known as 'the wild Irish'.

The size of the Pale (cf. *palisade* and *palings*) steadily shrank, as the Irish regained more territory, but after the Reformation, in the 16th century, the English occupiers re-focused their energies and crushed the old order. Lands were confiscated and the establishment of *plantations* (colonizing settlements) brought large numbers of English and later Scottish Protestant *planters* to the island as loyal supporters of the Crown. The history of Ireland from then on was dominated by revolts against a 'Protestant Ascendancy' imposed from London, in a struggle first for religion, then home rule, and at length independence—as well as for the language.

However, throughout the upheavals English grew stronger. By 1800, it was being used by around half the population; by 1900, a census recorded only 21,000 monolingual speakers of Irish; in 2002, the number of Gaelic monolinguals is zero, although some 100,000 people speak Irish as a co-mother tongue. The reasons for this massive transfer are complex; it has been said both that English 'murdered' Irish and that Irish 'committed suicide'. Although the emotions involved in any discussion of language can be strong, the main reasons for the virtually total displacement of Irish seem to have been socio-political rather than linguistic, and include the following five developments:

❶ The Plantations

A policy of large-scale planned settlement, which began in the 16th century under the Tudor rulers of England and continued in the 17th under both the Stuart kings and Oliver Cromwell.

❷ Legislation

Penal laws in the 18th century largely reduced the rural population to subsistence level and ensured that people could no longer hope to better themselves through Irish.

❸ Religion

The Roman Catholic Church in Ireland became increasingly reconciled to English at the same time as it became more wary than ever of Protestant proselytism in Irish, although it had in fact begun in Elizabethan times.

❹ Education

In 1831 the National Schools were introduced, in which English was the sole medium of instruction.

❺ Starvation and emigration

The famines of the mid-19th century, which resulted in large-scale loss of life, emigration, and a widespread belief that land and language alike were blighted. Ironically, on the eve of the potato famines of 1846–8, population growth had been so great that there were probably at that time more Irish-speakers than ever before but, as the famines and migrations proceeded, the position of English was further consolidated.

The decline of Irish accelerated so quickly that by the end of the 19th century there were few monolingual Irish left and bilingualism had become a way-stage to monolingual English, as was emigration to the United Kingdom, North America, and Australia.

The founding of the Gaelic League in 1893 initiated a wave of revivalism, but it came at a point when the language was gravely weakened. Indeed, leaders of the movement included such Dublin intellectuals as Douglas Hyde and Eoin MacNeill, whose Irish was acquired, not native. Worse, the League failed to engage the support of the dwindling number of impoverished and uneducated native speakers in the *Gaeltacht*, rural Irish-speaking enclaves in the west that were idealized and romanticized, yet also kept at a safe geographical, psychological, and cultural remove. Furthermore, Irish was often associated with an unyieldingly conservative Catholicism, in terms of which English was seen as the secular medium of progressive culture—despite the anomaly that the Church was itself promoting English in Irish-speaking parishes. The Gaelic League had considerable success in working for Irish in schools and in Trinity College Dublin, but it did not succeed in altering the language habits of the people at large, who freely used English despite their massive rejection of control from England.

The struggle for Irish autonomy culminated in the Easter Rising in Dublin in 1916, during the First World War. The partition of the island followed in 1920, establishing a Catholic-dominated Irish Free State in 1921 (which became the Irish Republic in 1949) and the Protestant-dominated six counties of Northern Ireland, which remained part of the United Kingdom. Often violent hostility continues there, despite decades-long efforts at peace and reconciliation, between 'loyalist' Protestants who wish to sustain the British link and 'nationalist' Catholics who seek a re-united autonomous Ireland within the European Union. The Republic is 95% Catholic by religion and has two official languages, Irish in principle and English in practice, whereas Northern Ireland has since the 18th century had a Protestant majority which as time passes becomes slimmer, with parity between the communities looming. As with the rest of the UK, there is no official language *per se*; English is simply taken as given.

When the Irish Free State was set up in 1921 and Irish was declared its 'national language', the heady rhetoric of a new dawn was accompanied by serious and often pessimistic concern. The government was then—and continues to be— accused of paying only lip service to the revival of the language. The task of revitalization was entrusted to the schools and it is in education that the most significant action has been taken, including compulsory Irish classes and making the acquisition of a secondary school leaving certificate conditional on a pass in Irish (a rule now rescinded). The massive decline has continued. Ireland today is an overwhelmingly English-speaking country, in which only 2% at most use Irish on a regular basis. Even in the Gaeltacht many parents bring their children up in English. Indeed, given the strong currents of English in everyday life, the schools have done surprisingly well in spreading a slim awareness of Irish throughout the land.

Northern Ireland or Ulster is different. Whereas 'Northern Ireland' is a clear-cut term (somewhat more political than geographical), the meaning and use of the name 'Ulster' are complex. Ulster is traditionally one of the four historic provinces of Ireland, along with Connaught, Leinster, and Munster, but its name has long since been applied to Northern Ireland, for which the traditional term 'province' is also in wide local use (although it covers less territory than the original undivided Ulster, which was intimately associated with the ancient Celtic epic stories of Cùchulain and Finn MacCumhail).

During the English conquest of Ireland, Ulster was the most rebellious province and was therefore the most heavily *planted* ('settled'), creating the famous/ infamous *Ulster Plantation* of Protestant English and Scots, the latter group coming to be called both *Ulster Scots* and *Scotch Irish*. The nine counties of the original Ulster are the most linguistically varied region of Ireland, with Gaeltacht areas in Donegal, Hiberno-English communities in counties Fermanagh and Tyrone, Ulster Scots in counties Antrim and Down, Anglo-Irish or Ulster English most notably in the southern areas, and RP speakers among the traditional Ascendancy (the Anglican gentry).

There is even less use of Irish in the North than in the South, but despite its decline, Irish Gaelic for a majority in the South and for Catholics in the North retains the symbolic value of a national flag, and is the key to a locked-up heritage that most Irish people cannot reach. There seems little likelihood that Irish will significantly revive, although there has in recent years been a growing demand in urban areas for Irish-medium education. That demand may or may not increase, but in the mean-time both the Englishing of the Irish and the Irishing of English are a *fait accompli*.

Irish English

The hybridity of language in Ireland is most marked in the Republic, which is officially bilingual. Irish and English appear together on public buildings, in official forms and documents, and most notably on road signs. Thus, English/Irish pairings on notice-boards at Dublin Airport include: *Shops/Siopaí*, *Bar/Beár*, *Snacks/Sólaistí*, *Post Office/Oifig an Phoist*, *Telephones/Telefón*, *Information/ Fiasrúcháin*. On road signs, the relationship of the two is deftly managed: English below, larger and capitalized, Irish above, smaller and in Celtic letters, as in:

> Cill Fhionnúrach
> KILFENORA
>
> An Carn
> CARRAN
>
> Baile Uí Bheacháin
> BALLYVAGHAN
>
> Lios Dúin Bhearna
> LISDOONVARNA

In many instances, the English names are Anglicizations of Irish names, the two corresponding fairly closely in visual terms and even in pronunciation, points that emphasize the un-Englishness of it all (adding to the brand image of Ireland as a distinctive tourist destination). In some cases, however, the names are very different, as when *Baile átha Cliath* (pronounced 'Bla-klee') is set above *Dublin*, although both names are Irish. *Dublin* derives from *Dubh Linn* ('Black Pool').

Although the leaders of England's original invasion spoke Anglo-French and the soldiers variously spoke Flemish, Welsh, and West Country English, the lingua franca was an English that became established in the Pale, and notably in County Wexford. In due course, this 'first' Irish English came to be known as *Yola*, a word that derives from West Saxon *yald* ('old'). Settlers from England in the 16th–17th centuries regarded Yola as quaint and archaic. *Holinshed's Chronicle* put it as follows in 1586: 'Howbeit to this day, the dregs of the old auncient Chaucer English are kept as well there [in Wexford] as in Fingall [North Dublin]'. Yola survived tenaciously in County Wexford into the 19th century, when in 'A Glossary of the old dialect of the Baronies of Forth and Bargy' (edited by the Dorset philologist-poet William Barnes, 1867), Jacob Poole provided the following piece of verse, entitled 'A Yola Song':

> Joud and moud vrem earchee ete was ee Lough.
> Zitch vapereen, an shimereen, fan ee-daff ee aar scoth!
> Zitch blakeen, an blayeen, fan ee ball was ee-drowe!
> Chote well aar aim was t'yie ouz n'eer a blowe.
> ['Throngs and crowds from each quarter were at the Lough.
> Such vapouring and glittering when stript in their shirts!
> Such bawling and shouting, when the ball was thrown!
> I saw their intent was to give us never a stroke.']

To the native Irish, the English-speaking remnant had long been known as *na Sean Ghaill* ('the Old Foreigners'), echoing both the term *Yola* itself and emphasizing the alienness of their speech. The descendants of the first settlers who continued to use English came to be known to the second wave of settlers, from the 16th century onward, as 'the Old English'.

Scholars in recent decades have used at least three terms in their discussion of English as it has developed in Ireland: *Anglo-Irish*, *Hiberno-English*, and *Irish English*. Of these, *Anglo-Irish* is the oldest, long associated with people of mainly English origin. As a result, the term is socially and historically ambiguous, and Irish people are often uncomfortable with it, except in such a phrase as *the Anglo-Irish poet Samuel Butler Yeats*. It does not therefore work well as a cover term for all usage in Ireland. The term *Hiberno-English* avoids this difficulty, but runs the other way: it tends to exclude the Anglo-Irish and disenfranchise the indigenized descendants of Protestant settlers. *Irish English*, however, although the phrase may sound paradoxical (even 'Irish'), has less of an academic ring, is transparent, and is unlikely to be misinterpreted.

It also comfortably fits into the set *American English*, *Australian English*, *Indian English*, etc., and for that reason is the generic term here. *Irish English* subsumes all the Englishes of the island, and the other terms stand for subvarieties. The two main politico-linguistic divisions are *Southern* and *Northern*, within and across which further varieties are *Anglo-Irish*, *Hiberno-English*, *Ulster Scots*, and the usage of the two capitals, *Dublin* and *Belfast*.

Anglo-Irish, Dublin, and echoes of the Ascendancy

The speakers of this largely but not exclusively middle-class variety can be found in modest numbers throughout the island and most densely in the Dublin area. Anglo-Irish derives from the usage of the more socially prominent 17th-century Protestants from England, members of what has been called the *Protestant Ascendancy*, or simple the *Ascendancy*, modified by contacts with Hiberno-English, Ulster Scots, and Irish itself. It is a continuum influenced by level of education and regional background. The usage of its more educated speakers blends into broadcasting norms while less educated speakers blend into the other varieties and are likely to use non-standard forms.

Pronunciation

1   The three main varieties are all perceived as 'Received Pronunciation'. RP as such is spoken by a small minority, mainly of men, educated in public schools in England, and by some people in the media. In the Republic, the more pervasive local variety in the Republic differs from RP in being rhotic, and is notable in the pronunciation on *Radio Telefis Eireann* (*RTE*: 'Irish Radio and Television'). The Northern Ireland variety is also rhotic, many BBC broadcasters speaking with a local accent and serving as more influential models than mainland speakers of classic RP.

2   The pervasive *r*-sound is retroflex, comparable to the Northern dialect in the US.

3   In working-class speech, such words as *leave* and *tea* sound like 'lave' and 'tay', *cold* and *old* sound like 'cowl' and 'owl', *bull* and *could* can rhyme with 'cull' and 'cud', and *which* and *whether* begin with 'hw', distinguishing them from *witch* and *weather*.

4   Also in working-class speech, in such words as *arm* and *film* a vowel often separates the consonants, producing an effect like 'arrum' and 'fillum', much as in the west Central Lowlands of Scotland.

5   In the South, such words as *thin* and *then* sound close to 'tin' and 'den', but are more breathy, while such words as *try*, *dry*, *butter*, and *under* sound close to 'thry', 'dhry', 'butther', and 'undher', features shared with Hiberno-English.

Grammar

Less standard forms of Anglo-Irish have the following four features also found outside Ireland, but appear to be more tolerated at higher social levels than in Britain.

1   *Done* and *seen* used for the simple past (*She done it because she seen me do it*), and some past participles (*He has div* 'He has dived'; *They've went* 'They've gone').

2   *Them* used as a demonstrative plural adjective and pronoun: *Them shoes is lovely*; *Them's the ones I want*.

3 Common plural forms of *you* vary regionally. In the South, they may be *ye* (rhyming with *he*), as in *Ye'll all get what's comin to ye*, or *youse* (rhyming with *whose*), as in *Youse kids better be quiet!* In the North, it is *yiz* (rhyming with *his*), as in *Yi'll all get what's comin to yiz* and *Yiz kids better be quiet!*

4 The use of plural *is*: *Me and Mick's fed up*; *Mary and the daughter's out shoppin*; *Yiz is late*; and *Themins (= those ones) is no use.*

Vocabulary

1 There are many distinctive words, such as: an *atomy* (from *atom*), a small, insignificant person: *Did you ever see such a wee atomy of a man?*; to *cog* is to cheat, especially by copying: *I wouldn't let just anybody cog my exercise*; to *thole* is to endure: *There was nothin for it but to thole* (similar to *thole* in Scots and *thoil* in Yorkshire dialect).

2 General words with distinctive senses include: *backward* ('shy'), *bold* ('naughty'), *doubt* ('to believe strongly'), as in *I doubt he's comin* (shared with both Scots and Scottish English).

3 Most regionally marked words occur in the speech of older, often rural people. It is for example unlikely that *biddable* meaning 'obedient', *feasant* 'affable', and *pishmire/pismire* 'ant' occur in the natural usage of people under 40.

Ireland has fewer urban dwellers than most Western European countries, but each city, including Armagh, Cork, Derry/Londonderry, Donegal, Galway, and Limerick, has its own forms and sphere of linguistic influence. The most powerful however are the foremost cities of South and North: Dublin and Belfast. The English name of the capital of the Irish Republic derives from Irish *dubh linn* ('black pool') while its Irish name is quite different: *Baile átha Cliath* ('Town of the Hurdle Ford', pronounced 'Bla-clee'). Dublin is the home of more than a quarter of the Republic's 3.6 million people. It pre-dates the 9th-century Scandinavian settlement and was central to the spread of English in Ireland. Indeed, some parts of the city have been English-speaking for almost 800 years.

The speech of middle-class Dubliners is Anglo-Irish and the norm for their peers throughout the Republic, while the speech of the majority of the working class mixes Anglo-Irish and Hiberno-Irish. Typically, *thin* and *this* sound like 'tin' and 'dis' (*Dere was tirty-tree of dem*), words such as *tea* and *peacock* sound like 'tay' and 'paycock', in words like *fat* and *fad* there is often an *s*- or *z*-like hiss ('fatss', fadzz'), in such words as *castle* and *glass* the *a* is short (as in Scotland and the North of England), in words such as *suit* and *school* there is a diphthong, so that for many people *suit* and *suet* have the same pronunciation, and words such as *tie* and *buy* sound almost like 'toy' and 'boy'.

Dublin is the birthplace of many writers in English who have attained worldwide fame and been intensively studied, including Jonathan Swift, Oliver Goldsmith, Richard Sheridan, Oscar Wilde, George Bernard Shaw, James Joyce, Sean O'Casey, Iris Murdoch, and Samuel Beckett. In the main, their approach to writing has been either standard in the British style, as with Wilde and Shaw, or highly individualistic, as with Joyce and Beckett. Although many such writers have introduced Irish usages into their writing for various purposes, there is no tradition of distinctness comparable to Scottish writers such as Burns and MacDiarmid deliberately sustaining a national tradition.

The Protestant Ascendancy, which lasted from the 17th to the early 20th century, and of which Dublin was the capital, has long gone. Its echoes, however, have reverberated in 'the Troubles' between the Irish Republican Army (IRA) and British police and soldiers both in Northern Ireland and on the British 'mainland', as well as in a national memory of 'the Black and Tans', a quasi-military force recruited by the British to fight the Sinn Fein nationalists just after the First World War. Recently, however, Irish, British, American, and Continental European leaders have met in Dublin's Fair City, attempting on the one hand to solve political problems within Ireland and on the other to further the interests of the European Union, membership of which has served the Republic well. An elegant Georgian capital, built to serve the ends of the old Ascendancy, now serves unanticipated new ends, which include not only political and economic change but also the good will of a vast world-wide—and English-speaking—Irish diaspora.

Hiberno-English and Irish Gaelic

This term covers the mainly working-class variety used by primarily Catholics whose ancestral language was Irish. It is strongest in rural areas and regions in the west where Irish is spoken. It preserves certain Gaelic features while many of its speakers approximate to local Anglo-Irish or Ulster Scots norms.

Pronunciation

1 Words such as *cat* and *garden* sound like 'kyat' and 'gyarden'.

2 Words such as *true* and *drew* sound breathy and close to 'threw' and 'dhrew', while *three* and *those* sound close to 'tree' and 'dose', and are also breathy, features shared with Anglo-Irish.

3 In such words as *pine*, *time*, *come*, the opening consonant is similarly breathy.

Grammar

1 An unstressed initial *and*-like word may introduce a question: *An' do you like it?* In Irish, such questions normally begin with an unstressed element which in the present tense is *an*, as in *An maith leat* e? 'Do you like it?'

2 Comparably, *well*, *sure*, and *sure and* are common openers: *Well, that's nice now*; *Well now, that's nice*; *Sure, he's a fine man*, and *Sure now, he's a fine man*; *Sure an' I'm just after doin' it.*

3 Certain noun usages originate in Irish: *I let a squeal out of me* ('I squealed'); *Give her the full of it* ('Fill it'); *He has a long finger on him* ('He's a thief').

4 Idiomatic constructions place a preposition and pronoun together: *His back's at him* ('He has a backache'); *She stole my book on me* ('She stole my book').

5 The pronoun *it* is used to foreground words and phrases: *It's a lovely girl she is now*; *It wasn't to make trouble I went.*

6 Comparable *it*-foregrounding is used for emphasis with reflexive pronouns: *It's himself was the brave runner*; *'Twas meself she came to see.*

7 Differentiating singular and plural *you*: *Sure, you're dead bate, child/Yiz is dead bate, childer* ('You're dead beat child/children').

8 Using *after* and *-ing* to indicate recently performed action: *Sure, I'm after doin' it this very minute.*

9 Using *a-* and *-ing* as a passive: *Where were you? You were a-lookin'* (= being looked for) *this last hour and more.*

10 Using *and*, a noun phrase, and *-ing* to show that two actions happen at the same time: *I went in an' me tremblin'; In he walks an' him whistlin'.*

11 Using religious phrases in secular situations: *In the name of God, did I rare an eejit?* ('Did I rear an idiot?'); *Oh Mother o' God, what on earth do we do now?*

12 Because Irish has no words for *yes* and *no*, many people tend to answer questions without them: *Will you go to Dublin with me?—I will; Is this car yours?—It is not.*

13 Using idioms (similes, proverbs, etc.) loan-translated from Irish: *She's as light on her foot as a cat at milking; There's a truth in the last drop in the bottle.*

14 Using emphatic devices equivalent to Irish usages, most notably 'at all at all', as in *I'm not tired at all at all* (loan-translating *ar chor ar bith* as in the original *Nil mé tuirseach ar chor ar bith*). Emphatic *at all at all* also occurs in Highland English and in Atlantic Canada.

Vocabulary

1 Nouns taken from Irish often relate either to food (as with *boxty*, from *bacstaidh* 'mashed potato') and the supernatural (as with *banshee*, 'fairy woman', from *bean sidhe*). Others are: *kitter* (a left-handed or clumsy person, from *citeóg*); *mass* ('respect', faith', from *meas*), as in *I've no mass in them things now; smig* ('chin', from *smeig*), as in *It was a blow to the smig that felled him.*

2 Gaelic influence on meanings can be seen in words such as *destroy* and *drenched*. These have the semantic ranges of their Gaelic equivalents *mill* 'to injure, spoil' (*He has the child destroyed with presents*) and *báite* 'drenched, drowned, very wet' (*You're drowned, child. Get all off you. There's not a dry inch to your clothes*).

Irishisms are particularly associated with Hiberno-English, and cover any usage, custom, or peculiarity, especially in language, considered to be quintessentially Irish. They include such shibboleths and stereotypes as the exclamations *begorrah* and *bejabers* (euphemistic variations of 'by God' and 'by Jesus') as well as such expressions as *a broth of a boy* ('a fine lad') and *The top of the morning to you* ('Good morning'). Such expressions are well known, and often overworked when the topic of Ireland comes up, in Britain, North America, and Australia. Currently, Irish people use them only when engaging in *stage Irish* for amusement or as a parody (cf. *Mummerset* and South West England). Phonological, syntactic, and lexical Irishisms occur in: *Divil the bit of a shtick could I find for to bate the baisht with* ('I couldn't find a stick to beat the beast/animal with'); *Will you be after havin a cup of tea?—I will, to be sure* ('Will you have a cup of tea?'—'Certainly'); *Wasn't it herself broke the plate?* ('Wasn't she the one who broke the plate?'). Rhetorical Irishisms are often plays on words (*He's teetotally obsnorious*, 'He's obnoxiously teetotal'), malapropisms (*That man's a confederate liar, so he is*, where the usual word would be 'inveterate'), and such Irish bulls as *Nuns run in that family* ('A lot of the girls in that family become nuns').

Northern Irish English, Ulster Scots, and Belfast

The distinctive English of 'the North' falls into four broad varieties:

1 *Ulster Scots*, also known as *Scotch-Irish*, brought to the area by 17th-century Protestant settlers from Lowland Scotland. The most northerly variety in the North, it is found in Antrim, Down, Derry/Londonderry, and in eastern and central Donegal in the Irish Republic.

2 *Anglo-Irish* (see) or *Ulster English*, introduced by 17th-century Protestant settlers from England. It stretches northward from Bundoran in the west to Dundalk in the east, has much in common with southern Anglo-Irish, and has been influenced by Ulster Scots.

3 *Hiberno-English* (see), notably in Armagh, Donegal, Fermanagh, and Tyrone, with a further pocket in the Glens of Antrim, where Irish Gaelic, reinforced by Scottish Gaelic, survived into the 1940s.

4 The distinctive speech of the city of Belfast.

Large numbers of speakers of Ulster Scots migrated to Pennsylvania and the valleys of the Appalachian and Ozark mountains in the US and to Ontario and other parts of Canada. The resulting 'Scotch-Irish' usage is associated both negatively with the term *hill-billy* and positively with country and western music. Since around 1950, *Scotch-Irish* has also been a less-used alternative term for *Ulster Scots*. The form *Scots-Irish* is part of a preference for the more traditional adjective *Scots*: 'The ingrained hostility between the Catholic community and the Scots-Irish in Northern Ireland' (*The Listener*, 21 Dec 1972). It is not, however, traditional in this particular phrase, and so *Scotch* is kept here although the conventional form *Scots* is kept in *Ulster Scots*.

Pronunciation
The extent of a person's distinctively Ulster Scots usage tends to depend on location, education, and social standing. The lower down the social ladder, the more likely the speaker is to roll the *r*s in *war* and *work*, lose the *l* in *fall* and *full*, rhyme *die* with 'me', *dead* with 'bead', *home* with 'name', *now* with 'you', and use the sound in Scottish *loch* in such *gh*-words as *Clogher, Drogheda, laugh*, and *trough*.

Grammar
Grammatical features include the negatives *no* ('We'll no be able to come'; 'Do ye no ken the man?') and *-nae/ny* added to auxiliary verbs ('A didnae think he would come'; 'Ye canny mean it'), and the demonstratives *thon* ('yon'), *thonder* ('yonder'), as in 'D'ye ken thon man?' and 'Thonder she is!').

Vocabulary

The Scottish and Northern Irish communities share such words as: *ava* ('at all');
bairn ('baby, child'); *brae* ('hill, steep slope'); *firnenst* ('in front of'); *greet* ('cry,
weep'); *ken* ('know'); *lum* ('chimney'); *message* ('errand'); *nor* ('than'); *oxther*
('armpit': Scots *oxter*); *peerie* ('spinning-top'), *tae* ('to').

Ulster Scots, the sole fully fledged variety of Scots beyond Scotland, is part of the
long debate on whether Scots is a distinctive and complex dialect of English or a
language in its own right, or somehow both. It has had a verse tradition since the
peasant poet James Orr in the 18th century, including the verse of G. F. Savage-
Armstrong and Adam Lynn in the 20th century. Its more limited prose tradition,
used primarily for comic purposes, includes W. G. Lyttle in the novel *Betsy Gray*
(1888). The following passage is from Savage-Armstrong's 'Death and Life' (1901):

> 'Puir Wully is deed!'—'O, is he?'
> 'Ay, caul' in his coffin he's leein'!'
> 'Jist noo A em muckle tae busy
> Tae trouble me heed about deein';
> There's han's tae be got fur the reapin'
> We're gaun tae the wark in the murn;
> An' A'm thinkin' the rain 'ill come dreepin',
> The-night, an' destroyin' the curn.
> [*puir* ('poor'), *deed* ('dead'), *caul'*
> ('cold'), *leein'* ('lying'), *Jist noo A em*
> *muckle tae busy* ('Just now I am much too
> busy'), *me heed* ('my head'), *han* ('hand,
> worker'), *gaun tae the wark* ('going to
> work'), *murn* ('morning'), *dreepin*
> ('dripping/dropping'), *the-night*
> ('tonight'), *curn* ('corn')]

The name of the city of Belfast derives from Gaelic *Béal Feirste* ('mouth of (the river)
Feirste'). The area was settled in the early 17th century with Protestant *planters*
mainly from England. The numbers of Scottish Protestants increased in the 18–19th
centuries and of Irish Catholics in the 19th, the often mutually hostile Protestants
and Catholics tending to settle in distinct parts of the city. The range of usage varies
according to education and background.

Such words as *true* and *drew* sound like 'thrue' and 'dhrew', while *good* and *cap*
sound like 'gyood' and 'kyap', *cheap* and *speak* sound like 'chape' and 'spake',
all with single vowel sounds as in Scots. *Push* and *took* have short vowels and
sound like *rush* and *luck*, *ever* and *yet* also have short vowels and sound close to
'ivver' and 'yit', while *deck* and *penny* sound rather like 'dack' and 'panny' and
berry/bury and *cherry* sound close to 'barry' and 'charry'. *Board* and *course* sound
like 'boored' and 'koorss', but tighter, *cold* and *hold* are like 'cowl' and 'howl', *bag*
and *can* sound like 'beg' and 'ken', and *off* and *shop* sound like 'aff' and 'shap'. The
form *Y'are not* is commoner than *you're not* and much commoner than *you aren't*.

None of the above features are exclusive to Belfast, but both their co-occurrence
and the rapidity of informal speech distinguish Belfast people from other speakers

of Irish English. All such features are associated with the vocabulary and general grammar patterns of non-standard Anglo-Irish (as described above). Elements of vocabulary have also been drawn from Ulster Scots, especially in the north and east of the city.

In 1996, Oxford University Press brought out the *Concise Ulster Dictionary*, edited by C. I. Macafee, with over 15,000 entries and more than 5,000 etymologies. The historical introduction by Michael V. Barry draws attention to four kinds of Ulster usage: Ulster Scots (or Scotch-Irish); Mid-Ulster English; 'the speech of those areas where Gaelic is either still in use or has died out relatively recently' (that is, local Hiberno-English); and the 'distinctive dialect' of Belfast. He notes that '[t]here is probably no clear concept of any regional standard or socially prestigious form of English in the North', as a consequence of which dialect is used, and considered respectable, 'much higher up the social scale . . . than in many other parts of the British Isles'. He notes, however, that in recent years local media usage has become influential and 'probably reflects the usage of educated Belfast speakers'.

Continental Europe

1994 It may well be . . . that we shall see an increased divergence in the Englishes spoken worldwide and the 'English' of England will become an increasingly minor variety of 'world English'. Certainly the English that is becoming rapidly the language used in conferences within the European Union is becoming a new variety of the language.
– Mike Heyhoe & Stephen Parker, *Who Owns English?* (Open University Press), p. xiv

2001 If 'Euro-English' is indeed an emerging variety as a European lingua franca, then it should be possible to describe it systematically, and eventually also to provide a codification which would allow it to be captured in dictionaries and grammars and be taught, with appropriate teaching materials to support this teaching. While many might (still) find it difficult to countenance such thoughts, very specific research efforts are currently under way to undertake these first steps required for an eventual description and codification.
– Barbara Seidlhofer, 'Towards making "Euro-English" a linguistic reality,' in *English Today* 68 (17:4), Cambridge University Press, 14

The spread of English in recent decades as a mainland European lingua franca (at all social levels) has been remarkable, and the emergence of the label 'Euro-English' was probably inevitable, to go along with such other forms as *Eurocentric*, *Eurodollar* and *euro* on its own as the name of a common currency for member states of the European Union.

There are few mainland Western European languages with which English does not have ties: of a shared Germanic origin (as with German), of such an origin plus close historical links (as with Dutch and the Scandinavian languages), or with a distinct origin but strong cultural and linguistic associations (as with Latin and

Greek), or distinct origins but a long-term process of acculturation (as with French and Italian). In addition, mainly because of the lingua-franca role of English at the present time, Anglicisms are flowing freely into all major mainland languages. To look at the links adequately, however, it is necessary to begin at the beginning, which was long before English as it is now known came into existence.

Latin and Latin in English

2001 Erasmus must be turning in his grave. The latest ploy in the campaign to promote Latin teaching in British schools is a mouse called Minimus, the hero of a beginners' course for seven-to eleven-year-olds ('the mouse that made Latin cool'). Concerns for the health of Latin are nothing new, of course. . . . But the claim is all the more plausible today for Classicists anxiously questioning the prospects of a subject which rests on the shoulders of Maximus the gladiator and Minimus the mouse.

– Llewelyn Morgan, 'The many deaths of Latin', *The Times Literary Supplement*, August

The Latin language has existed for some 2,500 years, during which it has passed through at least four phases. In the first two it was a living community language; in the second two it has been a medium used for religious, educational, and academic purposes. As such, it has generally been described as 'dead'. The phases are:

❶ An Italic dialect

From an unknown date to around the 5th century BC, Latin was a western Italic dialect spoken in Latium ('The Broad Plain': Italian *Lazio*), and especially the city of Rome. It was dominated by the now long-extinct language of the Etruscans to the north and influenced by the usage of Greek colonists to the south.

❷ The language of the Roman Republic and Roman Empire

From the 4th century BC to the 5th century AD, it was the language of Republic and Empire, greatly influenced by Greek, with a literary standard and latterly a range of vernacular forms throughout much of Western Europe, from which the present-day Romance languages derive.

❸ The language of Roman Catholicism

From the 3rd century to the present day, it has been the international medium of the Roman Catholic Church, and the learned language of Western Christendom, centred on the Vatican in Rome, where it is still a spoken medium.

❹ The foundation language of Western scholarship and science

Also known as *Neo-Latin* and *New Latin*, from the 15th to the early 19th century, the core cultural and educational medium of Renaissance and post-Renaissance Europe, rich in technical adoptions from Greek.

Most noticeably since the Renaissance, Latin has been the linguistic seed-corn for much of the cultural and technical vocabulary of the major Western European languages, both through direct loan words and indirect loan translations, and via these languages it has touched other languages worldwide, as with the many Latinate words in Malay and Japanese. Although itself a Germanic language, English has been massively receptive to Latin influence, as a consequence of Catholicism, the Norman Conquest and the influence of French, Latin scholarship in Medieval, Renaissance, and Enlightenment Europe, and more recently in the Greco-Latin scientific heritage.

Latin is a highly inflected language noted for compactness of expression. Thus, the one word *amabunt* translates as the three English words 'they will love', while the passive form *amabuntur* translates as 'they will be loved'. For centuries, formal education in England, Scotland, Wales, and Ireland has been closely associated with the teaching and learning of Latin. Most notably, in England, this training was provided in *grammar schools*, in which the term 'grammar' was in effect a synonym for 'Latin', and it is evocative that in Nigeria today 'grammar' is in effect a synonym for Standard English, a primary language of education in West Africa (a situation with many linguistic and social parallels to Europe in the 16th–18th centuries).

Indeed, the Latin-medium grammar schools of 16th-century England performed a comparable linguistic service to the English-medium schools set up since the 19th century in Nigeria, India, and similar locations and to the traditional grammar-translation styles of teaching English in Japan and Korea, which do not necessarily produce fluent speakers but create many competent readers and writers of English, much as happened in Europe with Latin. Indeed, in the recent past in Japan and Korea, learners of English had as little likelihood of needing to speak and understand English as grammar-school pupils and university students in Western Europe had of speaking Latin after the 17th century.

Both the terminology and style of the traditional grammatical study and teaching of English derive from the study and teaching of Latin, and the formal analysis of English grammar (widely taught until recent decades and continued in present-day linguistics at university level) continues to owe a great deal to a Latin model that derived in turn from a Greek model. Paradoxically, despite what many people suppose in the UK and the US (as a direct consequence of the massive decline throughout the 20th century of Latin teaching), the link with Latin remains unbroken. Indeed, the vast majority of users of English over the centuries only met Latin directly in such Anglicized phrases as *habeas corpus* and *ad infinitum*, and the majority of those who met it in the classroom kept little of it afterwards. Nonetheless, the influence has been everywhere, and indeed is built into the fabric of all the major Western European languages. It is difficult to break such links, which are in any case dynamic, not static.

Because no one has acquired it as a mother tongue for *c.*1,500 years, Latin is often called a 'dead' language. However, the unbroken (though nowadays much reduced) tradition of scholarly Latin, and of Latinisms used in many languages (even such small matters as the abbreviations *e.g.* and *i.e.*), makes it a lively corpse. Significantly, a large part of the world's written work in Latin and scholarly borrowing from it and from Greek took place centuries after it ceased to be a natural language, and was done by people who had acquired it more as a textual than a verbal language.

The use of Neo-Latin ('New Latin') in creating the terminology of botany, zoology, medicine, and other disciplines is part of the continuously evolving verbal apparatus of the medieval and modern worlds. This resource made possible the writing and dissemination of many of the foundation documents of Western science. The pioneering Swedish naturalist known to the world as Carolus Linnaeus rather than as Carl von Linné (1707–78) wrote his revolutionary works in Latin: in 1735 *Systema Naturae* ('Nature's Way'), in 1737 *Genera Plantarum* ('Kinds of Plants'), and in 1753 *Species Plantarum* ('Plant Species'). These works were roughly contemporary with the beginnings of the Industrial Revolution: that is *c*.1,700 years later than Pliny's *Historia naturalis* ('Natural History': 1st century AD).

In the 4th century AD, Jerome (later the patron saint of translators) translated the Bible into Latin, and Augustine of Hippo, a teacher of rhetoric later canonized, wrote such works as *Civitas Dei* ('The City of God'), in the course of time becoming models for Western European writing. In England, such scholars as Aldhelm (7th century), Bede (7th–8th), Alcuin (8th–9th), and Aelfric (10th–11th) followed their example, and translations from Latin by King Alfred of Wessex (9th) laid the foundation of prose writing in England. In addition, the fluid interplay of languages in Britain during the Middle Ages can be illustrated by three successive 12th-century works which dealt with the cycle of mythic and legendary material known in French as the *Matière de Bretagne* and in English as the *Matter of Britain*. Their successive creation also illustrates how one particular evolving genre of cultural writing began in Latin and then passed through French into English:

❶ Geoffrey's *Historia regum Britanniae* ('History of the Kings of Britain')

The Oxford cleric known in Latin as Galfridus Monemutensis and in English as Geoffrey of Monmouth was an Englishman with Welsh and Breton ties. Geoffrey wrote the Latin prose work *Historia regum Britanniae* (*c*.1135), claiming that he translated it from an ancient book 'in the British tongue' (Welsh). His *History* begins with the legendary settlement in Britain of Brutus (a great-grandson of the Trojan prince Aeneas, hero of the Roman poet Virgil's *Aeneid*), after whom the island was supposedly named. It ends with King Arthur, a legendary Celtic hero who was adopted as a legitimating predecessor by the Anglo-Norman monarchs of England.

❷ Wace's *Roman de Brut* ('The Romance of Brutus')

Geoffrey's *History* was then translated into French and further romanticized as the *Roman de Brut* (1155) by Wace, an Anglo-Norman from Jersey in the Channel Islands.

❸ Layamon's *Brut* ('The Brutus')

Wace's translation served in turn as the source for the *Brut*, a late 12th-century alliterative poem in Middle English by Layamon, a Worcestershire priest. His poem was the first of many versions down the centuries in English of the stories of Arthur and the Knights of the Round Table. It also included quasi-historical accounts of King Lear and King Cymbeline that had an influence on Shakespeare's plays *King Lear* and *Cymbeline*.

Latin was the pre-eminent language of scholarship throughout Britain until *c*.1700, by which time English was itself becoming a world language. Such scholars as William Camden (1551–1623) wrote in Latin by preference, considering that to use English was to write in sand. The poet John Milton (1608–74) was fond of Latin verse from an early age and wrote Latin as an official diplomatic secretary. Sir Isaac Newton chose Latin as the medium for his masterwork of early modern science *Philosophiae naturalis principia mathematica* ('Mathematical principles of natural philosophy', 1687), better known simply as the *Principia*. This work was not translated into English until 1729. However, Newton wrote his second major work, *Opticks*, in English, its date of publication (1704) marking the point at which significant scholarly writing began to appear in English first, then in Latin, and in due course in English alone.

A general upper- and middle-class familiarity with the Classics, however, meant that writers continued to use in English the imagery and phrases of ancient Rome, often only slightly adapted, to allude to topics that, until well into the 20th century, their readers could be expected to grasp without the help of editorial footnotes or A–Z cultural compendia like *Brewer's Dictionary of Phrase & Fable*. Many Latin quotations and tags continue in English, such as *ceteris paribus* ('other things being equal') and *nil desperandum* ('never despair'), their translations eventually operating in their own right as loan translations from Latin, a state of affairs of which many users are entirely unaware, and indeed do not need to be aware. In addition, a vast part of both everyday and technical English is Latinate; in this paragraph alone, the words taken from Latin are: *familiarity*, *Classics*, *continued*, *evoke*, *image*, *Rome*, *adapt*, *allude*, *fluent*, *century*, *editorial*, *numerous*, *Latin*, *quotation*, *extend*, *present*, *vast*, *part*, *vocabulary*, *origin*, *include* (plus the Anglo-Latinized Greek words *topic*, *phrase*, *technical*, and *paragraph*). Plus the neologism *Anglo-Latinized*. Plus *neologism.*

The pronunciation of Latin by speakers of English and of Latin words and tags used in English has had a special history. After the Norman Conquest, Latin was taught through the medium of French and as a result took on a French aspect: for example, both the *i* in *ius/jus* ('law') and the *g* in *gens* ('race, clan') had the *j*-sound in *just* and *gent*. After the 13th century, *c* before *e* and *i* came to be pronounced 's', and long vowels were shortened before two or more consonants, so that Latin *census* and *nullus* were pronounced like present-day English *census* and *null*. Speakers of Anglo-French and English (often the same people) pronounced Latin in much the same way as they pronounced French and English. In other words, for several centuries Anglo-French, Latin, and English had a more or less common pronunciation, facilitating the smooth transfer of Latin vocabulary into English.

In the 14th century, with the decline of Anglo-French, English slowly became the medium of instruction for Latin, largely as a result of the efforts of the educational reformer John Cornwall. Later, however, controversy was aroused throughout Europe when the Dutch scholar Desiderius Erasmus published *De recta Latini Graecique sermonis pronuntiatione* ('On the correct pronunciation of Latin and Greek') in 1528. This work discussed the diverse national accents of Latin, which were often mutually unintelligible and often led to confusion at international gatherings—a situation not unlike some world-English milieux today. Erasmus proposed that all national pronunciations be standardized on the basis of what was known or assumed about classical Latin speech, such as a hard *k*-sound for *c* ('kensus' for *census*, etc.), a hard *g* as in 'get' (for *gestum* etc.), and voiceless *s* between vowels (that is, no *z*-sound for the mid-position *s* in *Iesus*: cf. English *Jesus*).

Some responses to these mild proposals were explosive. Thus, when such progressive young scholars as John Cheke and Thomas Smith took up Erasmian ideas at Cambridge, they met fierce resistance from the university establishment. In

1542 an edict forbade Erasmian pronunciation there, on pain of beatings for under-graduates and expulsion for masters. In the view of the Chancellor who imposed the edict, Stephen Gardiner, speakers of Erasmian Latin were unintelligible to their elders. In 1558 the edict was repealed, but Erasmianism had also fallen foul of the Great Vowel Shift, which was taking place at the same time as the Latin controversy. Just as the GVS was changing the pronunciation of general English (and in the process creating many anomalies in spelling), so it was affecting the pronunciation of Anglo-Latin. Thus, the Latin long vowels *a*, *i*, and *e* acquired the values now found in English *same*, *fine*, and *been* (and the Anglicized Latin *radius*, *minus*, and *arena*). As a result, an Anglicized and thoroughly un-Erasmian Latin was the norm in England from the later 16th to the earlier 20th century. In effect, such Latin words as *radius* were not being Anglicized after they had entered English but were already so pronounced in Anglo-Latin. The Great Vowel Shift was in effect working on both English and Anglo-Latin as if they were the same language.

Around 1870, a reformed pronunciation of Latin was proposed at both Oxford and Cambridge universities, but did not become widely used until the early 20th century, and was resisted until the outbreak of the Second World War. One outcome of the ancient tension between native and classical/Erasmian pronunciations has been confusion regarding not only the pronunciation of Latin itself but also of Latin elements in English. These include the plural endings of such words as *formula* (*formulae*: Is it 'ay' as in *say*, 'ee' as in *see*, or 'y' as in *try*?) and *stimuli* ('y' as in *try* or 'ee' as in *see*?). Un-Erasmian Anglicization has long been the norm for everyday tags, as with *tempus fugit* ('tempus fewjit'), *bonafide* with a long *oh* and a weak vowel-ending in *bona* and an *i* as in *hide* in *-fide* (with alternative pronunciations 'fide' and 'fidee' in American and British respectively). In Scotland, in contrast to England, there has long been a preference for Erasmian pronunciation in teaching the language, with full vowel values and hard *g* and *c*. As a result, Scots with a background in Latin are more likely to be Erasmian than Anglican when pronouncing Latin words and phrases in English.

A large part of the word-stock of Latin entered English in two major waves: mainly religious from Old English to the Reformation, and mainly scientific, scholarly, and legal (slightly different in English and Scots law), from the Middle Ages onwards.

In the early 17th century, such pioneers of English dictionary-making as Robert Cawdrey and John Bullokar converted Latin words into English. To do this, they used a strong French lexical base in English to create a primarily written register of education and refinement in which such words as *fraternity* and *feline* were set lexically and stylistically above *brotherhood* and *cat(like)*. Their methods were straightforward: turn Latin word-endings into Anglo-French word-endings (a practice that has continued ever since, well-understood although seldom explicitly taught or even discussed). Examples:

1 *alacritas* became at first a French-like *alacritie* and later *alacrity*

2 *catalogus* (Greek in origin) became *catalogue* and later *catalog* in American

3 *incantatio* became *incantation*

4 *onerosus* became *onerous*

5 *puerilis* became *puerile*

6 *ruminare* through its past participle *ruminatus* became *ruminate*

This process accounts for thousands of words perceived around the world as English, learned as English, and adopted into further languages as Anglicisms. In addition, the relationships are highly regular between fully Latin words and the words derived from them in Spanish, Italian, Portuguese, French, and English, which in this regard is a kind of honorary Romance language. Such words are in effect 'translinguistic', a kind of international reserve currency for any language that needs or wants them.

Latin is not now a major subject in the secondary schools of the English-speaking world, although there are bastions where it still flourishes. This is the current outcome of a long, steady, but gradually accelerating process since the 18th century of removing direct instruction in and use of Latin from education and public life, essentially because the teaching of literacy spread beyond elite schools where Latin was a core subject. The heavens did not fall as a result, but a consequence has been the loan-translation of many long-standing Latin expressions into English. In this way, *Tempus fugit* became 'Time flies' and *Nil desperandum* became 'Don't despair' or 'Never give up'—the English forms now commoner but the Latin originals still used.

In addition, there has been a tendency to make words that have been taken unchanged from Latin behave in a more conventional way, so that the plurals of *cactus* and *referendum* are more likely now to be *cactuses* and *referendums* than *cacti* and *referenda*. In the train of such changes, and because the grip of Latin is still tenacious (*tenax* 'holding tight'), there is often uncertainty and friction (Latin *frictio* 'rubbing') regarding usage: as for example whether *data* and *media* (which in Latin are plural) are singular or plural in English.

Greek and Greek in English

Greek is not a Western European language. Its ancient location was the coastlands and islands of the Aegean and the neighbouring eastern Mediterranean, but with colonies to the west in the Italian peninsula (where a remnant of Greek-speakers persists in the south to this day), in Sicily, and in Massilia (Marseilles). Although Greek is a classical language of Europe (much of its vocabulary a lexical and conceptual seed-corn for that continent), it also served as a source of words for medieval scholarly Arabic. In addition, Greek was once a major North African language (Alexandria in Egypt was a classical centre of Greek learning), and through the Greek texts of the New Testament it has had both a direct and indirect influence on Christianity and culture at large worldwide.

Greek is also a member of the Indo-European language family, commonly divided into *Ancient* or *Classical Greek* (often thought of as a 'dead' language) and *Modern Greek*, the language of Greece and Cyprus (with Turkish), of enclaves in the Soviet Union and the eastern Mediterranean, and of Greek and Cypriot immigrants in Australia, Britain, Canada, the US, and elsewhere. It has one of the longest unbroken linguistic traditions in the world, nearly 3,500 years, divisible into some seven stages:

1 **Mycenaean** (14–12th century BC) the language of Mycenae and Linear B writing

2 **Archaic or Pre-classical Greek** (11–8th century BC) the language of the Homeric epics, Hesiod, and the early lyric poets

3 **Classical or Ancient Greek** (7–5th century BC) with several forms, notably Attic in Athens and Doric in the Peloponnese

4 **Hellenistic Greek** (4th century BC to 4th century AD), also known as *he koine dialektos* ('the common language'), or simply *he koine* (the adjective taken into English as a noun, pronounced 'koinee'), a vernacular or lingua franca (that includes *New Testament Greek*)

5 **Byzantine or Romaic Greek** (5–15th century), the language of the Eastern Roman or Byzantine Empire, centred on Constantinople/Byzantium

6 **Modern Greek**, for a long period divided into *Demotic* or *Dhimotiki* ('popular, demotic') and *Katharévousa* ('purified', a classicized language of education and culture), with considerable tension between the more aggressive proponents of the two styles

7 **Standard Modern Greek** (since the early 1980s), a homogenizing variety, based on the usage of moderately educated people in the large urban centres, primarily Athens and Saloniki.

The Greeks were the first Europeans to use an alphabet, to theorize about language, and to frame such categories as *ónoma* ('name', 'noun') and *phrásis* ('way of speaking', 'group of words', 'phrase'). Most of the literary genres of the Western world were either invented or formalized by the Greeks and many of the names they coined have passed with only minor adaptation to many successor languages, such as, in their English forms: *anachronism, anthology, archetype, biography, catharsis, comedy, criticism, elegy, epic, euphemism, hubris, irony, lyric, metaphor, mythology, poetics, rhetoric, sarcasm, symbolism, tragedy*.

The influence of Classical Greek on English has however been largely indirect, through Latin and French, with some orthographic and other consequences. For most speakers of English, Greek has been remote and esoteric, and their attitudes have been a mix of bafflement and enthusiasm: *It's all Greek to me* ('I can't understand it, and it may not be worth understanding anyway') and the *The Greeks had a word for it* ('What a rich language that was!').

Greek word-forming patterns, words, and word elements were adopted and adapted into Latin over *c.*1,500 years, from which many of them passed into many European and other languages, directly or indirectly, usually for scholarly and technical reasons, but with many items passing on into demotic use, especially in recent decades, as with the forms *hyper* and *mega*, used not only as word elements (*hyperbole, hypersensitive; megatherium, megastar*), but as adjectives in their own right ('He was really *hyper* last night' and 'It was a *mega* deal involving *mega* bucks'). Greek in English was at first limited and largely religious, as with *church* in English and *kirk* in Scots (both adapted from the first word in *kuriakón dôma* 'Lord's house'), then a more significant influx developed in the later Middle Ages and the Renaissance (*catalogue c.*1460, *rhetorical c.*1476, *stratagem c.*1489, *psalmodize c.*1513, and *analytical c.*1525, etc.) and has continued strongly to the present day.

Latin and French have shaped the spelling of Greek words in English, the classic succession being, for example, from Greek *kalligraphía* to Latin *calligraphia* to French *calligraphie* to English *calligraphy*. Occasionally, however, a more Greek look survives, as in: *kaleidoscope*, not the more likely **calidoscope* (but also not **kaleidoskope*); *kinetic*, not **cinetic* (allowing hard-*k kinetic* to be used in contexts unrelated to soft-*c cinema*. Synonym variants are rare, but do occur, as with *ceratin* and *keratin*, both from *kéras* ('horn'). Fossilized contrasts occur when a *k* survives in some usages but not in others: for example, *ceratosaurus* ('horned lizard', a dinosaur) but *keratogenous* ('producing horny tissue'); *cinematography* ('writing, i.e. making, moving pictures') but *kinematograph* (obsolete) a film/movie projector.

Although many Greek personal and place-names in English have the look of French or Latin about them (*Achilles, Alexander, Hercules; Athens, Crete, Rhodes*), they can if needed take forms closer to either classical (*Akhilleus, Alexandros, Herakles*) or Modern Greek (*Athinai, Kriti, Rhodos*). The use of *ph* as a marker of Greek words in Latin survives in English because French writers favoured it, the *ph* representing the Greek letter *phi*. Other Romance languages have managed things differently, so that French *philosophie* and English *philosophy* contrast with Italian and Spanish *filosofia*. However, English *neuralgia* and *neurosis* are closer to Greek than both French *névralgie* and *névrose* and Italian *nevralgia* and *nevrosi*, which have been influenced by the pronunciation of Modern Greek.

Because some loans (such as *diuretic, deontology*, and *dogmatism*) are close to their Greek originals, and others are virtually identical with them (*diphtheria, dogma*, and *drama*), both the effects of Latinization and the creation of hybrids have tended to be overlooked: thus, the words *rhetorical* and *analytical* are largely Greek, but they end with the suffix *-al*, an adaptation of Latin *-alis*. Scholars have tended to minimize such adaptations, because Latin and Greek are as it were equally 'classical', and often discuss Greek as if it were a self-contained and pure source of technical vocabulary for English (which it seldom is). The Oxford lexicographer Henry Bradley put it as follows:

> **1904** So well adapted is the structure of the Greek language for the formation of scientific terms, that when a word is wanted to denote some conception peculiar to modern science, the most convenient way of obtaining it usually is to frame a new Greek compound or derivative, such as Aristotle himself might have framed if he had found it needful to express the meaning.
> – *The Making of English*

This is true, but only partly so. A new formation is likely to be more Neo-Latin than Greek, and it was a combination of circumstance and cultural development rather than unique worth that made Greek a prime source of terms for European academic discourse. Other languages of learning, such as Arabic and Sanskrit, are equally rich in a potential for word-formation, but no such westward channels as Latin and French were open to them. Elsewhere, however, they have had a comparable impact, Arabic on Persian, Turkish, Hausa, and Berber, and Sanskrit on Hindi, Bengali, Tamil, and Malay.

The word-creating capacity of Greek, while prodigious, is therefore not unique, nor has it had a direct channel into, or a monopoly within, the Western European languages. Indeed, even rigorous scientific terminologies can be innovatively hybrid, as for example the names of geological eras, created—in English—as an extremely *ad hoc* system:

❶ Major eras

The names of major eras are formed from Greek elements for time and life: *Pal(a)eozoic* ('relating to old life'), *Mesozoic* ('relating to middle life'), *Cenozoic* ('relating to recent life').

❷ Lesser eras

However, most of the terms for periods within the Paleozoic and Mesozoic are Latinate and none are time-dependent. Three refer to rocks in Wales (*Cambrian*, *Ordovician*, *Silurian*), one each to rocks in England (*Devonian*: Devon), Russia (*Permian*: Perm), and France (*Jurassic*: the Jura), and three to physical features (*Carboniferous* to coal, *Cretaceous* to chalk, *Triassic* to three definitive layers of rock).

❸ Recent eras

The divisions of the Cenozoic return to Greek and to time, marking extremely vague degrees of recentness by turning the *cen(o)-* of *Cenozoic* (original Greek *kainos* 'recent') into the form *-(o)cene*. The results serve their purpose, but are quirky and more poetic than academic: *Paleocene* ('ancient recent'), *Eocene* ('dawn recent'), *Oligocene* ('few recent'), *Miocene* ('less recent'), *Pliocene* ('more recent'), *Pleistocene* ('most recent'), *Holocene* ('entirely recent').

❹ Subsidiary formations

The mix of Greek, Latin, and English is marked in such subsidiary formations as *Early Prepaleozoic, Infracambrian, Eocambrian, Upper Silurian, Permo-Triassic*. Such a system, constructed in an ad hoc fashion to serve the ends of geology, is typical of how Greek is used in Modern English.

The subsystem of *-cene* terms did not endear its creator, the 19th-century Scottish geologist Sir Charles Lyell, to the English usage critic Henry Fowler, who makes the following comment in his usage dictionary under the entry *barbarism*:

> **1965** A man of science might be expected to do on his great occasion what the ordinary man cannot do every day, ask the philologist's help; that the famous *eocene-pleistocene* names were made by 'a good classical scholar' shows that word-formation is a matter for the specialist.
>
> – *Dictionary of Modern English Usage* (Henry Fowler, ed. Ernest Gowers) (Oxford University Press)

More in sympathy than Fowler with the needs and practices of scientists and engineers, the English scholar Simeon Potter in 1950 noted that electricians had abstracted from *electron* a new noun-forming suffix *-tron*, for use in terms like *dynatron, kenotron, phanotron, magnetron*, and *thyratron*. He then observed:

> **1950/66** I once heard an unkind critic allude disparagingly to these neologisms as dog-Greek. To a lover of the language of Sophocles and Plato these recent coinages may indeed appear to be Greek debased. More appropriately, perhaps, they might be termed lion-Greek or chameleon-Greek. They are Neo-Hellenic in the genuine Renaissance tradition.
>
> – *Our Language* (London: Penguin)

Such flexible Greek material has been fully integrated into the lexis and word-formation of English, and is used more or less unreflectingly as a lexical quarry (with, notably, no sense that anyone should consult present-day Greeks: the system has in effect been universalized). The word element *bio-* demonstrates both flexibility and universalization: *biosphere* (all Greek); *bio-degradable* (Greek, Latin, and French, but in English); *biofeedback* (Greek and vernacular Germanic English). An additional dimension in recent times has been the ease with which both Latin and Graeco-Latin material has passed through English into further languages, as for example *elecronics*, *elevator*, and *plutonium* into Japanese as *erekutoronikkusu*, *erebeta*, and *purutoniumu*, and *calorific*, *harmony*, and *symphony orchestra* into Malay (Bahasa Malaysia) as *kalorifik*, *keharmonian*, and *orkestra simfon*.

Romance and English

The name of the Romance language family derives from two similar words of Medieval Latin: *romancium* and *romancia*, both meaning 'a Latin vernacular language', and these derive in turn from *Romanicus* ('Roman; of Roman origin'). Romance languages (and their creoles) are spoken by *c*.400 million people worldwide, but the precise number of those languages varies according to the criteria used to establish them:

❶ Status as a national language

Five languages: French, Italian, Portuguese, Romanian, and Spanish/Castilian—or six if Romansch or Rhaeto-Romanic (a language of Switzerland, now with relatively few speakers) is included.

❷ Possession of a literary tradition

Nine languages: the above, plus Catalan and Gallego (in Spain) and Occitan/Provençal (in France).

❸ Geographical or other distinctness

Fifteen languages: the above, plus Andalusian in Spain, Friulian, Ladin, Sardinian, and Sicilian in Italy, and Judaeo-Spanish/Judezmo/Ladino (the Romance equivalent of Yiddish).

❹ Extinct varieties

At least two languages: Dalmatian (Yugoslavia), Mozarabic (Christians in Moorish Spain).

❺ Romance pidgins and creoles

Including Haitian Creole French, Papiamentu (a Portuguese–Spanish–Dutch creole in the Netherlands Antilles), and Seychellois.

With the disintegration of the Western Roman Empire (3rd–5th centuries), regional forms of Popular (or Vulgar) Latin became the main means of communication in its many successor communities, often at the expense of earlier vernaculars, such as the Italic dialects in Italy and Celtic languages in Spain and France. In addition, Germanic invaders of Italy, Spain, and France did not retain their own languages, and even as late as the 10th century Scandinavian invaders gave up Norse in favour of French when they settled what came to be known as Normandy ('Northmanland'). Not long afterwards, when they invaded and conquered England, they took a distinctive Norman French with them.

For at least two centuries after the Norman Conquest, a Romance language dominated social, political, and cultural life in much of the British Isles and had such an impact on the vocabulary and writing of English that, like Albanian and Maltese, English has sometimes been called a *semi-Romance language*. As Owen Barfield put it in 1962, 'the English language has been facetiously described as "French badly pronounced"' (*History in English Words*, 59). Because of the powerful presence of French and Neo-Latin, English in fact shares a vast reservoir of lexis, concepts, allusions, and conventions with the Romance languages. As a minimal demonstration, the accompanying table lists 20 everyday English words and their equivalents in French, Spanish, Italian, and Portuguese.

English and Romance vocabulary

The table shows not only the similarity and even visual identity) of many items, but also (roughly in proportion to the various vocabularies) some patterns of dissimilarity. Three English words of non-Romance origin (*bed*, *garden*, *oak*) are included, one of which (*garden*) is an example of a Germanic word being adopted into Romance.

English	French	Spanish	Italian	Portuguese
art	art	arte	arte	arte
bandage	bandage	venda	fasciatura	venda
bed	lit	cama	letto	cama
date (fruit)	date	dátil	dattero	tâmara
eagle	aigle	águila	acquila	águia
garden	jardin	jardin	giardino	jardim
January	janvier	enero	gennaio	janeiro
February	février	febrero	febbraio	fevereiro
legal	légal	legal	legale	legal
magic	magie	magia	magia	mágico
mountain	montagne	montaña	montagna	montanha
oak	chêne	roble	quercia	carvalho
parcel/packet	paquet	paquete	pacco	pacote
poor	pauvre	pobre	povero	pobre
price	prix	precio	prezzo	preço
question	question	pregunta	domando	pergunta
round	rond	redondo	rotondo	redondo
solution	solution	solución	soluzione	solução
value	valeur	valor	valore	valor
war	guerre	guerra	guerra	guerra

French, English, and *franglais*

Governments in France have tended to promote and protect the French language, widely conceived as both the national language and a priceless patrimony. The standard language is based on a northern dialect associated with the Ile de France region, in which the capital Paris is situated. Not only was this variety originally in competition with other northern dialects; in the south, there were at least two other distinct Romance languages, Occitan/Provençal and Catalan.

The northern tongue was formerly known as the *langue d'oïl* ('the language of *oui*', the northern word for 'yes': from Latin *ille*, 'that'), while the major southern tongue was the *langue d'oc* ('the language of *oc*', the southern word for 'yes': from Latin *hoc*, 'this', which also provides the first element in *Occitan*). Occitan is closely related in turn to Catalan, spoken in both southern France and particularly northern Spain. Occitan/Provençal was a significant medieval language which declined after the northern annexation of the south. Occitan survives as a range of dialects, which benefited from the efforts and literary success of the Provençal poet Frédéric Mistral (Nobel Prize, 1904), and its relationship with French is similar to that of Scots with English. Occitan was a major element, with Italian, in the Lingua Franca ('Frankish/French language') used by soldiers, sailors, and merchants for many centuries throughout the Mediterranean.

Since medieval times, the language of the northern French has enjoyed considerable prestige in Europe, and in its modern form was from the 17th to the 20th century a key language of international diplomacy. In 1637, the Académie française was founded with a view to fixing (standardizing) the language and keeping *le bon français* ('good French', based on spoken court usage and the work of 'the best writers') as pure as possible. The French Revolution in the late 18th century reinforced French as the language of national unity, with the result that using the other languages of the French state—Basque, Breton, Alsatian, Flemish, Occitan, and Corsican—has generally been considered unpatriotic, divisive, and unsophisticated.

Much the same policy was pursued in French colonies worldwide, with a carry-over in attitude to those colonies which have become independent nations (as opposed to overseas departments of France). The French government pays close attention to the worldwide community of speakers of French, whose territories are collectively *La Francophonie*, a word that is difficult to translate into English, because for example the translation 'the French-speaking world' does not convey the intended sense of cultural solidarity. As a result the term is generally left untranslated in English. The closest analogue in English (though inadequate because of the absence of the United States) is the Commonwealth. The distribution of French worldwide is largely as follows:

❶ Europe

In addition to France, French is official in Belgium (with Flemish) and Switzerland (with German and Italian, and Romansch as a national language), and is spoken in Luxembourg, Andorra, Aosta in Italy, and the Channel Islands.

❷ The Americas

French is the official language of the French island department of St Pierre and Miquelon (off Newfoundland), the French Caribbean departments of Guadeloupe, Martinique, and Guiana. It is the official language of Haiti, an official language of Canada with English, and is spoken alongside English in Trinidad and Tobago, and Saint Lucia. It is spoken in the US in the states of Maine, Louisiana, and Florida.

❸ Africa

French is the official language of Benin, Burkina Faso (Upper Volta), Burundi, Chad, Congo, Côte d'Ivoire, Gabon, Mali, Niger, Rwanda, and Senegal, is widely used in Algeria, Morocco, and Tunisia, and to a less extent Egypt.

❹ The Indian Ocean

It is the official language of the French island of Réunion, and of the Comoros Islands and the Malagasy Republic, and is spoken in Mauritius and the Seychelles.

❺ West Asia

French is spoken in Lebanon and to a less extent Syria, and, decreasingly, in Cambodia, Laos, Vietnam, and the Indian territory of Pondicherry.

❻ Oceania

French is the official language of the French island of Nouvelle Calédonie/New Caledonia and an official language in Tahiti, Vanuatu, and other islands.

❼ Pidgins and creoles

There are French pidgins and creoles in Africa, the Caribbean, and the Indian and Pacific oceans.

Although French is technically classified as a 'Romance' language, and English as a 'Germanic' language, and although France and England were for centuries rivals and often at war, the two languages have been linked throughout their histories. When the Western Roman Empire began to collapse, the same Germanic peoples invaded both regions, the Franks south into the Roman province of Gallia ('Gaul'), changing its name to theirs (Latin *Francia*, German *Frankreich*), while the Angles and others moved across the Mare Germanicum (the 'German Sea') to southern Britannia ('Britain'), which they called by *their* name (Latin *Anglia*, Anglo-Saxon *Englaland*). However, whereas the Angles retained their Germanic speech in England, the Franks gave theirs up in favour of the Latin of Gaul, which duly took on their name, as *français* ('Frankish' or 'French').

While it is possible to discuss the history and nature of French since those times virtually without bringing in English until the 20th century, no one commenting on the history and nature of English can avoid French from the 11th at least until the 18th century. Although the Anglo-Saxons did not give up their language, their descendants opened their doors to nine centuries of French influence. In the last hundred years, however, the current has reversed, leaving many French people alarmed by the sudden and unexpectedly generous repayment of old linguistic debts.

In medieval England, first Norman-French then the Anglo-French of the Plantagenet kings was the elite language. As such, it had a powerful influence on the language of law and culture, and resulted in a massive range of adoptions that was the first stage in giving English its Romance dimension. Some examples:

❶ Animals and their meat

Famously, the animals tended by the Anglo-Saxon peasantry retained English names like *calf* and *sheep*, while their meat when eaten in the Norman castles became French *veal* and *mutton*.

❷ Young and adult animals

A young English *hare* is a French *leveret*, a young English *swan* a French *cygnet*, and a small English *axe* is a French *hatchet*.

❸ Fossils from French

Because of the long presence of the language in England, many French fossils survive in the strata of English: for example, an *s* lost by French is preserved in *bastard, beast, cost, escape, establish, (e)state, hostage, interest, master, paste, scout, tempest* (compare: *bâtard, bête, coûter, êchapper, êtablir, êtat, ôtage, interêt, maître, pâté, êcouter, tempête*).

❹ Two for one: bisociative pairs

Because of the French connection, English sometimes has a twofold vocabulary. People can *answer* or *respond* and *begin* or *commence* to seek *freedom* or *liberty*. Such pairs of near-synonyms often express stylistic differences, as with *kingdom* and *realm*, *sight* and *vision*, and *snake* and *serpent*. Others are further apart, as with *ask* and *demand*, *bit* and *morsel*, *heel* and *talon*, and *illegible* and *unreadable*.

The flow of words, ideas, and fashions from France has continued ever since, often with bouts of Gallomania in England and Anglomania in France. A telling development in England in 1530 was the first ever grammar of French, John Palsgrave's *Lesclarcissement de la Langue Françoyse* ('Making the French Language Clear'), written for English schoolboys and other learners.

Before the Renaissance, prolonged contact with French opened English to increased Latinization, just as French was itself re-Latinized. Consequently, the two languages share a common Neo-Latin technical vocabulary: French *homicide* (12th century) antedates English *homicide* (14th), but English *suicide* is recorded earlier (1651) than French *suicide* (1739), and *insecticide* is almost simultaneous in both (French 1859, English 1866). Curiously, however, Latinization has gone further in English than in French: *pedestrian* and *tepid* are closer to Latin than *piéton* and *tiède*, and many Latinate words in English, such as *abduct, connubial, equanimity, fulcrum, impervious*, and *odium*, are not found in French. On the other hand, many words borrowed into French from other Romance languages (especially Italian) have entered English in a more or less French form, as with *artisan, caprice, frigate, orange, picturesque, stance*, and *tirade*.

French loan-translations often underlie English expressions, as in *flea-market* (from *marché aux puces*), *ivory tower* (from *tour d'ivoire*), and *third world* (from *tiers monde*). Romance word structure can be found in such phrases as *chief of state* (from *chef d'état*) and *point of view* (from *point de vue*). The word order is French in such forms as *Governor-General, poet laureate*, and *treasure trove*.

English also contains many doublets in which the first item is French and the second taken direct from Latin: *constraint* and *constriction*; *custom* and *costume*; *frail* and *fragile*; *loyal* and *legal*; *marvel* and *miracle*; *poison* and *potion*; *sever* and *separate*; *straight* and *strict*. In some cases the Latinate form has no equivalent in French: *allow* and *allocate*; *count* and *compute*; *croissant* and *crescent*; *esteem* and *estimate*; *poor* and *pauper*; *royal* and *regal*; *sure* and *secure*. In other cases, the same word may have been borrowed more than once, with different meanings and forms: *chieftain* and *captain*; *corpse* and *corps*; *hostel*, *hospital*, and *hotel*; *pocket*, *poke*, *pouch*; *ticket* and *etiquette*; *vanguard* and *avant-garde*.

Borrowing from English into French has been widespread for two centuries, but when such borrowing takes place the item may have a specialized role: *un meeting* is political rather than general. Expressions may swap roles, such as *savoir-faire* in English and *know-how* in French. Waves of English words have been borrowed since the 18th century, especially in such areas as:

❶ Politics

congrès, majorité, meeting, politicien, sinécure

❷ Sport and horse-racing

baseball, basketball, football, goal, tennis; derby, outsider, steeplechase, sweep-stake, turf

❸ Rail travel

bogie, condenseur, terminus, trolley, viaduc, wagon

❹ Aviation

cockpit, crash, jet, steward

❺ Medicine

catgut, pace-maker, scanner

❻ Social life

bestseller, gangster, hot dog, leader, sandwich, strip-tease, western

On occasion, English words can be Gallicized by adapting their forms and changing their pronunciation and orthography: *boulingrin* ('bowling green'); *contredanse* ('country dance'); *paquebot* ('packet boat'); and *redingote* ('riding-coat'). Both *réaliser* and *ignorer* are now often used with their English meanings. Canadian French is especially open to such influences: *la ligne est engagée* ('The line is engaged'); *Ayez une bonne journée* ('Have a nice day'). Pseudo-Anglicisms have also arisen: *recordman* ('record-holder'), *shake-hand* ('handshake'), *tennisman* ('tennis player'), and forms in *-ing* such as *jogging* and *lifting* ('face-lift'). French *parking* and *smoking* are reduced from *parking place/lot* and *smoking jacket*, and *cargo*, *steeple*, and *surf* from *cargo vessel*, *steeplechase*, and *surf-riding*.

Loan-translations (calques) conceal the English origin of certain French words: *cessez-le-feu* ('ceasefire'), franc-maçon ('freemason'), *gratte-ciel* ('skyscraper'), *lavage de cerveau* ('brainwashing'), *libre-service* ('self-service'), *lune de miel* ('honey-moon'), prêt-à-porter ('ready-to-wear'), and *soucoupe volante* ('flying saucer'). The spread of the *-ing* suffix has prevented such borrowings as *doping*, *kidnapping*, and *parking* from being re-organized as *dopage, *kidnappage, and *parcage. However, some native coinages lead the resistance to Anglicisms, such as *baladeur* ('*Walkman*', itself an Anglo-Japanism), *cadreur* ('cameraman'), *logiciel* ('software'), *ordinateur* ('computer'), and *rentrée* ('comeback').

Some commentators argue that ancient exports coming back with a new sense should be welcomed, as with *budget, challenge, confort, intercourse, interview, nurse, partenaire, scout, sport,* and *toast.* Some such exports have returned with spellings unchanged since Old French: *barge, label, maintenance, nuisance, partition, record, suspense,* and *train. Champion* has always existed in French, but its currently frequent use in connection with sports dates from the 19th century. *Missile,* a 14th-century French borrowing from Latin, went back in 1960. Again, this phenomenon is common in Canadian French, in which English *bargain, beverage, car,* and *county* account for the preservation of *barguigner, breuvage, char,* and *comté.* In addition, the word *information* is now widely used because the traditional *renseignements* is not internationally understood.

The 1960s term *franglais,* blending *français* and *anglais,* was at first used pejoratively for French with too many loans from English. It now tends to be used to label a fact of life: English vogue words in the media and in commerce and hybridization among bilinguals, notably in Canada. The term was popularized by the French writer René Etiemble in *Parlez-vous franglais?* (1964), a work in which he condemned the spread of Anglo-Saxon culture and language since the Second World War. His target was American rather than British English: such terms as *call-girl, coke, drugstore,* and *strip-tease.* Etiemble's criticism combined linguistic purism with a distaste for anything *yanqui: capitalisme yanqui, cancer yanqui,* and hostility to the idea of Europe as *un protectorat yanqui.* The solution offered to deal with his critique has been the Gallicizing of Anglicisms, turning English *meeting, ticket,* and *rocket* into *métingue, tiquet,* and *roquette,* while loan translation could turn *surfing* and *flashback* into *rase-rouleaux* and *retour en arrière.*

The term has also been used facetiously for an artificial hybrid, notably as developed by the English humorist Miles Kington in *Parlez-Vous Franglais?* (1981), which exaggerates the school French of Britons abroad: 'Si vous êtes un first-time reader de Franglais, welcome! Franglais est comparativement painless et ne donne pas un hangover. En quantités judicieuses, il est mindblowing. Ayez fun.' However, tension between French and English is sometimes more likely than fun, in several spheres:

❶ In the Francophone/francophone world

In terms of world prominence, in which France has nursed *La Francophonie* (the French-speaking world community) within an organization of the same name with its headquarters in Paris, much on the model of the Commonwealth of Nations, with its Commonwealth Institute in London.

❷ In the European Union

In which Paris seeks to defend the interests of French as a major language, in the face of the spreading influence and use of English, increasingly in terms of a range of mainland European Englishes subsumed under the term *Euro-English.*

❸ In terms of 'Anglo-American' economic and cultural imperialism

In which individuals and groups in France have sought to present their country as a champion of liberty and diversity against the growing influence of the United States and the co-operation of the Americans and British (a Trojan horse within the EU) in seeking to advance a hegemonic Anglo-Americanism in terms of language, the media, and corporate style (as exemplified by McDonalds).

Protecting *la langue de Molière*

Since the 16th century, and accelerating in recent years, there have been many attempts in France and Quebec to defend French against the world in general and English in particular.

1539 The Ordinance of Villers-Cotterêts, in which King Francis I orders the replacement of Latin by French as the language of law.

1637 The *Académie française* ('French Academy') is founded.

1789 The French Revolution links the language to national unity and patriotism.

1794 The Abbé Grégoire presents a report to the National Convention on the need and means to root out the regional patois of France and make a standardized French universal.

1937 The *Office de la langue française* ('The Department of French Language') is formed by such linguists as A. Dauzat and F. Brunot. After the German invasion it disappeared, but was partly restored in 1957 as the *Office du vocabulaire français* ('Department of French Words'), especially under pressure from French Canadians.

1953 The organization *Défense de la langue française* ('Defence of the French Language') is formed under the auspices of the *Académie française*.

1964 The publication of René Etiemble's *Parlez-vous franglais* ('Do You Speak Frenglish?', Paris: Gallimard), a work warning his compatriots about the influx of Anglicisms into French.

1966 The *Haut Comité pour la défense et l'expansion de la langue française* ('High Committee for the Defence and Expansion of the French Language') is formed, directly responsible to the Prime Minister of the Republic.

1967 The *Association pour le bon usage du français dans l'administration* ('Association for the Good Use of French in Government') is formed, to regulate government language.

1975 The *Loi Bas-Lauriol* ('Bas-Lauriol Law') is passed on the use only of French in advertising and commerce. In 1982, a government circular extended its constraints to foreign exporters of goods destined for France.

1977 The *Loi 101/Bill 101* is passed in Quebec, Canada, making French the sole official language of the province, limiting access to English-medium schools, and banning public signs in other languages.

1983 In France, a decree is passed requiring the use in teaching and research of terms made official by specialist committees.

1984 The French *Haut Comité* of 1966 is replaced by the *Commissariat général de la langue française* ('General Commission for the French Language') to assist private groups and members of the public in the pursuit of violations of the Bas-Lauriol law.

1994 In France, the *Loi Toubon* ('Toubon Law') is passed, named for Jacques Toubon, Minister of Culture and Francophonie, stipulating that all documents relating to goods and services (including contracts and commercials) should be in French (or be accompanied by explanations in French), and that the medium of education should be French.

German, English, and *Deutschlish*

Known as *Deutsch* to its speakers (compare *Dutch*, also from an old shared word for 'people'), German is the official language of Germany and Austria, an official language of Switzerland (with French and Italian) and of Luxembourg (with French), and a minority language in Belgium, Denmark, France, Hungary, Italy, Liechtenstein, Poland, Romania, and Russia. It is widely used as a second language in Turkey and Yugoslavia, and is spoken in enclaves in North and South America, Africa, and Australia. The Jewish language Yiddish is an offshoot once spoken widely in north-central Europe. With nearly 100 million speakers, German ranks around tenth among languages in world terms and comes first in Western Europe in numbers of native speakers.

Because of their close genetic links, German and English share many features, as seen in the sentence: *Für rund 95 (fünfundneunzig) bis 100 (hundert) Millionen Menschen ist Deutsch heute Muttersprache* ('For around five and ninety to hundred million people is German today mother-speech': Today German is the mother tongue of about 95 to 100 million people). The difference in word order is great, but a close match can be made with *für*/for, *rund*/around, *fünf*/five, *neunzig*/ninety, *hundert*/hundred, *Mensch*/man, *ist*/is, *Mutter*/mother, and *Sprache*/speech (with *million* as a shared Romance borrowing).

German is structurally more complex than English, having inflectional endings for number, case, gender, person, tense, etc. In this it is closer to Old rather than Modern English. In its orthography, German gives an initial capital letter to its nouns, a practice that was common in English until the mid-18th century. Historically, it has been an amalgam of dialects that were slow in acquiring a standard language. The continuum ranges from the geographically 'low' German dialect of Westphalia in the north-west (mutually intelligible with Dutch), through those of Lower and Upper Saxony, the Rhineland, and Franconia, to the 'upper' German varieties spoken in Bavaria, Switzerland, and Austria.

Plattdeutsch ('Low German') is the usual name for the 'broad' dialects in the north and west, especially in Saxony and Westphalia. The English term 'Low German' can however be more complex, having also been used for:

1 All the West Germanic languages except High German and English, that is, for Dutch, Flemish, Frisian, and Plattdeutsch.

2 All the West Germanic languages except High German, and therefore including English with the others, as in: 'High German and Low German, the latter including certain German dialects, Dutch, Flemish, Frisian, and English in all the forms it has taken throughout the world' (Barbara Strang, *A History of English*, 1970 (London: Methuen), 405).

Ambiguities arise because of the various applications of the term, as when in the work just cited Strang also says: 'The debt of English to Low German (Dutch, Flemish, Saxon) chiefly reflects maritime relations' (123).

The distinction between *Niederdeutsch* ('Lower German') and *Oberdeutsch* ('Upper German') covers the same continuum. It is usually traced to the Second Sound Shift in the 8th century, in which the southern dialects became phonologically distinct from the northern, producing such south/north contrasts as *machen/maken* ('make') and *Schiff/skip* ('ship'). Confusingly, the geographical term *Hochdeutsch* ('High German') is applied to the outcome of this sound change, so that the term can refer both to all Upper German (geographically 'highland' and Southern) dialects and to an idealized standard German language which is 'high' in the social sense.

Even then, the division into Lower and Upper/High German is not the whole story, as language scholars generally recognize an intermediate variety: *Mitteldeutsch* ('Central' or 'Middle German'), stretching from Cologne to Frankfurt and Leipzig. Observers can draw attention either to such Low/High contrasts as *Junge/Bub* ('a boy'), and *Sonnabend/Samstag* ('Saturday'), or such Low/Middle/Upper contrasts as *ik/ich/i* (the pronoun *I*), and *Männeken/Männchen/Mandl* ('a little man'). The contribution of the Central and Southern dialects to a common *Schriftsprache* ('written' or 'literary language') is often acknowledged, as is the fact that more recently a supra-regional *Umgangssprache* ('colloquial semi-standard') has served to level out differences. Tensions, however, persist between unifying and separatist tendencies. *Schwyzertüütsch* is the common spoken German in Switzerland, a variety sharply different in speech from the German of written and printed usage, which is comparable to that in Germany and Austria.

More than in English, orthographic conventions have been standardized, largely because of the influential *Duden* spelling dictionary (*Vollständiges orthographisches Wörterbuch der deutschen Sprache*, Konrad Duden, 1880; *Duden*, vol. 1, *Die Rechtschreibung*, 19th edn, Bibliographisches Institut Mannheim, 1986). Local differences in pronunciation occur at all social levels, often to establish people's backgrounds. As with English, there is no single, supranational norm for pronunciation in German-speaking countries, although 19th-century Bühnendeutsch ('stage German') and 20th-century media and social mobility have promoted compromises between Lower/North and Upper/South speech. While 'all German-language countries have problems or dilemmas concerning nationhood or ethnicity' (Michael G. Clyne, *Language and Society in the German-Speaking Countries*, Cambridge University Press, 1984, xi), distinct varieties emerged in East and West Germany (prior to reunification in 1990), Austria, and Switzerland, especially in vocabulary, which have been partly codified in 'national' dictionaries.

German differs from English in having an equivocal relationship with loanwords (*Fremdwörter*: 'foreign words') which, since the late 17th century, have often been resented, and replaced with vernacular equivalents by purist grammarians, as with *Anschrift* for *Adresse*, *Bücherei* for *Bibliothek*, *Mundart* for *Dialekt*, and *Stelldichein* for *Rendezvous*.

Over the centuries, many German words have found their way into English, as with: Low German *brake*, *dote*, *tackle* and High German *blitz*, *dachshund*, *kindergarten*. Cultural acquisitions have been significant in such fields as food (*frankfurter*, *hamburger*, *hock*, *pretzel*, *sauerkraut*), mineralogy (*cobalt*, *feldspar*, *gneiss*, *quartz*), music (*glockenspiel*, *leitmotiv*, *waltz*), philosophy (*weltanschauung*, *zeitgeist*), and politics (*diktat*, *realpolitik*).

Contacts between English and German have been on the increase since the early 18th century, promoted by literary translation, diplomatic links, trade relations, language teaching, and the media. Loans have entered German from such fields as literature (*sentimental*, *Ballade*), sport (*boxen*, *Rally*), politics (*Hearing*; *Hochverrat*, loan-translated from 'high treason'), and technology (*Lokomotive*; *Pipeline*). Resistance is not as vociferous as during the time of the *Sprachgesellschaften* ('language societies') in the 17th century, and the anti-foreigner propaganda of the Nazis in the 1930s, but at the present time the sheer volume of Anglicisms has begun to alarm more traditional speakers of German, leading to the formation of several organizations to defend the language of Goethe. Creative comment has taken various forms, including wryly and humorously caricaturing a hybrid that has been variously labelled *Gerlish*, *Deutschlish*, and *Denglish*. The text that follows is from an article in the newspaper *Die Welt*, by Enno von Lowenstein, a deputy editor, which wryly pushes Anglicization to its limits:

> **1996** Unser Way of Life im Media business ist hart, da muss man ein tougher Kerl sein. Morgens Warm-up und Stretching, dann ein Teller Corn Flakes und ein Soft Drink oder Darjeeling Tea, dann in das Office—und schon Brunch mit den To-Leuten, Meeting zum Thema: Sollen wir die Zeitung pushen mit Snob Appeal oder auf low Profile achten? Ich habe den Managern ganz cool und businesslike mein Paper presentiert: Wir müssen News powern und erst dann den Akzent auf Layout und Design Lagen, auf der Front Page die Headline mehr aufjazz.
>
> – 'English Uber Alles', as presented in Suzanne K. Hilgendorf, 'The impact of English in Germany', *English Today* 47 (12:3), July.

English usages continue unabated. They are adopted and adapted as: loanwords such as *babysitten* ('babysit'), loan translations such as *Beiprodukt* ('by-product'), blends of loan word and loan translation, as with *Teamarbeit* ('team work'), semantic transfer, as in *Schau* ('show', meaning a theatrical event), and loan-related neologism, as in *Öffentlichkeitsarbeit* (literally 'work for the public', loosely based on 'public relations'). Most borrowing is at the word level, but occasionally idioms and syntactic constructions are transferred, as in *grünes Licht geben* ('give the green light') and *Ich fliege Lufthansa* ('I fly Lufthansa'). The influence of English is strong in advertising (*High Life*, *Image*) and information science (*Compiler*, *Feedback*). And, in general, American has a greater influence than British English.

Dutch, Flemish, Frisian, and English

Dutch is a Germanic language, is the national language of the Netherlands, is an official language of Belgium (where it has traditionally been known as *Flemish*), has a community of speakers in northern France, and is the ancestor of Afrikaans, a settler language of Southern Africa. It is known in Dutch as *Nederlands* ('Netherlandish'), meaning 'belonging to the low country'. Scholars use *Netherlandic* as a general, especially historical term for all varieties as spoken in the Netherlands, Belgium, north-western France, the Netherlands Antilles, Surinam, Indonesia, and elsewhere. The English name *Dutch* comes from Middle Dutch *duutsch*, cognate with Old High German *diutisc* ('of the people': as opposed to Latin, which was the language of the learned), and therefore also with *Deutsch*, the name in German for German.

With English and Frisian, Dutch belongs to the Low German branch of West Germanic, where 'Low' refers to terrain and not lack of prestige. All three are structurally similar. Such words as *lip*, *maken*, *open*, and *water* show that Dutch is closer to English than to German, whose equivalents are *Lippe*, *machen*, *offen*, and *Wasser*. Dutch was a significant language of commerce and empire from the 17th to the earlier 20th century, established at one time in North America (notably in the colony known first as *New Amsterdam*, then *New York* when it became British), in Southern Africa (where *Cape Dutch* became Afrikaans), in the Caribbean, and in Indonesia (formerly the *Dutch East Indies*). It has had an influence in Sri Lanka and, through early exploration, a role in place-name creation in Australasia (as in *Arnhem Land*, *Tasmania*, and *New Zealand*, after the Dutch province of *Zeeland*, 'Sealand'). It has also had an influence on the development of such creoles as Papiamentu in the Netherlands Antilles and Sranan in Surinam.

There was a considerable Low German influence on English from the later Middle Ages, through shipping, migration, and commerce (especially the English wool trade with Flanders), as testified by such nautical terms as *boom*, *deck*, *freebooter*, *sloop*, *smuggler*, and *yacht*. Dutch was widely known in mainland Europe in the 17th century, when the first English–Dutch dictionaries appeared and such Dutch-derived artistic terms as *easel*, *etch*, *landscape*, *maulstick*, and *sketch* entered English. Later, many Dutch loanwords entered American English, from which it passed to other varieties, as with *boss*, *coleslaw*, *cookie*, *dope*, *poppycock*, *Santa Claus*, *snoop*, and *spook*.

Because of purist sentiment in the 16th–17th centuries, Dutch kept more of its Germanic character and resisted Latin more strongly than did English. However, many Latinate words are now entering Dutch from English, such as *crucial* ('crucial'), *informatie* ('information'), and *educatie* ('education', co-occurring with Dutch *onderwijs*), along with many other Anglicisms, and English has been the dominant foreign influence since the Second World War. It is now widely used for scholarly publishing, is the first choice among foreign languages in schools, is a significant language at university level, and a major influence through the media, especially British TV. The effect is seen in borrowings (such as *management*, *research*, *service*), loan translations (*diepvries* from 'deep freeze', *gezicht-sverlies* from 'loss of face', *gouden handdruk* from 'golden handshake'), changes in the meanings of established words (*controle* in the English sense as well as an earlier Dutch sense of 'check, supervision'), and idioms (such as *je nek uitsteken* 'to stick your neck out'). The text that follows is an excerpt from an article which facetiously pushes the Anglicization of Dutch about as far as it can go (but is not entirely out of line with reality):

> **1995** *De Tactics-briefing*: Het gaat heren, om de tactics bij de hele campaign voor 'Limite', de niuwe after-shave. Het is een prachtige account. Uit de briefing is duidelijk geworden dat we een deadline hebben de ruimte geeft voor uitgebreid pretesten. Deze brainstorming is dan ook voornamelijk bedoeld om tot een totale copy-planning te komen. We hebben een visual, ontwerpen voor een brand-image met copy een duidelijk idée voor de aanpak van de client-service. Ik zal straks 't word geven aan onze account-executive.

> [Translation: The briefing on tactics: We are here, gentlemen, to discuss the tactics for the entire campaign for 'Limite', the new after-shave. It's a wonderful account. From the briefing it has become clear that we have a deadline which leaves room for extensive pretesting. Consequently, this brainstorming session is primarily intended to decide on a full-scale copy planning, We have a visual, designs for a brand image with copy and a clear idea for the approach to client service. Later I will hand things over to our account executive.]

> – from *Onze Taal*, no. 5, May 1989, quoted and translated in Susan Ridder, 'English in Dutch', *English Today* 44 (11:4, October), Cambridge University Press

The many English-speaking immigrants in the Netherlands come mainly from the UK, the US, and Ireland. In Amsterdam, they constitute the largest foreign community, and do not particularly need to learn Dutch. Many multinational Dutch companies now operate in English and hope that this practice will be extended within the European Union. The extent of the penetration of English into the lives of the Dutch is clear from the following comment by a Dutch language scholar based in London:

> **2000** In 1985, the Dutch made English a compulsory subject for all children from the last two years of primary school, and so one can predict that in thirty years time there will be no monolingual speakers of Dutch left.
>
> — Reinier Salverda, 'The other languages of the Netherlands', in *The Low Countries: Arts and Society in Flanders and the Netherlands 8*, papers published in English by the Flemish–Netherlands Foundation 'Stichting Ons Erfdeel', 248

Flemish in Belgium has in the past been widely regarded as a language in its own right but its standard is close to that of Dutch. It has been called both *Low Dutch* and *South Dutch*, and is sometimes described along with Dutch as two varieties of *Netherlandic*. There are some parallels in this situation with the relationship between English in England and Scots in Scotland. Together with French, Flemish is an official language of Belgium, spoken in the northern provinces. It is closely associated with Flanders, an ancient region now divided among Belgium, the Netherlands, and France. In English, the name *Flanders* is associated with the trench battles of the First World War (*Flanders field*, *Flanders poppy*) and since medieval times with Flemish cloth and weaving (*Flanders flax*, *Flanders lace*).

Contact between Flanders and Britain has traditionally been close, especially because its cloth industry once depended on English wool. Flemish weavers settled in both England and Scotland, sometimes with the surname *Fleming* (originally meaning 'a native of Flanders'). The Flanders link produced such loans as *cambric* (a fine white linen or cotton from Kamerijk or Cambrai, a town now in France), *dornick* (a damask cloth from Doornik or Tournai, a town in Belgium), and *spa* (a place for taking the waters, from Spa, near Liège). The region was important in the development of printing in the 15th century: William Caxton lived there for many years, spoke Flemish, and in 1476 printed the first book in English at his press in Bruges: *The Recuyell of the Historyes of Troye*.

Frisian is a Germanic language spoken in coastal regions and islands in the north of the Netherlands and in neighbouring western Germany to the Danish border, and the most closely related of the mainland European languages to English. Some scholars have supposed the existence of an *Anglo-Frisian*, an intermediate language before the Anglo-Saxons reached Britain in the 5th century. The two languages share such common phonological features as:

❶ Initial *ch* not *k*

The initial consonant in English *cheese*, *church*, *chaff* and Frisian *tsiis*, *tsjerke*, *tsjef*: compare Dutch *kaas*, *kerk*, *kaf*, and German *Käse*, *Kirche*, *Kaff*.

❷ Initial *s*

A front vowel in English *sleep*, *sheep* and Frisian *sliepe*, *skiep*: compare Dutch *slapen*, *schaap* and German *schlafen*, *Schaf*.

❸ Loss of *n*

The loss of *n* in words such as English *goose*, *us*, and Frisian *goes*, *ús*: cf. Dutch *gans*, *ons* and German *Gans*, *uns*.

The main variety is *Modern West Frisian*, spoken by some 400,000 people in and around the Netherlands province of Friesland. Since the 19th century, Frisian has revived as a literary language. A movement seeking independence from the influence of the province of Holland within the Netherlands has enhanced the legal status of the language and promoted its use alongside Dutch, especially in schools, where it was illegal until 1937. The Frisian Academy (founded in 1938) sponsors scholarly publications on Frisian history and culture, including a definitive historical dictionary.

The Scandinavian languages and English

There are at least four senses to the word *Scandinavia*: the peninsula inhabited by the Norwegians and Swedes; this plus the Danish peninsula; these plus the Faeroe Islands (Danish) and Iceland; Norway, Sweden, Denmark, plus Finland but not necessarily the Faeroe Islands and Iceland. Danish, Norwegian, Swedish (in Sweden and Finland), and Faroese (in the Faroes) are Germanic languages and Finnish and Lappish are Finno-Ugric languages. In linguistics, the terms *Scandinavian* and *North Germanic* refer to the same Germanic subgroup. In addition, the Scandinavian language Norn was spoken in Scotland until the 17th–18th centuries.

Originally, there was little variation in Scandinavian (often also called *Norse*, *Old Norse*, *Danish*, and *Old Danish*), the common language of the Vikings (9th–11th centuries AD). At the present time, in Norway, Sweden, and Denmark, educated people seldom have difficulty in communicating across frontiers using their own languages, although these languages are clearly different. Icelandic and Faroese, however, are more different still and no longer immediately intelligible to other Nordic peoples, even though they retain many features of the original common language. The justification for regarding Danish and Swedish as distinct languages is a 'modern' one: separate nationhood and distinct literary traditions, the latter dating from the 16th century. In Norway, however, as will be seen, the situation is more complex.

During the early Middle Ages, the Viking invasions led to settlements in Britain and Ireland: in the Northern and Western Isles, north-western coastal Scotland, parts of Ireland (including Dublin), the Isle of Man, and the large area of England that came to be known as *the Danelaw*. As a consequence, Norse was for several centuries a major language of Britain and Ireland, competing with Gaelic and English, on each of which it had a powerful impact. Scandinavian place-names are notably common in the Danelaw region, especially those ending in *-by* ('farm', 'town'), such as *Grimsby* and *Whitby*. By 1200, however, *Norse* had ceased to be spoken in England, but survived for centuries elsewhere: for example, in Scotland as *Norn*, principally in Orkney and Shetland.

In England, the long period of contact and ultimate fusion between the Anglo-Saxon and Danish populations, especially north of a line between London and

Chester, had a profound effect on the English language. Old Danish influence survives in the general vocabulary of English (as with the *sk-* words *sky*, *skill*, *skin*, *skirt*, *scrape*, *scrub* and such vernacular words of northern England and Scotland as *gate/gait* ('road') and *sark* ('shirt'). It is also present, remarkably, at the heart of the modern language, in the set of grammatical words *they*, *their*, *them*, *though*, and *both*. All are words of Scandinavian/Norse and not Anglo-Saxon provenance. Old Danish place-names are also common on the east coast of England and widely in Scotland, especially those ending in *-by/-bie* ('farm, settlement, town'): *Grimsby*, *Whitby* in England; *Lockerbie* in Scotland.

Present-day Danish is spoken principally in Denmark (where it is the national language), in parts of Schleswig (in North Germany), in the Faeroe Islands in the North Sea, and mostly as a second language among the Inuit of Greenland (a Danish territory). Danish therefore (like English, Spanish, and French) is both a European and a North American language, and it has been historically influential on both English and Norwegian.

Faroese or *Faeroese* is the language of the Faroe/Faeroe Islands, a self-governing region of Denmark located between Shetland and Iceland, and first settled by the Norse in the 8th century. It is similar to both Icelandic and the now extinct Norn of Orkney and Shetland in Scotland, but whereas Norn gave way to Scots in the 17th–18th centuries, Faroese survived, acquiring a written form in the 19th century. Danish is taught on the islands as a second language. Despite their proximity, Faroese and English have had little impact on one other.

Norwegian (called *Norsk* by its speakers), the language of Norway, became distinct when differences began to appear in *Old Norse* (AD *c*.1000), between *West Norse* in Iceland and Norway and *East Norse* in Denmark and Sweden. However, after the union between Denmark and Norway in 1387, the written usage of Norway took after Danish, and in due course the speech of educated Norwegians became Danish with a local accent and Norwegianisms (much as happened with Scots in relation to English after 1707). The union was dissolved in 1814, after which there was a much looser union with Sweden, then in 1905 Norway became distinct again from both its neighbours. The long union with Denmark, however, left its mark. Throughout the 19th century, most of the leading Norwegian literary figures, including Henrik Ibsen, wrote in a Danish-influenced Norwegian, and many had their books published in Copenhagen. They called their usage both *Norsk* ('Norwegian') and *Dansk–Norsk* (in English *Dano-Norwegian*).

This Dano-Norwegian, however, contrasts with a kind of Norwegian advocated from mid-19th century by Ivar Aasen, a self-taught philologist and the son of a farmer, who constructed a composite of various dialects that he called *Landsmaal* ('country language'). Speakers of Dano-Norwegian gave it a mixed reception, and a passage in Ibsen's *Peer Gynt* satirizes it as a 'primeval forest tongue'. Despite such opposition, however, Landsmaal developed a literature and in 1885 was recognized as an official language to be taught in school alongside Dano-Norwegian, which then came to be known as *Rigsmaal* ('state language'). Parents voted on the kind of Norwegian they wanted as their children's primary medium. The two terms, later spelt *Landsmal* and *Riksmal*, were replaced in 1929 by *Nynorsk* ('Neo-Norwegian') and *Bokmal* (book language).

There have been three official language reforms, in 1907, 1917, and 1938, aimed primarily at bringing Bokmal closer to Nynorsk. Despite protests, the reforms have narrowed the gap, but differences remain and it is uncertain whether a *Samnorsk* ('Pan-Norwegian') will develop. Since the Second World War, support for reform and for education in Nynorsk have declined, perhaps because of increased urbanization. Educated Danes and Norwegians communicate with ease in speech and writing, but whereas before 1907 there was a common reading public, a novel or play in one country must now be 'translated' to succeed in the other.

English influence, for centuries slight, began to increase in Scandinavia from *c.*1750. In the 20th century, especially after the Second World War, it became extensive in the media, computer technology, aviation, leisure activities, popular music, sport, business, advertising, and youth culture, all aspects of life in which US influence has been strong. The impact includes:

❶ Loanwords

Nouns are the largest group, followed by verbs and adjectives. Before *c.*1900, borrowings usually conformed to local conventions (English *strike* becoming Danish *strejke*, Norwegian *streike*, Swedish *strejk*), but recent loans generally undergo little or no modification.

❷ Loan translations

These include: *blood bank*, which has become *blodbank*; *self-service*, which has become Danish and Norwegian *selvbetjening*, Swedish *självbetjaning*. Phrasal verbs are a feature of Scandinavian as well as English and loan translations have been increasing: Danish *tone ned* ('tone down'); Danish *ende op med*, Norwegian *ende opp med* ('end up with').

❸ Idioms

Idioms such as *drag one's feet* and *conspiracy of silence* have entered Scandinavian usage in translation.

❹ Loan constructions

Such front-loaded structures as *wall-to-wall carpets* and *lovely 20-year-old X* are no longer foreign to Scandinavian usage, although older people may object to them.

❺ Semantic borrowing

As with *to sell* in the sense 'to convince people of the worth of (a product, idea, etc.)'.

❻ Vogue words

Fashionable expressions from English compete with adequate existing terms: while *personlighed* or *personlighet* is usual, an advertisement for a new car might claim instead that it has *personality*.

❼ Anglo-Latinisms

Many existing borrowings from Latin have gained in frequency under the influence of their use in English: *status*; Danish and Swedish *kommunikation*, Norwegian *kommunikasjon*.

In Iceland, English influence has had some colloquial influence, and has made some inroads in television, but a strong purist tradition generally sustains the written language, in which imports are indigenized, as with *hamborgan* (for the already

Germanic 'hamburger'). Faroese is comparable. In Scandinavia proper, English is compulsory in all schools with the result that it has become so much a part of life in school, work, and recreation that it can be like a second first language. Scholarly and scientific publications, as well as course books, are often in English, and university regulations usually allow doctoral theses to be submitted in English, German, or French as an alternative to a Scandinavian language. English has become a frequent choice.

Robert Phillipson, a British language scholar living and working in Denmark, reported in 2001 on the proceedings of a pan-Scandinavian conference held in Copenhagen in 1998 on the language situation in the region at large and especially in Denmark. Presentations were given in the various regional languages, but the published outcome is largely in Danish, and has the hybrid Hamlet-style title *Engelsk eller ikke Engelsk? That is the question: Engelsk indflydelse på dansk* ('English or not English? That is the question: English influence on Danish', 1999). Phillipson notes:

> **2001** The cover of the book portrays the Danish flag hemmed in
> by chunks of Union Jack, a curiously anachronistic image in view
> of the incontrovertible fact that the decisive forces behind the
> spread of English in Denmark over the past half-century have been
> the political, economic and cultural might of the United States. . . .
> American diplomats no longer bother to learn Danish, and instead
> of Danes resenting this, they feel flattered.
>
> – 'English or no to English in Scandinavia?', *English Today* 66 (17:2), April (Cambridge
> University Press).

The conference papers ranged over the international limitations of Danish and the other Scandinavian languages, hybridization with English, notably in Danish, and a full awareness that English infiltrates from both above and below, at the levels of schooling and academia on the one hand and kinds of youth solidarity on the other, with processes of commercialization at work in the population at large: 'Linguistically it means that a stuffy top-down school subject meshes with bottom-up youth culture, a productive synergy for individual and societal foreign language competence.' This is a potent mix.

Spanish and English

A Romance language of Western Europe, called by its speakers *español*, and spoken by *c.*250 million people worldwide. It is the official language of Spain (including the Balearic and Canary Islands), and of most Central and South American nations: Argentina, Bolivia, Chile, Colombia, Costa Rica, Cuba, Dominican Republic, Ecuador, El Salvador, Guatemala, Honduras, Mexico, Nicaragua, Panama, Paraguay, Peru, Uruguay, Venezuela. In Paraguay, official status is shared with Guarani, and in Peru with Quechua, both Amerindian languages. It has also been spoken by Sephardic Jews in North Africa, Turkey, and the Balkans, and is used on the Caribbean island of Trinidad. In Africa, it is the official language of Equatorial Guinea and is spoken in parts of Morocco and in the Spanish coastal Mediterranean enclaves of Ceuta and

Melilla. In Asia, it is spoken by a small minority in the Philippines. There have also been Spanish creoles in Colombia, the Caribbean, and the Philippines.

Spanish is widely spoken in the US, especially in the Southwest (Arizona, California, New Mexico, Texas), in Florida, in parts of Louisiana, and in such cosmopolitan cities as New York and Chicago, as well as in the Commonwealth of Puerto Rico. It is now so significant that its presence has led to the formation of organizations to defend American English (see *The United States*).

Historically, Spanish evolved out of Late Vulgar ('Common') Latin, with minor Germanic and major Arabic influence. Its history is divided into three periods: Old Spanish (*c.*750–1500), Renaissance Spanish (1500–1808, the beginning of the Napoleonic Wars in Spain), and Modern Spanish (since 1808). At the close of the Roman period (early 5th century), the Iberian Peninsula was overrun by the Vandals and Visigoths, Germanic invaders who contributed such war-related vocabulary as *brida* ('bridle'), *dardo* ('dart'), *guerra* ('war'), and *hacha* ('axe'). During the Muslim period (711–1492), when much of the peninsula was held by Moorish rulers, Arabic loanwords were absorbed into the local Romance dialects, such as: *aceituna* ('an olive'); *ahorrar* ('to save'); *albóndiga* ('a meatball'); *alfalfa*; *algebra*; *alquilar* ('rent'); *cifra* ('a cipher, zero'); *naranja* ('an orange'); *ojala* ('may Allah grant', 'may it happen', 'if only', 'some hope'). This influx of Arabicisms was facilitated by Christians in Moorish territories, who were known as *mozárabes* (from Arabic *mustarib*, 'Arabicized'). Many spoke both Arabic and the now extinct variety of Spanish known as *Mozarabic*. The national epic, *El poema/cantar de mío Cid* ('the Poem/Song of My Lord'), in which the word *cid* is of Arabic origin (*as-sid* 'lord'), is from the period of the Reconquest.

Works of literature first appeared in Castilian/Spanish *c.*1150 and a literary language was established by the 15th century. Three pivotal events came together in 1492:

❶ The Reconquest

'The Catholic kings', Ferdinand of Castile and Isabella of Aragon, completed the reconquest of Spain by taking Granada, the last Moorish kingdom.

❷ The crossing of the Atlantic

Christopher Columbus, acting on their behalf, sailed west to find China and India and instead discovered the Americas.

❸ The first modern European grammar

The first grammar of a modern standardizing European language was published: Antonio de Nebrija's *Gramática de la lengua castellana* ('Grammar of the Castilian Language'), which was duly followed by his dictionary and orthography.

A reunified Spain in a very short time became a world power and the centre of a vast empire. The new standard language of Spain and its empire was based on Castilian (the dialect of the kingdom of Castile), and for this reason continues to be referred to in Spanish as both *castellano* and *español*. Despite long efforts made by royalty, government, and the Roman Catholic Church, and notably during the period in power of Generalissimo Francisco Franco (1939–75) to establish Castilian Spanish throughout the land, other loyalties survive—notably for Catalan in Catalonia and Gallego in Galicia.

Because of the reintroduction of Greek learning to Europe by the Arabs in Spain and then the great wealth and power of the new empire, 16th-century Spain was a major centre of learning. Spanish was a language of high prestige throughout Europe, and in late 16th-century England was the subject of several linguistic treatises, notably Richard Percivall's *Bibliotheca Hispanica, Containing a Grammar, with a Dictionarie in Spanish, English, and Latine* (1591). The *Real Academia* ('Royal Academy') was founded in 1713, on the model of the French Academy (1637), in order to *limpia, fija, y da esplendor* ('purify, fix, and give lustre') to the language, according to the motto on the great seal of the Academy that appears on the spine and title-page of all volumes of the Academy's dictionary.

During the 16th and 17th centuries, Spain and England were competing to amass empires and influence, and Spanish had its first direct impact. Loanwords of the period include the orthographically unadapted words *armada, cargo, desperado, flotilla, mosquito, mulatto, negro, pec(c)adillo, sombrero*, and the adapted *ambush, cannibal, cask, cigar, comrade, jennet, parade, renegade, sherry*. Other loans have entered the language since then, such as the unadapted *albino, flotilla, hacienda, mesa, plaza, siesta*, and the adapted *barbecue, caramel, cockroach, corvette, doubloon, escapade, guitar, jade, lime, maroon, picaresque, quadroon*. Some Spanish loans have Arabic origins, such as *alfalfa* (Arabic *al-fasfasah*), *alcazar* (Arabic *al-qasr* 'the castle'), *alcove* (through French *alcôve*, from Spanish *alcoba*, from Arabic *al-qubbah* ('the vault').

In recent decades, English has had a strong influence on Spanish wherever the language is spoken, but particularly where Spanish- and English-speaking communities live as neighbours (such as the US–Mexican border regions) and where speakers of one language have migrated to the territory of another (such as Puerto Ricans in New York City, and British expatriate communities and facilities for holidaymakers along the Mediterranean coast of Spain). Gibraltar is also an intimate point of contact. All such contact has produced hybrid forms, for which casual names have arisen, notably *Spanglish* (see also *The United States*).

In general, the influence of English is lexical, especially in the borrowing and adaptation of technical and sporting terms. Many of these borrowings are accepted only grudgingly or until more Hispanicized equivalents are coined. Not all are current in all varieties of Spanish, but are clearly favoured in contact situations. Some expressions are borrowings, either unadapted or adapted, while others are Anglicisms in a more general sense: loan shifts resulting from English influence in the usage of traditional Spanish words, often cognates of English Romance-derived words. Examples of borrowings are:

❶ In sport

boxeo ('boxing'), *boxear* ('to box'), *nocaut* ('a knockout'), *noquear* ('to knock out'), *jonrón* ('a home run'), *jonronear* ('to make a home run'), *fútbol, criquet, basquetbol*.

❷ In cooking and eating

cake/queque ('a cake'), *panqueques* ('pancakes'), *bistec* ('a beefsteak'), *cóctel* ('a cocktail'), *hamburguesa* ('a hamburger').

❸ In politics

agenda, *boicot* ('a boycott'), *boicotear* ('to boycott'), *cartel*, *detective*

❹ In general usage

bus, *camuflaje*, *esmoking* ('a dinner jacket, tuxedo'), *esnob* ('a snob'), *esnobismo* ('snobbery'), *jazz*, *jet*, *microchip*, *parquear* ('to park'), *troca* ('a truck').

Loan shifts and loan translations may compete with established usages: the verbs *rentar* with *alquilar* ('to rent') and *clarificar* with *aclarar* ('to clarify'); the nouns *elevador* with *acensor* ('a lift, elevator'); *profesional* with *profesionista* ('a professional'). They may also provide a new sense for a traditional word: *carácter*, in the theatre, as opposed to *personaje*; *conductor*, of music, as opposed to *director*; *década* for a ten-year period, as opposed to ten of anything; *educación* for schooling, as opposed to manners. Sometimes they are entirely new: *perro caliente* ('a hot dog'); *escuela alta* ('high school'). Others, such as *filmoteca* ('a library of films'), are loan blends.

Portuguese and English

Portuguese is a Romance language of Western Europe. It is closely related to Spanish and was the earliest of the major West European trading and colonial languages. It is spoken by some 135 million people worldwide:

❶ In Europe

As the national language of Portugal (including the Azores and Madeira, islands in the Atlantic), with, in north-western Spain, a related medium known as *Gallego* (in English, *Galician*) sometimes regarded as Portuguese and increasingly in Spain as a distinct language.

❷ In the Americas

As the official language of Brazil.

❸ In Africa

As the official language of Angola, Cape Verde, Guinea-Bissau, Mozambique, and São Tomé and Príncipe.

❹ In Asia

In Macau/Macao, a special administrative region of China and formerly a Portuguese colony, and in such ex-colonial territories as Goa in India and East Timor in the Indian Ocean.

❺ As an immigrant language

In Canada, France, the US, and elsewhere.

Portuguese has given rise to or influenced pidgin and creole languages in many parts of the world, such as a Portuguese creole in Cape Verde and the mixed Creole Papiamentu (with Spanish and Dutch) in the Netherlands Antilles. Like Spanish, it was influenced by Arabic during the centuries of Muslim dominance in the Iberian peninsula.

Portuguese mariners in the 15th century were the first Europeans to explore the Atlantic coast of Africa and take the passage to Asia around the Cape of Good Hope. Portuguese settlers played a significant part in colonizing the northern part of South America and adjacent parts of the Caribbean. Although Portugal is the oldest ally of England (since the 14th century), the impact of its language on English has been slight. Adoptions and adaptations include *albino*, *auto-da-fe*, *ayah*, *caste*, *madeira*, *marmalade*, *molasses*, *palaver*, and *port* (wine, from the city of Oporto).

Many such words have reached English indirectly, as with *ayah* and *caste*, the outcome of Portuguese influence on English in India. Portuguese has also mediated words from other languages into English. *Albatross*, for example, is apparently an adaptation of obsolete *algatross*, a variant of *alcatras* ('the frigate bird'). This word in turn derives from Portuguese and Spanish *alcatraz*, a term applied variously to the frigate bird, pelican, gannet, and solan goose. Its origin is Arabic *al-ghattas* ('the diver': the white-tailed sea eagle), the substitution of *b* for *g* perhaps arising from an association with Latin *albus* ('white').

Italian and English, Italian in English, English in Italian

Italian is the official language of Italy and an official language of Switzerland, and is spoken by Italian communities in Argentina, Australia, Britain, Canada, the US, Venezuela, and elsewhere. The term refers to both a standard and literary language in contrast to the many dialects of Italy, some of which are mutually unintelligible, and most of which (as with some 'dialects' in France and England) have many of the features conventionally attributed to distinct languages. Indeed, some regional varieties, such as Friulian and Sardinian, are widely regarded as more or less distinct languages, without much scholarly dispute. Standard Italian is based on the medieval Tuscan dialect, and probably a majority of Italians use Italian for a range of wider public activities and their local vernacular for the more immediate world of family, friends, and matters of local interest.

The centuries-old influence of Italian on English is almost entirely in terms of vocabulary. Since medieval times, Italian has had a strong influence on French, and through French on English, as with *battalion* (16th century, from *battaglione* through *bataillon*), *caprice* (17th, from *capriccio* 'the skip of a goat', through *caprice*), *charlatan* (16th, from *ciarlatano* 'chatterer', through *charlatan*), *frigate* (16th: from *fregata* through *frégate*), *picturesque* (17th, from *pittoresco* through *pittoresque*, with assimilation to *picture*), *tirade* (*c.*1800, from *tirata* 'volley of shots' through *tirade*). Direct borrowings fall into four broad categories:

❶ Music

Terms from the centuries-old pan-European tradition of using Italian to discuss and describe music include: *adagio, alto, andante, arpeggio, bel canto, cello, coloratura, con brio, concerto, contralto, crescendo, diminuendo, divertimento, fortissimo, libretto, mezzosoprano, pianoforte, pizzicato, scherzo, solo, sonata.*

❷ Literature, architecture, art, etc.

Such terms as: *canto, conversazione, cupola, extravaganza, fresco, intaglio, novella, palazzo, piazza, stanza, tarantella.*

❸ Cuisine

Such terms as: *lasagne, minestrone, macaroni* (from *maccheroni,* earlier *maccaroni*), *mozzarella, pasta, pizza, ravioli, spaghetti, tagliatelle, vermicelli.*

❹ Social life

Such terms as: *alfresco, bambino, bimbo, bordello, bravo, confetti, fiasco, gigolo, ghetto, graffiti, imbroglio, mafia, mafioso, regatta, seraglio* (originally from Persian).

Some words have moved to a greater or less extent from their original area of application into wider use, as with *crescendo, extravaganza, piano,* and *solo.* Italian singular/plural inflections usually apply among terms restricted to musical, cultural, and culinary registers (*concerto/concerti, scherzo/scherzi*), but English inflections apply in general use (*concerto/concertos, scherzo/scherzos*).

The influence of English on Italian is essentially lexical and relatively recent. Noticeable in the 1930s, it has accelerated greatly since the 1960s, encouraged not only by the growing international use and prestige of English, but also by the adoption after the Second World War of English (to replace French) as the first foreign language in schools. Recent borrowings, often described as contributions to *Itangliano* (highly Anglicized Italian), include: *baby, boom, boy, budget, cartoon, catering, ceiling, club, control system, deadline, dee-jay, designer, egghead, fifty-fifty, flash, girl, happiness, identikit, killer, lady, leader, life-saver, market, partner, shop, shopping, show, spray, staff, standard, stop, style, target, trekking, trend.* The assimilation and use of many borrowings resemble the processes by which English is absorbed into French, including:

1 The adaptation of words to fit the gender and inflectional systems: *un bluff* ('a bluff'), *bluffare* ('to bluff'); *uno snob* ('a snob'), *snobbare* ('to snub'); *handicappati* ('the handicapped'). Compounds may be reversed to conform to Italian norms, *a pocket radio* becoming *un radio-pocket.*

2 The restriction and adaptation of senses: *un flirt* ('an affair'); *look* used only as a noun; *un mister* ('a sports coach').

3 The clipping of compounds: *un full* ('a full hand [of cards]'); *un night* ('a night club').

The term *itangliano* is a 1970s blend in Italian of *italiano* and *anglo,* on the analogy of *franglais.* It is a non-technical term for Italian that contains many English expressions, apparently first used by Giacomo Elliot in the Italian-language publication *Parliamo Itangliano* (Milan, 1977). Elliot commented on 400 words and phrases (such as *know-how, management,* and *moonlighting*) used both in the export business and in business in Italy itself. The influx of English has been discussed in the media, including the journal of current affairs *Europeo,* in articles with titles like *Scusi, lei parla Itangliano?* ('Excuse me, do you speak Itangliano?').

The application of Italian phonology to English words can produce distinctive effects, such as the pronunciation of *puzzle* (noun) as 'pootzlay'.

The Slavonic languages and English

The expression *Slavonic languages* tends to be British, while the expression *Slavic languages* tends to be American. Both refer to a branch of the Indo-European language family spoken primarily by the Slav peoples of Central, Southern, and Eastern Europe. Scholars usually divide it into *East Slavonic* (Russian, Ukrainian, Byelorussian), *West Slavonic* (Polish, Czech, Slovak, and Sorbian/Lusatian), and *South Slavonic* (Old Church Slavonic, Macedonian, Bulgarian, Serbian and Croatian—formerly linked as Serbo-Croat(ian)—and Slovene). There are some 300 million native speakers of these languages: Russian *c.*150 million; Polish *c.*37 million (with some 13 million diaspora Poles in Western Europe, North America, and Australasia); Ukrainian 35 million (with 600,000 in North America, two-thirds of them in Canada, and 100,000 in Poland); Serbian and Croatian *c.*12.5 million; Bulgarian *c.*8 million; Byelorussian *c.*7 million.

Slavonic languages divide into those using the Roman alphabet (western and southern, including Polish, Croat, Czech, Slovak, and Slovene) and those using the Cyrillic alphabet (eastern and southern, including Russian, Serbian, Ukrainian, and Bulgarian). The classical language Old Church Slavonic, originally used by evangelists among the South Slavs, has had considerable influence on both the South and East Slavonic languages.

The impact of the group on English has been slight. Loanwords include: *mammoth* (from 17th-century Russian *mamot*), *mazurka* (from Polish, after a regional name), *robot* (from Czech, from the base of *robota* 'compulsory labour', and *robotnik* 'a peasant owing such labour'), *samovar* (from Russian: 'self-boiling'), and *vampire* (through French from German from Serbo-Croat *vampir*). The especially American diminutive suffix *-nik* (mid-20th century) is Slavonic in origin, and has entered English along two paths: from Russian, as in *sputnik* (a space satellite), and through Yiddish, which adopted it from its Slavonic neighbours in Eastern Europe, as in *kibbutznik* ('a person who lives on a kibbutz'). The suffix as used in English refers to someone who exemplifies or endorses a way of life or an idea, as in *beatnik, no-goodnik, peacenik, refusenik*. It is often humorous or dismissive.

Loans from English into the Slavonic languages increased greatly in the late 20th century, with the collapse of the Soviet Union, especially in such areas as sport, as in Polish *faul* ('foul'), *faulować* ('to cause a foul'), *play-off, sprint, sprinter*, and *tennis*, and high technology, again as in Polish *bit, bajt, hardware*, and *software* (and the adjectives *hardwarowy* and *softwarowy*), *interface, joystick*, and *monitor*.

The European Union and Euro-English

The use of English in Continental Europe at the beginning of the 21st century has gone well beyond even such developments as: the flood of Anglicisms into individual languages; the expanding use of English in universities (including in some cases as a teaching medium); and its role as the official working language of major transnational companies, such as Royal Dutch Shell in the UK and the Netherlands and the Swiss–Swedish conglomerate Asea-Brown-Bovery (ABB). As a result, English is straightforwardly the lingua franca of both the Continent at large and of the European Union, whose peaceful emergence with a parliament and a common currency, the euro, is one of the most dynamic events in a thousand years of competition, suspicion, division, and warfare.

In 1993 the European Union subsumed the earlier European Community (EC), which was at an earlier stage known as the European Economic Community (EEC), which in turn came into being in 1967 through the merger of several earlier associations formed after the Second World War. Its fifteen members are Austria, Belgium, Denmark, Finland, France, Germany, Greece, the Irish Republic, Italy, Luxembourg, the Netherlands, Portugal, Spain, Sweden, and the United Kingdom, and a number of Eastern European nations are currently seeking membership. Its headquarters are in Brussels in Belgium, its Parliament mainly in Strasbourg in northern France, and there are significant institutions in Luxembourg. Some language-related features of the EU are:

❶ Official languages

The official working languages of the EU are English and French, and its official languages are Danish, Dutch, English, Finnish, French, German, Greek, Italian, Portuguese, Spanish, and Swedish. Officially these languages are known (with appropriate abbreviations) as Dansk (DA), Nederlands (NL), English (EN), Suomi (FI), Français (FR), Deutsch (DE), Elinika (EL), Italiano (IT), Português (PT), Español (ES), and Svenska (SV). There are two official scripts, Roman for the majority and Greek, and Greek texts are produced in both the Roman and the Greek scripts. (The looser, more cultural and less politically charged Council of Europe is an entirely different organization, with 43 members and a wide range of cultural and other interests. It has its own official languages: English and French as its working languages, plus German, Russian, and Italian. Delegates at its meetings are free to use other languages, with the provision of interpreters. All major European organizations have multilingual policies.)

❷ Translation and other language activities and services

All eleven EU languages are used in meetings, with simultaneous translation as a matter of course. This makes the EU a major consumer of language services, an estimated $300 million a year being spent on translation and interpreting. Official documents must be published in all the official languages, and considerable sums are spent on EUROTRA automatic translation.

❸ Minority languages

In addition to the national and official languages there are some 30 or 40 minority EU languages. Some are regional varieties of larger languages in neighbouring states (such as Alsatian German in France) while others are entirely distinct (such as Breton in France and Basque in Spain and France), while some have a somewhat ambiguous status (such as Scots in Scotland, closely related to English, Letzburgish in Luxembourg, closely related to German, and Gallego in Spain, closely related to Portuguese). All member countries save unilingual Portugal have EU-recognized regional minority languages, such as Basque, Breton, and Alsatian German in France and Gaelic, Scots, and Welsh in the UK. The European Bureau for Lesser-Used

Languages, set up in 1982 with its headquarters in Dublin, represents these languages, with the exception of the 'trans-European' minority languages Yiddish and Romany.

Despite or perhaps because of this linguistic variety, as well as its international nature and the influence of the United States, English has emerged as the unofficial lingua franca of the EU, in which representatives of smaller 'member countries' (the official term for EU states), such as Denmark and Greece, often give their press conferences. The French notably remain concerned to protect the position of their language within the Union, but otherwise there is no resistance to the growing use of English in EU communication at home and abroad, especially in such commercial and technical spheres as global business, computer use and the Internet, telecommunications, and scientific research. Finally, for most member countries English represents neutral ground, and might have been the EU lingua franca even if the UK and Ireland had not been members. English is the second language in all other EU countries in terms of education and employment prospects.

Within the next ten to twenty years, the vast majority of the inhabitants of certain countries, notably the Netherlands, Denmark, Sweden, and Finland, will be bilingual and biliterate in their national tongues and English, and in the longer term such balanced bilingualism could also be the case for large numbers of people in all mainland EU countries (whatever the size and composition of the Union might then be). It is currently estimated that $c.16\%$ of the EU population uses English natively and 31% use it as a second language, making 47% in all, the highest such figure in the Union. German has 32% and French 28%. The international strength of Spanish is not reflected in the EU, where its total is 15%, preponderantly in Spain itself. The figures suggest that within a decade or so English could be the unofficial 'federal' EU language: a remarkable role for an offshore language.

Commentators have for some years proposed various names for kinds of English used in the EU, notably as a bureaucratic jargon in Brussels, Strasbourg, and Luxembourg, where much of the institutional life of the EU takes place and most media attention has been focused. The four main terms have been *Eurospeak*, *Eurolish*, and *Minglish* on the one hand and *Euro-English* on the other. The first three are earlier, only *Eurospeak* has lasted, and may be fading out. The fourth is more recent, and its difference from the others is marked. Whereas *Euro-English* has serious practical aspects to it and appears to be increasingly seen as labelling something neutral and significant, the other terms have been humorous, facetious, and snide (as in *Eurospeak Desperanto*). A typical use of *Eurospeak* about a decade ago was:

> **1990** And as more and more magazines and newspapers view
> Europe as home territory, neologisms and borrowed words will
> undoubtedly emerge—as long as newspapers and magazines don't
> resort to bland Eurospeak.
> – *Journalist's Week*, 22 June.

Humour with a sting in its tail is seldom far off where such usage is concerned, but in recent years, running jokes of the 'Eurospeak Desperanto' type have mutated into something with an edge to it regarding the growing strength of English. This new development has parallels with the early satirical use of *franglais* (above). The new creation is *Europanto*, the work of Diego Marani, an Italian translator for the European Council of Ministers in Brussels. Like *Desperanto*, the term plays on *Esperanto*, the name given by the Polish/Russian Jewish physician Ludwik Zamenhof to the artificial language he created in 1888, formed from various European languages and offered to the world hopefully (cf. Spanish *esperanza* 'hope') as a universal language. Whereas, however, Zamenhof had high philanthropical aims, Marani's approach is playful, creative, cautionary, and has a sting in its tail. Some specimens (as variously reported):

1 Europanto is une melogia van der meer importantes Europese linguas.

 ('Europanto is a mix of the more important European languages'.

2 Que would happen if, wenn Du open your computerzo find eine message in esta lingua? No es Englando, no est Germano, no este Espana, no est keine known lingua aber Du Understande! ('What would happen if, when you open your computer, you find a message in this language? It isn't English, it isn't German, it isn't Spanish, it isn't any known language, but you understand it!').

3 Vamos enfantos del Europanto/
 Wir shall Englanto speakare not!'
 (Let's go, children of Europanto/
 We shall not speak Englanto!'
 [*La Marseillaisa*]

Marani sees Europanto as a recreational means through which the vast majority of people forced to use English can enjoyably vent their frustration. It is anarchic and its grammar more a gut response than a set of rules: an ultra-pidgin symbolizing for its creator the linguistic mess that necessarily attends on the unification of Europe. *Newsweek* (21 December 1998) notes that Marani was inspired not by anything *outré* but rather by his own multilingual, language-mixing children. He then 'began culling his favorite words from German, English, French, Spanish and Italian and combining them in sentences. The amalgam caught on, and Marani now writes regular satirical columns in the language and is about to publish a book of Europanto short stories.

The term *Euro-English* has gone in a different direction, and has nothing humorous, ironic, or hostile attached to it. Rather, language scholars interested in and concerned about adequate transnational communication in the EU have adopted it as a neutral term for use in research projects and discussions which have pedagogical implications in areas where English has as yet weak local roots. The emergence of a *Euro-English* of this kind allows one to think in terms of a continuum of English in the EU across three geographical zones:

❶ English as a native language

That is, English in two nations and some dependencies: the UK, the Irish Republic, Gibraltar, the Channel Islands, and the Isle of Man, with predominantly unilingual English-speaking populations.

❷ English bilingually paired with a native language

That is, English as one member of several bilingual pairs in north-western Europe. The most fully established of these are Dutch/English, Danish/English, and Swedish/English (with Norwegian/English nearby but not in the EU). The English/Finnish pair appears to be developing quickly, and something of the kind is also true for many people in Germany.

❸ English as a lingua franca: 'Euro-English'

That is, English used for communication in regions where it is widely taught in schools but has not been indigenized and institutionalized as extensively as in the Netherlands, etc. This appears to be the sense in which interested scholars are taking the matter up.

In this model, English in the EU bears a fair resemblance to English in India, where it has for generations been a mother tongue (for Anglo-Indians and others), one member in sets of pairs or more complex arrangements (as with Bengali or Tamil and English), and a lingua franca (with a pidgin dimension) used variously throughout the nation as a 'link language' and 'a window on the world'. Certainly, British and Irish English could only be kinds of Euro-English if the latter term came to mean 'English in all its forms as used in the European Union', but everyone concerned would know that English pre-dated the EU by centuries. Comparably, Dutch, Danish, and Swedish English are the successful outcome of educational programmes initiated long before the EU was thought of. In these terms, the only English that is, as it were, inherent to the EU is the novel kind of lingua franca that has developed in recent decades, within the framework of nations in which English in the past was not as intensively studied as in countries like the Netherlands: that is, it would be English as used by citizens of Spain, Portugal, France, Italy, Greece, and perhaps Austria, among themselves, with other EU member states, and with the rest of the world. Germany is a moot nation in this matter, but its close involvement with English in recent years has carried it nearer to the position of its fellow northern European members.

The safest basis to work on would appear to be that 'Euro-English'—if the term proves viable—is the English of all the EU countries except the UK and Ireland. Such a Euro-English is not however by any means homogeneous, and the major distinction is in effect, at the present time, between north and south. In many countries, notably the Scandinavian member states, the Netherlands, and Germany it is in relative terms close to 'native' English, while elsewhere it by and large has a fairly classic lingua-franca role. Such usage is likely to be influenced by both American and British, increasingly with American English predominating. Several commentators, including notably the American scholar Marko Modiano, domiciled in Sweden, have called the outcome 'mid-Atlantic', and it is evident that many younger mainland Europeans incline towards a General American speech style rather than the RP/BBC pronunciation once massively endorsed in Europe.

The nature of mainland European (and especially EU) English is currently in flux. Several traditions and influences have come together, and a main concern among interested scholars and teachers of English is to ensure that communication in English actually works. This concern has recently led to an interest among scholars at several European universities in analysing the patterns of pronunciation and the kinds of grammar common among users of 'English as a lingua franca' (ELF). At least one project, at the University of Vienna, seeks to create a corpus of spoken usage among non-native users of the language, entitled the *Vienna Oxford ELF Corpus*, so that teachers and others can have a principled awareness of the ways in which a Euro-English lingua franca is evolving or might evolve. The following comments come from articles by Jennifer Jenkins at Kings College London, and Marko Modiano at Gävle University in Sweden, and Barbara Seidlhofer at the University of Vienna on 'Euro-English' in *English Today* 68 (17:4), Cambridge University Press, October:

> **2001** Expressions which are commonplace in European
> languages are slowly making their way into 'Euro-English'. . . .
> In Swedish, for instance, if you want to neglect something, you
> say that you '*hoppa över* it' (in literal translation, this is the verb
> phrase *hop over*). . . . [O]ne can sometimes hear Swedes say [in
> English] that they are going to 'hop over' an activity, meaning that
> they refrain from doing something. An example would be, 'I am
> going to hop over lunch today.' . . . [A]s such usage becomes more
> commonplace, it could very well become accepted by users of
> English not familiar with the Swedish language.
>
> – Marko Modiano, 'Euro-English: A new variety of English'

> **2001** Speakers of the different varieties of 'Euro-English' will,
> through extensive exposure to each other's accents, be able to
> interpret their regional vowel quality differences to the same
> extent that speakers within L1 [mother-tongue] varieties of
> English are able to do so. Speakers of native varieties of English,
> who are less likely to have prolonged exposure to 'Euro-English'
> accents, will need to familiarise themselves with its regional
> vowel qualities if they wish to interact efficiently in 'Euro-
> English' contexts.
>
> – Jennifer Jenkins, ' "Euro-English" accents'

A viable comparison can be made between the situation in the mainland EU today and the acquisition of English in Wales, Ireland, and the Highlands of Scotland some centuries ago. This time, however, the changes are on an immensely larger scale. It is understandable that many mainland Europeans feel uneasy when confronted with the inroads that English has already made since the mid-20th century, without taking into account changes now under way and likely to accelerate. The care with which the three scholars have placed *Euro-English* in quotation marks indicates their caution in handling a subject that is likely to be highly controversial.

However, a later report in 2001 in *Business Week*, by Stephen Baker and Inka Resch in Paris, was considerably less restrained. Its lead-in runs: 'In Europe, speaking the lingua franca separates the haves from the have-nots' and the following quotations highlight the central points that these writers have sought to make:

> **2001**
> ● 'English is becoming the binding agent of a continent, linking
> Finns to French . . . as they move toward political and
> economic unification. A common language is crucial, says Tito
> Boeri, a business professor at Bocconi University in Milan,

> "to take advantage of Europe's integrated labor market. English, in short, is Europe's language." '

- ' "If I want to speak to a French person, I have to speak in English," says Ivo Rowekamp, an 11-year-old in Heidelberg, Germany. . . . The English-speaking children appear to be in charge, ordering food in English for their parents, and arranging early-morning taxis to the airport.'

– Business Week, European edn, 13 August.

Baker and Resch note that '[t]he need for a lingua franca is most pressing for global technology players', with striking results, as for example when such companies as Alcatel and Nokia 'embraced English as the corporate language'. The authors also point to a neutrality offered by English in certain increasingly common situations; an example is the coming together of the French company Rhone-Poulenc and the Germany company Hoechst as the futuristic-sounding new company *Aventis*. They set up the new headquarters of Aventis in Strasbourg, a Franco-German city in northern France—and 'further defused cultural tensions by adopting English as the company language.'

3 The Americas

1992 English came to North America and what eventually became the United States as part of the general movement of European languages and their speakers not only to the one 'new' continent but to almost all parts of the world. The type of English spoken during the period of exploration and colonization was important to the history of American English. So were the languages spoken by other groups—immigrants and native Americans. The first point has received recognition from the beginning of the study of American English. The second has tended to be overlooked. . . . English came to the New World in a context of language contact, and language contact is the salient feature of its early history.

– J. L. Dillard, *A History of American English* (London and New York: Longman), 1

Many European and other languages met and mixed on the high seas during and after the era of exploration that was set in train by the Genoese explorer Christopher Columbus while in the service of the Catholic Kings of Spain, Ferdinand and Isabella. The forms of the European languages that first went west were generally neither courtly nor scholarly, but the usage of sailors, soldiers, fishermen, traders, explorers, and farmers, most of whom could not read or write much or at all. They also did not usually know each other's languages well or at all, and yet they had to share information. As a result, they often used any mix of sound and gesture that would serve their purposes—both among themselves and with the inhabitants of the new continent.

A significant but little discussed forerunner to their usage was the ancient, variable, and unwritten Mediterranean patois known as both Lingua Franca (Italian: 'the Frankish tongue') and Sabir (Spanish: 'to know', a cousin of which is the casual English 'Savvy?', 'You savvy?', and 'Me no savvy'). The original Lingua Franca, based on Provençal and northern Italian (the kind of patois that a Genoese voyager and his crew would have known), drew varyingly on many sources and served a motley range of people not for a century or two at the time of the Crusades but for a thousand barely recorded years, vanishing away only at the beginning of the 20th century.

Sabir appears to have been the template for a range of Portuguese, Spanish, French, Dutch, and English trade jargons, pidgins, and creoles worldwide. In turn, it may well itself have been a continuation of an even older Mediterranean interlanguage dating from Greco-Roman times. Whatever the uncatalogued reality, such a free-flowing kind of sailor's talk was common when in 1620 the Puritan colonists established their settlement of Plimoth Plantation in what is now Massachusetts. A local 'Indian' called Samoset was able to speak to them in a pidgin English he had learned from sailors along the coast of what is now the state of Maine. Without Samoset's knowledge of that makeshift lingo the Plimoth colony might well have failed.

Although the serious exploration and colonization of the Americas by the Netherlands, France, and England began later than the activities of Spain and Portugal, the more northerly nations had been interested in the New World from the start. Merchants in the English city of Bristol in 1497 (five years after Columbus reached the Caribbean) commissioned another Genoese navigator, Giovanni Caboto (Anglicizing his name to 'John Cabot'), to explore further north, leading to the first landings in what is now Canada, which was however mistaken by Cabot for China. In 1504, the English settlement of St John's was established as a shore base for fisheries on an island named in English *New Found Land* (French *Terreneuve*, 'Newland'). In 1583, Humphrey Gilbert claimed the whole of that island for England. In 1584, Walter Raleigh established the colony of Roanoke in *Virginia*, a mainland territory named in Latin and claimed for Elizabeth I ('the Virgin Queen'). Gilbert's colony prospered, and survives as the capital of the Canadian province of Newfoundland, that now includes the mainland territory of Labrador. But Raleigh's settlement vanished without trace. There was no secure English toehold on the mainland until 1607, when the Jamestown colony was set up: named in English for Elizabeth's successor, James VI of Scots and I of England. If the Latin tradition had been followed, it might have been known today as *Jacobia*.

The United States

1936 When I became interested in the subject and began writing about it (in the Baltimore *Evening Sun* in 1910), the American form of the English language was plainly departing from the parent stem, and it seemed at least likely that the differences between American and English would go on increasing. This is what I argued in my first three editions. But since 1923 the pull of American has become so powerful that it has begun to drag English with it, and in consequence some of the differences once visible have tended to disappear . . . [T]he Englishman, of late, has yielded so much to American example, in vocabulary, in idiom, in spelling and even in pronunciation, that what he speaks promises to become, on some not too remote tomorrow, a kind of dialect of American, just as the language spoken by the American was once a dialect of English.

– H. L. Mencken, Preface to the 4th edn, *The American Language: An Inquiry into the Development of English to the United States* (Corrected, Enlarged and Rewritten) (New York: Knopf), p. vi

The population of the United States of America was reckoned in the 2000 Census to be just over 280 million, the vast majority of whom had English as their first or only language, outnumbering all other primary users of English everywhere by around 2 : 1, and those in the United Kingdom by around 4 : 1. This enormous demographic and social advantage has been augmented by the current position of the US as the world's only 'superpower' and its principal source of media- and computer-related products. As a result, American English has a global role at the start of the 21st century comparable to that of British English at the start of the 20th—but on a larger scale than any previous language or variety of a language in recorded history. Mencken may have been right in his 1936 prediction, above, but it took some four centuries for his 'American language' to reach its current condition. Any account of how this happened must be complex, but one way of making it manageable is to divide the topic into three historical periods:

❶ Colonial, 1607–1776

When a distinct variety or group of varieties of English emerged in a scattering of British North American territories.

❷ National, 1776–1898

When an autonomous variety or group of varieties of English emerged in the steadily expanding United States of America (which had throughout the period an unclear secondary international status in relation to the English of the UK and the British Empire).

❸ International, 1898–

During which American English has exerted an ever-increasing influence on other varieties of English and on other languages, becoming increasingly significant after the Second World War.

Old World, New World

Two colonies, named in English as Plimoth Plantation in 1620 and Maryland in 1634, were founded for mainly religious reasons, secular colonization beginning again in 1663 with the creation and settlement of the Carolinas (named in Latin after Charles II). In 1664 the Dutch, who had settled the island of Manhattan 40 years earlier, swapped 'Nieuw Amsterdam' for the more appealing English plantation colony of Surinam in northern South America. The English then gave the name 'New York' to both the ex-Dutch colony (which included parts of the mainland) and its key settlement on the island of Manhattan. In addition, although an enormous forested area to the south-west was already being settled by both the Dutch and the Swedes, the English Crown felt free to give William Penn and his Quaker colonists a charter for it in 1681. The region was then known as Pennsylvania (Anglo-Latin: 'Penn's Woodland').

Because settlers came to these and later colonies from many places, dialects of English in the British Isles were not transferred unaltered across the Atlantic, and the languages of migrants from other parts of Europe were not simply or quickly replaced by English, the present-day German-speaking Pennsylvania 'Dutch' being a case in point. Instead, the coming together of people of many language and dialect backgrounds set in train long-term processes of both homogenization and miscegenation, which in the end—paradoxically—produced a more uniform general spoken English in the United States than in the United Kingdom. Three factors in particular helped create such a usage:

❶ Isolation and distance

The slowness with which linguistic changes in the motherland reached these colonies resulted in a paradox: the survival of conservative forms alongside radical new local creations.

❷ Transfer from Old World to New

Old World words were applied to New World objects, activities, and processes, as with the American *robin*, a very different bird from its European namesake.

❸ Local adoptions

The adoption of words from three distinct groups of speakers of other languages:

- Native Americans: *tomahawk* ('cutting instrument', from the Algonquian usage of Virginia).

- African slaves: *voodoo* (through Louisiana French from such a West African source as Ewe *vodu* 'demon').

- Colonizing mainland Europeans: *boss* (from Dutch *baas* 'master'); *corral* (a pen for livestock, originating in a Spanish/Portuguese name for a defensive circle of wagons: cf. the parallel but distinct developments in South Africa with Dutch/Afrikaans *baas* and *kraal*.

As a result, although the settlers continued to rely on the educated and aristocratic élite of a faraway England for their perceptions about language and a developing standard for writing, print, and to some extent speech, they drew increasingly on their own resources, with varying degrees of uncertainty on both sides of the Atlantic about whether this was a good thing or not.

Manifest destiny

When the War of Independence (1775–83) brought the colonial period to a close, the citizens of the new United States of America faced a double challenge of which they only slowly became aware: to develop an autonomous English with a standard of its own that would be recognized both at home and abroad; and to extend the use of that standard throughout the nation as it grew larger and more complex. Foremost among those concerned with the education of the nation's children was Noah Webster (1758–1843), whose principal concerns were a consistent and distinctive spelling system and a dictionary through which the independence of the English of the United States from that of England could be established beyond argument.

The American counterweight to Samuel Johnson was born in Connecticut, educated at Yale College, and admitted to the bar in 1781. Instead of becoming a lawyer, however, he had a complex career as a schoolmaster, writer, editor, lexicographer, lecturer, and political lobbyist. His best-known works, noted for their linguistic patriotism, were *The American Spelling Book* in 1783, known simply as the 'Blue-Back Speller' (a perennial bestseller) and, published when he was 70 in 1828, *An American Dictionary of the English Language*.

Webster recommended spelling reforms as early as his *Dissertations* in 1789, basing them on the four principles of analogy, etymology, reason, and usage. The spelling of such words as *honor, center, defense*, and *public* can however be attributed simply to his preference for them over *honour, centre, defence*, and *publick*. Both sets of spellings were in use at that time on both sides of the Atlantic, such forms as *public* now however being standard in the UK as well as the US. Webster's lexicography began with *A Compendious Dictionary* (1806), which was marked in particular by two features: spelling innovations and the use of educated New England speech as a pronunciation model for all. Criticism of his innovations led in the 19th century to the 'dictionary wars' in which Joseph Emerson Worcester, who favoured British norms, led the opposition.

The first dictionary called *Webster's* was published in 1847 by George & Charles Merriam and called the *American Dictionary of the English Language*. The name was later used for Merriam editions in 1847, 1864, and 1890, the last having the title *Webster's International Dictionary*, the term *international* being used to imply 'non-' or 'more than British'. When the copyright of the 1847 edition expired, several companies published cheap dictionaries with the name *Webster's* in their titles. G. & C. Merriam sued for damages in several states, and in 1917 a federal court finally determined that the company did not have exclusive rights to the name and so anyone was free to publish a 'Webster'.

By the time of the Civil War (1861–5), when slavery was finally brought to an end, US territory extended from the Atlantic to the Pacific, a development that encouraged a sense of 'manifest destiny' first in the Americas then in the world at large. During this period, at least ten factors shaped both US society and what Webster had called 'Federal English':

❶ The Western frontier

The settlement and acquisition of frontier lands, extending ever further west, creates a potent dual symbolism of 'frontiers' (including novel technology and 'space: the final frontier', as in the TV series *Star Trek*) and an aspirational direction ('Go west, young man').

❷ The 'iron horse'

The application of the British invention of locomotives and coaches travelling on tracks (a *railway* transformed into a *railroad*) serves to 'open up' the country and particularly the West.

❸ Industrialization

A US industrial revolution first rivals then exceeds that of the UK (and is in part financed by UK interests). The British in fact have never stopped being culturally and financially interested in the United States.

❹ Organized labor

The creation of labor unions serves to defend the rights of workers and strengthen both the democratic ideal and the Democratic as opposed to the Republican political party.

❺ Technological innovation

Novel technical developments such as electricity, the telegraph, the telephone, the typewriter, and linotype printing are exploited to the full under the most open (and least restricted) system of competitive private enterprise ever known.

❻ Journalism

The growing vigour and influence of the press include the development not only of morning and evening dailies but also weeklies and in due course such distinctive weekly newsmagazines as *TIME* and *Newsweek*.

❼ Universal education

All kinds of training for life expand through the development of educational institutions at every level, all conceived and described as 'school', whether primary, secondary, or tertiary.

❽ Educational publishing

The importing and increasing creation of textbooks and school dictionaries, a key development for lexicography, in that prior to this point in Europe and notably Britain dictionaries had been self-help manuals for adults eager to strengthen their grasp of the standard language.

❾ Commercial influence and expansion

A political, commercial, and military interest in other lands and territories grows steadily stronger (despite an even greater inclination towards 'splendid isolation' than exhibited by the British), especially to the west (through California then Hawaii and the Philippines to East Asia) and the south (through Mexico and the Caribbean to South America).

❿ Military, political, and quasi-imperial expansion

The unintended extension of military activity from within the US itself and in its immediate vicinity led to foreign adventures in the Pacific, the Caribbean, and South America, then massive involvement in three linked crises: the First World War (1914–18); the Second World War (1939–45); and the Cold War (–1989). The outcome was a vast expansion of power and influence central to the worldwide economic and cultural process currently known as 'globalization'.

As a consequence of these and other developments, the US by 2002 had become both the so-called 'indispensable nation' and the primary engine of world English. Internationally powerful American companies, especially those with media and publishing interests, such as AOL–Time-Warner, have however (remarkably) tended not to see American English as the primary driving force behind world English but rather as distinct from it, so that—as for example with Microsoft—a product may be prepared in two versions: 'American' (for the home market and following US print usage) and 'World' (for everywhere else, and following UK usage).

Throughout the 19th century, Americans enlarged their territory, drawing in populations with languages other than English. Thus, in 1819 the US purchased Florida from Spain; in 1821, US settlers arrived in the Mexican territory of Texas, which under their influence declared its independence from Mexico in 1836 and became a state of the Union in 1845, which led to the re-absorption of these settlers along with many Mexicans; and in 1848, Mexico ceded vast areas of the West, including California, adding in the process further speakers of Spanish as well as a range of endangered Native American languages.

The action of the US Navy commander Matthew Perry in 1853 compelled the Japanese to open their harbours to Western trade, setting in train a long and complex relationship between the US and Japan, and between American English and Japanese. A major turning point, however, was 1898, the year of the four-month Spanish–American War. Spain ceded the Caribbean island of Puerto Rico and sold for $20 million dollars the Asian archipelago of the Philippines, regardless of the views of the Filipinos. In the same year, in a separate action, the US annexed Hawaii, through these two developments expanding its possessions, influence, and language to the far side of the Pacific. In a geopolitical sense, the US became in that year a kind of Asian nation just as, in the 20th century, through its involvement in two world wars and the North Atlantic Treaty Organization, it became a kind of European nation.

At the end of the nineteenth century, although no such phrase has ever been employed by the US government, a *de facto* American empire had begun to take shape, paralleling the *de jure* British Empire, at that time at the height of its power and influence. In the immediately following years, the US developed an Open Door policy towards China, mediated in the Russo-Japanese war, encouraged a revolution in Panama against Colombia (the US then building a canal comparable to the Suez Canal of the British in Egypt), intervened frequently in Latin American affairs (to secure American interests), and purchased from Denmark some of the Virgin Islands in the Caribbean. All such activities strengthened the presence of American English in Asia and Latin America, and as a result (especially through steadily increasing immigration) the US became a Latin American nation, with a burgeoning and widespread Spanish-speaking population, most notably in California, Texas, Florida, and New York State. There are major concentrations of Spanish-speakers in Los Angeles, Miami, and New York City.

From the First World War (1914–18) onward, as the US played an increasing role in world politics and economics, its scholars, writers, and media presenters increasingly confidently asserted their own educated variety of English as the equal of and an alternative to what they tended early in the 20th century to call 'Standard English' then more generally 'British English'. By the early 1920s, an acknowledged American Standard English, whatever name might be given to it, had come into its own at home and abroad, and—especially in the 1930s—Americanisms at all social levels became recognized worldwide as distinctive, although they were often frowned on as vulgar or outlandish, including often within their own borders.

At least the following five developments assisted in disseminating American usage and linguistic influence worldwide:

❶ Cinema and television

The growth and sustained popularity first of 'the movies', based in Hollywood, then of US TV programmes, including those which can be syndicated abroad.

❷ Popular music

Two notable influences on popular music have been African-American and country-and-western performers, each group with its own accents, performance styles, and body language.

❸ Warfare, ideology, and politics

The nation took part in the Second World War in Europe, Asia, and the Pacific, the Cold War with the Soviet Union and its surrogates (as the dominant member of the North Atlantic Treaty Organization: NATO), in the Korean, Vietnam, and Gulf wars, and in various lesser actions, overt and covert, throughout the world, disseminating US military usage and slang.

❹ International trade and publication

The US currently dominates world trade, including the global expansion, advertising, and products of such brand-name corporations as Coca-Cola, IBM, Kellogg, McDonalds, Microsoft, and Pepsi Cola, and such internationalized publications as *TIME*, *Newsweek*, the *Reader's Digest*, and the *International Herald Tribune*.

❺ Space-age and futuristic technology

The US currently dominates technological, military, and communicative developments that include spacecraft and space exploration, satellite communication, missile systems, the computer, and the Internet.

At the beginning of the 21st century, the US is the most powerful society ever known. As such, its language (whatever it might have been) is inevitably the foremost means of communication in the world. Had the dominant US language been Spanish, American pre-eminence might have been a body blow to the international standing of English, however influential the UK might have been. The emergence of the US on the world stage in the 20th century, however, only served to strengthen what was already (for good, for ill, or both) the world's foremost language.

General American

Since around 1950 there has been broad agreement that national news presenters in the US speak a more or less regionally neutral variety of American English, whereas broadcasters delivering weather and sports information are likely to represent a more local variety, in a pattern comparable to the BBC. The terms *General American* and *(the) network standard* have been widely used to refer to presenters' avowedly more neutral and national speech, but no one appears ever to have set out, or been expected, to acquire it, or to have expected listeners to be influenced by it. No special social value has been assigned to it and no claims are made that it represents—or should or could represent—the speech style of a majority of educated Americans.

The term *General American* (abbreviations: *GA*, *GenAm*) was introduced by the US linguist George P. Krapp in *The English Language in America* (1924), to refer to a form of speech without marked regional characteristics. The term was immediately denounced by his fellow American Hans Kurath, and has been controversial ever since. According to *The Random House Dictionary of the English Language* (1987 through 1998) it is 'no longer in technical use', but it has in fact continued in use among both language scholars and ESL/EFL teachers, especially outside the US.

Thus, the British phonetician John Wells has used a GA/RP contrast in his *Longman Pronunciation Dictionary* (1990), as have Peter Roach and James Hartman in the 15th edition of the Daniel Jones *English Pronouncing Dictionary* (Cambridge, 1997). More recently, however, there has been a tendency in UK-generated ESL/EFL publications to have the same GA/RP contrastive pronunciations as in the past but without using either of the traditional labels, instead favouring a blanket contrast between 'British' and 'American' pronunciation.

The expression *network standard* has been less contentious. It grew up strictly in relation to radio and TV, and is probably best defined negatively, as a variety without distinct regional features, that does not mark class, is not learned collectively in childhood, and has never been institutionalized or directly offered as a pronunciation model. There has also recently been an increasing tendency in both the US and the UK to use educated regional accents on national broadcasts, so that the wish or need for an anodyne would-be non-regional pronunciation appears to have become less important in both countries.

National radio and television announcers supposedly favour a national standard because it avoids (or appears to avoid) pronunciation features considered peculiar to specific groups—or simply peculiar. The network standard is typically rhotic (*r* being pronounced wherever it is spelled) and does not either diphthongize the vowel of *caught*, as in the South, nor pronounce it long and tense, as in the North-East. The terms *General American* and (*the*) *network standard* refer in the main to one dimension of language, pronunciation, and are likely to remain both controversial among language professionals and little known to the public at large. The phrase *General American English*, however, is at times used for the overall more or less standard language of the US, and as such covers grammar, vocabulary, writing, and print as well as pronunciation, as in: 'The educational system in the Philippines uses General American English as the norm' (from a seminar report by Philippines linguists, 1981).

The term *Standard/standard English* has been used in the US since the beginning of the 20th century to cover essentially the same range of usage as *General American English* and *American English*, two terms being often used loosely—especially in educational circles—with standardness in mind. The terms *American Standard English* and *Standard American English* (with much the same meaning) are less common, and when they occur, usually in specialist discussions, they are contrasted in particular with *British Standard English* and *Standard British English* (also both with much the same meaning), as well perhaps as *Australian Standard English*, *Canadian Standard English*, and increasingly *World Standard English* and *International Standard English* (*WSE, ISE*). The latter two terms by and large mean the same thing: a loose and somewhat varied, but nonetheless real, 'federative' standard for the language, especially as exemplified in the text of the major national and international newspapers of the English-speaking world.

'General' or 'standard' American usage is not therefore a monolith separated off from the many kinds of US English; rather, it is influenced by networks that include age group and peer group, social class and ethnic background, gender, occupation, education, and recreation. There are, however, two ethnic varieties that have gained national prominence and influenced usage from coast to coast (including the middle class). They are:

❶ African-American English

Long an instrument of social solidarity among Americans of sub-Saharan African background, African-American English has been widely used in popular entertainment and has spread in informal settings, especially among the young and with emphasis on trendy slang, verbal games, and such music-related activities as jazz and rap.

❷ Jewish English

Made more widely known through entertainers and writers, so that non-Jews are likely to have in their repertoires at least a sprinkling of adoptions such as *chutzpah*, *schmaltzy*, and *schmooze* and such expressions as *I should be so lucky* ('Something as good as that won't happen to *me*').

Because they have a high profile, such varieties are open to casual imitation, especially in jokes with enough shibboleths and clichés to identify the target easily. Other communities, though less widely known, exert similar constraints on their members and influence on their neighbours. They include: Cajun English in Louisiana, influenced by French and Caribbean Creole; the English of people of Finnish descent in northern Michigan; the German English of the Amish and Mennonites in Pennsylvania ('Pennsylvania Dutch'), Ohio, and Indiana; Native American or 'Indian' English, notably in Arizona and New Mexico; and the Polish English of such north-eastern industrial cities as Buffalo and Detroit.

Although *General American* and *American Standard English* are difficult terms and entities to pin down, they include at least the features listed below, which are widely regarded as nationally 'neutral'. These have for some decades been part of an idealized teaching model for foreign students, commonly referred to as 'American English' (often in contrast with 'British English'). Although the standardness of these varieties is generally taken as needing no further discussion, foreign learners, their teachers, and the publishers of teaching materials at times forget (or fail to make clear) that what they offer is often far removed from usage that foreign learners will meet (and probably therefore need) in the United States at large.

In the following lists, the vast range of pronunciation, spelling, grammar, and vocabulary more or less shared with the peoples of Britain, Ireland, and elsewhere is taken as given, and a selection of the generally agreed distinctions in American Standard English is provided. After them comes information concerning less standard and non-standard US usage. Because of the strong on-going influence of all such usage on other kinds of English, many US expressions have become so international as to be unexceptional: that is, American English supplies a major part of the 'default mode': that imprecise but developing entity increasingly known as 'International' or 'World' English (however perceived).

American pronunciation

1　Although the concept of 'nasality' is not easy to pin down in phonetic terms, American usage is generally regarded as more nasal than in most other English-speaking communities worldwide.

2　Apart from the South, eastern New England, and New York City, American speech is rhotic. US usage is therefore usually classed internationally (with appropriate exceptions) as fundamentally a rhotic variety, *r* being typically pronounced after a vowel, as in *worker*.

3   The American *r* is retroflex, the tip of the tongue curling back without touching the upper mouth.

4   The quality of the *a*-vowel is the same in such words as *pat*, *pant*, *path*, *cant*, *can't*, *dance*.

5   There is a *y*-sound in such words as *beauty*, *pew*, *few*, *view* ('byooty', 'pyoo', 'fyoo', 'vyoo'), and *cute*, *newt* ('kyoot', 'nyoot'), and in the second syllable of such words as *menu* ('menyoo') and *value* ('valyoo'), but there is no such sound in such words as *duke*, *duty*, *tune*, *new* ('dook', 'dooty', 'toon', 'noo').

6   The vowel sounds in such word pairs as *caught* and *cot*, *taught* and *tot* are likely to be the same.

7   A *d*-like sound typically occurs where the spelling has *t/tt* in such words as *atom*, *bitty*, *latter*, *metal*, which respectively sound much the same as *Adam*, *biddy*, *ladder*, *medal*.

8   There is generally no *t*-sound in such words as *winter* ('winner'), *intercourse* ('innercourse'), and *international* ('innernational').

American grammar

1   For the verb *get*, there are two contrastive past participles: *gotten* and *got*. *Gotten* generally indicates a process rather than a state or condition: *I've gotten it* ('I've acquired it'), as opposed to *I've got it* ('I possess it'). Similarly, *I've gotten to go* ('I've received permission or been given the opportunity to go') contrasts with *I've got to go* ('I'm obliged to go').

2   The forms *I will*, *you will*, *he will*, etc., are usual; *shall* is rare, and largely restricted to formal invitations (*Shall we dance?*) and emphasis (*I shall return*).

3   The simple past rather than the present perfect may be used for action that leads up to the present time, including with adverbs: *Did you ever hear that? —I already did* (as opposed to *Have you ever heard that?—I already have*).

4   In formal constructions where clauses follow verbs, adjectives, and nouns of requiring and urging, the present subjunctive is preferred to a construction with *should*, as in: *They insisted that he go with them*; *It is imperative that you be here on time*.

5   When the subject of a clause is a collective noun, a singular verb is generally used, in concord with form rather than sense: *The airline insists that increased fares are necessary*; *The committee is aware of the problem*.

American vocabulary

1   Direct adoptions from Native-American languages include *chipmunk*, *hickory*, *moccasin*, *pecan*, *skunk*, *squash*, *totem*, *wigwam*. Words taken indirectly from Native-American languages through French include *caribou* and *toboggan*.

2   Adoptions from other European colonial languages in North America include: Dutch *boss*, *coleslaw*, *cookie*, *Santa Claus*, *sleigh*, *snoop*, *waffle*, and probably *Yankee*; French *chowder*, *prairie*; Spanish *corral*, *lasso*, *ranch*.

3   Adoptions from immigrant languages include: West African *goober*, *gumbo*, *juke*, *voodoo*, *zombie*; German (including through Pennsylvania Dutch, a specific German-American dialect) *dumb* ('stupid'), *noodle*, *sauerkraut*, *snorkel*, and the elements *-fest* and *-burger* in *bookfest*, *cheeseburger*, etc.

4   Americanized foreign food terms include: Mexican Spanish *enchiladas*, Chinese *chop suey*, German *wiener*, Italian *pizza*, Japanese *sukiyaki*, Swedish *smorgasbord*, and Nahuatl-to-Mexican-Spanish *tamale*.

5   An old word put to a new use is *creek*, meaning 'a small stream' (as also in Australia) rather than for a narrow opening to the sea (as in Britain), probably because the term was first applied to the mouths of streams along coasts, then extended to the whole watercourse.

6   New words from old resources include: *lengthy* from *length*; *Briticism* (an expression peculiar to Britain, on the analogy of *Scotticism* and *Americanism*); *complected* as in *dark-complected* (having a dark complexion); *speechway* 'a pattern, style, or feature of spoken language shared by the people of a particular group or area' (*Random House Dictionary Unabridged*, 1996).

7   Some words have complex linguistic histories, as with *lagniappe*, a small present given by merchants to their customers, extended to signify any small extra benefit: a Southern adoption from Louisiana French, in turn from Spanish *lañapa* ('the gift'), in turn from *yapa* in Quechua, an Andean language (Peru and Bolivia).

8   There is a propensity for coining words that may then be adopted internationally, as with *airline*, *boondoggle*, *checklist*, *disco*, *expense account*, *flowchart*, *geewhiz*, *halfbreed*, *inner city*, *junk food*, *kangaroo court*, *laser*, *mass meeting*, *nifty*, *ouch*, *pants*, *quasar*, *radio*, *soap opera*, *teddy bear*, *UFO*, *vigilante*, *wholehearted*, *xerox*, *yuppie*, *zipper*.

9   The form *OK* or *okay* is probably the most intensively and widely used (and borrowed) word in the history of language. Its many would-be etymologists have traced it variously to Cockney, French, Finnish, German, Greek, Norwegian, Scots, several African languages, and the Native American language Choctaw, as well as a number of personal names. All are imaginative feats without documentary support. Its complex history has however been tracked down by the American lexicologist Allen Walker Read to two fads of the 1830s in the city of Boston, as follows: In the first fad, people used the initials for a phrase rather than the phrase itself (*OFM* 'our first men', *ng* either 'no go' or 'no good'), while in the second fad they favoured comic misspellings, such as *oll wright* ('all right'). The two came together to produce such initialisms as *OW* ('oll wright'), *KY* ('know yuse': no use), and *OK* ('oll korrect': all correct). *OK* would probably have gone the way of *OFM* and *OW*, except that it was taken up as a pun on *Old Kinderhoek*, the nickname of the politician Martin Van Buren (after the town where he was born in New York State). A political organization, the OK Club, was formed to support his political fortunes, and its first element caught on through heavy partisan use in the election campaign of 1840. Van Buren lost the election, but his catchword has gone from strength to strength. In addition to its two spellings, it has been shortened to *oke* and reduplicated to *okey-dokey*.

Despite the kinds of commonality just listed, the United States is vast, its usage is varied, and many linguistic opinions and stances are strongly held. New Yorkers know that other Americans generally regard their speech as uncouth, and may even at times agree, but this makes little or no difference to how they speak. Comparably, people from the Appalachians and Ozarks may, like outsiders, describe their speech as 'hillbilly', but this does not mean they plan to give it up; its value in reinforcing local solidarity and its prestige through country and western music outweighs any adverse judgements. Americans moving to parts of the US far from their place of origin may retain much or all of their home variety and, if there is a strong 'exile' community in the new locality, they may pass their usage on, as with Northernisms in Memphis and New Orleans and Kentuckyisms in parts of Chicago and Detroit. Such loyalties tend to be strong.

Local varieties (notably in traditionally defined dialect areas) can often be distinguished by synonym preference: thus, the term *crawfish* (though used nationally) is most common in the South and West, while *crawdad* is likely in the Midland region and to the west of the Appalachians, and in the North *crayfish* (also the British usage) is dominant. People in both the North and West are 'sick to their stomachs', while in Pennsylvania and southward along the Atlantic coast they are 'sick on their stomachs', and along the Gulf Coast and in the Southwest they are 'sick at their stomachs'. To pluralize the pronoun *you*, many Southerners—cultivated and otherwise—use *you-all* or *y'all*, while Northerners generally considered uncultivated may say *youse* (following Irish usage). The varieties in which such usages occur are often described within the US in terms of sound: Southerners 'drawl' and both New Englanders and Texans talk with a 'twang'—although to many outsiders *all* Americans drawl and talk with a twang.

Language scholars have broadly agreed that there are four dialect regions in the US: *Northern*, *Southern*, *Midland*, and *Western*. They usually also note, however, that *Midland* is an area of transition between Northern and Southern, for which reason its traditional sub-areas *North Midland* and *South Midland* are often assigned respectively to Northern as *Lower North* and to Southern as *Upper South*. Other names for South Midland/Upper South include *Hill Southern* (to contrast with *Coastal Southern*) and *Appalachian* (often also yoked with the *Ozarks*).

The North, New England, and New York City

Northern runs more or less due west from New England and New York, and has been shaped mainly by migration from Boston, New York, and their hinterlands. The Northern population was especially enlarged by three waves of migration: in the 1850s from northern Europe (especially Scandinavia and Germany), in the 1890s from eastern and southern Europe, and in the 1930s from the Southern states within the US.

Northern pronunciation

1 Western North is rhotic while New York and New England are non-rhotic, with intrusive *r* commonly occurring in New England in such expressions as *the idea/r of it*.

2 *Grease* tends to rhyme with *lease* in the North and West, and with *freeze* elsewhere.

Northern grammar

1 *All the* is followed by a comparative adjective, as in *That's all the farther I could go* ('That's as far as I could go').

2 *Dove* as the past of *dive* appears to be a development by analogy with *drive/drove* and *weave/wove*, is widely attested in Northern (and in Canadian) usage, and is spreading.

3 The use of *had ought* and *hadn't ought* has also spread, as in: 'If you don't like people, you hadn't ought to be in politics at all' (President Harry S. Truman).

Northern vocabulary

1 The following words are distinctively Northern: *American fries* (boiled potatoes sliced and fried in a pan); *bitch* ('to complain'); *bloodsucker* ('leech'); *cabbage salad* ('coleslaw'); *comforter* ('heavy quilt'); *ice-cream social* ('gathering for refreshments', often to raise money for a worthy cause); *nightcrawler* ('large earthworm'), *pitch* ('the resin of coniferous trees'), *sweet corn* ('maize grown for human consumption'), and *teeter-totter* ('see-saw').

2 Other languages have contributed: *babushka* (a kind of head scarf: from Polish and Russian); *cruller* (a small fried sweet cake: from Dutch); *frankfurter/forter*, *frankfurt/fort*, *frank* (a kind of cooked sausage: from German, and now both nationalized and internationalized); *quahog* (a kind of thick-shelled edible clam: from Narraganset, a Native-American language): and *schnozzle* ('nose': from Yiddish).

The term *New England*, unlike *New Zealand*, has no independent political significance, but has cultural significance because of its early settlements. It covers the six north-easternmost states: Maine, Vermont, New Hampshire, Massachusetts, Connecticut, and Rhode Island. The original colonies were largely settled by Puritans, mainly from East Anglia in England, a serious-minded and often hard-headed people with a strong work ethic and a social conscience based on the New Testament concern for charity towards others. Tension between puritanical ideals and a secular quest for gain, fame, and pleasure has long been a feature of American life and culture, together with an enthusiasm for hard work and educational success, for which New England's foremost colleges, Harvard (1636) and Yale (1701), remain archetypes.

New Englanders are noted for a laconic style and 'flat' accents. The terms applied popularly to present-day New England speech are often the same as those used in the 17th century to characterize the Puritans in England: a harsh and high-pitched nasal twang. In reality, however, New England has two dialects: *Eastern*, with Boston as its hub; and *Western*, which blends into upper New York State and is the source of the *Inland Northern* dialect. However, the original Puritan style has been linguistically augmented by a range of more recent arrivals that includes the Irish, French-Canadians, Italians, Greeks, Blacks from the South, and middle-class émigrés from New York City. But even so, the old Yankee style and usage survive.

New York City and its port occupy Manhattan and Staten Island, the western end of Long Island, and part of the adjacent mainland, all within New York State, but its conurbation extends into Connecticut to the north and New Jersey to the south. New York usage is therefore, despite the name, more widely spoken than in the immediate urban area. New York City embodies Israel Zangwill's concept of the United States as a 'melting pot' of peoples, having received through Ellis Island many waves of immigrants, notably from Europe. Many languages are spoken in the city, leading to a wide range of hybrid usage and distinctive influences on the local English.

New York, like London, is a megacity in terms of size and diversity. The two cities have long been closely associated culturally and commercially (from the French point of view as the prime citadels of 'Anglo-Saxon' civilization), and in recent years an increasing number of high-level professionals and others have tended to 'commute' between the two, in a way of life referred to as 'NYLon'.

Native New York speech, like eastern New England and the South, is non-rhotic, with both a linking and an intrusive *r*. When a word with a final unpronounced *r* is followed by one that begins with a vowel, linking *r* occurs: *gopher* is pronounced 'gofa', but in *The gopher ate everything*, the words are the same as 'The gofa rate everything'. An intrusive *r* occurs, however, where it is not etymologically or orthographically normal: in New York, *sofa* rhymes with *gopher*, and so there is an additional *r*-sound in *The sofa ris lost* (following the same rule). New York is also noted for a long, tense, round vowel, as in the local pronunciation of *coffee* ('cwawfee').

New York English (sometimes disparagingly 'New Yorkese') has low prestige even among its speakers. Their response to their own usage, sometimes described in terms of 'linguistic self-hatred', is unusual; in most other areas (as for example Cockney usage in London), local ways of speaking are usually taken to show that speakers are honest, friendly, and reliable. New Yorkers' discomfort with their own speech may reflect the low regard of the rest of the nation. Within New York usage, the most vilified variety is associated with Brooklyn (one of the city's five boroughs). Often called simply *Brooklyn*, it is also more pejoratively known as *Brooklynese*. A typical feature is the vowel that makes the local pronunciation of *earl* sound like 'oil', a form that also occurs in New Orleans in Louisiana. In stereotypical or 'stage' Brooklyn, the pronunciation of the two shibboleth words is reversed, so that *earl* is pronounced 'oil' and *oil* is pronounced 'earl'.

Yankees, Yanks, Wasps, and Anglos

The three more or less informal terms *Yankee*, *Wasp*, and *Anglo* are commonly used in the United States for kinds of people in various ways closely associated with the English language, a traditional Protestant culture, and a north-western European ethnic background, as well as the traditional Puritan heartland in such north-eastern states as Connecticut and Massachusetts. The origin of the informal name *Yankee* (and its shortened form *Yank*, with its slightly different associations) is uncertain, but the currently favoured origin is *Jan Kees*, a variant of Dutch *Jan Kaas* ('Johnny Cheese'), a nickname for the ordinary man that was mistakenly taken to be plural. Other proposed origins include the Dutch *Janke* ('Little John'), used as a derisive nickname in New England, and versions of *English* and *Anglais* in Native-American languages. Conceivably some or all of these could have contributed to the creation of the word, in a kind of multiple etymology. *Yankee* and *Yank* may or may not have an initial capital. There are three senses of *Yankee*, according to place of reference, emotional connotation, and user:

❶ Someone from New England

The oldest, narrowest sense appears in the Revolutionary War song *Yankee Doodle*, which satirized the supposedly naive and incompetent New England colonials. When those so satirized adopted the song as a marching tune, the term *Yankee* became an expression of pride, particularly after the defeat of the British.

❷ Someone from the northern states

This sense was particularly associated with the Civil War, when the names *confederate*, *rebel*, *reb*, and *Johnny Reb* were used for Southerners and *yankee* or *damn yankee* for Northerners. This wider reference is the most common in the US, although the strict limits of Yankee territory are not clear. For almost all Americans, however, *yankee/Yankee* applies to someone from the North-east: New England, New York State, New Jersey, and Pennsylvania. This was the area north of the old Mason Dixon Line, the boundary between Pennsylvania and Maryland named for the surveyors who laid it out, which was later taken as the dividing line between free soil and the slave states. For many people, however, Yankee territory extends westward through all the northern states that formed the Union during the Civil War. There is, however, uncertainty about how far west the term applies.

❸ Someone from the USA (*Also, more commonly, Yank*)

The most inclusive sense, as used by the British after the Revolutionary War and now almost exclusively by non-Americans. The sense became popular during the First World War: for example, in George M. Cohan's 1917 marching song *Over There*, with its line 'The Yanks are coming'. This usage is often pejorative (as in *Yankees go home!*), and is not used by Americans as a national term for themselves. Non-American uses of the term for all Americans are likely to conflict with its other meanings. It is particularly inappropriate, and will probably be offensive, if applied to a white Southerner.

WASP or *Wasp* is an acronym that emerged in the 1950s for *White Anglo-Saxon Protestant*: an informal, at times pejorative term for what is widely considered to be—or to have been—the dominant US cultural group. Hispanics in the Southwest talk casually about *Anglos* (English-speaking people) and African Americans about *whitey* or *Mr Charlie* (for white men or white people in general), but *WASP/Wasp* refers particularly to Protestant (mainly Anglican or Presbyterian) whites of British (or at least not notably other ethnic) origin. From the acronymic insect may come associations of irritability, pettiness, and an inclination to sting. Even so, however, Wasps are widely regarded as setting the national standard (and maybe agenda), including for language and education.

Anglo began in and around the Southwest as a clipping of Spanish *anglo-americano* or English *Anglo-American* or both, standing (at times pejoratively, but often neutrally) for a (usually white) speaker of English in contrast with the Spanish-related terms *Chicano* and *Latino*: 'Chicano norms always seem to be somewhat less formal than Anglo norms' (Fernando Peñalosa, *Chicano Sociolinguistics*,

1980). The term is now widespread and used outside the Americas. In Canada and especially Quebec, however, *Anglo/anglo* is a clipping in both French and English of *anglophone*, and means a speaker of English, as in *Anglo rights*.

The Pennsylvania Dutch

The term *Pennsylvania Dutch* was coined in the 1810s for a strict, conservative rural community descended from Anabaptist Protestants from Germany and Switzerland, who settled in the area in the seventeenth and eighteenth centuries. They are also known as both Mennonites (after Menno Simons, a sixteenth-century Frisian religious leader) and Amish (German *Amisch*, after Jakob Amman, a Swiss Mennonite bishop). The name is also used for their dialect, more accurately *Pennsylvania German*. The term *Dutch* is from *Deitsch*, a variant of *Deutsch* ('German'), and has nothing to do with the Dutch of the Netherlands. The dialect is spoken mainly in the eastern part of the state and there is strong interaction with English. The following points broadly describe the English usage of the Pennsylvania Dutch.

Pronunciation

1 The devoicing of voiced consonants: 'britches' for *bridges*; 'chutch' for *judge*; 'ice' for *eyes*; 'mate' for *made*; and 'ruck' for *rug*, and in the voicing of unvoiced consonants, as in 'bush' for *push* and 'bull' for *pull*.

2 The reversal of *v*- and *w(h)*-sounds, as in 'wisit' for *visit* and 'vistle' for *whistle*.

3 The replacement of a *th*-sound by an *s*- or *z*-sound, as in 'nossin' for *nothing*, 'sank you' for *thank you*, 'some' for *thumb*, and 'zis' for *this*.

Grammar

Such German-influenced structures as: 'Throw the cows over the fence some hay'; 'They live the hill over—way out where the road gets all'; 'It wondered me where you've been'; 'Come—we make the dishes away and set ourselves down and talk'; 'Go the hill over and the road a little up till it gifs a fork, then you take the one that gifs a britch'; 'Ach, such a pretty dress! Was it at the store boughten?'

Vocabulary

Such words from dialect German as: *bobble-mowl* ('a blabbermouth'); *butz* (*up*) ('to clean [up]'); *fershpritz* ('to spatter, splash' a person or thing); *greisle* ('to worry'); *knoatchin and schmutzin* ('hugging and kissing'); *friendschaft* ('relatives'); *rootsch* ('to squirm').

The Amish generally keep to themselves, farming in traditional non-mechanized ways, using their 'Dutch', and calling their neighbours 'the English'.

The South, New Orleans, Cajun, and Texian

Historically, Southern (also known as *Southern English*, *Southern American English*, *Coastal Southern*, *Lowland Southern*, and *Plantation Southern*) has centred on Virginia, the Carolinas, Georgia, Florida, and on along the Gulf Coast into Texas. These coastal areas are distinct from both the North and their own often mountainous hinterlands, the dialects of which have been variously called *South Midland*, *Upper South*, *Hill Southern*, *Inland Southern*, *Appalachian*, and pejoratively *Hillbilly*. Coastal Southern was formed in a time of plantation and ranch agriculture, while the way of life in the largely hilly interior was largely small towns and farming (often at or just above the subsistence level).

Plantation agriculture needed a large cheap labour force to grow cotton, tobacco, and rice, and for close on three hundred years (from the late 16th well into the 19th century) enslaved West Africans provided the main labour force. The extent of black influence on white Southern usage continues to be debated, and both have much in common. In addition, however, not all varieties of English in the South fit neatly into a broad scheme, as for example: the distinct and isolated dialect of Tangier Island in Chesapeake Bay; the English influenced by the black African creole known as Gullah around Charleston; Cajun English in Southern Louisiana; kinds of African-American usage in New Orleans; and Spanish-influenced usage in Texas.

Southern pronunciation

1   Southern is non-rhotic. However, where non-rhotic Northerners have a weak vowel in place of *r* in such words as *door* and *torn* (in New England, coastal New York state, and New Jersey north of Philadelphia), Southerners generally have only the preceding vowel, so that *door* sounds the same as *doe* and *torn* the same as *tone*. There is neither the linking nor intrusive *r*-sound (as in *She saw/r 'im* for 'She saw him'), as with other non-rhotic US varieties. Indeed, Southerners often lose an *r*-sound between vowels, as in *ve'y* for 'very' and *Ca'olina* for *Carolina*. Non-rhotic pronunciation differs widely in its prestige, depending on where it occurs: in the South, unlike New York City, *r*-lessness is universal in many areas at all social levels, and attracts no condemnation.

2   A syllabic *n* often replaces *ng* in *-ing* forms: 'comin' and 'runnin' for *coming* and *running*.

3   Diphthongs tend to become single vowels, *nice time* sounding like 'nahs tahm', and *hide* nearly rhyming with both *hod* and *hard*.

4   The word *greasy* is pronounced, as in Scottish English, with 'z' and not 's'.

5   Some word-internal consonant clusters can be captured by such spellings as 'bidness' for *business* and 'Babtist' for *Baptist*.

6   Merger of vowels occurs in such words as *pin*, *since* and *pen*, *cents* (to the vowel in the first pair), a feature that is spreading more widely.

Southern grammar

1   The inclusive plural personal pronoun *y'all* ('you all') is widespread: *Y'all comin tonight?*

2   The use of *all the* followed by an adjective in the positive degree, as in *That's all the fast Ah c'n run* ('That's as fast as I can run').

3   Invariant *be* is widespread, although more common among blacks than whites, and men than women, as in: *She be here tomorrow*; *Ah be pretty busy*; *That land don't be sandy*.

4   Scots-style double modal verbs occur in both Coastal and Hill Southern, as in:
    She might can do it ('She can probably do it'); *He might could come Friday*
    ('It's possible he could come on Friday'); *Could you may go?* ('Could you get
    permission to go?').

5   Coastal and Hill Southern also use *ain't* in informal contexts, and degrees of
    stigma attach to this usage, increasingly from the set phrase *ain't it* ('ainnit?')
    through its use for *are not* (as in *They ain't here*) to its use for *haven't*, as in
    You ain't seen nuthin yet.

Southern vocabulary

1   Many distinctive Coastal expressions are archaisms in other varieties of
    English, as with: *all-overs* (feelings of uneasiness); *antigoglin* ('askew,
    slantwise'); *(ap)preciate it* ('thank you'); *bank* (a storage heap of potatoes,
    other vegetables, or coal); *branch* ('brook, stream'); *carry* ('to escort'); *firedogs*
    ('andirons'); *green beans* ('string beans'); *gullywasher* (a violent rainstorm);
    hand ('farm worker'); *hull* (the shell of a nut); *kinfolk* ('relatives'); *lick* ('sharp
    blow'); *poke* ('paper bag/sack': from Scots); *Scat!* ('Bless you!' or 'Gesundheit!',
    a remark after someone sneezes); *slouch* (a lazy or incompetent person); *skillet*
    ('frying pan'); *snapbeans* ('string beans'); *squinch* ('to squint'); *tote* ('to carry');
    carry ('to escort').

2   Various languages have contributed to Southern: the Native-American
    languages of Virginia, with *hominy* ('hulled kernels of corn/maize'), *terrapin*
    (a kind of turtle); West African languages, with *cooter* ('turtle'), *gumbo* ('soup
    thickened with okra pods'); French, with *armoire* ('wardrobe'), *bayou* ('small
    creek or river'), *jambalaya* (a Provençal stew made with rice and various
    meats); and Spanish to the west, with *arroyo* ('brook, creek'), *llano* ('open,
    grassy plain'), *riata* ('lariat, lasso'), and *vaquero* ('cowboy').

The distinctive usage of New Orleans, in Louisana, derives from at least three
sources, each complex: its Spanish and French founders; West African through
Caribbean usage; and waves of migrants from Ireland, Germany, Italy, and most
recently Vietnam. Some characteristics of general 'Nawlins' speech come from
French, either as locally used or from past and on-going French-speaking areas in
Louisiana at large, such as obsolescent *banquette* ('sidewalk': British 'pavement')
and French-influenced *make the groceries* ('shop for groceries'), *make menage*
('clean [the] house'), and *save the dishes* ('put the dishes away'). The city has locally
well-understood stereotypes of race, class, and neighbourhood, across which
linguistic features move in complex ways. Typical grammatical features include
a widespread tendency to use *had* + past participle for the simple past (as in
Yesterday I had run into him) and the tags *no* (as in *I don't like that, no!*) and the
more general Coastal Southern *hear* (as in *I'm having another piece of pie, hear?*).
Four aspects of New Orleans life and language particularly stand out:

❶ Creole

With a two-fold significance in the city: (as defined by whites) white descendants of
early French or Spanish settlers; (as defined by blacks) persons of Afro-French

parentage. Whichever is the case, however, the term covers the language and culture of both groups.

❷ Yat

The most distinctive local variety of English, the name said to derive from the greeting *Wha' y'at?* 'What are you at?' (= What are you doing?). Associated with such working-class districts as the Irish Channel and old Ninth Ward, Yat is also heard elsewhere, including some suburban *parishes* (areas in Louisiana corresponding to *counties* in the US at large). Outsiders may confuse sounds in Yat with Brooklyn/New York usage, especially features represented facetiously in print as *berlin* ('boiling'), *earl* ('oil'), *mudder* ('mother'), and *taught* ('thought').

❸ Cuisine

Much of the city's characteristic culinary vocabulary comes from Louisiana French: *beignet* (pronounced 'bainyay') a square doughnut dusted with powdered sugar; *debris* ('pan gravy'); *étouffée* ('stewed'); *file* (pronounced 'fee-lay': a thickener for soups and stews derived from young sassafras leaves); *jambalaya* (a dish prepared with rice, seasoning and meat or seafood: see above, Southern vocabulary); *praline* (pronounced 'prah-leen': a confection made with pecans and brown sugar); *sauce piquante* (a condiment made from tomatoes and red pepper). Other terms are from English: *cajun popcorn* (deep-fried crayfish tails); *dirty rice* (spicy rice with chicken giblets); *king cake* (a ring-shaped coffee cake served from Epiphany to Shrove Tuesday); *po'boy* (a sandwich known elsewhere in the US as a *grinder*, *hoagie*, or *submarine*).

❹ Mardi Gras

Shrove Tuesday, celebrated in French and Latin-American style, has a technical vocabulary that has emerged into national consciousness as a result of US-wide TV broadcasts of the elaborate parades for *Mardi Gras* (French: 'Fat Tuesday': the last day of feasting before Lent): *krewe* (an organization sponsoring a parade float); *trow* ('throw': a trinket tossed by a parader to the streetside crowd).

The word *Cajun* derives from *Acadian* (like *Injun* from *Indian* and *Bajan* from *Barbadian*). It is associated with the state of Louisiana in the 'Deep South', and has three linked senses:

❶ Also Cajun French

A dialect of French in southern Louisiana, developed from the regional French carried there in the 18th century by migrants expelled from Acadia/*Acadie* (now part of Nova Scotia in Canada). It is one of three kinds of local French, the others being the more prestigious Louisiana French and less prestigious French Creole (also known as *Gumbo* and *français neg*, 'black French'). Cajun, Creole, and Southern are routinely spoken side by side and mixed.

❷ Also Cajun English

The English of the 23 parishes of Louisiana called Acadiana, where *c*.16% of the population still speaks Cajun French. Several characteristics are borrowings or translations from French, as with: *cher* ('dear': a term of affection); *make* (compare French *faire* as an auxiliary verb: *He made closed the door*); *hair* as a count noun

(*I have to wash my hairs*: compare French plural *cheveux* 'hair'), and the object pronoun used for emphasis at the beginning or end of a sentence (*Me, I'm going to the store*; *I was late, me*: compare French *moi*).

❸ *A Cajun*

A Louisianan descended from the original Acadian immigrants, especially in the area known as Acadiana and speaking both French and English. Cajuns are known for their Roman Catholicism, devotion to family, hunting, fishing, and 'passing' a good time. Their cuisine and music are regarded as realizing the Cajun motto: *Laissez les bons temps rouler!* ('Let the good times roll!').

Both the standard adjective *Texan* and non-standard *Texian* relate to the state of Texas. The English pronunciation of the state's name, with its 'ks' pronunciation, emerged in the 19th century, adapted through Spanish from *techas* ('allies, friendship' in Caddo, a Native-American language). The first Europeans to arrive and settle in the region in the 18th century were Spanish-speaking and until 1836 Texas was part of Mexico. Until the 1870s, there was some debate as to whether a citizen of the state should be called a *Texan* or a *Texian*, the latter formed by dropping the *c* of *Texican*, an earlier form that echoed *Mexican*. Although *Texan* became the established form, the others remain in use, usually for humorous purposes, as in 'Kin Ah Hep You to Talk Texian?', the title of an article about Texas usage by Robert Reinhold (*New York Times*, July 1984). The clipping *Tex* has been used as both a nickname (as with the cowboy hero *Tex Ritter*) and a combining form (as in *Tex-Mex* for varieties of language and cooking, and the town of *Texarkana* on the Arkansas border).

The terms *Texas English*, *Texas*, and *Texian* all refer to the English usage of Texas, a variety of Coastal Southern that is distinctly nasal, with diphthongs where others have single vowels: thus, 'hee-ut' for *hit* and 'ray-ud' for *red*. Some standard diphthongs are however single vowels in Texas, where *awl*, *white*, and *wire* have the same pronunciation as *oil*, *watt*, and *war*, *oil business* sounding like 'awl bidness' and *barbed wire* like 'bob war'. In addition, *rate* and *right* and *star* and *store* are almost homophones. Texas English is not however homogeneous: the usage of East Texas is more Southern and of West Texas more Midland and Western, while a growing Hispanic population has its own branch of Chicano ('Mexican') English known as both *Tex-Mex* and *Spanglish*.

Midland, the Scotch-Irish, and country and western

Some scholars treat the speech areas between the Northern and Southern dialects as a single region with two sub-regions: *Midland*, divided into *North* and *South Midland*. Others, however, consider such a region unnecessary and call the north midland area *Lower North* and the south midland area *Upper South*. The terms *Hill Southern* and *Inland Southern* are also used in South Midland (in contrast to *Coastal Southern*), as well as *Appalachian*, after the Appalachian mountains. A virtue of the term *Midland* is that it emphasizes a flow of settlement from Philadelphia in two directions: one westward through Pennsylvania into Ohio, Indiana, and Illinois; the other south-west into the hill country of Kentucky,

Tennessee, the interior of the Southern coastal states, Missouri, and Arkansas. A south-west flow brought settlers into contact with transportation routes northward from New Orleans along the Mississippi, Arkansas, and Ohio rivers, contacts which have left enduring linguistic traces.

The most influential settlers in Appalachia (parts of Kentucky, North Carolina, Tennessee, Virginia, and all of West Virginia) were the *Scotch-Irish* (sometimes *Scots-Irish*), Protestants who began arriving from Northern Ireland *c*.1640, some three decades after their immediate forebears had migrated from Scotland to Ireland as part of the Ulster Plantation. Because of relative isolation and the continued use of forms regarded elsewhere as archaisms, Appalachian (with its roots in Ulster Scots) has been widely but inaccurately regarded as a kind of Elizabethan English. It shares features with other kinds of American usage, particularly Southern and African-American English, and is often stigmatized as the language of poor, uneducated mountain people—'hillbillies' whose culture has nonetheless had a profound impact on the US in terms of country and western music, citizen-band radio among truck drivers, pilots, and others, and Hollywood road movies and TV series. Country music and its sad-edged songs have also become popular throughout much of the traditional English-speaking world, notably Canada, Scotland, Ireland, and England, with all of whose folk-music traditions it has strong associations. Some key regional features are:

Midland pronunciation

1 Midland is rhotic. Its focal area is Philadelphia, the only rhotic city on the Atlantic seaboard, its usage having influenced a hinterland that includes the cities of Pittsburgh, Columbus, Indianapolis, Springfield, and St Louis.

2 The merger of the vowels in *tot/cot* and *taught/caught* begins in a narrow band in central Pennsylvania and spreads north and south to influence Western, in which the merger is universal.

3 In the Ohio River valley westward to Missouri, the vowel in *fish* and *itch* is almost the same as that in *meek* and *speech*.

4 A diphthong resembling the non-rhotic pronunciation of the vowel in *beer* is found in such words as *bit* and *hill* ('beeit' and 'heeil'), a pronunciation that is beginning to spread among younger speakers in the inland North.

5 Appalachian (South Midland) has initial *h* in such usages as *hit* for *it*, *hain't* for *ain't*, and the ending distinctively written as *-er* instead of *-ow*, as in *feller*, *tobaccer*, *yeller*.

Midland grammar

1 The verb *to be* is often omitted, as in *That all right*.

2 Distinctive intensifiers, especially in Appalachian, are *right* and *plumb*, as in *She hollered right loud* and *The house burnt plumb down*.

3 Though increasingly archaic, *a-* prefixed to verbs in *-ing* is well known, especially in Appalachian: *She went a-visitin yesterday*; *They just kept a-beggin and a-cryin*; *Ah'm a-fixin to do it tomorrow*.

4 Appalachian has *done* as a marker of completion, as in *He done sold his house* ('He has sold his house').

5   The use of *anymore* (treated as a single word) in the sense 'nowadays' (without a preceding negative) is spreading to other regions: *My aunt makes hats all the time anymore*; *We use a gas stove anymore*.

Midland vocabulary

1   Distinctive words include: *blinds* ('roller window shade'); *fishing worm* ('earthworm'); *mango* ('sweet/bell pepper'); *woolly worm* ('caterpillar').

2   As with the other regions, some formerly limited usages have come into more general use: *bucket* ('pail'); *hull* ('to remove the outer covering of a bean); *off* (as in *I want off at the next bus stop*, as also in Scotland).

3   Many expressions, often of Scots origin, no longer found elsewhere in the US, continue to be used, as with: *donsie* ('sickly'); *poke* ('sack, bag'); and *redd* ('to tidy [up]').

Western and the power of California

> **2001** Populations are fluid, but demography is rigid. The census, which freezes the flow of humanity into categories, creates sharp points in what is really a steady process of change. California is marking, for the most part with pride, one such artificial landmark produced by the 2000 Census. Somewhere in the past ten years, the number of Californians who describe themselves as white fell behind the number who describe themselves as something else. . . . The change has happened fast; as recently as 1950, Hispanics were only about 6% of the population. Whites made up around 90%. The drop since then is steep and is accelerating.
>
> – The Lexington column (unsigned), *The Economist*, 7 Apr

The American West, which was first settled by speakers of English after the gold rush of the 1850s, is a difficult region to delineate and describe. For example, in the most extreme cases, it may or may not include Alaska (separated off by Canada) and Hawaii (in mid-Pacific), and it is by no means clear where, in the continental US, the linguistic West begins. Southern migration brought settlers to southern California from Missouri and Arkansas along both the Butterfield Stage Route through Texas, New Mexico, and Arizona, and the Santa Fe Trail by a slightly more northerly route. Northern trails, and later the railroads, took settlers either through Nebraska, Wyoming, and Utah into central California and the San Francisco Bay Area or by the Oregon Trail to the Pacific Northwest, a region generally regarded as part of the Northern dialect area.

Expressions from both the Northern and Southern dialects have distinct distributions in the West. Thus, the Northern term *curtains* (meaning 'roller window shades') is commoner from San Francisco northward, while the Southern term *arroyo* (Spanish: 'gully, watercourse') is traceable westward from Texas to Los Angeles, but not north to San Francisco. More significant, however, is the West itself—and particularly California—as a source of linguistic innovation. Although California was dialectally mixed in the past, it has for some time been a usage area in its own right, with a considerable and increasing capacity to influence first Alaska, Hawaii, Nevada, and the Pacific Northwest, then the rest of the United

States, then the world at large (both English- and non-English-speaking). This influence relates not only to pronunciation, grammar, and particularly vocabulary and slang, but also new and overlapping kinds of usage associated with three specific social areas:

❶ Motion pictures and television

Since the 1920s, the Hollywood motion picture ('movie') industry has had an immense influence on language, imagery, symbolism, music, and other aspects of life worldwide. Many movies have added words, phrases, and even whole sentences, to the repertoire of world English, as with the cornucopia of terms from *Casablanca* (1942), including: (*I'll round up*) *the usual suspects*; *Here's lookin' at you, babe*; *We'll always have Paris*; and the apocryphal *Play it again, Sam* (which was never actually uttered). Hollywood has often, especially in made-for-TV series and soap operas, made use of its own physical and social environment, including such speech styles as Los Angeles law-enforcement usage, Black urban slang, the laid-back sun-and-sand style of *Bay Watch*, and the eager fuzzy-edged informality of high-school slang, notably in such teen-oriented TV series as *Buffy the Vampire Slayer* and *Charmed* (about three nubile sister witches).

❷ Psychobabble

An informal, rather dismissive term for various linguistic styles that involve (and often blend): the usage of hipsters in the 1950s and hippies in the 1960s; 'New Age' expressions, including the terminology of non-conventional therapies and so-called 'feel-good' activities; a range of social-reform movements (notably feminism and gay liberation); and kinds of 'consciousness-raising', aimed at making people more aware of their potential and the true nature of things. The term originally related therefore to 'alternative' lifestyles, seen as distinct from, and often as cures for, a traditional acquisitive and materialistic Euro-American/Anglo-Saxon/WASP (sub)urban way of life. Psychobabble has included elements from such systems as yoga and related meditational and health practices originating in India, and Chinese, Japanese, and Korean martial arts and other cultural/therapeutic activities.

❸ Technobabble

An equally informal, often dismissive term notably relating to the usage of 'Silicon Valley' (the informal name for an area between San Francisco and San Jose, in the general area of Stanford University) as a centre for the development of computers and related equipment and services. Such usage is similar to, but wider than, *computerspeak* and *computerese*, covering both authentic high-tech and pseudo-technical language that baffles lay people. The term is also often used for the technical jargon of sci-fi movies and TV series, as in the series *Star Trek: Voyager* ('Lysosomal enzymes are often a sign of symbiogenesis'; 'Not according to your cortical theta ray readings'; 'The captain's consciousness may have phase-shifted out of our reality').

Indeed, the worldwide significance and impact of California and Hollywood can be illustrated with reference to Paramount Pictures' almost 40-year-old TV-and-movie series *Star Trek*. Thus, on a starship like the *Enterprise* or a station like Deep Space Nine (some four hundred years from now), an alien with power shoulders and pointed ears, seated on the bridge of a Romulan warbird, might appear on the viewscreen of a Starfleet starship. When the Romulan speaks, it is in a smoothed-out Californian English, courtesy of an unseen and never-explained 'universal translator'. In a real sense, Californian English is the default dialect of this particular space opera.

Romulans have never spoken their own language since the series began (when they had Latin-style names like *Decius* and titles like *centurion*), but another interstellar species, the Klingons, originally played as oriental, later as a kind of intergalactic biker, acquired a language carefully constructed by the linguist Marc Okrand, and this often operates in episodes despite the presence of the universal translator. Klingon has passed into real life among Klingon hobbyists after Okran wrote a teach-yourself textbook entitled *The Klingon Dictionary: The Official Guide to Klingon words and phrases* (Pocket Books, 1992). The Klingon for 'What do you want?' is *nuqneH*, 'It's not my fault' is *pIch vi-ghaj-BE*, and 'Beam me aboard!' is *HIjol*. When addressed in Klingon by some enthusiasts, Okrand had to admit that he had not in fact learned the language himself, only constructed it. Their reply might have been *veQDuj oH Dujllje* ('Your ship is a garbage scow').

Occasionally, *Star Trek* characters from Earth 'have accents', whereas the majority do not (that is, they are speakers of standard Hollywood American). Thus, in the original 1960s series Montgomery Scott, the chief engineer of the starship *Enterprise*, has a Scottish accent, as interpreted by an Irish Canadian, James Duggan. This is because Scots have long been associated with ships' engines. It is also appropriate that the ship's surgeon Leonard McCoy should sound like a country doctor from Missouri, because that is how he describes himself. It would, however, be wrong if Mr Spock (half-human, half-Vulcan) had a Southern or an East Coast Jewish accent (which would fit the Boston background of Leonard Nimoy, the actor who famously played the part). Spock, however, had to be vocally *undistracting*, because the rest of him (pointed ears and eyebrows, green blood, remote manner) were difficult enough. Only a neutral Network accent fit(ted) that bill, for both Americans and the world. In this, Hollywood inherited a tradition of accent typecasting comparable to the policy of the BBC in London from the 1920s to the 1980s.

The following are some points covering the usage of the diffuse but increasingly influential Western region:

Western pronunciation

1 In some respects, the West brings to completion processes begun elsewhere in the US, as with the merger of the vowels of *don* and *dawn*: virtually universal there and spreading east.

2 The vowel in such words as *measure* and *fresh* (which has the value of *bet* in much of the North-East) is increasingly given the more Southern sound of *bait*, so that *edge* and *age* have virtually the same pronunciation.

3 Though Westerners regard themselves as distinguishing the vowels in such words as *steel* and *still*, Easterners and others hear such pairs as identical (with the vowel of *sill* in both). Typically, therefore, the Western pronunciation of *really* sounds to outsiders like 'rilly'.

Western grammar

1 There are few if any distinctive regional grammatical usages, but particular communities and subgroups, such as inner-city Blacks, Hispanics, Las Vegas

professionals, Hawaiians, and Southern California teens have distinctive syntax:

2 Hispanic usage in East Los Angeles: *We all the time used to go outside* ('We used to go outside all the time').

3 San Francisco drug usage: *I bin trippin for three weeks* ('I've been high on drugs for three weeks', where the effect of a drug is conceived as a journey, and *have* has been omitted).

4 Hawaiian usage, as for example the foregrounding of the object of the verb in: *Moray eel you can spear it* ('You can spear Moray eel, for example').

5 Southern California teen talk: *She went, 'Hey, like, no biggie'* ('She said, 'Hey, that's no big deal': that isn't anything really important).

Western vocabulary

1 Some common Western terms are uncommon elsewhere, except in reference to Western language or culture, as with: *bar pit* (a ditch by the side of an ungraded road); *bear claw* (a large sweet pastry shaped like a bear's paw); *bush pilot* (a daring pilot of light aircraft used to reach remote Alaskan areas); *canyon* (a narrow, steep-sided valley, from Spanish *cañon*); *chesterfield* (a sofa: also in Canada); *gunny sack* (a burlap bag); *lug* (a field crate for fruit and vegetables); *parking strip* (a band of grass between sidewalk and curb [British *kerb*] on a city street, on which a car can be parked); *sourdough bread* (bread started with some fermented dough).

2 The most important language influence is Mexican Spanish, with many borrowings in southern California, Arizona, and New Mexico: *adios* ('goodbye'); *adobe* ('sun-dried brick'); *bronco* ('wild, mean, rough', for a wild or partly broken horse); *embarcadero* ('wharf'); *hombre* ('guy, fellow'); *Santa Ana* (a seasonal hot, dry wind in southern California).

3 Various terms for Mexican cookery, typical of the region, widely used there, and now found in English elsewhere in the US and the world, such as: *carne seco* ('chipped beef'); *frijoles* ('beans'); *langosta* ('crayfish, spiny lobster'); *tortilla* (a flat, thin, round piece of unleavened bread).

4 The region is cosmopolitan, and many languages have contributed to its usage. They include: Hawaiian, *aloha* (a greeting or farewell), *lei* (a garland of flowers); Native-American languages in the Pacific Northwest, *chinook* (a warm winter wind), *Sasquatch* ('Bigfoot', a large legendary hominid creature); Chinese, *dim sum* ('meat-filled dumpling'), *kung fu* (a martial art), *tai chi/Tai Chi* and *tai chi chuan/Tai Chi Chuan* (a regime of slow balletic physical exercises); Japanese, *honcho* ('strong leader, boss'), *karaoke* (club-like entertainment in which people sing along with pre-recorded music, a hybrid from *kara* 'empty', *oke*, short for *okesutora* ('orchestra').

Many such expressions have been internationalized as a consequence of business, advertising, fashion, and media influence, others are in the process of internationalization, and others coming into use will most probably also in due course be internationalized.

African-American English, Gullah, Ebonics, and rap

A variety of names have been used over at least the last three centuries for Americans descended wholly or in part from slaves shipped across the Atlantic from Africa. At one extreme is the once widespread, often dismissive, and much detested *nigger* (an adaptation of Latin *niger* 'black', fossilized in controversial phrases such as *Nigger Minstrel Show*, in the Al Jolson musical tradition), and sometimes used as a playful pseudo-insult among African Americans themselves seldom acceptable from whites, however friendly. More acceptable but now rare is *negro/Negro* (Spanish 'black'), with the female form *negress/Negress*, long since abandoned. *Negro* however continues in such set phrases as *a Negro spiritual* for a kind of hymn.

During the period of slavery and for a time afterwards a range of labels served to calibrate the degree of someone's 'blackness' and 'whiteness'. They have included: *mulatto* (from Spanish *mulato* 'young mule') for someone half-African, half-European; *quadroon* (from Spanish *cuarterón* 'quarter') for someone with one-quarter African 'blood'; and *octoroon* (from Latin *octo* 'eight', by analogy with *quadroon*) for someone with one-eighth African blood (who could also have been referred to as having 'a touch of the tar brush'). These usages were almost entirely abandoned over the second half of the 20th century.

Earlier in the 20th century, the euphemisms *colored man/woman/person* etc., were preferred among Americans of full or part African background, and were institutionalized and perpetuated in the title of a leading civil-rights organization, the National Association for the Advancement of Colored People (NAACP). They were replaced by *Negro* (capitalized, first vowel as in *league*, second as in *go*, and not the common Southern pronunciation 'Nigra', which was too close to 'niggah'). *Negro* was replaced in later decades by *Black/black* (in contrast to *White/white*), and, more recently still, especially for formal and politically correct purposes, the euphemism *person of color* has emerged, with the intention of satisfying egalitarianism in both ethnicity and gender. Perhaps the broadest change has been in the introduction and spread first, briefly, of *Afro-American* (sometimes in contrast to *Euro-American*), then more successfully to *African American*, on the analogy of *Irish American*, *Jewish American*, *Swedish American*, and the like. This last seems to have stabilized.

Such changes have had corresponding effects on the names for the kinds of English used by African Americans. Among academics at the present time, the general term is *African-American Vernacular English* (*AAVE*). A reduced version of this, *African-American English*, has been adopted for this text, on the grounds that there is no clear-cut contrasting term or condition that can be labeled *African-American Standard English*, the standard usage of African Americans apparently being much the same as that of most other subgroups of Americans. Some years ago, scholars used *Afro-American English* and in the 1980s a briefly popular term was *Black English Vernacular* (*BEV*). The variety is also known as *American Black English*, and more commonly within the US (and coincidentally in South Africa) simply *Black English*. However, among some commentators who have sought a name that marks its distinctive nature strongly, and without reference to past usages, the preferred term is *Ebonics* (a blend of *ebony* and *phonics* coined in the mid-1970s: see below).

There has often in recent years been intense debate about whether African-American English should be an accepted classroom medium leading to and co-existing with American Standard English, or something separated off as at best casual usage and at worst slang and street talk. Older African Americans have been among the strongest opponents of any suggestion of the co-equal use of the two varieties in schools, usually because it is regarded as a brake on people's socio-economic progress (which includes the fluent use of mainstream English). The nature, origin, and development of African-American English have long been controversial matters among scholars, and indeed the existence of such a discrete variety has been fiercely questioned by a number of American academics, regardless of their own ethnic background.

African-American English is a consequence of the massive enslavement and shipment to the Americas of Africans between the late 16th and mid-19th centuries, followed by black migration from the southern states to what became in most instances racial ghettos in large cities elsewhere. According to J. L. Dillard in 1972, some 80% of black Americans at that time spoke the vernacular, and he and other commentators (including in the Anglophone Caribbean) have stressed its African origins and associations.

Gullah is the name of both a member of an African-American community on the Sea Islands and in the coastal marshes of South Carolina, Georgia, and north-eastern Florida, and the English-based creole spoken by that community. The name has been speculatively linked with the Gola of Liberia and Angola in South-west Africa. Gullah (also known as *Sea Island Creole*), which is generally not used or discussed in front of outsiders, developed on 18th-century rice plantations after British colonists and their slaves arrived in Charleston from Barbados in 1670. The Creole is the outcome of an encounter among such African languages as Ewe, Hausa, Ibo, Mende, Twi, and Yoruba, the English of plantation overseers from England, Ireland, and Scotland, and the pidgin used in West Africa and on board ships. Gullah therefore shares features with both Caribbean Creole and West African Pidgin English. Some major points about Gullah and related speech forms are:

❶ Tense and aspect

The use of distinctive words to indicate the tense and aspect of verbs: *He duh come* (both 'He is coming' and 'He was coming'); *He bin come* (both 'He came' and 'He had come'); *He done come* (both 'He has come' and 'He had come'); *He go come* (both 'He will come' and 'He would come'). In addition, *He come* may mean 'He came', 'He has come', 'He comes', but *not* 'He will come'.

❷ Pronouns

Pronouns that are more inclusive than in conventional English: *He see um* ('He/She saw him/her/it'); *He see she* ('He saw her') and *he see we* ('He or she saw us'). A pronoun also usually has the same form whether subject or possessive: *He ain see he brother* (both 'He hasn't seen his brother' and 'He didn't see his brother').

❸ Subordination

Subordinate clauses introduced by *say* (functioning rather like *that*) as in *Uh tell you say he done come* ('I told you that he has/had come') and by *fuh*, as in *Uh tell um fuh come* ('I told him/her to come'). Both particles can be left out: *Uh tell you he done come*; *Uh tell um come*.

❹ A usage continuum

There is a continuum between Gullah and local varieties of American English, much as in: *He duh come—He duh comin—He comin—He's comin.*

❺ Africanisms

English words of African origin that may have come wholly or partly through Gullah include *goober* ('peanut', compare Kimbundu *nguba*) and *juke* ('bawdy and disorderly, compare Bambara *dzugu* 'wicked'), as in *juke house* ('a brothel, cheap roadhouse') and *jukebox.*

❻ Geechee

Geechee is the name for Gullah as spoken in Georgia along the Ogeechee River: 'Among the negroes living on the Ogeechee River a patois, developed in ante bellum days, has persisted . . . [T]he 'Geechee' negro speaks in a sort of staccato and always seems excited when talking' (*National Geographic Magazine*, Sept 1926).

❼ Afro-Seminole

A creole related to Gullah and Geechee, formed in the 18th century when plantation slaves escaped to Florida and traded and intermingled in the wetlands with Seminole Indians, themselves runaways from the Creek Federation further north. Their descendants, often part-Seminole, are known as *Black Seminoles*. In the First Seminole War (1817–18), US forces led by Andrew Jackson forced the mixed population farther into the swamplands. When Spain sold the territory to the US in 1819, the Seminoles resisted a government decision to re-locate them to Indian Territory (Oklahoma), bringing on the Second Seminole War (1835–42). Some chose to hide and others were dispersed to Oklahoma, Texas, Mexico, and the Bahamas. Afro-Seminole is spoken today by several hundred people in Bracketville, Texas, near the border with Mexico, and in Nacimiento de los Negros ('Negro Nation'), 200 miles south of the border, and may still spoken in Florida and the Bahamas. In Bracketville, it is used mainly by older people, who also speak Spanish or English; in Nacimiento, they also speak Spanish. The Seminoles of present-day Oklahoma include Black Seminoles in their number, and the issue of allocations of money to registered 'Indians' has recently raised the issue of whether Black Seminoles are in fact (despite the passage of so much time and their long unquestioned presence in Seminole bands) 'true' Indians who should be registered and therefore eligible for such allocations.

Slave labour in the South led to a wide range of usage influenced by indentured servants from all parts of the British Isles, whose menfolk often became overseers on plantations. Slavery as an institution was disrupted first by the Industrial Revolution then the Civil War, promoting African-American migration within the US. As a result, the speech forms of slavery were passed from Southern plantations to the factories of the North and Midwest. When smokestack industries grew, so too did urban employment for black Americans, but the segregation maintained so rigorously in the South was sustained in other forms elsewhere in the country, continuing in less blatant but still vigorous forms today.

At the present time, the forms of African-American English furthest from American Standard English are those used by poor people with limited education and restricted dealings, while those whose speech is nearest to, or part of, standard usage are generally influenced by regional norms, especially in pronunciation. The Standard English of educated African Americans in the South is different from that in the North, each variety blending with the colloquial usage of the educated population in the same areas. Considerable style-shifting occurs between blacks talking to non-blacks and informally to one another, with variation in pronunciation, intonation, grammar, slang, and idioms, including intense ritualized verbal encounters, especially among younger black men. The main constituents of African American English include:

African-American pronunciation

1   Like general Southern usage, African American is non-rhotic: *cah* ('car'); *pahty* ('party').

2   The *l*-sound is absent in such word-final consonant clusters as in *hep* ('help') and *sef* ('self').

3   Both *are* and *will* are absent in such usages as *We comin* ('We're coming') and *We be here* ('We'll be here'), features which can also be interpreted as grammatical reduction (see below).

4   An *n* commonly replaces *ng* in *-ing* forms: *comin*, *runnin* ('coming', 'running').

5   In word-final consonant clusters, the closing consonant is dropped: *des*, *tes*, *col* ('desk', 'test', 'cold'), and the *d*-sound of past-tense endings as in *look*, *talk* ('looked', 'talked').

6   Word-initially, there is often a *d*- rather than a *th*-sound: *dat day*; *dis house*.

7   Word-finally, there is often an *f*- rather than a *th*-sound: *bof*, *souf* ('both', 'south').

8   There is often heavy initial stress in disyllabic words: *pólice* for *políce*, *défine* for *defíne*.

African-American grammar

1   Multiple negation is common, especially for strong emphasis: *No way no girl can't wear no platform shoes to no amusement park* ('There is no way that any girl can wear platform shoes to an amusement park').

2   Existential *it* replaces *there*: *It ain't no food here* ('There is no food here').

3   Inflected forms such as plural, possessive, and singular *-s* and past *-ed* are variably omitted (as illustrated for pronunciation, above), as is the verb *to be*: *He got tree cent* ('He's got three cents'); *Dat ma brudda book* ('That's my brother's book'); *Dey talk* (= They talked) *all night*.

4   Auxiliary *do* can be used in a negative statement: *It don't all be her fault* ('It isn't all her fault'); *Ah don got none* ('I don't have any'/'I haven't got any').

5   Auxiliary *be* is often used to indicate habitual occurrence: *Dey be fightin* ('They are always fighting'); *He be laughin* ('He laughs all the time').

6   Stressed *been* conveys long-standing events with remote pasts: *Ah been see dat movie* ('I saw that movie long ago'); *She been had dat hat* ('She has had that hat for some time').

7   Intention is sometimes expressed by the particle *a*: *Ah'm a hep you* ('I'm going to help you'). Compare South Midland/Appalachian *Ah'm a gonna hep you* ('I'm going to help you').

8 *Steady* is used (with heavy stress in sentence-final positions) to indicate habitual (persistent, consistent, or intense) behaviour: *We be steady rappin*, *We steady be rappin*, *We be rappin steady* ('We are always talking'); *Dey steady be good, Dey be steady good, Dey be good steady* ('They are always good').

9 *Come* sometimes functions as a semi-auxiliary verb: *He come tellin me some story* ('He told me a lie'); *Dey come comin in here like dey own de place* ('They came in here as if they owned the place').

10 Adverbial use of *like to* meaning 'almost': *Ah like to die when she tol me dat* ('I almost died when she told me that'); *He like to hit his head on dat branch* ('He almost hit his head on that branch').

African-American vocabulary and idiom

1 Many terms, including *goober* ('peanut'), *yam* ('sweet potato'), *tote* ('to carry'), and *buckra* ('white man'), can be traced to languages in West Africa, as can the grammatical functions of habitual *be* and aspectual *steady* (above).

2 Several terms are used to refer to intimate associates or to other African Americans at large: for example, *homeboy* began with convicts who served prison terms with other 'boys from home' (convicts from the same neighbourhood). The bond between homeboys is stronger than that between other *brothers* or *bloods* (black men) who had no relationship prior to imprisonment. The term travelled from prisons to communities where ex-convicts lived and from there into the general community. The plural is generally *homies* and the female equivalent is *homegirl*.

3 Pejorative ethnic terms for whites include *honkie* and *whitey* for all whites, and *redneck* and *peckerwood* for poor and/or rural and/or Southern whites, especially overt racists such as members of the Ku Klux Klan.

4 Established slang includes significant changes in the senses and applications of words: *bad* used for 'good' (*Hey, dat a b-a-a-d cah!* 'That's a marvelous car!'); *cool* and *hot* used with equal intensity for 'very good', and now part of internationalized slang (*Dat cah real cool/hot!* 'That car's really great'); *crib* for an apartment or other place where one lives, including a federal housing project; *ride* and *short* for an automobile: *Homeboy be steady drivin dat short/ride!*

5 Everyday idioms include: *stepped-to*, subject to a physical advance by an opponent before a likely exchange of blows, as in *So Ah said, 'What's goin down* [what's happening]?' *an Ah got stepped-to'*; the phrase *upside the head* (against the head), as in *He got hit upside de head*; the derivative *ashy*, referring to a dry skin that looks slightly discoloured, as in *His skin always be so ashy*.

6 Many African-American expressions have 'crossed over' into mainstream colloquial usage, including beyond the US, such as: *hip* (less commonly *hep*) referring to someone knowledgeable about popular (and especially inner-city black) culture; *dude* as a generic for any male, as in *Hey, dat dude be crazy*.

Many styles of speaking go back to African traditions: for example, *the dozens* (verbal insults directed at an opponent's mother); *rappin* (a voluble, rhythmic eloquence that includes both the language of seduction and the lyrics of popular music: see below); *shuckin* and *jivin* (deceiving whites through verbal trickery); *soundin* (engaging in verbal duels). The *men and women of words*, who embody the community's oral traditions, are common in most black communities, among them preachers, poets, musicians, and political radicals who sustain rhetorical forms derived from both African tradition and Biblical English. Such African-American forms of art and ritual as Negro spirituals, jazz, dance, poetry, rap, and even elaborate handshakes have all substantially 'crossed over' into popular culture in the US and elsewhere, regardless of the ethnicity of the participants, and the presence of black usage in US literature is comparable to that of literary Cockney in England. The earliest official and literary presentations appeared well before the end of the 18th century:

> **1972** Attestation (recorded literary examples) from Crèvecoeur, Cotton Mather, Benjamin Franklin, the court records of Salem, Massachusetts, and several other sources may be found before the 1790's—and all without any recourse to fictional sources. The wealth of material after that date is simply astonishing. There is, in fact, a very great deal of pre-Civil War literary Negro dialect.
> – J. L. Dillard, *Black English*, Random House, New York.

In making this observation, Dillard was responding to such statements by the journalist and social commentator H. L. Mencken as:

> **1936** The Negro dialect, as we know it today, seems to have been formulated by the song-writers for the minstrel shows; it did not appear in literature until the time of the Civil War; before that . . . it was a vague and artificial lingo which had little relation to the actual speech of Southern blacks.
> – *The American Language*, 4th edn, Knopf, New York.

Minstrel shows were however usually written and performed by whites, involving stereotypes which have (often inadvertently) served to perpetuate language myths. By contrast, contemporary African-American writers such as Maya Angelou, Langston Hughes, Toni Morrison, Alice Walker, and Richard Wright have approached African-American English in ways that blend the language and experience of African Americans into the standard language and American literature at large.

In 1975, Robert L. Williams wrote *Ebonics: The True Language of Black Folks* (Institute of Black Studies, St Louis, Missouri, 1975), its novel term a blend of *ebony* and *phonics*. The usage remained largely unnoticed for some twenty years, when it became briefly prominent in California, then nationwide, then internationally, for some months after 18 December 1996. On that date, the board of Oakland Unified School District, California, resolved that Ebonics was *not* a dialect but the mother tongue of most African-American children. They took the view therefore that English (in whatever form) was for them a second language, and should be taught as such, an assertive announcement 'making [Oakland] the first district in the nation to give the dialect official status in programs targeting bilingual students' (Mary Curtius, in 'California Educators Give Black English a Voice', *Los Angeles Times*, 20 Dec 1996).

Reports of the Oakland resolution generated considerable instant media attention and prompted a brief national debate, much of it hostile, as a result of which the board in mid-January 1997 issued a re-statement from which the assertion that Ebonics is a distinct language was removed. The widespread outrage arose largely from a belief among many Americans of all backgrounds that the board wanted to focus on black rather than standard usage while also seeking additional government funds by presenting English as a second and not a mother tongue—just as funds were being provided to help Hispanic children. In the process, it was assumed by critics, the board would misuse tax dollars at the same time as it deprived children of a solid grounding in Standard English, the sole key to social and educational advancement.

The Oakland board certainly sought more money, but it also wished to emphasize that under-achieving African-American children need help to bridge the gap between vernacular and standard. One way of doing this in the classroom would be to highlight the differences between the two kinds of language constructively while also encouraging use of the standard. Whatever the politics and economics of the situation, or the truth about language, the nine-day wonder of Ebonics briefly reminded Americans of the linguistic inequities with which they continue to live.

An entirely different phenomenon within the complex of African-American usage is *rap*. The term itself has been informally used since the 1960s (as both verb and noun), extending a century-old US slang expression meaning 'chat freely'. It is currently closely associated with both black inner-city neighbourhoods and popular radio and television, and has at least the four following senses:

❶ As a verb

Talking rapidly, rhythmically, vividly, and boastfully, as part of competing for prominence among one's peers and impressing one's listeners. The 1960s versifying of the American boxer Cassius Clay (later known as Muhammad Ali) was an early form of rapping, as in:

> Only last week
> Ah murdered a rock
> Injured a stone
> Hospitalized a brick
> Ah'm so mean
> Ah made medicine sick

❷ As a noun

The ritualized repartee of (especially younger) black men, associated with *hip* or *cool* street talk, traditionally known as *soundin, cappin,* and *playin the dozens*. It includes brash assertions, clever taunts, and calculated insults. Rapping has also been associated with *hip hop*, a flamboyant youth style originating in the streets of the South Bronx in New York City in the early 1970s, including graffiti-style art, break-dancing, and Afrocentric ways of dressing.

❸ As a verb

Performing a rhyming and usually improvised monologue against a background of music with a strong beat to which the style and rhythm of speech conforms. In a street, the music was often in the 1980s and 90s from a portable radio/cassette-player (a *ghetto-blaster* or *boom-box*), or played in a broadcasting studio from a background of recorded music or as a heavy bass beat produced by a drum machine or synthesizer.

❹ As a noun

A song or poem performed in this way, the performer being a *rapper*, the outcome *rap music*. On television, the background to raps may be series of fragments of music and/or video scenes.

The journalist Jon Pareles has noted:

> **1990** Ask most pundits about rap music, and they'll describe it as rude, jumbled noise. A few others may consider it million-selling post-modernism in audible form—songs as mix-and-match collages that treat the history of recorded music as a scrap heap of usable rubble and, often, trade narrative and logic for a patchwork of bragging, storytelling, speechifying and free-form rhymes. . . . It had to happen, sooner or later, that popular music would reflect the ubiquity of television—and it's true to American musical history that a black subculture picked up the new rhythms first. . . . To say that rap reflects television doesn't discount its deep roots in black culture; the networks didn't invent rap, ghetto disk jockeys did. Rap comes out of the story telling and braggadocio of the blues, the cadences of gospel preachers and comedians, the percussive improvisations of jazz drummers and tap dancers. It also looks to Jamaican 'toasting' (improvising rhymes over records), to troubadour traditions of social comment and historical remembrance, and to a game called 'the dozens,' a ritual exchange of cleverly phrased insults.
> – 'The Etymology of Rap Music', *The New York Times*, January

Pareles considers that rap's chopped-up style reflects the impact of television, in which programmes are accompanied and interrupted by commercials, previews, snippets of news, and using a remote control to 'zap' from channel to channel. He quotes as an example the following lines from 'Bring the Noise', by Carlton 'Chuck D' Ridenhour of the group Public Enemy:

> Bass! How low can you go?
> Death row. What a brother knows.
> Once again, back is the incredible the rhyme animal
> the incredible D, Public Enemy No. 1
> 'Five-O,' said, 'Freeze!' and I got numb
> Can I tell 'em that I never really had a gun?
> But it's the wax that Terminator X spun
> Now they got me in a cell 'cause my records, they sell!
> [*brother* (a fellow black man), *Five-O* (a reference to the TV cop
>   show *Hawaii Five-O*), *the wax* (an LP record), *spun* (played),
>   *Terminator X* (a disc jockey)]

Word-play is prevalent not only in rap but also in the names the performers give themselves, which have tended to have at least the following four aspects: alliteration, often focused on the consonants of *dee-jay* (DJ: 'disc jockey'), as in *Chuck D*, *Jazzy Jeff*, *LL Cool J*, and *Jam Master Jay*; coolness and hipness, as in *Ice T*, *Ice Cube*,

Kid Frost, *Easy E*, and *Mellow Man Ace*; the dramatization of menace, as in *Red Alert*
and *Terminator X*; providing an African connection, as in *Afrika Bambaataa*
and *Queen Latifah*. The explosion of interest and participation in rap both in and
beyond the African-American community in the 1990s includes a fertile, febrile,
brash, and showy creativity in the use not only of Black English but also in the
language of reviews of popular music and entertainment. Eclecticism rules. Some
comments and examples from the press are:

1994:1 Ice-T's 'DIE PIG DIE'

Home Invasion specifically set out to 'infect white kids with black
rage,' while Body Count's debut, a fairly blatant appeal to the
millions of whites buying Guns N' Roses and Nirvana, included
not only Cop Killer ('I'm about to kill me somethin'/a pig stopped
me for nothin'/DIE PIG DIE') but KKK Bitch, a song boasting about
the band's white groupies, citing a Grand Wizard's daughter and
Tipper Gore's 12-year-old nieces. And now he's lecturing the
nation's schoolkids . . . 'America is a vicious killing machine,' he
tells the students, 'based on rip-offs, lies, cheating and murder . . .
The pilgrims were some corrupt muthafuckers.'

– Jim Shelley, 'Ice-T's new look', *The Guardian Weekend*, 13 August

1994:2 Millions of 'wiggers'

They are certainly listening to him: millions of them, usually
under the age of 20, from coast to coast. Most listeners, however,
are not the dispossessed black ghetto-dwellers he portrays, but
white suburban adolescents who wouldn't know one end of an
Uzi from the other. According to *Newsweek* magazine, the largest
segment of the rap audience is white—'wiggers', in the
vernacular, wannabe white niggers.

– Ben Macintyre, 'Shooting from the Lip', *The Times Magazine*, 19 March

1996 Count Bass D

Dwight Farrell a/k/a Count Bass D is one of those rare rappers who
is a musician too. . . . Bass D's first album 'Pre-Life Crisis'
(Work/Sony), a rap record for people who don't like rap, features
breezy horn lines over his own drums, bass and keyboards. Riffs
infer blues, jazz, bossa nova, gospel and funk music. His raps are
hard-hitting but mellifluous, minimum-expletive and laugh-
sprinkled. . . . There is . . . a loser's dirge about being 'so broke
I can't even pay you no mind' and a reverbed round from '*Frère
Jacques.*'

– Mike Zwerin, 'Count Bass D: Rap for People Who Like Music', *International Herald
Tribune*, 14 February

1997 Salt-N-Pepa 'n' Da Brat

It's 4 o'clock on a rainy Wednesday afternoon at the MTV studios
in New York, and Cheryl (Salt) James and Sandi (Pepa) Denton are
quietly making their way through wardrobe and makeup. The
group's deejay, Dee Dee (Spinderella) Roper, is taking a nap in the
green room. The Queens of Rap just released their first album in
four years, appropriately titled 'Brand New'. But here in the
tiresome round of publicity and promotion, it's just the same ol'
same ol'. . . . Although the group members are only in their late
20s . . . , Salt-N-Pepa are the godmothers of rap, young women
who opened the door for such acts as Queen Latifah, Li'l Kim and
Da Brat.

– Veronica Chambers, 'Rapping on Their Own: Salt-N-Pepa have a new CD and newfound
faith', *Newsweek*, 3 November

The influence of rap is now international and has affected various other kinds of popular performance poetry and song.

Yiddish, Hebrew, and Jewish English

The term *Jewish English* refers to kinds of English used by Jews anywhere in the world but, after Israel, the US is probably the most significant place for Jewish English usage, and within the United States the city of New York. Although both the concept and the term are recent, kinds of Jewish English have existed for as long as Jews have been speaking the language, both in and beyond their own communities. At present, the most common variety is an English influenced by Yiddish and Hebrew and used chiefly by Ashkenazim (Jews with a Central and Eastern European background). This variety has introduced many words into both American and British English, many of them more colloquial than standard, as for example *maven, nebbish, nosh,* and *shlep.* The following list primarily describes American Ashkenazic English, which is representative of American Jewish English at large.

Pronunciation

1 Certain features are still heard of the New York English of the first generations of Jewish immigrants from Eastern Europe (*c.*1880–1940), including the pronunciation of such words as *circle, nervous, first* as something close to 'soikl', 'noivis', and 'foist'.

2 A widespread feature is the replacement of final *e* in words of Yiddish origin in *pastrame, khale, shmate, tate,* and *Sore* with *-i,* as in *pastrami, khali* ('Sabbath loaf'), *shmati* ('rag'), *tati* ('daddy'), and *Sori* ('Sarah').

3 Numerous features of speech, including pitch, loudness, tone, voice quality, and speed, reflect an expansive and vigorous Yiddish conversational style.

Grammar and idiom

1 Some verbs are used in a non-standard absolute way: *Enjoy, enjoy* ('Enjoy yourself'); *Go figure* ('Work it out for yourself'); *I'm entitled* (to have or do something).

2 The use of inversion for emphasis and wry comment: *A roof over our heads we have*; *Well, OK, he can write, but Shakespeare he is not.*

3 The frequent use of Yiddish constructions, spreading into especially New York colloquial usage: *You want I should go?* ('D'you want me to go?'); *He's a boy is all* (= that's all); *Again with the complaints!* ('Complaining again!'); *Enough with the talk* ('Enough talking'); *Begin already!* ('So begin/Get started!'); *They don't know from nothing* ('They really don't know anything').

4 Anglicized Yiddish idioms have spread into general US usage, and further: *Get lost!*; *Eat your heart out*; *I need it like a hole in the head*; *I should live so long* ('I would need to live a long time to see that'); *You should be so lucky* ('You are never going to be so lucky').

5 The use of rhetorical questions (usually translations from Yiddish) is frequent and similarly spreading: *Who needs it?* ('This is a problem I/we don't need');

What's with all the noise? ('Why all this noise?'); *So what else is new?*
('Everybody knows that'); *What's to forgive?* ('There's nothing to forgive').

Vocabulary and usage

1 Yiddish and Hebrew loanwords integrated into English in four ways:

- by dropping infinitive endings (*davn* 'pray', from Yiddish *davnen*), then
  giving the verb English inflections (*davns, davned, davning*).
- by replacing Yiddish and Hebrew plural forms (*shtetlekh* 'small towns',
  Shabatonim 'Sabbath social gatherings') with English plurals (*shtetls,
  Shabatons*).
- by forming new derivatives with English affixes (*shlep* 'drag, move or go
  with difficulty': *shleppy, shleppily, shleppiness, shleppish, shleppishly*).
- by extending the function of loans: for example, the Yiddish interjection
  nebish 'a pity' (with the spelling *nebbish*), used as an adjective meaning
  'pitiful, unfortunate' (*a nebbish character*), and as a noun meaning
  'unfortunate person, poor devil' (*What a nebbish!*).

2 Many Yiddishisms and Hebraisms relating to Jewish life: *shadkhn*
('matchmaker'); *hesped* ('eulogy'); *kanehore* ('preserve us from the evil eye');
halevay ('would that it were so').

3 Hybrid compounding of Yiddish and Hebrew words with English words: *matse
balls* ('round dumplings'); *shana tova card* (a Jewish New Year card), *sforim
store* (a Jewish bookstore).

4 Semantic shifts in English words because certain Yiddish words are similar in
form but not meaning: *learn* ('study (the) torah' (the law), from Yiddish *lernern*
'to study'); *give* meaning 'take', from *gebn* ('take'), as in *Give a look*; *by* meaning
'with', from *bay* ('with'), as in *The money is by him*.

5 Abbreviations for: vulgarisms of Yiddish origin, as with *TL* ('sycophant') from
Yiddish *tokhes leker* ('ass/arse-licker'); pejorative terms with English
components, such as *JAP* ('Jewish American Princess'); traditional Yiddish
and Hebrew expressions (*B'H* 'with God's help'; the acronym *zal*, meaning
'of blessed memory').

6 Several Yiddish word elements have become more widely productive:

- The element *shm-* in many dismissive reduplicative constructions: *Oedipus-
  shmoedipus, so the boy loves his mother!* ('This doesn't involve the Oedipus
  Complex!', referring to the misuse of psychoanalysis); *Rich-shmich—money
  isn't everything*.
- The suffix *-nik*, for a person, as in: *beatnik, Freudnik, kibbutznik, peacenik,
  real-estatenik, spynik*.
- The diminutive of endearment *-ele*, often appended to English given names
  (*Stevele, Rachele*), sometimes with a doubling of diminutives, as *-inkele* and
  -chikele (*Debbiinkele, Samchikele*), and sometimes with common nouns
  (*roomele, roomkele, boyele, storele, storkele*).

In addition, speakers and writers of Jewish background often replace terms which
have un-Jewish (and particularly Christian) connotations with others that are more

neutral or comprehensive: preferring *first name* or *given name* to *Christian name*; preferring *CE* ('Common Era') and *BCE* ('Before the Common Era'), both Jewish English coinages, to *AD* and *BC*; avoiding idioms that allude to Christian themes and practices, such as *cross one's fingers, knock on wood/touch wood, the gospel truth, Christ! Jeez!*; shunning usages with anti-Semitic denotations or connotations, such as *Hymietown* (New York City), *jew down* ('to bargain sharply with'), *Shylock*, and *Yid.*

Jewish English has played an important role in the works of many American (as well as British, Canadian, and South African) writers of Jewish origin, among them Saul Bellow, Joseph Heller, Dan Jacobson, Bernard Malamud, Mordecai Richler, Philip Roth, and Israel Zangwill (who coined the phrase 'melting pot' to describe the USA).

Spanish, English, and Spanglish

> **2001** *?Entiende Ud. Español?* If your answer to, 'Do you understand Spanish?' is 'no,' get ready to be left behind. With the astonishing surge over the last decade in the Hispanic population in the United States, speaking Spanish is becoming more of a necessity than a choice in many parts of the country. From feed lot managers in Nebraska to New York City stockbrokers, Americans are scrambling now to learn a language spoken by many of the 35.3 million Hispanics in the United States.
>
> – 'Si usted no habla español, puede quedar rezagado (If you don't speak Spanish, you might be left behind): Spanish study booms in USA', Deborah Sharp, *USA Today*, 9 May

Spanish has in fact been spoken longer than English in what is now the USA. The Spanish settlement of San Agustin, Florida, dates from 1565, various areas in New Mexico were settled in 1598, and settlements in California were established from 1769. As the English-speaking US expanded, it incorporated territory originally held by Spain (Florida), France (the Louisiana Purchase), and Mexico (the Southwest and extreme West, from Texas to California and Nevada), in all of which Spanish was in use. Although statehood for the Territory of New Mexico was delayed until 1912 at least in part because of lack of English-speaking citizens, Spanish was later granted legal status there along with English. Puerto Rico became associated with the US in 1898 and currently has Commonwealth status, Puerto Ricans having US citizenship. As a consequence of such social and political complexity, however, Spanish-speaking residents in the US may share the same mother tongue but are far from homogeneous, including communities and individuals from every part of the Spanish-using world, notably Mexicans and Central Americans in the West, Central Americans and Puerto Ricans in New York City, and Cubans in Florida.

In the United States, the term *Hispanic* has become generic for people of Spanish-speaking Latin-American (and often indigenous 'Indian') background and their culture and traditions, especially if they have established or are seeking to establish themselves in the US. This meaning has gained priority over the more traditional international use of the word as an adjective to cover all Spanish-related culture anywhere and at any time (as in *Hispanic civilization*). It is used as both a noun (as in *local Hispanics*) and an adjective (as in *Hispanic/hispanic cuisine*); the first use here has a capital, but the second may (following English orthography) or may not (following Spanish orthography).

There has been a steady flow of two kinds of borrowing from Spanish into American English since the nineteenth century, mainly in the Southwest:

❶ Unadapted Spanish words

Well-established words unchanged from Spanish mainly relate to life in the Southwest, as with *arroyo, bronco, cantina, chaparral, corral, gringo, mesa, patio, rancho, rodeo, tequila, vaquero*. More recent adoptions fall into two further broad categories: social usages, such as *jefe, macho, machismo*, and more pervasively such culinary terms as *burrito, chiles rellenos, flautas, frijoles, frijoles refritos* (also 'refried beans'), *nacho, pan dulce, salsa, taco, tortilla*. Hybrid compounds are common, as with *taco sauce* and *tortilla chips*, and many terms have become international.

❷ Adapted Spanish words

Adapted words include: *alligator* (from *el lagarto* 'the lizard'); *buckaroo* (from *vaquero* 'cowboy', perhaps influenced by African-American *buckra* 'white man'); *chaps* (abbreviating *chaparajos*, a probable blend of *chaparral* and *aparejos*, 'gear for the bush'); *lariat* (from *la reata* 'the means of tying up, a lasso', *lasso* itself being from Spanish *lazo* 'noose', and generally pronounced 'lassoo' in English); *mustang* (from *mestengo* 'a stray beast'); *ranch* (a straight adaptation of *rancho*, a term also sometimes used in the Southwest).

The lists indicate that some doublets have come into existence, as with *rancho* and *ranch*, *vaquero* and *buckaroo*, with only slight differences in meaning. In addition, some Anglicized Hispanic usages that are now international are Native-Americanisms, as with *avocado, chocolate, coyote*, and *peyote*, all from Nahuatl (the language of the Aztecs and the main indigenous language of Mexico): *ahuacatl* (also meaning 'testicle'), *chocolatl, coyotl*, and *peyotl*.

An informal blend of Spanish and English emerged in the 1960s, initially referred to pejoratively as *Spanglish* (now a fairly everyday name for the variety), probably on the analogy of *franglais*, which runs *français* and *anglais* together). Although the term is not confined to the US, it is more common there, referring to all or any of several mixtures of Spanish and English, from the use of adopted words and loan translations to code-switching among bilinguals. Occasionally, the term appears in Spanish as *el espanglish*, and the reverse condition, in which Spanish is influenced by English, is called *el englañol*. English-influenced Spanish is often referred to humorously but negatively in the Southwest as both *español mocho* ('chopped-off Spanish', from *mochar* 'to cut limbs off trees') and *español pocho* ('stunted Spanish', from Nahuatl *potzi* 'short, tailless'). At its broadest, the term *Spanglish* covers:

❶ Learner Spanish

The pidgin-like Spanish of some English-speakers, including so-called 'Learner Spanish'

❷ Anglicized Spanish

A non-standard Spanish containing adoptions from English (such as *wachar* 'to watch', *pushar* 'to push') and English senses attached to traditional Spanish words, as with *asistir* ('to assist, help') and *atender* ('to attend [school]').

❸ Calques

Loan translations such as *llamar pa(ra) (a)tràs* ('to call back' on the telephone).

❹ Hybridization

Code-switching, such as *Sàcame los files for the new applicants de alla!* ('Get me the files for the new applicants from over there').

In effect, a continuum exists between full conventional Spanish and full conventional English. The Puerto Rican linguist Rose Nash has identified four points along this continuum as *espanõl*, *englañol*, *Spanglish*, *English* while the Chilean linguist Lucía Elias Olivares has for the Spanish dimension alone the five points *standard Spanish*, *popular Spanish*, *mixed Spanish*, *Caló*, and *code-switching*. In this model, *mixed Spanish* contains loans and loan translations from English, and *Caló* is a hybrid secret language descended in part from the *germanía* ('brotherhood', the argot of the Spanish-using underworld) and associated mainly with adolescent boys in gangs, who rapidly alternate Spanish and English.

Now a common noun and adjective in American English, *Latino* is an adoption of the Spanish word for 'Latin' as used in the Americas for either a person of Latin-American background or descent (especially if Spanish-speaking and domiciled in the US) or anything relating to such a person and background. Although usually written with a capital *L*, it also occurs as *latino*. The masculine plural form is *Latinos/latinos* and a feminine form is often used for women: *Latina(s)/latina(s)*.

Latino was first used by US-born Hispanics in the Southwest to refer—often pejoratively—to recent immigrants from Mexico, as opposed to longer-established and more Americanized Hispanics who in their turn have been known to Mexicans —often pejoratively—as *Pochos* ('Shorties', meaning 'locals': see above). *Chicano* is a clipping of the Spanish *mexicano* ('Mexican'), with a local pronunciation like 'metshicano', and is written both with and without a capital. *Chicano* became popular in the 1960–70s during the US civil-rights movement in the Southwest as a means of encouraging Hispanic ethnic pride: that is, not to see oneself or be considered by others Spanish or Mexican or American, but a unique combination of all three.

To some, the term implies militancy or radicalism, as a consequence of which they may prefer *Mexican-American* or the more generic *Latino/latino* and/or *Hispanic/hispanic*. The terms *Chicano English* and more formally *Mexican-American English* refer both to English learned as a second language by people of Mexican background and to the usage of Mexican Americans at large, regardless of whether they are bilingual or have shifted wholly or mainly to English. The variety is affected and characterized in at least four ways: through carry-overs from Spanish, institutionalized learners' errors, contact with various American English dialects, and novel developments within the community. It is therefore difficult to distinguish between contemporary and historical interference from Spanish in a community that includes first-generation learners, bilinguals of varying competence, and near-monolingual English-speakers of Hispanic descent. Some Chicano highlights are:

Chicano pronunciation

1 The vowel sound 'ee' for short *i*, as in 'sheep' for *ship*.

2 The use of *s* for *z*, as in 'present' for *present*.

3 The use of 'sh' for *ch*, as with 'sheeken' for *chicken*.

4 A tendency towards a rising sentence-final intonation for statements.

Chicano grammar

Mass nouns often used as count nouns, as with *vacations* in *Next week we have vacations* and *applause* in *Let's have an applause for the speaker*.

Chicano vocabulary

The many unchanged adoptions from Spanish within the community include *quinceañera*, a special party for a 15-year-old girl, *comadre* ('godmother') and *compadre* ('godfather').

The term *Tex-Mex*, a rhyming blend of *Texas* and *Mexico* coined in the Southwest in the 1940s, is applied informally and at times pejoratively both to anything considered a combination of Texan and Mexican (commonly in food, cultural traditions, and language, especially along the common 1,200–mile border) and to anything of Mexican origin either in Texas or along the border (and often considered by Americans at large to be not as good or authentic as something that is 'really' Mexican).

Tex-Mex food includes *enchiladas* (rolled and filled *tortillas* with *chilis*), *frijoles refritos with salsa picante* (refried beans with a piquant sauce), and *tacos* prepared in the Northern Mexican style. In music, the term refers to Northern Mexican *ranchera* music adapted to modern themes, to North American life, and to electronic instrumentation, often with some English in the lyrics. In politics, the *pachanga* (a gathering featuring food, drink, and speeches) is an important Tex-Mex event. In language, the term refers to any of several varieties of Spanish (sometimes collectively known as *Border Lingo*) that may or may not show English influence, as well as to hybridized Spanish/English among speakers of Mexican Spanish, as in:

1986

Husband	Que necesitamos?
Wife	Hay que comprar pan, con thin slices. [to sales clerk]
	Donde está el thin-sliced bread?
Clerk	Está en aisle three, sobre el second shelf, en el wrapper rojo.
Wife	No lo encuentro.
Clerk	Tal vez out of it.

– Lorraine Goldman, 'Tex-Mex', *English Today* 5, January (Cambridge University Press.)
[*H* What do we need? *W* We have to buy bread, with thin slices. Where's the thin-sliced bread? *C* It's in aisle three, on the second shelf, in the red wrapper. *W* I can't find it. *C* Maybe we're out of it.]

Finally, and at some distance from the Southwest, the casual and almost facetious term *New Yorrican* or *Nuyorican* (with stress on the *ri*) blends *New York* and *Puerto Rican*, and has two linked meanings:

1   Among Puerto Ricans at large it is an informal and at times pejorative and dismissive term for Puerto Ricans who live in New York City or return to Puerto Rico from New York, as in: 'The New Yorrican students . . . seem to have plenty to say about their island brethren. "A lot of snotty people," said one high school student at the Padre Juan Rulfo School in San Juan' (*International Herald Tribune*, 17 February 1990).

2   In the form *Nuyorican*, it is the name given in 1975 by the Puerto Rican poet Miguel Algarín to a hybrid of Puerto Rican Spanish and New York English, as in *Aquí your credito is good* ('Here your credit is good'). This version of the usage seems to have grown popular.

Immigration from Latin America in recent decades has made Spanish the second most widely spoken language in the US. The influx of Cubans into Florida beginning in 1960 turned the Miami/Dade County area into a centre of Hispanic language and culture. In the Southwest, immigration from Mexico increased during and shortly after the Mexican Revolution (1912–15), after the Second World War, and again from the 1980s onward. Immigration from Central America also increased rapidly in the 1980s, because of difficult local conditions. The increasing Hispanic population has given some areas outside the Southwest and Florida a decidedly Latin-American flavour, including parts of New York and Chicago.

In all areas, programmes of bilingual education have been implemented as a method for bringing new immigrants to fluency in English in the shortest possible time. In reaction, however, many people (including some Hispanics and members of other immigrant groups) have supported the US English campaign, favouring a constitutional amendment to declare English the official federal language and eliminate bilingual education. They would prefer children from their communities to be educated entirely in English from the start, as was the case with most immigrants in the past, in an essentially monolingual melting pot. Others equally vehemently defend and extol the advantages of multilingualism.

The figures for the US census in 2000 make the general trend clear: the number of Hispanics of all backgrounds in the US is now roughly equal to that of the African-American community: *c.*35.3 million (*c.*3 million more than the Census Bureau had predicted). The black population is now between 34.4 and 34.7 million, the second figure bringing in those who (as the Census for the first time allowed) classified themselves as mixed (black and another race). A strict comparison between the two groups is not, however, a straightforward matter, because Hispanics can be of any race, as a result of which a proportion of them would also be counted in the Census as blacks, whites, Asians, and indeed Native Americans.

Two things, however, are clear. First, the growing Hispanic population has changed many things in many places, from marketing and advertising (notably on Spanish-language television) to kinds of political campaigning, all of which must now in many parts of the country include provision for Spanish as well as English. Secondly, the Hispanic population, like much of the so-called 'black' population of the United States is in fact genetically mixed. Together, despite tensions between them in inner-city neighbourhoods, the black and the Hispanic populations constitute *c*.70 million people (more than the population of many large countries). They are also, massively, speakers of distinctive varieties of English that do not correspond to the traditional 'American English' norms. When the total population of the United States (over 280 million) is cited as a major indicator of how many native speakers of English there are in the world, this figure of 70 million poses at least two questions: What kind of English is intended when such figures are cited, and how many of the 70 million cannot be cited as native speakers?

For some years there has been a controversy about the official use in the US of languages other than English, both at the state and federal levels, not so much as a matter of general principle but focused on the actual or possible use of Spanish in three areas: as a medium of instruction in public schools; as an aid to voting in elections; and for governmental and other official activities. Pressure for the official or semi-official use of languages other than English comes in the main from communities which wish to maintain their linguistic identity and culture, and has generated an often vehement counter-pressure to declare English the official language at the federal level, as it is already in a number of states. The movement variously known as *US English*, *English for US*, *English First*, and *Official English* is the present-day equivalent of the 'Federal English' campaign of the early Republic, the aim of which was to establish a single standard national language. US English has often been labelled xenophobic by its opponents, many of whom favour a multilingual and multicultural United States, or argue that such a state of affairs already exists and should be accepted, not suppressed.

The English Language Amendment (ELA) and US English

The ELA is a proposed amendment to the constitution of the US that would make English the official language of the republic. The aim of its proponents is to ensure that English retains its leading—indeed massively dominant—role in US society, most particularly in response to the increase in the number of speakers of Spanish in the country. As in the UK, and despite a widespread assumption to the contrary, English has no official status in the US at the federal level. For over two centuries, however, it has been the *de facto* national language, into which the vast majority of non-English-speaking immigrants have been assimilated.

In 1981, Senator Samuel Hayakawa, an American of Japanese background, from Hawaii, introduced a constitutional amendment to make English the official language. Hayakawa did not succeed in his aim, but founded with John Tanton in 1983 an organization called *US English*, to support and promote the proposed amendment. US English is a nationwide, non-profit-making, non-partisan organization, with several hundred thousand members and a board of advisers that has included the writers Jacques Barzun, Saul Bellow, and Gore Vidal, and the US-domiciled British journalist and media figure Alistair Cooke. It promotes English as a common bond integrating America's diverse population, and tends to view official French/English bilingualism in Canada (and the politics of Quebec versus the rest of Canada) as a source of disharmony that Americans should heed and seek to avoid.

In addition to its concern that English be made official, US English holds that every effort should be made, especially through education, to help immigrants acquire the language. At the same time, however, it rejects linguistic chauvinism, nativism, and xenophobia, encourages foreign-language study, supports individual and private rights to use and maintain languages other than English, and does not propose to prohibit forms of bilingual education intended to ease children into a fluent use of English.

Both John Tanton and Linda Chavez (a former president of the organization) have explained why US English was founded when it was: in the past, of the many languages in or brought to the US, none had the capacity to threaten English. They have argued that this state of affairs has changed, however, with the influx of Spanish-speaking immigrants, especially in southern Florida, the Southwest, and New York City. Members do not favour a change in bilingual education from an emphasis on transition (in which English replaces the mother tongue) to an emphasis on maintenance (in which a heritage language is retained alongside English). They also oppose the provision of bilingual Spanish/English ballots and comparable bi- or multilingual services.

There appears to be considerable popular and political support for the idea of 'Official English', 'English for US', and 'English First', as the primary aim of the movement is variously known. A 'sense of the Senate' measure declaring English official has been passed three times in recent years as an attachment to immigration legislation, but such declarations do not have the force of law. However, twenty-three states of the Union made English their official language in the 20th century:

> Louisiana 1912, Nebraska 1920, Virginia 1950, Illinois 1969,
> Hawaii 1978 (with Hawaiian), Indiana 1984, Kentucky 1984,
> Tennessee 1984, California 1986, Georgia 1986, Arkansas 1987,
> Mississippi 1987, North Carolina 1987, North Dakota 1987, South
> Carolina 1987, Arizona 1988, Colorado 1988, Florida 1988,
> Alabama 1990, Montana 1995, New Hampshire 1995, South
> Dakota 1995, Wyoming 1996

Public-opinion polls in a variety of locations have shown support for English as an official language at both state and federal level. Many of these have, however, been fairly casual, often conducted by newspapers, radio, and television, but some have been taken by reputable survey organizations.

US English has since the outset faced opposition. Many academics and ethnic leaders have seen it as a nativist organization pandering to the prejudices and entrenched attitudes of unilingual whites. A president of *La Raza* (a Hispanic political movement) has compared US English to the Ku Klux Klan, and the journalist James Crawford has linked the group to allegedly racist funding agencies—through organizations called *US Inc.* and the *Federation for American Immigration Reform* (*FAIR*), the latter also founded by Tanton. These agencies include the *Pioneer Fund*, created in 1937 to promote 'racial betterment' through eugenics. Crawford has written about a leaked memorandum by Tanton which expresses fear of Hispanic control over America and lists such dangers as Roman Catholicism, large families, and a tradition of bribery. Linda Chavez resigned as president when she learned of this statement.

American organizations that have either explicitly or indirectly opposed US English include: the National Education Association (NEA: a teacher's union), the National Council of Teachers of English (NCTE), Teachers of English to Speakers of Other Languages (TESOL), the Linguistic Society of America (LSA), and the Modern Language Association (MLA). Many see it as promoting an English-only policy rather than simply Official English, despite claims to the contrary. The English Plus pressure group (formed in 1987) has encouraged Americans to be bilingual: English plus one or more other languages. Supporters of its position have proposed a constitutional amendment of their own: the Cultural Rights Amendment, which would give legal backing to the preservation and promotion of ethnic and linguistic diversity. The Spanish-American League Against Discrimination (whose acronym SALAD offers an alternative to the melting-pot concept) also works for a more liberal approach to language issues in the US.

However, as the figures of the 2000 Census suggest, ethnic, social, and linguistic diversity within the United States is already immense, perhaps too large and widespread for organizations such as US English to serve as more than a rearguard action.

Canada

> **1997** When Margaret Attwood received a medal recently in New York, Robert MacNeil (co-author of *The Story of English*), said as he introduced her: 'She makes me feel my Canadianness. . . . Her characters misbehave on chesterfields, not sofas.' . . . [Many] people—even many Canadians—assume that their English is identical to American English. In fact, it is not: Canadian English is a variety of English in its own right. In the past, however, Canadians seeking information or advice on their language had to look to either British or American dictionaries and usage guides, neither of which reflected the distinctiveness of Canadian English.
>
> – Margery Fee and Janice McAlpine (eds), *Guide to Canadian English Usage* (Toronto: Oxford University Press)

The Breton explorer Jacques Cartier was the first to use the name *Canada*, in 1535, when he applied it to regions at the mouth of the St Lawrence River that later came to be known as the Gaspé and Saguenay. The story goes that when he asked for the name of the land in which he found himself, an Iroquois guide pointed to a nearby settlement and said *kanata* ('village'). *Canada*, the French version of the Iroquois word, was then applied to all the French territories along the St Laurent/St Lawrence. After the American War of Independence (1775–83), these lands became known in English as *Lower Canada*, in contrast to *Upper Canada*, the newer British settlements to the west. The two areas are now, in essence, the provinces of *Quebec/Québec* and *Ontario*.

After the conquest of Quebec, the various British and ex-French colonies north of the US came to be known as *British North America*, until Confederation in 1867, after which the official title of the land was the *Dominion of Canada*. However, for many years after that date, the people of the Maritime provinces—the ex-colonies of Nova Scotia, New Brunswick, and Prince Edward Island—continued to regard 'Canada' as a place off to their west. And later still, when the very distinct British colony of Newfoundland became a province of the confederation in 1949, many of its people persisted in thinking of, and referring to, 'Canada' as entirely another place—the mainland.

Mosaic, not melting pot

In 1996, the Canadian population was reckoned at close to 30 million, some 45% British and Irish in origin, 29% of French provenance, 24.5% other immigrant groups, and 1.5% Native Peoples. Whereas, in the neighbouring United States, the world's ethnicities go into a melting pot, Canada fits its 'New Canadians' into a mosaic. Such metaphors never quite fit, but the contrast of *mosaic* with *melting pot* expresses a subtle and serious difference north of the border.

At the federal level, English and French—the languages of the two avowed 'founding peoples' of Canada—are co-official, co-existing delicately one with the other as well as a multitude of 'heritage languages' that are either indigenous, like Inuktitut and Ojibwa, or imported, like Cantonese and Ukrainian. Currently, about half the schoolchildren in Vancouver and a quarter of those in Toronto speak English as a second language. In addition, because distinctive groups have tended to concentrate in particular areas, vernacular hybrids are common, as for example *Italese* in Toronto (created over generations of contact between Italian and English) and the ancient mix of English, French, and Native Indian spoken among the Métis (French: 'mixed people', mestizos). In 1970, William Kilbourn described the nation as a 'two-cultured, multi-ghettoed, plural community' (in *Canada: A Guide to the Peaceable Kingdom*), in which all kinds of language adaptation and accommodation have taken place. This condition is even more apparent at the start of the 21st century.

The Official Languages Act of 1969 confirmed the bilingual nature of Canada at the federal level and set up in Ottawa the Office of the Commissioner of Official Languages, who oversees the implementation of the Act and deals with complaints concerning the infringement of individual and collective language rights. Each of its publications is in both languages, bound as a single document. In a typically Canadian way, the section for each language is so printed as to look as though it comes first, the English an inverted addendum to the French, and vice versa.

Canadians whose first—and perhaps only—language is English have tended to say and write little about linguistic nationalism in their homeland, and in this they differ from Americans, Australians, Icelanders, Malaysians, and indeed from *French* Canadians, for most of whom the recognition and use of their language (as both French and *Canadian* French) is a matter of cultural and even ethnic security and survival. In addition, some thirty years ago, David Haberley succinctly put the English Canadian view of language and national feeling as follows:

1974 The normal and natural development of linguistic
nationalism has apparently been blighted by the peculiar
condition of Anglo-Canadian culture, caught between the
Scylla of England and the Charybdis of the United States.
– In 'The Search for a National Language,' in *Comparative Literature Studies* II, 87

The point is significant, yet no more so than the French Canadian dimension. Nationalism expressed through a single language is natural and straightforward only if it does not risk fragmenting a multilingual community that (by and large) seeks to be a nation in spite of language difficulties. In Canada, there is always the risk that a full-blown English-language nationalism might risk just that. Canada may in many ways be Kilbourn's 'peaceable kingdom' (above), but not always where French and English are concerned.

The relationship between English, French, and the communities that use them dominates the linguistic and often the political scene nationwide, even though there are areas of English Canada where French hardly reaches, and areas of French Canada where English is a rather distant drum. In the 1986 census, English was listed as the mother tongue of 61% (15.3 million people) and French of 24% (6.2 million people). However, English is spoken in the home by many for whom it is not a mother tongue, so that altogether some 16.6 million people speak English and some 5.8 million speak French at home. The proportion of speakers of French has been declining since 1951 (when they represented 29% of the population), but the proportion in the province of Quebec has remained stable at 81% while its English-speaking population dropped from 14% in 1941 to 10% in 1986. This is a typical Canadian paradox.

New Brunswick is the only officially bilingual province, while Ontario and Manitoba provide some services in French. Since the passage of Bill/Loi 101 in 1977, French has been Quebec's sole official language, but even so anglophones have their federal services in English, and their own hospitals, school system, universities, and other distinctive institutions, although public signs in English must remain discreet, and preferably off the street and out of the shop fronts. Nonetheless, English/French bilingualism has been increasing throughout Canada for several decades, assessed at 13.4% of the population in 1971, 15.3% in 1981, and 16.2% in 1986, but such bilingualism is in fact commonest in Quebec at 34.5%. Across Canada, over 250,000 English-speaking children are enrolled in French immersion programmes in which all teaching, except for English studies, is done in French.

Of the 2.9 million people (11% of the total) who in the 1986 census reported as their mother tongue languages other than English and French, 2.1 million listed European languages (the commonest being Italian, German, Dutch, Portuguese, Polish, and Greek) and 634,000 reported Asian languages (Chinese, primarily Cantonese, being the most common). The Native population is estimated at 756,000, *c.*3% of the total population: 331,000 Indians (with various languages), 27,000 Inuit (speaking Inuktitut), and 398,000 Métis (people of mixed European and Native origin), and people of mixed Native origin. Approximately 175,500 people reported one of 53 indigenous languages as a mother tongue, the majority listing Algonquian languages (116,820 speakers), then Athapaskan/Dene languages (17,080 speakers), then Inuktitut (22,210 speakers).

The most linguistically stable Native communities are the Cree, Ojibwa, and Inuit (Eskimo); in many others, the traditional languages are spoken only by a few elderly people. Native Canadians (the phrase is another paradox, as it is used only for a small percentage of the citizens of Canada) have suffered from a long-established national policy of educational assimilation, which created strains in their communities and weakened their languages and cultures. This policy has only been significantly challenged since the 1970s. Currently, by and large, Native Canadians speak hybrids of their own languages and English.

Canadian content, the United States, and French

Relations with the US have long (but not always) been peaceful, and are usually friendly, though from time to time ambivalent and prickly, especially on the Canadian side. Canadians often assert that Americans take them for granted and pay little or no attention to their interests, needs, wishes, and aspirations, a state of affairs that they also ruefully recognized as a kind of compliment: Americans perceive them, to all intents and purposes, as slightly quirky members of the same family (and large numbers of Canadians comfortably live and work in the US). A sense of domination has however regularly surfaced down the years:

> **1921** The United States makes a rule today and we follow it tomorrow; or, to put it differently, they take the snuff and we do the sneezing.
> – Samuel Jacobs, Canadian House of Commons, *Debates*, 30 March

> **1981** Ours is a sovereign nation
> Bows to no foreign will
> But whenever they cough in Washington
> They spit on Parliament Hill.
> – Joe Wallace, in *The Maple Haugh Forever*

Because of the similarity of American and Canadian accents, English Canadians when travelling abroad are generally resigned to being taken for American. It should be noted, however, that although they seem to be 'indistinguishable from the Americans, the surest way of telling the two apart is to make the observation to a Canadian' (Gerald Clark, *Canada: The Uneasy Neighbour*, 1965).

In addition to a cross-border prickliness there is an internal itch. The social, cultural, linguistic, and imperial tug of war between Britain and France included religious and social differences. Where English, Scottish, Northern Irish, and Welsh settlers have been mainly Protestant, the French and southern Irish have been mainly Catholic, a situation that once raised hackles but has now lost much of its force. More recently, in Quebec (by far the largest and most vigorous of the French communities, formerly with a powerful Church hierarchy), the *indépendantiste* movement has been largely secular, insisting on the province's nature as *un pays* ('a country') both in its own right and as the heartland of French Canada. Demands for kinds of independence have frequently been made, one form of which in recent years was called 'sovereignty-association'—a loose confederal liaison regarded by the rest of Canada as having one's cake and eating it.

Prominent for some decades in the vocabulary of language politics are three French terms ending in *-phone* and, following the French convention, generally beginning with a lower-case letter: *anglophone*, referring to someone able to speak English and to anything relating to English (as in *the anglophone minority in Quebec* and *anglophone objections*); *francophone*, the equivalent term for French (as in *the francophone minority in Ontario* and *francophone concerns*); and *allophone* ('other speaker'), an umbrella term for any native speaker of any other language, whether Italian, Mohawk, or Cantonese.

A third aspect of life is the sheer size of Canada, felt even in the cities strung out just north of the US border, but especially in the vast spaces of the sub-Arctic and Arctic. Northern images and descriptions have a significant place in Canadian literature, much like 'the bush' and 'the Red Centre' in Australia. Most Canadians may directly experience little of 'the Great White North', but it is archetypal alongside such stereotypes as the Mounties (the Royal Canadian Mounted Police/ *Gendarmerie Royale du Canada*) and huskies pulling sleds.

The term *Canadian* originated, like *Canada*, in the 16th century, deriving from and co-existing with the French *canadien*, and with three distinct historical senses. Initially, and well into the 19th century, it served to name not settlers but the indigenous peoples, as in:

> **1872** John was not a pure blooded micmac. His father was a
> Canadian belonging to some of the tribes along the St Lawrence.
>
> – as cited in the *Dictionary of Newfoundland English*, ed. G. M. Story *et al.* (Toronto:
> University of Toronto Press, 1982)

From the 17th century, however, *Canadian* was the name for French settlers along the St Lawrence, and from the later 18th it was extended to British colonists in both Lower and Upper Canada. In a Canadian context, the terms 'French' and 'English' tend to refer more to language than ethnicity, people being labelled 'English' if English is their language in Canada (whether they are English, Scottish, Caribbean, Italian, Ukrainian, or other) and 'French' if French is their language in Canada (whether they are French, Belgian, Mauritian, Haitian, or other). Only secondarily, and in identified contexts, do *English/anglais* and *French/français* refer to England and France.

In addition, and parallel to the use of *American* in the US, but less commonly, the term *Canadian* has been used as a name for English in Canada, and not only by Canadians:

> **1925** What language is spoken in the Dominion of Canada?
> Canadian.
>
> – James D. Gillis, *Canadian Grammar*, 3

> **1996** A new Canadian Dictionary of English, the first in more
> than a decade, was published this fall, and another, the Oxford
> Canadian Dictionary, is due out soon. . . . To those who chart such
> things, there is little question that, despite British roots and
> American influence, Canadian has arrived.
>
> – from an article by Howard Schneider of the Washington Post service in the *International
> Herald Tribune*, 11 November

Significant numbers of English-speaking settlers began to enter Canada after the signing of the Treaty of Paris of 1762, which ceded New France/*La Nouvelle France* to Great Britain. Most of them were from the already established colonies of New England and went to what later became the provinces of Nova Scotia ('New Scotland'), New Brunswick, and Prince Edward Island. During and immediately after the American War of Independence (1776–83), some 50,000 settlers—the so-called *United Empire Loyalists* (*UELs*) or simply 'Loyalists'—arrived from the newly established United States. Government promotion of settlement also resulted in the arrival from the US of at least 80,000 'late Loyalists' after 1791. By 1812, Upper Canada (with a population of *c.*100,000, 80% of American background) consolidated its values by fighting against attack from the US during the War of 1812. By 1871, the population of Ontario alone had risen to 1.6 million.

Although there are subtle arguments among Canadian linguists about the similarities and differences between Canadian English and Northern US English, it is clear that the Loyalist influx had a powerful effect. Broadly speaking, both Northern US and Canadian English have a common origin in the New World mix of British dialects, Canadian however apparently having a stronger association with the North of England, Scotland, and Northern Ireland. In addition, the Loyalists were by no means linguistically homogeneous: some had been in the US for generations, but others were more recently arrived, including many speakers of Gaelic. Since children generally adopt the usage of their peers rather than their parents, later British settlers had to accept the assimilation of their children's speech to a local norm:

> **1869** Listening to the children at any school, composed of the children of Englishmen, Scotchmen, Americans, and even of Germans, it is impossible to detect any marked difference in their accent, or way of expressing themselves.
> – William Canniff, *The Settlement of Upper Canada*

Some immigrants may indeed have embraced a North American style as a token of their rejection of England and its dominant values. As Catharine Parr Traill observed:

> **1836** Persons who come to this country are very apt to confound the old settlers from Britain with the native Americans; and when they meet with people of rude, offensive manners, using certain Yankee words in their conversations, and making a display of independence not exactly suitable to their own aristocratic notions, they immediately suppose they must be genuine Yankees, while they are, in fact, only imitators. . . . You would be surprised to see how soon the newcomers fall into this disagreeable manner and affectation of quality, especially the inferior class of Irish and Scotch; the English less so.
> – in *The Backwoods of Canada: Being Letters from the Wife of an Emigrant Officer*

In 1857 the Reverend A. Constable Geikie argued that Canada's 'newspaper and other writers should abstain from the attempt to add new force to the English tongue by improving the language of Shakespeare, Bacon, Dryden and Addison'. In saying this, however, he was resisting a process of adaptation already well advanced. Canadian writing in English began with such works as Frances Brooke's *The History of Emily Montague* (1769), John Richardson's *Wacousta* (1832), and the sketches of Thomas McCulloch and Thomas Haliburton in the 1820s and 1830s. In addition, there were exploration narratives, travel books, and early immigrant journals, marking the beginning of the act of possessing through naming that Geikie feared would produce 'a language as unlike our noble mother tongue as the negro patua, or the Chinese pidgeon English' (in 'Canadian English,' *Canadian Journal of Industry, Science and Art*, 2, 1857).

As a consequence of the major settlement patterns, the English of Ontario became the dominant (though not uncontested) variety in Canada, especially westwards through Manitoba, Saskatchewan, and Alberta to British Columbia, largely because settlement in the west was led by Ontarians, who provided the bulk of the middle and professional classes. It was also government policy to ensure that non-English-speaking immigrants conformed to the values of Ottawa and Southern Ontario, a policy mainly accomplished through education.

The debate on the possibility of a distinctive literary Canadian has been going on since the 1820s. Assertions began with Charles Mair's generation in the 1880s, and by the mid-20th century the writer Roy Daniells felt able to describe 'elements of style that may safely be called Canadian':

> **1947** No conscious Latinity, no marked or cumulative rhythm, no pronounced idiom or flavour in the diction, no hint of the grand manner or of rhetoric; on the contrary, a distrust of the sublime, the heroic and the pathetic [i.e., giving human attributes to nature]. . . . Above all it is *wary* and exploring. Life is unpredictable; facts are strange things: the words must move humbly and alertly to adapt themselves to the matter, whatever it may be.
>
> – 'Canadian Prose Style,' *Manitoba Arts Review* 5

Two years later, Lister Sinclair described literary Canadian English as characterized by 'the still small voice' of irony, noting that 'our famous calculated diffidence can be used as the final stroke of irony to make our small voice influential' (in 'The Canadian Idiom,' *Here and Now*, 4, 1949). These were hardly clarion calls.

However, English Canadian writers gained unprecedented attention in national and international terms at Canada's centennial celebrations in 1967. Change in educational, publishing, theatrical, and governmental institutions stemmed from and reinforced nationalist sentiment, including support for the development of a national literature—and readership—in English. Margaret Laurence became a key figure after the publication of *The Stone Angel* (1964), as she fulfilled her desire 'to take the language and make it truly ours, to write out of our own familiar idiom' ('Ivory Tower or Grassroots?', 1978). Concurrently, Margaret Atwood, Robertson Davies, and Alice Munro enjoyed unprecedented publication and attention, and increasing international awareness of English-Canadian writing has followed.

But bilingualism is never far away, whether it is a matter of what is printed on bilingual cornflakes boxes or the names of linguistic, literary, and other organizations. For the latter, in an English setting the English name comes first, as with

Canadian Linguistic Association/Association canadienne de linguistique (founded 1954), and in a French setting the French is first, as in *La Revue canadienne de linguistique/The Canadian Journal of Linguistics*. The *Literary Translators' Association/Association des traducteurs littéraires* was founded in 1975, and its abbreviations are mirror images: *LTA/ATL* (or the reverse). Because of Canada's high rate of immigration and large French minority, teaching English as a second language has been a major concern in schools, universities, and adult education. In the 1970s, several provincial language organizations were founded, including *SPEAQ* (*Société pour la promotion de l'enseignement de l'anglais, langue seconde, au Québec*: 'Society for the Promotion of the Teaching of English as a Second Language in Quebec'), in which the Frenchness of Quebec is fully displayed but at the same time mildly subverted by the acronym.

In order to reach and unite its far-flung communities, Canada has developed one of the most advanced broadcasting systems in the world. Radio and television in both official languages reach almost every part of the country. While the *Canadian Broadcasting Corporation* (*CBC*) operates national radio and TV networks in English and French, the privately owned *Canadian Television Network* (*CTV*) operates nationally in English only. In Quebec, in addition to CBC (known there as *Radio-Canada*), private French-language TV networks are operated by *TVA/ Télémetropole*, *Telemedia Communications*, and *Quatre Saisons*. The Quebec government operates *Radio Québec*, a French educational TV network. Private French-language radio stations and English-language TV and radio stations also operate in the province. There are CBC French-language TV production centres and radio stations in British Columbia, Alberta, Saskatchewan, Manitoba, Ontario, and New Brunswick. In addition, in Toronto, the private company Multilingual Television broadcasts to local ethnic communities.

The English of the CBC is more conservative than that of most Canadians, and the organization takes pride in the pronunciation and usage of its announcers and newsreaders. From 1940 to 1989, it maintained an *Office of Broadcast Language*, which from 1975 to 1983 produced 100 issues of an advice sheet called *You Don't Say*, promoting pronunciations such as *schedule* with 'sh' and not 'sk' and favouring many British over American pronunciations. However, the relative ease with which Canadian announcers can move to US networks demonstrates that there is little difference between network accents and styles in the two countries.

Both public and private broadcasting are regulated by *the Canadian Radio-Television and Telecommunications Commission* (*CRTC*). This government agency has the role of ensuring that the system 'should be effectively owned and controlled by Canadians so as to safeguard, enrich and strengthen the cultural, political, social and economic fabric of Canada' and that programming be 'of high standard, using predominantly Canadian creative and other resources' (Act, 1968). However, most Canadians live within receiving distance of US television and radio signals, and the CBC and independent stations have always had to compete for their audience share with US networks.

The CRTC has found it difficult to insist on rules for 'Canadian content' that run counter to general demand and might even drive private stations out of business. Nonetheless, it requires that the broadcasts of private stations provide 60% Canadian content; 50% between 6 and 12 p.m. The major source of programming has traditionally been the CBC. In 1985–6, Canadian content reached 77% on the English and 79% on the French television network. However, of the 24.2 hours per week that Canadians spent watching television in 1986, 64% was devoted to foreign programming. CBC Radio attracts 10% of the potential audience. Now that 80% of Canadian homes have access to radio and to TV signals on cable, which deliver many American and Canadian educational, public, and commercial channels, the CBC has to work hard to sustain a distinctive profile.

Kanajan, eh?

Canadians often use the particle *eh* (as in *It's nice, eh?*) where Americans use *huh*. Although this state of affairs is borne out by both research and general observation, until more comparative work is done, the view of Walter Avis (in 'So *EH?* is Canadian, eh?', in the *Canadian Journal of Linguistics* 17, 1972) that it is not uniquely Canadian must stand. As elsewhere, *eh* is used in Canada to mean *Could you repeat what you said*, but more commonly it is a question tag, as in *You do want to go, eh?* (= don't you?), or serves to elicit agreement or confirmation (*It's nice, eh?*) and to intensify commands, questions, and exclamations (*Do it, eh?*). It is also common in anecdotes and informal reports: *He's holding on to a firehose, eh? The thing is jumping all over the place, eh? And he can hardly hold on to it, eh? Well, he finally loses control of it, eh? And the water knocks down half a dozen bystanders.* This last use, anecdotal *eh*, is the most stigmatized.

Canadian words

Vocabulary that is distinctively English-Canadian has three main sources: the extension and adaptation of traditional English words to new ends; adoptions from indigenous languages; and adoptions from French.

❶ The extension and adaptation of traditional English words

Many British words have had their meanings extended and adapted to conditions in North America. Canadian therefore shares with American many usages relating to landscape, social life, and so forth, together with a range of usages uniquely its own, such as: the distinction between *prime minister* (federal chief minister) and *premier* (provincial chief minister); the use of the terms *province* and *provincial* to refer to the major political divisions of the country, most of them once distinct British colonies; the term *reeve* (formerly a chief magistrate in England) used in Ontario and the Western provinces for the elected leader of the council in a town or rural municipality; the term *riding* for a political constituency (compare the old divisions of Yorkshire into its *North*, *West*, and *East Ridings*, originally *thridings* 'thirdings'); the term *Native* (capitalized) as a non-pejorative noun and adjective for the indigenous peoples of Canada (*the Native Peoples*); the term *status Indian* (someone officially registered as a Canadian Indian); and *reserve*, contrasting with American *reservation*, as a term describing an area of land reserved for Native peoples.

❷ Adoptions from indigenous languages

There are two sources: the Canadian Indian languages (such as Abenaki, Cree, Dene, and Ojibwa: sometimes sharing expressions with the US) and Inuktitut (the language of the Inuit, perhaps sharing expressions with Alaska and Greenland). Such words tend to relate to flora and fauna, economic and social activities, travel, and survival, and may be divided into those that are now widely known elsewhere and those that are known only nationally or locally:

- **Internationally known borrowings**

    From Indian languages: *chipmunk* (a terrestrial squirrel, from Ojibwa); *husky* (a shortening of Algonquian *(h)usquemau*, the same source as for *Eskimo*, originating in the first element of the phrase *husky dog* 'Eskimo dog'); *moose* (a large elk-like animal, from Abenaki); *muskeg* ('boggy, mossy land', from Cree); *toboggan* (from Micmac *tobagan* 'sled', through French *tabaganne*). From Inuktitut: *anorak* (a kind of jacket, from *anoraq* in Greenlandic); *kayak* (a kind of boat, from *qayak*).

- **Locally known usages (virtually unknown in the rest of Canada or elsewhere)**

    In the Lower Mainland area of British Columbia (the city of Vancouver and its hinterlands), from Indian languages: *cowichan* (a vividly patterned sweater); *kokanee* (land-locked salmon); *saltchuck* ('ocean'); *skookum* ('big, strong'); *tyee* ('chief, boss'). In the Arctic North, from Inuktitut: *angakok* ('shaman'); *chimo* (a greeting or a toast before drinking); *kabloona* (a non-Inuit, a white person); *ouk* (a command to a sled-dog to turn right); *tupik* (a tent of animal skins). In the Prairies, from Cree: *kinnikinik* (a smoking mixture including sumac leaves and tobacco); *saskatoon* (an edible berry and the shrub on which it grows); *wachee* a greeting (from *wacheya*, in turn a Cree adoption from archaic English *what cheer*, parallel to Cockney *wotcha/wotcher*).

❸ Adoptions from French

In addition to the ancient legacy of French expressions in English at large, a range of distinctively North American and especially Canadian usages includes: the name *Métis* (a person or people of 'mixed' blood, the 's' not pronounced in the singular but pronounced in the plural); *portage* (the carrying of canoes past rapids); the terms *coureur du bois* (a French or Métis trader or woodsman); *voyageur* (a French-Canadian canoeman in the service of the fur companies; someone travelling the northern wilderness); *caboteur* (a ship engaged in coastal trade); *cache* (a place for storing supplies, a supply of goods kept for future use); *mush* (from French *marcher*, a call used to get sled dogs moving); *tuque* (a knitted cap); such contemporary terms as *anglophone* and *francophone* (usually without an initial capital, in the French style), and *caisse populaire* (a credit union, a bank-like institution, especially in Quebec).

Many expressions are common in particular regions (often for environmental or occupational reasons) and may not be nationally known at all or are known because they are special to a particular area. Thus, in the West, *boomsticks* are 66-foot logs connected by *boom chains* in order to hold back floating logs that will be towed to a mill; in the Prairies, *Calgary redeye* is beer with tomato juice added and a rodeo is a *stampede* (most notably the internationally famous *Calgary Stampede*); in the Ottawa Valley a *snye* is a side channel, specially one that by-passes rapids (from French *chenail*); in Quebec, *whisky blanc* is a colourless alcoholic drink (cf. American *white lightning*); and in Newfoundland, an *outport* is a coastal settlement other than the capital St John's.

The existence of the two official languages has led to various distinctive usages, including the use of *Canada* in the names of government departments, crown corporations, and national organizations (often with French word order, the attributive following the noun): *Canada Post*, *Revenue Canada*, *Air Canada*, *Loto Canada* (a lottery). French and English often officially mix, as in names like the *Jeunesses Musicales of Canada* and such formulaic hybrid signs as *Postes Canada Post*. During the Canada Games (in French: *Jeux Canada*), some anglophone announcers referred to them as the *Jeux Canada Games* as if *Jeux* were an English word that needed saying and not part of the official bilingual formula from which one takes only the part that fits one's language.

Quebec and the rest of Canada

Quebec/Québec is the name of both the largest province of Canada in physical terms (home to the largest French-speaking community in North America) and its capital city (founded by Samuel Champlain in 1608). The two are distinguished in French by masculine gender for the province (*au Québec* 'in Quebec province') and feminine for the city (*à Québec* 'in Quebec city'). Out of a population of some six million, 82% speak French and 16% English, with Italian and Greek notable among many immigrant languages and Cree and Mohawk notable indigenous languages. The first Europeans to settle in the region were the French in the 17th century; their colony was known as *La Nouvelle France* ('New France') until well into the 18th century. In its heyday, the French empire in North America stretched from the valley of the St Lawrence down the Ohio and Mississippi rivers to the Gulf of Mexico, limiting British westward expansion. In the late 20th century, however, Quebec is the only major French-speaking community in North America, although there are sizeable francophone communities in New Brunswick and Ontario in Canada, and in Florida, Louisiana, and Maine in the US.

French usage in Quebec descends from the speech of 17th-century Normandy and Picardy. Distinctive and varied, it has a broad form known as *joual* (pronounced 'zhwal': a variant of *cheval* 'horse'). The traditional standard of education and the media has been that of Paris, often however referred to as *le français international* ('International French'). Local French of all varieties and at most social levels has long tended to be stigmatized in France and in Quebec itself as a patois marred by accent, archaisms, and Anglicisms. As a result, many Québécois have had experiences similar to those reported by the writer Léandre Bergeron, who in the 1980s responded to the negativism of the French abroad and purists at home by treating Quebec usage as a language in its own right:

> **1982** 'You don't speak *real* French in Quebec.' This often heard
> pronouncement, said either with scornful condescendence or,
> even worse, with matter-of-fact naiveté, has always struck me.
> What can you say to it? How can you reply to someone who rubs
> you off the map with one sentence? To make matters worse, we get
> this not only from English Canadians but from Frenchmen as well.
> The two main cultural influences in our lives tell us that the
> language our parents taught us was not a *real* civilized language,
> but a peasant patois, a primitive gibberish.
> – from the preface to *The Québécois Dictionary*

British Empire Loyalists from the US, the first English-speakers in Quebec, founded the Eastern Townships to the south-east of Montreal. By 1831, anglophones of British descent were in the majority in Montreal itself, but an influx of rural francophones, who filled the ranks of the urban working class, had by 1867 reversed that trend, and by 1981, 66% of the city's population was French-speaking. Such facts explain why English as used in Montreal (and more generally in Quebec) is not as homogeneous as other Canadian Englishes. Rather, it exists as a continuum, from long-established unilingual anglophones similar to anglophones in Ontario through bilinguals of various kinds to francophones using English as a second language. Until 1970, Montreal was the economic capital of Canada, but many anglophone companies relocated, especially to Toronto, as a result of separatist pressures in the 1970s and early 1980s, notably under the government of the secessionist Parti Québécois (1976–85).

Much has been written in French on the effects of English on French in Quebec. In such works, the dominant role of English in North America has generally been viewed as pernicious, and francophones have often been urged to *éviter les anglicismes* ('avoid Anglicisms') and not *commettre un anglicisme* ('commit an Anglicism') in their French. The French of Quebec and Canada as a whole, however, is heavily influenced by both Canadian and American English, as with *bienvenu(e)* as the equivalent of *You're welcome* (in response to *merci* 'thank you'), rather than the *de rien* ('It's nothing') of France. There has been little comparable concern about the effects of French on English in Quebec. For socio-economic reasons, English was until *c.*1975 regarded in both communities as the language of prestige. In the last three decades, however, under the impact of pro-French legislation, French has gained in prestige and strength.

Quebec English has inevitably been heavily influenced by French. Many French usages have simply moved into local English, as with *autoroute* ('highway'), *caisse populaire* ('credit union'), *dépanneur/depanneur* ('convenience store, corner shop'), and *subvention* ('subsidy'). Anglophones who routinely speak French tend to use such loan-translated expressions as *give a conference* ('give a lecture', from *donner une conférence*), *sc(h)olarity* ('schooling', from *scolarité*), and *syndicate* ('trade union', from *syndicat*). The Gallicisms of francophones when speaking English range from such easily grasped expressions as *collectivity* ('community') and *annex* (the appendix to a document) to a commonplace misuse of such *faux amis* ('false friends') as *deceive* in 'I was deceived when she didn't come' (from *décevoir* 'disappoint'), *reunion* in *We have a reunion at 5 o'clock* (from *réunion* 'meeting'), and *souvenir* in *We have a good souvenir of our trip to Louisiana* (from *souvenir* 'memory').

The language situation in Quebec has been highly politicized for decades. In 1977, the passing of Quebec's Bill 101 (the Charter of the French Language) required among other things that public signs be in French only. This led to deliberate violations of the law, especially in English-speaking areas of Montreal, and the consequent imposition of much-resented fines. As part of the so-called 'battle of the signs', the English language rights group Alliance Quebec/Alliance Québec organized and financed the defence of five merchants accused of violating the law. The 'Chaussure Brown' (Brown Shoes) case went to the Supreme Court of Canada, which declared in 1988 that the section of Bill 101 dealing with signs was unconstitutional.

The Quebec government responded by passing a new law, Bill 178, which has allowed non-French signs inside stores but not outside—an ordinance mocked by some anglophones as 'the inside outside law'. To pass this law, the provincial government used a provision in the Canadian Constitution Act (1982) that allows provinces to pass and enforce laws that contravene the constitution for periods of up to 5 years. In the furore that followed, three anglophone ministers resigned from Quebec's Liberal government. A subsequent election brought four new anglophones into the predominantly francophone legislature, all members of the Equality Party, founded to support minority language rights in Quebec. By and large, the province's francophones support the language law with its ban on non-French signs, while anglophones are either against it or ambivalent.

In May 1980, a referendum was held in Quebec to decide whether the province would remain a part of Canada or seek a more independent status called 'sovereignty-association'. The referendum rejected the latter option, opening the way for Ottawa to seek the patriation of the Canadian Constitution: the British North America Act of 1867. Renamed the Constitution Act, and incorporating a new Charter of Rights and Freedoms, the Act was 'brought home' from Britain in 1982. René Levesque, the separatist Parti Québécois premier at the time, was however the sole provincial premier to refuse to sign the national agreement to patriate the constitution. In the years since then there has been a kind of mildly fluctuating stalemate between Quebec, the federal government, and the other provinces, the population of Quebec tending to vote in ways that have effectively played off Quebec City and Ottawa against each other. There is no majority in the province for absolute separation from the rest of Canada.

In 1987, the federal and provincial governments drew up the Meech Lake Accord in order to resolve the differences that led to this refusal and to establish a more generally acceptable association between Quebec and the rest of Canada. Robert Bourassa, the Liberal Party successor to Levesque as Quebec premier, put forward five requirements, among which was recognition of Quebec as a 'distinct society'. This point was accepted by the Prime Minister, Brian Mulroney, and all provincial premiers, although the premiers of several provinces had cited what they saw as Quebec's suppression of English language rights as a reason for resisting Quebec's demands.

Once agreement was reached, the accord had to be ratified by every province by the 23 June 1990. During the last-minute debate on the accord, however, the premier of Manitoba, Gary Filmon, insisted on holding hearings and putting acceptance of the accord to a vote in his legislature. Elijah Harper, a Native member of the Manitoba Assembly, blocked debate until time ran out, on the grounds that aboriginal rights had been inadequately served. The premier of Newfoundland, Clyde Wells, had insisted on presenting the accord to his legislature for a free vote, but, angered by federal pressure to ratify it before the deadline, adjourned his legislature without voting. The deadline passed and the accord died. As a result, amid a steady subsequent series of charges and countercharges, the constitutional and emotional gulf between Quebec and the rest of Canada remains unbridged.

Atlantic Canada: the Maritimes and Newfoundland

The coastal Atlantic provinces of mainland Canada are New Brunswick, Nova Scotia ('New Scotland', including Cape Breton Island), and Prince Edward Island. When Newfoundland is added, the collective term is *the Atlantic Provinces*. Although the traditional regional accents of the Maritimes differ considerably from usage to the west, the urban accents of Fredericton, Halifax, and other centres of population are part of the continuum of General Canadian. The territory is roughly the region called *acadien* (*Acadian*) by the French. In the seventeenth century, it was also claimed by the English and settled by both, changing hands several times until 1713, when it was ceded to the new union of Great Britain. A complex settlement history explains its variety of rural dialects, some of which were influenced by Acadian French, some by German (in Lunenburg County, Nova Scotia, settled in 1753), some by Gaelic (Cape Breton Island, settled 1802–28 by 25,000 Highlanders during the Clearances in Scotland), as well as various dialects of England. In 1783, the arrival of Loyalists after the American War of Independence almost tripled the English-speaking population.

A well-known shibboleth of local pronunciation is mentioned by a character in Margaret Atwood's novel *Lady Oracle* (1977): 'Being from the Maritimes, he said *ahnt* . . . whereas I was from Ontario and said *ant*' (for *aunt*). Regional grammar includes the use of *some*, *right*, and *real* as intensifiers, as in *It's some hot*, *It's right hot*, and *It's real hot*. Regional vocabulary shares some terms with Newfoundland and some with New England, and includes: *banking* (storing illegally trapped lobsters until the season opens), *barachois* (small ponds near the sea, which is held back by a narrow causeway, and by extension the causeway itself: from Canadian French *barachoix* 'sandbar', in Newfoundland also *barrasway*); *bogan* 'backwater'; *grayback* (a large ocean wave); *make* as in *make fish* and *make cod* (to dry fish or cod); *malpeque* (a famous local variety of oyster, from Malpeque Bay, Prince Edward Island); *sloven* (a long low wagon with a specially low back axle, to make loading easier); and *tern* (a three-masted schooner).

Newfoundland, whose local nickname (like Gibraltar) is *The Rock*, was England's first colony, as a result of which English has been spoken there for some 500 years. The capital, St John's, was founded as a base for English fishermen in 1504 and Sir Humphrey Gilbert claimed the entire island in 1583. In 1855, the colony of Newfoundland became self-governing, and in 1949, after two close votes, it was united with Canada, becoming a province that includes the adjacent mainland area of Labrador. Its population in 1981 was 567,681. Its languages are English and French, together with the Amerindian languages of Labrador. There are no Native languages on the island, because (as with Tasmania in Australia) the indigenous people, the Beothuk, were exterminated.

Newfoundland usage is the oldest variety of English in the Americas, a fact that is not currently well recognized. It derives from the speech of early settlers from the English West Country and later Ireland, and is the outcome of long, stable settlement and relative remoteness. The isolation, however, should not be overemphasized: 'The women in these communities were isolated, while the men were not, because they travelled to find seasonal work sealing, logging, and cod-fishing' (*Dictionary of Newfoundland English*, 1982). Many Newfoundland *townies* have features of pronunciation, grammar, and vocabulary distinct from the rest of Canada, and the varied dialects of the *baymen* are probably the most distinctive in the country. The English of Newfoundland is therefore more than a dialect of Canadian English: it is a variety with dialects and a standard of its own. Harold Paddock, in *Languages in Newfoundland and Labrador* (1982), delineated five main dialect areas on the island. In a survey by Sandra Clarke, the residents of St John's ranked six accents in terms of prestige: British Received Pronunciation, upper-class St John's Irish, Standard Canadian, St John's 'Anglo-Irish', and a regional dialect of the southern shore.

Pronunciation

1 Newfoundland speech is mainly rhotic, reflecting both an English West Country and an Irish influence. The West Country is exhibited in initial 'v' for 'f' and 'z' for 's' (as in 'a vine zummer' for *a fine summer*), the Irish in 't' and 'd' for kinds of 'th' (as in 'Dere was tree of dem altogedder' for *There were three of them altogether*).

2 Initial 'h' is unstable, sometimes added before the vowels of stressed syllables (as in 'helbow' for *elbow*), sometimes dropped (as in 'eel' for *heel*). Final consonant clusters are often simplified ('a soun in the loff' for *a sound in the loft*), and certain conventional vowel distinctions are commonly not made (*boy* being pronounced like *buy*, *speak* rhyming with *break*, and *port* with *part*).

Grammar

1 The use of *is* and *m* for present forms of the verb *be*: either *I is, you is, he is, we is, they is* or *I'm, you'm, we'm, they'm*.

2 The negative forms *baint'e* ('be ain't thee/ye') for 'aren't you', *idden* for the negative verb elements in 'I'm not', 'you aren't', 'he isn't', and *tidden* for 'it isn't', reflecting the influence of the West of England.

3 Distinctive forms of *do*, *have*, and *be*, as in 'They doos their work', 'I haves a lot of colds', 'It bees cold here in winter', and 'Do Mary work here?', 'Have she finished?', and ''Tis cold here now'.

4 In some areas, *-s* in all simple present-tense verb forms (*I goes, he goes, we goes*, etc.).

5 Weak rather than strong forms in some verbs that are regular in the standard language, as in 'knowed' for *knew*, 'throwed' for *threw*.

6 Four possible variants for the perfect: *I've done, I've a-done, I bin done,* and *I'm after doin*.

7 *He* and *she* used as substitutes for inanimate countable nouns: *We'd have what we'd call a flake-beam, a stick, say, he'd be thirty feet long.*

8 Expressions from Irish English, deriving ultimately from Irish Gaelic: *It's angry you will be*; *It's myself that wants it.*

Vocabulary

1 Expressions that are archaic or obsolete elsewhere: *angishore* or *hangashore* for a weak, miserable person (from Irish Gaelic *ain dei seoir*); *brewis* (from Scots, pronounced 'brooze') stew made from a mix of soaked ship's biscuits, salt codfish, and pork fat.

2 Words for natural phenomena, occupations, activities, etc., such as terms for seals at various stages of development: *bedlamer, dotard, gun seal, jar, nog-head, ragged-jacket, turner, white coat.*

3 *Screech*, a Scots word for whisky used for a potent dark rum.

4 A *livyer* ('live here'), a permanent inhabitant; a *come-from-away* (sometimes shortened to *CFA*), a mainlander or outsider.

The terms *Newfie* and *Newf* are informal names throughout Canada for a person born in Newfoundland and for Newfoundland English. The so-called *Newfie joke* (a version of the ethnic or regional put-down) became popular across Canada from the late 1960s. The Newfoundlander Robert Tulk published two collections of such jokes (*Newfie Jokes*, 1971; *More Newfie Jokes*, 1972), including: 'What is black and blue and floats in the bay?—A Mainlander, after telling a Newfie joke.'

Double-standard English and General Canadian

The United Kingdom has profoundly influenced the social institutions of Canada, as witness the monarchy, the Houses of Parliament in Ottawa, and the Canadian Broadcasting Corporation (CBC). Kinship ties with the UK remain strong, despite significant immigration from parts of the world where the British connection has been weaker (as with South Asia, the Caribbean, and Hong Kong) or non-existent (as with Vietnam). The generation that fought alongside the British in the Second World War has almost gone, the Governor-General is no longer appointed from London, and, where Britain's economic interests now focus on the European Union, Canada's lie principally with the North American Free Trade Area, in which the United States is dominant.

The Canadian population is highly urbanized and mobile, 80% living within easy reach of the US border. In response to the inevitable dominance of US usage, some Anglo-Canadians have tended to stress the British connection while others have concluded that to do so is pretentious, defensive, and/or confesses to another kind of dominance. However, studies of Canadian usage inevitably compare it with both the US and UK; in the past, they often did little more than that, but more recently the view that only highly distinctive varieties can be national languages with their own standard has been changing. In his essay in *The Canadian Oxford Dictionary*, J. K. Chambers notes:

> **1998** For an entire century, until the 1950s, Anglo-Canadian attitudes enjoyed a special prestige. The most abiding result for Canadian English . . . is the double standard. Wherever British and North American practices differ from one another in vocabulary, pronunciation or spelling, Canadians usually tolerate both. Not only can Canadians vary their pronunciation of *either* and *leisure* without arousing any comment, but different regions sometimes maintain different norms, as, for instance, Ontarians prefer the spellings *colour* and *neighbour* but Albertans prefer *color* and *neighbor*.

Here, Chambers typically says '*North American* practices', where commentators in both the US and the UK would probably have settled on '*American* practices': Canada drawing the short straw yet again. As far as the British and the Americans are concerned, if they think about such matters at all, the dual pressures on Canada come from two outside sources, not one source, the UK, pressing on a shared US and Canadian ('North American') usage. From the British and American perspectives, Canadians are free to make their own choices, but it is no surprise to anyone that the greater longer-term influence has been from the United States.

In terms of speech, Canadian usage is fairly homogeneous, the strong exceptions being the Maritimes and especially Newfoundland, with some distinctiveness in Quebec as a consequence of French. At least the five following observations can be made about a more or less pan-Canadian pronunciation:

❶ Canadian Raising

It is a shibboleth that Canadians pronounce words like *house* and *out* differently from Americans. The term *Canadian Raising* (J. K. Chambers, 1973) labels a raised position for certain double vowels (diphthongs) whose tongue position is lowered in most other varieties of English. In Canadian, the tongue is raised higher to produce the diphthong in such singular word forms as *bite*, *knife*, *tribe*, and *house*, *lout*, *mouth* than in their plural forms *bites*, *knives*, *tribes* and *houses*, *louts*, *mouths*. Studies of the spoken English of Montreal, Ottawa, Toronto, Vancouver, and Victoria show that Canadian Raising is a majority usage (over 90% in Vancouver, over 60% in Ottawa), but that there is also a trend towards Northern US values, especially among women under 40. This suggests that Standard American rather than Standard British or Standard Canadian is becoming the prestige variety. If so, linguistically at least, Americans are right about Canadians.

❷ The *cot/caught* distinction

Many phonological features shared with Northern US English are distributed distinctively in Standard Canadian: for example, the low back vowels have merged, so that most English Canadians have the same vowel sound in such pairs as *cot/caught*, *Don/Dawn*, *caller/collar* (although the quality of this sound varies). This merger is also widespread in the US (notably eastern New England and western Pennsylvania) and is spreading in the Midwest and West, but—curiously—a distinction in such pairs is maintained in US areas bordering on Canada.

❸ *T-flapping* and *t*-deletion

Especially in casual speech, many Canadians, like many Americans, pronounce *t* as *d* between vowels and after *r*, a feature known as *t-flapping*. Such pairs as *waiting/wading*, *metal/medal*, *latter/ladder*, *hearty/hardy* are therefore often homophones, Ottawa, for example, being generally pronounced 'Oddawaw'. In addition, as in the US, *t* is not usually pronounced after *n*, so that *Toronto* is generally 'Trawna'.

❹ Pronouncing *wh-*

Speakers of Standard Canadian tend more than speakers of Standard Northern US to drop the distinction between 'hw-' and 'w-', making homophones out of *what/watt* and *which/witch*.

❺ UK-related holdouts and variations

Some speech forms associated with Standard British appear to be holding their own and even gaining ground. Examples: *been* rhyming with *seen* and not *sin*; *anti-*, *semi-*, and *multi-* ending like 'ee' and not 'eye'; words ending in *-ile*, such as *fertile*, rhyming with *Nile* and not *nil*. However, different regional and social groups vary as regards the pronunciation of some words. Examples: *lever* (either like *fever*, UK-style, or *level*, US-style); *schedule* (with either a British 'sh-' or an American 'sk-'); *aunt* (with either the RP long *a* or the GA short *a*); and *route* (either rhyming with 'loot', UK-style, or with 'lout', a widespread US pronunciation).

In addition, Canadian English has a salient feature unknown to US usage, and one that distinguishes it from all other major varieties. It is, however, something about which Anglo-Canadians might feel ambivalent: the co-occurrence, at the federal/national level, of English and French. Although *spoken* French is concentrated in Quebec, New Brunswick, and eastern Ontario, *printed* French appears alongside English everywhere: from signs in post offices to packaged articles in supermarkets. In addition, where in the past in English-language broadcasts simultaneous translation displaced spoken French, recent CBC news broadcasts have let French speakers be heard, relying on commentators to make the message comprehensible to those with a limited or no knowledge of French.

A cardinal feature of Canadian English is therefore co-existence (or co-occurrence) with Canadian French, much as a cardinal feature of South African English is co-existence (or co-occurrence) with Afrikaans and such African languages as Zulu and Xhosa. Even so, however, there continues to be a tendency among English Canadians to see themselves as *the* Canadians. French Canadians find this particularly frustrating, as when a book in English that purports to discuss 'Canadian literature' does not mention any works in Canadian French.

Despite the dominance and wide distribution of English, it has not been easy for scholars to delineate and agree on regional aspects of Canadian English, and no statement about them is likely at present to be free from dispute. A long-established approach has, however, proposed a large area in which there is one more or less uniform variety, stretching from Ontario to British Columbia, balanced by several other distinct varieties to the east. The widespread central and western variety has commonly been referred to as *General Canadian* (a name analogous to *General American* and therefore tending to focus on pronunciation). It is also often used in a sense close to *Canadian Standard English*. The eastern varieties are all however long-established and distinctive, and pose necessary questions as regards how general General Canadian is or should or can be. They include the rural usage of the Ottawa Valley, the English of Quebec (both mother-tongue and as a second language), and the distinct and long-established speech forms of the Maritime Provinces and Newfoundland.

The heartland of General Canadian is Southern Ontario, largely centred on the Toronto conurbation. The middle-class variety of this dialect has long been perceived as the representative or standard form of Canadian English as a whole, in effect therefore the national standard variety. The distinctive Ottawa Valley dialect is spoken by mainly country people along the banks of the Ottawa River, from northwest of Montreal through Ottawa and north to Algonquin Park. It strongly reflects Irish usage from both Ulster and the South, with influences from Lowland Scots, Highland English, Gaelic, German, and Polish. A shibboleth of the accent is the local place-name *Carp*, pronounced 'Kerp'. Syntax includes *for to* as an infinitive complement: *She wants for to go*, and local vocabulary includes *(cow)byre* ('cowshed, cow barn'), *moolie* ('cow without horns'), and *weight-de-buckety* or *weighdee* (British 'seesaw', general North American 'teeter-totter').

Both scholarly and public perceptions continue to change. A recent consensus among scholars sees the term *General Canadian* as applying not so much to a traditional Southern Ontarian dialect as to a largely urban variety of educated speech, writing, and media usage that operates across the nation. Broadly in line with this approach, and more generously still, the term *Canadian Standard English* is increasingly likely to be interpreted as neither Ontario- nor indeed urban-specific, but as a synthesis (with appropriate minor variations) of educated professional usage across the nation. And in all cases, despite the mighty neighbour to the south and stresses and strain at home, this synthesis has the requisite Canadian content.

The Caribbean and Latin America

1996 It is now 500 years since the Caribbean first disclosed itself to Columbus and submitted its indigenous peoples and cultures fatally to European misjudgement. An emptiness of population followed while European adventurers made tentative calls, Englishmen among them. . . . Sir William Courteen's ship 'found' an empty Barbados in 1625 and his English settlers followed in 1627. So settled the English tongue permanently in the Caribbean, in the company of others. The many-faced generations of replacement peoples who followed through the centuries developed, though unrespected and ill-documented, ways of life . . . out of which evolved today's Caribbean culture. . . . As home-made, the Caribbean linguistic product has always been shame-faced, inhibited both by the dour authority of colonial administrators and their written examinations on the one hand, and by the persistence of the stigmatized Creole languages of the labouring population on the other.

– Richard Allsopp (ed.), *Dictionary of Caribbean English Usage* (Oxford: Oxford University Press), p. xvii

Many languages have been spoken in the islands and coastlands of the Caribbean and the Gulf of Mexico: indigenous, such as Arawak, Carib, Chibcha, and Maya; Atlantic European, such as Spanish, English, French, and Dutch, introduced from 1492 onward by explorers, merchants, and plantation managers; western African, such as Ashanti, Efik, Ewe, and Yoruba, spoken by slaves brought by Europeans to work their 'West Indian' plantations; local creoles that are in effect Euro-African hybrids; and Asian, such as Hindi, Chinese, and Javanese, spoken by indentured labourers, traders, and storekeepers.

The islands and rimlands of the Caribbean

Because the many languages of the region have interacted widely and richly over five centuries, the current situation is difficult to discuss without bringing in a great deal of detail, and harder still to discuss without controversy. However, from the perspective of the Western European languages and their creoles, and of English in particular, the situation can be broadly structured in terms of a varying 'surface' continuum of Spanish, English, French, Dutch, and even Danish (and some Portuguese) along with an equally complex substrate of influences from western Africa and indigenous languages, some extinct and some in use in several mainland regions (or 'rimlands', as Allsopp, above, has called them), by and large as follows:

❶ Spanish and Spanish Creole

On the mainland (Mexico, Central America, and South America), Spanish is the predominant language, and, with Spanish Creole, co-exists and mixes with Amerindian languages, most notably in Mexico, Guatemala, Costa Rica, Honduras, Colombia, Venezuela, Peru, and Paraguay. It is also present in Belize. On both the mainland and the islands, Spanish and Spanish Creole co-exist and mix with English creoles as follows:

- in Colombia, on the islands of San Andres and Providencia (formerly the British colonies of St Andrews and Providence)
- in the Dominican Republic, with Samaná English (originally imported as the language of freed slaves from the Southern US)
- in Honduras, especially on the Bay Islands
- in Nicaragua along the Miskito Coast
- in Panama, among immigrants from the Anglophone Caribbean.

Spanish is the norm in Cuba. In both Puerto Rico and Panama, it is dominant but co-exists and mixes with American English, which is also influential in the US Virgin Islands, the Bahamas, and throughout Latin America. In the Cayman Islands, Spanish co-exists and mixes with English. In addition, the varieties of Latin American Spanish contrast with European Spanish and with one other.

❷ English and English Creole

In the immediate Caribbean area, a mix of English and English Creole is the key usage in Anguilla, Antigua and Barbuda, the Bahamas, Barbados, Jamaica, Montserrat, St Christopher/St Kitts and Nevis, the Turks and Caicos Islands, and the British and US Virgin Islands.

- In Belize, this combination is dominant, but co-exists and mixes with Spanish, Maya, and Carib.
- In the Cayman Islands, it co-exists and mixes with Spanish.
- In such territories as Dominica, Grenada, St Lucia, and St Vincent and the Grenadines, it co-exists and mixes with French Creole.
- In Trinidad and Tobago, it is dominant, but co-exists and mixes with Bhojpuri/Hindi, French and French Creole, and regional Spanish.
- In Guyana, it is dominant, but co-exists and mixes with Bhojpuri/Hindi/Urdu and Amerindian languages. In the Netherlands Antilles it has some, mainly tourist-related use.
- In Puerto Rico, it co-exists and mixes with local Spanish, which is the primary language.
- In Colombia, Costa Rica, Honduras, Nicaragua, and Panama, minority English creoles co-exist and mix with Spanish and other languages.
- In the coastal southern states of the US, English is dominant, but co-exists and mixes with minority French and French Creole in Louisiana (notably in Cajun usage), and with kinds of Spanish (notably from Cuba) and French (notably from Quebec) in Florida. There are also Creole-related forms in some black communities in the southern states, as for example Gullah in the sea islands of Georgia and the Carolinas.

There is also competition in the region between British and American English as external influences whose standard varieties have variously served as reference norms.

❸ French and French Creole

The combination of French and French Creole is the majority usage in French Guiana, Haiti, and the French island *départements* of Guadeloupe and Martinique. French Creole mixes with English and English Creole in Dominica, Grenada, St Lucia, and St Vincent and the Grenadines.

❹ Dutch and Dutch Creole

In the Netherlands Antilles, Dutch co-exists and mixes with Papiamentu, a Portuguese-based creole with Spanish elements, and English has some use; in Surinam, Dutch and Dutch Creole co-exist and mix with several long-established and highly distinctive English Creoles (principally Sranan, Ndjuka, and Saramaccan) as well as with Hindi, Javanese, and Chinese. There is also a Dutch Creole in the US Virgin Islands.

❺ Danish and Portuguese

Danish was formerly used in the US Virgin Islands (earlier name, the Danish West Indies), but was displaced as the official language by American English in 1917. Anomalously, both a Dutch and an English Creole have been traditional there. Portuguese has also had some influence in the Netherlands Antilles and Surinam.

As the above list indicates, an intricately varied, class-related Caribbean continuum stretches from the high-prestige standard varieties of Spanish, English, French, and Dutch (as appropriate) to low-prestige 'deep' creoles (whatever their provenance). Creoles and near-creole mixes are the majority speech forms (technically, basilects at the bottom and mesolects in the middle of the social pyramid). Increasingly, 'deep' creoles are regarded by scholars as languages in their own right, part of a complex multilingual phenomenon known to the general population and those scholars alike simply as 'Creole', whatever the associated European language or languages in any given territory.

Consequently, and often confusingly, the capitalized form *Creole* on its own (as in *They speak Creole here*) can refer: (1) to any creole in any territory, as with *(Jamaican) Creole (English)* and *(Haitian) Creole (French)*; (2) to all the creoles of a single European language taken collectively, as with *English Creole, Creole English*, or simply *Creole*; (3) to all the creoles of all the relevant European languages looked at collectively, because of shared natures and histories regardless of any degree, or lack, of mutual intelligibility. Viewed from this perspective, language and people's perceptions of language in the Caribbean defy tidy traditional Euro-American models for the identification, classification, and discussion of language at large, and of any language on its own or in a 'family'. This situation suggests that in such regions as the Caribbean, West Africa, and India, traditional models of language are not comprehensive and flexible enough to handle everyday reality.

From Carib to Caliban

The word *Caribbean* derives from *Carib*, the name of the dominant Amerindian inhabitants of the Lesser Antilles when Europeans first arrived there. The Caribs were warlike and had absorbed or driven out many of the more peaceful Arawak communities shortly before the arrival of Columbus, whose first encounter was with the Taino, an Arawak group on the island of Hispaniola (today divided between the Dominican Republic and Haiti). The Caribs provided the English name for the region, first called the *Caribees* (from *Caribes*, the plural of Spanish *Caribe* 'Carib'). A notable feature of Carib life was that the men spoke Carib while the women spoke Arawak, probably because Arawak slave-wives were commonplace. *Black Carib* is the name of a language still spoken in parts of Central America by people of mixed Carib and African descent, transported there from the Lesser Antilles. Black Carib, which derives from Carib, contains borrowings from English, Spanish, and French.

The original Caribs ate human flesh. Through a scribal error that turned an *r* into an *n*, the Spanish word *Caribal* ('a Carib') entered English as *canibal* and in due course came to be written as *cannibal*. In the play *The Tempest* (first performed *c*.1611), Shakespeare's name for a character who is part-human, part-beast is *Caliban*, an anagram of *canibal*. In the play, apart from the sprite Ariel, Caliban is the only inhabitant of a desert (= deserted) island that might have been anywhere from the Mediterranean to the Caribbean. When the magician Prospero, the erstwhile Duke of Milan, is shipwrecked there, Caliban and Ariel become his slaves. Both want their freedom, but Ariel co-operates while Caliban grows steadily more resentful and angry. He asserts that Prospero treated him well at first ('Thou stroakst me, & made much of me'), then took the island from him and penned him on a rock. Prospero answers that at first he had indeed been kind to Caliban, but had imprisoned him because he tried to rape Miranda, Prospero's daughter.

> *CALIBAN*. Oh ho, oh ho, would't had bene done:
> Thou didst preuent me, I had peopel'd else
> This Isle with Calibans.
> *MIRANDA*. Abhorred slaue,
> Which any print of goodnesse wilt not take,
> Being capable of all ill: I pittied thee,
> Took pains to make thee speak, taught thee each houre
> One thing or other: when thou didst not (Sauage)
> Know thine owne meaning; but wouldst gabble, like
> A thing most brutish, I endow'd thy purposes
> With words that made them knowne: But thy vild race
> (Tho thou didst learn) had that in't, which good natures
> Could not abide to be with; therefore wast thou
> Deseruedly confin'd into this Rocke,
> Who hadst deseru'd more then a prison.
> *CALIBAN*. You taught me Language, and my profit on't
> Is, I know how to curse: the red-plague rid you
> For learning me your language.
> (Act 1, Scene 2)

Caliban rebels and helps Prospero's enemies, but their plot fails, and when the play ends Prospero frees Ariel, everyone departs, and Caliban is left alone to brood.

In the late 20th century, Caliban has been seen by some black writers in English as representing both Africans and West Indians, symbolizing their enslavement and debasement. Discussing the situation of writers in the black Commonwealth, David Dabydeen has observed:

> **1991** The pressure is to become a mulatto and house-nigger
> (Ariel) rather than stay a field-nigger (Caliban) . . . [but] . . .
> Caliban is [now] tearing up the pages of Prospero's magic book
> and repasting it in his own order, by his own method, and for
> his own purpose.
> – in 'On not being Milton: Nigger Talk in England Today', in Christopher Ricks and Leonard Michaels (eds), *The State of the Language* (London & Boston: Faber), 9

Many names were misapplied during and after the voyages of Columbus and other explorers in the 15th–16th centuries. Alongside *cannibal* and *Caliban*, and ultimately much messier in world terms, have been names associated with the assumption that the Americas and other remote lands were in fact India. Most notable is the word *Indian*, which has been used not only (appropriately) for natives of India but also for the indigenous peoples of the Americas (often also commonly known in the past as 'Red Indians') and even for a time of Australia. The name did not survive for the Australian Aborigines, but for many Americans the primary meaning of *Indian* is 'native American', associated with tomahawks and scalping.

The islands of the Caribbean have been commonly referred to as the *West Indies* (on the assumption that they were part of the *Indies*—also formerly the *Indias*— islands of an archipelago in the Indian Ocean which was as a result re-named the *East Indies*. The terms *West Indies* and *West Indian* have however become fixtures for the territories and inhabitants of former or continuing British Caribbean colonies, and their descendants elsewhere. Notable present-day uses of *West Indies* include the cricket team that represents the region (called *the West Indies* but nicknamed the *Windies*, from the abbreviation *W. Indies*) and the *University of the West Indies*, whose campuses are distributed among several territories. The ultimate irony is that the majority ethnicity in the West Indies today is neither East nor Red Indian, but of western African origin.

Caribbean English

Although English is the official language of the Commonwealth Caribbean (and of CARICOM, a common market for a number of English-speaking Caribbean territories), for most people in the region the standard internationalized forms of the language are more or less remote, acquired to varying degrees through schooling, the media, and activities in which their use is common and accepted, such as church-going and professional and business life, including tourism. Standard British has traditionally been the reference norm for the Commonwealth Caribbean, but the influence of US media and tourism has made Standard American a compelling region-wide alternative, in part because it is already significant in Panama, Puerto Rico, the US Virgin Islands, and the Bahamas. The political independence of a majority of Caribbean territories, and the self-awareness that goes with it, have been equally influential in reshaping attitudes towards standard usage of any kind—both inside and outside the region and in individual territories within the region.

In its broader geographical sense, the term *Caribbean English* covers the English of both the archipelago and the adjacent areas of Central and South America. The term may include the more northerly archipelago of the Bahamas, but does not include Bermuda, an island and British colony in the North Atlantic, despite similarities and historical links. In its narrower geographical sense, the term centres on the Lesser Antilles and Guyana, and perhaps Belize (formerly British Honduras), the region traditionally known as 'the West Indies' and formerly part of the British Empire.

In its broader linguistic sense, the term *Caribbean English* covers both conventional and creole usage; in its narrower linguistic sense, it refers not to regional English at large, with all its variations, but only to the part considered 'standard'—although there may be considerable debate about how standard the standard is in any Caribbean Anglophone territory and where the line is to be drawn between usage that is standard enough from an international point of view and usage that is markedly local and inclined towards Creole. It is only at the extreme ends of the continuum that English and Creole are decisively separated off, as in such a contrast as standard *The child is sick* and Jamaican Creole *di pikni sik.*

In writing and print demarcation is easy: the mass of such usage is as standard as anywhere else in the world. Texts in Creole are rare, largely restricted to humorous and/or satirical social comment, to expressions of local solidarity, and to literary and occasional formal texts, many of an experimental nature. In recent years, language scholars and others have developed distinctive conventions for Creole, as with *di pikni sik* (as opposed to, say, 'de picky sick', cf. *piccaninny*). Such customized orthographies remain contentious and are not widely used (see p. 236).

An already difficult state of affairs has been further complicated by the traditional classification of creoles as 'dialects' and/or 'creole dialects' of English. Younger scholars in the region tend to stress the differentness of the creoles from dialects of English in the UK and US, and tend to favour the collective, unifying, and capitalized singular form 'Creole'. In addition, Caribbeanists born earlier in the 20th century have generally used the term 'English' to cover both the standard and the creole, as in Frederic G. Cassidy and Robert B. Le Page's *Dictionary of Jamaican English* (1967, 1980) and John A. Holm and Alison W. Shilling's *Dictionary of Bahamian English* (1982).

In the approach followed by such scholars, the term *Caribbean English* tends to embrace everything from varieties of the standard language (such as *Standard Jamaican English* and *Barbadian Standard English*) to the creoles known collectively and variously as *Caribbean English Creole, Caribbean Creole English, Creole English, West Indian Creole*, and simply *Creole/creole*, and individually by such names as *Barbadian Creole* and *Trinidadian Creole.* Some Creoles, however, also have distinctive local names, as with *Patwa/Patois* in Jamaica and *Bajan* in Barbadoes (from *Barbadian*).

Following on from this model, it can be said that the use of English in the Caribbean ranges from local standard and near-standard varieties (known to linguists as *acrolects* or 'high' varieties) to creoles (*basilects* or 'low' varieties), with a spread of *mesolects* between. In addition, the English-cum-Creole usage of the region is affected by three further processes: indigenization, regionalization, and internationalization. These processes may often conflict, may operate differently in each locality, and may affect the degree of standardization of the varieties used, much as follows:

❶ Indigenization

Between 1962 and the early 1980s, most of the British Caribbean colonies became independent, with accompanying changes in the evaluation of local culture and institutions. These changes have included a reassessment of Creole and other speech forms, such as the usage of Rastafarians. An increasingly positive re-evaluation of the vernaculars has affected—and continues to affect—opinions about the standardization of local forms of English, the distinctness of creole vernaculars, the extent to which these should be valued and preserved, and the social and professional acceptability of switching and mixing. Generally, the result has been an increasing acceptance of, pride in, and ease with regard to all kinds of local usage, paradoxically alongside a powerful residue of doubt about the worthiness of Creole.

❷ Regionalization

A sense of regionality has been stimulated by intra-Caribbean travel, the spread of local art forms (especially music), the sharing of higher education (notably through the campuses of the University of the West Indies), and the existence of the Caribbean Examinations Council (CXC), providing secondary-level certification across the Commonwealth Caribbean. Procedures for marking scripts transnationally have exposed teachers to the written work of students throughout the region. CXC guidelines have been established with a notable sensitivity to local forms of English, helping to modify teachers' perceptions of the acceptability of particular usages. At the same time as they have recognized that no single local form merits greater respect than any other, teachers have grown conscious of region-wide commonalities, as a result of which they appear to have become more receptive to the idea of a flexible regional standard for the language.

❸ Internationalization

The degree of acceptability of Standard British English as a norm for the region continues to depend on sensitivities dating from colonial experience, and the degree of comfort with Standard American English depends on whether in any territory the US is perceived as primarily benevolent or malevolent. There is pressure for the unequivocal adoption of an internationally recognized regional standard, which in essence means staying with the British or opting for the American norm. More equivocally but perhaps more realistically, it might mean letting the two standards run side by side as part of an emerging World Standard English while providing a more generous space for localisms, mainly through 'promoting' elements of Creole.

The third option has the advantage of accepting the centrality of the mesolects. These tend to be characterized by variation in the usage of both the same speakers on different occasions and different speakers on the same occasions. Thus, in Trinidadian Creole, the sentence *It have plenty people in the park* is equivalent to the Standard *There are plenty of people in the park*. Within the mesolect, however, *they have* is widely used with the same meaning: *They have plenty people in the park*. All three usages may occur in the speech of the same person depending on whether the social context is more formal or more casual: or any one of the three may be preferred by different speakers for most if not all occasions. Below are some significant points regarding the Standard-to-Creole usage of the region.

Pronunciation

1 The different territories are similar but not identical: thus, Barbadian, Guyanese, Jamaican, and Trinidadian all having distinct intonation patterns, but enough shared features exist to identify a general West Indian accent.

2 Rhythm tends to be syllable-timed: thus, all or most syllables are equally stressed, as in *ré-gú-lár* rather than *RE-gu-lar*. Creole is fully syllable-timed, by and large reflecting the rhythm of West African languages, the vowel in each syllable getting its full value. Caribbean shares this feature with African-American English and Gullah in the US, and much of the usage of West Africa.

3 The major difference in pronunciation relates to *r*. Usage in Barbados, Jamaica, and Guyana is rhotic, but in the Bahamas, Belize, Trinidad and Tobago, and the lesser Antilles it is non-rhotic. Rhotic speakers pronounce *r* in all positions in such words as *run*, *art*, and *worker*; non-rhotic speakers pronounce *r* in *run* but not in *art* and *worker*.

4 There is greater lung and mouth pressure than in US and UK speech, often accompanied by more emotional expression and stronger facial movements, gestures, and body language.

5 There is a tendency to use *t* or *d* for *th*, as in *tree of dem* for 'three of them'.

6 Final consonant clusters tend to be reduced to the opening consonant only in all but the most careful speech, as in *han* for 'hand'.

7 There are relatively few diphthongs. The general equivalent of the RP diphthong in *face* is a single vowel as in Scots, although in Jamaica and the Leeward Islands there is a distinctive diphthong producing an affect like 'fee-ess'. The vowel in *goat*, etc., is generally long, again comparable to Scots.

Grammar

1 Where British and American have the simple past, as in *At yesterday's meeting the committee prepared a public statement*, there is a tendency to use the past historic, making it *At yesterday's meeting the committee had prepared a public statement*.

2 *Yes/no* questions with a declarative word order and rising intonation are commoner than questions with inverted word order, as with *You are coming?* rather than 'Are you coming?'

3 The key syntactic difference between Caribbean English and International English lies in the influence of Creole (see below), in which the differences are great.

Vocabulary

1 Local senses of general words: in many places, *miserable* ('mischievous'); in Jamaica, *tall hair* ('long hair'); in Trinidad, *fatigue* as in *give someone fatigue* ('to tease or taunt someone with a mixture of half-truths and imaginative fabrications'), and the intransitive verb *lime* ('to hang around, loiter, or be a casual observer of an event').

2 Distinctive local words: in Belize, *Cannabal Day* ('Carnival Day': Ash Wednesday); in Jamaica, a *higgler* (a person selling fruit, vegetables, and other small items of food by the roadside); in Trinidad, *catspraddle* ('to send

(someone) sprawling with a blow'; 'to fall in an indecorous way'), *jort* ('a snack'), and *touchous* ('touchy, short-tempered'); in the US Virgin Islands, *dumb-bread* (a heavy bread baked without using yeast and sometimes made with cornmeal).

3 Words from West African languages include: *bakra, bukra, backra, buckra* ('a white man/person': cf. Southern US), from Efik *mbakara* ('master'); *catta, cotta, kata* ('a head-pad to go under a load carried on the head'), from Twi and Kikongo *nkata*; *duppy* ('an evil spirit'), probably combining several sources, such as Fante *adopi* ('an ape') and Kikongo *ndoki* ('a sorcerer or person who takes lives through witchcraft'); *fufu* (a dish made by pounding boiled plantains, yams, or cassava in a mortar to form a smooth, firm mass that may be cut and served), from Twi *fufuu*.

4 Loan translations from West African languages: *sweet mouth* ('to flatter, a flatterer'), from Yoruba *soro didun-didun fun e* ('say word sweet-sweet give you'); *eye-water* and *cry-water* ('tears'), from various languages such as Yoruba *omi l'oju* and Igbo *anya mmili*, both with the same translation; *door-mouth* ('doorway' or 'entrance' to a building)', from various languages such as Nupe *eko misun* and Igbo *onu uzo*, both with the same translation.

5 Loanwords from French Creole: generally, *lagniappe* (cf. Southern US: 'something extra given by a vendor to a buyer for the sake of good will, a small gift or a bonus'); locally, for example in both Trinidad and St Lucia, *macafouchette* ('leftovers'), and in Trinidad alone, *ramajay* ('to warble, twitter, make an extravagant display').

6 Loanwords from regional Spanish and Spanish Creole: *parang*, from *paranda*, referring to a number of musical rhythms, song types, and festivities associated with Christmas in Trinidad and parts of Venezuela; in Jamaica, *frutapang* ('breadfruit': from *fruta* 'fruit' and *pan* 'bread'), *mampala* ('an effeminate man': from *mampólon* a common cock, not a fighting cock); *scaveeched fish* ('pickled fish', from *escabeche*, 'pickling brine').

It is, however, by no means easy to draw a dividing line between the vocabulary of 'proper' English in the Caribbean and that of Creole. Such words as *parang* and *mampala* belong as much in one as the other, in effect emphasizing the ultimate unity of the two varieties.

Caribbean English Creoles

This variety or language is—or these varieties or languages are—the outcome of contact between the British and various West African peoples as a result of the sea-borne expansion of various Western European nations, their colonization of the Americas, and the Atlantic slave trade. The usage of English-speaking sailors and settlers was the prime source of vocabulary for an English-based Creole, together with many loanwords, loan translations, and grammatical patterns derived from various European and West African languages. Indeed, despite regional Caribbean differences, all varieties of Creole have common features, among which are the following grammatical features in English creole:

1   Tense, mood, and aspect are expressed through the presence or absence of particles derived from English words, as in the Jamaican *Im waak* (no particle) 'He/she walked'; *Im a waak* (with *a*, from *have*) 'He/she walks/is walking'; *Im bin waak* (with *bin*, from *been*) 'He/she walked, He/she had walked'.

2   Marking the plurals of nouns by particles derived from English words and not *-s*, as in Jamaican and Guyanese *di daagdem* (the dog-them) 'the dogs', and Trinidadian *di dog-an-dem* (the dog-and-them) 'the dogs'.

3   Foregrounding in order to disambiguate, emphasize, or contrast, as in Trinidadian *Iz mi mudduh tel mi du it* (Is my mother tell me do it) 'My mother told me to do it (not anybody else)', and Jamaican *A tief im tief di goat* (A thief him thieve the goat) 'A thief stole the goat (he didn't buy it)'.

4   Reduplication, usually for emphasis, as in Jamaican *poto-poto* 'very slimy or muddy', *fenky-fenky* 'very puny, cowardly, fussy', *batta-batta* 'to beat repeatedly'.

5   Differentiation of singular and plural second-person pronouns (cf. archaic *thou* and *you*), as in Barbadian *yu* and *wuhnuh*, and Trinidadian *yu* and *all-yu* (cf. Southern US English *y'all* 'you all').

6   Possession shown by placing unmarked nouns side by side, as in Trinidadian *mi fada kuzn hows* ('my father's cousin's house').

With an increasing sense of regionalism and nationalism, Caribbean English Creole has been gaining in prestige. It is commonly the form of speech into which people relax, while individuals who are opposed for any reason to Standard English may make a point of using Creole as much as possible or all the time.

Jamaican Creole (also known as *Jamaican English Creole*, *Jamaican Creole English*, *Jamaican*, and *Patwa/Patois*) has the most extensive and longest-standing literature and the widest media and artistic use, and is also the most fully studied. In addition, the appeal of Jamaican music and dub poetry, as well as of Rastafarianism, has spread Patwa throughout the region and beyond, especially to parts of the UK, the US, Canada, and Panama. Its influence is particularly noteworthy in the UK, where it dominates other Creole varieties and has been a major element in the evolution of British Black English (as *Jamaican* or, in particular, *London Jamaican*). Although a consensus has evolved on the artistic value and distinctness of Patwa, its use nonetheless continues to be stigmatized. It is commonly viewed as an obstacle to education, a view countered by those who urge that the obstacle is the failure to develop strategies for teaching English in a Creole environment: one can compare this situation with the emotive public debate about Ebonics (African-American English) in the US in 1997 (see p. 194).

Even so, the use of Creole for literary purposes is growing, and it is the norm for popular drama and local song lyrics, notably reggae in Jamaica. *The Dictionary of Jamaican English* (1967, 1980) helped stabilize spelling in the national press and encouraged a fuller use of Creole by Jamaican writers, with a knock-on effect in radio and television, where Creole is an established medium for popular entertainment, for programmes with public participation, and in advertisements, again notably in Jamaica. The news is however generally read in Standard English, and in newspapers Creole is minimal, usually in special columns.

In the early 1980s, the Barbadian poet and scholar Edward Kamau Brathwaite coined the term *Nation Language* in the hope of presenting Creole in a positive light, especially in artistic and literary terms, notably in his *History of the Voice: The Development of Nation Language in Anglophone Caribbean Poetry* (London: New Beacon, 1984). Brathwaite's concern was to escape from the dominant traditions of speakers of conventional English in the Caribbean and elsewhere. Although he developed his concept in terms of English, he has intended it for all the regional creoles. While acknowledging the lexical resources from English in his own creole, he has affirmed the Africanness of its rhythms and perspective, and put forward the view that Creole is as valid and capable as any other kind of language. Even so, however, advocates of Creole (in essence the majority speech of the Anglophone Caribbean) have felt the need to go on sounding warnings with regard to élitist exclusionism. Hubert Devonish has for example observed:

> **1986** On the attainment of political independence, English
> became the sole official language of the countries of the
> Commonwealth Caribbean. The diglossia involving, on the one
> hand, Creole as the language of everyday informal interaction for
> the mass of the population, and English as the written, public-
> formal, and official language, on the other, continued. The new
> political elite, with a command of English not possessed by the
> Creole-speaking mass of the population, were and continue to
> be the beneficiaries of the prevailing official language policies.
> The new flag and the new national anthem signalled, for the
> monolingual Creole-speaking mass of the population, a continued
> denial of their language rights.
> – 'The decay of neo-colonial official language policies: the case of the English-lexicon
> Creoles of the Commonwealth Caribbean', in Manfred Görlach and John A. Holm, *Focus
> on the Caribbean* (Amsterdam & Philadelphia), John Benjamins, 24

As with many disdained vernaculars, the issue of viability ties in with education and particularly the use of a language for printed works, most prestigiously kinds of literature. The earliest example of writing in English about the Caribbean is Sir Walter Raleigh's *The Discovery of the Empyre of Guiana* (1596), an account in fact of his search for Eldorado. Similar narratives continued to be written, mainly by British authors, until the end of the nineteenth century, when local writers emerged, such as the Jamaican poets Tom Redcam and J. E. Clare McFarlane, and Egbert Martin in British Guiana. Well into the mid-20th century, the novels of H. G. DeLisser of Jamaica provided a mix of adventure, terror, and romance in the Gothic style. By the 1950s, however, local settings and styles had emerged, in for example the work of George Lamming, Samuel Selvon, Roger Mais, and V. S. Naipaul, and many such writers migrated to Britain to find outlets for their work. Currently, however, the writing of fiction and poetry is strong in the region itself, notably in Jamaica, Trinidad, Barbados, Belize, and Guyana. Derek Walcott, a native of St Lucia, has wryly observed:

> **1988** You start off as a colonial writer, you get promotion to
> Commonwealth writer, West Indian writer, then maybe to the
> international club by the people who run this thing called English
> literature. The horrific thing for them is that English literature is
> out of their control.
> – quoted in 'Conquering English', *South*, July

There have since the 19th century been many attempts to represent Creole in print, essentially (as elsewhere) by adapting the techniques for representing vernaculars first used by Walter Scott, Thomas Hardy, and the Brontë sisters. Generally, adaptation has been casual and informal, but in recent years linguistically principled approaches have emerged. Below are specimens from two of these, from Guyana and Belize. They share a convention by which single vowel symbols (*a, e, i, o, u*) represent 'short' and double symbols (*aa, ee, ii, oo, uu*) represent 'long' sounds. The Guyanese specimen is rhotic (*ordinary* for example being 'ardinarii') and the Belizean specimen is non-rhotic (*northern part* being adapted as 'naadan paat'). Both extracts are from Marlis Hellinger, 'On writing English-related Creoles in the Caribbean', in the collection *Focus on the Caribbean*, edited by Manfred Görlach and John A. Holm, John Benjamins, Amsterdam & Philadelphia, 1986.

1979 Den fain Kriol pipl chruuout di Karibian iina di Greeta an Lesa Antiliz, iina di Bahamaz, pan di ailan aafa di koos a Jaaja an Sout Karolaina, an pan di naadan paat a Sout Amerika. Wen i kom to rees an kolcha, Kriol den da di rizolt a wan intamikscha bitween di Yuuropian an Afrikan den we di Yuuropian den mi bring da di Nyuu Wol az sleev. Da Biliiz, di Kriol den da wan mikschaa di British an Afrikan we da mi boot sleev an friiman, we mi kom da Biliiz moosli fan Jameeka fi wok ina di faris.

[*Transliteration*: You can find Creole people throughout the Caribbean in the Greater and Lesser Antilles, in the Bahamas, on the islands off the coasts of Georgia and South Carolina, and on the northern part of South America. When it comes to race and culture, Creoles are the result of an intermixture between the Europeans and Africans when the Europeans brought them to the New World as slaves. In Belize, Creoles are a mixture of British and African when they were both slaves and freemen, when they came to Belize mostly from Jamaica to work in the forests.]

– Belizean Creole: an excerpt from a textbook composed for American Peace Corps volunteers learning Belizean Creole as a foreign language: part of a lesson titled *Pipl an langwij a Biliiz* ('People and Language in Belize') by Jon P. Dayley (1979)

1981 Wa dis peepa trai fo shoo fos is how di kain a langwij palisii wa wii gat doz mek om hard for ardinerii piipl tek part in nof ting wa gai-in aan in dem oon kontrii. Insaid di skuul, dem larnin yu fo riid an rait in Ingglish, an if yu een no dis Ingglish langwij ting an yu een eebl wid it yu sok salt fo riid and rait.

[*Transliteration*: What this paper tries to show first is how the kind of language policy that we have makes it hard for ordinary people to take part in enough things that are going on in their own country. In school, they teach you to read and write in English, and if you don't know this English language thing and you aren't able with it you suck salt as regards reading and writing.]

– Guyanese Creole: part of the summary of a linguistic paper by H. Devonish, 'Language policy in the creole-speaking Commonwealth Caribbean'

The following list of culturally complex terms in English/Creole has been adopted and adapted principally from Richard Allsopp's *Dictionary of Caribbean English Usage* (Oxford University Press, 1996).

anancy, anancy-spider, nancy, nancy-spider

A large brown house spider: from Twi *ananse* 'spider'. *Anancy* (also *Boro Nancy*, *Bo Anancy*, *Brer Anancy*) is also the rascally but amusing trickster hero of tales that derive from West African and especially Ashanti folklore concerning *Ananse*, a mythic spider being. He takes on human form, is greedy, selfish, and often outwits his opponents or barely escapes them, but is also often caught in the web of his own cleverness. By extension a tricky and untrustworthy person: *Look here, boy, don't get me out! If you spen' twenty cents out a dollar, how di change could be fifty cents? You di try play Anaansi 'pan me!* (from a Belize manuscript story).

ball-bush

A name in Barbados and Jamaica for a wild plant about four feet tall, with leaves and ball-like spiky growths, used for medicinal and ornamental purposes, and also known as: *ball-and-thread* (Anguilla), *ball-head (bush)* (Jamaica, St Vincent, Tobago), *ball-head cashie, bird-honey* (St Vincent), *candle-bush* (Dominica), *chandilyé, chandelier* (Trinidad), *Christmas candlestick* (Bahamas, Jamaica), *governor-balls* (Barbados), *gwoponpon* (St Lucia), *gwo tèt* (Dominica), *hop-bush* (St Vincent), *la-lavinton* (Antigua), *lion-bush* (Guyana), *lion's-tail* (Barbados, Virgin Islands), *man-piaba* (Barbados, Guyana), *pomp-pomp* (St Vincent), *rabbit-food* (St Kitts), *reeler-bulb* (Turks and Caicos). Allsopp shows that in Barbados alone this plant is known as *ball-bush, governor-balls, lion's tail*, and *man-piaba*.

custos

In Jamaica, the chief magistrate of, and also the Governor-General's representative in, a parish. From Latin *custos* 'guardian' (cf. *custodian*).

dhan

In Guyana and Trinidad, unmilled rice still in the brown husk, used especially as poultry feed. From Bhojpuri and Hindi *dhaan*, with the same meaning.

hototo, hoe-toe-toe

In Trinidad and Grenada, 'very much/big' (*She gave me a hototo plate o rice and peas*: Trinidad) and 'plentifully' (*Man, they had mangoes hoe-toe-toe in the market*: Grenada). From French Creole, probably *ho* ('great amount') and *to* (from *trop* 'too much').

Mashramani

In Guyana, a week of annual national festivities and celebrations surrounding Republic Day, 23 February. From Arawak *masaramani* ('voluntary work done co-operatively').

nation

Notably in Guyana, Jamaica, and Trinidad, people of especially non-European descent: (1) Those identifying themselves as descendants of a particular ethnic group before enslavement: for example, the people of the village of Mayo in Trinidad, who see themselves as part of the Yoruba nation in Nigeria; (2) A race or community, especially if non-European: *the African nation, the Black nation, a Chinee nation, an East Indian nation*. High- and low-caste Indians are *high nation* and *low nation* ('Dem is high nation people, Brahman people'). In Guyana, *no-nation* is a pejorative term for someone dark-skinned of several ethnic backgrounds or a lineage that is hard to determine; (3) People of some kind, especially if unpleasant: *I is accustom to female behaviour; dey is a nation a man got to expect anything from.*

rangatang

In Grenada, Guyana, and Jamaica, a pejorative and sometimes jocular term for a coarse, ill-disciplined, and belligerent man or woman, from *orang-utang* (a South-East Asian ape). In Trinidad the form is *rango* and in Guyana *kangalang* is a variant.

santapee-band

In Guyana, the name for what is more generally known as a *masquerade-band* and in Barbados a *tuk-band*. Such a band, with drums, flutes, triangles, and rattles, goes through the streets at festivals, usually accompanied by dancing masqueraders. *Santapee* is from 'centipede', the movements of the performers suggesting centipedes.

sweet-eye

Generally, a sexy or lustful wink, usually by a man. To *get sweet-eye* (said of a woman) 'to get affectionate or sexually suggestive glances':

> *Dey was faithful to duh husbans,*
> *Faithful to de en'*
> *Even when duh get sweet-eye*
> *From de husban' bes'-frien'*
> – in *The Pelican*, the magazine section of *The Nation*, Barbados, 11 Nov 1977

yard, Yard

In historical terms, the *Negro Yard* was the area in a Jamaican sugar plantation where the slaves lived. Currently, by extension, a *yard* is a house or home (including its garden, etc.), especially of a poor person or family in a town, and especially in Kingston, the capital: *I can tell you that you won't find no looters or no stolen goods either: this is a respectable yard.* In general usage, a *yard-boy* is a man employed to do general outdoor domestic chores: cf. US *yardman.* In Barbados, a *yardfowl* is a political lackey whose services are available in return for favours. In Jamaica and elsewhere, Jamaicans informally refer to their home island as *Yard*, and generally in the Caribbean, North America, and Britain, a *Yardie* is either a Jamaican or a member of a criminal gang that has its base or origins in Jamaica.

Rasta Talk and reggae

Rasta Talk is the general informal name for the argot of the Rastafarians, a religious group that originated in Jamaica. *Rasta* abbreviates *Rastafarian*, which in turn derives from *Ras Tafari*, the title in Amharic ('Prince to be Feared') by which Haile Selassie was known until 1930, when he became Emperor of Ethiopia. *Talk* here is an informal word for language or usage, as in *baby talk* and *girl talk*. In the form *tok*, it labels kinds of pidgin English, as in *Tok Pisin* in Papua New Guinea and *Kamtok* in Cameroon. Other names for the argot are *Dread Talk*, *Iyaric*, *I-lect*, and *Rasta*.

While the usage of Rastafarians in the Caribbean, the UK, the US, and elsewhere derives from Jamaican Creole, it also incorporates elements from the Old Testament and the black consciousness movement in the US, as well as possessing its own distinctive features. The movement, known also as *Rastafarianism* and *Rastafaria*, and informally as *Rasta* and *Ras*, originated among the Jamaican poor in the 1930s. Haile Selassie is regarded as the incarnation of *Jah* ('God', from Hebrew), through whom—despite his unanticipated death in 1975—the faithful of the black African diaspora will be taken out of *Babylon* (the oppressive white power system) to the promised land (Ethiopia). Since the 1960s, middle-class people have also been included among its numbers.

The usage of Rastas, who reject both Standard English and Creole, emerged in the 1940s as an argot among alienated young Jamaican men, became a part of local youth culture, and has been a potent factor in the growth and spread of dub poetry and reggae. A major difference from both Standard English and Creole is the use of the stressed Standard English pronoun *I* to replace Creole *mi* (normally used for both subject and object in a sentence, as in *He tell me* and *Me come*). The form *me* is seen as a mark of black subservience that makes people objects rather than subjects, and as such its use in any role in English or Creole is undesirable. The form *I and I* may be used for emphasis and solidarity and stands for both *we* and the Rasta movement at large, as in:

> **1973** I and I have fi check hard . . . It change I . . . now I and I [eat]
> jus' patty, hardo bread, from Yard.
> — *New York Magazine*, 4 November
>
> [I was greatly affected . . . It changed me . . . Now I only eat
> patties, hard-dough bread, from Jamaica—a reference to Rasta
> vegetarianism.]
>
> **1984** At the same time I fully know why leaders of societies have
> taken such a low view of I n I reality. They hold Rasta as
> dangerous to their societies.
> — Jah Bones, 'Rastafari: A Cultural Awakening,' appendix to E. E. Cashmore, *The Rastafarians*, Minority Rights Group Report 64

Because of its significance as a mark of self-respect and solidarity, *I* often replaces elements in mainstream words: *I-lect* ('Rasta dialect'); *Iyaric* (by analogy with *Amharic*: 'Rasta language'); *I-cient* ('ancient'); *I-man* ('amen'); *I-nointed* ('anointed'); *I-quality* ('equality'); *I-sanna* ('hosanna'); *I-thiopia* ('Ethiopia'). Other items of vocabulary are: *control* ('to keep, take, look after'); *dreadlocks* (hair worn long in coils, to signify membership of the group); *dub* (a piece of reggae music, a rhythmic beat); *queen* ('girlfriend'); *Rastaman/Rasta man* ('an adult Rastafarian'); *reason hard* ('to argue'); *sufferer* ('a ghetto-dweller'); *trod* ('to walk away, leave'); and both *weed of wisdom* and *chalice* (by analogy with Holy Communion: 'marijuana, pot, ganja', regarded as a sacred herb). Rasta word-play includes the interpretive etymology *Jah mek ya* ('God made here') for Jamaica, and such preferred adaptations as *blindjaret* (for 'cigarette', in Jamaican 'see-garet') and *higherstand* (for 'understand').

The term *reggae* dates from the 1960s and probably derives from Creole *rege* 'rags, ragged clothes' (referring to slum origins), probably also echoing the US word *ragtime*, formerly used to describe jazz. *Reggae* is music with a heavy four-beat rhythm, accented on the first and third beat rather than the second and fourth as in rock music. Reggae began in Kingston, Jamaica, and currently has cultural, social, and political implications in the Caribbean, the UK, the US, West Africa, and elsewhere. The lyrics propose solutions to black problems ranging from social revolution to redemptionist prophecy, and are often a vehicle for Rastafarianism, as in:

> Babylon system is the vampire
> Sucking the children day by day.
> – Bob Marley, 'Babylon System', 1979
>
> I hear the words of the Rasta man say
> Babylon your throne gone down, gone down.
> – Bob Marley and the Wailers, 'Rasta Man Chant'

Rasta lyrics are sung in Jamaican English and Creole, or a mix of the two, 'often expressing rejection of established "white-man" culture' (F. G. Cassidy & Robert Le Page, *Dictionary of Jamaican English*, 1980) and are 'a major, if not sole, source of information (or focal point of information) about Jamaica for North Americans' (Lise Winer, 'Intelligibility of Reggae Lyrics in North America: Dread ina Babylon' (in the journal *English World-Wide* II:I, 1990). They are also sung in French in Quebec and Senegal, and in Hausa, Lingala, Soninke, and Twi in West Africa.

Bahamian, Samaná, englañol, Sranan Tongo, and Saramaccan

Although every locality in the Caribbean is a special case, most communities fit the model of conventional English on one side and 'deep' Creole on the other, with mixing in the middle. There are, however, four areas in which the situation is markedly unusual: the Bahamas; the Dominican Republic; Puerto Rico; and Surinam. Three are distinctive because of their links with the US (but in each case a different link); the fourth is special because the ties between English and a range of local English-based creoles were broken three hundred years ago.

The Bahamas The term *Bahamian English* refers, like comparable labels elsewhere in the region, to the continuum of usage from creole to standard. Here, however, although the archipelago is an independent nation whose head of state is, as with many Anglophone Caribbean nations, the British monarch, the standard language tilts towards the US. Indeed, if matters had gone a little differently in the American War of Independence, the Bahamas could have been part of the Union. Close historical ties with Georgia and the Carolinas have included migration from the mainland of people of both European and African descent (including Loyalists at the time of the War of Independence, much like those who went to Canada, and former slaves). Trade has always been significant between the two, and the crucial Bahamian tourist industry is primarily geared to the US market. In this, the archipelago resembles the British colony of Bermuda to the north, from which the first European settlers in the Bahamas set out in 1647.

The Dominican Republic Spanish is the official language of the republic, which shares the island of Hispaniola with Haiti. There is, however, on the Samaná Peninsula a black community whose language is known as *Samaná English*, which is not directly linked with Caribbean English at large (conventional or creole), but is the offshoot of a creole once spoken on plantations in Georgia and the Carolinas, in the US. In the same way that some freed US slaves went to the newly created West African country Liberia ('Freedom Land') from 1922 onward, so others went to the Dominican Republic, whose Haitian rulers at the time wished to counter the local strength of Spanish.

Samaná English is currently spoken by some 8,000 people, and despite the isolation of the community is considerably decreolized. The precise nature of the language taken to the Samaná Peninsula and the extent to which it had begun to lose its Creole features before its speakers' departure from the US are issues that scholars continue to debate. Decreolization may have been well advanced in some parts of the US before the break-up of the plantation system, and this may be one reason for Samaná being close to conventional English. The older generation was schooled mainly in English and tends to be monolingual, but younger members of the community are generally bilingual in Spanish and English, and tend to intermarry with the general population. Many Spanish terms have been borrowed or converted into Samaná, as for example the expression *to gain money* rather than 'to make money', taken by loan translation from *gañar dinero*.

Puerto Rico The island was formerly better known in English as *Porto Rico*, a name often still casually used in the US. It is the easternmost of the Greater Antilles, lying between the Dominican Republic and the US Virgin Islands. Its capital is San Juan, its currency is the US dollar, its ethnicity is African, European, and mixed, and its official languages are Spanish and English. Originally inhabited by both Arawak and Carib Indians, the island was visited by Columbus in 1493 and was a Spanish colony until ceded to the US in 1898 after defeat in a brief war. In 1952, Puerto Rico became a semi-autonomous Commonwealth in association with the US, and its people are US citizens. The endless debate about whether the island should become a state of the Union, should seek independence, or should remain as it is dominates local politics. The English of Puerto Ricans on the island and the US mainland ranges from second-language to native speaker, and there is no indigenous English creole.

Puerto Rican usage ranges through four points on a continuum demarcated as follows by the researcher Rose Nash: a conventional Latin-American Spanish: *Englañol*, a hybrid in which English items occur in Spanish (as in *Se solicitan dos clerk typists* 'We need two clerk typists'); *Spanglish*, a hybrid in which Spanish items occur in English, either directly (as in *He has that special manera de ser* 'He has that special something', literally 'way of being') or through false friends from Spanish, as with *Please prove the car* (where the influence is Spanish *probar* 'to test') and *I assisted to the reunion* (where the influences are *asistir* 'attend' and *reunión* 'a meeting'); and conventional American English. Such a range of usage is so common as to be unremarkable, much like English, Frenglish, *franglais*, *français* in Quebec. The Spanglish of the large Puerto Rican community in New York is informally known as *Nuyorican*. The range of usage available to Puerto Ricans at home and in the mainland US is a major element in Spanish and Spanglish in the United States.

Surinam The Republic of Surinam (or Suriname, formerly Dutch Guiana) has a population of some half a million at home and in diaspora; it is mainly of Asian and African origin, with a small number of people of Amerindian and European background. Some 10 per cent of the Surinamese of African descent are Morron and Bosneger ('Maroons' and 'Bush Negroes'), the descendants of slaves who escaped from English plantations established by colonists from Barbados in 1651, and it is among the Maroons that several English creoles emerged. The Dutch gained the colony in 1667 in a treaty of colonial re-adjustment in which they gave their northern colony of Nieuw Amsterdam to the English, who re-named it New York. The official language is Dutch and such other languages as Hindi, Javanese, and conventional English are spoken, but the territory is remarkable in the almost total separation of its English-based creoles from English. The most notable of these 'long-lost' creoles are *Sranan*, *Ndjuka*, and *Saramaccan*. As the Surinam-born linguist Herman Wekker has put it:

> **1996** Sranan and Saramaccan are two of the half-dozen
> Anglophone creoles spoken in Surinam. These languages arose
> as a result of intensive contact between Englishmen and West
> Africans during the slave trade. The linguistic influence of the
> Dutch and other European languages has only been small. At the
> end of the seventeenth century, Surinam had already started to be
> a multilingual society, with several stable *new* languages.
> – 'The English-based creoles of Surinam,' *English Today* 48 (12:4), October

Sranan ('Surinamese') is also known as *Sranan Tongo* ('Surinamese Tongue') and *Taki-Taki* ('Talky-Talky', especially formerly and now regarded as an offensive label), and in Dutch as *Surinaams* ('Surinamese') and formerly *Neger-Engelsch* ('Black English', also now regarded as offensive). Sranan has long been used as a lingua franca among the coastal population at large. Its vocabulary is mainly from English, with some Dutch-derived items, and elements from Portuguese, African, and Amerindian languages. It is the first or second language of about a third of the population, and almost the entire population is acquainted with it as a language of national communication with its own literature. The national anthem as sung in Sranan begins:

> *Opo kondreman un opo!*
> *Sranan gron e kari un.*
> *Wans ope tata komopo*
> *We mu seti kondre bun.*
> ['Rise, countrymen, you rise!
> Surinam your country is calling you.
> Wherever our ancestors came from
> We must put the country right.'
> *Bun* from Portuguese *bon* 'good'.]

Ndjuka has been spoken since the eighteenth century by the Eastern Bush Negroes (whose two groups are the Ndjuka or Aucan and the Boni or Aluku, with their own related creole). Ndjuka is a language of runaway plantation slaves and is related to Sranan, but the two have limited mutual intelligibility. Ndjuka is remarkable, however, in having its own writing system, which is syllabic, not alphabetic, and strongly resembles indigenous West African scripts.

Saramaccan is spoken by the Central Bush Negroes (the Saramaccans and the Matuari). It is generally taken to be the oldest of the group and, unlike any other regional English-based creole, a significant part of its vocabulary derives from Portuguese. Saramaccan has also retained relatively many Africanisms (especially from Kikongo). It developed among 17th-century runaway slaves who may have spoken a Portuguese pidgin as well as their own West African languages before encountering English in the local plantations. They evidently escaped from the plantations before contact with English affected their speech to the same degree as those whose speech in due course developed into Sranan and Ndjuka. The extreme otherness of Saramaccan is well illustrated by Wekker's citation *Gaama, mi o-go náki lúku* (Literally: Grand-man, me go hit look) 'Chief, I am going to try to hit it.'

The Caribbean linguistic scene is complex, and the case of Surinam and Saramaccan illustrates this in a truly extreme and remarkable form. Sranan and Ndjuka have a degree of mutual intelligibility, but Saramaccan is foreign to both, and all are foreign to conventional English beyond the Caribbean. At the same time, however, as Wekker points out, 'Jamaican creole and Sranan are to a large extent mutually comprehensible.' This intelligibility on one hand and unintelligibility on the other is a matter entirely of circumstance: speakers of Saramaccan were long isolated in the bush, whereas speakers of Sranan lived on the coast and were open to a wider world. They shared in that massive centuries-long movement of ships and people which began with what the Barbadian scholar Richard Allsopp calls (as quoted at the beginning of this section) the original 'European misjudgement' in settling these islands and coastlands. The result has been both loss and gain in one of the most linguistically intricate regions on earth.

English and Latin America

1992a Although it is a topic of continuing debate, there can be little doubt that English is the most widely-spoken language in the world, with significant numbers of native speakers in almost every major region—only South America falling largely outside the net.

– Richard M. Hogg, General Editor's Preface, *The Cambridge History of the English Language: Vol. I. The Beginnings to 1066* (Cambridge: Cambridge University Press)

1992b In the end perhaps the most serious potential challenge to World English will come from outside. In the age of the New Pacific should we not consider those two historical rivals to English: Spanish and Chinese? The economic power of Latin America, many experts believe, has yet to be fully deployed. The Hispanic question is now on the minds of many Americans. Might Spanish not mount a serious challenge to the hegemony of American English?

– Robert McCrum, William Cran, and Robert MacNeil, *The Story of English: New and Revised Edition* (London: Faber; and BBC Publications (2nd edn) 1992), 374

1997a English is the second most widely spoken language in Argentina. It reaches us through a varied range of teaching methods and teaching institutions and through the influence of the media—cable television, music and advertising. This influence and its globalised use have transformed the learning of English from a 'need' into a 'must'. . . . Year after year, there has been a significant increase in the number of candidates sitting for the TOEFL and Cambridge examinations. . . . Argentina perseveres in strengthening its connection with the English-speaking world, equally hosting British and Americans in a permanent effort to overcome the language barrier.

– Graciela Clelia Moyano, 'English in Argentina', *English Today* 49 (13.1) (Cambridge: Cambridge University Press), 38–9

> **1997b** In Brazil, two varieties of English are used at the same time
> and taught in parallel: British English and American English. . . .
> The case of Brazil is significant because it is a huge source of
> potential speakers of English as a Foreign Language (EFL). . . .
> Only the members of the middle and upper middle class have
> access to education and to the media in which English is very
> present. The status of English in Brazil needs to be studied as it is
> of major relevance for communication with the rest of the world,
> where Portuguese is not commonly spoken. French used to be the
> first foreign language taught at school. . . . Nowadays, English has
> taken its place.
>
> – Annick Rivens Mompean, 'Pronouncing English in Brazil', *English Today* 49 (13.1),
>   Cambridge University Press, 28–9

It is entirely true that South America, as a continental mass, has remained 'largely outside the net' of English, as Hogg puts it (above), but as with so much of the geopolitics of language, the matter is not simple. McCrum *et al.* are also entirely right in supposing that Spanish and Chinese are the only two language complexes that offer any alternative in terms of numbers to world English. And, indeed, if there is an area that has escaped the net of English, it is South America—or rather Latin America in its entirety.

Most significantly, however, as Mompean points out, Spanish is not alone in the region. The massive presence of Portuguese in Brazil greatly complicates matters, even though Portuguese is close kin to Spanish: there is much less linguistic solidarity in Latin America than the name and the history of the region might suggest. The pattern of Iberian exploration, exploitation, and settlement was powerful and extensive enough for the rest of the world to accept the name 'Latin America'. The Latin grip, as it were, extended from Tierra del Fuego ('the Land of Fire') in the farthest south all the way, at its fullest reach, to Florida, California, Texas, and New Mexico. Much of the present United States has been 'Latino' longer than 'Anglo'.

It was only through a strong combination of warfare and treaty-making that the French, the British, and then the Americans were able to take over so much territory in North America and the Caribbean, the Americans becoming the most and the French the least successful in keeping what they took. But when the Americans pushed Latin America back it was only as far as the present border with Mexico, and since then there has been a reversal of flow, making Miami a kind of Latin-American extra-territorial capital.

Central America is largely Spanish-speaking, but with an overlay of American English notably in Panama but also in Costa Rica, El Salvador, Guatemala, and Nicaragua. Argentina and Brazil are also not alone in South America as regards their interest in English and indeed in Anglo-Saxon ways: the issue of the 'dollarization' of national economies has become a major talking point again since Ecuador abandoned its own hard-pressed national currency in favour of the Yanqui dollar, a policy that others (notably Argentina) have also from time to time considered. Along with the economic strength of the United States, American English has become a significant second presence in the entire region. Manifestly foreign, it has nonetheless made itself at home, which (curiously enough) Spanish has also been doing in recent years in *los Estados Unidos*.

4 American and British

1987 The nature of the relationship between British and American English has been the subject of debate (often heated) for years. *Webster's Seventh New Collegiate Dictionary* defines British English as 'English characteristic of England and clearly distinguishable from that of the United States . . .' Evelyn Waugh's amusing dedication page in *The Loved One* reads in part: 'My thanks are due to Mrs. Reginald Allen who corrected my American; to Mr. Cyril Connolly who corrected my English.'

– Norman W. Schur, Introduction, *British English A to Zed* (New York and Oxford: Facts on File)

The standard varieties of British and American English are touchstones for all other varieties and all learners of English worldwide; in terms of pronunciation, spelling, grammar, vocabulary, usage, slang, and idiom they are the reference norms, and seem likely to remain so for the foreseeable future. However, comparison and contrast are difficult matters, as people throughout the world know when they seek to follow one or other norm consistently, or at least to know what it is. Indeed, the Americans and the British are not themselves clear on just where the dividing lines run; in some parts of the world blends have grown up, traditionally for example in Canada and more recently in the mainland countries of the European Union.

National and international standards

Much of the widespread uncertainty (with its attendant mixing of UK and US practices) arises because there are at least six ways in which American English and British English relate to, and differ from, one another:

❶ As national varieties

Both British English (BrE) and American English (AmE) have many subvarieties, regional or national, formal or informal, and in a general sense anything any Americans do linguistically is representative of American usage and anything any British do represents British usage, but only parts of what they may do belong in the core areas of standard usage, British or American.

❷ As national standard varieties

Both British Standard English (BrSE) and American Standard English (AmSE) are generally regarded as distinct from other varieties within their respective national ranges, such as dialect or slang. However, norm-sustaining varieties in real life share an imprecise border area with 'non-standard' or 'sub-standard' or 'dialect' varieties, whose elements can also on occasion migrate into a standard text for stylistic or other effect.

❸ As national prestige varieties

Although AmSE and BrSE are only one part of the range of English within the two nation-states, they are without contest the most prestigious part, closely identified with good social, educational, and professional standing: that is, with an elite or range of elites that comfortably use them at home or abroad. In this sense, by no means everything that Americans or Britons say and write is acknowledged to be socially and educationally 'good usage', although all registers (including cursing and swearing) are good for something.

❹ As international varieties

Each variety is an integral part of the life of its nation-state. On occasion, however, each may be regarded as subsuming national varieties beyond its borders (in a well- or ill-defined way), American for example being taken to include Canadian English and British to cover Irish English (whether or not Canadian or Irish people object).

❺ As international standard varieties

Following from this, the standard varieties of AmE and BrE may be regarded as subsuming other *standard* national varieties, each serving (in a more or less clear-cut fashion, and to a greater or less extent) as a reference norm for users of English in these other locations. In addition, whether Standard British and Standard American are taken to be national or more-than-national entities (or both), there is so much intercommunication between them that novel usages pass easily and quickly from one to the other, and it can sometimes be hard to decide where a particular novel usage began. At present, a large but unquantifiable mass of items passes from American to British and other varieties worldwide, and some are standard and some are not.

❻ As the parts of an international dual standard

Furthermore, since both standards are used as models for schools in, and as vehicles in the media of, other territories (cf. British English in Singapore and American English in the Philippines), they have in fact a powerful role beyond the limits of the UK or US. In this they are not so much separate standards as parallel streams within (paradoxically) a global *dual standard*, notably for the editing of print, free writing, and (least easily and consistently) for speech.

The fuzziness at the edges of the terms *American English* and *British English* is reflected in the organization of mainstream English dictionaries. When, for example, a dictionary labels an item *British*, users can safely assume that it has more currency in Britain than in the US, but cannot be sure of at least four other things: (1) whether it is restricted to Britain and if used elsewhere is recognized as a 'Briticism'; (2) whether it is used throughout Britain or only in a region or regions and/or only or mainly in certain groups; (3) to what extent (if any) it is used or could be used in the US, and if so when and where and by whom; (4) whether or how it is used in any other English-speaking territory, such as Canada, Australia, or New Zealand. All too often, the lexicographer who applies the label does not know the answer to any or all of these or similar questions, and may not know how to find the answer.

Inevitably, dictionaries reflect the very vagueness and uncertainty that attends the easy transfer of usages from one major variety to the other, and from them to other national varieties, notably through sensibly qualifying *Am/Amer/American* or *Br/Brit/British* with *chiefly* or *mainly* or *esp(ecially)*, which is an increasingly common practice. The first edition of the *American Heritage Dictionary* in 1969 used both *British* and *Chiefly British* as labels, but the second edition in 1982 used only *Chiefly British*. By and large, interest in the differences between British and American reflects an underlying confidence that the similarities in standard varieties are much greater than the differences. Even though Americans and Britons are said to be 'divided by a common language', standardness is something they largely share with each other and with other varieties worldwide.

Contrasts in pronunciation

Three points can be borne in mind when comparing the speech patterns of American and British:

❶ Idealization

Because of diversity within both varieties, there is no easy way in which the two kinds of pronunciation can be compared and displayed, and there is little benefit in directly contrasting, say, Coastal Southern with Yorkshire or New York with London. The comparisons are actually made between two idealized (even sanitized) 'standard' accents, known as *General American* (*GA* or *GenAm*) and *Received Pronunciation* (RP). In US dictionaries, pronunciations are generally shown through re-spelling in a would-be phonetic style, except in dictionaries for foreign learners (as published by the New York branches of UK publishing houses), in which the pronunciations are given in phonetic symbols. In UK dictionaries, pronunciations may be either re-spelling or IPA (International Phonetic Association) symbols, which are the norm for dictionaries for foreign learners, without the hint of a *gonna* or a glottal stop. Millions of people in both locales do not have accents that fit such idealizations.

❷ *R*-sounds

GA is rhotic and RP non-rhotic: that is, in GA, *r* is pronounced in all positions in the words *rare* and *rarer*, but in RP it is not pronounced unless a vowel follows, and is therefore present in the word *rare* in the first but not the second position, and in *rarer* in the first and second positions but not the third (unless followed by a word beginning with a vowel, as in *a rare item* and *a rarer item*. Generally, *r* is a retroflex consonant in GA (the tip of the tongued curled back) and an alveolar consonant in RP (the tongue touching the alveolar ridge behind the upper teeth). In broad terms, GA represents the rhotic (*r*-pronouncing) accents of English and RP the non-rhotic accents.

❸ *A-sounds*

In about 150 words where the sound represented by the letter *a* comes before a fricative (a rubbing sound, as in *pass, laugh, bath*) or a nasal (a sound in the nose, as in *chance, sample*), GA has a short *a* and RP a broad *a*, a shibboleth for the difference being *I can't dance*. In RP, in the pronunciation of the broad *a*, there are many traps for the unwary: thus, *grant* and *slant* have the broad *a* but *grand* and *hand* do not, while such words as *translate* and *telegraph* may or may not have it, and *telegraphic* does not.

Contrasts in spelling

Most of the spelling differences between American and British do not mark differences in pronunciation, but serve in the main as emblems of linguistic nationalism, and it is primarily spelling that indicates whether a text is British or American in origin. By and large, in the 19th century especially, the adoption of certain spellings in American ensured that, if they were being used at the time in Britain, people would soon stop doing so: *-or* spellings as in *color* were once available in the UK as alternatives to *-our*, but the option died out after the US adopted them as its sole usage. The key spelling differences between the two varieties are minor but significant. There are two ways in which they can be classified: as *systemic* and *non-systemic* and *exclusive* and *non-exclusive* (divisions formulated by the UK-domiciled US lexicographer Robert Ilson in the early 1990s, and used in 1992 in the *Oxford Companion to the English Language*):

❶ Systemic and non-systemic (i.e. part or not a part of a system or pattern)

If a difference is *systemic*, it runs through a whole system or class of words; if it is *non-systemic*, it affects only one or a few words. The difference between UK *colour* and US *color* is systemic, because many words are involved (such as *hono(u)r, favo(u)r, neighbo(u)r,* and *vigo(u)r*), but even so exceptions occur (as with UK *languor, stupor, torpor,* and US *Saviour*). However, the UK variant *gaol* (contrasting with shared UK/US *jail*) is non-systemic, because no other words are spelt that way except its own 'family': *gaols, gaoler, gaolbird*. Occasionally, variants are systemic and therefore acceptable in both varieties, as with *abridg(e)ment, acknowledg(e)ment,* and *judg(e)ment*.

❷ Exclusive and non-exclusive (i.e. no choice or some choice)

Usages are exclusive when they can only be spelt one way in the UK or US: thus, when writing the word *colo(u)r*, either US *color* or UK *colour* must be chosen: the usages are mutually exclusive. In the case of *gaol/jail*, however, there is a choice between UK *gaol* and shared *jail*. In the case of *ax(e)*, the shared variant *axe* coexists with *ax*, which is now American alone, although it was at one time used in Britain. In 1884, the *OED* favoured *ax*, but, in 1989, the *OED2* went over to *axe*.

❸ Permutations and combinations

All permutations and combinations of these categories are possible: (1) *Colour* and *color* are systemic exclusive variants: one or other must be chosen; (2) The suffix forms *-ise* and *-ize* are systemic non-exclusive variants in British: either is possible, but only *-ize* is normally possible in the US; (3) *Gaol/jail* are non-systemic, non-exclusive variants in British usage: either can be chosen, but only *jail* is normally possible in the US; (4) *Axe/ax* are non-systemic, non-exclusive in American: either can be chosen, but only *axe* is normally possible in the UK; (5) In banking, *cheque* and *check* are non-systemic exclusive variants: they are one-off differences and each country asserts its own spelling.

The most significant systemic expressions fall into nine groups:

❶ The *colo(u)r* group

Most words of the type *color/colour* are from Latin or French: *arbo(u)r, armo(u)r, endeavo(u)r, favo(u)r, flavo(u)r, hono(u)r, humo(u)r, labo(u)r, odo(u)r, rigo(u)r, savo(u)r, tumo(u)r, valo(u)r, vigo(u)r*. Universally, *u* is not used in words—apart from *neighbo(u)r*—that refer to people, as with: *actor, author, emperor, governor, survivor, tenor*. There are, however, anomalies: UK *error, mirror, pallor, terror*, and *tremor*; US *glamor, savior, savor* co-exist with *glamour, saviour*, and *savour*. In American, the group has *-or-* in inflections (*coloring*), derivatives (*colorful, coloration*), and compounds (*color-blind*). British is more complex: *u* before vernacular suffixes (*armourer, colourful, flavoursome, savoury*) and French-derived *-able* (*honourable*), but not before Latinate suffixes (*honorary, honorific, humorous, humorist, coloration, deodorize, invigorate*). But there are anomalies: British *colourist*; and American can have *savoury* and may favour *glamour* over *glamor*.

❷ The *centre/center* group

In this type, British exclusively has *-re*, American *-er*: *centre/center, fibre/fiber, goitre/goiter, litre/liter, meagre/meager, mitre/miter, sabre/saber, sombre/somber, spectre/specter, theatre/theater*. Agent *-er* (as in *writer*) and comparative *-er* (as in *colder*) are unaffected. Many words in both varieties have *-er* (*banter, canter*) and *-re* (*acre, lucre, massacre, mediocre, ogre*). In the second group, *-er* would suggest a misleading pronunciation (therefore no *acer, *lucer, etc.). British distinguishes *metre* (unit of measurement) from *meter* (instrument for measuring; prosody), but American uses *meter* for both. Though *theater* is the preferred US spelling, *theatre* is common as part of a name. Generally, the differences are preserved in inflections (*centred/centered*) and compounds (*centrefold/centerfold*), but usually vanish in derivatives through loss of *e* (*central, fibrous, metric/metrical, theatrical*).

❸ The *(o)estrogen* group

In words of Greek origin (in which an original *oi* became a Latin *œ*), British has *oe* in exclusive variants, American *e* or less commonly *oe*, typically in non-exclusive variants: *am(o)eba, diarrh(o)ea, hom(o)eopathy, (o)esophagus, (o)estrogen, (o)estrous*. The differences are maintained in all inflections, derivatives, and compounds. Two words of Latin origin have been assimilated into this class, *f(o)etus* and *f(o)etid*. In both varieties, all trace of the earlier forms *oeconomy, oeconomical, oecumenical* has gone (in *economy, economic/economical, ecumenical*, etc.). Within a word, *(o)e-* is pronounced 'ee' in both varieties; at the beginning, it is pronounced 'ee' in British and may be so pronounced in American, although *e-* tends to be pronounced as in *neck*. The pronunciation of British *oestrogen* is therefore 'ees-', of American *estrogen* is generally 'ess-'.

❹ The *(a)esthetic* group

In words of classical (and ultimately Greek) origin in which a Neo-Latin æ passed into English as first æ then *ae*, British has tended to keep *ae* as an exclusive variant and American has had *e* and *ae* as non-exclusive variants: *(a)eon, arch(a)eology, gyn(a)ecology, (a)esthetics, an(a)emia, encyclop(a)edia, h(a)emophilia, h(a)emorrhage, medi(a)eval, pal(a)eontology*. The spelling differences are maintained in inflections, derivatives, and compounds. In the case of *(a)esthete* and its derivatives, the spelling can signal a difference in pronunciation: beginning in British with the vowel in *seed* or *send* and in American only in *send*. Elsewhere in this class, however, *ae* is pronounced as in *seed* in both varieties. One classical form keeps *ae* in both varieties: *aer-* as in *aerate, aerobics, aerodynamics, aerosol*. In both varieties, *encyclopedia* and *medieval* are commoner than *encyclopaedia* and *mediaeval*, but where British pronunciation typically begins 'meddy', American often begins 'meedy'. There is now a tendency for *e* and *ae* to become non-exclusive variants in British in such words as *co-eval, primeval* and *archeology, gynecology*.

❺ The *instil(l)* group

In such words, British has a single written vowel plus *-l* and American has a single written vowel plus *-ll*, and the exclusive variants are all disyllabic verbs stressed on the second syllable: *distil(l), enrol(l), fulfil(l), instil(l)*. Uniquely, *extol* prevails in the US over *extoll*. Verbs like this but with *a* in the second syllable belong to this class in American: *appall, enthrall, install*. In British, the preferences vary: *appal, befall, enthral, install*. The verb *annul* has single *l* in both varieties.

❻ The *final -l/ll* group

In British, verbs that end in a single written vowel plus *-l* or *-ll* keep them before *s* (*travels, fulfills*), have *-l* before *-ment* (*instalment, fulfilment*), and have *-ll* before a suffix beginning with a vowel (*travelling, fulfilling*). In American, verbs that end with a single written vowel plus *-l* or *-ll* keep them before *-s* and *-ment* (*fulfillment, installment*); before a suffix beginning with a vowel, the verbs ending with *-ll* keep both letters (*fulfilling*), but the verbs ending with *-l* either have *-ll* as in British (*compelling, cavilling*) or more usually follow the general rules for doubling final consonants (*compelling, caviling*). Sometimes the result is the same for both varieties: *compel, compels, compelled*. Sometimes it is different: *travel, travels, travelled, traveller* shared by both, but American generally has *travels, traveled, traveler*. *Parallel* does not usually double its final *-l* in either variety.

❼ The *-ise/ize* group

Some verbs can only have *-ize*: *capsize, seize*. In some, only *-ise* is possible: *advise, surprise*. In many, both *-ise* and *-ize* are possible, as in *civilise/civilize, organise/organize*, and the *s* or *z* is preserved in derivatives: *civilisation/civilization*. For such verbs, American has a systemic, exclusive *-ize*, and British has both *-ise* and *-ize*. In Australian, *-ise* is preferred. British publishers generally have their own house styles: among dictionary publishers, *-ize* is preferred by Cassell, Collins, Longman, Oxford, *-ise* by the Reader's Digest (UK). Chambers has *-ise* for its native-speaker dictionaries, *-ize* for its EFL learners' dictionaries, intended for an international public. There is no infallible rule identifying the verbs that take both, but they generally form nouns in *-tion*. With the exception *of improvise/improvisation*, verbs that take only *-ise* do not generally have a noun ending in *-ation*: *revise/revision*, *advise/advice*. However, some verbs that allow both forms do not form nouns in *-tion*: *apologise/ize*, *apology*; *aggrandise/ize*, *aggrandisement*, *aggrandizement*.

❽ The *-lyse/ze* group

In such verbs as *analys/ze*, *catalys/ze*, and *paralys/ze*, British prefers *-lyse* and American *-lyze*. The variants are systemic and have been mutually exclusive, but recently *analyze* has begun to appear in the UK. The difference disappears in corresponding nouns: *analysis*, *catalysis*, and *paralysis* are international, as the z of the verbs becomes s in the nouns.

❾ The *-og(ue)* group

Although in words like *catalog(ue)*, *dialog(ue)*, *monolog(ue)*, *pedagog(ue)*, *prolog(ue)*, American sometimes drops *-ue*, only *catalog* is a widely used American variant. Thus, such spellings are systemic, non-exclusive variants in American. *Analog(ue)* is a special case: the spelling *analog* prevails in contrast with *digital* when referring to such things as computers, but that is true not only in American but also in British, where American spellings are generally used in the register of computing.

At least the following three conclusions can be drawn from these points:

❶ Length

Where differences exist, American spellings tend to be slightly shorter than British: *catalog*, *color*, *councilor*, *counselor*, *jewelry*, *jeweler* as opposed to *catalogue*, *colour*, *jewellery*, *jeweller*, *councillor*, *counsellor*. Exceptions however exist, among them American *instill*, *installment*, *skillful*, *thralldom* against British *instil*, *instalment*, *skilful*, *thraldom*.

❷ Acceptability

In general terms, a spelling used in Britain is more likely to be acceptable in America than vice versa, but is unlikely to remain uncorrected by proof-readers for texts to be published in the US. There is a mild but perhaps growing tendency however for US spellings to dominate in certain areas, most notably the usage of computer technology (as with *dialog* and *program*).

❸ Homophony

There is a tendency in British English to use spelling to distinguish homophones, as with *tyre* and *tire*, *cheque* and *check*, and *kerb* and *curb*. American English does this rarely, as for example with *vice* (a moral condition) and *vise* (a tool).

Contrasts in grammar

Below are twelve notable grammatical contrasts between American and British standard usage:

❶ *Shall* and *will*

Shall is even less common in American than in British, and the only significant differences concern two of the least common British uses. The first concerns second-person questions and the second the use of the contraction *shan't*, both as in *Shall you be at the embassy reception?—No, I'm afraid I shan't*. Both are virtually unknown in American. Two of the British uses of *will* are also much less likely in American: *will* used for inferences (and roughly equivalent to *must*), as in *That will be the postman at the door*; and stressed *will*, indicating a disagreeable habit or practice, as in *He WILL keep telling us about his operation—I wish he wouldn't*.

❷ *Should* and *would*

In polite first-person statements (such as *We should be happy to comply with your request*), *should* is rarer in American than in British, particularly in advice-giving formulas (such as *I should dress warmly if I were you*). *Would* is primarily British in uses that parallel *will* (as above): for inferences, as in *That would have been the postman at the door*; stressed, as in *He WOULD keep telling us about his operation— I wish he wouldn't*. However, *would* seems to be primarily American as an initial equivalent of *used to*: *When I was young, I would get up early*, though as a subsequent replacement for *used to* it is shared: *I used to get up early and before breakfast I would go jogging*.

❸ *Can* and *may*

Both varieties use *can* freely for permission, a usage formerly discouraged on both sides of the Atlantic, as in *You can see him now*. When used for permission, *may* tends to be more formal. Where a negative inference is involved, British tends to use only *can't* and *couldn't* (*If you got wet, you can't/couldn't have taken your umbrella*), while American allows these and *mustn't*, which is very unlikely in British. See next.

❹ *Must* and *have (got) to*

A positive assertion such as *This has (got) to be the best novel this year* is more likely in American than British, although it is becoming an alternative in British to the shared *must* in *This must be the best novel this year*. A negative sentence such as *If you got wet, you mustn't have taken your umbrella* is American rather than standard British, which uses *can't*.

❺ *Let's not—Don't let's—Let's don't*

The negative form as in *Let's not argue* is shared, co-existing with the chiefly British variant *Don't let's argue* and the American variant *Let's don't argue*, often reproved in the US as non-standard.

❻ Subjunctives

After words like *demand*, several constructions are possible: *I insisted that he should (not) leave* (more British than American), *I insisted that he (not) leave* (more American than British, especially with *not*), and *I insisted that he left/didn't leave* (much more British than American).

❼ Perfectives

With *yet* and *already*, such perfective sentences as *Have you eaten yet?* and *They've already left* are shared usages. Such alternatives as *Did you eat yet?* and *They left already* are virtually exclusive to American, where disagreement may arise about whether they are standard or not.

❽ Time expressions

The form *Monday to Friday inclusive* is shared, while the synonymous *Monday through Friday* is American. *Monday through to Friday* is British, and may be ambiguous as to whether Friday itself is included. The forms *a week from today* and *a week from Friday* are shared, while *a week today*, *a week on Friday*, and *Friday week* are British. The form *half past six* is shared, and co-exists with the informal British *half six*. The use of *past* in time expressions (as in *10 past 6*, *(a) quarter past 6*) is shared; the corresponding use of *after* (as in *10 after 6*, *(a) quarter after 6*) is chiefly American. The form *ten (minutes) to six* is shared, while *ten (minutes) of six* is strictly American.

❾ Some collocations

The collocations *go to church/school/college* and *be at church/school/college* are shared, but *go to university/be at university* and *go to hospital/be in hospital* are British (and specifically England), while American requires *the* as in *go to the university/hospital* (shared with the Scots). The form *do a deal* is British and *make a deal* is American. *Take a decision* is chiefly British, though *make a decision* is shared.

❿ Vocabulary and idiom

As with differences in spelling, lexical differences can be divided into the exclusive (such as British *windscreen*, American *windshield*, and the non-exclusive. The non-exclusive differences subdivide into those in which the shared variant coexists with an exclusive usage, such as: shared *editorial*, British *leader*; shared *autumn*, American *fall*; and those in which a shared variant coexists with both a British variant and an American variant, as with shared *socket*, British *power point*, and American *outlet*. Systemic differences in vocabulary are due to two factors: source and subject. Notably, in the vocabulary of computing, US spellings are used in the UK, as with *program*, *disk*, while British *programming* is used in American.

⓫ Some slightly different idiomatic phrases

The two varieties sometimes have slightly different expressions, such as:

British	American
a home from home	a home away from home
leave well alone	leave well enough alone
a storm in a teacup	a tempest in a teapot/teacup
blow one's own trumpet	blow one's own horn
sweep (something) under the carpet	sweep (something) under the rug

⓬ Some differences in the use of prepositions

Prepositional usage is often different: Americans live *on* a street while Britons live *in* a street; they cater *to* people where Britons cater *for* them; they do something *on* the weekend where Britons do it *at* the weekend; are *of* two minds about something while Britons are *in* two minds; have a new lease *on* life where Britons have a new lease *of* life. American students are *in* a course and British students *on* a course. Americans leave Monday or *on* Monday, but Britons can leave only *on* Monday.

Contrasts in vocabulary:
An A–Zed/Zee of differences

In the following list, items in the extreme left-hand column are: *either* shared spellings of words that have different pronunciations (as with *clerk*) *or* square-bracketed notes intended to clarify the contexts of the contrasted items (as with [of radios, etc.] beside *antenna* and *aerial*, [anatomy] beside *ass* and *arse*, and [slang: *to vomit*] beside *barf* and *puke*). The lists are representative and not exhaustive; they present the information and contrasts broadly, without subtleties of use. Many pairs do not require notes.

Note	American	British
[in law etc.]	accept, agree to	agree, accept
	acclimatize, acclimate	acclimatise, acclimatize
	accommodation(s)	accommodation [no plural]
[abbreviation: *advertisement*]	ad	advert, ad
[of insurance claims]	adjuster	assessor
	adz, adze	adze
[media commercials]	'after these messages'	'after the break'
	airplane	aeroplane
	aluminum	aluminium
[of radios etc.]	antenna	aerial
	apartment	flat, apartment
	artifact, artefact	artefact
	artsy-craftsy, arty-crafty	arty-crafty
[part of anatomy]	ass	arse
[insult]	asshole	arsehole, asshole
	automobile, auto, car	car, motor car, *rare* automobile
	ax, axe	axe
	baker's shop, bakery, bakeshop	baker's (shop)
[slang: to vomit]	barf, puke	puke
	bartender	barman, bartender
	billboard	hoarding
	business suit	lounge suit
[of a phone line]	busy	engaged
	candy	sweets
[on a train]	car	carriage
	carcass, carcase	carcass, carcase
[used in burials]	casket	coffin
	charge account	account
[money]	check	cheque
[board game]	checkers	draughts
	checkerboard	draught(s)board
	checkroom	cloakroom
[religion]	church aisle	aisle
clerk	*rhymes with 'jerk'*	*rhymes with 'dark'*
[in a shop/store]	(sales)clerk	(shop) assistant
	clothes-pin	clothes-peg

Note	American	British
	collar button	collar stud
	commutation ticket	season ticket
	comfort station, restroom	public convenience/toilet
	cookie	biscuit
	corn	maize
	cotton batting, cotton	cottonwool
[law]	court sessions	assizes (England and Wales)
	crematory, crematorium	crematorium
	custom-made clothes	made-to-measure clothes
[at roadside]	curb	kerb
[of playing cards]	deck	pack
Derby	*rhymes with 'Herbie'*	*rhymes with 'Barbie'*
[in a hotel]	desk clerk	receptionist
	dessert	sweet, afters, dessert
[of air, liquid, in water, etc.]	draft	draught
[– beer]	draft beer	draught beer
[of a document, etc.]	draft [noun and verb]	draft, draught [noun and verb]
[a written order, etc.]	draft	draft
[military: noun]	the draft	conscription
[military: verb]	to draft	to conscript
[letting in air]	drafty, draughty	draughty
	druggist, pharmacist	chemist, pharmacist
[rough equivalent]	drugstore, pharmacy	chemist's (shop), pharmacy
[of intelligence]	dumb	stupid
	eggplant	aubergine, eggplant
	elevator	lift, elevator
[rail travel]	engineer	(engine) driver
[taxation]	exemption	allowance
	fall, autumn	autumn
	faucet	(water) tap
fertile	*sounds like 'fertle'*	*ends like 'tile'*
[in buildings]	first floor, second floor . . .	ground floor, first floor . . .
	freight train	goods train
	funeral director, mortician,	undertaker
	funeral parlor/home	undertaker's
	garden party, lawn party	garden party
	gas(oline)	petrol
[rough equivalent]	grid(iron)	football/soccer field
[metal equipment]	hardware	ironmongery
	hardware store	ironmonger's
	highway	main road
	hog [young hog = pig]	pig [hog: castrated male; feral pig]
	pigpen, pigsty, hogpen	pigsty, piggery
[of people's looks]	homely, plain	plain
[of a vehicle]	hood	bonnet
hostile	*sounds like 'hostel'*	*ends like 'style'*
	janitor	caretaker, doorkeeper (Scotland: janitor)
	jeweler	jeweller

Note	American	British
	jewelry, jewellery	jewellery
	kerosene	paraffin
lieutenant	'loot-'	'left-'
[informal]	mad, angry	angry
	mail	post
	mailbox, mailbag, etc.	postbox, postbag, etc.
missile	sounds like 'missal'	ends like 'smile'
[adhesive]	mucilage	gum, glue
	multiple plug	adapter
	normalcy, normality	normality
[sewing items, etc.]	notions	—
[leg coverings]	pants	trousers, pants (under US influence)
[police]	patrolman/woman	constable (on the beat)
[road surface]	pavement	roadway
[punctuation]	period, full stop	full stop, period
	pitcher	jug [pitcher: large jug]
	porch	veranda(h)
	program	programme (computers: program)
	public school	state school [public school: a kind of private school]
[a woman's]	purse	handbag
	railroad	railway
[increase in pay]	raise	rise
[of lawyers]	represent (a client)	act for (a client)
	restroom, comfort station	public convenience/toilet
	reservation	booking, reservation
	round-trip ticket	return ticket, return
[in politics]	run (for office)	stand (for election)
	scratch pad	note pad, scribbling block
[road vehicle]	sedan	saloon (car)
	shoestring	shoelace
[lacking in]	shy of, short of	short of
	sidewalk	pavement
[in business]	silent partner	sleeping partner
	sports	athletics, sports
	store, shop	shop [store: large shop]
[in buildings]	storey/storeys	story/stories
	streetcar, trolley (car)	tram(-car)
[rail travel]	subway	tube, underground (Scotland: subway)
	sundown, sunset	sunset
	sunup, sunrise	sunrise
[for men]	suspenders	braces
[rail travel]	switch	points
[TV: proprietary names]	Teleprompter	Autocue
	thumbtack	drawing pin
	ticket office	booking office

Note	American	British
	trailer	caravan
	trailer truck	articulated lorry
	truck	lorry, truck
[rail travel]	trunk line	main line
	tuxedo, *informal* tux, dinner jacket	dinner jacket, *infml* DJ
	undershirt, undervest	vest
	vest	waistcoat
[conversation]	visit (noun, and verb + with)	–
	washcloth	facecloth
[washing dishes]	–	the washing-up
[generic use]	whiskey	whisky
	zee	zed

Conclusion

There is currently no certainty about the extent to which the usage of non-American and non-British English-speaking countries reflects American or British standard practice (or indeed their other practices, such as slang and special terminology). It is also impossible to be sure to what extent there is, especially in the European Union, a wish for a mid-Atlantic compromise (or fudge). This lack of certainty, however, has no implications for worldwide educated English usage. All national standards are closely related, indeed markedly so in their print forms and Internet and Web practices, and confusion between UK and US norms is not a hanging offence.

The 'New Englishes' of nations that have emerged since the Second World War in Africa, Asia, the Caribbean, and Oceania add to a general awareness of diversity that has existed for decades, if not in some cases centuries, without much serious and systematic discussion and description until the last two decades. Although the range of the English language is enormous, international native and non-native usage still tends to centre/center on a surprisingly uniform standard US/UK complex, but with a shift throughout the 20th and into the 21st century away from British towards American norms. It is still possible, however, to think of the international print standard as a single entity with two major aspects, American and British, which, though different, are not in conflict.

In addition, we see emerging a number of other standard varieties buttressed by national dictionaries and strong media and publishing industries. Australia, Canada, and New Zealand are at the present time the most prominent and successful of these, but it seems likely that other nations will follow, such as South Africa, the Philippines, and perhaps Singapore—and the European Union may in the not-far-distant future have its own views of English as a European lingua franca, taking account of UK and Irish needs and norms while at the same time paying attention to the needs and even the norms that make sense in other member states (where for example the printing of English might follow certain traditional practices for national languages rather than either the UK or the US).

The fuller international linguistic presence of such nations and associations of nations would lead to something beyond the 'dual standard' just discussed, which has in effect dominated the international scene for decades. An evolving standard for the 21st century would therefore be in some sense federative, although even in a democracy of world Englishes some varieties are likely to go on being more equal than others. The pecking-order model cannot be entirely set aside, society being what it is, but at the same time a greater synthesis and balance among varieties and standards seems likely to emerge in the next twenty or so years. Certainly, it is already becoming harder for the dictionary and textbook publishers of any one English-speaking country to avoid reporting what is happening in other English-speaking countries, and indeed wherever else English is being used.

5 Africa

The word *Africa* began as a Latin adjective, as in *Africa terra*, 'Land of the Afers', an ancient people about whom almost nothing is known, although they may have been the ancestors of the present-day Afars of the southern Red Sea coast. For the Romans, *Africa* as a noun had two senses: first, the entire land mass south of the Mediterranean: secondly, an imperial province between *Mauretania* (Greek: 'Blackland') in the west and *Aegyptus* (Egypt) in the east. Roman Africa therefore covered much of present-day Algeria, Tunisia, and Libya. To its south lay an inde-terminate region that the Greeks called *Aethiopia* ('Land of the Burnt Faces'), with which the story-telling slave Aesop has traditionally been linked. If so, he might well have been, as it were, the Uncle Remus of the ancient world.

On European maps (16th–19th century), the name *Africa* was applied to a continent whose general extent and shape were known but whose interior was largely uncharted. By that time, the land-mass to the south of the Sahara had three names of its own: *Aethiopia/Ethiopia*, *Nigritia* (Latin: 'Blackland'), and *Kaffraria* (Latin-cum-Arabic: 'Land of the Infidels'). In the 19th century, the third of these names was also used for part of Cape Colony, in tandem with the white South African term *Kaffir*, applied indiscriminately and dismissively to all black Africans. In Europe, in the meantime, an on-going mix of ignorance, mystery, and romance encouraged phrases such as the *Dark Continent* and *Darkest Africa*, which chimed with Joseph Conrad's novella about the horrors of the Belgian Congo, *Heart of Darkness* (1902).

By then, however, exploration had dispelled much of the ignorance and added to an awareness in Europe of the continent's natural wealth. As a result, in the wake of the Berlin Conference of 1885, the 'great powers' engaged in what came to be known as 'the scramble for Africa'. Before that point, European languages had been largely confined to the coasts, but with the creation of large colonies, many of them with arbitrary straight-line boundaries, these languages moved inland, establishing a novel patchwork continent-wide. At the same time, many speakers of the same indigenous languages found themselves on the opposite sides of borders suddenly and opportunistically imposed by outsiders.

In the same period, in both Europe and North America, the mystery-and-romance view of Africa encouraged speculation about 'lost' kingdoms such as Great Zimbabwe and the homeland of the legendary Christian ruler Prester John. In travel writing and in fiction, missionaries, explorers, gold- and diamond-miners, colonial officers, and white hunters were represented as performing on a vast and savage stage, against a backdrop of jungle, desert, animals, Arab traders, and Negro tribes. Public interest was fed by (and in turn guaranteed the success of) such novels as: Henry Rider Haggard's *King Solomon's Mines* (1886) and *She* (1887); Edgar Wallace's *Sanders of the River* (1911); John Buchan's *Prester John* (1910); and Edgar Rice Burroughs's *Tarzan of the Apes* (1914). Such novels and the motion pictures that later drew on them helped shape general Western views of Africa and its peoples, in a cast of pith-helmeted *bwanas*, loyal bearers, savage warrior tribes, proud Arabs, treacherous half-castes, lost cities, and missing links.

In the 1930s, a parallel Messianic enthusiasm for Africa emerged in Jamaica, centring on Ethiopia and its emperor Haile Selassie in the role of an imminent saviour. One of the emperor's titles was Ras Tafari, from which the movement took the name *Rastafarians* (duly shortened to 'Rastas'). Its menfolk began to wear their hair in 'dreadlocks' to emphasize their distinctness from others (black and white), and Rastafarianism has survived and grown as a significant black-consciousness movement of the Western hemisphere, greatly influencing kinds of culture and belief not only in the African diaspora of the Caribbean, the US, and the UK, but also in sub-Saharan Africa itself.

For almost 200 years, the names of regions, peoples, and states in Africa have been unstable, largely as a consequence of European colonization and exploitation from the 1880s to withdrawal after the 1950s. British involvement included: a West African colony, the *Gold Coast*, which on independence became the Republic of *Ghana* (reviving the name of a medieval regional empire); the southern colonies of *Northern Rhodesia* and *Southern Rhodesia* (named after the imperial adventurer Cecil Rhodes), which became *Zambia* and *Zimbabwe*. *Nyasaland* is now *Malawi*,

Bechuanaland now *Botswana*, *South West Africa* is now *Namibia* (after the Namib Desert), and *Tanganyika* and *Zanzibar* were unified as *Tanzania* ('Tan-zan-EE-a'). Radical anti-apartheid activists gave the name *Azania* to the Republic of *South Africa* (which in 1994 ceased to be an international pariah state with a white, mainly Afrikaner, apartheid regime). In the unification of British and Italian Somali colonies, the British name *Somaliland* was dropped in favour of *Somalia*, vernacular -*land* typically giving way to the Latin -*ia*, but elsewhere old and new co-exist: for example, *Ovamboland* in *Namibia*; *Mashonaland* and *Matabeleland* in *Zimbabwe*. In Southern Africa, the former British protectorate of *Basutoland* is now *Lesotho*, but *Swaziland* has retained its colonial name.

A key sound and letter in the geopolitics of Africa has been z, as in *Zaire*, *Zambezi*, *Zambia*, *Zande/Azande*, *Zanzibar*, *Zimbabwe*, *Tanzania*, *Azania*, *Swazi*, *Swaziland*, *Zulu*, and *Zululand*. Some of these names are happenstance (no more pregnant with meaning than *Zapata* and *Zapotec* in Mexico) but some, such as *Azania* and *Zanzibar*, echo Arabic *zanj* ('black').

Africa's African languages

The peoples of many parts of Africa use several languages as a matter of course: one or more home languages; one or more lingua francas; one or more languages of religion, education, and administration—all mixing and adapting. The post-medieval European concept of one nation-state with one (preferably sole) language has not done well (mainly because of the haphazard shapes of many countries), but the concept of a language for each ethnicity (formerly thought of as a 'tribal language') is entirely normal.

Hausa, spoken by some 30 million people in the Sahel region of West Africa, illustrates how a major non-national language is likely to be used. Not only is it part of a web of regional languages that includes Fulani and Yoruba, but its speakers have long been in daily contact with three 'world languages': Arabic as the language of Islam (Hausas generally being Muslim), and English and French as languages of Christianity, imperialism, Westernization, globalization, and in the case of Nigeria national and regional unity. Scholars do not entirely agree on how many African languages there are or how they should be grouped, but four families appear to account for something like a thousand distinct languages. They are:

❶ Hamito-Semitic/Afro-Asiatic

Which combines the Hamitic and Semitic groups as subfamilies. Hamitic includes Berber in the Maghreb, Coptic in Egypt, Gallinya in Ethiopia, and Somali in the Horn of Africa. Semitic includes Amharic and Tigrinya in Ethiopia, Arabic in North Africa and West Asia, and Hebrew in West Asia.

❷ Nilo-Saharan

Which includes Dinka in Sudan, Lango in Uganda, and Luo in Kenya.

❸ Niger-Congo

This immense family ranges from West to South Africa, including the vast Bantu subfamily, among whose members are Bemba, Kikongo/Kongo/Congo, Kimbundu, Kiswahili/Swahili, Xhosa/isiXhosa, and Zulu/isiZulu. The word *Bantu* in its international scholarly sense identifies over 300 widely distributed but closely related languages, and *c*.60 million people of various ethnic backgrounds who speak them. Included are Douala in Cameroon, Ganda in Uganda, Kongo in Congo (formerly Zaire), Nyanja in Malawi, Shona in Zimbabwe, Ndebele in Zimbabwe and South Africa, Sotho in Lesotho and South Africa, Tsonga in Mozambique and South Africa, Tswana in Botswana and South Africa, Siswati in Swaziland, and Xhosa and Zulu in South Africa. The most widely used Bantu language is Swahili, a lingua franca of East and Central Africa strongly influenced by Arabic and more recently English.

❹ Khoisan

A small family whose name combines *Khoi* (formerly *Hottentot*) and *San* (formerly *Bushman*), spoken by small groups in South Africa and larger but still small populations in Namibia, of whom the largest are the Namas (*c*.45,000).

There have been at least two enormously significant developments in the history of the sub-Saharan languages: the first internal to the African continent, and more or less evolutionary, the second externalizing and immensely fractured. The first relates to migrations involving the Bantu subfamily of languages, the second to slave trading on the Atlantic coast. The following list covers significant aspects of the spread of the Bantu languages:

❶ The Bantu migrations

Epic migrations south and east from west and central Africa helped to create, among other developments, the major element in the pattern of present-day Southern Africa's language complex. The original Bantu-speaking peoples appear to have originated in the region of Cameroon (west/central Africa). In the structure of these languages, bases and affixes play a pre-eminent role: thus, from the base *Tswana* are formed *Batswana* (the Tswana people, formerly known in English as *Bechuanas*), *Motswana* (an individual Tswana), *Botswana* (the land of the Tswana), and Setswana (the language of the Batswana: a form increasingly used in English as more appropriate than simply *Tswana*). Among Bantu words in English are: the animal names *impala* and *zebra*; *boma* ('a thorn-bush enclosure'); Zulu *impi* ('regiment') and *indaba* ('gathering, conference'); and Swahili *uhuru* ('freedom').

❷ Borrowings into Bantu languages and English

English words associated with Bantu can be etymologically deceptive: thus, Swahili *bwana* ('master, boss') is from Arabic *abuna* ('our father'); *assegai* ('spear, lance') passed from Berber in North Africa into Arabic and thence to South Africa; *kraal* is from Portuguese *curral* through Dutch/Afrikaans, and is a doublet of Spanish-derived *corral*. Bantu languages have borrowed more extensively from English than English from them, most particularly in South Africa: for example, Zulu *ikhalenda* (from *calendar*), *ukheroti* (from *carrot*), and *ukholiflawa* (from *cauliflower*); Xhosa *ibhentshi* (from *bench*), *ikati* (from *cat*), and *ukubhaptiza* (*to baptize*).

❸ Bantu languages in South Africa

Two distinct groups of Bantu languages have emerged in South Africa, referred to by scholars as the *Nguni* and *Sotho-Tswana* families. Nguni (with over 15 million speakers today) includes over six million each for Zulu (isiZulu) and Xhosa (isiXhosa), and about a million for Swazi (Siswati/Swati). Sotho-Tswana includes about two million speakers of Sesotho (also called South(ern) Sotho), about three million speakers of Sepedi (also called North(ern) Sotho), and about three million speakers of Tswana (Setswana: formerly called both Sechuana and Bechuana).

❹ Nguni and Sotho-Tswana: possibilities of standardization

There is a considerable degree of mutual intelligibility among speakers of the Nguni languages, and somewhat less among the Sotho-Tswana languages. There could in principle be single planned standards, initially in writing and print, for Nguni as a whole and for Sotho, but language loyalty and inter-communal rivalry may act against such developments.

❺ Lingua francas

Zulu is a lingua franca in some areas of South Africa, and there are many 'township colloquials': hybrid varieties in black urban areas, such as *Flytaal* (an English/Afrikaans hybrid with links to the Bantu vernaculars, the name meaning 'fly language': *fly* in the sense of 'clever').

❻ 'Bantu', 'bantustans', and apartheid

During the period 1964–78, the indigenous population of South Africa was officially known as *Bantu*, as in the terms *Bantu Affairs* and *Bantu Education*. Before this period, the term was *Native* and in post-apartheid times the term has been *Black*. In apartheid times, one person was *a Bantu* and more than one were *Bantus*, terms generally detested by Black South Africans on both social and linguistic grounds: 'In South Africa today, the word Bantu has become a swear word . . . part and parcel of the apartheid structures. . . . There is no such thing as "a Bantu"' (*Voice*, 9 May 1982). A key element in the official policy of 'separate development' (Afrikaans: *apartheid*) was the creation of ten 'Bantu homelands', circumscribed territories set aside for specific groups. The hybrid term *bantustan* (combining Zulu *bantu* and Hindi/Persian *-stan*, as in *Afghanistan*) was used facetiously in South Africa for these homelands, especially in the English-language press, and was then widely supposed internationally to be a standard government term. The 'Bantu' homelands were: Bophuthatswana, Ciskei, Gazankulu, KaNgwane, KwaNdebele, KwaZulu, Lebowa, QwaQwa, Transkei, and Venda. Some were granted quasi-autonomous status but none was recognized outside the country. They no longer exist.

The second and external exodus was precipitated by the slave trade across the Atlantic, and included massive language transfer and change.

❶ The Middle Passage

Slave-trading was for centuries indigenous to Africa, a situation which European traders adapted to and then took advantage of, extending it to the plantations of their New World colonies. The shipment of millions of slaves to the Americas (16th–19th centuries) via 'the Middle Passage' (an eastern and western movement, midway between the northern and southern Atlantic regions) did not affect the languages of those who were not taken, but first disintegrated then re-created the usage of the slaves, leading to entirely new speech forms among their descendants.

❷ A half-hidden heritage

Slaves were actively discouraged from speaking their own languages, and members of the same language groups were often separated for commercial convenience or to prevent communication that their masters could not understand. Even so, however, the original languages left their mark on the new usage, a feature long disregarded (even disbelieved) by European and US language scholars.

❸ European languages in the Americas affected by African languages

The languages variously affected by African usage include: Portuguese in Brazil; English, French, Spanish, and Dutch in the Caribbean; Spanish and English in Central America; and English and French in the USA (notably in Louisiana, Georgia, and the Carolinas, but also in African-American English at large).

❹ Full circle: The speech of emancipated slaves 'returns' to Africa

In the course of time, the English slave patois that first developed in West African trading depots and then more fully on North American plantations returned in two forms to West Africa with groups of freed slaves: one to become Krio in Sierra Leone, the other to become Merico in Liberia. Krio in due course influenced West African Pidgin English at large.

In recent decades, many governments of post-colonial sub-Saharan states have had difficulty deciding which of their languages to standardize in the Western style and how to manage such languages alongside any Africanized European language also used in their territories. Such states have generally retained one or more ex-colonial language in official roles, for example: English in Nigeria; French in Benin; French and English in Cameroon; English in second position to the East African regional language Swahili in Kenya; and English and Afrikaans in South Africa alongside nine indigenous languages. At least four arguments have emerged in favour of retaining a former imperial/colonial European language as an official language:

❶ The *status quo* argument

The language was already in use for administration and education: Why change something that works and with which people are familiar, however unsatisfactory the history behind it?

❷ The anti-rivalry argument

Such a language poses fewer problems of loyalty and rivalry than any local language: everybody is equal in having to acquire it, and no community language is likely to gain untrammeled pre-eminence.

❸ The unification argument

Such a language could serve as a unifying medium in areas of great sociolinguistic diversity.

❹ The *lingua franca* argument

English and French were already lingua francas, especially if their pidgin varieties are included. Even if the standard varieties of the ex-colonial languages were not adopted as official usage, the pidgins would continue to be widely used. The existence of the 'proper' language at the national level might encourage people to improve their pidgin usage and perhaps ultimately abandon it.

The issue of the uses and interfaces of indigenizing European languages on the one hand and local languages on the other continues to be controversial. Some observers (African and other) have argued that the use of European languages for national purposes de-Africanizes the people who use them, while others contend that these languages are themselves being more and more Africanized. From one point of view, they continue to be alien impositions; from another, they are as much languages of Africa as Spanish and English are languages of the Americas. From a third (paradoxical but very human) point of view, they manage to be *both* alien impositions *and* Africanized languages, predicated on how people feel and what they want or need at any time.

There is in any case nothing new about non-African languages being used in Africa. West Asian and European languages have been successively introduced into Africa from the earliest recorded times:

❶ Phoenician, Greek, and Latin

Phoenician in Carthage; Greek in Egypt and Libya; Latin as the language of first the Roman Empire, then the Roman Catholic Church

❷ Arabic

Introduced in the early Middle Ages, the primary proselytizing language of Islam, empire, and trade, and long part of the linguistic fabric of the continent. Varieties of Arabic have been spoken for centuries from Morocco to Egypt, and been significant as a lingua franca in the Sahel and on the east coast, notably in and around Zanzibar.

❸ Atlantic European languages

Portuguese, Spanish, English, French, and German (five major ship-borne languages) were introduced during the 16th–19th century, two results of which are pidginization and hybridization.

❹ Asian languages

Immigrants from the Indian subcontinent introduced Gujarati, Hindi, Urdu, and other languages into mainly British territories in the 19th–20th centuries, but (as in the Caribbean) these have remained almost entirely the preserve of localized South Asian Hindu and Muslim communities.

All the evidence suggests that the language situation in Africa has long been varied and fluid, and has required great adaptability and range on the part of its peoples, especially since so much of the interplay has been entirely spoken, within a rich and diverse oral tradition.

Africa's European languages

Paradoxes abound with regard to European languages established in sub-Saharan Africa, despite (or because of) their use as official languages, as with Portuguese in Angola, French in Senegal, and English in Nigeria. A mix of ambivalence, frustration, determination, and even optimism is noticeable among writers and scholars who (though they may vigorously seek to resist the influence of ex-colonial languages and to strengthen indigenous languages) continue to write in these 'elite languages' and in West Africa (most ironically) to use Pidgin as a channel for protest. African European languages fall into several overlapping types:

❶ Settler languages

The languages of long-established colonizing communities, notably in Southern Africa: Portuguese from the 16th century, Dutch from the 17th century (morphing into a new language, Afrikaans, in the 19th century), and English from the 18th century.

❷ Africanized languages

Such indigenized languages as Portuguese in the Cape Verde Islands (off the West African coast) and American English in Liberia ('Freedom Land').

❸ Post-colonial languages of government and management

National, official, administrative, and legal languages, as with English in Nigeria, French in Senegal, and Portuguese in Angola.

❹ Cultural and educational languages

Such as English and French in churches, schools, colleges, publishing houses, and other institutions, roles comparable to the use of Arabic for Islamic purposes.

English has been in Africa since the 17th century and at the beginning of the 21st century is the continent's single most widely used language. In North Africa, the foremost European colonial and post-colonial language has been French (with English, Italian, and Spanish in less extensive roles), but in the rest of the continent the foremost European post-colonial, missionary, and educational language has been English (with French, Portuguese, Dutch, Spanish, and German in less extensive roles, by and large in that order).

In addition, two languages of European origin are native to the continent: Afrikaans, whose status as an autonomous local language in and around South Africa was established at least a century ago (after resistance within the Cape Dutch community itself), and West African Pidgin English (WAPE, Pidgin English, Pidgin), whose status and uses remain controversial. It nonetheless manifests all the signs of an independent language, including three cardinal features of any language: (1) 'dialects' of its own in a continuum across West Africa; (2) the possession of an orthography (variable across the region); (3) a growing literature (often mixed with more conventional English). The closest thing to a social and historical nucleus is Krio, the speech of North American slaves taken back to West Africa, who settled in Freetown in what became Sierra Leone.

African English

The use of the phrase *African English* is now common. In principle, it should mean 'the English language as used in Africa' but, as with other such labels, matters are not straightforward. If, logically, the term covers all English from Cairo to the Cape, then it would include English in the Arabic-speaking countries of the North (such as Morocco and Egypt), the English of speakers of, for example, Yoruba, Igbo, and

Hausa in Nigeria in West Africa, Swahili and Kikuyu and Luo in East Africa, and of Xhosa, Afrikaans, etc., in South Africa—alongside the post-settlement English of British colonists.

In practice, however, the term is not so widely applied. Thus, Egyptians in Cairo and South Africans of European or Asian backgrounds in Cape Town are seldom if ever said to speak *African* English. A minority of Egyptians is commonly regarded as speaking (in addition to their everyday Arabic and Coptic) an Egyptian English comparable to the Englishes of other Arabic-speaking countries in North Africa and West Asia (such as Libya and Lebanon). Such usage is not, however, normally linked or compared with, say, Nigerian or Zimbabwean English—both of which are incontrovertibly regarded as kinds of *African English*. Secondly, in the case of South Africans of European background, those of British origin have English as part of a pre-African ethno-cultural inheritance. Their usage has also traditionally been called *South African English* when discussed both in its own right and alongside *American*, *British*, *Canadian*, and *Australian English*, etc.

In addition, many Afrikaners (alongside Afrikaans and any other language) speak an 'Afrikaans English' that is both influenced by their mother tongue and intimately linked with (British settler) South African English, and both varieties are distinct from the usage of Black South Africans. Indeed, in South Africa, the more or less synonymous terms *African English* and *Black English* contrast implicitly and explicitly with *White English*. Like so many other things in South Africa, the kind of English one speaks tends to be tied to race, and to have political echoes. Indeed, the case is often made in South Africa that the country has two kinds of English: *White English* (British-derived and Afrikaans-influenced) and *Black English* (the Africanized usage of the majority, with British and Afrikaans associations)—with some uncertainty about where to locate Coloureds and Asians. White usage is generally regarded as prestigious and linked with education, and Black with brokenness and the impoverished African townships.

For the continent as a whole, *African English* is a Black language, sometimes labelled for clarity's sake a 'Black African language', although the term *African* is often taken to imply 'black', and to exclude, say, Arabs and others in the North (although there is no absolute reason for this to be so). As such, 'Black African English' is partnered by the 'Black English' of the Caribbean, of most African Americans, and of young Afro-British people (especially in London). Many speakers of Black English in South Africa do not identify with the English of White South Africans or the rest of the world, and their usage is linguistically, socially, and often politically associated with 'Black consciousness', 'Black culture', and 'Black pride', in contrast to 'White' domination, exploitation, and racism in South Africa, the US, the UK, and elsewhere.

Traditionally, there has been some sociopolitical solidarity with Black 'brothers and sisters' elsewhere, but in the years since apartheid this has by no means been consistent. In the severe competition for jobs in the RSA, Black South Africans have at times proved highly unsympathetic towards migrants from north of their border when they have come south looking for work, nor have matters always been positive between them and the small numbers of Black Americans who, after apartheid, went to South Africa to work and/or show solidarity with the recently liberated— nor indeed are relations always good among the different Black communities in 'the rainbow nation' itself.

Contentiousness does not end there. For some commentators, the term *African English* includes all indigenized sub-Saharan English since trading posts were set up in the 17th century, notably including the trade jargons and pidgins. For others, it refers only to standard and near-standard forms spoken and written by educated Africans after territories began to be administered as colonies by the British, some of these territories being settled by them (as with Kenya, Zambia, Zimbabwe, and South Africa), others not (as with Ghana and Nigeria). If all forms are included (notably Pidgin in West Africa), then the English language has been used in Africa for almost 400 years: that is, much the same length of time as in North America, the Caribbean, and Asia. If, however, the second, narrower, and 'higher' sense is adopted, then English in Africa dates only from the earlier 19th century—just under 200 years.

Whatever the interpretation, the reality and integrity of a comprehensive African English (with such subvarieties as Kenyan English, Nigerian English, and South African Black English) remain controversial matters. Kinds of English are in daily use for many purposes throughout the continent, including as an inter-state high-level political and economic lingua franca, reflecting all manner of local, regional, and international distinctions. It is taught as a second language in the Arabophone North African countries and such Francophone countries as Côte d'Ivoire (Ivory Coast) and Senegal, as well as Lusophone countries such as Angola and Mozambique (the latter recently accepted into the Commonwealth). As a result, it is *the* universal African lingua franca. That lingua franca is not, however, simply (Black) *African* English as just discussed, but part of the general international continuum within which (Black) African English has a place alongside all other Englishes. Four levels are in fact involved—local, national, intra-continental, and global.

The situation is not simple, but it would seem from all of this that English in Africa is a continuum, from ancient and thriving Pidgin varieties and a range of hybrids through local and national varieties to service as an international (indeed cosmopolitan) medium for all the peoples of Africa from Cairo to the Cape. Within this array, such a pan-African English is neither homogeneous nor can it be tidily marked off from either indigenous 'White' South African usage (which has African aspects that other 'white' Englishes do not possess) or from English as used in the Arabic and Arabic-and-Berber regions.

That said, however, the focus of 'African English' has for many reasons been sub-Saharan and indigenous, and many issues remain to be resolved within that frame of reference alone (regardless of 'other Africas'). Despite the difficulties, some broad general statements can be made—with care and provisos—about the vast variety south of the Sahara.

Pronunciation

1 Black African English is universally non-rhotic and is generally syllable-timed. In this, it is comparable to English and English Creole in the Caribbean, and most African-American groups. When *r* is pronounced, it is often trilled ('rrr').

2 The schwa (or weak vowel) typical of unstressed syllables in the rhythm of traditional English is generally replaced by a full vowel: 'stu-dent' for *student* and 'qui-et-ness' for *quietness.*

3 West African speakers tend to have antepenultimate overall word stress (that is, the emphasis falls two syllables before the last, as in *CONdition*), while East and Southern African speakers tend to have penultimate word stress (one syllable before the last, as in *mainTEnance*, applying a Bantu stress pattern). [Native-speaking communities and Afrikaners largely follow UK norms, with the exception of Liberia, where US norms prevail.]

4 In West Africa, intonation is influenced by the tonal systems of the indigenous languages.

5 Vowel systems of no more than five to seven sounds often lead to sets of homophones such as *beat/bit*, *had/hard*, *fool/full*, and *cot/caught/court/cut* (all with more or less the pronunciation of the first word in each of these sets).

6 The two sounds of *th* are usually realized in West Africa as *t* and *d* ('tree of dem' for *three of them*) and in East Africa as *s* and *z* ('sree of zem').

Grammar

1 There is a tendency to make traditionally uncountable nouns countable: *firewoods* ('bits of firewood'); *furnitures* ('pieces of furniture'); *correspondences* ('letters').

2 Words are often repeated for emphasis and effect: *Do it small small* ('Do it slowly, bit by bit'); *What you say, you say*; *My friend, I see what I see*. At times there may be a biblical or oratorical and repetitive dimension: *They blamed them, they blamed them for all the troubles that have befallen us.*

3 The use of resumptive pronoun subjects is common: *My daughter she is attending that school*; *My father he is very tall.*

4 Simple verbs are often used instead of their phrasal-verb derivatives: *crop* rather than 'crop up' ('I hope it won't crop again'); *pick* for 'pick up' ('We'll pick you at three').

Vocabulary

1 The same broad patterns of word formation and use (local and regional borrowings; hybrid expressions, especially compounds; loan translations; and distinctive adaptations) are universal, but even major regional items have not spread more widely.

2 Local and regional borrowings: West African *buka* ('foodstand') from Hausa; *danfo*, *oga* ('minibus', 'master, boss'), from Yoruba; East African *pombe* ('beer', from Swahili); Southern African *madumbi* ('tubers', from Zulu); more general, *bush meat* (meat from game animals).

3 Hybrid compounds: West Africa, *kente cloth*, *bodom beads* (Ghana); *akara ball* ('bean cake'), *juju music* (Nigeria); East Africa, *mabenzi people* and *wabenzi* ('people with a Mercedes-Benz, by implication rich and influential', from English/German and Swahili); Southern Africa, *lobola-beast*, from Nguni *ukolobola* ('to give a dowry'), someone who uses a bride price as a means of exploitation while feigning friendship; *kwela music*, from Xhosa *kwela* ('to get moving'), penny-whistle music (South Africa).

4 Loan translations from local languages: West African *chewing stick* (a piece of wood used as a toothbrush); *cornstick* ('corncob'); *tight friend* ('close friend');

enstool ('to enthrone (a chief)'); *destool* ('to overthrow or remove (a chief)'), with derivatives *enstoolment* and *destoolment*.

5   English words used in distinctive ways: Nigerian/Cameroonian *in state* ('pregnant'); Nigerian *have long legs* ('to wield power and influence'); West African *high life* (local music similar to jazz); Kenyan *thank you* (as a reply to 'goodbye'); East African *beat me a picture* ('take my photograph'), and *It's porridge* (slang: 'It's a piece of cake').

Style

1   A narrative style (in public speaking, works of fiction, and the media) that is characteristic of oral rhetoric, using proverbs, figures of speech, titles, praise words, and special epithets: *My brother, son of my fathers, you have failed*; *Do you blame a vulture for perching over a carcass?*; *Father, isn't it true that a wise man becomes wiser by borrowing from other people's heads?* Such a traditional style closely parallels Biblical and Quranic usage, which both have links with traditional orality.

2   Kinds of hybridization, with or without glossing, as exemplified by these excerpts from three West African novels: 'He paraded me to the world, l'ogolonto' (Igbo 'stark-naked', in Wole Soyinka's *Kongi's Harvest*, 1967); 'Each feared onwana wa rikutene—a bastard child' (in Abel Mwanga's *Nyangeta: The Name from the Calabash*, 1976).

3   Such mixing may include Pidgin in West Africa: *'He no be like dat,' said Joseph. 'Him no gentleman. Not fit take bribe'* (Chinua Achebe, *No Longer at Ease*, 1960).

Works of literature have been produced in English in the sub-Saharan countries that were part of the British Empire. The first widely acknowledged novels by Black Africans have been Nigerian, including notably Amos Tutuola's *Palm Wine Drinkard* (Faber, 1953), Cyprian Ekwensi's *People of the City* (Hutchinson, 1956), and Chinua Achebe's *Things Fall Apart* (Heinemann, 1958). Ngugi wa Thiong'o's *Weep Not, Child* (Heinemann, 1964) is Kenyan. Achebe's novel (its title from T. S. Eliot's 'The Wasteland', 1922) has become a world classic and a yardstick for subsequent African-English fiction. Since 1960, there has been a flow of novels, plays, poetry, and short stories, many adapting into literature the style and content of traditional orature. Drama, myth, story, song, dance, and poetry (often of epic proportions) are part of indigenous culture, elements of which were maintained and adapted by slaves carried to the Americas.

The non-African origin and nature of English was a matter of heated debate both before and after the emergence of independent sub-Saharan states. Obiajunwa Wali in Nigeria and Ngugi wa Thiong'o in Kenya have argued that the use of English as a literary medium is an elitist colonial remnant, a vehicle of Westernization, and a threat to local languages. Such writers and their supporters have favoured the use of local languages but even so been constrained to make their point *in* English, at home and elsewhere. Others, including Achebe, have supported English, emphasizing four points: its international status and readership; its importance as a unifying medium within Africa; the ease with which it can be moulded to reflect African culture and tradition; and the role it has played in liberation movements.

Like their Caribbean counterparts, African writers have recalled Shakespeare's Caliban, arguing that English is now part of the African repertoire: 'You taught me Language, and my profit on't/ Is, I know how to curse: the red-plague rid you/ For learning me your language' (*The Tempest* 1: 2). Many West African writers use Pidgin as part of their spectrum. In Nigeria, Achebe has used it in prose, Aik-Imoukhuede in poetry, and Ola Rotimi in drama. Literature is also being provided through radio and television, broadcasting poetry, plays, stories, and serials by local writers who often write in both English and their mother tongue. In its turn, their English uses specific linguistic and cultural backgrounds to express universal themes, as part of the tradition of Walter Scott, Thomas Hardy, the Brontë sisters, Rudyard Kipling, Mark Twain, James Joyce, R. K. Narayan, and Derek Walcott.

West African English

The term *West African English* (*WAE*) primarily covers six countries, among which Cameroon, Gambia, Ghana, Nigeria, and Sierra Leone are former British colonies, while Liberia has a unique American connection. English is official in each, in Cameroon alongside French. It is typically acquired as a second, third, or fourth language, and the line between Standard English as used by a small elite and the more widely used *West African Pidgin English* (*WAPE*) can be hard to draw. English-speakers generally understand each other, but there are differences inside each territory. The continuum of *WAE* and *WAPE* also includes hybridization with local languages, such as Wolof, Ashanti, Hausa, and Igbo as well as with French and français petit-nègre ('Little Black French': Pidgin French) in neighbouring francophone territories. Some interaction has also occurred with Spanish in Equatorial Guinea, Portuguese in Guinea-Bissau and Cape Verde, and German formerly in Cameroon.

WAPE in its various forms (dialects?) is the outcome of long-term trading between Africans and Europeans, and has played an enduring role in the development of English creoles in the US, the Caribbean, and Central America. The trans-Atlantic forms have in turn influenced it, notably through Krio in Sierra Leone and Merico in Liberia, both of which have origins in the usage of liberated slaves returning from North America. *WAE*, on the other hand, evolved out of the formal teaching of the language during the colonial era, when grammatical and literary studies began to be central to educational success (indeed, 'grammar' is often used as a kind of synonym for 'English', much as it was once used in England as a synonym for Latin).

Inevitably, as with standard French, Portuguese, and Spanish in other African colonies, Standard English became both a necessity for communication between administrations and their educated subjects and a prized vehicle of upward mobility. As a result, it became the elite medium of the post-colonial establishment, while various lingua francas—including Pidgin—served the immediate needs of the majority. Contact between WAE and such lingua francas added to its complexity and distinctness. In addition, both creative writers and publishers willing to take them on have contributed to the emergence of a literary English that made plenty of room for WAPE. As the Nigerian novelist Chinua Achebe put it over thirty years ago:

> **1965** My answer to the question, can an African ever learn English well enough to be able to use it effectively in creative writing? is certainly yes. If on the other hand you ask: Can he ever learn to use it like a native speaker? I should say: I hope not. It is neither necessary nor desirable for him to be able to do so. The price a world language must be prepared to pay is submission to many different kinds of use. The African writer should aim to use English in a way that brings out his message best without altering the language to the extent that its value as a medium of international exchange will be lost.
> — *Transition* 18

The late Nigerian writer Ken Saro-Wiwa used the term 'rotten English' for the first-person narrative in his 1985 novel *Sozaboy* ('Soldier Boy'). As described in his preface, it is 'a mixture of Nigerian pidgin English, broken English, and occasional flashes of good, even idiomatic English. This language is disordered and disorderly. Born of a meagre education and severely limited opportunities, it borrows words, patterns and images freely . . . To its speakers, it has the advantage of having no rules and no syntax. It thrives on lawlessness.' Whether any intelligible flow of speech can be as anarchic as that is moot, but Saro-Wiwa's 'lawlessness' is evident enough in the following excerpt from *Lomber Eighteen* ('Number' or Chapter 18):

> To talk true, I was not thinking of all these things. I was just thinking of my mama and my young wife Agnes. If my mama die, what will I talk? If that sozaman have pregnanted my young darling or even sef killed her because she no gree 'am, what will I say? Ah, God no gree bad thing, God no gree bad thing. I must to find my mama and my wife. We must to all return to Dukana and build fine house to live inside.

This usage is a literary rendering of a rough-and-ready area between Standard and Pidgin: confused, but hardly chaos. The narrator is clear in recounting the reasons for his pain, and his style, strength, and fluency suggest that to separate WAPE surgically from WAE would be a futile enterprise.

WAPE is spoken in a geographical continuum from Gambia to Cameroon (including enclaves in French- and Portuguese-speaking countries) and in a vertical continuum with WAE at the top. Among the local varieties are *Aku* in Gambia, *Krio* in Sierra Leone, *Settler English* and *Pidgin English* in Liberia, *Pidgin* (*English*) in Ghana and Nigeria, and *Pidgin* (*English*) or *Kamtok* in Cameroon. It originates in 16th-century contacts between West Africans and English sailors and traders, and is therefore as old as so-called 'Modern English'. Some WAPE speakers, especially in cities, do not speak any traditional African language: it is their sole means of expression.

Because many of its features are close to those of creoles in the Americas, some researchers have proposed a family of 'Atlantic creoles' that includes Pidgin in West Africa, Gullah in the US, and the various patois of the Caribbean. However, like them, and despite its usefulness, vigour, and wide distribution, Pidgin tends to be regarded as debased English. The following points indicate its nature and how it appears in print:

WAPE pronunciation

1   It is non-rhotic and syllable-timed.

2   Its vowels and consonants have the same values as in the languages around it.

3   Clusters of consonants tend to be reduced to single sounds, as in *tori* ('story') and *mash* ('smash'), or to be opened up by an inserted vowel, as in *sipia* ('spear') and *sikin* ('skin'), with stress on the syllable containing the conventional vowel.

WAPE grammar

1   Individual words may function as different parts of speech in ways untypical of English: *plenti* as an adjective (*plenti pikin* 'plenty of children'), a verb (*Pikin plenti* 'There are plenty of children'), a noun (*Plenti pwel*: 'Many are spoilt'), and an adverb (*I get pikin plenti*: 'He has plenty of children').

2   Tense and aspect are non-inflectional and deduced from context. The element *bin* ('been') denotes both simple past and past perfect (*Meri bin lef* 'Mary left', 'Mary had left'); *de/di* the progressive generally (*Meri de it* 'Mary is eating', 'Mary was eating'); *don* ('done') the perfective (*Meri don it* 'Mary has eaten', 'Mary had eaten'). Other forms are: *A bin go* ('I went'); *I go go* ('He/She will go'); *Wuna di go* ('You *plural* are going'); *Yu sabi chop* ('You *singular* eat all the time', literally 'You know eat').

3   Depending on context, *Meri it* can mean 'Mary ate' or 'Mary has eaten', and *Meri laik Ed* means 'Mary likes Ed' or 'Mary liked Ed'.

4   Serial verbs are common, such as *ron go* ('run go'), as in *I ron go rich di haus* ('He/She ran as far as the house').

5   Adjectives are used without the verb *to be* when in the predicate position: *Meri sik* ('Mary is sick'). In *Meri de sik* ('Mary is falling/getting sick'), the progressive *de* marks transition. Adjectives and verbs function in much the same way: *A big* ('I'm big'); *A go big* ('I'll be big'); *Som big man* ('A big man'); and *A waka* ('I walk'), *A go waka* ('I'll walk'), *som waka man* ('a walker, someone walking').

6   Plurality is assumed from context (*tu pikin* 'two children') or indicated by the element *dem* ('them': *ma pikin dem* 'my children'; *arata* 'rat'; *arata dem* 'rats'). *I bin kil di arata dem kwik-kwik* ('He/She killed the rats quickly').

7   Questions are marked either by intonation alone (*I no go kam?* 'Won't he/she come?') or by a question initiator followed by a statement form (*Usai i bin go?* '(You say) Where did he/she go?').

WAPE vocabulary

1   Although most words derive from English, many have adapted meanings and uses, as with: *han* (both 'hand' and 'arm'); *fut* (both 'foot' and 'leg').

2   Compounds with figurative meanings include: *dei klin* ('day clean': dawn); *drai ai* ('dry eye': 'brave'), both common in Krio.

3   Most words are from English, but the meanings of many have widened in the process: *buk* ('book, letter, anything written'); *savi buk* ('know book': educated).

4   Loanwords from local languages tend to relate to culture and kinship: *ngombi* ('ghost, spirit of the dead'); *danshiki* ('tunic-like shirt'); *mbanya* ('co-wife in a polygamous family'); *njamanjama* ('green vegetables').

5 There are many loan translations from local languages, as in: *krai dai*
   ('cry die' = a wake or funeral celebration); *tai han* ('tie hand' = meanness).

The following review focuses on English, Pidgin, and local languages in Gambia,
Sierra Leone, Liberia, Ghana, Nigeria, and Cameroon.

Gambia became a British colony in 1807, gained its independence in 1965, and
became a republic within the Commonwealth in 1970. English is the official language, Pidgin is widely used, and the local languages include Mandinka, Fula, and
Wolof. Arabic is also used, especially in Quranic schools. Also traditionally known
as *the Gambia*, the country is geographically unusual, consisting of long narrow
strips of territory along both banks of the Gambia River. With the exception of
a short coastal strip, it is entirely surrounded by Senegal, which therefore has no
direct access to the river. The official language of Senegal is French. In 1982, Gambia
and Senegal formed the Confederation of Senegambia, which brought English,
French, and the local languages into a relationship comparable to Cameroon, but
the arrangement collapsed in 1989, and was replaced in 1991 by a treaty of co-
operation. The local Pidgin is known as Aku and Aku Talk, and is so similar to
the Krio of Sierra Leone that it is also called Gambian Krio.

Sierra Leone is similarly multilingual, its ethnic groups including the majority
Mende (over 30%), the Temne, Kono, Fulani, Bullom, Koranko, Limba, Loko,
Kissi—and the Krios. English is the official language and Mende, Temne, and the
pidgin known as Krio ('Creole') are widely spoken. The first Europeans in the region
were Portuguese then English slave-traders. In the 1780s, some British philan-
thropists bought land from local chiefs in order to establish settlements for freed
slaves, whence the name of the capital, Freetown. The coastal settlements became
a British colony in 1807 and the larger hinterland a protectorate in 1896. Sierra
Leone became independent in 1961 and a republic in 1971. It is a member of the
Commonwealth. A multi-party political system was approved by referendum in
1991 but it was prevented from functioning by a military coup in 1992, since which
there has been often horrific violent turmoil leading to intervention by Nigeria in
1998 and UN and UK forces at the turn of the millennium.

  The first Krios (sometimes *Creos*) were transported from both Britain and Nova
Scotia in 1787 and 1792, bringing with them the English slave vernacular of North
America, often at that time known simply as *Creole*. Christian and often literate,
they were valued as teachers and clerks along the anglophone West African coast,
and Krio settlements grew up in Gambia, Liberia, Ghana, Nigeria, and Cameroon. As
a result, their everyday usage, also known as Krio, has had a formative influence on
all WAPE except *Merico* in Liberia. Krio is a mother tongue to some 250,000 people
in and around Freetown, and second language to many more. The 'bilingual'
Krio–English Dictionary, edited by C. N. Fyle and Eldred Jones, has both marked it
off from WAE and elevated its status. Krio is the most standardized form of WAPE,
with translations of parts of the Bible, Shakespeare, and other works. WAE and Krio
shade into one other and into the local languages.

  WAE is the language of government, education, newspapers and magazines,
and 95% of television and cinema. It has such a high status that 'using an African
language at a wedding reception or even a private party is unheard of, because it is

considered a debasement of the value of the occasion' (Joe Pemagbi, 'Still a Deficient Language? The New English of Sierra Leone', *English Today* 17, Jan 1989). Distinctively Sierra Leonean vocabulary includes:

1 Extensions in word meanings, such as: *apprentice* (a young man who loads and unloads vehicles); *to bluff* ('to be elegantly dressed': *She's really bluffing today*); *cookery* cheap food (eaten outside the home); *to foolish someone* ('to make someone appear stupid': *The shopkeeper was foolished and felt bad*); *woman damage* (money paid to a husband by another man as compensation for having sexual intercourse with his wife).

2 Borrowings from local languages, such as: *agidi* (a paste made from fermented cornflour); *akara* ('beancake'); *bondo* (a secret society for women); *fufu* (grated and fermented cassava cooked into a paste and eaten with soup or sauce); *nono* ('buttermilk'); *woreh* ('cattle ranch').

Liberia (Latin: 'Freedom Land') has over twenty Niger-Congo languages, of which Kru and Mande are the most prominent. The region was mapped by the Portuguese in the 15th century and later visited by the Dutch, British, and other Europeans looking for gold, spices, and slaves. A homeland for freed slaves in this area was set up by a group of philanthropic societies in the US (including the American Colonization Society), influenced by the creation by the British of Freetown in Sierra Leone. Monrovia, the Liberian capital, was founded in 1822 and named for US President James Monroe. Until 1841, the governors of Liberia were white Americans, and in that year a black Virginian, Joseph Jenkins Roberts, took over, declaring in 1847 the 'Free and Independent Republic of Liberia'.

Liberia is the only Black African country in which English is a native language. Freed slaves migrated from the US until the end of the Civil War in 1865, and African-Americans settled there in small numbers for decades afterwards. Liberia did not, however, become the peaceful and progressive haven and homeland that its founders hoped for. The descendants of the ex-slaves (known formally as *Americo-Liberians* and colloquially as *Mericos* and *Congos*) established the centrality and prestige of American English in their new country, which they dominated politically and economically, especially through the True Whig Party, until a coup in 1980, led by Sergeant Samuel Doe, a non-Merico. The US-style constitution was suspended and a People's Redemption Council established, with a new constitution in 1984. Civil war broke out in 1990, leading to famine, and more or less ended in 1996 when Charles Taylor took control of the country after elections in 1997, but conditions in and around Liberia have remained volatile, chaotic, and violent.

Currently, the English of Liberia is a continuum from high to low prestige, with Liberian American English at the top: widely regarded as a token of good education and being civilized, and used on radio and TV. Below it comes *Vernacular Liberian English*, then at the base of the pyramid four distinct varieties, the first contrasting sharply with the others. It is known as both *Merico* and *Settler English*, and has echoes of Southern US usage before the Civil War. The others can all be regarded as varieties of WAPE. One arose out of contacts from the 17th century on between native speakers of both British and American English and such coastal peoples as the Kru, and is known as *Kru Pidgin English*. Another is a later cousin, *Liberian*

Interior English, used mainly by speakers of Mande. The third is *Soldier English*, a pidgin used since the early 20th century by and with non-English-speakers in the army. To add to the complexity, Sierra Leone Krio has also been influential.

In terms of pronunciation, Liberia's usage ranges from a rhotic (associated with General American usage) to more conventional West African non-rhotic pronunciations influenced by Kru and Mande. The following list provides examples of middle- and low-prestige grammatical usages and contrasts and some distinctive vocabulary items:

❶ Non-standard auxiliaries

He done come ('He has come'); *A was not know* ('I didn't know'); habitual *do*, as in *I do see boy all de time* ('I see the boy all the time'); progressive *de*, as in *I de go* ('I am going').

❷ Uninflected verbs

You see da man? ('Did you see the man?'); *A know dem* ('I knew them'); *Dey kesh grahapa* ('They caught grasshoppers').

❸ Kinds of Pidgin

The distinction between Merico/Settler and Kru Pidgin can be seen in Merico *Da pekin cryin* and Kru *Di pekin de krai* ('The child is crying'), and Settler *I ain see him* and Kru *A neva siam*.

❹ Local vocabulary

Distinctively Liberian words include: *bugabug* ('termite'); *dumboy* ('boiled, pounded cassava'); *to favour* ('to resemble': compare US usage); *fresh cold* ('a runny nose, a head cold'); *groundpea* ('peanut, groundnut'); *jina* ('spirits'); *kanki* (a measurement for rice, around two cups); *kwi* ('foreigner'); *outside child* (a child acknowledged although born outside marriage).

Although, traditionally, the standard language has been emphasized and other varieties disparaged, much as in the rest of Anglophone West Africa, as a consequence of civil unrest in recent years, compromise forms have been gaining ground in the media and as expressions of political and social solidarity. Notably, the mid-level usage in Monrovia has been spreading.

Ghana (formerly *the Gold Coast*) has a population of some 20 million, and a wide range of languages. English is official, Pidgin (with no distinctive local name) is widely used, and indigenous languages include Ashanti, Ewe, Fanti, and Ga. The territory came under British influence in 1874, and present-day Ghana comprises the former British colonies of the Gold Coast and Ashanti, the protectorate of the Northern Territories, and the United Nations trusteeship of British Togoland. When it gained independence in 1957 within the Commonwealth it was the first British colony in Africa to do so. Although for most of its subsequent history it was under military rule, it is currently a democracy. Ghana is one of the world's major producers of cocoa, and is also noted for cotton and rubber.

Ghana has probably had a more intimate and longer contact with speakers of English than any other West African country. The English established a fort at Cormantine in 1631 and had four forts in the area by 1670. Indeed, English seamen and merchants and their local wives appear to have formed a nucleus of English-speakers in Ghana more than a century before there were settlements in Liberia and Sierra Leone. Although well-educated Ghanaians take a pride in the quality of their English and like to consider that quality representative of their nation, there is (as in other West African countries) a continuum of usage from Standard Ghanaian to Pidgin English. As Kofi Sey, himself a Ghanaian, has observed regarding the existence or not of a distinct 'Ghanaian English':

> **1973** The linguist may be able to isolate features of Ghanaian English and describe them. But once these are made known to him, the educated Ghanaian would strive to avoid them altogether. The surest way to kill Ghanaian English, if it really exists, is to discover it and make it known.
> – *Ghanaian English: An Exploratory Survey* (Macmillan), 10

Even so, however, there is a great deal of distinctive usage in Ghana, including words and grammatical forms common across anglophone West Africa. Among them are: *balance* ('change': as in *The balance you gave me is not correct*); *chop box* ('food box': as in *Put the yam in the chop box*); *themselves* ('each other', as in *Those two really love themselves*); *an airtight* ('a metal box'); *a cover shoulder* ('a kind of blouse'); *enskin* ('to enthrone' a chief, using a ceremonial animal skin); *an outdooring* ('a christening'); uncountable nouns often used countably, such as *equipments* and *furnitures*; and hybrid compounds formed from English and local words, such as *kente cloth*, *donno drum*, *bodom beads*.

There has also since independence been an informal and mainly spoken hybridized variety of English in schools, on university campuses, and increasingly among younger people at large. It draws: on Pidgin, as in *I no sabi* ('I don't know') and *Is that your pickin?* ('Is that your child?'); on words and styles from local languages, as in *He is an akuafo* ('He is a farmer'), *She tear-tear her shirt all* ('She tore her shirt to shreds'), and *I don't like mouth-mouth* ('I don't like boasting and bragging'); and on hybridisms, such as *dondology* (the study of music and dance, from *dondo*, a kind of drum), *Manu afaili* ('The man failed'), and *He loves abigism* 'He puts on airs'), The Ghanaian scholar Samuel Ahulu notes:

> **1995** [I]t may not be surprising that H[ybridized] E[nglish in] G[hana] has generated so much debate in the country. Combining features that are associated with Standard English, the Ghanaian languages and pidginization, HEG means different things to different people. To some parents and educationalists, it is nothing more than pidginization, and should not be allowed on Ghanaian campuses. . . . Others see it as resulting from students' inability to use Standard English, and, therefore, a sign of deterioration in educational standards. To some people, it reflects linguistic ingenuity and eclecticism.
> – 'Hybridized English in Ghana', in *English Today* 44 (11:4) (Cambridge University Press), 36

Ghanaian Writers in English include C. Ama Ata Aidoo, Joseph W. Abruquah, Aye Kwei Armah, Kofi Awoonor, and J. Benibengor Blay. Kofi Annan, a Ghanaian, is currently in his second term as general secretary of the United Nations Organization.

Nigeria, with some 150 million people, is the most populous country in Africa, its name based on that of the river Niger (Latin: 'black'). Lagos (Spanish, 'the Lakes', but pronounced 'Lay-goss') is its largest city and was its capital until 1991, after which it was the new custom-built city of Abuja. The country's ethnic groups are, in descending order of numbers, the Hausa, Yoruba, Igbo, Fulani, Tiv, Kanuri, Ibibio, Edo, and others. English is official at the national level, and along with the main language of each state at the state level. The three most widely spoken of the *c.*400 languages are, in descending order, Hausa, Yoruba, and Igbo. English is the language of education after the first three years of primary school and WAPE is widely used.

The Portuguese established the first trading posts along the Guinea coast in the 15th century, after which other European sea-going nations traded in the area for gold, ivory, and slaves. British contacts with the region date from the 16th century and varieties of English were well enough established in coastal areas in the 18th century for Antera Duke, an Efik chief in Calabar, to keep a diary in it. An excerpt: '[A]bout 6 am in aqua Landing with small Rain morning so I walk up to see Esim and Egbo Young so I see Jimmy Henshaw come to see wee and wee tell him for go on bord' (D. Forde, ed., *Efik Traders of Old Calabar: The Diary of Antera Duke*, 1956).

British missionaries began to teach English in the Niger region during the first half of the 19th century, but relations between Britain and parts of what became Nigeria were not formalized until 1861, when the Lagos settlement was declared a colony. The Berlin Conference of 1885 recognized Britain's claim to the *Oil Rivers Protectorate* created in 1882 in the delta. This stake was enlarged and renamed the *Niger Coast Protectorate* in 1893. Official use of the Latinate name *Nigeria* came in 1900 when the *Protectorate of Southern Nigeria* and the *Protectorate of Northern Nigeria* were created from territories controlled by the Royal Niger Company. These became the *Colony and Protectorate of Nigeria* in 1914, gaining independence in 1960 as a republic within the Commonwealth in 1961 (becoming federal in 1963).

The spectrum of English in Nigeria ranges from Standard English through a more general English whose structures are influenced by the mother tongues, by the Indian English of many traders and teachers, and by WAPE, which is sometimes acquired as a mother tongue in such urban areas as Calabar and Port Harcourt, usually along with one or more local languages. Its many forms reflect both mother-tongue and WAPE influence. Although a number of Pidgin dictionaries have been compiled, it has not yet been standardized. Pidgin has been used in prose by many writers, including Chinua Achebe, as a vehicle for poetry by Frank Aig-Imoukhuede, and for drama by Ola Rotimi. Some distinctive points:

Pronunciation

1   Nigerian English is non-rhotic and largely syllable-timed. Although RP is no longer the norm for the media, it continues to have prestige and to influence pronunciation. The tendency towards syllable-timing becomes more pronounced along the continuum from Nigerian Standard English to Pidgin.

2   Vowel contrasts are limited, and there is usually no distinction between *cheap* and *chip*, *pool* and *pull*, and *caught*, *court*, and *cot*.

3   The pronunciation of consonants tends to differ across the country. *Thin* and *then* tend to be 'tin' and 'den' in Igbo- and Yoruba-influenced English, and 'sin' and 'zen' in Hausa-influenced English.

Grammar

1 Nouns that are countable elsewhere are often treated as countable: *I had only fruits to eat*; *I am grateful for your many advices*.

2 Definite articles are sometimes used as if the rules of Standard English have been reversed: *Lorry was overcrowded*; *What do you think of the Structuralism?*

3 The use of prepositions can differ from UK and US norms: *He came to my office by four o'clock* (= at four o'clock); *She is the best teacher for our school* (= in our school).

4 Phrasal verbs include *cope up (with)*, as in: *He couldn't cope up with any more money worries*. There are also constructions in which the phrasal-verb particle is dropped: *Pick me at the corner* (no *up*).

5 The modal verbs *could* and *would* are often used instead of *can* and *will*, as in: *He has assured me that he could come tomorrow*; *They say that he would be attending our next meeting*. Conversely, *will* is sometimes used for *would*, as in: *I will first of all like to thank you*.

7 The form *themselves* is often used instead of 'each other' with *like/love*: *The husband and wife loved themselves dearly*; *They really like themselves*.

Vocabulary

1 Borrowings from local languages: *danshiki* (from Hausa: 'male gown'), *oga* (from Yoruba: 'master, boss'), *obanje* (from Igbo: 'spirit child').

2 Loan-translations from local languages: *to have long legs* ('to exert influence'); *to throw water* ('to offer a bribe').

3 Conventional items of vocabulary given local meanings or coined for local purposes: *You've come!* ('Welcome!'); *decampee* (a person who moves to another political party); *hear* ('to understand'), as in *I hear French*; *senior* ('elder'), as in *senior sister*.

Cameroon has a history that amply illustrates the linguistic intricacies of life in West Africa. The full names of the country are the *République Unie du Cameroun* and the *United Republic of Cameroon*, reflecting the official roles of French and English (with documents being legally binding only if in French). The very large number of indigenous languages includes Bamileke, Douala, Fang, Fulani, and Hausa. The first Europeans in the area were Portuguese in the 15th century, who established a trade in slaves and passed it on in the early 17th century to the Dutch. The British declared this trade illegal in 1807 and policed the regional waters until slavery came to an end in the 1840s.

Although the British established settlements, the territory became by European agreement the German protectorate of Kamerun in 1884. In 1919, however, as a consequence of the First World War, the region was taken from Germany and divided into French and British zones, which became League of Nations mandates in 1922 and United Nations trusteeships in 1946. French Cameroon became an independent republic in 1960 and the southern part of British Cameroon voted to join it in 1961, while the remainder was incorporated into Nigeria.

In addition to official co-existence with French, conventional English blends with Cameroonian Pidgin, also known as Kamtok ('Cameroonian Talk'), a variety of WAPE in use for at least a century and with relatively high prestige. All Cameroonian post-primary students receive a bilingual education in French and English, and English is the first language of local government and education in western Cameroon. *Kamtok* is a media term coined in the 1980s to stress Pidgin's local value. When the Germans annexed the region in 1884, they found Pidgin English so well established that they produced a phrase book in Pidgin for the use of their soldiers. It is a mother tongue on plantations and in some urban settlements, and is used in families where the parents speak different languages. Rarely the only language in use, it takes various forms, depending on the age, education, regional background, mother tongue, and linguistic ability of its users. Its written use is complicated by three systems of orthography: semi-phonetic as in *Wi di waka kwik kwik*; English-based as in *We dee walka quick quick*; and French-based as in *Oui di waka quouik quouik.*

Cameroonian Pidgin has been semi-institutionalized in the media, in Bible translation, in creative writing, and for general religious purposes. Such uses may well lead to a form of standardization comparable to Krio in Sierra Leone, especially as there is a controversial view that Pidgin would be a better medium than conventional English when children start school:

> **2001** The present writer recognizes the value of English in Cameroon education. He does, however, argue the case that because for the vast majority of Cameroonians in the North West and South West provinces (formerly British Cameroon) the L1 [first language] is Pidgin English, the best medium for teaching children at the initial stages of their education should be Pidgin English.
>
> – Paul Mbufong, 'Pidgin English in anglophone Cameroon education', in *English Today* 67 (17:3), (Cambridge University Press)

Pidgin is widely favoured for informal purposes by different ethnic groups, and has been useful in easing the transition from village to city life. Distinct varieties include *Grassfield* (more usually *Grafi*) among the Bamileke, *Pidgin-Maqueraux* ('Mackerel Pidgin') a kind of street slang, and an offshoot of Krio in Limbe (formerly Victoria) as well as in the African Baptist Church, in which Krios played a prominent role in the 19th century.

East African English

The English language as used in East Africa is an outcome of British involvement in Kenya, Malawi (formerly Nyasaland), Tanzania (formerly Tanganyika and Zanzibar), Uganda, and perhaps also in Somalia and Sudan (although the precise condition in these countries is unclear, as a consequence of long-term civil strife). Rwanda (traditionally a Francophone African country) has unexpectedly become a special case: the return home of Tutsi soldiers and refugees long resident in Uganda has led to English being declared official alongside French. English in East Africa at large co-exists in conventional and hybrid forms with a range of local languages, most notably region-wide Swahili (a language of Bantu origin influenced by Arabic). The use of English in the region includes an expanding body of literature by such writers as John Mbiti, Ngugi wa Thiong'o, Peter Palangyo, J. P. Okot p'Bitek, and David Rubadiri.

When English came into use in East Africa, Swahili was an established lingua franca, as a consequence of which (unlike West Africa) Pidgin English did not develop. The current choice of a regional language is between Swahili (with more informal associations) and English (with associations of formality and authority). Because the two languages occupy slightly different roles, the wrong choice of language may cause offence: if English is chosen, the people being addressed may lose face because they cannot reply; if Swahili, the implication may be that the people being addressed are not well enough educated to know English. In addition, linguistically mixed marriages, such as between a Luo and a Kikuyu in Kenya, may make English the first language of a family. Some general features are:

Pronunciation

1 East African usage has been influenced by Swahili (over the entire region), and such languages as Kikuyu in Kenya, Chichewa in Malawi, Luo in Kenya and Tanzania, and Shona in Zimbabwe.

2 It is non-rhotic and has a five-vowel system, as a result of which there are more homonyms than in West African English or in English at large: 'bead' for *bead/bid*; 'bad' for *bad/bard/bird/bud*; 'bod' for *bod/board/bode*.

3 A vowel, usually close to schwa, is often inserted in consonant clusters: 'conifidence' for *confidence*, 'diginity' for *dignity*, 'magginet' for *magnet*.

4 Consonants are often devoiced: 'laf' for *love*, 'sebra' for *zebra*.

5 Nasal sounds may be introduced before stop consonants: 'mblood' for *blood*, 'ndark' for *dark*.

6 A distinction is not always made between *l* and *r* for speakers of some mother tongues: speakers of Lozi often use 'long' for *wrong*; in Bemba, the name for *oranges* is both 'olanges' and (with a Bantu plural prefix) 'ma-olanges'.

Grammar

1 Because many people are multilingual, hybridization is common, as in the Swahili/English Tanzanian sentence *Ile accident ilitokea alipolose control na akaoverturn and landed in a ditch* ('The accident occurred when he lost control and overturned and landed in a ditch').

2 The omission of an adverb (*more, less, worse*, etc.) in comparative constructions can occur: *This university is successful in its training program than yours*; *They value children than their lives*.

3 Use of the blanket question tags *isn't it?* and *not so?*: *He came here yesterday, isn't it?*; *She is a married lady, not so?*

Vocabulary

1 Loans from local languages: Swahili *boma* ('enclosure, administrative quarters'), *duka* ('store, shop'), *ndugu* ('brother, friend'), *piripiri/pilipili* ('red-pepper sauce').

2 Loan translations from local languages: Kenya *clean heart* ('pure'), *elephant ears* ('big ears': often sarcastically of someone who does not listen), *word to come into one's throat* ('a word on the tip of one's tongue').

3   Extensions in the senses and uses of general words, many well established, some more or less ad hoc: *come with* ('bring'), as in *I will come with the kitenge* ('I will bring the women's cloth': Swahili); *medicine* ('medical'), as in *She is a medicine nun*; *duty* ('work'), as in *He is at his duty now*.

4   Hybrid compounds: *magendo whisky* (Swahili/English: 'black-market whisky').

Kenya is known formally in Swahili as the *Jamhuri ya Kenya* and in English as the *Republic of Kenya*: *jamhuri* from Arabic, *republic* from Latin. It is a member of the Commonwealth whose population of *c*.36 million consists in the main of the Kikuyu, Luhya, Luo, Kalejin, Kamba, Kisii, and Meru ethnic-cum-linguistic groups. Swahili is its official and English its second language.

British control of Kenya was established by the Berlin Conference of 1885, and the *British East African Protectorate* was established in 1895, opening the way to European settlers, especially in the area known as the *White Highlands*. In 1920, Kenya officially became a British colony and in 1944 African participation in politics was permitted. The Mau Mau rebellion, most notably among the Kikuyu, lasted from 1952 to 1960, and Kenya gained its independence in 1963. English was the official language immediately after independence, but a constitutional amendment in 1969 instituted the use of Swahili in the National Assembly, and Swahili replaced English as the official language in 1974. At the time, President Jomo Kenyatta stated:

> **1974** The basis of any independent government is a national language, and we can no longer continue aping our former colonizers. . . . I do know that some people will start murmuring that the time is not right for this decision; to hell with such people! Those who feel they cannot do without English can as well pack up and go.
> – public address, Nairobi

English has, however, remained the language of higher education and attendant professional and social prestige, and is used by most senior administrators and military officers. The curriculum of 1967 focuses on mathematics, science, and English, which is valued as the language of modernity and mobility, often used to express authority, even at the family level. A complex hybridization of English, Swahili, and indigenous languages is common. The Voice of Kenya radio service and Kenyan TV broadcast in both Swahili and English. Although the authenticity and homogeneity of English both in East Africa at large and the nation in particular are controversial matters in Kenya, the following points can be made:

Pronunciation

1   The two sounds of *th* are generally replaced by *t* and *d*: *tree of dem* ('three of them').

2   The sounds *ch* and *j* tend to be adapted as *sh* and *ss*: 'inrisht' for *enriched*; 'hwiss' for *which*; 'joss' for *judge*.

3   The consonants *b* and *v* are often devoiced: 'laf' for *love*; 'rup' or 'rop' for *rub*.

4 The sounds *f* and *p* are commonly replaced by *v* and *b*, *laughing* and *loving* having the same pronunciation, as 'lavin'.

5 Final *l* is often deleted: 'andastandebu' for *understandable*; 'loko' for *local*; 'pipu' for *people*.

Grammar

Usually uncountable nouns are often countable: *Thank you for your many advices*; *We eat a lot of breads*; *I held the child on my laps*; *A lady with big bums is attractive*.

Vocabulary

1 The meaning of some words has been extended: *dry* (of coffee: without milk or sugar); *medicine* (chemicals at large); *hear* ('to feel' someone's pain, 'to understand' language).

2 Loanwords and loan translations from indigenous languages are common: *panga* ('machete'); *sufuria* ('cooking pot'); *sima* ('cornmeal paste'); *clean heart* ('without guile').

Sudan (also, especially formerly, *the Sudan*) is at the northernmost limits of East Africa, with some *c.*33 million people, just over half of whom are classed as Arab and the remainder as Dinka, Lokuta, Nuer, and Shilluk. Arabic is official. In the early 19th century, northern Sudan was controlled by Egypt, and in 1899 the entire region became a condominium of Britain and Egypt known as the *Anglo-Egyptian Sudan*. It became independent in 1956. The division between Arab and Nubian Muslims in the north and pagan and Christian peoples in the south has been a source of low-level warfare for years, mainly in the south. English was widely used in the 19th and earlier 20th centuries, but currently it has no status. Of all the African countries associated historically with Britain, Sudan has had the least interest in maintaining English. It is, however, more used in the non-Muslim Black African south than the Arab north, currently in the main as a vehicle for communication with international aid services.

Uganda is a landlocked nation, with a population of *c.*19 million. It is a member of the Commonwealth, and its major ethnic groups are the Baganda, Banyoro, Bagisu, Banyankole, Turkana, Iteso, Bachiga, and Lango. Its main languages are English (official, and the language of education and the media), Swahili (as a lingua franca), and Luganda, and most of its languages belong to the Bantu group. Uganda was visited by Arab traders in the 1830s, by the British explorer John Speke in the 1860s, and in 1888 was granted by the British government to the Imperial British East African Company. When the company withdrew in 1893, the territory was administered by a commissioner, and after treaties with the four Ugandan kingdoms the territory became a protectorate, becoming independent in 1962. Because local Bantu languages generally have only two fricative ('rubbing') consonants, *f* and *s*, other English fricatives tend to be obscured: *very* pronounced as 'ferry', *sure as* 'sueh'. Many speakers do not distinguish *r* and *l*: 'rorry', 'lolly', and 'rolly' are all pronunciations for *lorry*. Consonant clusters tend to be broken up by an inserted vowel (as with 'sittering' for *string*) or reduced (as with 'lenss' or 'lents' for *length*).

Tanzania (pronounced 'Tan-zan-EE-a') combines the former British colonial territories of Tanganyika (mainland) and Zanzibar (several off-shore Indian Ocean islands). Its population is *c*.29 million. It is a member of the Commonwealth, and its main ethnic groups are the Chaga, Luo, Makonde, Masai, and Nyamwezi. The territories united on independence in 1964. English was a co-official language with Swahili until 1967, when Swahili became the sole official language. English remains important for higher education, the media, and international relations, while Swahili dominates for general education, and internal business and communication. Germany colonized Tanganyika from the late 19th century to 1920, when it became a League of Nations mandate and later a United Nations trust territory administered by the British. In the early 19th century, the Sultanate of Zanzibar was the hub of an Arab-Shirazi Indian Ocean trading empire, dealing mainly in slaves and ivory. The British ended the slavery and divided the island-and-mainland territories of Zanzibar with the Germans. Arab-Shirazi commercial dominance continued through the British period but ended on union with Tanganyika.

Malawi has a population of *c*.9.5 million and is a member of the Commonwealth. It is landlocked and almost totally dependent on Mozambique (an ex-Portuguese territory) for access to the sea. Its principal ethnic groups are the Chewa, Nyanja, Lomwe, Sena, Tombuka, and Yao. English and Chichewa are both official. The first European contact was made in 1859 by the Scottish missionary David Livingstone. In 1878, the *African Lakes Company* was formed, and in 1883 Britain appointed a consul to the Kings and Chiefs of Central Africa, the territory in due course becoming the protectorate of Nyasaland in 1891, part of the Federation of Rhodesia and Nyasland in 1953, and independent as Malawi in 1964. English is the principal internal link language, the language of education from the fourth year of schooling, and, with Chichewa, of the media.

Southern African English

The term *Southern African English* is rare, but is useful in two ways: as a third term in a set with *West African* and *East African English*, and as a means of distinguishing the English of the continental south from that of the Republic of South Africa (RSA) which, though massively dominant, is not the whole story. The region covered is not however clear-cut geographically or linguistically: Zambia and Zimbabwe are variously regarded as East African, as transitional between East and Southern, and as Southern. Here they are taken as Southern.

The first Europeans to reach southern Africa were the Portuguese in the 15th century, followed much later by Dutch settlers in 1652 and Huguenots in 1688, committed Protestant groups that were well established and integrated into a single Afrikaner community by the time the British took the Cape in 1795. Bantu-speaking peoples appear to have been moving from the north, displacing or absorbing the indigenous San (formerly known as Bushmen) and Khoikhoi (formerly Hottentot) at about the same time as the Dutch began colonization from the south. In turn, British settlers first landed at Port Elizabeth on the Indian Ocean in 1820, in the Eastern Cape.

Later, to escape increasing British control—and keep their slaves after the abolition of slavery in the British Empire in 1833—many Boers (Dutch-descended

Afrikaner farmers) made the Great Trek beyond the Orange River, establishing their republic of Natal in 1839 (which was duly annexed by the British in 1846), then Transvaal ('Across the Vaal river') in 1852, and the Orange Free State in 1854 (the British initially leaving these settlements alone). The modern sociolinguistic history of southern Africa relates to the interaction of the Portuguese in Angola and Mozambique with the British and Afrikaners, as well as with the wide range of mainly Bantu-speaking peoples who were establishing themselves in the region at much the same time as the Europeans.

The term *Southern African* as used here covers Zambia, Zimbabwe, Botswana, Lesotho, Malawi, Namibia, Swaziland, and the RSA. It enables the further term *Southern African English* (for a division of Black African usage) to contrast with *South African English* (a label traditionally centred on White usage, but of necessity also including Black, White, Coloured, and Asian usage in the RSA). The technically precise term for Black English in the RSA should logically—if clumsily—be 'South African African English' (cf. the useful oddness of 'English English' as a label for the English of England). For most people in the RSA and elsewhere, 'South African English' is not a subcategory of 'African English', although 'African English' in the RSA can be a subcategory of 'South African English'. For White South Africans, any 'African English' has traditionally been secondary to their usage. Six Southern African territories are discussed in this section, while South African English (because of its range and complexity) is described in the next section.

Zambia was formerly the British colony of *Northern Rhodesia*, gaining its independence in 1964. It has a population of close on 10 million and is a member of the Commonwealth. English is the official language, and its seven recognized vernaculars include Bemba, Nyanja, and Tonga. About 1% of the population is of European background. It is one of the most urbanized Southern African countries, and the mix of languages in its towns emphasizes the need for a link language. English is used exclusively in education from the first year and is important in the media. Zambian English is hybridized, even to the extent of adding Bantu affixes to English roots, as in: *maolanges* ('oranges', where *ma-* is a Bantu plural prefix and *l* replaces *r*), the word having in effect two markers of plurality; *cipoto* ('pot'), where *ci* is a Bemba prefix marking nouns; *awashes* ('he/she washes') and *adriver* ('he/she drives'), where *a-* is a subject prefix. Examples of innovations in using adverbial particles are the omission of *up* in *I'll pick you at half eight*, its addition in *cope up with*, and a reassignment of use in *I'm fed up* ('I'm full', meaning 'I have eaten enough'). An innovation is *movious* ('always on the move'). Cultural influences are evidenced in the questions: *How have you stayed the day?* ('How have things gone since this morning?'); *How are you suffering?* as a greeting to someone who has suffered a misfortune ('How are you managing?' or 'Are you doing all right?'), and a young man addressing an older man as *uncle* or *father* and being addressed in turn as *son* or *nephew*.

Zimbabwe was formerly the British colony of *Southern Rhodesia*, and gained its independence as *Zimbabwe* in 1980 after some years of resistance by a White settler government at odds with the UK. It has a population *c*.11.5 million people and is a member of the Commonwealth. Its ethnic divisions are *c*.70% Shona, 16% Ndebele, 11% other indigenous peoples, and 2% European. English is the official language and Shona and Ndebele may be used in the Senate. Towards the end of the 19th century, English was introduced into the region through the colonial and commercial ventures of Cecil Rhodes and in schools set up by missionaries. In recent years tension has grown between the government of Robert Mugabe and a slowly shrinking White community, principally large-scale farmers, numbers of whom have been forcibly evicted from their lands by avowed veterans of the struggle for liberation against minority White government in the 1970s. As a result, numbers of Whites have been leaving the country. In Zimbabwean English there is a five-vowel system which leads to reduced contrasts: thus, 'men' is the pronunciation of both *man* and *men*, 'fit' of both *fit* and *feet*. Syntactic structures are often attributable to transfer from local languages: *He (has) grown up in my eyes* ('I saw him grow up'); . . . *when the rain is in the nose* ('. . . when the rainy season approaches'). Loans from local languages include *shimiyaan* (home-made liquor, using treacle) and *muti* ('medicine'), as well as words of various origins common in Southern Africa, such as *kraal* ('village') and *veld* (high open grassland). Local usages include *head-ring* (a marker of elder or high status), *impi-line* (a Zulu warrior unit), *love-muti* (a love charm), and *now-now girl* (a modern young woman).

Lesotho is a landlocked country entirely surrounded by the Republic of South Africa, where about half of its adult male population works. Its currency consists of the *loti*, divided into 100 *sente* ('cents'): plurals *maloti* and *lisente*. Its population of just under 2 million is mainly Basotho (formerly written *Basuto*). The Lesothan languages are Sesotho and English (both official). The first Basotho arrived in the area in the 16th century. In 1854, the territory was incorporated by the Boers into the Orange Free State, but in 1869 it became the British protectorate of *Basutoland*. The territory gained internal self-government in 1955 and independence as the kingdom of Lesotho in 1966. It is a member of the Commonwealth.

Swaziland is a landlocked country between Mozambique and the Republic of South Africa. Its currency, whose name forms are Bantu and English, is the *lilangeni* (plural emalengeri) divided into 100 *cents*. Its population of just under 1 million is mainly Swazi. The national languages are Swazi and English. The area was first occupied by the Swazi in the mid-18th century. It was a South African protectorate from 1894 and came under direct British rule after the second Anglo-Boer War in 1902. In 1968 it became the fully independent kingdom of Swaziland. It is a member of the Commonwealth.

Namibia is a coastal Atlantic country with a population of just under 2 million, its ethnic groups: 50% Ovambo, and less than 10% each for Kavango, Damara, Herero, Nama, Caprivian, Afrikaner, San (Bushman), German, and Basters ('Bastards', mixed). English, Afrikaans, and German were all official until independence, when English was declared the sole official language, although few people speak it fluently. Afrikaans is more widely used. Because of the size and hazards of the Namib Desert, British and Dutch missionaries did not penetrate the region until the late 18th century. The Germans colonized it as *German West Africa* in 1892–3, but lost it during the First World War to South Africa, which governed it from 1920 as *South West Africa*, under a League of Nations mandate. The United Nations sought to make it a trusteeship after 1946, but South Africa refused to cooperate. In 1966, the UN mandate was withdrawn. In 1968, the territory's name became Namibia. South Africa governed it without international recognition until independence in 1990.

South African English

The southernmost, richest, and most technologically advanced country in Africa is known in formal terms in English as the *Republic of South Africa* and in Afrikaans as the *Republiek van Suid Afrika*, both abbreviated as the *RSA*, and has often been referred to by Black activists as *Azania*. Uniquely, the RSA has three capital cities: Pretoria for administration; Bloemfontein for the judiciary; and Cape Town for legislation. Its population is close to 42 million: *c.*70% Black, 18% White, 9% Coloured (mixed race), 3% Asian. In 1910, English and Afrikaans became the official languages; in 1994, the number of official languages expanded to eleven, English, Afrikaans, and nine largely regional African languages. In their variant names and spellings these are:

> Ndebele or isiNdebele
> Pedi or Sepedi or sePedi or North Sotho or Northern Sotho
> Sotho or Sesotho or seSotho or South Sotho or Southern Sotho
> Swati or Setswati or Siswati or siSwati or Swazi
> Tsonga or Xitsonga or Shangaan
> Tswana or Setswana
> Venda or Tshivenda
> Xhosa or isiXhosa
> Zulu or isiZulu.

The earliest inhabitants of the region appear to have been the San (widely known as Bushmen) and the Khoi Khoi (traditionally but inaccurately referred to as Hottentots), speakers of the Khoisan languages (this technical term combining their two names). Hindi, Tamil, Telugu, Urdu, and other South Asian languages are (decreasingly) spoken by descendants of immigrants from South Asia. The RSA is a special case in the English-speaking world for at least the following four reasons:

❶ The 'rainbow nation'

It is a complex land with a majority of indigenous African peoples and a minority of people of European, Asian, and mixed origins, speaking (and routinely mixing) a large number of local languages, including African English (Black), South African English (White and other) and varieties of Afrikaans (White, Black, and Coloured).

❷ Apartheid

Most Black South Africans suffered discrimination and often deprivation in the years of apartheid (Afrikaans: 'separateness') under the Afrikaner-dominated Nationalists (*c.*1961–91).

❸ British South Africans

There has been an English-speaking settler community since the late 18th century, mainly but not exclusively British in origin, whose members have had significant roles in the economy and the professions.

❹ Afrikaner South Africans

A colony of mainly Dutch settlers in the mid-17th century evolved into the Afrikaner community, which speaks Afrikaans (a language of Africa in its own right descended from Dutch) and usually also English as a second language. The community has had a history of serious political, social, and linguistic tension with both the British (including the two 'Anglo-Boer' wars) and the indigenous population (culminating in the rise and fall of the 'apartheid' political system).

The mosaic of English in South Africa is unique. The RSA resembles the UK in the core ethnicity and culture of its anglophones and in aspects of its standard speech and writing. It resembles the US in having a history of racial tension and kinds of 'Black' and 'White' English, except that the population proportions are reversed. It shares with Canada a bicolonial history, resulting in a tense relationship between two long-established settler communities: English and French in Canada, English and Dutch/Afrikaans in South Africa. It is like Australia and New Zealand in aspects of its southern-hemisphere English and in degrees of tension with indigenous peoples and their languages—but on a far larger scale than with the Aborigines of Australia and the Maori of New Zealand, the oppressed greatly outnumbering the oppressors. In addition, its European-derived minorities once shared a great deal with settler communities in Kenya, Zambia (formerly Northern Rhodesia), and Zimbabwe (formerly Southern Rhodesia). Despite their relative security, the English- and Afrikaans-speaking White communities in the RSA are sensitive to major past retreats in Kenya and Zambia, and an on-going retreat in Zimbabwe.

English is the first language of $c.10\%$ of the South African population, about two-thirds of whom are White and most of the rest Indian or Coloured (of mixed descent: African, European, and other). Many Afrikaners speak English fluently or adequately, and a significant though small Black élite speaks it as a kind of second first language. As a lingua franca, English is used with varying proficiency by millions of Blacks whose mother tongues are not English, and is commonly mixed with them in terms of pronunciation, grammar, vocabulary, and rhetoric.

The presence of Europeans in Southern Africa goes back over three centuries, to a settlement at the Cape of Good Hope established by the Dutch East India Company in 1652. When the British seized this colony in 1795, during a war with revolutionary France, they took control of a long-established society with its own administration and culture. That community was already diglossic, using metropolitan Dutch for religious and government purposes and Cape or Colonial Dutch for everyday purposes, the latter acquiring official recognition as a distinct Afrikaans ('African') language between 1875 and 1925. Afrikaans, also known emotively as simply the *Taal* ('the Language'), was considerably influenced by *Vreemdelinge-Nederlands* ('Foreigner Dutch'), a variety spoken by many German and French Protestant colonists, the local indigenous population, and slaves, with some influence from Malay in the Dutch East Indies.

When the British took control of the Cape, discrimination against Dutch by the new colonial authorities created a strong protectionist movement from the mid-1870s called *Die Eerste Afrikaanse Taalbeweging* ('The First Afrikaans Language Movement'), also the first occasion when the word *Afrikaans* appeared in print with the sense of a distinct way of speaking. The distinctness of this African Dutch—especially as the language of the *Boers* (Afrikaner farmers)—had begun to be recognized, but reluctantly by many who valued the cultural traditions of the Netherlands and disdained the Taal as debased and promiscuous usage. Afrikaans texts at the time included tracts for Islamic schools (such as the Moslem Theological School in Cape Town, founded in 1862) and a translation of the Bible (begun in 1872 and published in 1933).

Afrikaans continued to be resisted, and in 1910 English and Dutch became the official languages of the Union of South Africa, by which time however most Afrikaner patriots felt that the Taal was no longer Dutch while at the same time English was *die vyand se taal* ('the enemy's language'). In 1914, after years of bitter and emotive struggle, Afrikaans became a medium of instruction in schools, in 1925 it replaced Dutch as an official language, and today it is the official language of the Dutch Reformed Churches in Southern Africa. A great deal of time, money, and effort has been expended on its promotion, including a national dictionary project at the University of Stellenbosch. Even so, however, attitudes have tended to be defensive, in terms of both Dutch and English, and the protection, survival, and acceptance of the *Taal* remained a key matter for the Afrikaner community.

In the 19th century, the rivalry of British and Boer was sharpened by the discovery of both gold and diamonds, factors which contributed to the Anglo-Boer wars of 1880–1 and 1899–1902, both of which were won by the British, who also engaged in hostilities with the Zulu nation. In 1910, Cape Colony, Natal, Orange Free State, and Transvaal became provinces of the Union of South Africa, a dominion of the British Empire. In 1931, South Africa became independent within the Commonwealth and in 1961 the by then Afrikaner-dominated Republic of South Africa left the association because criticism of its racial politics by the other members made a continued presence too difficult. On a limited electoral base, the National Party governed without a break from 1948 to 1994, maintaining a policy of *apartheid* ('apartness', 'separation', 'separate development') for four categories of people: Europeans, Africans, 'Coloureds' (those of mixed ethnicity), and Asians. Voting rights were restricted to European South Africans until 1983, when the franchise was minimally extended to Coloureds and Asians. Afrikaans was closely identified with apartheid over the next 30 years.

The compulsory use of Afrikaans as a medium in many Black schools was a primary cause of a violent uprising in 1976 in Soweto ('South West Township'), a vast Black shanty town on the edge of Johannesburg. Even so, however, under the apartheid regime, a 'resistance Afrikaans' developed and recent work on a 'People's Afrikaans' has helped to rehabilitate the language among Blacks and others. Afrikaans is currently the mother tongue of about 6 million people in Southern Africa, principally Afrikaners and Cape Coloureds, and it continues to serve as a lingua franca for millions of South Africans and Namibians, regardless of ethnic or social background.

Since the end of the 18th century, and despite alienation and warfare, speakers of English have generally been in close contact on broadly equal terms with Dutch/Afrikaans people, resulting in much intermarrying, and with speakers of African languages, largely as servants, with whom such interlanguages as *Kitchen Kaffir* and *Fanakalo* were mainly used—pidgin-like vernaculars widely disliked by their Black users. Competent bilinguals and multilinguals have been numerous and influential (notably between English and Afrikaans, but also with these and one or more African language, such as Xhosa or Zulu), and conditions have favoured complex interplay and hybridization. There is a large body of published writings in English by authors also writing in other languages, such as Sol Plaatje (Setswana) and Andre Brink (Afrikaans).

Fanakalo (or *Fanagalo*) is a pidgin whose name derived, in the mid-20th century, from Zulu *fana* ('to be like'), the adverbial particle *ka*, and *lo* ('this'), as in *Khuluma fana kalo* ('Speak like this'), with stress on the last syllable, the Zulu *k* sounding close to an English *g*. A pejorative English name for it was *Mine Kaffir* (using *Kaffir*, a detested Afrikaner term, taken from Arabic, for an African). Fanakalo was taught as a lingua franca for use in the mines, between workers of different language backgrounds and between workers and their bosses. It combines the basic sentence structure of English with a vocabulary mostly from Zulu and Afrikaans. Strongly associated with discriminatory racial policies in the past, it has been condemned by the National Union of Mineworkers as offensive and inadequate.

Another Black vernacular is Tsotsitaal/tsotsitaal, a term originating in the 1940s, from *tsotsi* and *taal* (Afrikaans: 'language'). A totsi was a flashily dressed African street thug, the name deriving from *potso-tso* ('stove-pipe trousers'), which may have been an Africanized adaptation of the US slang term *zoot-suit*. Tsotsi-taal began as an argot or street language based on Afrikaans and used by members of young Black urban gangs: 'Black lawyers are required to be fluent in English, Afrikaans, Latin, Zulu, Venda and Tsotsi-taal whose vocab changes annually from place to place and depending on which gangs are in power' (O. Musi, *Drum*, January 1987). In the course of time however it extended to become a kind of lingua franca in and around the Black townships.

A development of Tsotsitaal is *Fly taal* (English) or *Flaaitaal* (Afrikaans), a term that may have emerged in the 1950s, from English slang *fly* ('cunning, smart') and *taal*. It emerged as young street radicals rejected Tsotsi-taal because others besides tsotsis were now using it. Fly taal has increasingly shifted to using African languages rather than Afrikaans as its base, and includes a range of English loanwords. It too, however, has widened its base, and its many names include both *Town Talk* and in township usage *isileng* ('slang'). It varies from area to area, depending on the local language mix and the inclinations of its speakers. Although formerly in-group slang, it too has become widely known and understood, and appears in dialogue in Black literature and drama in English. Its vocabulary includes such former in-group words as: *sharp* ('good', 'right'); *groove* ('enjoy'); *dlas* ('house', from Zulu *idlala* 'temporary hut'), and *dikota* ('marijuana or dagga', from Sotho *dikota* 'dry wood'). Flytaal has many terms for money, clothing, and drugs, and many modes of address, of which the most popular is *bra* or *bla* ('brother'), often used as a title, such as *Bra Victor*.

Such usage has moved towards literature. Literary writing by Blacks was once rare, nurtured only by churches and mission schools and drawing heavily on British models, but in the 1950s writers associated with the Black magazine *Drum*, centred in Johannesburg, were publishing material for readers in the townships. A new style developed that was impressionistic, energetic, racy, though it still largely conformed to British/American norms. In the late 1950s and 1960s, however, both political protest and Black writing were suppressed, and many writers went into exile, where they continued to produce a largely poetical or autobiographical literature, such as Ezekiel Mphahlele's *Down Second Avenue* (1959). Oswald Mtshali's collection of poetry, *Sounds of a Cowhide Drum*, signalled the flowering of Black poetry in the 1970s in tandem with the ideology of Black Consciousness. It became a matter of principle to reject Western culture, associated with the oppressor, to represent Black standards, and to assist in consciousness-raising.

Fostered by *Staffrider* magazine in Johannesburg, a new form of English emerged, especially among those whose facility in the standard language had been destroyed by the policies of Bantu education. It has used Tsotsi-taal as a lingua franca of the townships, Afrikaans, Americanisms, and jazz rhythms, and mingles traditional African epic and oral techniques in a rhetoric of protest. In ideology and practice, it is similar to the radical poetry of West Indian immigrants in England, where much of the writing is conceived as performance.

There is no South African standard as such for English. Traditionalists look towards the BBC and RP, while American English has had the same kind of influence in the RSA as elsewhere. At the same time, however, there is a recognized range of usage that fits the label *'educated' South African English*. The following lists seek to cover part at least of this range, especially where it is more colloquial and conversational, from South Africans of largely British descent through a minority of others raised within the same linguistic and sociocultural traditions, to speakers of Afrikaans, Indian languages, and the indigenous languages who are comfortably fluent in English.

Pronunciation

1 South African usage is non-rhotic, but may become partially or even fully rhotic in speakers strongly influenced by Afrikaans, in which case *r* is a tap or trill, as in Scots.

2 Variations in accent usually depend on education, social class, domicile (rural or urban), and an effort to accommodate to speakers of other varieties.

3 Conservative middle-class accents remain close to RP, though typically with the adaptation of the vowel in RP *bit, pin* to a central position, often sounding like a tightly pronounced 'beet, peen'. This is widely regarded as the characteristic South African vowel.

4 In many instances, such words as *ham* and *trap* may sound to outsiders like 'hem' and 'trep', and *park the car* like 'pork the caw'.

5 In such adoptions from Afrikaans as the interjection *ga* (expressing disgust) and *gedoente* ('fuss, bustle'), most speakers realize the *g* as the sound in Scots and German *ach*.

Grammar

1 Colloquial usage includes opening expressions such as affirmative *no*, as in *'How are you?'—No, I'm fine'* (which is probably from Afrikaans) and the emphatic negative *aikona*, as in *Aikona fish* ('No fish today'), which is of Nguni (Bantu) origin. The common informal answering phrase *Ja well no fine* ('Yes well no fine') has been adopted in solid form as an affectionate expression of ridicule for broad usage ('jawellnofine'), and has served as the name of a TV programme.

2 *Busy* is used as an indication of continuity with certain verbs, such as *wait*, in *We were busy waiting for him*, often with a non-animate subject, as in *The rinderpest was busy decimating their herds*.

3 The all-purpose response *is it?* closely parallels the Afrikaans *is dit?*, as in *She had a baby last week.—Is it?*

4 There is extensive use of the Afrikaans adverb *sommer* ('just'): *We were sommer standing around, waiting*.

5   The phrase *and them* is common, as in 'We saw *Billy and them* in town', meaning 'Billy and the others'.

Vocabulary

1   Some South African words have become part of general English, as with *trek* and *veld*, both of Dutch/Afrikaans origin, and English *concentration camp*, coined by the British during the second Anglo-Boer War.

2   In topography there is a high proportion of words from Dutch/Afrikaans, such as *drift* ('a ford'), *klip* ('a rock'), *kloof* ('a deep valley; ravine'), *land* ('a cultivated piece of ground, usually fenced', from Cape Dutch), and *veld* ('open country') and part-translated expressions such as *backveld* ('back country, outback', from Dutch *achterveld*).

3   Compound nouns drawing on both Afrikaans and English are common: *veld management* ('management of the veld or open, undeveloped country'); *veld sickness* ('a potentially fatal disease of livestock resulting from malnutrition, and occurring particularly when animals raised in a sweetveld area are moved to sour-veld pastures': from *A Dictionary of South African English*, Oxford University Press, 1996).

4   Kinds of trees with Dutch-related names include the flowering *keurboom*, the hardwoods *stinkwood* and *yellowwood* (translating *stinkhout* and *geolhout*), and *silver tree*, a coinage dating from early travellers' accounts of the Cape (cf. Dutch *wittebome* 'white trees').

5   Animal names include the antelopes *eland* (Dutch: 'elk'), *kudu* (probably Khoisan), *impala* (Zulu), and *tssebe* (Tswana).

6   Kinds of people include *predikant* or *dominee* (Dutch/Afrikaans: a minister of the Dutch Reformed Church) and *sangoma* (Nguni: 'diviner').

7   Some words of English origin have acquired new senses, as with *location*, originally (as in Australia) an area allocated to White settlers, later 'a district set aside for Blacks', and still later 'a segregated urban area for Blacks', typically with strongly unfavourable connotations (as in: 'the usual mess, the location, of sacking and paraffin tins'). In this sense, *location* has largely given way to the equally euphemistic *township*.

8   Items of African-language origin include: *karroo* ('semi-desert', from Khoi); *donga* ('eroded watercourse, usually dry', from Nguni).

9   Artefacts range from *kaross* (Khoisan via Afrikaans: 'skin blanket') through *Cape cart* (mistranslating Afrikaans *kapkar* 'hooded cart') to *bakkie* (from Afrikaans: 'basin, container'), a common name for a light truck.

10   Liquor includes: Nguni *tshwala* brewed with malted grain or maize (formerly called *Kaffir beer*, now often *sorghum beer*); *mampoer*, a brandy distilled from peaches and other soft fruits, perhaps named after the Sotho chief Mampuru; and *mahog(a)*, a brandy as served in township shebeens (many now legalized as *taverns*), possibly from English *mahogany*.

11   Foods include *boerewors* (Afrikaans: 'farmer sausage'), a centrepiece of a *braaivleis* (Afrikaans: 'barbecue') and *sosaties* (curried kebabs, probably from Malay). At outdoor parties, the focal dish may be *potjiekos* (Afrikaans), a stew made in a three-legged pot over an open fire.

12 African township culture has generated a large vocabulary that includes: *matchbox* (a small standardized dwelling); *spot* (a shebeen or tavern); *tsotsi* (a black street thug).

13 Three distinctive items are *muti, larney*, and *lekker*. The first, from Zulu, originally designated traditional African medicines and other remedies, but has passed into general White colloquial use as in *The pharmacist gave me a special muti for this*. *Lahnee*, of unknown origin, appeared first in local Indian English and is now in general colloquial use, usually as *larney*, meaning 'smart, pretentious', as in *a hell of a larney wedding*. *Lekker* is an informal term meaning 'pleasant, excellent, delicious' (as in *lekker sunshine* 'nice warm sunshine', and *the lekkerest ladies in London*.

The English of native speakers of Afrikaans is a major feature of South African life, with an inevitable influence on the usage of native speakers of white South African English. Some of its aspects are:

Pronunciation

1 Afrikaans English is generally rhotic, characterized by a trilled *r* similar to that in Scots, and distinct from the non-rhotic RP-related pronunciation of native English-speaking South Africans.

2 Initial *h* is often dropped, so that the phrase *red hair* may be heard as 'red air'. Conversely, there is often an intrusive *h* between vowels: 'cre-haytion' for *creation*; 'i-haytus' for *hiatus*.

3 Final voiced consonants tend to be devoiced: 'dok' for *dog*, 'piecess' for *pieces*.

4 Because Afrikaans verbs are not marked for third-person singular, confusion of concord is common, including in the media, particularly with *is/are, has/have, does/do*.

Grammar

1 The use of prepositions is influenced by Afrikaans: *He's by the house* (= at the house); *She's not here on the moment* (= at the moment); *They're waiting on their results* (= for their results).

2 Many usages are carried over from Afrikaans: *I rode (= drove) all over town looking for my shoes but didn't find it* (cf. *dit*, the Afrikaans pronoun for 'them' when referring to inanimate objects). A frequently heard phrase is *Is it?*, from Afrikaans *Is dit?* ('Really? Is that so? Are they?', etc.).

3 A number of Afrikaans expressions have been assimilated, such as: *He's lazy to get up* ('He's too lazy to get up'); *The tree is capable to withstand frost* ('The tree is capable of withstanding frost'), *He farms with wine grapes* ('He grows grapes for wine'); *The village boasts with beautiful vineyards* ('The village boasts beautiful vineyards').

The third variety of English in South Africa, and the majority form, is the African English of the majority population, often influenced either by the mother tongue of the speaker or by contact vernaculars in the townships. At present, young Black

South Africans learn through their mother tongue for the first four years of schooling, English being one of their subjects, and from the fifth year English becomes the sole medium of instruction. The change is usually abrupt, resulting in a high failure and dropout rate. In the intense debate about educational policy, some advocates propose a choice of medium: either mother tongue or English throughout one's school career.

There are two arguments against earlier English: a shortage of trained teachers and the inherent difficulty of acquiring many new concepts and skills without also having to grasp them through a foreign language. There are two arguments in favour of earlier English: that it has to be mastered at some time, and one might as well get on with it, and that not all African languages have terms for the concepts to be learned (such as multiplication and division). In practice, however, teachers (as elsewhere in the world) often use the mother tongue in a mixed mode with English, and in recent years there have been moves towards extending the indigenous languages, a policy that includes the creation of dictionaries and the expansion of vocabulary (inevitably including quantities of loan material from English comparable to the flow of Latin into the new national languages of Western Europe in late medieval times).

In addition to its many distinctive features, the English language in South (and Southern) Africa has a unique institution: the English Academy of Southern Africa (EASA). No other Anglophone country or region has had such an institution: such academies are not part of the tradition of the English-speaking world. The EASA is not, however, like the Académie française. That institution and others like it are associations of eminent (generally elderly and male) littérateurs, academics, and others officially appointed to sustain, defend, refine, and strengthen the high literary and public form of a language, usually as part of the cultural apparatus of a nation-state. Such Academicians have tended to be prescriptive, proscriptive, puristic, nationalistic, and socially remote; and, where nations with academies have possessed empires and colonies, they have tended to lay down the law regarding the sociolinguistic primacy of the mother country, its elite, their literature, and their ways of speaking and writing the language in question. The EASA in its nearly forty years of existence had its prescriptivist and purist dimension, but has lacked statutory role and recognition that consolidate élitism.

The prime mover in creating the EASA was Professor Gwen Knowles-Williams of the University of Pretoria. It came into existence in 1961 in response to sociopolitical pressure perceived as dangerous for the status and security of English as an official language—most particularly in terms of Afrikaans. Its members were therefore more reactive and defensive than reactionary and authoritarian, although memories of empire and kin, and awareness of the international role of English, may have played a part in their attempts to sustain BBC English in South Africa in much the same way as the Queen's English Society has extolled it in the UK. The QES, however, is a grass-roots group that lacks support from scholars of language, whereas scholarly participation has always been central to the activities of EASA. Its mission statement in a recent conference handbook notes:

> **1998** The English Academy of Southern Africa is concerned
> with all forms and functions of English in southern Africa and
> internationally, and with all literatures written in English. It
> exercises this concern by interesting itself in English in education;

promoting research and debate; organizing lectures; making representations; presenting awards; and in other ways fostering the creative, critical and scholarly talents of users of English. It does this while respecting the multilingual heritage of southern Africa.

The conferences of the Academy have already reached out beyond Southern Africa to other parts of the continent. Among language scholars in South Africa itself the organization remains controversial, but at the same time it represents an intra-African development of significance that emerged during the apartheid years. The role proposed in the mission statement has significant integrative and empowering potential, given the interest throughout sub-Saharan Africa in English as a vehicle of prosperity and international communication and not of oppression and personal aggrandisement. It fits well with the role adopted by the African majority in the Republic of South Africa in its long encounter with institutionalized racism.

6 Asia

1976 When, in the twentieth century, Western Europe forfeited her ecumenical hegemony by waging two fratricidal wars, the leading role passed to the United States. At the time of writing, it looked as if the American ascendancy in the Oikumenê [world order] would be as short-lived as the Mongol Ascendancy had been. The future was enigmatic, but it seemed possible that, in the next chapter of the Oikoumenê's history, the lead might pass from America to Eastern Asia.

– Arnold Toynbee, *Mankind and Mother Earth: A Narrative History of the World* (Oxford: Oxford University Press), 37

1997 But there are at least three possible linguistic scenarios. . . . One is that English will remain the preferred language of international communication within Asia, since the investment in English may be regarded as too great to throw away, or the social elites who have benefited from English in the past may be reluctant to let their privileged position become threatened. A second scenario is that Mandarin becomes regionally more important . . . , The third scenario is that no single language will emerge as the dominant lingua franca in Asia.

– David Graddol, 'Rival languages', in *The Future of English? A guide to forecasting the popularity of the English language in the 21st century* (London: The British Council), 58

2000 When it comes to Internet Data Centers and Hosting in Asia iAsiaWorks for you. . . . iAsiaWorks' Pan-Asian footprint of world-class data centers provide the highest quality speed, peering relationships and local expertise in 11 Asia-Pacific countries and the USA, giving you the opportunity to host right where your customers do business. . . . And with 24 × 7 support and expert on-site technicians, you can rest assured that your online presence is secure with us.

– advertisement, *South China Morning Post*, Hong Kong, 13 October

The ancient Greeks had a word for the vast lands on the sunrise side of the Aegean, and they were probably also the first to highlight conflict between 'Asia' and 'Europe' and indeed 'East' and 'West'. Homer was the first, with his epic picture of an archetypal war between the Greeks and the Trojans, Herodotus ('the father of history') followed in the 5th century BC with an account of Greek resistance to the Persian Empire, after which Alexander the Great of Macedon successfully took the contest in the opposite direction.

When the Greeks began to use the word *Asia*, they applied it to two matters now largely forgotten: one mythical, the other geographical. In their history of the cosmos, Asia was a titan, one of whose sons, Atlas, was a rebel whom Zeus condemned to supporting the western sky on his shoulders (and whose name survives in collections of maps, a range of mountains in Africa, and the ocean between Europe and America). Another son was Prometheus, later a symbol of human, and Western, creativity and daring. He challenged Zeus by stealing fire from heaven to give it to his suffering people on earth, and for this impertinence the king of the gods hung him on a cliff-face in the Caucasus, under an eastern sky, where an eagle came every day to feast on his liver.

In immediate geographical terms, however, *Asia* had a more modest start, as the name of a city on the eastern shore of the Aegean. Inland from it lay a region the Greeks called *Anatolia* ('Land of the Rising Sun'), whose Latin near-equivalent *Oriens* ('rising') became in English 'the Orient', as used in the title of the detective-fiction writer Agatha Christie's novel *Murder on the Orient Express*, a train whose destination was Istanbul, gateway to the East.

By the time the Romans controlled the eastern Mediterranean, Asia had become as titanic as the mother of Atlas and Prometheus. By then the Aegean coastal region and Anatolia were simply *Asia Minor* ('Lesser Asia'), with an awesome *Asia Major* stretching all the way to Sinae, which was later known in English as *China*. Perhaps under pressure from inquisitive Europeans, the inhabitants of this huge region began to see themselves as inhabiting a single continent from the Aegean to the Pacific and the Arctic to the Indian Ocean. For Europeans, this enormous 'other' has remained mysterious, glamorous, paradoxical, and risky, a view of things about which the Palestinian-American literary critic Edward Said has observed:

> **1978** Orientalism is a style of thought based upon an ontological and epistemological distinction between 'the Orient' and (most of the time) 'the Occident'. Thus, a very large mass of [European] writers, among whom are poets, novelists, philosophers, political theorists, economists, and imperial administrators, have accepted the basic distinction of East and West as the starting point for elaborate theories, epics, novels, social descriptions, and political accounts concerning the Orient, its peoples, customs, 'mind', destiny, and so on.
>
> – *Orientalism: Western Conceptions of the Orient* (London: Routledge & Kegan Paul)

The matter of West and East is culturally and emotionally charged, as a consequence of which a range of European expressions, including in English *Asiatic*, *Oriental*, and *Eastern*, has acquired negative implications. Such phrases as 'the Royal Asiatic Society', 'Oriental cuisine', and 'Eastern mysticism' have remained viable, because they are well established, familiar, and uncontentious, but such expressions as 'Asiatic politics', 'Oriental businessmen', and 'Eastern economic problems' are impossible or unlikely, while the phrases 'Near East(ern)', 'Middle East(ern)', and 'Far East(ern)' are increasingly regarded as territorially unclear and altogether too Eurocentric to have lasting roles. The neutral term *Asian* now serves, but even with *Asian* there are points to be noted: in the UK, the term commonly refers to Indians and Pakistanis, whereas in the US it tends to refer to Chinese, Japanese, and Koreans, in both cases because of immigration patterns.

If naming is difficult, delimitation is worse. Where does Asia begin and end? Arabia, India, China, and Japan (among other territories) are unequivocally 'Asian', as are their languages, literatures, and the like, but Russia raises questions, because it extends over vast tracts of both North-Eastern Europe and North and East Asia. Some cartographers are currently careful about Russia, as for example the editors of the *Reader's Digest Illustrated Atlas of the World* (UK edn, 1997), who divide their spreads of the 'Old World' into: Northern Europe; Southern Europe; Central Europe; Russia and its Western Neighbours; Central and Eastern Asia; South-East Asia; the Middle East and the Gulf; the Indian Subcontinent and its Neighbours; and Oceania. Here, Russia entirely escapes continental classification. And at the other end of Asia, what is to be said about Australia, in recent years virtually re-created for reasons of trade and good neighbourliness as an Asian country (while still remaining firmly fixed in a psycho-cultural 'West')?

Russian is certainly a language *of* or *in* Asia, as is English, but both have been carried to the region from elsewhere, one by land, the other by sea. Does their long-established presence make them *Asian languages*, in the way that English is both an *Australasian* and a *Southern African language* (though historically invasive in these regions)? In practical reality, Russian and English are in some sense Asian languages, but in traditional terms they are alien, although the alienness seems to be decreasing as the years pass. For better or worse, three centuries of use have made them part of the social ecology of the largest continent.

The transcontinental use of languages is hardly unusual. Ancient Greek was for centuries spoken in Eastern Europe, Western Asia, and Northern Africa, a distribution later dwarfed by the spread of Arabic through much of Africa, across Asia at least as far as the Malay islands, and well into Europe: in Spain for centuries; in the Balkans with the Turks, and currently in Western Europe, notably in France with North African and Britain with South Asian immigrants.

Whereas Russian long ago established itself as both a language of Russians and others in northern Asia and a lingua franca for others still, the distribution and use of English in Asia has not involved settlers and has been more uneven. However, although no significant settlement by British and Irish people occurred in Asia, their influence has been enormous, as a consequence of which communities exist in which English is (often massively) used as a second or third language or even indeed as a first or 'second first' language. The British commentator David Dalby has identified four major planetary language complexes—English, Chinese, Spanish, and Hindi-Urdu—and uses a graphic image to demonstrate their range:

> **2000** The relative importance of each of these four spoken
> languages currently alternates during the course of each day.
> When the sun is over the western Pacific, the national language
> of China is the most in use, but when the sun is over the Atlantic
> and China sleeps, English takes the lead. The world's second most
> spoken language also alternates daily, between Hindi+Urdu and
> Spanish respectively.
>
> – 'The Linguasphere', in *The Linguist* (London, 39:4)

Dalby's imagery is striking, and historically appropriate, but the demographics of the use of English changed so profoundly in the last 50 years that the situation is not entirely what it was. English has long been a key spoken and written language of the Indian subcontinent, both in its own right and mixed with (among others) Hindi and Urdu, so that the major language complex in South Asia can also be described as Hindi–Urdu–English. English has also for decades been a 'link language' throughout South Asia, and, although a common estimated figure for fluent users of English in India is *c.*50 million out of a billion people, the figure for people using kinds of English regularly could be *c.*250 million. Additionally, something over 200 million mainland Chinese are acquiring English at the present time. It is likely therefore that by AD 2020, a majority of the world's regular users of English will be in Asia. Dalby's sun does not in fact set on English as a major Eastern and Western language.

The unevenness of the distribution of English in Asia is nonetheless striking. There is little of it in the north and centre, where Russian has long been both a national language and a lingua franca, and, while English has recently been making headway in the new Central Asian republics, the demographics of its use are likely to remain limited. English is highly significant in West Asia, but in no country does it have a strong population base, except perhaps Israel, which is small. In South Asia, however, the picture is different, with a high but uncertain number of millions of regular users from the Himalayas to Sri Lanka and a widespread more or less officially acknowledged status. South-East Asia is harder to quantify, but has four notable features: English is co-official with Pilipino/Tagalog in the Philippines, where perhaps as many as *c.*40 million people use it; it is predominant among the four official languages of Singapore; it is significant in Malaysia; and ASEAN (the Association of South-East Asian Nations) uses it as the working language of its linguistically highly disparate members. In East Asia, there is no territory with a consistent widespread internal everyday use of English, not even the Hong Kong Special Administrative Region of China. At the same time, however, the language is a crucial part of Hong Kong life, education, and business, and is being massively acquired throughout the region as a lingua franca for both Asian and world purposes and as a language of computation, education, science, and the media.

West Asia

For many centuries, four languages—Hebrew, Arabic, Persian, and Turkish—have been predominant, especially in cultural terms, in West Asia, a region formerly more commonly known in English in part as 'the Near East' and in part as 'the Middle East', the second term slowly squeezing out the first as its area of coverage drifted further west. Hebrew and Arabic belong to the Semitic branch of the Hamito-Semitic language family, Persian (Farsi) is Indo-European, and Turkish is Ural-Altaic, and Central Asian in origin. Although English is a language of significant and increasing importance in West Asia, and has long had contact with its languages, it has not significantly developed as a language of local use, a state of affairs that to some extent aligns West Asia with Latin America.

The only territory in the region where English is regularly used on an everyday basis is Cyprus, which is however nowadays generally regarded as an extension of Europe rather than an Asian island (despite its closeness to Turkey, Lebanon, and Israel). There are, however, many places traditionally and Eurocentrically called the 'Near East' and 'Middle East' where English is firmly established in higher education (for example Jordan), the oil business (for example Kuwait and Bahrain), and air travel (for example the United Arab Emirates). The current status of English in Iran is uncertain, with the exception that it is known to serve there as a widely valued window on the world.

Arabic and English

Arabic is the most widespread and culturally significant language in present-day West Asia, a world language also massively present in North Africa and influential elsewhere in Africa and in both South and South-East Asia. It originated in the Arabian peninsula in the early first millennium AD. Known to its speakers as *al-'Arabiyya*, its name in English derives from the Latin adjective *Arabicus* ('relating to the Arabs'). It is the mother tongue or a national language of *c.*150 million people in Algeria, Bahrain, Chad, Egypt, Iraq, Jordan, Kuwait, Lebanon, Libya, Mali, Mauritania, Morocco, Oman, Qatar, Saudi Arabia, Sudan, Syria, Tunisia, the United Arab Emirates, and Yemen, as well as significant in many communities elsewhere in Asia, Africa, increasingly Europe, and to some extent in the Americas. The most notable European Arabic-speaking community is in France, which has played a colonial and cultural role in the Arabophone countries of the *Maghreb* (the Arab 'West': western North Africa: Morocco, Algeria, and Tunisia). There is also a considerable Arab community in London.

Because of its role as the scriptural language of Islam, Arabic has also had an enormous cultural and linguistic influence on non-Arabic-speaking Muslims, in Afghanistan, Albania, Bangladesh, Bosnia-Herzegovina, India, Indonesia, Iran, Kazakhstan, Kyrgyzstan, Malaysia, Nigeria, Pakistan, the Philippines, in various republics of Russia, Somalia, Tajikistan, Turkey, Uzbekistan, and in Western countries where there are significant Muslim communities (Arab or otherwise), notably Canada, France, Germany, the UK, and the US. Arabic has influenced such languages of southern Europe as Italian, Portuguese, and Spanish, and such Asian languages as Persian, Urdu, Punjabi, Kashmiri, and Malay. It was formerly a mainland European language, spoken for *c.*400 years in the medieval Iberian peninsula, was influential in medieval Sicily, and continues to be represented by *Malti* (Maltese), an Arabic variety influenced by Italian and English and regarded as a language in its own right by the European Union.

Arabic is generally divided into *classical* and *colloquial*. The classical or literary language includes, and is based on, the Arabic of the *Quran* ('Recitation'), the text of the teachings of the Prophet Muhammad in the 7th century AD, regarded by Muslims as divine revelation. Colloquial Arabic is not monolithic, but a range of often very distinct 'dialects', some of which are mutually intelligible, others not. They fall into several groups, principally in Arabia, Egypt, the Maghreb, Iraq, and Syria. Classical Arabic is, however, uniform and immensely prestigious throughout the Arab world, and all colloquial varieties have been influenced by it, and may have standard varieties that incline to a greater or less extent towards it. However, just as there are Muslims who do not speak Arabic, so there are speakers of Arabic who are not Muslim, notably Christian Arabs in West Asia. Some key features of Arabic at large are:

Pronunciation

1 Arabic has a series of consonants formed in the velum (the soft palate at the back of the mouth), and pronounced with a tightening of the pharynx (the cavity immediately behind the mouth) and a raising of the tongue. It also has a group of uvular and pharyngeal fricatives (rubbing sounds at the back of the mouth) that give the language a throaty (guttural) quality.

2 The glottal stop serves as a consonant, represented in Arabic script by the letter *alif* and in Roman transliteration by the lenis symbol (') or the apostrophe ('): *'ana* ('I'), *sa'al* ('he asked'). The sign *hamza* also represents a glottal stop and is transliterated in the same way. In the transliteration of the letter *ain*, a voiced pharyngeal fricative, the asper symbol (') or the turned comma (') is used, as in *'amiyya* ('colloquial'), *shar'ia* (Islamic law).

3 There are three short and three long vowels, transliterated as *a, i, u* and *ā, ī, ū*.

4 Words start with a consonant followed by a vowel and there are no clusters of more than two consonants.

5 Arabic script, which probably developed in the 4th century, is the next most widely used writing system after the Roman alphabet. It has been adapted as a medium for such non-Semitic languages as Malay, Persian, Spanish, Swahili, Turkish, and Urdu. It has 28 letters, all representing consonants, and runs from right to left.

Grammar and word-formation

1 Arabic syntax and word-formation centre on a system of *triconsonantal roots* that provide the basic lexical content of words: thus, the root *k-t-b* underlies words relating to writing and books, and *s-l-m* underlies words relating to submission (to the will of God), resignation (to one's fate), peace, and religion. Such roots are developed in patterns of vowels and affixes: words formed from *k-t-b* include the nouns *kitab* ('book') and *katib* ('one who writes', a clerk or scribe); words formed from *s-l-m* include *aslama* ('he submitted'), *islam* ('submission to the will of God, Islam'), *muslim* ('one who submits'), and *salam* ('peace, safety, security': also used as a greeting).

2 Nouns in Arabic are often preceded by forms of the definite article *al*, often carried over into English as part of the word itself, as in *albatross, alchemy, alcohol, algebra, alcove, alembic, alfalfa, algebra, alhambra, alkali, almanac*.

Loanwords in English

1 Contacts between Arabic and English date from the Crusades (11th–13th centuries). Though often individually significant, such borrowings into English have never been numerous. Loanwords from the 14th century include *admiral, alchemy, alkali, bedouin, nadir, syrup*; from the 16th, *alcohol, algebra, magazine, monsoon, sheikh, sultan*; from the 17th, *albatross, alcove, assassin, ghoul, harem, jinn, mullah, sofa, zenith*; from the 19th, *alfalfa,*

jihad/jehad, majlis, safari, yashmak; from the 20th, *intifada* direct from Arabic, and *ayatollah, mujahedin* through Persian.

3 Arabic words in English tend to relate to three sociocultural areas: Islam (*ayatollah, mullah*); Arab society past and present (*alcove, bedouin, sultan*); and kinds of learning (*alchemy, alkali*), including mathematics and astronomy (*algebra, nadir, zenith*).

4 Many words have come into English through a mediating third language: *admiral* through French, *albatross* through Portuguese and Spanish, *safari* through Swahili, *ayatollah* through Persian.

5 Some Arabic words have more than one spelling in English. Of these, the older, more traditional forms, usually for reasons of rivalry and animosity between Christians and Muslims, have taken little account of Muslim sensibilities. As a result, vernacular and academic orthography are often sharply different, the latter having strict conventions for transliterating Arabic into Roman script. Forms of the name of the Prophet include the obsolete and highly pejorative *Mahound* (equating him with a devil, false god, or idol), the archaic *Mahomet* (greatly disliked by Muslims because *ma-* is a negative Arabic prefix), *Mohammed* and *Mohamed* (currently common among Muslims), and *Muhammad* (used principally by scholars). Similarly, a believer in Islam has been a *Mahometan* or *Mohammedan* (on the analogy of *Christian*, disliked by Muslims because the usage emphasizes the Prophet and not God), *Moslem* (widely used), and *Muslim* (used standardly by scholars and now common in general writing).

6 Names for Islam have included the obsolete and offensive *Mahometry* and *Maumetry* (meaning 'false religion') and the more recent *Mahometanism* and *Mohammedanism*, focusing on the Prophet and not God, neither of which are acceptable to Muslims.

7 The name for the Islamic scriptures has variously been *the Alcoran* (archaic, redundantly incorporating the Arabic definite article: in effect 'the the Koran'), *the Koran* (in general use), and *the Qur'an* (especially among scholars). In the following excerpt, the Arabic words are transliterated using current scholarly conventions: 'The Shāfiʿī school traces its founding to Abū ʿAbdallah Muhammad ibn Idrīs al-Shāfiʿī, a Meccan of the Quraysh, who taught in Egypt in Fusṭāṭ (now part of Cairo). He died there AH 204/AD 920' (J. E. Williams, *Islam*, 1962).

Many English words have been borrowed into both spoken and written Arabic. In Egypt, for example, where the British had a quasi-colonial presence for 72 years (1882–1954), loans from English span many registers, including the formal, technical, and colloquial, and general terms such as *aftershave, ceramic, shampoo*, and *spray*, architectural terms such as *motel, roof garden, shopping centre*, and *supermarket*, items of clothing such as *cap, overall*, and *shorts*, foodstuffs such as *grapefruit* and *ice cream*, and sports such as *football, half-time, match*, and *tennis* (with their attendant technical terms).

The question of how to adapt especially scientific and technical terms into written Arabic has long been hotly debated. Innovators advocate directly borrowing and nativizing terms where there are gaps, while purists urge the coining of equivalents, in most cases loan translations but in many situations nativizations of the concept but not the usage. By and large, therefore, the Arabicization of words from English and other Western languages takes three forms:

❶ Loan adaptations

These give an Arabic look to foreign borrowings from all sources, so that the equivalent of Greek *philosophía* and English *philosophy* is *al-falsafa*, and the linguistic technical term *morpheme* is *al-murfim*.

❷ Loan translations

These create new Arabic forms, the Anglo-Greek term *semiotics* for example becoming '*ilm al-rumūz*'.

❸ Loan concepts

These use the system of Arabic roots and derivatives, as in *aḍā'a* ('to broadcast'), *iḍā'a* ('broadcasting'), and *mūdī'* ('broadcaster').

Although direct European colonial and regional power ended in the 1950/1960s, the English and French spheres of linguistic influence continue. French, however, has for some years been giving ground to English, and British English to American English. In the early 21st century, English is a significant additional language in most (if not all) Arabic and part-Arabic-speaking countries, notably for business, technical matters, and higher education.

Hebrew and English

The Hebrew language has existed in at least three forms over more than three millennnia: as the Semitic language of the ancient Israelites; as its scholarly textual and chanted descendant (no longer used as a mother tongue, but serving as a classical vehicle of religious texts and debate); and in a deliberately revived living form in modern Israel. Hebrew is closely related to Aramaic (still, barely, a living West Asian language) and Phoenician (long defunct, though once significant throughout the Mediterranean world), as well as, more distantly, to the Arabic language complex. One of the world's oldest on-going languages, it is best known traditionally as the medium of the Hebrew or Jewish Bible (the Christian Old Testament). In Biblical times, it was called *yehudit* ('Jewish') and in post-Biblical rabbinic literature *lashon kodesh* ('Holy Tongue').

Scholars divide it historically into four phases: *Biblical* Hebrew *c*.12th century BC to *c*. AD 70), *Mishnaic Hebrew* (*c*. AD 70–500), *Medieval Hebrew* (6th–13th century), and *Modern Hebrew* (from the late 19th century). The fourth phase is known to its speakers as *ivrit*, a revived form developed chiefly in Palestine by European Jewish settlers, especially after 1880. It became the predominant language of the state of Israel after 1948 and with Arabic is one of its official languages. It is often referred to as *(Modern) Israeli Hebrew*. The alphabet consists of 22 letters, all consonants. Hebrew is written from right to left with or without vowel signs above and below the consonants. Currently, it has *c*.4 million speakers, most of whom live in Israel.

Because of the influence of Bible translations, there have since Anglo-Saxon times been words and names of Hebrew origin in English. They include *amen*, *babel*, *behemoth*, *camel*, *cherub*, *gehenna*, *leviathan*, *manna*, *rabbi*, *Sabbath*, *shekel*, and *shibboleth*. In addition, a number of religious and cultural terms were introduced during the Renaissance through the works of scholars, such as *Cabbala*, *Talmud*, *Sanhedrin*, *Mishnah*, and *mezuzah*. Since the 19th century, Yiddish has been an indirect source of Hebraisms in English, notably in the US and especially in New York City, and in the UK, notably in London, including such colloquialisms as: *kosher* ('ritually fit, all right, satisfactory, legitimate'); *mazuma* ('money, cash'); *chutzpah* ('impudence, gall'); *goy* ('a gentile'); *megillah* ('a long story'). In the 20th century, terms taken from Modern Hebrew, used mainly by English-speaking Jews, included *kibbutz* (a collective Israeli farming community, plural usually *kibbutzim*); *hora* (a Romanian and Israeli round dance); *moshav* (a cooperative Israeli farming community, plural usually *moshavim*); *sabra* (a native-born Israeli, named after the prickly pear, tough and sharp outside but soft and sweet inside); *aliya* (Jewish immigration to Israel), and *Knesset* (the Israeli parliament).

The English language was intimately part of the creation of the state of Israel, where many languages other than Hebrew and including English continue in daily use: note the influential *Jerusalem Post*. In 1922, after the collapse of the Ottoman (Turkish) Empire, the League of Nations gave Britain a mandate to govern Palestine and establish a Jewish national home there, and during the period of British rule (1917–48) English was an official language. When the state of Israel was created in 1948, the position of English, though no longer administrative, was to a great extent sustained by the settlement of many English-speaking Jews, especially from the US. In addition to the two official languages, English is currently in wide use, as are Yiddish, Russian, and other languages. English has also been a significant international lingua franca for the Palestinians in their efforts to re-create a homeland. Generally, British English has been the dominant influence, including on Hebrew, as with *karavan* (a light mobile home) and not American *trailer*, and *tships* ('chips') and not *french fries*, but American English is now immensely popular and influential, leading to such colloquialisms in Hebrew as *okey* ('OK'), *hay* ('Hi'), and *bay-bay* ('bye-bye').

Persian and English

The speakers of Persian refer to it as *Farsi* (after *Fars*, the heartland province of the classical Persian Empire, which the Greeks called *Persís*, from Old Persian *Parsa*). It is an Indo-European language of West Asia, is the official language of Iran, and is widely used in Afghanistan where it is also known as *Dari*. Persian has been culturally significant in both West and South Asia, and noted for its literary and poetic tradition. Although part of a much older language tradition than English, the development of the two languages runs parallel in at least the five following ways:

1   Scholars divide it into three stages, each with its own writing system: *Old Persian*, early first millennium BC to *c.*3rd century BC (written in cuneiform script); *Middle Persian*, 3rd century BC to 9th century AD (in Aramaic script); and *Modern Persian*, 10th century to the present day (in Arabic script).

2 Modern Persian has lost most of the complex inflections of the older stages, much as Modern English has lost most of the inflections of Old English.

3 Just as English contains a vast lexical inheritance from Latin, Persian has absorbed, under the influence of Islam, a great number of Arabic loanwords.

4 Just as English has acquired many literary and rhetorical practices from Latin and ultimately Greek, Persian has acquired equivalent practices from Arabic and ultimately Greek.

5 Both languages have been widely used in the Indian subcontinent and have greatly influenced its vernaculars. Used officially by the Moghuls (16th–18th centuries), Persian was the imperial language of India immediately before English.

Persian loanwords in English have usually been mediated by other languages, as with:

❶ Persian—Arabic—French—English

Azure, through Old French *azur*, through Arabic *al-lazward*, from Persian *lajward* or *lazhward* ('lapis lazuli'), the colour blue.

❷ Persian—Greek—Latin—French—English

Magic, through Old French *magique*, through Late Latin *magica*, from Greek *magiké (tékhné)* ('magic (art)'), from *mágos* (Latin *magus*), from Old Persian *magu-s* a member of the priestly caste, perceived as a sorcerer; *paradise*, through French *paradis*, through Latin *paradisus*, through Greek *parádeisos*, from Old Persian *pairidaeza* ('enclosure, park, pleasure ground, used by Christians to mean both the Garden of Eden and heaven), from *pairi* ('around'), *diz* ('to mould or form').

❸ Persian—Turkish, Urdu, and others—English

Pilaf, pilaff, pilau, pillau, pilaw, pillaw, pilao, pulao, etc.: through the usage of a variety of languages and localities, such as Turkish *pilâv* and *pilâf* and Urdu *pilao* and *palao*, from Persian *pilaw*, colloquial *polo* ('boiled rice (and meat)').

❹ Persian—Indo-Portuguese—French—English

Turban, through French *turban*, probably through Portuguese *turbante* (acquired in India), with an *l/r* change from Persian *dulband*.

❺ Persian—Indian languages—English

In loanwords that have passed, often unchanged, through Indian languages, the possessive linking vowel of Modern Persian (the *ezafeh*) appearing as -*i*-, as in *koh-i-noor* or *kohinoor*, the name of an Indian diamond in the British Crown Jewels, from Persian *koh-i nur* (*koh* 'mountain' *nur* 'light'); *khaki*, through military usage in Urdu from Persian *khaki* ('dusty, dust-coloured'), from *khak* ('dust').

In the reign of Mohammed Reza Shah Pahlavi (1941–79), English replaced French as the key language of Westernization in Iran, British usage at first dominating, then American. However, the Shah was overthrown in 1978, in a revolution which resulted in an Islamic Republic led by the Shi'a cleric Ayatollah Khomeini, and went into exile. Since that time, although Western influences have been suspect, English has remained the nation's primary window on the world.

Turkish and English

The Turkish language is the best known and most extensively used member of a group of closely related languages referred to by scholars as *Turkic*, spoken from former Eastern Turkestan (now the Chinese province of Xinjiang, formerly Sinkiang) through various parts of Central Asia to Azerbaijan and Turkey. The Turkic languages in turn belong within the Ural-Altaic language family which also includes Hungarian and Finnish in Europe and Mongolian and the Tungusic languages in East Asia. Turkish itself is spoken in Turkey and the Turkish-controlled part of Cyprus and in diaspora groups elsewhere, notably Germany.

Turkish is an agglutinative language, in which word elements behave as if glued together in succession, as in *evlerde* (*ev* 'house', *ler* 'plural element', *de* 'in': 'in the house'). English has taken relatively few words from Turkish and other Turkic languages, and these include *bosh*, *caftan/kaftan*, *caique*, *coffee*, *Cossack*, *divan*, *horde*, *khan*, *mammoth*, *pasha*, *turkey*, *turquoise*, and *yogurt/yoghurt/yoghourt*. English has also generally had little influence on Turkish and the related languages of Azerbaijan, Kazakhstan, and Turkmenistan, but in recent years this has changed greatly, in Turkey through NATO membership and other links with the West, and in the Central Asian republics after the dissolution of the Soviet Union. English teaching programmes have increased in all the Turkic regions.

South Asia

> **1614** James, by the grace of Almightie God . . . , King of Great Britaine, France and Ireland . . . To the high and mightie Monarch the Great Mogor, King of the Orientall Indies . . . Greeting. We hauing notice of your great fauour toward Vs and Our Subjects, by Your Great *Firma* to all Your Captaines of Riuers and Offices of Your Customes, for the entertaynment of Our louing Subjects the English Nation with all kind respect, at what time so euer they shall arriue at any of the Ports within Your Dominions, and that they may haue quiet Trade and Commerce without any kind of hinderance and molestation. . . .
> – James I of England and VI of Scotland, to Jehangir, the Moghul Emperor in India

In 1600, when Shakespeare was at the height of his career, English traders (following the Portuguese and Dutch, and with the blessing of their queen) set up 'the Company of Merchants of London trading to the East Indies', better known as simply 'the East India Company', fully endorsed as above by Elizabeth's successor.

From the 16th to the 18th centuries, the forms *India* and *Indias* both served in English to name not only large parts of southern Asia (much larger than India today) but also the 'new world' of the Americas. Although the conviction of Christopher Columbus in 1492 that he had reached India by a western sea route was soon dispelled, a range of skewed 'Indian' expressions emerged, survived, and continues to flourish in the western hemisphere (hardly touched by the 'politically correct' movement). Most prominent among these are: *(Red) Indian* and the casual form *Injun* for most of the indigenous peoples (especially in the northern hemisphere); the *West Indies* for islands in the Caribbean; and *East Indian* as a term for someone from India (to contrast with *West Indian*, which refers mainly to people of African origin in the Caribbean). The term *East Indian* has also survived in South and South-East Asia, particularly for Eurasians of Portuguese-Indian background, most of whom (and paradoxically) live on the west coast of India.

Even sixty years after it was entirely clear that there was no India across the Atlantic, the name lingered on, as in Richard Eden's book (1553), *A treatyse of the newe India, with other new founde landes and Ilandes*. But unlike later 'new' terms (such as *New England* and *New York*) the title and concept *New India* did not endure, because it had no emotive 'home country' value for Europeans intent on building new and better versions of their old world. However, the choice of *East* to refer to the 'old' India sustained the conceit that there are two parts of the world where kinds of *Indian* live until the associated usages became taken for granted, treated as 'true' because they had become routine. Historically, therefore, the only link between Asia's Indians and America's Indians is a European linguistic slip.

Once the East India Company was established, and although its heartland was the Indian subcontinent, it traded wherever in Asia it could make a profit. The parallel Dutch East India Company had no base in India as such, but focused its attention on the Malay archipelago, its colonies there coming to be known collectively as the *Dutch East Indies*. These 'spice islands' are now part of *Indonesia*, a country whose Greco-Latin name means 'Land of the Indian islands' (although no one today thinks of the peoples living there as Indians). There is also nearby, however, a region called *Indo-China*, considered as located more or less between India and China; for a time, it was known in English as *Further India* (although no community in the area either then or later has regarded itself as Indian).

By 1612 the English traders in the east had established themselves in the coastal town of Surat, in Gujarat in western India proper, by 1637 they had reached the southern coast of China, in 1640 they established a trading 'factory' at Madras on the east coast, in 1674 Charles II received the territory of Bombay on the west coast from England's ancient ally Portugal (as part of the dowry of Catherine of Braganza), and in 1690, a further factory was established at Calcutta in Bengal.

In the early 18th century, the empire of the Moghuls began to fail and by 1757 the East India Company became the power behind the government of Bengal. In 1774, the British Regulating Act placed both the Bombay and Madras trading areas under the control of Bengal, and the Company was in effect launched as an extension of the state, with an army of its own (locally recruited but with British officers). From 1786 it had its own governors-general, a state of affairs that continued until the revolt of the sepoys ('soldiers') in 1857: dubbed *the Indian Mutiny* by the British and known today in India as *the War of Independence*. After that date, the company continued to trade but no longer ruled or controlled soldiers.

Before that stage was reached, however, Thomas Babington Macaulay (a member of the Supreme Council of India) wrote his 'Minute on Education', through which the British, as rulers of India from the Himalayas to Cape Comorin, endorsed English as a medium of education for a select minority of Indians. In it, he noted:

1835 [W]e are free to employ our funds as we choose; that we ought to employ them in teaching what is best worth knowing; that English is better worth knowing than Sanscrit or Arabic; that neither as the languages of law, nor as the languages of religion, have the Sanscrit and Arabic any peculiar claim to our engagement; that it is possible to make natives of this country thoroughly good English scholars, and that to this end our efforts ought to be directed. . . . We must at present do our best to form a class who may be interpreters between us and the millions who we govern; a class of persons, Indian in blood and colour, but English in taste, in opinions, in morals, and in intellect. To that class we may leave it to refine the vernacular dialects of the country, to enrich those dialects with terms of science borrowed from the Western nomenclature, and to render them by degrees fit vehicles for conveying knowledge to the great mass of the population.

In the early years of trading in India, the English used a form of Portuguese current in the region (Portugal having acquired the west coast territory of Goa in 1510) and only slowly began to use their own language and local languages. Missionaries became important in diffusing English in the 18th century, especially through the establishment of English-medium schools, in Madras (1715), Bombay (1719), and Calcutta (1720).

By the 1830s, an influential group of Indians was sufficiently impressed by Western thought and culture, and by its scientific advances, that—like Macaulay—they wished to encourage the learning of English as a means through which the people of the subcontinent could gain a knowledge of such things. In particular, the Bengali Hindu social reformer Raja Rammohan Roy (1772–1833) wanted European gentlemen of 'talents and education to instruct the natives of India in mathematics, natural philosophy, chemistry, anatomy, and other useful sciences, which the natives of Europe have carried to a degree of perfection that has raised them above the inhabitants of other parts of the world'. In the long official controversy over the nature of the medium of education for Indians, the so-called *Anglicists* supported the 'transplant theory' while the *Orientalists* favoured the 'nativist theory', and it was Macaulay's Minute that settled the matter in favour of English without denying the vernaculars space in which to extend themselves.

In 1857, the first three of many subsequent Western-style universities were established at Bombay, Calcutta, and Madras. By 1928, English was (as Macaulay hoped) the language of a subcontinental élite, and after the independence of India and Pakistan in 1947, and then the emergence of Bangladesh in 1971, its diffusion increased rather than diminished.

South Asian English

1982 I shall use the term South Asian English to refer to the variety of English used in what has traditionally been called the Indian subcontinent. The label *South Asian English*, unlike *English in South Asia*, suggests a parallel with variety-oriented terms such as *American English* or British English and implies a historical tradition and institutionalisation, as well as distinct

formal and functional characteristics. . . . South Asia comprises
about one fifth of the total human population and is culturally and
linguistically pluralistic. The number of languages and dialects
spoken in the region is very large, and the sociolinguistic situation
is complex.

– Braj B. Kachru, 'South Asian English', in Richard W. Bailey and Braj B. Kachru, *English as a
World Language* (University of Michigan Press), 353

Kachru's term has become standard among scholars of world English, and has
proved useful and acceptable for at least four reasons:

❶ Loss of agreement about the use of the term 'Indian subcontinent'

After the partition of British India in 1947 into India and Pakistan, and then of
Pakistan into Pakistan and Bangladesh, there was no traditional mutually acceptable name for the region, the term *Indian subcontinent* no longer being acceptable
to non-Indians.

❷ The need to cover territories beyond the traditional subcontinent

Nepal, Bhutan, and Sri Lanka were never part of India and are at the very limits of
the concept of a South Asian 'subcontinent'.

❸ By analogy with other comparable regions

By general though unofficial agreement the region came to be known as *South Asia*
on the analogy of *South-East Asia* and as part of the set *West Asia*, *Central Asia*,
South Asia, *East Asia*, *South-East Asia*, and increasingly in recent years *North-East
Asia*.

❹ Shared features

The varieties of English used throughout the region so designated have shared features that in the past would have fallen under the heading *Indian English* regardless
of locale. It was practical therefore to bring them together as varieties of *South Asian
English*, whether or not there is a comparably broad range of English in other Asian
regions.

The South Asian countries covered by the term are Bangladesh, Bhutan, India, the
Maldives, Nepal, Pakistan, and Sri Lanka. Their combined population is $c.1,400$
million, with a billion people in India alone, in all about a quarter of the human
race. To use local terms, English is the primary 'link language' and 'window on the
world' for that entire population, a state of affairs that is, by and large, the outcome
of British commercial, imperial, educational, and missionary influence since the
17th century. During that period, only Nepal, Bhutan, and the Maldives remained
outside the British Raj, but all three had close long-term involvement with it.

The South Asian countries are linguistically and culturally diverse, with two
major language families, Indo-Aryan (part of the Indo-European family) and
Dravidian (a distinct subcontinental grouping), as well as a shared cultural, political, and religious history, common literary and folk traditions, and pervasive strata
of Sanskrit, Persian, Arabic, and/or English in their languages and literatures. At
least the following six factors have operated in favour of the spread of English in
South Asia:

❶ Commerce

Trade by the East India Company from 1600 onward.

❷ British officials

The involvement of agents of government in the region since the 18th century.

❸ Missionaries

The work of Christian missionaries, both Roman Catholic and especially Protestant. Although the missionaries did not achieve the hoped-for mass conversions, their network of English-medium schools has had a great impact and remains intact, although now somewhat secularized.

❹ Education

Demand from local leaders for education in English, so that their countries could benefit from trade, technology, and scientific knowledge.

❺ Imperial government policy

A decision by the government of British India to make English the official medium of education, broadly though varyingly sustained subsequently in India, Pakistan, Bangladesh, and Sri Lanka (formerly Ceylon).

❻ Post-imperial government policy

Decisions by the various national governments to use English as, in the commonly used Indian term, their 'window on the world'.

In 1835, Lord Macaulay's Minute led to the use of English as the language of education in British India. Its proposals split the administration of British India, the attendant controversy still continuing in present-day South Asia. Although Macaulay's opponent, H. T. Princep, considered the Minute 'hasty and indiscreet' (and many South Asians have agreed with him), language policy in the Indian states has in fact sustained Macaulay's programme. Before his Minute, each Indian princely state had its own policy for language in education, and Hindi, Urdu, Sanskrit, and Persian were the languages of wider communication. Affluent Hindus, Muslims, and Buddhists generally sent their children to their respective scriptural schools. Afterwards, education in English was, even in Christian schools, increasingly secular and general, although there was a thin wash of Christian ethics and a bias towards English literature and European culture.

In 1857, the three English-medium universities of Bombay, Calcutta, and Madras were founded. The new policy emphasized the use of vernacular languages instead of Sanskrit and Arabic, and indicated that English should be taught only where there was a demand for it. However, it continued as an important component of education, administration, and law, as well as in personal use among the educated elite (across linguistic, political, and religious boundaries) until 1947, when the British departed, and afterwards. The diffusion and impact of the language has not in fact slackened; indeed, its spread continues to increase both in range and depth.

There is now in effect a general educated South Asian English, used for internal, pan-regional, and international purposes: historically, by and large, it is Indian English with national variations. Its use is affected by three factors: level of education and proficiency; the characteristics of an individual's first or dominant language; and ethnic, religious, and/or other cultural background. In practical terms, it is the third most significant English grouping after the British Isles and North America, underlined by the fact that many Indians and others from the region routinely teach English elsewhere in the world, most notably in West Asia, East Asia, and parts of Africa. It could well, by the mid-21st century, contain the largest concentration of regular users of English in the world.

English in India

> **1973** I am Indian, very brown, born in
> Malabar, I speak three languages, write in
> Two, dream in one. Don't write in English, they said,
> English is not your mother tongue. Why not leave
> Me alone, critics, friends, visiting cousins,
> Every one of you? Why not let me speak in
> Any language I like? The language I speak
> Becomes mine, its distortions, its queernesses
> All mine, mine alone. It is half English, half
> Indian, funny perhaps, but it is honest,
> It is as human as I am, don't
> You see?
> – Kamala Das, from *The Old Playhouse and Other Poems*
> (New Delhi: Orient Longman)

The word *India* has a long pedigree: through Latin from Greek from Persian *hind* and Old Persian *hindu* (cognate with Sanskrit *sindhu*). A common origin therefore underlies the three terms *India*, *Sind* (now the name of a province of Pakistan, associated with the river known in English as the *Indus*), and *Hindu* (formerly written *Hindoo*). This last term refers to a range of peoples united through adherence to a religious and social system known in Sanskrit as the *sanatana dharma* ('the eternal law/faith') and more prosaically in English as *Hinduism* (a term with no original in any Indian language). The Latin name *India* was used unchanged in Old English, but Middle English used the French adaptation *Ind(e)*, which survived in later centuries mainly in poetry. The form *India* was re-adopted into English in the 16th century, as part of the Latinization of English. Its uses have been complex, and in its four major senses it has several synonyms:

❶ Also *Hindustan, Hindusthan*
Originally used for the plain of the river Indus, then extended to the entire Indo-Gangetic plain, then to the southern peninsula.

❷ Also *the Subcontinent/subcontinent (of India)* and *the Indian Subcontinent/subcontinent*
The South Asian land mass bounded to the north-west by Iran and Afghanistan, to the north by Tibet, and to the north-east by China and Burma. The term currently covers five mainland states (Bangladesh, Bhutan, India, Nepal, and Pakistan) and two island states (Sri Lanka and the Maldives), and appears to be giving way to *South Asia*.

❸ Also *British India*, and more politically *the British Raj* ('Realm'), and *the Raj*

That part of the subcontinent once controlled by the British, made up of directly governed areas such as the Bombay Presidency and indirectly controlled princely states such as Gwalior and Jaipur. The term *undivided India* is retrospective, prompted by Partition in 1947.

❹ Also officially *Bharat*, sometimes unofficially *Hindust(h)an*

Associated with a heroic legendary Indo-Aryan people, the Bharatas. The Republic of India, a member of the Commonwealth, population *c*.1 billion (2000), whose official language is Hindi and associate official language English, with 15 national or major languages (including Hindi and English), and many smaller languages. The rough proportion of the population using major regional languages is: 35% Hindi, 7% Bengali, 7% Marathi, 7% Telugu, 6% Tamil, 5% Gujarati, 5% Urdu, 4% Oriya, 3% Kannada, 3% Malayalam, 3% Punjabi, 1% Assamese, 1% Kashmiri. The Republic was formed after Partition.

The term *Indian English* has two applications: one broader and less precise, the other narrower but by no means simple. The broader meaning covers the whole area of the old undivided India (India, Pakistan, and Bangladesh), often together with Sri Lanka, Nepal, and the Maldives: a term of convenience for kinds of English that share many features. By and large, however, this term has been superseded among scholars by the Indian language scholar Braj B. Kachru's term *South Asian English*, as noted above, largely so as not to disturb the sensibilities of the millions who are not *Indian* in a present-day political sense. The narrower sense covers India alone.

However, even in its narrower sense the term remains controversial. Some commentators maintain that *Indian English* refers to an established range of usage in present-day India within which there is an incipient or partly established standard, while others contend that the kinds of English in India are too diverse both socially and geographically, and often too deviant or delimited, to be lumped together as one variety (except perhaps in the broadest and vaguest general sense). Some have also argued that, since no detailed across-the-board linguistic description has been made of this variety, the term is misleading and ought not to be used, at least in scholarly discussions. Still others, however, maintain that the sheer length of time in which English has been present in India (*c*.350 years), its national significance, and the medley of varieties within the country, make the term inevitable.

It is by no means clear how many Indians regularly use English. The estimate offered in the *Oxford Companion to the English Language* in 1992 was 30 million (4% of the population at that time), and enough to make India the third largest English-speaking community in the world. The number excluded the millions who have a limited range in the language, speak kinds of Pidgin English, and/or mix English words into their other languages. However, the number given then was probably an underestimate and needs reconsideration and upward revision in 2002. India's current population is just over one billion and there may well be *c*.100–200 million people using the language regularly, including young people nationwide with a creative and slangy style of their own. Certainly, an expanding middle class increasingly uses it, and seeks it for their children, and for that group 10% of the population is not an unlikely base figure. In addition, and quite regardless of statistics, however vague, English has 5 institutional roles in India:

❶ As associate official language

English is the associate official language alongside Hindi, the official language. A key, usually unstated reason for this role is that English is more acceptable than Hindi to many South Indians, who are in the main speakers of Dravidian languages. Many of them regard Hindi, an Indo-Aryan language, as an unnecessary northern imposition. In the South, English is now generally considered to be a necessary pan-Indian medium long since shorn of its imperial associations.

❷ As an official state language

English is the official language of five north-eastern states: Manipur (1.5 million people), Meghalaya (1.33m), Nagaland (0.8m), and Tripura (2m). None of the major indigenous languages of India could serve the needs of these small enclave states, either because they are not used in the north-east or are associated with the kinds of socio-economic exploitation by larger regional communities that led to their formation in the first place.

❸ As the official language of Union territories

English is the official language of 8 Union territories: the Andaman and Nicobar Islands; Arunachal Pradesh; Chandigarh; Dadra and Nagar Haveli; Delhi; Lakshadwip; Mizoram; and Pondicherry. For various historical reasons, English is neutral in these areas in relation to other languages used in and around them.

❹ As a part of a 'three language formula'

English is one of the languages included in the 'three language formula' adopted in the 1960s for educational purposes: a state language, such as Marathi; Hindi; and English (often described as a 'window on the world'). Where Hindi is already a state language, the formula is reduced to two.

❺ As a legal, administrative, military, and media language

English is used in the legal system, in pan-Indian and regional administration, in the armed forces, for national business at home and abroad, and in the media. English and Hindi are regarded as 'link languages' in a complex multilingual society where English is also both a 'library language' and a 'literary language' (recognized as having a national literature by the Sahitya Akademi/National Academy of Letters).

There are few places in the world where the continuum of English is so complex, the numbers involved are so great, and the direct and indirect influence of the language is so overwhelming.

Sanskrit and English, Sanskrit in English

Just as Latin has been the classical language underpinning the culture and religion of Western Europe, so Sanskrit has been the pre-eminent cultural base for many present-day languages in India. Like Latin, Sanskrit is generally regarded as 'dead', in that it is no one's mother tongue, but as with Latin its death has been greatly exaggerated. Also like Latin, it has an on-going relationship with English. In Sanskrit, the word for 'Sanskrit', *samskṛta*, means 'put-together, composed, well-formed, perfected', especially as a vehicle for the chants and rituals of the brahmin caste (associated primarily with priesthood and learning). It was, however, also a significant language for the kshatriyas (members of the warrior, governing, and teaching caste), who have for centuries disputed primacy of position in the order of castes with the Brahmins.

Sanskrit is the oldest known Indo-European language, and with its 'cousin' Pali is also a sacred language of Buddhism. It is primarily written in the Devanagari script, which like the Roman script runs from left to right, but hangs rather than sits on the line. It has two major, and successive, historical forms: *Vedic Sanskrit*, the medium of the Vedas and Upanishads, *c*.3,000-year-old texts jointly known as *daivi vak* ('the speech of the gods': compare *daivi* with 'divine' and *vak* with 'vox' and 'vocal'); *Classical Sanskrit*, pre-eminent among whose texts are two epic poems, the *Mahabharata* (of which the foremost text of Hinduism, the *Bhagavad-Gita*, is only one section), which was reputedly created by the sage Vyasa, and the *Ramayana*, reputedly created by the sage Valmiki. The *Iliad* and *Odyssey* of ancient Greece are modest works compared with these vast creations.

The Vedic language grew out of ancient oral priestly traditions; the grammarian Panini reputedly systematized the classical language in the late first millennium BC. Much as Latin influenced European languages, so Sanskrit has influenced many languages in South and South-East Asia. Since the 19th century, it has also provided loans to such European languages as English, French, Spanish, and German. The best known of these relate to religion, philosophy, and culture, such as *ahimsa*, *chakra*, *dharma*, *guru*, *karma*, *kundalini*, *mahatma*, *pundit*, *swami*, and *yoga/yogi*. Less obvious loans, borrowed through other languages, include *carmine*, *cheetah*, *chintz*, *chutney*, *juggernaut*, *jungle*, and *jute*.

It is striking, however, that a number of Sanskrit words that are central to religion and social authority have tended to have a cynical and dismissive aspect in English, especially in the media and business, as with *guru* (traditionally in India a respected teacher, especially of spiritual practices) in the phrase 'management guru', and *mantra* as in 'endlessly repeating the mantras of globalization'. Such slanted usages recall a time when many Europeans doubted the integrity of such words and concepts, even when apparently taking them seriously.

All major present-day Indian languages (Indo-Aryan and Dravidian) have Sanskritized registers or levels, used in both religious and secular contexts; Indian English is no exception, especially where commentary on Hindu religion and philosophy are concerned. In addition, Indian writing in English often makes use of such conventions from Sanskrit as the repetition of main themes in paragraphs and an abundance of compounds and embedded clauses. Sanskrit words appear in English texts in two forms: fully Anglicized, as with the variants *pundit* and *pandit* (through Hindi *pandit*); and in a style of transliteration intended to serve the phonology of the language, noted in particular for diacritical marks, as with *paṇḍita*, the Sanskrit source of 'pundit'. A representative scholarly text using full transliterations is:

> **1964** In the *Bṛhad-āraṇyaka Upaniṣad* (3.9.1) we are told that, when Śākalya asked the sage Yājñavalkya what was the number of the gods, the sage gave a cryptic answer.
> – Alain Daniélou, *Hindu Polytheism*, Bollingen Series LXXIII (New York: Pantheon Books (Random House))

Differences in meaning and use often match the styles in writing, print, and speech: thus, *paṇḍita* means a learned *brahmin*, *brahman*, or *brāhmaṇa*, as discussed in a serious treatise; *pandit* has much the same meaning but a wider social distribution, serving notably as a title, as in *Pandit Jawaharlal Nehru*, the first prime minister of independent India. The form *pundit*, which is more integrated into English at large, may have the same meaning and use, but commonly refers to an expert, specialist, or academic whom the writer perhaps considers suspect in some way: 'Nobody dared to predict how long the financial upheaval would last, but every dealer and pundit agreed that it reflected international anxiety and not the economy' (*International Herald Tribune*, 22 Dec 1990).

Other religion-related terms are: *mahatma* ('great soul'), for a pre-eminent spiritual leader, such as *Mahatma Gandhi*; *ahimsa* ('non-violent behaviour', both in yoga and as part of the passive resistance to British rule as advocated by Gandhi prior to independence); and *satyagraha* ('spiritual passive resistance' to injustice). All three have the same positive associations in English as in both Sanskrit and the vernacular Indian languages.

The Hindi-Urdu-English language complex

Hindi is an Indo-Aryan language, spoken by over 250 million people in India and by people of mainly north Indian origin in Canada, Fiji, Guyana, South Africa, Surinam, Trinidad, the UK, the US, and elsewhere. Hindi is the official language of India, one of India's 15 major indigenous languages, and the state language of Bihar, Haryana, Himachal Pradesh, Madhya Pradesh, Rajasthan, and Uttar Pradesh. It is written in a form of the Devanagari (Sanskrit 'divine urban') script, and its literary tradition is a millennium old. Hindi has traditionally had three stylistic forms: an especially Sanskritized variety used in the higher law courts, administration, legislation, journalism, literature, philosophy, and religion; an especially Persianized variety used in lower law courts, in certain genres of literature, and in films; and an especially Anglicized variety in day-to-day administration, on college campuses, and in scientific and technical registers.

The lower-level vernacular variety *Hindustani* (formerly also *Hindustanee*) exhibits strong English influence. Mahatma Gandhi advocated the adoption of Hindustani as the national language of India, because it was very much a language of the ordinary people. However, although the Indian National Congress adopted it as a symbol of national unity in 1925, it never became a language of literature, academia, or journalism. As a result, after independence in 1947, Hindustani lost its potential role to Hindi in India and Urdu in Pakistan.

Urdu is also an Indo-Aryan language, particularly associated in the subcontinent with the Moghul Empire, in which Persian was the court language. The name derives from Persian *zaban-i urdu* ('the language of the camp'), from Tatar *ordu* ('camp'), whence also Russian *orda* ('clan, crowd, troop'), Polish *horda*, and English *horde*: compare *the Golden Horde*, a Tatar people in Central Asia in the 14/15th centuries. Urdu is spoken in Pakistan and India as a first language by over 30 million people and as a second language by over 100 million more, as well as by people of Indo-Pakistani origin in Canada, Fiji, Guyana, South Africa, the UK, the US, and elsewhere. It is used especially by South Asian Muslims, is written in a variant of Perso-Arabic script, and its vocabulary is heavily Persianized and Arabicized. In

India, it is the official language of the state of Jammu and Kashmir, and the associate state language of Uttar Pradesh. The literary tradition of Urdu dates from the 16th century in the region of Hyderabad in south central India, from which it spread north to the cities of Delhi and Lucknow (now in India) and Karachi and Lahore (now in Pakistan).

The term 'Hindi-Urdu' has become common in recent years for the two languages conceived as a continuum, in spite of at least the following four differences: Hindi is written in the Devanagari script and Urdu in the Perso-Arabic script; Hindi is strongly associated with Hinduism and Urdu with Islam; Hindi is the official language of India, a secular state, a majority of whose citizens are Hindu, while Urdu is the national language of Pakistan, an Islamic state, the vast majority of whose citizens are Muslim; and Hindi is not significant in Pakistan, while Urdu is a significant language among Muslims throughout India, but mostly in the north.

A comparable linguistic complex is Serbo-Croat(ian) in the Balkans in Europe. Although both Hindi and Urdu have been strongly influenced by other languages, Hindi looks to Sanskrit for its script, technical vocabulary, and literary conventions, while Urdu looks to the Perso-Arabic script, usage, and literary conventions. Comparably, Serbian uses the Cyrillic alphabet and looks east to the traditions of Orthodox Christianity while Croat(ian) uses Roman and looks west to the traditions of Roman Catholicism.

Despite such differences and difficulties, speakers of the two languages manage well on an everyday basis. There is, however, a third element in this intricate situation. Both languages have extensively borrowed from English and hybridize with it in many situations. Many of their users also know English, as a result of which there is a continuum of Hindi-English and Urdu-English—and thence of Hindi-Urdu-English—across the two countries but especially in India. There appears not to be a word for such mixing in Pakistan, but in India the variants *Hindlish* and *Hinglish* are used: casual, humorous, slightly rueful names for such expressions as *city kotwali* ('city police station'), *relgari* ('railway train': literally 'rail coach/car'), and *Mai apko batati hum, he's a very trustworthy fellow* ('I tell you, . . .'). The continuous flow is not easily captured, but the following extract provides a graphic and light-hearted illustration of what it is like to be hip in contemporary colloquial Hindlish:

> **2001** I am telling you, no—these people these days! Arey akkal nahin hai, yaar! The other day only, one fellow is asking: Is English Indian language or what? Kyaa, rey! Movies nahin dekhta, kyaa? Aaj kal hero banna boley toh English aanaa, rey. Old movies antey even if you don't know English boley toh no problem. Aaj kal toh yeh crucial ho gaya rey yaaron. If you are wanting to say 'I love you' to the heroine boley toh kyaa Hindi mein bolta, rey? English aanaa!
>
> [I am telling you, really—these people these days! They just don't have any brains, yaar ['man, mate, pal']! Only the other day someone asked me whether English is an Indian language. Hey, man! Do they never see movies? These days, if you want to be a hero, you have to know English. In the movies of old, even if you didn't know English, that was no problem. These days it has become absolutely crucial. If you want to say 'I love you' to the heroine, will you do it in Hindi? You must know English, man!]

– From Rakesh Chaudhary, 'Aati kyaa New York?', in *English Today* 65 (17:1), January Cambridge University Press

Although the text is playful, it demonstrates the dynamism and immediacy of the Hindi-Urdu-English complex, one of the world's most potent Anglo-hybrids.

Indian English and Indian Pidgin English

> **1998** If the British have the right to misconstrue a term like 'Full Monty' into removing every piece garment, I could always . . . mix-and-match my Indianness with the language I have grown up with—English. There may be a thousand errors that professors of English would take great pleasure in dissecting. But don't bother me. I am speaking a living language and writing one too. I don't hate Bob Marley's English anymore than Paul McCartney's. Paul's got rain and snow in his way of speaking and Bob's got sun and sand in his speech. I have the monsoon, the mystic, religions, castes, poverty, the Queen . . . the list is long, in mine.
>
> – Santanu Bora, journalist, *Maharashtra Herald*, 9 April (quoted in Jean D'souza, 'Contextualizing range and depth in Indian English', *World Englishes* 20:2, 2001, 150

Many factors affect the use of English in India, where it can be a first, second, or third, etc., language, a language of education and/or work but not of the home or the social circle. The use of English can be profoundly affected by the immediate linguistic background of the user, which may depend on other languages in a family, a neighbourhood, and/or a place of religion, as well as in school, college, or university (or whether indeed schooling is available, minimally or at all).

Relevant social factors include: (1) *ethnicity, caste, and class* (an immensely varied matter that covers a majority in the north identified as 'Indo-Aryan', a majority in the south identified as 'Draridian', distinctive hill peoples in and near Assam, significant thinly distributed minorities such as the Parsis, and small Eurasian communities such as the Anglo-Indians and East Indians); (2) *socio-religious dimensions* (among religions, as with Hindus, Muslims, and Christians; within religions, as with Hindu and other caste and sectarian groupings, including large numbers of *Dalits*—formerly called in English 'untouchables'—at the lowest end of the Hindu social spectrum; individuals and groups favouring ecumenism, secularism, and/or communism; (3) socio-economic groupings (upper-middle, middle, lower, and lowest) either blending into or at odds with traditional caste distinctions and attitudes).

There is also a range of minimal and more or less fluent usage traditionally known by such names as *Boxwalla(h) English* (used by *boxwallahs*, 'pedlars'), *Butler English*, *Bearer English*, and *Kitchen English* (used by domestic helpers), and *Babu English* (as used by *babus*, especially lower-level officials and clerks, whether formerly employed by rajahs or the Raj, or currently in government offices, etc.). All can be subsumed under the much discussed and disputed term *Indian Pidgin English*, depending on how the term 'pidgin' is conceived. This usage varies from person to person and place to place, and according to mother tongue, but is manifestly focused on English while often blending in elements from other languages. Indeed, blending English with one or more other languages at various socio-cultural levels is not only common in India but entirely unremarkable, from highly erudite discussions in Sanskritized English to haggling in bazaars, for which any combination of any available languages will serve. The examples below were noted in and around the city of Benares/Banaras/Varanasi, and are taken from Raja Ram Mehrotra, 'Indian Pidgin English: myth and reality' (*English Today* 63 (16:3), (Cambridge University Press, 2000), 49):

A taxi driver

'Hello! Where going, Sir? River Ganges two hundred rupees go back wait. How much give you money? Nice scene pilgrim morning time. Much like the tourist Sarnath. Buddha temple look. Deer Park look.'

A boatman on the Ganges

'Dead body burning place. Everyday twenty four hour burn the body. Dom Raja dead body burning place incharge [supervisor]. He first take money. No money pay, no fire. After he buying fire, they wash the body in the Ganges. After three hour, body will finish and less piece of body throw in the Ganga river.'

A temple priest

Upper god Rama. Lower erotic carving sex. Middle side man, both side woman. Back side position. Here gymnastic position sex. Yoga. This side man this side woman. Here rubbing her breast another woman friend. This one carving here in monkey position sex.

Mehrotra observes that such India-wide usage adequately meets certain criteria for establishing a pidgin: (1) the language is reduced and simplified; (2) it is no one's mother tongue; (3) it is restricted to trade and services; (4) it is primarily oral; (5) it derives its linguistic features 'from English and the other Indian languages in contact'; (6) neither person involved speaks the other's language (adequately or at all); (7) it is not used for in-group communication; (8) its speakers generally have lower prestige; (9) it is not the primary means of communication of its speakers; (10) its role is instrumental and interactional, not instructive, regulative, or used with creative intent, and has no emotional overtones. He adds that 'it serves as India's Esperanto of sorts'.

Regional varieties of English, on the other hand, are often defined with reference to either the state language or mother tongue (or both) of a particular speaker (as with *Bengali English*, *Gujarati English*, *Tamil English*, etc.) or in terms of a larger language family (*Indo-Aryan English*, generally in the north, and *Dravidian English*, generally in the south). In this broad but serious sense, there are as many kinds of Indian English as there are languages and social situations in India.

Certain common features do however serve to identify speakers of Indian English across the many varieties that are linked with 'background' vernacular languages. One such set of features, common throughout India, does not have a specific name in its own right but derives from traditional *Anglo-Indian English*, which emerged in the 18th and 19th centuries among the 'Anglo-Indian' families of rank-and-file British soldiers and others on one side and lower-caste Indian women on the other. Anglo-Indians were often disliked and disdained on both sides, and referred to disparagingly as *Chee-chees/Chi-chis*. The term is a reduplication of *chi*, a common multilingual interjection expressing disapproval or disgust, said to have been common among Anglo-Indians themselves, but manifestly also associated with the disdain of others towards them. As a result, their distinctive English (often described as 'sing-song', shared with other Eurasians, such as the East Indians, and sometimes said to resemble speakers of Welsh when using English) has been called both *Chee-chee twang* and, only slightly less negatively, *Chee-chee English*. The Anglo-Indian community in India is now much reduced through emigration since independence, but continues in small usually middle-class communities India-wide.

In spite of a negative inheritance, the position of the Anglo-Indians, with their strong aspirational values and Christian background, was reinforced by a venerable nationwide system of English-medium private schools generically known as *Anglo-Indian schools*. These became a direct concern of the community after independence, and of their representatives in national government and elsewhere, and served to raise the general level of the community's standing. Because of the quality and style of their (usually Anglican- or Presbyterian-based) education and their use of English as a teaching medium, the schools grew in status. Many upper-middle-class and upwardly mobile Hindu, Muslim, Parsi, and other families made—and continue to make—considerable efforts to ensure that their children attend them. As a result, the term *Anglo-Indian* has for many years tended to refer to a variety of English at the upper end of the spectrum rather than to the old Chee-chee twang.

Parallel with the Anglo-Indian schools and Anglo-Indian English are the Roman Catholic schools and *Convent English*. The use of the word *convent* indicates that attention has been focused more on schools for girls traditionally run by nuns, but the style of English relates to all Catholic schools and is close to that of the Anglo-Indian schools. Most such schools once operated within a network of both local and foreign missionaries who have tended to be involved in matters of education and health as well as religion. In India, Sri Lanka, parts of South-East Asia, parts of Africa, and elsewhere, such schools generally date from the 18th and 19th centuries. Originally intended to provide an education centred on Christianity, they have become increasingly secular, serving paradoxically as both exemplars of quality in the non-state educational sector and providers of an additional social cachet for the children of the élite.

Two ethnic groups traditionally associated with the Catholic schools, which can be found throughout India, are the Goans and the East Indians. The ancestors of the Goans were Hindus of the Konkan region of the west coast who were mass-converted to Catholicism by the Portuguese in the 16th–17th centuries, after they had set up their major Indian colony, Goa, south of Bombay. The East Indians are the Portuguese equivalent of the Anglo-Indians, most of whom originate in Bombay/Mumbai (originally a Portuguese colony). Roman Catholicism in India focused on English in its schools, and in Bombay in particular there is a tradition of Goan school-teachers, mostly women, fluent in Convent English and working with children of all backgrounds in many kinds of private English-medium schools from kindergarten upward. As a result, many well-to-do Indians, and most notably women, have accents immediately associated with both Convent and Anglo-Indian schooling.

However, the staffs of both the Anglo-Indian and Convent schools have for years represented a spectrum of educated Indian English usage from all social and religious backgrounds; both the illegality of discrimination in employment on grounds of religion and a shortage of Anglo-Indian and Goan teachers assures this variety in usage. To a high degree, therefore, as with the public school accent (Received Pronunciation) in England, the maintenance of a Convent school accent, especially among girls, is a matter of peer-group reinforcement more than adult example. Currently, a 'convent-educated' woman is taken to have a modern outlook within a traditional ethical frame of reference, to be comfortable and even relaxed and fluent in English, and likely to have a pleasing 'lilt'. In Indian matrimonial advertisements in English-medium newspapers the kind of bride sought is often therefore described as 'convent-educated' (a stipulation with no Christian or monastic implications whatever) and the phrase may be juxtaposed with a statement of her even more relevant caste and subcaste, if Hindu.

Anglo-Indian English and Convent English have jointly contributed to the standard for the media and other public activities in English on an India-wide basis, although their effect has been minimal to non-existent in state-supported local-medium schools, in which accent is usually conditioned by the state language, such as Marathi in Maharashtra, Hindi in Bihar, or Telugu in Andhra Pradesh. The two kinds of 'Christian' school have therefore, as an unintended by-product, helped provide a framework for pan-Indian communication that dates from well before independence in 1947. Their élitist dimension is a decided advantage in middle-class circles. Among the masses, however, an English-medium education is entirely beyond reach and a matter therefore of suspicion and envy. As a result, the use of English is often resented among the disadvantaged, notably in the 'Hindi Belt' of northern states, from Rajasthan to Uttar Pradesh.

Both British and American English have had an influence on Anglo-Indian and Convent English, which are part of—but by no means the sole yardstick for—an Indian Standard English that is slowly consolidating itself. The issue of whether such a standard exists is contentious, but many of the doubts about the actuality, possibility, or desirability of such a thing appear to have ebbed in recent years, especially as fluency in English is manifestly useful in many new kinds of employment available to Indians, notably the electronic and information-related industries and international service-call centres. Some highlights of Indian English pronunciation, grammar, vocabulary, and usage are provided below.

Pronunciation

1 Any discussion of the pronunciation of Indian English at large must take into account both the more pan-Indian and the more regional features in speakers' linguistic backgrounds. In terms of users of English at large in India, only a small minority of people have the accents of the Anglo-Indian and Convent schools.

2 Despite the long-standing influence of Received Pronunciation and other generally non-rhotic British accents, English in India is almost universally rhotic: that is, r is pronounced in all positions.

3 Despite British stress-timed models and varying degrees of stress-timing in Anglo-Indian and Convent usage, Indian English is generally syllable-timed, all vowels tending to have their full value.

4 Word stress does however exist, and distinctive stress patterns occur in different areas: thus, *available* is often stressed in the North on the last-but-one syllable, *avaiLAble*, and in the South on the first syllable, *AVailable*.

Generally, however, where no contrastive stress is required, the tendency is towards equal stress in all syllables, as in *ún-réad-í-néss*.

5 A *y* or *i* at the end of a word tends to be pronounced 'ee': *So sorree! That is reallee funnee! He was wearing a khakee shirt.*

6 The consonants *t* and *d* are retroflex, with the tip of the tongue curled back, while *th*-sounds are generally aspirated *t* and *d*, so that *three of those* sounds like 't^hree of d^hose'.

7 *F* is often pronounced as an aspirated *p*, so that *fellow* sounds like 'p^hellow'.

8 In such words as *old* and *low* the vowel generally has the same value as in Scots.

9 Among speakers of Indo-Aryan languages, such consonant clusters as *sk*, *sl*, *sp* tend to have an epenthetic (extra) vowel, *school* for example being pronounced 'iskool' by Punjabis and 'sekool' by Kashmiris.

10 The distinction between *v* and *w* is generally neutralized to a *w*, so that both *wine* and *vine* are 'wine'.

11 Among speakers of Dravidian languages (mainly in the South), some initial vowels tend to be preceded by a *y* sound (as in 'yell, yem, yen' for the names of the letters *l*, *m*, *n*) and a *w* sound (as in 'wold' for *old* and 'wopen' for *open*).

12 South Indians also tend to geminate ('twin' or 'double') certain consonants, as in 'Americ-ca' and 'hum-man'. Because such gemination is common in Dravidian languages, double consonants in written English are often assumed to require it, producing 'sum-mer' for *summer* and 'sil-lee' for *silly*.

13 Certain distinctive kinds of pronunciation serve as shibboleths for different kinds of Indian English, Bengalis for example using *b* for *v*, turning *vowel* into 'bowel'; Gujaratis commonly using *j* for *z* (converting *zed* into 'jed', *zero* into 'jero') and sometimes *z* for *j* ('jebra' for *zebra*).

Grammar

1 There is great grammatical variety, from native-speaker fluency to a limited command of many constructions and the use of substitute constructions from Indian languages. The following list covers a widespread middle level of usage.

2 Interrogative constructions often do not have subject/auxiliary inversion: *What you would like to buy, please? Where is he wishing to go?*

3 The definite article is often used as if the traditional conventions have been reversed: *It is the nature's way; Office is closed today.*

4 *One* is commonly used rather than *a*: *He gave me one book.*

5 Verbs that do not usually have progressive forms elsewhere are often given them in India: *Lila is having two children; Surely you must be knowing my cousin-brother Mohan.*

6 Word reduplication is used both for emphasis and to indicate a distributive meaning: *I bought some small small things; Why you don't give them one one piece of cake?*

7 *Yes* and *no* are commonly used as question tags: *He is coming, yes?; She was helping, no?*

8   The use of *isn't it* is common as a generalized question tag, particularly in the south: *They are coming tomorrow, isn't it? She knows him very well, isn't it?*

9   *Only* is widely used for emphasis: *They live like that only* ('That is how they live'); *He is working there only* ('He really only works there').

10   The present perfect is often preferred to the simple past: *I have bought the book yesterday.*

11   The present continuous is sometimes used for past actions: *He is doing it yesterday, sir.*

Vocabulary 1: Adoptions from various languages

1   Loanwords and loan translations from other languages have been common since the 17th century, often moving into the general worldwide vocabulary of English.

2   Loanwords from Portuguese include *almirah, ayah, caste, peon,* and from local languages through Portuguese include *bamboo, betel, coir, copra, curry, mango.*

3   Among words and their elements from indigenous vernacular languages, some are earlier and more Anglicized in spelling while others are later and have spellings that suggest their languages of origin. Some are also internationalized while others remain relatively local.

4   Words established internationally include: *bungalow, cheetah, chintz, chit/chitty, jodhpurs, juggernaut, mulligatawny, pukka, pundit, rupee, sahib, wallah.* Note: *rickshaw wallah*, combining Japanese and Hindi).

5   Words that have recently become more internationally known include: *basmati (rice), chapatti, dak bungalow, dacoit, samosa.*

6   Words that are widely used in Indian English but are less well or not at all known elsewhere include: *achcha* ('all right': used in agreement and often repeated: *Achcha achcha, I will go*); *crore* (a unit of 10m or 100 lakhs: *crores of rupees*); *goonda* ('ruffian, petty criminal'); *jawan* (a soldier in the present-day Indian Army); *lakh* (a unit of 100,000: *lakhs of rupees*); *lathi* (a lead-weighted bamboo stick carried by policemen); *masala* (spices: *garam masala* 'hot spices'); *paisa* (a coin, value 100th of a rupee); *panchayat* (a village council); *Shri/Shree/Sri* and *Shrimati/Shreemati/Srimati* (Mr and Mrs).

7   The suffix *-ji* (also *-jee*, especially formerly) often comes with personal names and titles, as a token of respect, especially when addressing a person: *Gandhiji* and *Mahatmaji* for M. K. Gandhi; *Shivaji* as the name of a Maratha hero (combining the god's name *Shiva* with *-ji*); *sahibji* ('respected sir/lord').

8   Loan translations from local languages: *dining-leaf* (a banana leaf used to serve food), *cousin brother* (a male cousin), *cousin sister* (a female cousin), *co-brother-in-law* (a man who is also someone's brother-in-law).

9   Words from Arabic and Persian through North Indian languages, used especially during the British Raj: *dewan* (chief minister of a princely state), *durbar* (court of a prince or governor), *mogul* (a Muslim prince, and in the general language an important person, as in *movie mogul*), *sepoy* (a soldier in the service of the East India Company and the British Indian Army), *shroff*

(a banker, money-changer, clerk dealing with money, also used elsewhere in Asia in the third sense, notably in Hong Kong, as in *car park shroff*), *vakeel/vakil* (a lawyer), *zamindar* (a landlord).

10 Words taken more or less directly from the Indian classical language Sanskrit, usually with religious and philosophical associations, some well known, some restricted to such contexts as yoga: *ahimsa* ('non-violence'); *ananda* ('spiritual bliss'); *chakra* (a mystical centre of energy in the body, one of a number); *guru* ('a (spiritual) teacher', now also, in general English, a quasi-revered guide, as in *management/political guru*); *nirvana* ('release from the wheel of rebirth'); *samadhi* ('spiritual integration and enlightenment'); *yoga* ('a system of physical, mental, and spiritual self-development'); *yogi* ('one who engages in yoga, especially if considerable achievement is easily seen or is asserted').

Vocabulary 2: Distinctive hybrids, compounds, adaptations, and idioms

1 A variety of mixed and adapted usages exists as part of Indian English and as a consequence of widespread code-mixing between English and especially Hindi.

2 Hybrid usages, one component from English, one from a local language, vernacular or classical, are commonplace: *brahminhood* (the condition of being a Brahmin); *coconut paysam* (a dish made of coconut); *goonda ordinance* (an ordinance against goondas); *grameen bank* (a village bank); *kaccha road* (a dirt road); *lathi charge* (noun) a charge using lathis; *lathicharge* (verb) to charge with lathis; *pan/paan shop* (a shop that sells betel nut and lime for chewing, wrapped in a pepper leaf); *policewala* a policeman; *swadeshi cloth* (home-made cloth); *tiffin box* (a lunch-box).

3 Local senses and developments of general English words, often in compounds, are common: *batch-mate* (a classmate or fellow student; *body-bath* (an ordinary act of having a bath); *by-two coffee* (in the south, a restaurant order by two customers asking for half a cup of coffee each); *communal* (with reference to Hindus and Muslims, as in *communal riots*); *condole* (to offer condolences to someone); *England-returned/UK-returned* (used of someone who has been to England or the UK, for educational purposes, a 'been-to'); *Eve-teasing* ('teasing or harassing young women'); *Foreign-returned* (used of someone who has been abroad for educational purposes); *four-twenty* (a cheat or swindler, from the number of a section of the Indian Penal Code); *head-bath* (washing one's hair); *interdine* ('to eat with a member of another religion or caste, with whom one might be presumed not normally to eat'); *intermarriage* (a marriage across different religions or castes); *issueless* ('childless'); *out of station* (not in one's town or place of work); *prepone* (the opposite of 'postpone'); an *undertrial* (someone being tried in a court of law).

4 Words more or less archaic in British and American, but used in Indian English: *dicky* (the boot/trunk of a car); *needful* ('Please do the needful, Sri Patel'); *stepney* (a spare wheel or tyre); *thrice* ('I was seeing him thrice last week').

5 The many idiomatic expressions include: *to sit on someone's neck* ('to watch a person carefully'); *to stand on someone's head* ('to supervise a

person carefully'); *Do one thing, Sri Gupta* ('There is one thing you could do, Mr Gupta'); *He was doing this thing that thing, wasting my time* ('He was doing all sorts of things, wasting my time').

Usage

1 It is by no means always easy to separate English from the general multilingual flux. In addition to hybridization, other languages are constantly drawn into English discourse and English into the discourse of other languages. In the English-language press, hybrid headlines are common: *JNU karamcharis begin dharna* ('Activists in the JNU political party begin dharna'), *The Statesman*, New Delhi); *Jhuggis gutted* ('Fire destroys shanty town'), *The Hindustan Times*, New Delhi).

2 Matrimonial advertisements in the English-language press tend to follow a pattern that covers religion and community (with caste and subcaste if Hindu), may raise the matter of complexion (especially if the subject's skin is lighter than the caste norm), and often includes an indication of education and expectations (commonly asking for a horoscope for purposes of comparison): 'Wanted well-settled bridegroom for a Kerala fair graduate Baradwaja gotram, Astasastram girl, subset [of caste] no bar. Send horoscope and details'; 'Matrimonial proposals invited from educated, smart, well settled, Gujarati bachelors for good looking, decent, Gujarati Modh Ghanchi Bania girl (25), B.A., doing her M.A.'; 'Tall, beautiful, Convent educated girl between 18 and 21 Non Bharadwaj Vadama Brahmin required for well placed Air Force pilot from a well-to-do and respectable family. Write with horoscope and particulars.'

However, by no means all uses of English in India have been pragmatic, social, and confined to everyday issues. During India's campaigns for independence, both journalism and political writing in English were highly significant, including such writers as: Rammohan Roy (1772–1833); Mohandas K. Gandhi (1869–1948); Bal Gangadhar Tilak (1856–1920); and Jawaharlal Nehru (1889–1964). The first literary works in English about India were however by British writers generally referred to in the UK and India as 'Anglo-Indian'. They included Rudyard Kipling (*Plain Tales from the Hills*, 1888; *The Jungle Book*, 1894; *Kim*, 1901), E. M. Forster's *A Passage to India* (1922–4), John Masters's *Bhowani Junction* (1954) and *The Venus of Konpara* (1960), and Paul Scott's *The Raj Quartet* (1966–75). The charter statement for a counter-balancing 'Indo-Anglian' literature (and other 'New English' literatures elsewhere) was made by the publisher and novelist Raja Rao:

> **1938** [T]he telling has not been easy. One has to convey in a language that is not one's own the spirit that is one's own. One has to convey the various shades and omissions of a certain thought-movement that looks maltreated in an alien language. I use the word 'alien,' yet English is not really an alien language to us. It is the language of our intellectual make-up—like Sanskrit or Persian was before—but not of our emotional make-up. We are all instinctively bilingual, many of us writing in our own language and in English. We cannot write like the English. We should not. We cannot write only as Indians. We have grown to look at the large world as part of us. Our method of expression therefore has

to be a dialect which will some day prove to be as distinctive and
colourful as the Irish or the American. Time alone will justify it.
– Raja Rao, Preface to the novel *Kanthapura*

Indo-Anglian literature is established 'not only as an academic discipline in the
universities but as one of our own literatures recognized by the Central Sahitya
Akademi [National Academy of Letters] which has honoured our writers in English
like those in the regional languages' (C. D. Narasimhaiah, 1987, below). The first
extant works by Indians in English are Cavelly Venkata Boriah's *Account of the
Jains* (1809) and Rammohan Roy's translations of four of the ancient Hindu scriptural writings the Upanishads (1816–20). The first creative writing includes the
work of two Bengali writers, Kashiprasad Ghosh's *The Shair and Other Poems*
(1830) and Lal Behari Day's novel *Govinda Samanta: Bengali Peasant Life* (1874).

Indianization has taken place not only in the themes of this growing body of
writing, but also in innovations of style and discourse, as in: Mulk Raj Anand,
Untouchable (1935), *Coolie* (1936), *Across the Black Waters* (1940), *Lament on the
Death of a Master of Arts* (1967); Anita Desai, *Cry, the Peacock* (1963), *Voices in the
City* (1965); G. V. Desani, *All About H. Hatterr* (1948); Manohar Malgonkar, *A Bend
in the Ganges* (1964); Kamala Markandaya, *Nectar in a Sieve* (1954), *A Handful of
Rice* (1966); R. K. Narayan, *Swami and Friends* (1935), *The Bachelor of Arts* (1937),
The English Teacher (1945), *Waiting for the Mahatma* (1955), *The Man-Eater of
Malgudi* (1962); Raja Rao, *Kanthapura* (1938), *The Serpent and the Rope* (1960);
Nayantara Sahgal, *Storm in Chandigarh* (1969), *Rich Like Us* (1985); Khushwant
Singh (b. 1915), *Train to Pakistan* (1956).

In recent times, Indian writers have been in vogue internationally, a development
primed by Salman Rushdie, an expatriate Indian of Muslim background. His novel
Midnight's Children (1981), dealing with a group of characters all born at the
moment India became independent, was a considerable bestseller. *Satanic Verses*
(1988) made him both famous and notorious because of its daring approach to
certain verses in the *Quran*. This prompted a fatwa (proclamation) by Iran's
religious leader Ayatollah Ruhullah Khomeini, urging good Muslims to kill this
blasphemer. Rushdie was protected by British police for some years until the fatwa
was lifted. Further international bestsellers by Indian writers include Vikram Seth's
A Suitable Boy (1993) and Arundhati Roy's *The God of Small Things* (1997), both of
epic proportions.

Popular fiction is not however the only way in which globalization has been
putting Indian English to use in the wider world. The electronics and computing industries have been expanding in recent years, notably in Bangalore and
Hyderabad, and companies in the UK have begun to outsource their telephone call
centres, a case in point being the department store Harrods in London, which for
reasons of economy has moved its telephone store-card operation from Leeds to
Delhi. As Luke Harding has put it in the *Guardian Weekly*:

> **2001** British unions are starting to complain. They object, in
> particular, to the fact that some Indian call centers encourage
> their staff to change their names to sound more, well, English.
> Thus Siddhartha might become Sid, and Gitanjali could be Hazel,
> not Gita. At Spectramind staff keep their original names, Roy

> explains: 'It is not a disadvantage to be called Ramakrishna these
> days.' It is no secret within the industry that 'agents' are taught to
> minimize their Indian accents, to speak more slowly, and to watch
> the BBC news. 'We don't try to teach our staff to speak with British
> accents. But after talking to British people they do start to sound
> like them.' A manager, Viswanathan, admits. . . . Most of
> Spectramind's new recruits have been educated at English-
> orientated schools, and spend Friday nights watching British
> programmes on Star TV, India's most contemporary channel.
> – 'Delhi calling', 15–21 March

A great deal of this 'remote processing' is being done in India not only for the UK but for the US, on the principle that (as one organizer put it) 'geography is history . . . distance is irrelevant' in a world of 'global servicing resources'. According to Harding, responses to advertisements for work are flooding in by the thousand: 'With the industry doubling in size every couple of months, India is fast becoming the call centre capital of the world—with a turnover, analysts predict, of $3.7bn by 2008.'

Pakistani English

The official title of Pakistan in Persianized Urdu is *Islámi Jamhúríya-e Pákistán* and in English is the *Islamic Republic of Pakistan*. Urdu is both the national language of Pakistan and a co-official language with English; other indigenous languages include Panjabi, Sindhi, Pashto, and Baluchi, in terms of whose numbers of speakers Urdu is a minority mother tongue. English is spoken as a second language by a national minority of $c.3$ million in a population of $c.133$ million.

The name *Pakistan* was coined during the struggle for independence in British India by Chaudhary Rahmat Ali and other Muslim students at Cambridge University in England in 1933. In Urdu, the name means 'Land of the Pure' (a reference to Islam), but it does double duty as an acronym of Punjab, Afghania (the North West Frontier), Kashmir, perhaps also Islam, and Sind, plus the last syllable of Baluchistan, representing its intended constituent parts. Before independence it was a collective term for the predominantly Muslim regions of British India, without East Bengal and Hyderabad. Mohammed Ali Jinnah's Muslim League adopted it in 1940, in the course of the Second World War, when Britain was under pressure from the Japanese, during the initial process of bargaining for a Muslim state entirely separate from India.

The Indian Independence Act of 1947 created two post-imperial states: India and Pakistan. In the first phase of its existence, Pakistan had two wings: *West Pakistan* in the north-west of the subcontinent (consisting of Baluchistan, North West Frontier, Sind, and West Punjab) and *East Pakistan* in the north-east (consisting of East Bengal). In 1948, Pakistan occupied part of Kashmir, in the Indian state of Jammu and Kashmir, giving it the name *Azad Kashmir* ('Free Kashmir'). In 1956, Pakistan became an Islamic republic. In 1971, civil war in East Pakistan led to the independent successor state of *Bangladesh*. The influence of Islam, an uneasy relationship with India (three wars, much skirmishing, and many mutual threats), and the alternation of civilian and military governments have been major factors in the history of the country.

The English language as used in Pakistan is a variety of South Asian English close to that of northern India, and is generally known as *Pakistani English*. Although English has had co-official status with Urdu since independence, the constitution of 1959 and the amendments of 1968, 1972, and 1985 have recognized Urdu as pre-eminent and sought to restrict the use of English, with a view to its eventual replacement. In 1981, the president appointed a study whose report recommended that 'Urdu should continue to be the only medium of instruction at the school level, with no exception' (1982), but that English and Arabic should be introduced as additional languages from class six (age 11).

English is nonetheless an important medium in a number of key educational institutions, is the main language of technology and international business, has a major presence in the media, and is a key means of communication among a national élite. The constitution and the laws of the land are codified in English, and the Pakistan Academy of Letters recognizes works in English for its literature award. English has also had a considerable influence on the nation's languages. As one writer has put it:

> **1983** [T]he use of an English word is believed to add a note of
> refinement and elegance to conversation in the 'lower' languages.
> – S. Hands, *Pakistan: A Country Study*, 4th edn (Washington, DC: American University Press)

Hybridization between English, Urdu, and the various other languages is common.

Pronunciation

1 Pakistani English is rhotic, tends to be syllable-timed, and shares many features with the English of northern India.

2 Some pronunciation features are typical of speakers of regional languages. Speakers of Panjabi/Punjabi and Urdu have difficulty with such initial consonant clusters as *sk* and *sp*, but respond to them differently, Panjabi-speakers saying 'seport', 'sekool' (*sport, school*) while speakers of Urdu say 'isport', 'iskool'. Pashto-speakers however follow neither pattern, but tend to replace *f* with *p* as in 'pood' for *food* and *pun* for 'fun'.

Grammar

Distinctive grammatical features relate to uses of the verb, article, relative clause, preposition, and adjective and verb complementation, all shared with northern Indian English (see).

Vocabulary

1 Borrowings from Urdu and the regional languages include: *atta* ('flour'); *tehsil* ('district'); *ziarat* ('religious place').

2 Loan translations from these languages are also common, as with *cousin-brother* (a male cousin) and *cousin-sister* (a female cousin).

3 Many terms are shared with Indian English, as with the quantities *crore* ('ten million') and *lakh* ('one hundred thousand'), and -*wallah* as a word element denoting 'one who does something as an occupation', as with *policewallah*.

4   Hybrids of English and local languages are common and often shared with northern Indian English: *biradarism* ('brotherism': favouring one's clan or family); *gheraoed* ('surrounded by protesters') in an office or similar place and unable to leave; *goondaism* ('hooliganism, thuggish behaviour').

5   Local compound words include: *age-barred* ('over the age for' particular work); *time-barred* (referring to loss of validity after a specific period); *load-shedding* ('intermittently shutting off a supply of electricity').

Pakistan has a strong English-language press. Most major cities have daily and weekly newspapers, and there are many fortnightly, monthly, and quarterly publications, such as *The Muslim, Dawn, Morning News, Star, Pakistan Times*, and *Khyber Mail*. The educated variety of English used by Pakistan radio and television serves as the model for teaching and learning the language throughout the country. Pakistani literature in English has developed various genres, and several writers have acquired international recognition, such as Ahmad Ali, Bapsi Sidhwa, Zulfikar Ghose, A. Hashmi, and Hanif Kureishi.

Bangladeshi English

The official titles of Bangladesh are Bengali *Gana Prajatantri Bangladesh* and English *People's Republic of Bangladesh*. Its population is *c*.120 million and its religion Muslim with very small Hindu and Buddhist minorities. The official language is Bengali, and English has been used in the region since the establishment of a trading 'factory' by the East India Company in Bengal in the 17th century.

In 1947, British India was divided into India and Pakistan, which had two parts, a larger entity *West Pakistan* and a smaller entity *East Pakistan*, which bordered on the Indian states of Bengal and Assam. Despite their sharing Islam, the motive force behind the creation of Pakistan, relations between the widely separated parts were seldom good, and after a brief war of secession in 1971 the eastern (and poorer) territory seceded, becoming *Bangladesh* ('Bengal Land'). Prior to secession, Urdu was the national language and English the official second language, used for administration, higher education, and as a link language between speakers of Bengali and Urdu (who in the main did not know each other's language). Bengali however came third, causing resentment and a prolonged and violent language movement.

In 1987, the *Bangla Procolon Ain/Bengali Implementation Act* was passed, Bengali became the main language of education, and English ceased to be the second official language. It continues, however, as a language of education, in the higher law courts, and for general South Asian communication, and has a place in radio and television, as well as a number of newspapers and magazines. In 1989, as concern about falling levels of education increased, English was made a compulsory language for primary and secondary schools, and a school-leaving pass in both Bengali and English is mandatory. Since Bengali is spoken in the Indian state of Bengal and in Bangladesh, and much of the linguistic history of Bengal and Bangladesh has been shared, the English usage of the two territories is similar, and Bangladeshi English usage shares much with Indian English at large. Notably, there are tendencies to pronounce English *v* as 'b' and *z* as 'j' (as in 'bijit' for *visit*) and to have the vowel of words like *bet* in words like *bat*.

Nepalese English

Nepal, to the north of India, with a population of some 24 million, mainly Nepali and Tibetan, has as its official language Nepali/Gurkhali, an Indo-European language and the mother tongue of some 60% of its people. Other major languages are Bhojpuri, similar to Hindi, and Gurung, a Tibeto-Burman language. English is classed as the country's primary foreign language, giving it precedence over Hindi in India, Urdu in Pakistan, and Putonghua in China, and it is in fact more extensive within Nepal than this role suggests. Although considerably influenced by the UK and with a special relationship with the British Army because of the provision of Gurkha soldiers (as also to the Indian Army), Nepal was never part of the Empire. Nepalese English is therefore unique in that it is not a direct by-product of either imperialism or missionary activity.

Until 1950, Nepal was a closed kingdom run by hereditary prime ministers, but a tradition of education in English came from India, in whose universities most Nepalese teachers were educated. Since the 1960s, Nepal has opened its doors, as a result of which English has become a key language of travel, tourism, and communication. In 1951, as part of a process of democratization, use of English in the media received some support; as a result, by 1985 there were 417 Nepali- and 32 English-language periodicals. English is widely used in advertising and there is a small body of creative writing in it. Radio and television have contributed to the diffusion of English, and hybridization between Nepali and English is common. Nepalese and Northern Indian English are part of a single continuum of usage.

Sri Lankan English

The name *Sri Lanka*, dating from the 1970s in English, derives from *Lanka*, the traditional Sanskrit and Sinhala name for the island (formerly known to the Western world as *Ceylon*), preceded by the honorific *sri* (in Indian English also *shree*). Equivalents in Tamil are *Ilam/Eelam* and *Ilankai*. Arab traders used the name *Serendip/Serendib*. This word entered literary English in the title of a Persian fairy tale, 'The Three Princes of Serendip', from which the writer Horace Walpole in 1754 formed the noun *serendipity* (the faculty of happily discovering one thing while diligently looking for another, something that came naturally to the heroes of the tale). Both *Serendip* and *Ceylon* (the name used throughout the British colonial period) derive from Sanskrit *Simhala-dvipa*, meaning 'island of the Sinhala', a people also known in English as *Sinhalese*, *Singhalese*, *Cingalese*, and *Ceylonese* (although the last term has tended to cover all the people of Ceylon).

The population of Sri Lanka is just over 18 million and its ethnicity is complex: an overwhelming majority of Sinhalese and a minority of Tamils, together with small groups of Moors/Muslims, Burghers/Eurasians, Veddahs (aboriginals), and Malays. Its religions include a Buddhist majority and Hindu, Christian, and Muslim minorities. Its languages are Sinhala and Tamil (both languages official and national) and English (with no official status but often used in government and spoken by some 10% of the nation, including especially the Burghers). English has also traditionally been a lingua franca between the Sinhala and the Tamils, each group's English usage being influenced but its mother tongue.

The island, often described as a physical paradise, has been much fought over; indeed, it is depicted in the ancient Hindu religious epic *The Ramayana* as a dangerous place to which the Indian god-prince Rama tracks the demon Ravana. The first Europeans in the island were the Portuguese (1505), who built a fort at Colombo, now the capital. They were forced out by the Dutch (1658), who failed however to gain control of the whole island. The Dutch were in turn defeated by the British (1796), who established the colony of Ceylon (1802), to which Tamil labourers were brought from South India to work on tea and coffee plantations, adding to a small Tamil population already there. Ceylon became a Dominion of the British Empire in 1948 and the independent republic of Sri Lanka in 1972. The island has therefore had successive, layered involvements with three European nations, languages, and cultures, in addition to tensions between the majority Sinhalese and minority Tamils (the latter concentrated in the north and east, with a focus on the peninsular city of Jaffna). Tensions led in the late 1980s to a bitter on-going civil war. Many Tamils wish to set up their own state, and the seemingly unending strife has at times seriously involved India, including the assassination by a Tamil of the Indian prime minister Rajiv Gandhi in 1991.

Education in English in Ceylon first centred on the work of Christian missionaries. It began in 1799, when the Reverend James Cordiner, chaplain to the British garrison in Colombo, became principal of the settlement's schools. In 1827, Sir Edward Barnes set up the Christian Institution, whose aim was 'to give a superior education to a number of young persons who from their ability, piety and good conduct were likely to prove fit persons in communicating a knowledge of Christianity to their countrymen'. In the early 1830s, when the government took control of education, there were 235 Protestant schools in the island, and until 1886 Christian schools and colleges predominated in education. English in Sri Lanka has a range of subvarieties based on proficiency in its use and the language background of its users. It shares many features with Indian English.

One result of the missionary tradition was the emergence of two broad and at times hostile classes: a Sinhala-educated majority, mostly Buddhist, and an English-educated minority, mostly Christian. Until 1948, the three languages were used side by side, with English as the language of administration and higher education, and a link language between the Sinhalese and the Tamils. In 1956, however, a socialist Sinhala-dominated government replaced English with Sinhala, which led to riots and greatly reduced the role of English for decades. The Sinhala-only policy also resulted in 'the sharp cleavage between Sinhalese and Tamils, most of whom are monolingual in their own tongues and therefore have no means of communication with members of the other community' (Rajiva Wijesinha, *An Anthology of Contemporary Sri Lankan Poetry in English*, Colombo, The British Council, 1988). More recently, a three-language policy was proposed seeking equality for Sinhala, Tamil, and English, and to restore to some extent the position of English, whose national role was greatly reduced after 1960.

Currently the position of English has strengthened. Sri Lanka has a number of daily and weekly English-language newspapers, including the *Ceylon Daily News*, the *Ceylon Observer*, *The Island*, the *Sun*, and the *Sunday Weekend*. Sri Lankan prose writers in English including J. Vijayatunga, Punyakante Wijenaike, James Goonewardene, Raja Proctor, Rajiva Wijesinha, and Savimalee Karunaratne, and poets include George Keyt, Patrick Fernando, Lakdasa Wikkramasinha, Yasmine Goonaratne, Ashley Halpe, and Anne Ranasinghe.

The Maldives, the Seychelles, BIOT, and Mauritius

The island territories of the Indian Ocean historically associated with the British and the English language tend also to have had links with other sea-faring and trading peoples, notably the Arabs in the Maldives (and in Zanzibar: see Tanzania), the French in the Seychelles, BIOT, and Mauritius, and the Sinhala in the Maldives.

The Maldives constitute a small country of nineteen atoll clusters, officially known as *Divehi Jumhuriya* in Divehi and both the *Republic of the Maldives* and the *Maldivian Republic* in English. Traditionally the islands have been known as the *Maldive Islands* or simply the *Maldives*. From 1887 to 1965 the Maldive sultanate was a British protectorate, and today the Republic is a member of the Commonwealth. The capital is Malé. Its population is *c.*266,000, an ethnic mix of Sinhala, South Indian, and Arab, and its religion Sunni Islam. Its official language is Divehi, also known as Maldivian, which is related to Sinhala in Sri Lanka, and therefore an Indo-European language. Its script derives from Arabic. English is widely used in government and tourism, and broadly follows the South Asian English pattern.

The Seychelles constitute a country of the western Indian Ocean of over a hundred islands. It is a member of the Commonwealth. The capital is Victoria and the population *c.*76,000. Its languages are Seychellois (a French-based Creole often simply called *Creole*, spoken by *c.*95% of the population), English, and French (all official). The islands were a French colony from 1768, a British colony from 1814, and became independent in 1976. The Seychellois are largely descended from French colonists and their freed African slaves, with smaller numbers of British, Chinese, and Indians.

The British Indian Ocean Territory (BIOT) is a British dependency in the Indian Ocean, comprising the Chagos Archipelago, annexed from France in 1814 and administered from Mauritius until 1965, when the Territory was established as a UK/US naval base, focused on the island of Diego Garcia. The traditional inhabitants, *c.*1,500 *Ilois* (French: 'Islanders') are descended from African slaves who once worked the islands' copra plantations. They speak a French-based Creole comparable to Seychellois. The entire population was resettled reluctantly under pressure by the UK government on Mauritius. After years of petitioning London, they recently won the right to return. As the islands are heavily committed to both British and American military use, such a return will not be easy.

Mauritius is an Indian Ocean island country and member of the Commonwealth, capital Port Louis. It lies some 500 miles east of Madagascar. The economy is based largely on sugar, tea, tobacco, textiles, and clothing. The island was a French colony from 1715 until it was ceded to Britain in 1810, during the Napoleonic Wars. It became an independent Dominion in 1968 and a republic in 1992. Its population is *c*.1,140,000, and its ethnicity *c*.68% Indian (Indo-Mauritian, both Hindu and Muslim), 27% African, and 3% Chinese (Sino-Mauritian). Its languages are English (official, legal, and in education), a French Creole called *Morisiè* ('Mauricien'), French, Hindi-Urdu-Bhojpuri, and the Hakka vernacular of Chinese, with some Cantonese. The Creole minority (*Gens de Couleurs*: 'coloured people', cf. South African 'Coloureds') is descended from African slaves and French settlers, while the Indo-Mauritian majority is descended from indentured labourers brought to the islands from India by the British after the abolition of slavery in 1833. Although English is the language of major aspects of national life, it is not the mother tongue of any traditional Mauritian community, and is the third language for many people (with Hindi or Creole and then French coming first and second). Texts in English and French may appear side by side in print, as for example in a newspaper, and the two languages and Creole are often hybridized in speech, including in the teaching of English in school. '[T]hose who are literate in English and French are those who have positions of power in Mauritian society' (Joseph Foley, 'English in Mauritius', in *World Englishes* 14:2, 1995, 222).

Such territories are both relatively small and isolated, but must be counted among a number of staging posts for shipping that were formerly important in the spread of both British and American influence and the language they share. Without staging posts such as Saint Helena and Ascension Island in the Atlantic, and Gibraltar, Malta, and Suez in the Mediterranean, English would not have travelled so far or fared as well as it has.

South-East Asia

Many languages are indigenous to South-East Asia, and a significant number of them belong to the *Malayo-Polynesian* language family (also known as *Austronesian*, 'belonging to the Southern Islands'), which extends to the Pacific islands and New Zealand. The home ground of such languages in the region are mainly insular and peninsular, as a result of which they were easily encountered by Western Europeans as they sailed in southern Asian coastal waters from the 16th century onward, looking for trading opportunities. The successive linguistic waves were first Portuguese and Spanish, then Dutch, then English (the British from the west and the Americans from the east, across the Pacific).

There are between 300 and 500 Malayo-Polynesian languages (depending on what one counts), and in South-East Asia they are found in Cambodia, Indonesia, Malaysia, the Philippines, and Vietnam. Elsewhere, they are spoken in Taiwan, Melanesia, Micronesia, Polynesia, and Madagascar. Their distribution makes it clear that earlier speakers of languages from Malay to Maori were skilled sailors and navigators.

English has been in South-East Asia since the 17th century, and currently falls into two broad types: second-language and foreign-language. The second-language varieties are found in the 5 countries that were formerly colonies or protectorates of an English-speaking power: the UK in the case of Brunei, Burma/Myanmar, Malaysia, and Singapore, and the US in the case of the Philippines. There is a continuum of use across the group, from large-scale involvement in Singapore, the Philippines, and Brunei through lighter public use in Malaysia (but heavy use as source material for Malay), to virtual abandonment in Burma after independence in 1948. The foreign-language varieties are found in Cambodia/Kampuchea, Indonesia, Laos, Thailand, and Vietnam. In this group, Thailand was never subject to a European power, and English is used there as an international language of business and a lingua franca for its high-octane tourist industry. Laos, Cambodia, and Vietnam were formerly colonies of the French, and like Thailand incline towards American usage. In recent years, their use of English for trade, tourism, and other purposes has been steadily increasing. Indonesia was formerly a colony of the Dutch, but after independence it rejected Dutch and favoured English, moving more and more towards its use as both a regional and a global lingua franca.

The Association of South-East Asian Nations (ASEAN, Asean) was formed in 1967, comprising Brunei, Indonesia, Malaysia, the Philippines, and Singapore, to which Burma/Myanmar, Cambodia, Laos, Thailand, and Vietnam were in due course added, with Australia, Canada, France, Germany, and New Zealand as associate members. English serves as the bridge language of the Association, whose member nations would otherwise have serious problems of communication. In 1968, within ASEAN, the Southeast Asian Ministers of Education Organization (SEAMEO) founded the Regional English Language Centre (RELC), with its headquarters in Singapore, their aim being to improve the teaching of English as a second or foreign language in the member countries. In 1977, its role was expanded to assist them in developing all language education, and its name was changed to Regional Language Centre, while retaining the acronym. RELC provides training and study programmes that lead to postgraduate diplomas and degrees, as well as related research and development, seminars, publications, and information services. It also provides consultancy and advisory services and arranges exchanges of personnel. Its Library and Information Centre is a clearing-house of language-related information for the region.

Malay, Malaysia, Malaysian English, and Manglish

> **2000** Malaysia recently opened a tourist campaign called
> 'Truly Asia,' with television commercials showing people in
> various traditional costumes swaying to the beat of ethnic drums.
> Visitors lured to Kuala Lumpur by those ads are quite likely to
> be disappointed: 'Truly Western' is perhaps a better way of
> describing the capital. . . . Residents have always loved sitting
> outdoors at tea stalls; these days they sip cappuccino at Starbucks.
> — Thomas Fe, 'East Morphs Into West,' *International Herald Tribune*, 8 December

The Malay language belongs to the Western branch of the Malayo-Polynesian family, and is used in both the Malay Peninsula and many of the islands of the countries now known as Malaysia, Indonesia, and the Philippines. Although the original *orang Melayu* ('Malay people') probably came from coastal Borneo, the usage of the southern Malay Peninsula serves as the basis of both the Standard Malay of Malaysia (*Bahasa Malaysia* 'the Malaysian language', *bahasa* deriving from Sanskrit *bhasha* 'language') and the Standard Malay of Indonesia (*Bahasa Indonesia* 'the Indonesian language'), which are the sole official languages of Malaysia and Indonesia respectively.

In its various forms, Malay is spoken by *c.*60 million people. By no means all are ethnic Malays, and many citizens of Malaysia and Indonesia use it as a second language, while ethnic Malays in Thailand and the Philippines have it as a native vernacular and need another language for national purposes. Malay, like English, has been notably open to loans and usages from other languages, including Thai, Javanese, Sumatran, Sanskrit during the Malay Hindu period, Arabic since the general conversion to Islam, and Chinese and English in recent times. Although the two national standards are similar, they use slightly different versions of the Roman alphabet. Both can also be written in Arabic script. *Bazaar Malay* is the name of a Malay-based pidgin used in market-places and traditionally by servants. For some years, under government supervision, both of the national standards have been undergoing rapid lexical expansion, drawing especially on English for the vocabulary of technology. Both Malay and English are the official languages of the independent Sultanate of Brunei on the island of Borneo. Loans from English into Bahasa Malaysia include:

Orthographically adapted words

ais ('ice'); *famili* ('family'); *kempen* ('campaign'); *terompet* ('trumpet'); *traktor* ('tractor'); *variasi* ('variation'); *wayar* ('wire'); *wiski* ('whisk(e)y'); *zeng* ('zinc').

Adaptations of trade names

beraso ('Brasso'); *klorox* (Chlorox); *termos* ('Thermos'); *zeroks* ('Xerox').

Hybrid expressions

bom waktu ('time bomb'); *tenaga solar* ('solar energy'); *antikerajaan* ('antigovernment').

Loan translations

bulan madu ('honeymoon'); *meja bulat* ('round table'); *papan hitam* ('blackboard'); *pelum berpandu* ('guided missile'); *pasar gelap* ('black market').

Until the 1960s, the term *Malaysia* was used only among geographers, and referred to all lands inhabited by Malays, including Indonesia and the Philippines. It is now restricted to one nation, whose formal title in English is the *Federation of Malaysia*. It is a constitutional monarchy (a king being elected for 5-year periods from among the sultans of the constituent Malay states), and a member of the Commonwealth. It has a population of over 20 million: ethnicity 47% Malay, 32% Chinese, 8% South Asian, 3% Iban, 3% Kadazan, 7% others. Its main languages are: Bahasa Malaysia (the official language, national link language, and medium of education); English (a compulsory second language in education); Chinese vernaculars (mainly Hokkienese/Fujianese and Cantonese); Tamil; Punjabi, and Iban.

From the 16th century, the British competed with settlers from the island of Sumatra, the Dutch, and the Portuguese for control of the Malay Peninsula. In 1826,

Singapore, Malacca, and Penang were incorporated into the *British Colony of the Straits Settlements*, and from 1874 British protection was extended over the sultanates of Perak, Selangor, Negeri Sembilan, and Pahang, which became in 1895 the *Federated Malay States*. Further treaties were made with the sultans of Johor, Kedah, Perlis, Kelantan, and Terengganu, which were known as the *Unfederated Malay States*. After the Second World War, Singapore became a separate colony, the island of Sarawak became a colony, the colony of North Borneo was formed, and the *Malay Union* created to unite the peninsular Malay states with the Straits Settlements of Malacca and Penang. In 1948, the *Federation of Malaya* was formed, and in 1957 (after the defeat of a long-drawn-out Communist insurrection) it became independent. In 1963, when Sabah (North Borneo) and Sarawak joined the group, the *Federation of Malaysia* was formed. In 1965, Singapore left the federation and became an independent republic. The Malay state of Brunei in Borneo also chose to remain distinct.

English-medium schools were established in the 19th century (in Penang in 1816, Singapore 1823, Malacca 1826, and Kuala Lumpur 1894), at the same time as Malay-, Chinese-, and Tamil-medium schools were set up, each linguistic interest group seeking in essence to look after its own. English-medium education, however, became manifestly a path to better-paid employment and higher education, leading to careers such as medicine and the law as well as proving useful in business. The greater the spread of English, the more useful it became and the greater the ease with which it could be used across communal groups, resulting in its ever greater indigenization, especially in Singapore and Penang. The now-defunct term *Anglo-Malay* was used to describe a Malay-tinged English that emerged during colonial times among both expatriates and the local élite, the conduit through which such words as *amok/amuck*, *compound/kampong*, *durian*, *orang utan*, and *sarong* passed into general English.

Those members of the various ethnic groups educated in English-medium schools came to use English increasingly in their occupations and their daily life, the 1957 census report noting that *c.*400,000 people (6% of the population) claimed to be literate in the language. When the British began to withdraw in the late 1950s, English was the dominant language of the non-European élite, and with independence it became the 'alternate official language' to Malay. The National Language Act of 1967, however, established Malay (whose standard variety had been formally renamed *Bahasa Malaysia* in 1963) as the sole official language, with some exceptions in such areas as medicine, banking, and business.

Even so, English-medium education expanded after independence, and there were nearly 400,000 students in such schools when, in 1969, the Ministry of Education decided that all English-medium schools would become Malay-medium. By the early 1980s, the process through which Bahasa Malaysia became the language of education was virtually complete, although the shift prompted concern that proficiency in English was declining and would decline further. To prevent this happening, English was retained as the compulsory second language in primary and secondary schools. Some 20% of the present population (*c.*3.4 million) understands English and *c.*25% of city dwellers use it for some purposes in everyday life. It is widely used in the media and as a reading language in higher education and for professional purposes. There are also a number of English-language daily newspapers (combined circulation over half a million). English remains, however, an urban middle-class language, virtually all of whose users are bilingual, and code-switching between Malay and English is routine. Given the initial official distaste for English when Malaysia came into existence, its continuing relative strength is remarkable. However, in the change of linguistic climate at government level, Malaysians are often exhorted to do better:

> **1995** KUALA LUMPUR—Malaysian Education Minister Datuk Seri Najib Tum Razak has warned that Malays stand to lose if they shun the English language. He said that Malays must know at least two languages to excel in the world, according to a report in the Malaysian Star. 'The English language is vital for the survival of a nation, and it must be able to master the language or else it will be left behind,' he said. 'Bahasa Malaysia is also as important as English and Malays must have control of both languages,' Datuk Najib told reporters after a Raya Haji thanksgiving at Kuala Pahang.
>
> – From the *El Gazette*, July, taken in turn from *The Straits Times*, date not given.

Malaysian and Singaporean English have much in common, the main difference being the strong influence of Malay on English in Malaysia. Both languages have also been influenced by local Chinese vernaculars. In formal situations, the English of educated Malaysians (and Singaporeans) is marked mainly by accent, but in more informal situations an innovative use of words includes both loans from Malay and the Chinese vernaculars and local modifications in the meanings of English words. Grammatical structure also shows the influence of local languages. In colonial times, most of the students at English-medium schools were Chinese; after independence, Malay-medium education increased. Malay is the main medium in primary schools and the only medium in secondary schools. English remains a compulsory subject but, as intended, its role has been considerably diminished. By contrast, Brunei has a bilingual Malay/English education policy, earlier primary-school classes using Malay alone, with an increasing use of English until in the senior secondary school it is the medium for 80% of class time. Some key features of Malaysian English usage are:

Pronunciation

1 There is a strong tendency towards syllable-timed rhythm.

2 The simplification of word-final consonant clusters is common, as in 'He live there lass year' for *He lived there last year*. Distinctive colloquialisms include words with such adaptations in sound, as with *bes* (from *best*: 'great, fantastic') and *relac* (from *relax*, meaning 'take it easy').

Grammar

1 Some usually uncountable nouns are used countably, as in 'Pick up your chalks' and 'A consideration for others is important'.

2 There are innovations in the use of phrasal verbs, as in *cope up with* rather than *cope with*.

3 Reflexive pronouns are commonly used on their own for emphasis, without the verb *to be*: *Myself sick* ('I am sick'); *Himself funny* ('He is funny').

4   Several Chinese interjections and particles are in common use, as in Singapore
    and Hong Kong: *aiyah* as an expression of surprise and/or displeasure, as in
    Aiyah, it's no good!; *ah* as an interrogative marker at the end of phrases and
    sentences, as in *How you going ah?*; *I say man, you crazy ah?*; *lah* at the end
    of phrases and sentences as a token of informal intimacy: *Sorry, can't come
    lah—too busy lah.*

Vocabulary and usage

1   Typical borrowings from Malay are: *bumiputra* (from Sanskrit, 'son of the soil':
    a Malay or other indigenous person); *dadah* ('illegal drugs'); *dangdut* (a kind of
    local music); *ikan bakar* ('grilled fish'); *rakyat* ('the people, citizens'); *Majlis*
    (from Arabic, 'Parliament'); *makan* ('food').

2   Hybrid compounds are common, as with: *bumiputra status* ('indigenous
    status'); *dadah addict* ('drug addict').

3   Abbreviated place-names, as with *KL* for *Kuala Lumpur*, *KB* for *Kota Baru*,
    KK for *Kota Kinabalu*, and *JB* for *Johor Baru*.

4   Distinctive uses of English words on their own or in combination include:
    crocodile ('a womanizer'); *go outstation* ('to travel to outlying areas': compare
    the Indian English phrase *be out of station* 'not be in one's usual place of work,
    probably because travelling on duty'); *girlie barber shop* (a hairdressing salon
    that doubles as a massage parlour or brothel); *sensitive issues* (as defined in the
    Constitution: issues that must not be raised in public, such as the status of the
    various languages used in Malaysia and the rights and privileges of the
    different communities); *banana leaf restaurant* (a South Indian restaurant
    where food is served on banana leaves).

Hybridization in the form of code-switching and code-mixing is common, as in the
following dialogue from a popular TV soap opera:

> A: Thanks, Ita, for house-sitting for me.
> B: No problem. Apartment kau lebih cantik darpada apartment
>   apu. Anyway, it's all yours again.
> A: Thank you. Selama aku tak ada, ada sesiapa telefon tak?
> B: Takde.
> A: Takde?
> [Translations: 'Your apartment is much more beautiful than
>   mine'; 'When I was away, did anyone call?'; 'Nobody']
>
> – from *Idaman*, 25 July 1999, as quoted at greater length in Andrew Preshous, 'Where you
>   going ah?', *English Today*, 65 (17:1), January 2001 (Cambridge University Press)

The term *Malaysian English* is sometimes informally contracted to *Malenglish* and,
with or without intended irony, *Manglish*, names which tend to refer to a more
or less controversial colloquial variety, comparable to the difference between
Singapore(an) English and *Singlish*. The essence of Manglish has been distilled in
the cartoon captions of K. H. Boon in the *Malaysian Post*, as in: 'Myself so thin don't
eat, can die one, you know?' Exhortations to use English more fastidiously have
been common, but during the years of strengthening Malay there was little incentive

to sustain an international level of use. In recent years, however, memories of colonial times have faded and, with globalization as an incentive, efforts have been made to re-energize and sustain the country's Standard English tradition, now regarded as less of a curse and more of a blessing.

Singapore, Singapore(an) English, and Singlish

1997

- As the millennium approaches, so too does Singapore's self-imposed deadline to become an 'Intelligent Island.' To this end, an ambitious program called IT2000 aims to transform the nation through extensive use of computers and information technology. Mr. [Stephen] Yeo [chief executive of the national Computer Board] thinks that Singapore already has the best IT infrastructure in the region, if not the world. 'This is not because we are exceptionally bright, but because it's a small place that is easy to wire.'

- A recent speech by Prime Minister Goh Chok Tong illustrates the dilemma. While telling community leaders that Singapore should aim to be one of the world's ten richest countries in the next century (it is currently number 11), Mr. Goh cautioned that citizens should not become obsessed with becoming wealthy: 'I want a Singapore with a soul. Rich, but not materialistic, competitive but compassionate.'

– Julia Clerk, 'Built for business: Singapore', sponsored section, *International Herald Tribune*, 28 April

The name of the city (and city state) of Singapore comes from Sanskrit *Simhapura* ('Lion City', a translation sometimes used as an alternative name, especially in the media). The official titles of the state are in English the *Republic of Singapore*, in Mandarin *Hsin-chia-p'o Kung-ho-kuo* (in the Wade-Giles transcription and not Pinyin), in Malay *Republik Singapura*, and in Tamil *Singapore Kudiyarasa*. Singapore is a member of the Commonwealth. If a distinction is needed, the nation is referred to as *Singapore* and its capital as *Singapore City*. In a population of just over 3 million, the ethnic breakdown is: Chinese $c.76\%$; Malay $c.15\%$; South Asian $c.7\%$; others $c.2\%$.

There are four official languages: English, Mandarin Chinese, Malay, and Tamil, with English the language of the law courts, government administration, and education. Because, however, few members of any one ethnic community speak a language of the other communities, English has since independence served as the everyday lingua franca, becoming in effect the primary language of the nation. This has raised the question of whether Singapore has become, or will become, an English-speaking nation comparable, say, to the Irish Republic.

Singapore was originally part of the Sri Vijaya kingdom of Sumatra. The British trader Sir Stamford Raffles leased the island from the Sultan of Johore in 1819, and with Malacca and Penang it became in 1826 (under the East India Company) the *Straits Settlements*, which became a British colony in 1867. The island was taken by the Japanese in 1942 (during the Second World War), became British again in 1945, obtained self-government in 1959, was part of the *Federation of Malaya* from 1963 to 1965, then became an independent state. Its relations with Malaysia since that time have from time to time been uneasy. In the early 1990s, Singapore dramatically raised both its standard of living and its international profile by becoming a key Asian financial, commercial, travel, and communications centre.

The English of Singapore, widely known as *Singapore* or *Singaporean English*, serves as both a means of uniting the country and an international medium. In 1947, 31.6% of students in the colony studied in English-medium schools, while others studied in Chinese- and Tamil-medium schools. Since 1987, however, English has been the sole medium of Singaporean primary, secondary, and tertiary education. It is the main language of business and commerce, internally and externally, and its influence extends beyond the boundaries of the state. Educated Singaporeans of Indian (mainly Dravidian-speaking) background and Singaporean Malays seek to retain their community languages while conforming to the government-led pattern. Straits-born Chinese (locally known as the *Baba Chinese*) traditionally spoke *Baba Malay* rather than a Chinese vernacular, but have tended increasingly to favour English over other languages. Other Chinese, the national majority, tend to sustain their vernaculars and also commonly wish their children to acquire Mandarin. Here too, however, the convenience and usefulness of English, both locally and globally (or, as the Singaporean language scholar Anne Pakir puts it, 'glocally') tends to outweigh all other considerations.

A fundamental feature of Singapore English is its social continuum. At the higher end is a government-backed normative variety based on British Standard English, spoken with a near-RP accent, used by the *Singapore Broadcasting Corporation*, and increasingly influenced by American usage. At the other end is a home-grown colloquial variety to which the name *Singlish* has long been attached (although it is also at times used for all local English usage). For some, Singlish is a cause for despair, for others delight, and for the same reason: it serves the young in particular as a vehicle of solidarity, is vigorous, slangy, and creative, and draws upon the hybrid linguistic and cultural background of the city and the region.

Many Singaporeans comfortably shift along the continuum from a standard usage that serves international business and professional purposes (and is entirely clear to outsiders) to a racy, relaxed local style and usage (that are often opaque to people from beyond Singapore, Malaysia, and Brunei). Many Singaporeans of Chinese, Malay, and Indian background have traditionally relaxed into their own languages, and continue to do so, but the younger generation (which is far more integrated than its elders) finds that Singlish is also a means of relaxing and being oneself, and tend to identify increasingly with it. The government and other concerned parties continue, however, to speak out against this home-grown patois, castigating the use of anything that might be labelled 'Singlish', but it appears to be flourishing. Below is a list of some defining features of Singapore usage. Lee-Wong Song Mei of the Nanyang Business School puts the case for the defence as follows:

> **2001** To deny the functionality of Singlish in the speech
> community is to be at odds with a situation where users are
> adapting a foreign language to a local communal culture. No
> doubt, steps can be taken to improve the standard of English,
> particularly at elementary schools, but, beyond the walls of formal
> learning, it is up to the individual to decide how s/he wishes to
> speak and in what manner . . . [I]t is undeniable that Singlish

represents a strong unifying force across ethnic boundaries and
socio-economic groups, among both the well- and less-educated.
– in 'The polemics of Singlish', *English Today* 65 (17:1) (Cambridge University Press) 44

She also points out that in a survey which she conducted in 1999, 68% of respond-
ents were inclined to be positive about Singlish, and two typical responses were:
'Gives us a unique sense of *identity* as Singaporeans. Should be encouraged', and
'Speaking Singlish doesn't mean we don't know the "actual" (standard) English.
Those "la", "leh" allow us to *express ourselves better*.' The following example of the
particle *la* in full local flow comes from Lee-Wong's article:

> A: How's the project going?
> B: . . . Like this *la*.
> [Asked how A was getting on with his project]
> A: Ok *la*.
> [Asked about B's work]
> B: Stressed *la*.

The Chinese particles *la(h)* and *aa/ah* are commonly used to convey emphasis
and emotion (as also in Malaysia, Brunei, and Hong Kong), in effect replacing the
intonational features of mainstream English: for example, *la(h)* as a token of informal
intimacy (*Can you come tonight?—Can lah/Cannot lah*); *aa/ah* in *yes-no* questions
(*You wait me, aa?* 'Will you wait for me?'; *I come tonight, ah?* ('Should I come
tonight?'); *You think I scared of you, aa?* Chinese-style interjections include: *ay
yaah!* (also *aiyah*, to express surprise or exasperation); *ay yor!* (to express or suggest
pain, wonder, or both); *ay yer!* (indicating a reaction to something unpleasant and
maybe unexpected); *che!* (expressing irritation or regret). Below are some further
highlights of Singaporean English usage:

Pronunciation

1 English in Singapore is non-rhotic and tends to be syllable-timed, despite the
   official aim of achieving a British-style stress-timed rhythm. It places more or
   less equal stress on all syllables, usually with the final syllable of phrases
   slightly lengthened.

2 There is generally no contrastive stress (as in *DON'T go!* versus *Don't GO!*).

3 Final consonants are often unreleased, resulting in glottal stops at the end of
   such words as *take*, *step*, and *hit* (much as in Chinese English at large, and
   similarly common in Hong Kong).

4 Final consonant clusters are generally reduced to one spoken consonant,
   such as 'juss' for *just* and 'tol' for *told*. Singaporeans will for example often
   write *s-l-e-p-t* but say 'slep'.

5 The vowels in such words as *take*, *so*, and *dare* are often single vowels, as in
   Scottish English and not diphthongs as in RP.

Grammar

1 There is a tendency to omit: articles, as in *You have pen or not?* and *He went to
   office yesterday*; the plural inflection *-s*, as in *I got three sister and two brother*;

the present-tense inflection *-s*, as in *This radio sound good* and *My mum, she come from China many year ago*; the past-tense inflection *-ed/-t*, as with 'ask' for *asked*, 'slep' for *slept*, 'He live there' for *He lived there*; and the *be* before adjectives used predicatively, as in *This coffee house cheap*.

2   *Already* in final position is used to mark completion: *Eight years she work here already* ('She has been working here for eight years').

3   *Would* is commonly used for future events rather than *will/shall* or the present tense: *We hope this would meet your requirements* ('We hope this meets/will meet your requirements').

4   Direct and indirect objects are often highlighted by being placed first: *This book we don't have*; *Me you don't give it to* ('You didn't give it to me').

5   The all-purpose tags *is it?* and *isn't it?* are common: *You check out today, is it?*; *They come here often, isn't it?*

6   *Also* is preferred over *too*, notably at the end of a sentence: *But we are supposed to learn Chinese also*.

7   Informal ways of checking that someone agrees or disagrees, or can or cannot do something, include: 'Are you coming? Yes or not?'; 'Like it or not? 'Are you going? Can or not?'; 'Enough or not?'; 'Got or not?'

Vocabulary

1   Words borrowed from regional languages include: (Malay) *makan* ('food'), as in *Let's have some makan*; (Hokkienese/Fujianese) *ang pow* ('red packet', a gift of money traditionally presented in a red paper packet).

2   Everyday words of English with significantly re-applied meanings, common in both South and South-East Asia: *send* in the sense of 'take', as in *I will send you home*; *open* meaning 'put on', as in *Open the light*, and *close* meaning 'put off', as in *Close the light*; *take* suggesting 'eat, drink, like', as in *Do you take hot food?* ('Do you like spicy food?'). The particles *off* and *on* can be used as verbs, as in *to off/on the light*), and *off* can be a noun meaning 'time off', as in *We had our offs changed to Thursdays*.

3   Formal and informal registers are less distinct from one another than in British and American (etc.) usage, with the result that a mix of highly colloquial and highly formal usages may co-occur, as in: *her deceased hubby* rather than 'her dead husband'.

Singapore usage shows many features comparable to the indigenization of English in Ireland and the Highlands of Scotland, except that where forms of one language, Gaelic, constituted the local substrate, a whole spectrum of local language influences provide the substrates and companion languages in Singapore, notably from such Chinese vernaculars as Fujianese/Hokkienese and Cantonese to Malay and Tamil. It seems very likely that its social flexibility will ensure that English becomes more and more firmly grounded in Singapore, and its range of usage from 'broad' Singlish to the standard language will make it, in twenty years or so, very much like any other English-speaking country.

Brunei and English

The independent sultanate of Brunei, officially known as *Brunei Darussalam* (Arabic, 'the abode of peace'), is situated in the north-west of the island of Borneo (a variant of the same name). Its capital is Bandar Seri Begawan and its economy mainly oil and natural gas. Its population of some 300,000 consists of a Malay majority, a small proportion of other indigenous groups such as the Dusun and Belait, with *c.*20% Chinese, others being foreign workers from neighbouring countries and the West. Malay and English are both official, and various minor local languages and Chinese vernaculars are in use. Brunei was a British protectorate from 1888 until independence in 1984. Radio Television Brunei (RTB) operates both Malay and English sections. Whereas education was formerly streamed in English- and Malay-medium schools, in 1985 a system of bilingual education (the *Sistem Pelajaran Dwibahasa*) was introduced in order to balance the two languages and improve proficiency in both. Malay predominates in the earlier primary system, and in the later primary and secondary stages religious knowledge, civics, and Malay are taught in Malay, while science, mathematics, geography, and English are taught in English.

A distinctive feature of local usage, taken from Brunei Malay, is the particle *bah*, used among other things to indicate agreement ('You want to come with me?'—'Bah') and opening a conversation ('That girl is very talkative, ah?'—'Au bah. So noisy.') and closing it ('See you.'—'Bah.'). It does not appear to clash with the Standard English exclamatory use of *bah* to express indignation and rejection.

Brunei English has much in common with the English of both Malaysia and Singapore: the present tense is commonly used where the simple past is usual in Standard English situations ('I come to see him yesterday'); distinctions between countable and uncountable nouns are relaxed ('Many student go there'); and the indefinite article is regularly dropped ('This is very interesting book'). In 'The English language in Brunei Darussalam' (*World Englishes* 13:3, Oxford: Blackwell, 1994), Graeme Cane lists a selection of usages that Bruneians share with Malaysians and Singaporeans, suggesting the existence of a single variety of English (with minor variations and some specific local slants) throughout the region. In the following mildly adapted list, local usage is followed by a standard international gloss in parentheses:

1 *Can I follow you?* ('Can I go with you?').

2 *I'm frus because unable to solve my problems* (an informal clipping of 'frustrated')

3 *Please on the light* (= 'turn on': opposite *Please off the light*)

4 *You're still schooling, of course* (= 'still going to school')

5 *They will scold you for that* (= 'criticize, reprimand')

6 *Can someone send me to Tiong Hin?* (= 'take me')

7 *You sleep early but we sleep late* ('You go to bed early but we go to bed late')

8 *Which part of Lambak do you stay?* ('Which part of Lambak do you live in?').

This last may have developed under the influence of Scottish expatriates. The form *Where do you stay?* ('Where do you live?') is straightforwardly standard in Scotland.

Cane offers the suggestion that similarities in the English usage not only of Malaysia, Singapore, and Brunei (which all embody influences from Malay and Chinese) but also the Philippines and Papua-New Guinea may rest not so much on shared features in the relevant mother tongues (which are many and varied across such a large region) as on 'a pan-linguistic grammatical simplification process'.

Indonesia

The formal title of Indonesia in Bahasa is *Republik Indonesia* and in English is *Republic of Indonesia*. It is a nation of islands and parts of islands, whose main areas are Sumatra/Sumatera, Java/Jawa, Kalimantan (two-thirds of Borneo), Sulawesi, and Irian Jaya (the western half of New Guinea). Its population is just over 198 million and its ethnicity *c.*77% Malay, including *c.*45% Javanese, *c.*14% Sundanese, *c.*8% coastal Malays, *c.*8% Balinese, Batak, Dayak, Madurese, and Moluccan, etc., and 2% Chinese. Its official and link language is Bahasa Indonesia or Indonesian, a form of Malay, and Javanese, English, and Dutch are widely spoken. The many local languages include Madurese and Sundanese, and some Chinese vernaculars continue to be used.

The Portuguese were the first Europeans to set up trading posts in the region, in the 16th century, and were followed by the Dutch and the English in the early 17th century. When the Dutch had driven out the English, they established the Dutch East Indies, which they controlled until independence in 1945–50. There were only two breaks in the long period of Dutch control: during the Napoleonic era, when first the French then the British briefly occupied the islands, and the Second World War, when the Japanese held them (1942–5). On declaring their independence in 1945, the Indonesians rejected Dutch as an official medium and made English the primary foreign language of the new country, as a result of which it is extensively and variously used in ways similar to Malaysia and Singapore.

As in Malaysia, the adaptation of English words has played a large part in enriching Indonesian Malay, such loans often being preferred to loan translations and Malay coinages: for example, *efisien* ('efficient') being preferred to *berdayaguna*. Typical of the many words borrowed from English into Bahasa are *antena, baterai, biskuit, dokter, helikopter, interkom, kabin, kompas, mesin* ('machine', extended to *mesin-jet* for 'jet engine'), *pelikan, pilot, radio*, and *stetoskop*. The vast majority of imported books are in English and thousands of private language schools offer EFL courses. The influence of both British and American English is pervasive (through printed matter, films, tourism, and pop music) and many educated people use the language among themselves.

The Philippines, Tagalog, and English

The official titles of the Philippines are, in Pilipino/Filipino/Tagalog, the *Republika ng Pilipinas*, in English the *Republic of the Philippines*, and in Spanish

República de Filipinas. The nation consists of an archipelago of more than 7,000 islands, the most prominent of which are Luzon, Mindanao, Samar, Palawan, Mindoro, Panay, Cebu, Negros, and Leyte. The capital is Manila, on Luzon, and the population is *c*.71,750,000, consisting mainly of Malays, with many mixed descendants of Malays, Spanish, Chinese, and Americans and a small Chinese community. Both Pilipino/Filipino/Tagalog and English are official, and larger local languages included Cebuano, Ilocano, Hiligaynon, Waray, and Bicol, as well as some Spanish and Chinese.

Ferdinand Magellan claimed the islands for Spain in 1521, and the name *Philippines* was given to them in honour of Philip II. Spanish control lasted almost 400 years, until the islands were ceded to the US at the Treaty of Paris in 1898, after the Spanish–American War. The islands became a self-governing Commonwealth in 1935: compare Puerto Rico, also acquired by the US in 1898 and currently with Commonwealth status. The Philippine islands were occupied by the Japanese during the Second World War, and very quickly after they were liberated the country gained its independence, in 1946. Since then, there have been recurring periods of social and political instability, with sudden changes of government and also conflict between Muslims and Christians, including the emergence in recent years of armed Muslim groups using kidnapping for ransom as a means of raising money to buy weapons to fight for the independence of the mainly Muslim south.

English-medium education began in the Philippines in 1901 after the arrival of some 540 US teachers. English was made the language of education and as its use extended it became indigenized through the inclusion of vocabulary from local languages, the adaptation of English words to local needs, and modifications in pronunciation and grammar. English was also adopted for newspapers and magazines, the media, and literary writing. After independence in 1946, the national language Tagalog (later called Pilipino) was made an official language along with English and Spanish. With increasing nationalism, the role of English diminished and in 1974 a bilingual education policy was implemented, with English as a school subject at primary level but as the medium for science and mathematics at secondary level. At tertiary institutions it remains the principal medium of instruction.

Filipino experience of Western colonialism and its linguistic impact has been unique, in that two very different kinds of colonialist were successively involved: monarchical Catholic Spain from the 16th century and a republican, paternalistic, and quasi-imperial United States from 1898. English spread rapidly, notably to the detriment of Spanish (except in the on-going use of Spanish personal names), because it was the new language of government, preferment, and education, and incentives to learn it included: recruitment into the civil service; opportunities to study in—and migrate to—the US; and the use of English for business beyond the islands. American teachers were brought in to support English as the medium to be used in the new colonial government's elementary-school system.

After independence, the national name *Pilipino* (in local pronunciation) and *Filipino* (in Spanish and English) was given to the language commonly known as *Tagalog* (pronounced with the stress on the second syllable: 'Ta-GA-log'), in order to lend it dignity and associate it with the entire nation, whereas it has traditionally been a language associated almost exclusively with the Metro-Manila area in Luzon. The Tagalog community numbers *c*.10 million, is the largest ethnic group, and makes up a majority of the population of Manila. Although most are farmers, the importance of Manila has given the urban Tagalog a leading position in manu-facturing, business, and the professions. The term *Taglish*, which emerged in the 1960s, blends *Tagalog* and *English*, and refers to a hybrid also known as *Mix-Mix*. The entire continuum is sometimes represented as *English—Taglish—Engalog—Tagalog*. It is extensively used in local motion pictures and on radio and television. Two examples from a movie gossip column:

> **1** 'Peks man,' she swears. 'Wala pang nangyayari sa amin ni Marlon. We want to surprise each other on our honeymoon.' [Translation: 'Cross my heart,' she swears. 'Nothing yet has happened between Marlon and me. . . .']

> **2** Donna reveals that since she turned producer in 1986, her dream was to produce a movie for children: 'Kaya, nang mabasa ko ang Tuklaw sa Aliwan Komiks, sabi ko, this is it. And I had the festival in mind when finally I decided to produce it. Pambata talaga kasi ang Pasko,' Donna says. ('That is why when I read the story 'Snake-Bite' in the Aliwan Comic Book, I told myself, this is it. . . . Because Christmas is really for children').

The mix may also occur (sometimes quite unevenly and in long alternating sections) in formal texts, both in and beyond the Philippines. Two examples are, from finance-related texts:

> **1988** Pwede kayong magbayad three months after arrival. Pwede pang i-extend up to two years ang payment. At sa pinakamababang interest rate pa.'
>
> – quoted by Lily V. Kapili, in 'Requiem for English?', *English Today* 16, October, Cambridge University Press
> [Translation: 'It is possible to pay three months after arrival. It is possible to extend payment up to two years. And the interest rate is the lowest.' The word *pwede* is from Spanish *puede* ('it is possible').]

> **1994** (from a text identified as Tagalog in a bilingual English/Tagalog leaflet provided by the Hongkongbank for Filipinas working in Hong Kong)
> *Arrange to pay in regular amounts* May tatlong paraan para maisaayos ang paghulog ng pera sa inyong Cash Card account:
> a. Mag-deposito ng pera mula sa ibang Hongkongbank account, at any Hongkongbank ATM, using your Cash Card. . . .
>
> – quoted by Tom McArthur in *The English Languages*, 1998, Cambridge University Press, 13
> [Translation (ignoring the English): '. . . . You can arrange to pay money into your . . . in three ways:
> a By depositing cash or cheques, or transferring money from another . . .']

There are some 85 Malayo-Polynesian languages in the islands, many of them mu-tually unintelligible and serving as substrates for regional Englishes. The English of the Philippines at large is known as both *Philippine English* and *Filipino English*. Filipinos whose English ranges from sufficient to fluent may constitute *c*.65% of the population, and for *c*.10% it is a first language, or first equal with another language, pre-eminently Tagalog, Cebuano, or Ilocano. Hybridization is routine. The follow-ing are some key aspects of Philippine English:

Pronunciation

1 It is rhotic, but the local *r* is an alveolar flap (against the ridge behind the upper teeth) and not an American retroflex (with the tongue tip curled back).

2 It is syllable-timed, following the rhythm of the local languages, full value being given to unstressed syllables. The weak vowel in the second syllable of such words as *bullet* and *sudden*, for example, is usually realized as a full vowel: 'boo-let', 'suh-den'.

3 Certain polysyllables have distinctive stress patterns, as with *elígible*, *éstablish*, *ceremony*.

4 Intonation is widely characterized as 'singsong'.

5 Educated Filipinos aim at an American accent, but have varying success with the vowel contrasts in *sheep/ship*, *full/fool*, and *boat/bought*.

6 For most Filipinos the vowel sound in, for example, American *mask* does not come easily. They are therefore more likely to use the vowel in, for example, American *father*.

7 The distinctions between *s*, *z* and *sh*, *zh* are not made: *azure* is therefore 'ayshure', *pleasure* 'pleshure', *seize* has the same sound at the end as at the beginning, and *cars* are likely to be 'karss'.

8 The sounds for *th* in *three of these* are likely to be 'tree of dese'.

Grammar

1 Loss of the singular inflection of verbs: *One boy give a report to the teacher every morning.*

2 Using the present perfect for the simple past (*I have seen her yesterday* rather than 'I saw her yesterday') and past perfect for present perfect (*He had already gone home* rather than 'He has already gone home').

3 Using continuous tenses for habitual aspect: *He is going to school regularly* rather than 'He goes to school regularly'.

4 Using the present-tense forms of auxiliary verbs in subordinate noun clauses rather than their past-tense forms, and vice versa: *He said he has already seen you* ('He said he had already seen you'); *She hoped that she can visit you tomorrow* ('She hoped that she could visit you tomorrow'); *He say that he could visit you tomorrow* ('He says that he can visit you tomorrow').

5 There is often a reversal of the mainstream uses of the definite article: *He is studying at the Manuel Quezon University; I am going to visit United States.*

6 Verbs that are generally transitive are commonly used intransitively: *Did you enjoy?—Yes, very much*; *I am not going to buy it—cannot afford*; *Do you like pork?—No, I don't like.*

Vocabulary and idioms

1 From Spanish: *asalto* ('a surprise party'); *bienvenida* ('a welcome party'); *despedida* ('a farewell party'); *Don/Doña* (a title for a prominent man/woman); *estafa* ('a fraud, scandal'); *merienda* ('afternoon tea/refreshments'); *plantilla* (faculty assignments and deployment in an academic department); *querida*

('a mistress'); *viand* (from *vianda* 'provisions for a journey': a dish served to accompany rice in a Filipino meal).

2   Loans from Pilipino/Tagalog: *boondock* (from *bundok* 'mountain': now common in the USA and elsewhere as *the boondocks* 'the back of beyond'); *carabao* (from *kalabaw* 'a water buffalo'); *kundiman* ('a love song'); *sampaloc* (from *sampalok* 'the fruit of the tamarind'); *tao* ('a man', as in *the common tao*).

3   Loan translations from local languages: *Open the light/radio* ('Turn on the light/radio': compare Indian English); *since before yet* ('for a long time'); *joke only* ('I'm just teasing you'); *You don't only know . . .* ('You just don't realize . . .'); *He is playing and playing* ('He keeps on playing'); *making foolishness* (especially of children: 'misbehaving'); *I am ashamed to you* ('I am embarrassed because I have been asking you so many favours').

4   Local neologisms include: *aggrupation* (from Spanish *agrupación* 'a group'); *captain-ball* ('a team captain in basketball'); *carnap* (a word blend: 'to steal or 'kidnap' a car); *cope up* ('to keep up and cope with (something)'); *hold-upper* (someone who engages in armed hold-ups); *jeepney* ('a jeep converted into a small bus: a blend of *jeep* and *jitney*, American English for a small bus).

Because of the influence of reading and writing and the academic context in which English is learned, many college-educated Filipinos speak the way they write, in a formal style based on prose models that may take their inspiration from English a century ago. Comparably, spelling pronunciations are common, such as 'lee-o-pard' for *leopard*, 'subtill' for *subtle*, and 'wor-sester-shire sauce' for *Worcestershire sauce* ('Wooster-'). The formal Filipino style in English has been called the *classroom compositional style*, and either accidental or deliberately playful clashes of style may occur, as in: 'The commissioners are all horse owners, who at the same time will appoint the racing stewards who will adjudicate disputes involving horses. Neat no?' (from a newspaper column); 'Now the tandem ["pair"] is making its dreams come true, so it's not Goin' Bananas forever for Johnny' (from a gossip column).

English currently competes in some domains with a spreading and developing Pilipino, in a process of register-building sometimes called *intellectualization*. Pilipino/Tagalog is still in the process of standardization and the development of a fully academic style, notably in the sciences, and the debate continues on its use instead of English for school work and official purposes. There is also conflict between learning Pilipino for symbolic purposes and learning English for utilitarian purposes. However, where English dominates the print media, Pilipino dominates television, radio, and local movies.

The Englishes of the Philippines and Malaysia have similar patterns of development and constriction *vis-à-vis* the promotion of Pilipino and Malay, and in some ways the Philippines has been moving in the opposite direction to Singapore. From a situation in which a premium is placed on learning and using English, the nation has moved to using English only in academic discourse, international relations, the tourist business, and the like. Philippine English has nonetheless developed a vigorous literature, and is itself in the process of standardization, including a variety no longer marked by accents associated with regional languages but one that originates in Manila, and is propagated largely through the schools and the media.

The trends are not clear. On one side, code-switching becomes code-mixing and adds to English/Pilipino hybridization; on the other, the demands of globalization, the dominance of the print media, and the on-going use of English in education may exercise a standardizing role, making Philippine English, as it were, a more effective international currency. Or the present system of bilingual education may be converted into a monolingual Pilipino programme in which English is taught as a foreign language that becomes fully available only to an elite.

Following the introduction of English-language education, short stories appeared in college magazines from 1910, and the first novel in English, Zoilo M. Galang's *A Child of Sorrow*, was published in 1921. Since then, a considerable body of work in all literary genres has developed in a nation that regards itself as having the world's third largest English-speaking population. However, creative writing in English suffered in its first 50 years from the association of that language with material and social development as opposed (in the minds of the intelligentsia at least) to Spanish as a language of culture. Much English writing has been art in the service of social protest and bolstering national pride. This approach, which was championed by Salvador P. Lopez, was countered by another characteristic of Filipino writing in English, an 'art for art's sake' formalism developed by the poet José Garcia Villa. Other traits are: a tendency to sentimentality and romance (with roots in both Spanish and indigenous traditions), a concern for identity in the face of colonial discontinuities, the blending of East and West, a focus on rural life (people against nature, village childhood, the pull to the city), dramatized questions of social justice, and the 'war of the sexes'. Key names include Linda Ty Casper, N. V. M. Gonzalez, Nick Joaquin, Bienvenido Santos, and Edilberto Tiempo.

In terms of strengthening a national cultural identity, English as a literary medium has always been under attack by advocates of self-expression in local languages. They argue that English is not only the tongue of foreign colonialists but also the vehicle of a privileged indigenous elite. Vernacular writing has been supported by recent generations of social activists who have had considerable success in promoting their views. In response, supporters of English have continued to claim that it is their natural means of expression and that, as an international language, it both offers access to a world literary tradition and protects against insularity.

East Asia

1997 The Roman soldiers guarding the east coast of Britain in the fifth century could not have foreseen that the language of the Saxon pirates would eventually be used all over the world not only by people but also by inanimate machines. With this precedent, we can predict that some organization will assume the power to control the English language. In the late 1990s the most likely contenders are native speakers not of English but of the languages of East Asia.

– Gerry Knowles, *A Cultural History of the English Language* (London: Arnold)

It is a long way, physically and imaginatively, from the dialects of ancient Saxon marauders to English in East Asia in the 21st century, but Knowles's observation is less bizarre than might be supposed. The phrase 'the power to control the English language' is startling, especially because there has throughout the history and use of English been almost no overt legislative or other control. There has been a great deal of social and political influence worldwide, but surprisingly little explicit management. The only 'English Academy' that has ever existed is in South Africa: a voluntary organization with limited ambitions and reach. Knowles's comment is, however, thought-provoking when considered in terms of the present and probable future demographics of English in East Asia, and whether East Asian nations might ever seek for any reason to limit or adapt it. At the present time, the very opposite seems to be happening: English in East Asia is expanding freely wherever one looks.

The centrepiece to this expansion is the People's Republic of China, and estimates of the number of English users and learners there range as high as 300 million; the number of professional teachers of English alone is probably the greatest for any single country in the world—perhaps around a million. John Platt and Heidi Weber, writing about English in East Asia in *The Oxford Companion to the English Language* in 1992 considered that 'in the next decade there will be an ever-increasing number of people (anywhere between 300 and 500 million) with varying degrees of competence in English, because of its position as an international medium'. Their guesstimate has proved accurate.

What could not have been predicted in 1992 was the precise form the explosion would take: notably, the immense number of Chinese now using the Internet both nationally and internationally, often sending one another emails that mix English and Putonghua. Below are examples in which the Chinese is expressed in Pinyin, sometimes with numbers to indicate tones. The punctuation follows the originals, and editorial notes are in square brackets.

2000

1 From Li Lan, 'Email: a challenge to Standard English', *English Today* 64 (16:4), October

- will meet you at the airport. Bu2 jian4 bu2 san4!!! ['Wait until we meet!']
- I do not mean to ban1 men2 nong4 fu3 ['show one's proficiency before an expert'],
  but I think your essay can be improved in the following way.
- You won't be able to finish it if you have three hearts two ideas [loan-translating *san1* xin1 er4 yi4, meaning 'shilly-shally']

2000

2 From Li Yongyan, 'Surfing e-mails', *ET* 64 (16.4), October

- I do like the film, *Bridges of Madison County*. Meryl Streep plays the woman, and is especially good. *Wo ke bugandang!* [A Chinese Pinyin phrase equivalent to 'It's more flattery than I can take', in response to my own joking comment that the writer looks like Robert Kincaid (Clint Eastwood) in the film.]
- [Email] Subject: xie xie nin ['thank you']
  Crystal, how are you? Thankyou so much for the mail. . . .

2001

3 From Gao Liwei, 'Digital age, digital English', *ET* 67 (17:3), July

- OK, I'll go home and eat *dan4chao3fan4* ['rice fried with eggs']
- If we have many students show up, we'll *wei4 ta1 men chen2 fan4cheng2 cai4* ['fill their bowls with rice and dishes'].

A variation on this theme is the recent explosive use among Hong Kong university students of ICQ ('I seek you'), an Internet chat service developed in the US. In their approach, Cantonese particles are added to otherwise fairly typical English e-mail usage, as in:

> **2001**
> GARY i know she is not lazy and I also believe that she got her own reason for skipping lectures, let m try my best to take notes for her *la*.
> PHILIP ha ha . . . something want to ask you *ar* . . . ha ha . . . it is much better to ask through icq *wor*.
> GARY just ask
> PHILIP ha ha . . . nothing *la* ask u later
>
> – from Gregory James, 'Cantonese particles in Hong Kong students' English e-mails', *ET*67 (17:3), July
> [Here, the particles *la, ar,* and *wor* occur. *La* is persuasive, suggestive, and advisory; *ar* is an Anglicization of *a*, which has a questioning role that may soften a statement; and *wor* is an Anglicization of *wo*, which can have a reminding or prompting role.]

This apparently up-to-the-minute ICQ style in fact reflects a long-standing element in everyday Hong Kong speech, in which Cantonese particles are added at the end of English sentences, as also happens in Singapore and Malaysia. Comparable to the mainland Chinese use of Putonghua and Pinyin in emails, it carries into a new medium the mixing that takes place widely in speech, as for example between English and Irish, Hindi, and Malay. It is both a long way and no distance at all from how matters developed when Westerners first went to China.

Throughout the second half of the 20th century, the use of English expanded not only in mainland China but also in Hong Kong, Macau, and Taiwan, as well as in Japan and South Korea. However, there is no significant community of speakers of English as a more or less first language in any East Asian country: nothing comparable to Singapore English. The British and other expatriates working in Hong Kong and the US military stationed in Japan, South Korea, and Guam are significant users of English, but they are few in number, have little linguistic impact, and by and large constitute a population of transients. It is therefore their own interests that have turned East Asians towards English in such large numbers and with such dedication.

At the same time, however, a tradition of teaching English formally through grammar, translation, and literature may have helped many to read English, but has for decades limited their capacity to speak it clearly and fluently. Because of limited opportunities to practise with native speakers, the East Asian spoken English has generally been hesitant, stilted. and bookish, and likely to have a syllable-timed rather than a stress-timed rhythm. In recent years, more practical teaching techniques for the spoken language have had an effect, but the very different natures of the regional languages and English (including very different writing systems) have made progress slower than many had hoped. Even so, however, the region has made a larger investment in and commitment to English than anywhere else in the world (in terms of public and private teaching, government planning, teacher training, student effort, and the sheer numbers involved), and this investment appears only now to have begun to pay off.

China, Chinese, and English

The first traders from the west on the South China coast were Arabs, whose centuries-old dominance was ended in the early 16th century by the Portuguese, followed by the Dutch and the English about a century later. When the first English traders arrived in 1637, like their predecessors they traded in the delta of the Chu Chiang ('Pearl River'), establishing a 'factory' in 1685 in a city they called *Canton*. In the 18th century the French, the Americans, and others joined the Western trading community of 13 such factories (harbour-side business buildings and residences).

The name *Canton* may serve to illustrate the complex historical interplay over many generations between spoken, written, and printed forms of English and Chinese. *Canton* derives not from the actual Chinese name of the city itself but from the province of which it was (and is) the capital. A brief discussion of the names of the province, the city, and some other expressions in Chinese may illustrate some of the linguistic issues that have arisen in the nearly 4-centuries-old interface between Chinese, English, and variations of the Roman alphabet.

❶ Alphabetic and logographic writing

Since the 16th century there have been difficulties in representing Chinese words by means of the Roman alphabet, which was constructed (by and large) to represent sounds, whereas traditional Chinese writing is logographic, each character (by and large) representing a whole word or concept, with no direct link to spoken language.

❷ Adopting the alphabetic principle for Chinese

There have been many attempts to represent Chinese in Roman letters. Currently, two systems are dominant: Wade-Giles and Pinyin. The first is more general, and was created by Westerners, while the second is specific to the People's Republic of China (PRC), though now widely used elsewhere. Older spellings of Chinese names in Roman have been broadly and inconsistently based on speech, but are still widely used (see list, below) for well-established Chinese names in English. The Wade-Giles system was created by the British diplomat and Sinologist Sir Thomas Francis Wade and developed and modified by the Cambridge scholar Herbert Allen Giles in his *Chinese–English Dictionary* (1912). The *Pinyin* system (often written *pinyin*, paralleling *roman* and *italic*) was officially adopted in Beijing in 1958, and is the only system officially recognized and used in the PRC.

❸ *Guangdong* and *Canton*

The Chinese name for the southern province of which Canton is the capital was formerly written in Roman letters as *Kwangtung*, in the Wade-Giles system is *Kuang-tung*, and in Pinyin is *Guangdong*. It is from this name that *Canton* derives. The Chinese name for the city of Canton is *Kuang-chou* in Wade-Giles, and *Guangzhao* in Pinyin.

❹ Interpretation

Chinese people who can read the roman alphabet straightforwardly interpret transliterated Chinese words in terms of their own pronunciation. However, for non-Chinese who do not know Chinese the different kinds of romanization tend to prompt different pronunciations, and unschooled outsiders encountering the three forms *Canton*, *Kuang-tung*, and *Guangdong* may be forgiven for assuming that they refer to three different places. The greater consistency of Pinyin tends to eliminate such problems and provide a better guide to pronunciation (especially if numbers are added to represent the four contrastive tones). See accompanying table.

Chinese names in roman letters

	Traditional	**Wade-Giles**	**Pinyin**
Places	Nanking	Nan-ching	Nanjing
	Peking	Pei-ching	Beijing
	Shansi	Shan-hsi	Shanxi
	Shantung	Shan-tung	Shandong
	Sian	Hsien	Xian
	Sinkiang	Hsin-chiang	Xinjiang
	Suchow	Hsu-chou	Xuzhou
	Szechwan, Szechuan	Ssu-ch'uan	Sichuan
People	Chou En Lai	Chou En-lai	Zhou Enlai
	Mao Tse Tung	Mao Tse-tung	Mao Zedong
	Teng Hsiao Ping	Teng Hsiao-p'ing	Deng Xiaoping
Other	tai chi chuan	t'ai chi ch'uan	tai ji quan

In its English-language publications, the Beijing government prints all Chinese personal and place-names in Pinyin, and assumes such forms will be used worldwide, both for the media and diplomatic and official purposes. In Taiwan, however, Pinyin is not recognized as a replacement of Wade-Giles, and elsewhere it may or may not be accepted or used consistently. It has not always been widely or consistently used in the PRC, although it is important in teaching Putonghua to children across the nation. Pinyin poses problems of distinguishing homographs, as for example in the 24 etymologically unrelated forms all spelt *lian*, which in traditional ideography has a distinct character for each.

A useful aid in Pinyin is the addition of a number after each syllable to indicate which of the four tones of Mandarin/Putonghua is required: as with *ma1* and *yi1* for the level tone, also shown as a macron above the vowel, as in *mā* ('mother') and *yī* ('clothing'); as with *ma2* and *yi2* for the rising tone, also shown as an acute accent above the vowel as in *má* ('linen') and *yí* ('suitable'); as with *ma3* and *yi3* for the falling and rising tone, also shown with a cup symbol as in *mǎ* ('horse') and *yǐ* ('chair'); and as with *ma4* and *yi4* for the falling tone, also shown with a grave accent as in *mà* ('to scold') and *yì* ('leisure'). The numbering device works well (as above) in emails, where diacritics are (at the present time at least) impossible.

The development of trade and other contacts between Westerners and the peoples of southern China was restricted for more than a century, and it was not until 1842 that other Chinese 'treaty ports' besides Canton, such as Shanghai and Amoy (now Xiamen) were opened, as an aggrieved concession by the imperial court after a Chinese defeat in the first Opium War (1839–42).

In the same year, the island of Hong Kong in the delta of the Pearl River was ceded by China to Britain in perpetuity as a Crown colony, to match (and in due course exceed in power and influence) the longer-established neighbouring Portuguese colony of Macau/Macao. From that period, English (in both its British and American forms) has been intermittently significant in China, although, throughout the Cold War period (from 1947 to 1989), Russian, as the primary vehicle of Communism, was the Western language with the lion's share of attention in the People's Republic (but virtually none in Taiwan, Hong Kong, and among the Overseas Chinese). In 1997, Hong Kong was returned by Britain to China and in 1999 Macau was returned by the Portuguese, each territory becoming a 'special administrative region' (SAR), in accordance with the formula 'one country, two systems' (a Communist mainland and two capitalist enclaves).

The official title of mainland China in Putonghua and Pinyin is *Zhonghua Renmin Gongheguo* and in English the *People's Republic of China* (*PRC*). Its precise population, despite a census in 2000, remains uncertain, but may be *c*.1.3 billion, over 90% of whom are Han (ethnic Chinese) and the rest a total of 55 minorities, including Manchus, Mongols, Koreans, Tibetans, and Uighur Turks. No Western language has established itself as a mother tongue in the PRC, but English is used in Hong Kong alongside spoken Cantonese and written Chinese, as a language of business, education, and recreation, and Portuguese and English are used alongside Cantonese in Macau. More significantly, however, English is massively the principal foreign language taught (and sought after) in the PRC, where it has high status as the global medium of education, travel, entertainment, e-communication, and business.

The term *Chinese* is straightforward when applied to ethnicity (the Han) and nationality (all citizens of the PRC, including the two SARs, but with the people of Taiwan in a more ambiguous political category). The term *Chinese* is, however, more difficult when applied to language, beyond the neutral academic view that 'Chinese' (the speech of the Han) is part of the Sino-Tibetan language family. The American scholar of Chinese, Jerry Norman, has noted:

> **1988** Chinese is . . . one of a very few contemporary languages whose history is documented in an unbroken tradition extending back to the second millennium BC. At the same time, in its numerous dialectal forms, it has more speakers than any language spoken in the modern world. This vast extension in time and space has imparted to the study of Chinese a complexity hardly equalled elsewhere. . . . Few language names are as all-encompassing as that of Chinese. It is made to serve at once for the archaic inscriptions of the oracle bones, the literary language of the Zhou dynasty sages, the language of Tang and Song poetry and the early vernacular language of the classical novels, as well as the modern language in both its standard and dialectal forms. And this list is by no means exhaustive.
> – *Chinese* (Cambridge University Press), pp. ix, 1

Norman goes on to consider why so many distinct historical stages and geographical variants have been subsumed under a single name. He notes that 'the modern Chinese dialects are really more like a family of languages, and the Chinese of the first millennium BC is at least as different from the modern standard language as Latin is from Italian and French'. Although the differences manifestly exist, and are generally conceded, behind them there is nonetheless a sense of 'the profound unity of Chinese culture', transmitted without a break over nearly five thousand years. He adds:

> Even in periods of political disunity at various times in the past, the ideal of a single, culturally unified Chinese empire has never been forgotten. The Chinese language, especially in its written form, has always been one of the most powerful symbols of this cultural unity. The aptness of language as a symbol of cultural and even political unity was facilitated by the use of a script that for all practical purposes was independent of any phonetic manifestation of their language, allowing the Chinese to look upon the Chinese language as being more uniform and unchanging than it actually was.

In contemporary terms, the name *Chinese* in English is both a noun and an adjective and has at least the following senses, or points along a continuum of usage:

❶ As in *Chinese art*

Meaning: 'Relating to a region that has been identified over most of its history as an empire with a succession of dynasties, centring on the *Han*.'

❷ As in *Chinese dialects*

Meaning: 'Relating to the speech of the Han, a complex in which two categories have long been identified: a high cultural language and a range of regional vernaculars traditionally referred to in English as 'dialects', many of which could as easily be classified as distinct languages.' The high language has long been known in English as *Mandarin*, from Portuguese *mandarim*, through Malay from Sanskrit *mantri* ('thinker, adviser'), and cognate with *mantra* ('thought', 'repetitive phrase'). In Mandarin, its name is *Kuan-hua* (in the Wade-Giles transcription) and *guanhua* in Pinyin, and means 'civil-servant language'. The form that the high language currently takes in the People's Republic is known in Wade-Giles as *Kuo-yu* and Pinyin as *Guoyu* ('national language'), and generally referred to in the PRC as *Putonghua* ('common speech'). Putonghua derives from, or is most closely related to, the dialects of Beijing, and is the sole official usage. The Han dialects generally fall into distinct groups, as for example (1) the Wu dialects, and (2) the main dialect of the province of *Fujian* (its Putonghua/Mandarin name), which is then known in English as *Fujianese*, or (if the local name *Hokkien* is used for the province) is known in English as *Hokkienese*. Both terms are in common use outside China, and may lead to confusion. Dialects that belong to the same groups are more or less mutually intelligible; dialects from different groups are more or less mutually unintelligible.

❸ As in *Chinese characters*

Meaning: 'Relating to the written language of China, which traditionally consists of up to *c.*40,000 characters and has had immense prestige and served as a powerful force for cultural unity.' The characters constitute the primary form of writing in mainland China, where they have been somewhat simplified, the number reduced to *c.*8,000, and officially associated only with Putonghua. In Taiwan, they relate to Mandarin, and in Hong Kong they are related in general practice to both Cantonese and Putonghua and/or Mandarin.

The term *Chinese* can therefore be applied: to a single widely spoken high-prestige language, the key version of which today is Putonghua; to a venerable ideographic writing system of thousands of characters made up of patterns of strokes, intimately associated with Mandarin and Putonghua; to both the high language and the writing system, the latter often seen as only readable in terms of the high spoken language; and to both the high language (with its writing system) and the dialects, with the proviso that the dialects do not have a written form (although some classic literary texts have had techniques through which dialects have been portrayed). The spoken words of the high language are often interpreted and explained in terms of the characters to which they relate, although those characters represent concepts and not sounds.

Although they are not usually thought of in such a way, Chinese characters can in principle serve any language. One proof of this is their use in Hong Kong without the intercession of Putonghua by speakers of Cantonese, which has traditionally been defined as a dialect and therefore as non-literate. Its speakers, however, routinely read Chinese script in terms of Cantonese with or without reference to Mandarin or Putonghua. Another proof is a venerable stratum in the complex writing system of Japan that consists of several thousand kanji ('Chinese') characters, which have both Chinese and Japanese readings, all accessible and meaningful to educated Japanese and allowing a wide range of associations and wordplay. A third proof is the interpretation of Chinese characters as Korean words in Korea.

The case of Cantonese is noteworthy, in that although it has traditionally been classed as a dialect there is widespread and probably increasing acceptance—gracious or otherwise—that it is a fully functioning language. Cantonese is widely spoken by millions in mainland China, the Hong Kong SAR, the Macau SAR, Malaysia, Singapore, elsewhere in South-East Asia, and in a worldwide diaspora centred on the provision of Chinese (mainly Cantonese-style) food. Cantonese and Mandarin/Putonghua are by and large mutually unintelligible, in much the same way as Spanish and French, although both are Romance languages. The BBC World Service has for years routinely handled difficulties when broadcasting to Chinese listeners in what it approaches as 'two languages in one': Chinese as Mandarin and as Cantonese. Although differences are primarily a matter of speech, they may also affect the interpretation of writing. As Rodney Mantle has noted:

> **1990** Uniquely among the vernacular services, the BBC Chinese
> Section has to cope with two languages in one. In principle
> written standard Chinese is one language. In practice (quite apart
> from pronunciation problems), the differences between Cantonese
> and Mandarin can mean that [English-language] scripts translated
> by Mandarin speakers may be difficult for Cantonese speakers to
> read for the microphone without recourse to the English original;
> and scripts translated by Cantonese speakers often present even
> more difficulty for speakers of Mandarin.
>
> – 'Speaking with One Voice in Thirty-Seven Languages', *The Linguist* 29:6

There are well over a billion speakers of varieties covered by the term *Chinese*, whether they are traditional Han dialects, Putonghua as the national language of the PRC (for both Han and non-Han), more or less traditional Mandarin, as in Taiwan or Singapore, or the distinctive case of Cantonese. Demographic statistics are often produced for various purposes by publishers worldwide to demonstrate (among other things) that more people 'speak Chinese' than any other language, but the range of speech among the Chinese (Mandarin/Putonghua, Cantonese, Fujianese/ Hokkienese, Hakka, Hsiang, Kan, Min, Wu, etc.) includes a range of forms as distinct from one another as any of the languages of the European Union. The statistics need therefore to be interpreted with care.

In the first contacts between speakers of the English and Chinese languages in the 17th century an additional dimension was added in the form of a trade jargon that saved each side from trying to learn the other's language. This was the original 'Pidgin English', which developed in and around the South China coast. As a consequence of this, language scholars and others have discussed it under such names as (*Chinese*) *Pidgin English* and (*South*) *China Coast Pidgin* (*English*). This usage, influenced by an earlier Pidgin Portuguese among the Cantonese and Portuguese traders in both Canton and Macau, was used aboard ships of any nation with Chinese workers on board. Unsurprisingly, it developed as a ship-borne lingua franca over a vast area that included Australia and the islands of the Pacific, significantly influencing the form of English-based pidgins used in the Queensland canefields, Papua New Guinea, the Solomon Islands, Vanuatu, Hawaii, and elsewhere. As regards the origin of South China Coast Pidgin, a Chinese scholar has noted:

> **1982** The Chinese held the British, like all 'foreign devils,' in low
> esteem, and would not stoop to learning the foreign tongue in its
> full form. The British, on the other hand, regarded the 'heathen
> Chinee' as beyond any possibility of learning, and so began to
> modify their own language for the natives' benefit.
>
> – Chuan Cheng, 'Chinese Varieties of English', in Braj B. Kachru (ed.), *The Other Tongue:*
> *English Across Cultures* (Urbana: University of Illinois)

Pidgin spread in China when the Treaty Ports were established for trading purposes in 1843, but declined there towards the end of the 19th century, as a more standard English began to be taught in new schools and universities. It is now extinct in the PRC, but survives in part at least in the English of Hong Kong, especially where a knowledge of English among speakers of Cantonese and other vernaculars of China has been slight. Pidgin, though useful and practical, has generally been looked down on; a disparaging but revealing nickname for it in the late 19th century was *Coolie Esperanto*. An example from its heyday is: 'Tailor, my got one piece plenty hansom silk. My want you make one nice evening dress.'

In the earlier 20th century, teachers of English in China used the British model and taught largely through literature, continuing after the establishment of the Communist regime in 1949, because the new Chinese educational policy was influenced by that of the Soviet Union, for which Standard British usage was also the model. For many years, China and the United States had limited relations, as a result of which American English only became a serious target for Chinese learners towards the close of the 20th century, when significant numbers of students were able to study in the US. Some traditionalists have continued to favour the British model as a kind of 'Mandarin English', but younger people generally incline towards American usage.

Currently, there is vast interest in English in the PRC: *c*.250 million out of *c*.1.3 billion seek to learn the language in various ways at various levels, and for most Chinese in the PRC, Hong Kong, Macau, Taiwan, Singapore, Malaysia, and the diaspora of 'the Overseas Chinese', English is simply the global language and therefore essential. Traditionally, however, in the PRC its use has included the rote memorization of fixed and formal expressions and a stilted old-fashioned style in both speech and writing. Chuan Cheng (above) has called this style 'Sinicized English', particularly as used in such official PRC organs as the English edition of the *Beijing Zhoubao* (in English the *Beijing Review*, formerly the *Peking Review*). Such publications have tended to lace their English with loan translations from Putonghua, as with *running dogs* for 'lackeys' (from *zou gou*) and *capitalist roaders* (from *zou zi pai*).

In the PRC, the influence of English on Chinese has been mainly lexical, in the adoption of technical terms. There has been a mild influence on the morphology of Putonghua, in that the acquisition of both direct loans (such as *modeng* 'modern', *moteer* 'model') and loan translations (such as *shehui* 'society', *yuanliang* 'excuse') has created polysyllabic words in a basically monosyllabic language. In syntax, translation from English and the study of English grammar appears to have led to an increase in the passive voice, entailing the use of the co-verb *bei* (a development paralleled in South Korea). Chinese has provided English, directly and indirectly (for example through Japanese and South China Coast Pidgin), with a vivid range of expressions, some with intricate etymologies and intriguing associations. They may be described under three headings:

❶ Food, health, and medicine

For example: *chopsticks*, a hybrid compound from English *stick* and Pidgin English *chop*, probably from Cantonese *gap* ('quick, urgent'); *chow* (slang) 'food', from Pidgin *chow-chow* ('food, mixture'), also the name of a tangy sweet mix of fruit peel in syrup, from *cha* ('mixed'); *chow mein*, from Mandarin *chao mian* ('fried noodles', with chopped meat and vegetables); *ginseng*, from Mandarin *renshen* ('man herb', probably because the plant's shape suggests a body and two legs): the double loan *ginseng tea* (with *tea* probably through Dutch *tee* from Fujianese *te*, although in this instance the 'tea' does not come from the tea plant).

❷ Behaviour and activities

For example: *chop-chop* (slang) 'quickly', from Pidgin, in turn probably from Cantonese *gap gap* ('quick quick'); *gung-ho* 'ready to fight, very enthusiastic', as in *a gung-ho attitude*, from *honghe* ('work together'), the motto of the US Marines in Asia in the Second World War; *kung fu* a quasi-monastic martial art (from *gongfu* 'merit master'); *tai chi* or more fully *tai chi chuan* (a regime of slow and meditative physical actions, taken to be beneficial to health and mental composure). The 1970s US term *chopsocky*, referring to the style of kung fu movies, combines the *chop* of *chop chop* for speed (and also suggesting a chopping hand movement) and *chop-suey* to suggest Chineseness with English *sock* meaning 'punch hard'.

❸ Objects and processes in the world

For example: *kaolin* a fine white clay used in medicine and making porcelain and ceramics (from *gaoling* 'high hill', naming the kind of hill where it is found); *sampan* a small flat-bottomed boat (from *sanban* 'three-plank'); *taipan* a foreigner in charge of an undertaking in China, and especially a business tycoon (from Cantonese *daaibaan*); *tycoon* a rich and powerful person in the business world (through Japanese *taikun* 'great lord, shogun', from Chinese *da jun* 'great prince'); *typhoon* a violent Asian tropical storm (partly from Cantonese *tai fung* 'big wind', and partly through Portuguese *tufao* from Arabic *tufan* from Greek *tuphon* 'whirlwind' (also found as *Typhon*, a chaos monster in Greek mythology).

English and Chinese constitute two of the most powerful language complexes on earth and it seems highly likely that their influence on one another in future will transcend anything that has so far transpired between them.

Hong Kong, Cantonese, and Hong Kong English

> **1997** On the surface Hong Kong appears to be a multilingual society where English and Cantonese coexist and function in different domains. Cantonese is the language of the home and intimacy while English is the principal means of communication within the administrative, legal and business worlds and is the ostensible medium of instruction in secondary and university education. . . . English was claimed to be the first language by 2.2% of the population and Putonghua, the standardized oral form of modern Mandarin, by 1.1% although nearly 32% professed to speak English and 18% said they could communicate in Putonghua. . . . English however is the 'language of success'.
>
> – Ken Hyland, 'Language attitudes at the Handover: Communication and identity in 1997 Hong Kong', *English World-Wide* 18.2 (Amsterdam and Philadelphia: John Benjamins)

Officially known as the *Hong Kong Special Administrative Region* (*Hong Kong SAR*, *HK SAR*), Hong Kong is an autonomous region of China that was a British colony from 1842 to the Handover in 1997, a transformation to which both China at large and the people of Hong Kong are continuing to adjust. The population of the enclave is *c*.98% Chinese: mainly Cantonese, but with other communities whose originating members have arrived at various times from 'the mainland', a common term in the English of Hong Kong for the People's Republic of China.

In 1842, by the Treaty of Nanking/Nanjing, imperial China ceded the island of Hong Kong in perpetuity to Britain, followed by the mainland peninsula of Kowloon in 1860, and the leasing of the mainland New Territories (NT) for 99 years in 1898. The colony was occupied by Japan in the Second World War. Under the Sino-British Declaration of 1974, it was agreed that Hong Kong would return in its entirety to China in 1997, the date of expiry of the NT lease. Today, the HK SAR, with a population of *c*.6.5 million, is the world's eighth-largest trading economy and third-busiest financial centre (with the world's busiest container port), and has among the world's highest office rents. Hong-Kongers tend to regard both the port city of Shanghai in the PRC and the city state of Singapore in South-East Asia as their major rivals, as a consequence of which they seek to project Hong Kong as pre-eminently 'Asia's world city'.

English is prominent in the media and advertising, omnipresent visually along-side Chinese, and crucial as the lingua franca of business, but is not widely used as an everyday spoken medium, and there have been debates for years in the English-language media and elsewhere about a decline in standards. In real terms, however, more Hong-Kongers today know more English (and use it more) than ever before, and the employment sections of the *South China Morning Post* list dozens of high-level vacancies that seek applicants able both to speak English, Cantonese, and Mandarin/Putonghua and write English and Chinese (paralleling the HK govern-ment's long-term plan for a 'trilingual and biliterate' population).

Joint recorded Cantonese and English announcements are routine on the trains of the MTR (Mass Transit Railway) and KCR (Kowloon-Canton Railway); street names are provided in English, highway directions are bilingual, and many parts of the territory have English names, such as *Happy Valley* (the location of the main race course of the Hong Kong Jockey Club) and *Clear Water Bay* (near the town of *Sai Kung*). Bilingual signs are common and mixed advertisements routine. Certain locations have names in both English and Cantonese (people referring to them in their language of choice or the language of the moment): for example, the areas on Hong Kong Island known in English as *Admiralty* and *Central* are *Gàmjùng* and *Jùngwàahn* respectively in Cantonese. Within families, even if some older members are stronger in other kinds of Chinese, Cantonese tends to dominate. Younger family members may use another Chinese vernacular with parents, relatives, or others, but use Cantonese or English or a mix of the two with one another and their peers.

Most primary education is in Cantonese. Secondary education was formerly provided in both *Anglo-Chinese schools* (in which English was the medium of instruction except for Chinese subjects) and *Chinese middle schools* (in which Cantonese was the medium except for the subject English). Currently, some schools are primarily English-medium (much favoured by parents) while others are Cantonese-medium. For decades there were two universities, Hong Kong University (English-medium) and the Chinese University of Hong Kong (ideally Chinese-medium, using Cantonese, Mandarin/Putonghua, and English). After 1990, higher education was greatly expanded; today there are eight universities, in-cluding the HK University of Science and Technology (modelled on MIT), the Open University, and upgraded technical colleges, liberal arts colleges, and a teacher-training college. Of some 40 newspapers, two are English-medium, the *South China Morning Post* and *The Hongkong Standard* (each with *c*.80% Chinese readers).

There has for some years been (at times heated) debate over whether there is a Hong Kong English (HKE) as such. The widespread view that there is no such thing ties in with frequent assertions that English is little used in Hong Kong, is bad, and is getting worse. The increasingly favoured view that there is indeed an HKE, and that it has its own dynamics, takes into account at least the following points:

❶ Long-term institutional use

English has been used in administration, education, entertainment, tourism, and business since the mid-19th century, is widely regarded as an asset for 'Asia's world city', and inevitably has its own distinctive aspects.

❷ Localization

Local English contains many Chinese and other Asian features and expressions comparable to, and sometimes shared with, the English of Singapore and Malaysia.

❸ A British Asian legacy

Local usage retains items from a one-time widespread British Asian vocabulary, many of its usages originating in the Indian subcontinent. Such expressions can be regarded as aspects of an English adapted to Asian ends or Asian items absorbed into the English of the British Empire in Asia and retained because of their familiarity and utility.

❹ A close association between Cantonese and English

The Cantonese-speaking majority tend, according to circumstances, to carry English into their Cantonese and Cantonese into their English, resulting in considerable hybridization, including the use of Cantonese phrase- and sentence-final particles, as in *Can you come?—Sorry, can't lah* (cf. the English of Singapore and Malaysia). Cantonese speakers range from comfortable and fluent in English to hesitant and inclined to use English words with Cantonese syntax, at times echoing the usage of South China Coast Pidgin. Features commonly ascribed to English as used in Hong Kong include:

Pronunciation

1 HK people of Chinese background have for decades had RP and the usage of the BBC as their model. A very small group (sometimes described as an elite) have RP or near-RP accents, and others approximate to it (or, increasingly, to General American, or mix the two), but most speak English with a Cantonese accent and style.

2 Like all 'Chinese English', Hong Kong speech is non-rhotic: that is, *r* is not pronounced in such words as *art*, *door*, and *worker*.

3 Word-final glottal stops are common, notably with *p*, *t*, and *k*, as in *cap*, *hat*, and *week*, sometimes producing a staccato effect, as in *Let me get you big bit of cake*.

4 Consonant clusters are routinely reduced, for example omitting word-final *k* and *t*, as in *tass force* ('task force'), *fiss moment* ('first moment'), *ness time* ('next time'). As a result, distinctions between present and past may not be clear, as in *They often ass me to come* (?'They often ask/asked me to come').

5 Such spoken forms can affect written usage, as with a note on the shelves of a university bookshop, stating that the titles are 'Arrange by author'.

Grammar

1 Present tense forms of the verb *to be* are often omitted: *This fiss time you here?* ('Is this the first time you've been here?').

2 The present tense is commonly used when describing events in the past and future, often leaving another word or phrase to cover the dimension of time: *I tell him this morning to do it* ('I told him this morning to do it'); *When she see me lass week she tell me to come* ('When she saw me last week she told me to come').

3 The pidgin-like quality of some kinds of spoken HK usage can be transferred to both informal and formal public notices: (at a ticket counter) 'Sorry! HK$500 & $1000 not accept'; (sign at waterside, Sai Kung) 'Swimming hereat is dangerous and swimmer take their own risks. The government of HKSAR.'

4 The foregrounding of the subject of a sentence may occur: 'Passengers who take the ferry service from Ma Liu Shui, they can enjoy a free ride from Tap Mun to Wong Shek' (notice).

Vocabulary

1 There are three sources of distinctive vocabulary: direct adoptions from Chinese sources, such as *dim sum* and *yam cha*; loan-translations from such sources, as with *dragon boat*; and usage common to former British Asian colonies, such as *godown* and *shroff*. See below.

2 Words and phrases from a general Chinese background that are known and used elsewhere but are notably common in Hong Kong include: *dai pai dong* ('big arranged counter': a streetside food stall); *dim sum* ('little heart': snacks, especially as served in Chinese restaurants); *fung shui* ('wind-water') geomancy used in deciding the sites, orientation, and design of buildings; *pak choi* ('white vegetable': Chinese cabbage); *siu mai* ('heated for sale': a steamed dumpling, of pork and shrimp).

3 Distinctive Cantonese words and phrases typical of Hong Kong include: *yam/yum cha* (an occasion for eating dim sum, especially in a restaurant); the racist terms *gweilo* ('ghost person', for someone white or European, especially a man) and less commonly *gweipor* (a white or European woman); *hong* (a large usually long-established British-Chinese trading company, such as Jardine-Matheson); *mafoo* (a stable hand); *taipan* (the head of a hong).

4 Loan translations from Chinese: *dragon boat* (a long canoe-like boat for racing at annual *dragon boat festivals*, supplied with a dragon-like head for the occasion); *snakehead* (a smuggler of illegal immigrants).

5 Expressions from other languages: *amah* (Portuguese: 'maid'); *godown* (Malayalam: 'warehouse'); *nullah* (Hindi: 'watercourse'); *shroff* (from Arabic *sarraf* through Hindi-Urdu and Anglo-Indian English): a cashier or person receiving payment in a government office or other public place, as in *Metro City Phase 2 Car Park Shroff Office*.

6 Distinctive abbreviations: *Exco* ('Executive Council'); *Legco* (with a soft *g*: 'Legislative Council'); *IIs* (pronounced 'eye-eyes': illegal immigrants, also called *illegals*).

7 Local uses of general English words: *short week* (a work schedule in which one works on Saturday morning every second week); *triad* (world use) a secret criminal society, as in *They are triad members*, (additional local use) a member of a triad, a gangster, as in *The police caught three triads last night*.

8 Local names often combine Cantonese and English, as in: *Po Lin Monastery*; *Cheung Chau Bun Festival*; *Lee Chum glutinous rice balls*; *Hello Kitty doll dim sum*; *Tseung Kwan O ParkNShop supermarket*. A typical list in a local publication runs: 'Rock carvings found at Shek Pik on Lantau Island, Kau Sai Chau, Po Toi, Cheung Chau and Tung Lung Islands, and at Big Wave Bay and Wong Chuk Hang on Hong Kong Island' (*Hong Kong: Our world in colour*, 2000).

An additional and often under-estimated element in the use of English in Hong Kong is the thousands of Filipina 'domestic helpers' (formerly known as 'maids'), many of whom spend a great deal of time looking after the young children of middle-class Cantonese families. They communicate more or less wholly in English with the children, partly because their own Cantonese is limited, and partly because the parents wish them to do so. In a serious sense, such helpers constitute a corps of auxiliary teachers of English in Hong Kong, using an established Asian 'brand' of English.

Although Hong Kong has never had a large permanent native English-speaking community, an influential group of native and near-native users of the language (civil servants, legislators, lawyers and senior police officers, business managers, academics, medical professionals, media professionals, and the like, and both Chinese and non-Chinese) have been using English alongside Cantonese for over a century, influencing the lives and languages of generations of local and in-migrating Chinese and others. For these and other reasons, the Hong Kong government is likely to continue emphasizing the local importance of English, especially when the language has such a central role in Singapore and has become phenomenally popular on the mainland (notably in Shanghai, a second major economic rival). Efforts to promote the official SAR formula of trilingualism (Cantonese, Putonghua, and English) and biliteracy (Chinese and English), however ambitious and demanding, are likely to continue.

Korea, Korean, and English

In the 19th century, the name of the country was usually spelt *Corea* and only occasionally *Korea*, but the *K* usage was fixed during the Japanese occupation of the country (1910–45), avowedly because *K* comes after *J* in the roman alphabet, which was acceptable, but *C* precedes *J*, which was not. Korea has been divided into *North Korea* and *South Korea* since the stalemate that ended of the Korean War in 1953. The Korean language, also spoken by communities in China, Japan, and the Soviet Union, is agglutinative, and usually regarded as a member of the Ural-Altaic language family.

Ancient Korean was written in a script called *idu*, in which Chinese characters were used to represent both sounds and meanings (not unlike present-day Japanese *kanji*). In the 15th century, an indigenous alphabet of 11 vowel and 17 consonant symbols (later reduced to 10 and 14) was devised and used for popular literature, while classical Chinese writing continued in use for official and scholarly purposes. Formerly called *onmun* ('common script'), this alphabet is currently known as *hangul* ('Korea alphabet'). Banned during the last decade of the Japanese occupation, Hangul is currently used either on its own or to a lesser degree in a mixed script with Chinese characters read as Korean words.

English has had a considerable influence on the structure of the modern language. Over the last 40 years, English has generally been assigned as many school hours as Korean for students aged 12–18, and serves in the main as an analytical exercise that has spilled over into the study and use of Korean, resulting in adjustments made to some Korean constructions so as to align them more closely with English: notably, greater use of the optional plural particle *-tul*. Although this is not a strict equivalent of the English plural inflection *-s*, many think that it either is or should be. Also under the influence of English and other Western languages, the convention of writing each word unit separately was adopted for Korean in the 19th century, a procedure which has not been followed for either Chinese or Japanese.

English was first taught in the 1880s by American teachers, when the royal government opened a school for the sons of the nobility. Around the same time, missionary schools began to provide instruction to commoners. During the occupation, Japanese teachers of English dominated the new school system and emphasized parsing. The end of the Second World War brought US soldiers to Korea, an event which largely accounts for the dominance of American over British English in Korea, but despite the acknowledged importance of spoken English the emphasis on texts and grammatical analysis continued. Koreans tend to regard English as a highly subtle language, its grammar subsumed under 5 basic structures and sustaining such categories as the subjunctive mood and the future perfect progressive tense.

After the Korean War and Partition, the need for English declined steeply in North Korea and massively increased in the South, where it has been the main foreign language. Almost all students there have three years of it, and the 80% who attend high school have six. There are many private English institutes, of which there are two sharply different kinds: one for students preparing for college entrance examinations, emphasizing parsing at deeper levels than in high school, and another for people who want to speak the language. Formal education rarely allows students to experience spoken English, and the minority who speak it generally say that they owe little to their schooling. The dismissive informal term *Konglish* has been used for non-standard usage among those Koreans with little opportunity to experience natural educated English directly.

The limited teaching of English in North Korea is slanted ideologically towards Marxism and a Stalinist cult of the leader.

Economic expansion has been rapid and often uneven in recent years in South Korea. As in other territories in East Asia and elsewhere, South Koreans regard English (predominantly in its American form) as vital for keeping pace with technology and communication with trading partners, with the result that reforming and streamlining teaching methods are widely regarded as essential.

Japan, English, Japlish, *gairaigo*, and *wasei eigo*

Since at least the 7th century, the Japanese have referred to their country as *Nippon* or *Nihon*, variant pronunciations of two written characters derived from Chinese and separately meaning *sun* and *origin*, whence the epithet in English 'Land of the Rising Sun'. However, Chinese readings of the same characters have traditionally yielded the spoken form *Jipangu*, which was adopted by the 13th-century Venetian traveller Marco Polo (among others), and is apparently the form from which the Western name *Japan* derives.

Japan is markedly homogeneous in ethnic terms, exceptions being a small community of indigenous Ainu in the northern island of Hokkaido and small long-established communities of Koreans and Chinese elsewhere. In recent years, however, the country has experienced an increase in migrant workers from many parts of the world, and, because of such workers, and increasing numbers of visitors formally trained in Japanese, the population is becoming more accustomed to *gaijin* ('foreigners') speaking their language. Japanese (locally known as *Nippongo* or *Nihongo*) has many regional varieties. The national standard, based on the middle-class usage of Tokyo, is the medium of instruction throughout the country. Although the writing system is complex and multiform, literacy is reckoned at 99%.

Japanese borrowed extensively from Chinese, notably in the 6th/9th centuries, and from various Western languages from the 16th century onward, including Portuguese, Spanish, Dutch, French, German, and both British and American English. The earliest Europeans to make contact were Portuguese merchants and Spanish Jesuits, followed by Dutch and then English traders in the 17th century. The first Japanese dictionary of English (in 1862) was Tatsunosuke Hori's *A Pocket Dictionary of the English and Japanese Language* [*sic*], in Japanese *Eiwa-taiyaku-shuchin-jisho* (1862). Hori's approach was both practical and ingenious. He based his compilation on the English/Dutch part of the 1857 second edition of H. Picard's *A New Pocket Dictionary of the English–Dutch and Dutch–English Languages*, buttressed by the 1858 edition of the *Nagasaki-haruma*, a Dutch/Japanese dictionary originally compiled (*c.*1812) in Nagasaki by Japanese interpreters with the encouragement of Hendrik Doeff, the Dutch trading *capitao* ('captain' in Portuguese). In effect, Hori used Dutch as a bridging language between English and Japanese. Once he had the dictionary he wanted, he removed the bridge.

As a reaction against Christian missionary activity, the rulers of Japan discontinued contacts with all Western nations except the Dutch until the 1850s, when US naval ships under Commander Matthew C. Perry forced a reopening of the country to international commerce. After the Meiji Restoration in 1868 (when direct imperial rule replaced rule by shoguns claiming to act on behalf of the emperors), Westernization became rapid and extensive. The impact of Japan's push to absorb (and improve on) Western ideas and practices has been marked, both in general and in linguistic terms. Whereas Australia and New Zealand are 'Western' because of ethnic and cultural links with Britain and Ireland, Japan has acquired a quasi-Western status through sustained economic, social, and cultural effort. The following quotations address the issue of the 'Westernness' of Japan:

> **1987** Despite its Asian roots, Japan has become suspended in the Western world. The West has long lost its purely geographical definition, and the west European cultural tradition is similarly no longer an exclusive starting point. Shared political and economic values and structures can provide the common ground between western Europe, North America and Japan (and some other non-European countries).
>
> – editorial, 'Japan's uneasy Western role', *The Independent*, London, 24 August

> **1990** The request comes amid an unusually high level of tension between the West's two biggest economic competitors. American corporate executives and members of Congress have complained that Japan has acted as a sponge for technologies developed in the United States.
>
> – David Sanger, 'U.S. Asks Japanese To Invest $2 billion In Supercollider', *International Herald Tribune*, 1 June

Japanese is typologically close to Korean and the Ural-Altaic language family and entirely distinct from Chinese, despite its use of large numbers of Chinese characters and adoption of many Chinese words. Although there are many regional varieties, the standard language is generally understood and widely used. Present-day Japanese vocabulary contains a majority of native words (*wago*), a significant minority of words of classical Chinese origin (*kango*), and a shifting and apparently ever-increasing range of foreign adoptions, mainly European and in recent years predominantly English (*gairaigo*, 'outside come language'). The members of all of these groups conform to a syllable pattern that ends in vowels or a syllabic *n*. Japanese writing has four scripts that can be regarded as distinct or as subsystems within a single overall writing complex. They are:

❶ Kanji

The most venerable, which uses full Chinese characters, each with a Chinese and a Japanese value or reading, as with *Nihon* (above).

❷ The kana: hiragana and katakana

Two native syllabic scripts derived from kanji, and known as the *kana*, the older of which is *hiragana* and the younger *katakana*. Hiragana is used for writing grammatical elements attached to kanji and for some native words. Katakana, which is more angular and simpler, is mainly used for onomatopoeic native words, transcriptions of foreign words and names, and foreign adoptions. Its function is not unlike italic letters in English when used for words from French and other languages.

❸ Romaji

A system of Roman letters, known as *romaji*, with at least five uses: for foreign words in their unmediated forms; for loans written as initials (such as *NATO* and *UNESCO*); for Japanese words and names that are likely to be read by non-Japanese (such as a company or product name); as a classifying device in some libraries; and for seating in some theatres and transport systems.

In addition, *Hebon* is the standard system for Romanizing Japanese words, named for the US physician and missionary J. C. Hepburn, who used it in the 1880s in his Japanese–English dictionary. It represents consonants according to English ortho-graphy, whereas official *kunrei* spellings are influenced by the Japanese syllabary: compare *ta chi tsu te to* (Hebon) with *ta ti tu te to* (kunrei). Long vowels are repres-ented by a superscript macron in Hebon, by a circumflex in kunrei, or sometimes informally, as for example long *a*, which can be represented by either *ah* or *aa*. Numbers are written in either Chinese or Arabic symbols. The layout of lettering in traditional Japanese books, magazines, and newspapers is generally vertical (top to bottom, opening from the right), and words in Romaji occurring in a vertical text are written on their side. Japanese scientific, technical, and official writing runs horizontally from left to right, Western style.

Japanese English-language company names such as *National*, *Sharp*, *Citizen*, *Brother* are written in romaji and/or in katakana. Japanese-language company names are sometimes written in romaji, and roman abbreviations of names from either language are common, as with *JAL* (Japanese Air Lines) and *NHK* (*Nihon Hoso Kyokai*). Western-style shops, cafés, apartment blocks, and office buildings often have foreign names shown in romaji, such as the Sunshine City commercial building in Tokyo.

Official research into Japanese is conducted by the *Kokuritsu Kokugo Kenkyujo* (The National Language Research Institute, established in 1948), a department of the Ministry of Education, and language reforms are under the direction of the *Kokugo Shingikai* (National Language Council, established in 1934). New compound words and recently adopted loans are listed and defined in both the comprehensive annually updated lexicon *Gendai Yogono Kiso Chishiki* ('Basic Information on Current Usage') and in large directories of general information, such as *Imidas*, whose name both combines *imi* ('meaning') and *dasu* ('to take out') and serves as an acronym of its English title *Innovative Multi-information Dictionary Annual Series*. There are many dictionaries of loanwords, with headwords in katakana script and explanations in Japanese, such as the *Zukai Gairaigo Jiten* ('Illustrated Loanword Dictionary'), published by Kadokawa, and *Katakana-go no Jiten* ('Dictionary of Katakana Words'), published by Shogakukan. Partly because of the emphasis on translation and reading comprehension in English-language education, dictionaries that explain English words in Japanese tend to be best-sellers; they include *Lighthouse* (Kenkyusha) and *Progressive* (Shogakukan).

By and large, the ties between Japanese and English are extensive, close, useful—and often intensely frustrating. Hard reality shows itself in the position of Japan in the international league table for scoring in the TOEFL/Toefl ('Test of English as a Foreign Language'), a global examination administered by a US company, the Educational Testing Service. An individual score of over 500 is necessary for a place in many American and Canadian universities. Each year, around a quarter of a million Japanese take this 2-hour ETS test. In 1995, the top-scoring nation was the Netherlands, average score 607 out of a possible 677, while mainland China averaged 549. The average for Japanese candidates was 490: the 152nd position out of 171 entrant locations that year.

English has long had a key role in Japan, especially through the reading and translation of Western works. There were calls by some radicals after the Meiji Restoration for English to be adopted as the national language, in order to promote Japan's development. These were unsuccessful, but remarkable in themselves. There have also been three waves of eagerness to learn English in more recent Japanese history: after the Second World War, at the time of the 1964 Tokyo Olympics, and in recent years in relation to the information-technology revolution and globalization. In January 2000, the *Commission on Japan's Goals in the 21st Century*, reporting to the then prime minister Keizo Obuchi, suggested that, over time, English might become Japan's second official language, a quasi-recommendation that sparked off heated debate.

Three issues appear to be crucial in such recent discussions: an awareness of the inescapable importance of English to Japan; a concern that Tokyo may be less attractive as an Asian financial centre than, say, Singapore or Hong Kong, because English is not a working language there; and a wish not to lose face, especially in East Asia, as for example in the TOEFL test scores. Part of the problem is an on-going sense of isolation from the world's mainstream, despite economic success and no matter how much effort is made. The following grimly realistic observation comes from an article whose author nonetheless considers the Commission's recent recommendation unrealistic:

> **2000** Academic papers, no matter how excellent their contents, will not be evaluated adequately internationally unless they are written in English.
> – Takuma Kiso, 'English? Who needs it?' *Insight Japan* 9:1, July

Kiso notes that this reality cannot be contested: '[W]hen it comes to business people and academics who have to communicate directly with non-Japanese, English is indispensable', but he argues that this does not require the entire population to develop an everyday working knowledge of English. He also considers that for reading and writing the world's lingua franca at a professional level the preparation offered by the current system is an adequate base to build on, but should be strengthened further. It is, as he and many others have observed of both Japan and Korea, in the management of natural spoken English that the system should be improved.

Efforts have been made to improve Japanese skills in English since the late 19th century. During the 1920s/1930s, the British EFL specialists Harold E. Palmer and A. S. Hornby worked in Japan, the first as adviser to the Ministry of Education, with a special interest in oral teaching methods and graded vocabulary, the second as a teacher and with E. V. Gatenby and H. Wakefield creating a novel learner's dictionary, *The Idiomatic and Syntactic English Dictionary*, before having to leave Japan because of imminent war. In 1942, Kaitakusha in Tokyo published the dictionary. After the war, the *ISED* was re-published by Oxford University Press as *The Advanced Learner's Dictionary of Current English* (1948, 1963), all three men listed as its creators, after which Oxford published a 3rd edition (1974) with the name adapted to the *Oxford Advanced Learner's Dictionary of Current English*. A 6th edition with CD-ROM was published in 2000, in which the Hornby 'brand name' posthumously continues. The link between the *ISED* in Japan in 1942 and the *OALDCE* (1948–2000) is not indicated in any edition.

Although the vast majority of Japanese seldom use or need English as such, they use many of its words on an everyday basis in the form of *gairaigo* and commercial names. When English itself is used there is a kind of carry-over effect from *gairaigo*, in that features of Japanese pronunciation, grammar, vocabulary, and social style are likely to occur. They include:

❶ The pronunciation of *l* and *r*

There is difficulty in distinguishing between and pronouncing *l* and *r*, the nearest Japanese sound being between the two, so that *really* may sound like 'rearry' and *learn* like 'ren'.

❷ Acknowledgement *yes*

Yes is commonly used, like its Japanese equivalent *hai*, to confirm that something has been understood or to acknowledge a question, with or without further development.

❸ Japanisms

Usages that adapt Japanese into English are also common, as in 'go to shopping' for *go shopping*, and the use of *silent* to translate *shizuka*, which has a wider meaning of 'silent, quiet, peaceful'.

❹ All foreignisms regarded as English

There is a tendency to assume that all or most expressions in Japanese that come from other languages are from English or are comprehensible in English, and that the Japanese use of such words reflect their use in English, as in 'I have an arbeit', where *arbeit* represents *arubaito* ('part-time job') an adaptation of German *Arbeit* ('work').

❺ Made-in-Japan English

For most Japanese, the term *Japanese English* does not refer to English as spoken by Japanese to foreigners, but to *wasei eigo* ('Made-in-Japan English'): local expressions drawn from English but used in distinctively Japanese ways, such as *imeji-appu* ('image up') 'improving one's image'.

Japan has four major English-language daily newspapers: the *Japan Times* (established 1897), the *Daily Yomiuri* (1955), the *Mainichi Daily News* (1922), and the *Asahi Evening News* (1951). All but the first are sister publications of Japanese-language newspapers. Large bookstores such as Kinokuniya and Maruzen stock a wide range of English-language books, and there are specialist English-language bookshops in the main cities.

Some private kindergartens and elementary schools provide English instruction. Regular study normally begins in the first year of lower secondary school, and continues at least till the end of upper secondary school. Traditional approaches, such as reading comprehension and grammar-translation, may be supplemented by oral work, sometimes with native speakers. Knowledge of English vocabulary and grammar is important in the selection of candidates to higher education, and an English-language paper is included in the national examination for university entrance. Tokyo and Osaka have public universities that specialize in foreign studies, some technical colleges specialize in English-language instruction, and there are many language schools. The educational channel of Japanese TV broadcasts regular foreign-language-learning series, including English, and there is daily English-language instruction on the radio, teaching mainly colloquial American. The two most prominent organizations for language teachers are the *Japan Association of Language Teachers* (*JALT*) and the *Japanese Association of College English Teachers* (*JACET*).

English words are sometimes included in their original form within Japanese texts (such as advertisements and in some scientific writing), but are normally transcribed phonetically by katakana, a custom that has encouraged the growth of English-derived *gairaigo*. Many Japanese products have English names written in their original form, often with katakana transcription, or given only in katakana, and English words and phrases are often used in advertising to draw attention to a product, and give it an attractive, fashionable image.

English is ubiquitous as decoration on Western-style personal items such as clothes, fashion accessories, toiletries, and stationery: part of a fashion that has spread in East Asia and beyond and is sometimes called *Decorative English* (see also p. 422). Goods for young people commonly feature such characters as Mickey Mouse, Alice in Wonderland, Snoopy, Beatrix Potter animals, and the local Hello Kitty, with appropriate phrases beside them, or sport English proverbs, mottos, and would-be inspirational slogans such as *Let's sing a song with me!* Goods may also be decorated with quotations or reproductions (not always accurate) from an English text (where the overall theme may be appropriate but the content may not, as when a floral design is accompanied by instructions for bedding a plant).

Decorative English is meant to be seen rather than read, eye appeal taking precedence over accuracy and appropriateness. The cosmopolitanism of Roman script conveys a mood more than a message, while the content is likely to reflect such themes as youth, health, vitality, joy, and freedom, as in: (on a packet of tissues) *for someone who seeks a long relationship with things nice*; (on a spectacles case) *This case packs my dream and eyeglasses*; (on a pencil box) *tenderness was completed a pastel*. English composed *by* Japanese *for* Japanese often translates Japanese: comprehensibly (as on a chocolate wrapper, *enjoy superb combination of almond and chocolate*) or obscurely (for hair conditioner, *soft in one*). The following examples are typical of the English used on casual bags: *ReSpice Enjoy fashion life*; *Nice to Heart and Just Impression*; *The New York City Theatre District is where you can and us, anyone*. Since the Second World War, English has become particularly associated with US culture, and its use as part of the design of Western-style goods reinforces their role as symbols of both modernity and America.

Foreign words have been borrowed increasingly from the 16th century onwards, beginning with such words as *tabako* ('tobacco': from Portuguese) and *kohi* ('coffee': from Dutch). The re-opening of Japan to the West during the 19th century led to the absorption of an unprecedented number of foreign terms, mainly from German, French, and English. Attempts to exclude such words followed growing resistance to imported culture during the 1930s, but since 1945 thousands of terms have entered the language, mainly from English. Borrowing from different European languages can have etymologically complex outcomes, as with *karuta* (a type of playing-card: from Portuguese *carta*), *karute* (a medical record: from German *Karte*), *arakaruto* ('à la carte': from French), and *kado* ('identity, credit, greetings (etc.) card': from English *card*). Such terms are freely used in everyday Japanese conversation and writing, the users often not aware of the languages from which they have come. Indeed, non-Japanese may also fail to recognize many of them because of adaptations in form and/or meaning.

Because katakana represents Japanese syllables (such as *sa* and *ke*), the transliteration of foreign words generally leads to phonetic change. Final consonants tend to be followed by a vowel, and consonant clusters are often broken up, as in *erekutoronikkusu* ('electronics'), *kurisumasu* ('Christmas'), and *purutoniumu* ('plutonium'). Sounds that do not exist in Japanese are converted to the nearest Japanese syllables, as in *takushi* ('taxi'), *chimu* ('team'), *tsuna* ('tuna'), *rabu* ('love'), *basu* (both *bus* and *bath*). Or they may be represented by katakana combinations created to allow foreign words to be closer to their original pronunciation, as happens with *hanbaga* ('hamburger'). Loanwords may undergo semantic as well as phonetic change, as with *manshon* ('high-class block of flats': from *mansion*), *konpanion* ('female guide/hostess': from *companion*), *sumato* ('slim': from *smart*), *baikingu* ('buffet meal, smorgasbord': from *Viking*), and *moningusabisu* ('morning service': a set breakfast). The density of foreign matter in some katakana-cum-gairaigo phrases is considerable, as for example *kurismasu sizun no romantikku dezato* (literally 'Christmas season of romantic dessert' = a romantic dessert for the Christmas season).

Clippings and other abbreviations are common, as with *terebi* ('television'), *apato* ('apartment building'), *pato* ('part-time work'), *engejiringu* ('engagement ring'), *masukomi* ('mass communication'), *wapuro* ('word processor'), as if *wordpro*. Clipped foreign words often combine with Japanese words: *haburashi* ('tooth-brush': from Japanese *ha* 'tooth', English *brush*), *kuropan* ('black bread', from Japanese *kuro* 'black' and the Portuguese for 'bread'). Words from different foreign languages can also come together: *rorupan* ('bread roll': from English *roll* and the Portuguese for 'bread'). In addition, two or more words from English are sometimes combined in new ways: *pureigaido* ('play guide': a ticket agency), *bakkumira* ('back mirror': rear-view mirror). Such usages are known in Japanese as *wasei eigo* ('Made-in-Japan English').

In general terms, *gairaigo* words have a modern, Western, and sophisticated image, sometimes competing with native equivalents: thus, *depato* ('department store') has almost replaced the corresponding Japanese word. English is tending to replace the combining of Chinese-derived root-words as the main resource for describing new concepts and things in Japanese: compare the older Chinese-derived *denwa* ('electric talk') for *telephone* and the more recent *terehon kado* ('telephone card'). All such adoptions, notably from English, are used especially in the media and to describe Western science, technology, ideas, arts, fashion, food, sports, leisure activities, and lifestyle.

The term *pidgin* has often been applied informally, and pejoratively, to several varieties of English associated with Japan. One was a pidgin spoken from the early 20th century by Japanese immigrants to Hawaii, distinct from the other pidgins and creoles used in the islands. Another, *Bamboo English*, was used after the Second World War between some Japanese and the US forces of occupation. American military involvement in other parts of East Asia later caused this pidgin to spread to Korea, the Philippines, Thailand, and Vietnam. Many of its usages have become well known, as with *mama-san* (originally an older Japanese woman, especially if in charge of geishas, from *mama* 'mother' and *san*, an honorific title), often applied to any bar hostess, and *ichiban* ('most, number one'), meaning 'the best'. A humorous text in what was called *Korean Bamboo English* survives from the Korean War, apparently written by a US soldier. It tells an old European story using elements of Japanese (and to a lesser extent Korean) with army slang. It begins:

> **1960** Taksan years ago, skoshi Cinderella-san lived in hootchie
> with sisters, . . . ketchee no fun, hava-no social life. Always
> washee-washee, scrubee-scrubee, make chop-chop. One day
> Cinderella-san sisters ketchee post cardo from Seoul. Post cardo
> speakee so: one prince-san have big blowout, taksan kimchi,
> taksan beeru . . . Cindy-san sisters taksan excited, make
> Cinderella-san police up clothes.
> – Grant Webster, *American Speech*

The informal terms *Japlish*, *Japalish*, *Janglish*, and *Japanized English* have been applied to the thousands of English words used in everyday speech in Japan and meant as it were for Japanese eyes and ears only. Many such *wasei eigo* usages are not necessarily obvious to, or even detectable by, native speakers of English. Thus, *dokuta sutoppu* ('doctor stop') is a prohibition on certain activities, such as smoking, made by a physician. The title of a recent best-selling novel, *Bajin Rodo* ('Virgin Road'), refers to the aisle a bride walks down in a church. A productive example is *sandoichi* ('sandwich'), usually shortened to *sando* and commonly compounded, as in *eggusando* ('egg sandwich'), *hamusando* ('ham sandwich'); *mikkususando* ('mixed sandwich': a plate of various kinds of sandwiches), *tsunasando* ('tuna sandwich'), and *hottosando* (a toasted sandwich of any kind).

The terms *Japlish* and *Japalish* have been widely used since the 1950s for any blend of Japanese and English, the first term risking local disapproval by using the element *Jap* (regarded since the end of the Second World War as an ethnic slur), while the second is probably intended to by-pass this risk by adding another letter from *Japan*. The term *Janglish* both sidesteps the slur and picks up the linguistic dissonance with *jangle*. All three terms are informal, wry, and inclined to be pejorative. They refer both to Japanese spoken or written with an admixture of English and to English that shows a strong Japanese influence, and have been in use for decades: 'A great many Japanese speak English nowadays (or at least 'Japlish', as the American colony calls it)' (*Harper's Magazine*, Jan 1963); 'Japanese sometimes sounds like Japlish: *masukomi* for mass communications, *terebi* for television' (*Time*, 22 July 1966).

Although Japanese words have entered English since the 16th century, they have been relatively few. There has been a modest but steady flow of words relating to life and culture, such as *bonze* in the 16th century, *sake* and *shogun* in the 17th, *Mikado* and *Shinto* in the 18th, *geisha* and *jinricksha* in the 19th, and *aikido*, *bonsai*, *origami*, and *pachinko* in the 20th. Areas of special interest include: the civil arts (*bonsai*, *haiku*, *ikebana*, *kabuki*, *kakemono*, *koto*, *Noh*, *origami*); the martial arts, war, and sport (*aikido*, *bushido*, *harakiri*, *judo*, *jujitsu*, *kendo*, *sumo*); cuisine (*nori*, *sashimi*, *satsuma*, *soba*, *sushi*, *tempura*, *teriyaki*, *tofu*); religion (*koan*, *Shinto*, *zazen*, *Zen*); kinds of people (*geisha*, *mikado*, *ninja*, *samurai*, *shogun*, *yakuza*); furnishings, clothes, etc. (*futon*, *kimono*, *obi*, *shoji*, *tatami*); entertainment (*go*, *karaoke*, *Nintendo*, *pachinko*); language (*hiragana*, *kanji*, *katakana*); and words taken from English, used in a special way in Japanese, and then returned to English with their Japanese sense (*homestay*, from *homosutei*, from *home* and *stay*, and *salaryman*, sometimes in the original Japanese form *sarariman*, from *salary* and *man*).

A form of Japanese linguistic creativity that includes borrowing from English and elsewhere and has a high international profile is the naming of cars. The patterns, which are highly neologistic, run much as follows:

❶ Company name and symbolic English name or name elements

Examples: *Honda Civic* (suggesting a town car whose driver behaves well); *Mitsubishi Colt* (echoing cowboy films, horses, and guns), with the variant *Mitsubishi Colt Spacestar* (blending sci-fi and roominess); *Isuzu Trooper* (offering the dash of a cavalryman and/or suggesting a good solid worker); *Mitsubishi Lancer* (with cavalry esprit); *Mitsubishi Space Runner* (suggesting ample room, endurance, the future, and speed); *Nissan Bluebird* (a streamlined high flier); *Nissan Stanza* (poetry in motion?); *Subaru Justy* (enigmatic Decorative English, touching on soundness and lustiness); *Suzuki Swift* (alliteratively suggesting speed and a streamlined and beautiful bird); *Toyota Hiluxe* (a *gairaigo*-style syncopation of 'high' and 'deluxe/luxury').

❷ Company name and symbolic classical or pseudo-classical name

Examples: *Mitsubishi Carisma* (combining 'car' and Greek 'charisma', suggesting prestige and power while ensuring that the second word is pronounced *k* and not *tch*); *Toyota Carina* (combining 'car' and Latin feminine ending *-ina*, and/or perhaps adopting for aesthetic rather than semantic reasons Latin *carina* 'keel'); *Toyota Corolla* (Latin: 'little crown', usually referring to part of a flower, and perhaps regarded as feminine and therefore attractive); *Nissan Micra* (Greek for 'small', in its feminine form); *Nissan Primera* (suggesting 'primary, prime, premier' while using Spanish *primera* 'first-class' and, less helpfully, 'first gear'); *Nissan Serena* (Latin 'serene', also suggesting *serenade*); *Subaru Impreza* (suggesting Italian or Spanish and touching on both *impressive* and *empress*).

❸ Japanese company name and international computer-linked neologisms

More recently, notably with the development of computer-generated forms with no prior dictionary meanings, more radical departures have become common, either invented, as with the *Toyota Celica* (suggesting *coelia/celia*, Latin for 'heavenly', and 'celestial', while sounding and looking soft and smooth), and *Suzuki Vitara* (perhaps echoing Latin *vita* 'life', and *vitality*).

Non-Japanese companies appear to have followed Japan's lead, including in the use of computer-generated word-like entities. Examples include: France's *Citroen Xantia* and *Citroen Xsara* (perhaps using *X* for mystery, the first rather meaninglessly suggesting Greek *xanthos* 'yellow', and pronounced 'Zantia' in English, whereas the second is usually pronounced 'zara' and may benefit from having no prior meaning at all); Germany's *Mercedes Elegance*; Italy's *Fiat Tempra* (enigmatically suggesting 'time' and touching irrelevantly on 'temper', 'temperature', and 'temporary'); *Vauxhall Corsa* (suggesting both 'corsair' and 'courser', each implying adventure, action, and surging motion). In this area, Japan appears to have been well ahead of the general game.

7 Australasia, Oceania, and Antarctica

1997
- Today Australia is a prosperous, primarily urban society. . . . Apart from Canberra—the federal capital—all the main cities are coastal.
- An ice cap thousands of metres thick covers isolated Antarctica. If it melted, the freed waters would drown all the world's coastal cities.
- The thousands of islands scattered across the Pacific Ocean form three main groups: Melanesia, Micronesia and Polynesia. Most are ringed by coral reefs. Much of Australia's interior is flat desert, whereas New Zealand and Papua New Guinea are mountainous and green.

– from *Reader's Digest Illustrated Atlas of the World*, 208, 226

Australia (Latin for 'Southern Land') is the name for an immense island widely regarded as a continent in its own right. That island, however, along with New Zealand and other island groups, technically belongs in *Australasia* (Latin for 'Southern Asia'), a continental region also known in Greek as the *Antipodes* (a place set 'against the feet' of northerners). The two classical European languages Latin and Greek have played a surprisingly strong role 'down under', but the words *Australia*, *Australasia*, and *Antipodes* no longer serve to express the kind of baffled wonder that the first European explorers felt when they came upon this second 'new world'. In talking about an 'Austral Asia', such men were (for convenience) simply stretching *Asia* much as their predecessors had stretched *India* to cover lands lying to the east of the Bay of Bengal—or as Columbus had misapplied it entirely to the far side of the Atlantic. But if these Dutch, British, and French explorer-exploiters had not assumed they were still in Asian waters, they would have been hard pressed to make sense of the regions they found themselves in.

Once they had made use of *Austral-*, the original meaning of -*Asia* could safely fade away. The previously imagined *Antipodes* now existed in their own right, and Australians and New Zealanders did not need to think again about being or not being part of Asia until the closing years of the 20th century—and then, once more, for the same kind of reasons of trade and gain that inspired the first explorers.

While the name *Australia* labels a single, clear-cut, self-contained 'island continent', and *Australasia* has a general if rather vague catch-all quality, the term *Oceania* (the Latin version of an earlier French *Océanie*, variously pronounced in English as 'Ohsee-AH-nia', 'Ohsee-AY-nia', and 'Oh-SHEE-nia') broadly covers all the islands of the Pacific Ocean, and overlaps with *Australasia*. It has, however, usually been taken to include three island groups labelled by Europeans in Greek: *Melanesia* ('the place of black islands'), *Micronesia* ('the place of small islands'), and *Polynesia* ('the place of many islands'). The *New Oxford Dictionary of English* (1998) defines it as covering 'the islands of the Pacific Ocean and adjacent seas', the *Encarta World English Dictionary* (1999) as the 'geographical region consisting of most of the smaller islands of the Pacific Ocean, sometimes including Australia and New Zealand', and the *Reader's Digest Illustrated Atlas* (1997, quoted above) includes both Australia and New Zealand within the circle of Oceania.

The mid-19th-century term *Melanesia* has been described (for example by the *Encyclopaedia Britannica* in 1986) as an 'ethnogeographic grouping', which means that both the colour of the skins of the peoples inhabiting the region and the fact that it is an archipelago were taken into account when formulating an apparently dispassionate scientific term. Greek is a lexical source that has at times been used not so much for scholarly precision as for draping modest classical robes over things that are too rough in the vernacular. As the *OED* puts it (1989): 'The name, modelled after *Polynesia*, was intended to mean "the region of islands inhabited by blacks." ' The same scholarly approach, applied to the islands off Western Europe, would have produced **Leuconesia* ('the region of islands inhabited by whites').

Antarctica lies well beyond both Australasia and Oceania. In physical terms, it is classed as the fifth in size of the world's continents. In Greco-Latin, *Antarctica* is an 'anti-Arctic' place: at the South and not the North Pole, and frozen land rather than frozen water.

A key characteristic, however, of the entire Antarctic–Australasian–Oceanian region is not only its own distances and its distance from the rest of the world, but its small populations and the thinness of their distribution by land and sea. A second characteristic is that so much has happened to those populations in linguistic terms. There is a danger that the rest of the world will overlook not only what has been happening to the indigenous languages of the region but also the antipodean fate of the colonial-cum-settler languages. Portuguese, Spanish, Dutch, and German have largely vanished from the scene, but French is still there, especially and ironically in New Caledonia/La Nouvelle Calédonie, as also a range of immigrant European languages in Australia. Otherwise English is the lingua franca of the Pacific. Indeed, quite apart from the influence of Australia and New Zealand, the United States influences a swathe of islands from Guam to Hawaii. The Pacific Ocean has in many ways become an English lake.

The roll-call of Oceania proper is long, redolent with island names that echo many places and realities. In Melanesia, *New Guinea* echoes the old Guinea coast of Africa; the *Admiralty Islands* nod towards the Royal Navy's headquarters in London; the *Bismarck and Louisiade archipelagoes* touch on both German and French imperialism; the *Solomon Islands* recall an ancient Hebrew king; *New Caledonia/Nouvelle Calédonie* echoes Scotland, in English and French; the *Santa*

Cruz Islands recall Spain and its holy cross; *Norfolk Island* (in Australian territory) expresses nostalgia for an English county; and the *Loyalty Islands* express a colonial aspiration. The only local names are *Vanuatu* (which replaced the *New Hebrides*), *Fiji*, and *Tuvalu*. In Micronesia, the *Federated States of Micronesia* (which include the *Caroline Islands*) have an American sound to them, while the *Northern Mariana Islands*, *Guam*, *Palau*, the *Marshall Islands*, and *Wake Island* all belong to the US. *Kiribati* and *Nauru*, however, are on their own. In Polynesia, *Tokelau*, *Tonga*, and *Samoa* survive as indigenous names, alongside *American Samoa*, the eponymous *Cook Islands* belong to New Zealand, and the rest is French. Some details:

Samoa Formerly *Western Samoa*, a country and kingdom of Oceania and a member of the Commonwealth, consisting of a group of nine islands in the South-western Pacific, with a population of *c.*167,000 and an economy based on agriculture, forestry, fishing, and tourism. The current head of state is HH Malietoa Tanumafili II and the prime minister Tofilau Eti Alesana. The first Europeans to visit the region were the Dutch, it was a German colony from the late 19th century, became a League of Nations mandate in 1920, then after the Second World War a United Nations trust territory administered by New Zealand. It gained its independence in 1962, and its languages are Samoan and English, both official.

Tonga Formerly known as the *Friendly Islands*, a country and kingdom in Oceania and a member of the Commonwealth, consisting of 170 islands due south of Western Samoa, with a population of *c.*100,000 and an economy based on agriculture, tourism, and some manufacturing. The current head of state is King Taufa'ahau Tupou IV and the prime minister is Baron Vaea of Houma. The first Europeans to visit the islands were the Dutch. Tonga was a British protectorate from 1900 until independence in 1970. Its languages are Tongan and English, both official.

Kiribati Pronounced 'Kiribas', with the stress on the first syllable: a republic in the south-west Pacific and a member of the Commonwealth, formerly known as the *Gilbert Islands*, and including the Line Islands and the Phoenix Islands. Kiribati was part of the British protectorate, then colony, of the *Gilbert and Ellice Islands*, and gained its independence in 1979. Its phosphate deposits have been virtually worked out and its economy now depends largely on copra, fish, and aid from the UK. Its currency is the Australian dollar. Its population is just under 82,000, its ethnicity 90% Micronesian, and its languages Kiribati (Gilbertese) and English, both official.

Tuvalu A small country of Oceania and a member of the Commonwealth, consisting of nine islands. Its currency is the Tuvaluan dollar, and the Australian dollar is also legal tender. Its population is just under 9,500, its languages are Tuvaluan and English, both official, and its economy is based on fruit, fishing, and Tuvaluan postage stamps. Formerly known as the *Ellice Islands*, it was part of the British colony of the *Gilbert and Ellice Islands*, gaining its independence in 1978.

Nauru An island of 21 square miles, an independent republic, and a member of the Commonwealth, using the Australian dollar as its currency, in an economy mainly of mining and agriculture. Its population is *c.*10,600, its ethnicity *c.*58% Nauruan, 25% other Pacific Islanders, 8% Chinese, and 8% Caucasian. Its languages are Nauruan (official) and English. It has little fertile land, most of its food and drinking water have to be imported, and its economy depends entirely on the extraction of phosphates. Annexed by Germany in 1888, it became a League of Nations mandate administered by the British in 1920 and later a UN trust territory administered by Australia, gaining internal self-government in 1966 and independence in 1968.

Today, fast aircraft simplify travel, but for centuries these populations have been linked one to another and to the rest of the world by the same medium that isolates them: the ocean. All the languages now used in Australasia and Oceania travelled there in fragile vessels. The voyages of those Polynesians who took Maori from Tahiti to Aotearoa were formidable achievements in open outrigger canoes. For those who took English from Britain to Australia, both as convicts and their over-seers, the journey has been described as the nearest thing humanity has known to colonizing another planet. Today, however, because of climatic change worldwide, many of the lower-lying islands in the region could well disappear beneath a rising sea level.

Australasian English

There have been at least three names for the English of Australia and New Zealand taken together: *Antipodean English*, *Austral English*, and *Australasian English*. All three have been popular in the past as means of reflecting the similarities between Australian and New Zealand usage, but have largely fallen into disuse, whereas *Australian English* and *New Zealand English* have in recent years become successful stand-alone (and standard) terms. The similar histories of the two countries have however led to similarities in their English, justifying such an umbrella term as *Australasian English*.

Both varieties are non-rhotic (that is, no *r* is pronounced in words like *art* and *worker*), are largely based on the late 18th- and 19th-century English of southern England, and the vocabulary of each has been heavily influenced by immigration from many parts of rural Britain. There are elements of Irish English in Australia and Scottish English in New Zealand, but the differences between the two countries has never been substantial enough for outsiders to be sure they are guessing right when trying to distinguish their speakers. Indeed, as late as 1970, Australians could only volunteer that the speech of New Zealanders was more 'English', while some New Zealanders saw Australian English as 'broad'. Speakers of British and American have normally been able to do little more than recognize them as distinct from the English of white South Africans of British provenance (which shares some features). Language scholars have tended therefore to discuss the two varieties together in the same publications, under such headings as 'English in Australia and New Zealand'.

Since *c*.1970, however, Australian and New Zealand English have been becoming discernibly distinct in their phonology, a development due almost entirely to a shift in the pronunciation of short front vowels in New Zealand, which have been raised and retracted. One effect of this change has led Australians to characterize New Zealanders as eating 'fush and chups', while New Zealanders return the compli-ment by hearing Australians say 'feesh and cheeps'. Graffiti near Bondi Beach in

Sydney, Australia, have included the phonologically inspired NEW ZEALAND SUCKS, AUSTRALIA SEVEN. The merging of two other vowels, so that for most NZ speakers *ear* and *air* are homophones, further reduces the range of contrasting vowel sounds (the phonemic inventory) of New Zealand English.

Such changes have been so recent and rapid that there is a distinctive age-grading in the phonology of New Zealanders. Speakers over 50 cannot often be identified as either New Zealanders or Australians, but for those under thirty the notion of a uniform spoken 'Australasian English' no longer holds true. Some Australians may be following the New Zealand lead in this vowel shift, but even so there does appear to be increasing divergence.

Even if there is a degree of recent divergence, Australian and New Zealand English together serve as a focus of mother-tongue English for the entire Asia-Pacific region west of Hawaii—one of the largest language constituencies on earth. For the already large and rapidly expanding middle classes of East Asia, English is already the lingua franca, and commentators have begun to talk uncontentiously about 'English as an Asian language': Malaysians talking to Chinese and Koreans, Thais meeting with Japanese and Filipinos, all need the language and want fluency in it for their children. With such a target in mind increasing numbers have been turning to Australian and New Zealand educational and other institutions and, aware of both the actual and the potential market, such institutions have begun to court them assiduously in return.

Terra Australis, Australia, and the legacy of Latin

> **1991** The status of the English language in Australia is today, and has been since British colonization, that of THE national language. It overwhelmingly dominates the linguistic landscape, both demographically and functionally. This is not to say that Australia is a monolingual country; on the contrary, a large number of languages are spoken within its borders. But the English language dwarfs all others in terms of both number of speakers and the social roles it is used for.
>
> – Gregory R. Guy, 'Australia', in *English Around the World: Sociolinguistic Perspectives*, ed. Jenny Cheshire (Cambridge University Press), 213

For over 40,000 years there were many languages in Australia, evolving apart from the rest of the world. English, on the other hand, has been in the region only since just before Jane Austen was born, in 1775. Present-day Australia (which might have been called 'Southland' if Latin had not been used) originated as a group of British colonies, the first of which was founded in 1786. In 1901, these colonies (which by no means always saw eye to eye) became a single self-governing Dominion of the British Empire, evolving into an independent federal nation whose sole (rather uncertain) constitutional tie with the United Kingdom today is the monarchy. For much of its existence, 'Australia fair' has been on the psychological as well as phys- ical rim of the English-speaking world, but in recent decades developments in transport and communication, as well as changes in the global mindset, have brought about a new assessment both by Australians and the rest of the world of who and what they are and how they speak and write.

During this period of development, however, the indigenous languages have done badly. About 50 are extinct, about 100 are dying out, and some 50 continue as first languages, mainly along the north coast and in the western and central interior (that is, far from major population centres). In every case, the number of speakers is low, as with the few thousands who use Aranda and Pitjantjatjara. Indeed, there are more Aboriginal speakers of such adaptations of English as *Roper River Creole* (also known as *Kriol*) and *Torres Strait Creole* (also known as *Broken*) than of Aboriginal languages properly so called.

The indigenous languages, the English language, and the creoles are not, however, the only languages in contemporary Australia. English is the first and only language of over 80% of its nearly 20 million people, but the list of Australian languages includes Italian, Greek, Chinese, Arabic, and German, all spoken by more than 100,000 people each. The overall dominance of English has long been recognized, but the distinctiveness and vigour of Australian usage has only recently been accepted both at home and in the world at large. The first recorded instance of the term *Australian English* dates from 1940 (although the term *Australian* on its own was applied earlier to fluent local swearing, especially involving the word *bloody*). Since the end of the Second World War, however, Australian English has steadily gained in prestige both abroad and more warily at home, until at the beginning of the 21st century (with its own media, dictionaries, and style guides) it stands third in numbers and burgeoning self-confidence in the international pecking order of English.

However, the English language in Australia has a short history: some 200 years of settlement and less than 60 years during which it has had serious recognition as a national variety in its own right. The first recorded use of the term *Australian English* is 1940. It has been a slow uphill struggle since then for the variety it names to become respectable, rather than serve as evidence of decline from the norms of England and as justification for a 'colonial cringe'.

The name *Australia* is Latin, an adaptation of the phrase *Terra Australis* that in turn comes from *terra australis incognita* ('unknown southern land'), the name for a theoretical continent that some geographers considered should exist to the south of Asia and Africa (although no one had yet either proved or disproved the theory). As exploration finally established, however, there were *two* land masses, now known as *Australia* and *Antarctica*. In the mid-17th century, the Dutch charted the western coastline of a land mass they called *New Holland*, and much later, in 1707, Captain James Cook charted what was later recognized as the eastern coastline of the same mass, to which he gave the name *New South Wales*. However, the explorer Matthew Flinders favoured *Australia* as the name for what came to be seen as a distinct 'new' continent. Promoted by Lachlan Macquarie, the Scottish governor of New South Wales (1809–21), this usage became from the 1820s the cover term for all the British colonies in the continent. The wider term *Australasia* ('Southern Asia') was sometimes used for the same area but currently refers to Australia, New Zealand, and an uncertain range of adjacent islands.

Latin as a language for naming things scientifically has a strong tradition in Australia, despite the nation's widespread anti-cultural image. In addition to *Terra Australis*, *Australia*, and the *Nullarbor Plains* ('plains with no trees'), the early settlers adopted and adapted the Latin phrase *aborigines* (as used in classical times, in the plural, for the indigenous people of Italy and Greece) and applied it to the age-old inhabitants of their new land, much of which they declared *terra nullius* ('no man's land'): that is, land to which no one had a prior claim in law, and which could therefore be straightforwardly appropriated—a view much later reassessed as legally invalid. From the plural *Aborigines* the early settlers back-formed first *Aborigine* as its singular, then the now widely disliked clipping *Abo*.

The world at large knows the indigenous people of Australia through the Latin name given to them, which oddly chimes in syllable structure and sound with words adopted from the people it names. Aborigines play the *didgeridoo* (*didjeridu*, in a language of Arnhem Land), eat *witchetty grubs* (called *wityu* in Adnyamathanha), and have *corroborees* ('social gatherings', from *garaabara* in Dharuk). The uneasy, unequal interplay between the settlers and the native peoples has been a defining experience for both white and black Australians, marked by these and such other archetypal Aussie words as *billabong*, *kangaroo*, *kookaburra*, and *wombat*. Yet, for all their historical and etymological interest, biological relevance, and symbolic significance, such adoptions are scant: some names for flora and fauna, cultural items, and places. These words and names tend to be written with a 19th-century penchant for double letters, as in the place-names *Murrumbidgee*, *Wagga Wagga*, and *Woomerah*. Or, as Rudyard Kipling put it:

> **1902** This is the mouth-filling song
> Of the race that was run by a Boomer,
> Run in a single burst—only event of its kind—
> Started by Big God Nqong from Warrigaborrigarooma,
> Old Man Kangaroo first: Yellow-Dog Dingo behind.
>
> **–** from the *Just So Stories for Little Children*

The bulk of the settlers during the heyday of Empire are now commonly referred to as *Anglo-Celtic*, a distinctive term for *migrants* (formerly, and elsewhere, *immigrants*, although this Australianism is increasingly in use worldwide) from Britain and Ireland. Distance and isolation (both in terms of the world and within the country) have been fundamental features of Australian life and language.

For a century, the colonists explored and worked a vast land veneered with exotica, in which Anglo-Classical and Anglo-Aboriginal names were haphazardly given to such flora and fauna as the *duck-billed platypus* (Anglo-Greco-Latin: 'duck-billed flat-foot'), the *koala* or *native bear* (not a bear at all, and *koala* taken from Dharuk), *spinifex* (Latin 'thorn maker'), and *eucalypt* (Greek: 'well-covered'). The Greco-Latin word *marsupial* ('pouch-like') became an everyday term, especially in such combinations as *marsupial cat*, *marsupial mole*, and *marsupial mouse* as analogies were drawn between these creatures and those at *Home*. Where possible, both settler and 'Abo' engaged in such *pastoral* occupations as sheep farming, but in ways that had little to do with farming in *the Old Country*, where sheep graze in flocks, not *mobs*, and on farms, not *stations*.

A well-established abbreviation of *Australia* in books and elsewhere is *Aus*, which (like *Aussie*) tends to be pronounced with a z- rather than an s-sound. This form may have been influenced by the phrase 'the Land of Oz' in the US journalist Lyman Frank Baum's children's book *The Wizard of Oz* (1900). It is now widely used as an informal and conveniently short name for Australia, notably in newspaper headlines, and such phrases as *a trip to Oz* and *the Oz Olympic team*. The usage was formerly neutral, but currently tends to have a positive slant. It was first recorded in 1908 (cf. the date of Baum's book) became common in the Second World War, and popular from the 1970s, probably as a result of its use as the title of a satirical Sydney magazine, diverting the epithet *the Land of Oz* to Australia rather than somewhere magical that was *not* in Kansas.

Australian English

In the early 21st century, however, although the life and industries of the *Outback* still go on, Australians are predominantly coastal city-dwellers, concentrated largely in the south-east. Australia's towns and cities have in recent decades become increasingly *multicultural* and *ethnic*, expressions that refer not to Anglo-Saxons, Celts, and Aborigines, but to migrants from Asia and Continental Europe. These add a leavening of internationalism and even political correctness to a society whose governments formerly had a rigid 'White Australia' policy. Within that frame of reference, Australian English was notably a frontier variety with a mythology of *the Bush* and *mateship* (solidarity among men who worked, played, and drank together; now more flexible), but the key influences at the start of the 21st century are cosmopolitan and urban (even urbane), involving computing and surfing on the one hand and global deal-making on the other.

Australian English is strikingly homogeneous from coast to coast, largely lacking the differences in accent and dialect found in the British, Irish, American, and Canadian varieties. A single speech continuum runs through the nation, within which however three areas have been identified, each receiving from linguistic observers a faintly damning name:

❶ Cultivated Australian

A minority accent and style so closely—and determinedly—patterned on RP that some phoneticians call it 'Near-RP'. However, for many Australians it is a snobbish, effete, and subservient form of speech long associated with high status, or pretensions to such status.

❷ Broad Australian

At the other end of the spectrum, an accent and style with features often identified internationally as Australian, as when outsiders hear (or claim that they here) such a question as '*Did you come here today?*' as 'Did you come here to die?' It is especially associated with mateship and the no-nonsense values of the traditional Australian working-class and lower middle-class male.

❸ General Australian

The wide band between 'cultivated' and 'broad', a majority usage, especially in the cities, where it receives the same kind of middle-class approval as *General American* and *General Canadian* in North America. There is no equivalent in the United Kingdom.

It is generally assumed that the Australian accent derives from the mixing of British (English, Scottish, and Welsh) and Irish accents in the early years of settlement.

However, although most convicts and other settlers came from London, the Midlands, and Ireland, the degree of influence of the accents originally most prominent cannot be conclusively established. The upper levels of society did however seek to sound like the upper classes in the Home Counties in England, while others lower on the social scale have often been compared to Cockneys. The present spectrum of accents was however probably established by the early 19th century.

The first Australian settlements were penal colonies, and until 1868, when *transportation* (the technical term of the period for sending people to penal colonies) came to an end, the life of the convicts and their overseers was discussed in a vocabulary comparable to that of a slave society in the Caribbean or the American South. Long-established noun/noun compounds include *convict colony* (a penal settlement), *convict servant* or *convict slave* (a convict assigned as a servant), and *cattle/sheep station* (a large farm raising mainly cattle/sheep). There was in the early days a distinction between *bond* and *free*, as in *bond labour*, *bond list*, *bond stockman*, *bond population* on the one hand and *free labourer*, *free emigrant*, *free native*, *free settler* on the other, and also between *free* and *freed*, as in *Free British Subject* as opposed to *freed convict*.

Reinforcing the slavery analogy, the use of *emancipated* arose as a euphemism for *freed*, as in *emancipated convict* and *the Emancipated* collectively, as well the terms *emancipist* and *emancipationist* for a freed or pardoned convict. The older settlements were populated in part by convicts and in part by free settlers (a group that included the military who guarded the convicts). Though convicts who had served their sentences or received pardons became free in terms of the law, they often could not escape the stigma of their earlier condition and obtained only a measure of freedom, because many of the *exclusives* or *exclusionists* (those who had never been other than free) now simply called them *free convicts* or *freed men*.

During the transportation period, the land was explored and opened up for settlement and stock-raising. *Squatters* (stock-raisers or *graziers* occupying large tracts of Crown land under lease or licence) moved inland from the *limits of location* (the frontier of settlement) into the *back country* or *back of beyond* in search of land suitable for *runs* (tracts of grazing land) or *stations* (ranches). The squatters looked for *open* land (free from forest or undergrowth), seeking *open forest* or *open plains*, and using words like *brush* (dense natural vegetation), *bush* (the distinctive natural vegetation), *mallee* or *mulga* (forms of natural vegetation giving their name to their habitat), and *scrub* (generally, poor vegetation) to describe features of an unfamiliar environment.

The stock industry employed *overseers* or *superintendents* (both convict-related terms), *stockmen*, and *rouseabouts* (general hands). *Drovers* 'travelled' stock long distances *overland*, the original *overlanders* driving stock from New South Wales to South Australia. The importance of sheep in opening up the country and establishing a frontier society was such that the occupational vocabularies of droving and shearing figure largely in Australian literature. Gold was discovered in the 1850s, leading to movement between the Californian, Australian, and New Zealand goldfields. *Rushes* (an expression first used of the sudden escape of numbers of convicts and then of the sudden movement of numbers of miners to a particular place or *goldfield*) followed when a *prospector* (*gold-finder*, *gold-hunter*, *gold-seeker*) made a *find* and established a *claim*. A number of such mining terms originated in Australia, but many are shared with other varieties of English, and the importance of the discovery of gold, and of the gold rushes that followed, lies in the mobility they encouraged and their influence on the homogeneity of the Australian accent.

Some primary features of pronunciation, grammar, and vocabulary are listed below.

Pronunciation

1 A relatively slow rhythm, with evenly spaced stress and fairly 'flat' intonation, as compared with RP (whose tonal range is wide) and the accents of Wales, the Caribbean, and the Philippines (often identified as 'singsong').

2 Australian English is non-rhotic, with no *r*-sound in such words as *art*, *hair*, and *worker*.

3 Many Australians call the sound and letter *h* 'haitch', a practice originating among people of Irish-Catholic background.

4 The vowel in *can't dance* is closer to that in 'kent dense' than in the RP 'cahnt dahnce'.

5 The weak central schwa vowel is common, occurring in unaccented positions where RP has a short *i*, as in the closing syllables of *boxes*, *dances*, *darkest*, *velvet*, and *acid*.

Grammar and style

1 Remarkably, no features of grammar distinguish Australian from British usage, standard or non-standard.

2 By and large, written and printed English is much the same in Australia as elsewhere. The authoritative style guide is the Australian Government Printing Service's *Style Manual for Authors, Editors and Printers*, first published in 1966. The manual was intended to set standards for government publications, but is widely used and has received input from the community at large through the annual *Style Councils* organized by the Macquarie publishing house associated with Macquarie University in New South Wales, near Sydney.

3 Where UK and US spelling norms differ, British is preferred: *honour* (but *Labor* as the name of the political party), *centre*, and *licence*. As also in New Zealand, the *-ise* spelling, as in *realise*, is generally preferred to *-ize*.

Vocabulary

1 Most of the many distinctively Australian words have not spread internationally, although a number are more widely known (and in some cases used) as a result of the success of Australian films and TV soap operas. Such expressions include *G'day* ('Good day') and the informal abbreviation *journo* ('journalist').

2 The largest and earliest demand for new words related to flora, fauna, and major occupations such as stock-raising, as a result of which Australianisms are predominantly nouns and noun-related. Single nouns include: *mulga* (Aboriginal: a kind of acacia tree); *mullock* (British dialect 'rubbish', narrowed to mean 'mining refuse'); *muster* (in world usage often military, but here 'a round-up of livestock').

3 A growing sense of national identity was fostered by involvement in the First World War. The line between formal and informal usage is perhaps less rigidly drawn in Australia than elsewhere, colloquialisms being more admissible than in Britain. In informal usage, the suffixes *-ie* or *-y* and *-o* or *-oh* are freely attached to short base words: *roughie* ('a trick'); *tinnie* ('a can of beer'); *bottle-oh* ('a bottle merchant'); *plonko* ('an addict of *plonk* 'cheap wine'); *smoko* ('a work break'), and clippings (*Aussie* 'an Australian'; *arvo* ('an afternoon'); *barbie* ('a barbecue'); *Chrissy* ('Christmas'); *compo* ('workers' compensation'); *derro* ('a derelict or down-and-out'); *reffo* ('a refugee').

4 The following list highlights some of the processes through which Australian usages have come into existence: (1) *balander/balanda*, from Aboriginal English, in turn from Malay *belanda*, adapting *Hollander*, a white man: 'Friends in the Northern Territory, both Aboriginal and Balanda'; (2) *hotel* a pub: *I'm going round to the hotel*; (3) *jackeroo/jackaroo* from the Aboriginal language Jagara *dhugai-iu*, 'a wandering white man', Anglicized like *kangaroo*: obsolete uses are a white man living beyond the bounds of close settlement, and a young man (usually English) seeking experience working on a sheep or cattle station; currently, someone working on a sheep or cattle station to get practical experience. Humorously, the female is a *jilleroo/jillaroo*, and the short form for both is a *roo* (cf. *kangaroo*); also used as verbs, *to jackeroo/jilleroo* 'to work in this capacity'; (4) *spruik* colloquial, 'to hold forth like a showman; to talk to attract customers', as in *spruik[ing] outside strip-tease joints* and *spruikers in braided uniforms strutted up and down*.

Until quite recently, Australia was straightforwardly assimilationist: all immigrants, whatever their background, would (or should) blend into the community as quickly as possible. With the need for immigrants and their arrival in recent years from many ethnic backgrounds, the term 'multicultural' has gained an iconic status, as a kind of signpost to the future. Such immigrant languages as Greek and Italian are now officially accepted as 'community languages', and the government now encourages kinds of bilingualism. Even so, however, the impact of these languages on Australian usage has to date been negligible.

Nonetheless, the arrival of so many immigrants from southern Europe, many parts of Asia, and elsewhere, is slowly converting a conservative 'Anglo-Celtic' society into a multilingual and multicultural community that is increasingly tolerant of difference. A major development was the publication (1987) of Joseph Lo Blanco's *National Policy on Languages*, a report commissioned by the Commonwealth Department of Education (1986). This has proved to be a key document for federal and state initiatives intended to do three things: improve the teaching of English as both a first and second language; to promote bilingualism (especially in those whose only language is English); and to preserve and foster the teaching of community languages (including Aboriginal languages). The increased prominence of Aboriginal English has been significant.

Despite a new-found sense of independence, including the export of Australian films and television series, Australian usage is subject to the media-borne influences of both British and, increasingly, American usage. By and large, because of traditional ties, there is less resistance to UK than US usage, particularly in pronunciation and spelling, but the balance appears to be tilting slowly towards the US. In addition, although it is 1,200 miles away, New Zealand is considered to be a close geographical, cultural, and linguistic neighbour, and the constant movement of working people between the two southern-hemisphere nations ensures an ongoing interchange of features in their similar but variously distinctive usage.

Swearing, slang, strine, and stereotypes

The use in Australia of the expletive *bloody* has attained such mythic proportions that, although it is also widely used in Britain, Ireland, and New Zealand, it has acquired the home-grown title 'the great Australian adjective', used not only before nouns but inside them, as in 'Shootin' kanga-bloody-roos/At Tumba-bloody-rumba' (W. N. Scott, *Complete Book of Australian Folk Lore*, 1976). Two comments on *bloody* from the 19th century are:

> **1847** I had once the curiosity to count the number of times that a bullock driver used this word in the course of a quarter of an hour, and found that he did so twenty-five times. I gave him eight hours in the day to sleep, and six to be silent, thus leaving ten hours for conversation. I supposed that he had commenced at twenty and continued till seventy years of age . . . and found that in the course of that time he must have pronounced this disgusting word no less than 18,200,000 times.
>
> – A. Marjoribanks, *Travels in New South Wales*

> **1899** The sunburnt——stockman stood
> And, in a dismal——mood,
> Apostrophised his——cuddy;
> 'The——nag 's no——good,
> He couldn't earn his——food,
> A regular——brumby'
>
> – from 'The Great Australian Adjective', W. T. Goodge, *Hits, Skits and Jingles*

Slang is also a significant, even pervasive part of Australian usage, sometimes called *Australian slanguage* or even *slangwidge*. Again, from Goodge, and a later commentator:

> **1899** And our undiluted English
> Is a fad to which we cling,
> But the great Australian slanguage
> Is a truly awful thing.
>
> – Ibid.

> **1983** 'Actually, Australian slanguage is well stocked with words and phrases to describe those who are a bit slow off the mental mark.'
>
> – *Weekend Australian*, 27 August

Australian usage has also attracted comic stereotyping at home and elsewhere in the English-speaking world. The term *strine/Strine* refers to a kind of stage Australian (cf. 'Mummerset' in the West of England), whose vowels are distorted and syllables reduced, as in the word *strine* itself, collapsing the four syllables of *Australian* into one, and in *Emma Chisit*, the enigmatic female created out of the Australian pronunciation of 'How much is it?'

The word was coined by Alistair Morrison in 1964. Writing under the pseudonym Afferbeck Lauder ('Alphabetical Order') and as the putative Professor of Strine Studies at the University of Sinny (Sydney), Morrison published a series of humorous articles in the *Sydney Morning Herald*, some of which were later collected under the title *Let Stalk Strine* (1965). The series made much of such features as elision, assimilation, metanalysis, and syncope in Broad Australian, as with: *money* ('Monday'); *ass prad* ('house proud'); *tan cancel* ('town council'). The term has had considerable local and international success as a humorous stereotype of the laid-back spoken style of many Australians. Examples like *Gloria Soame* ('glorious home') and the title of a second collection, *Nose Stone Unturned* (1966), demonstrate the importance of the eye in creating the desired effect.

The style and usage of the comedian Barry Humphries (b. 1934), created by exaggerating aspects of Australian pronunciation, delivery, and usage, mixes the residue of a long-standing deference to British norms along with an exuberant recognition of national identity. Humphries has contributed both to colloquial idiom and a widespread international perception of Australian English as casual and vulgar. His characters include Dame Edna Everage ('Average'), a Melbourne housewife turned megastar, Sir Les Patterson, an Australian 'cultural ambassador' (an oxymoron from Down Under), and Barry McKenzie, an *ocker* ('boorish chauvinistic Australian': *Encarta World English Dictionary*, 1999) in a comic strip in the British satirical magazine *Private Eye*.

More recently, however, international awareness of Australian English has taken two distinct forms. The first relates to the impact of such daily TV soap operas as *Neighbours* and *Home and Away*, notably in the UK, where some observers consider that Australian vowels have had an effect on the speech of young Britons, most particularly in shaping 'Estuary English' in the London area. The second is more academic, relating to the publication of dictionaries of English specifically for Australia, initially by Macquarie in Sydney then by Oxford University Press in Melbourne. The worldwide profile of Australian usage has been raised in the process. More recently, Macquarie has gone two steps further, in collaboration with publishers in the Philippines and Singapore. In the first instance, the Macquarie school dictionary has been somewhat de-Australianized, then Americanized, Philippinized, and re-named; in the second, it has been somewhat de-Australianized, then Briticized, Singaporeanized, and re-named. The philosophy behind these moves, formulated primarily by the lexicographer Susan Butler, has been to create out of the Macquarie database customized dictionaries of English as an Asian language.

Aboriginal English

Turning the Latin phrase *ab origine* ('from the beginning') into the plural *Aborigines* started long before it could be applied to anyone in Australia. It originated in Latin as the name for the first inhabitants of Greece and Italy, went from there to refer to the first peoples in many parts of the world, but in English it became focused first on the original inhabitants of both Australia and New Zealand, then on 'the first Australians'. There are two singulars, the back-formation *Aborigine* and the adaptation *Aboriginal*. In Australia, the forms *Aborigine* and *Aborigines* are the singular and plural preferred by standardizing agencies, though *Aboriginal* and *Aboriginals* occur and tend to be favoured by people who wish to get away from any possible suggestion of disparagement. It was by no means the only contender in naming the native peoples of Australia; early European settlers were eclectic, calling the indigenous inhabitants *Australians*, *Blacks*, *Blackfellows*, *Indians*, and *Natives*.

Aborigines appears to have become the preferred term by the 1820s, when local-born whites began to refer to themselves as both *Australians* and *natives*, and the inappropriateness of *Indians* had been accepted. *Blackfellow* has frequently been used, especially in Pidgin, and is offensive if used by whites, as is the short form *Abo*. *Black*, in use since the beginning, has recently gained new strength in Australia as elsewhere, as a consequence of black activism in North America and Africa. Associated in Australia with a land-rights movement that began in the 1960s, this activism has led to the concept of *Aboriginality*, one element in which has been the use of indigenous names, such as *koori* from the Awabakal language, *murri* from Kamilaroi, and *nyoongah* from Nyungar, as alternatives to *Aborigine*. None has made much headway nationally.

Aboriginal English is the technical name for a continuum of varieties of English between Australian Standard English and Australian English Creoles, which are often referred to by their speakers as *Blackfella English* or *blackfella talk*. In some parts of Australia, the transition from a traditional language to Aboriginal English has occurred within four generations in the 20th century, and the variety is used by Aborigines both among themselves and with non-Aborigines. Most varieties are intelligible to speakers of Australian Standard English, though certain norms are very different: for example, direct questions are typically not used to elicit information. There are also considerable differences in both pronunciation and grammar.

Some of the features of Aboriginal English are shared by non-standard varieties worldwide, as with the use of past and participial forms of certain verbs (*brang*, not *brought*), and double negatives (*He hasn't got no toys*), indicating that the form developed in contact with unschooled native speakers of English. Others are more characteristic of creoles, such as the non-occurrence of the verb *to be* (as in *His name John*, not 'His name is John') and lack of plural *s* (as in *two bird*, not 'two birds').

In areas where speakers continue to use traditional languages, such as Warlpiri and Pitjantjatjara, features from those languages occur in their English: as for example when *chicken* is pronounced 'tjicken'. There are also differences in vocabulary, including words borrowed from such languages, and distinctive uses of English words: thus, *granny* can be used in the South-West to refer to any male or female relative of someone's grandparents' generation. Some words can be used with a different grammatical function: *grow up* and *growl* may be used transitively, as in *My mother grew me up* and *She growled him*. Although the variety is generally stigmatized by white Australian society, it nonetheless functions as a symbol of Aboriginal identity. In addition, hybridization between English and Aboriginal languages is commonplace, as in the following excerpts from a magazine published in the Warlpiri language:

2001
- Yanulu August-rla Brisbane-kirra Yurrampi craft-wardingki-patu second National Indigenous Business Conference. ('In August, Yurrampi Crafts travelled to Brisbane to attend the second NIBC').
- September-rla-rnalu meeting wangkaja, wali natirli yanurnu committee member-patu panu purda-nyanjaku. ('During September, we attempted to hold an AGM, but many committee members were unable to attend.')

– quotations provided by Alexandra Welsch, in Gerhard Leitner, 'Australian Linguistics: a module in Australian Studies', in *Australian Language Matters (ALM)*, Jan–Mar, 12–14

Leitner also highlights a multilingual heritage that has traditionally been common among Aborigines, quoting the statement of Ngalawurr, an Aboriginal Australian:

1996 My language is Djapu, it's my father's language. My mother's language is Gumatji. My mother's mother's language is Gälpu. My mother's grandmother's language is Dhal'wangu. Rirratjingu were the women who delivered me. Birany Birany is my mother's land. The people who own the land there speak Gumatji. Gumatji men who belong to that land, their children speak Gumatji, and their mothers speak Djapu.

– (source as above), excerpt from *Australia's Aboriginal Languages*, Senior Secondary Assessment Board of South Australia, Canberra

To such already complex linguistic situations Aboriginal and Australian English are added. Prominent among varieties of Aboriginal English is *Roper River Creole*, also known as *Roper River Kriol*, *Kriol*, and *Roper Pidgin*. It is spoken in northern Australia from Queensland across the Barkly Tablelands and Roper River Basin through much of upper Northern Territory into the Kimberley Mountains of Western Australia. At first a contact language between Aborigines and outsiders, it is currently used by over 20,000 people in over a hundred communities, and for at least half of them it is the main language. Its continuum ranges from *Hebi Kriol* ('heavy creole': the basilect) to *Lait Kriol* ('light creole': the acrolect). Hebi Kriol is used mostly by mother-tongue speakers of an Aboriginal language while Lait Kriol is close to conventional Australian English.

A word in Kriol may have several different pronunciations along the continuum from heavy to light: thus, *policeman* is *balijiman* in the basilect, *blijiman* in the mesolect, and *plisman* in the acrolect. Most of the vocabulary is from English, in some cases with meanings altered to parallel equivalent words in Aboriginal languages: *kukwan* ('cooked one') means both 'cooked' and 'ripe'. There are also Aboriginal words in Kriol, such as *munanga* (a person of European descent). It has much in common with English-based pidgins and creoles in the Pacific, and some of its syntactic features are:

Grammar

1 The form of the transitive marker on verbs is *-im/-um*, as in *kilim* (from *kill him*: 'to hit'), *kukum* ('to cook'). Compare *kilim*, *kukim* in Tok Pisin in Papua-New Guinea.

2 The auxiliary *bin* ('been') marks completion: *Ai bin rid det buk* ('I have read the book').

3   Most of a minimal morphology relates to the verb, five prepositions covering grammatical relations: *blonga* ('belong'), as in *Aibin gibit im mani blonga daga* ('I been give it him money belong daga': I gave him some money for food); *longa* ('long'), as in *Imbin bogi longa riba* ('Him been bogi long of river': He swam in the river); *fo* ('for'), as in *Deibin hambagam mi fo daga* ('They been humbugging me for food': They pestered me for food); *from* ('from') as in *Olubat bin kaman from deya* ('All-about been coming from there': They came from there); and *garram* ('with'), as in: *Melabat kaan go garram yumob* ('Me-others cannot go with you-mob': We can't go with you people).

In addition to its distinct orthography, Kriol has a growing literature. In 1975, a school in Bamyili, where Kriol is a major means of communication, was allowed to introduce it as the pre-school language of instruction. In 1979, permission was sought and obtained from the Northern Territory Department of Education to introduce a bilingual Kriol/English programme, despite opposition from critics who did not accept Kriol as a real language.

New Zealand/Aotearoa

The Maori are the *tangata whenua* ('traditional people') of *Aotearoa* ('the Land of the Long White Cloud'), a name which has in recent years gained some international currency as an alternative for *New Zealand*, which was not in fact the first name given to the islands by Europeans. The Dutch explorer Abel Tasman (for whom the Tasman Sea and the Australian island of Tasmania are named) was the first European to reach (but not land in) Aotearoa, in 1642. He gave it the name *Staten Landt*, after the *Staten* (the legislative Estates General or parliament) of the Netherlands: compare *Staten Island* in New York, also once Dutch. The second name was also Dutch, *Nieuw Zeeland*, after the province of Zeeland: compare *Nieuw Amsterdam*, the original name of *New York*. In the 18th century, the British adopted the second name, anglicizing it to *New Zealand*. Many Maori and their sympathizers prefer *Aotearoa*, on occasion the two names come together as the combination *New Zealand/Aotearoa*, and *Aotearoa* is slowly becoming better known internationally.

The British explorer James Cook visited the islands in 1769, and the first European settlement was created by seal-hunters in 1792. When whaling stations were established and trade began with the colony of New South Wales in Australia, the territory became first an administrative extension of New South Wales, then a colony. In 1840, by the Treaty of Waitangi, the Maori ceded *kawanatanga* ('governorship', interpreted as 'sovereignty' by the British) to the British Crown. Subsequent disputes, especially about land, led to war in 1860–70. The relationship between Maori and *Pakeha* (the Maori term for Europeans, meaning both 'white' and 'strange') has been better than in many lands first settled then taken over during the Western European diaspora, but it continues to be uneasy, especially as regards land ownership and cultural and linguistic assimilation of Maori by Pakeha. Although ties between New Zealand and Britain have traditionally been strong, despite the distance, New Zealanders tend increasingly to see their future as 'Euro-Polynesian' rather than as an offshoot of Britain 'down under'.

New Zealand consists of *the North Island*, *the South Island*, and many small nearby islands. Wellington, the capital, and Auckland, the largest city, are both in the North Island. The head of state is the British monarch, represented by a governor-general, as in Canada and Australia, and New Zealand is a member of the Commonwealth. It has a population of *c.*3.6 million and an ethnic distribution of *c.*88% European, *c.*11% Polynesian (mainly Maori, but also from Western Samoa, Niue, and Rarotonga), and 1% others. Its languages are English and Maori (both official in courts of law), and other Polynesian languages. In New Zealand English traditionally, and in consequence in English at large, the name *Maori* when used as a noun can be pluralized, although there is no plural distinction in Maori. Traditionally, therefore, New Zealanders of European origin have referred to more than one Maori as *Maoris*, and many still do, whereas the Maori people and their sympathizers prefer *Maori* for both one and many.

New Zealand English

English has been used in New Zealand for over 200 years. Captain Cook recorded some Maori words in his diary, such as *pah* ('a fortified village') and *pounamu* ('greenstone, nephrite'). However, a more realistic starting-point for a distinctive New Zealand variety of English is the signing of the 1840 treaty, after which settlers from Britain and Ireland began to arrive in growing numbers, bringing many kinds of English with them. Parallels have often been drawn between Australian and New Zealand English and, although the two are by no means identical, to outsiders they often seem indistinguishable. The following points are significant in any discussion of general New Zealand usage:

Pronunciation

1   New Zealand English is non-rhotic, with the minor exception of the *Southland burr* among some speakers in Southland and Otago, South Island: an *r* in words like *afford* and *heart*, which most probably derives from Scots, since Otago was a predominantly Scottish settlement.

2   Although the traditional norm for educated spoken usage in New Zealand has been Received Pronunciation there are few 'straight' RP-speakers, but, as in Australia, there are many Near-RP speakers.

3   For some phoneticians there is a social-historical continuum in which there are three kinds of pronunciation: *Cultivated New Zealand*, *General New Zealand*, and *Broad New Zealand*. This again makes New Zealand English similar to Australian, in which similar categories have been established. Other phoneticians, however, regard the matter as unproved.

4   Many New Zealanders share with many speakers of Australian and Canadian English a rising tone in declarative sentences, often regarded as tentative by non-New Zealanders (as if inviting confirmation). As elsewhere, this pattern serves to check that a listener is still following what is being said and to invite agreement and sympathy when replying.

5   A distinction is often maintained between *wh* and *w* in words like *which* and *witch*. In words like *wharf*, however, where no near-homonym **warf* exists, aspiration is less detectable.

6   Such words as *ham*, *pen* sound to outsiders like 'hem' and 'pin'.

7   Short *i* is centralized to the weak vowel (schwa), so that to outsiders *fish and chips* sounds close to 'fush and chups' (and is often stigmatized as such), whereas in General Australian the sound is more like a tight version of 'feesh and cheeps'.

8   The weak vowel is also used in most unstressed syllables, as for the *i* in *rubbish* ('rubbesh'), and *affect* and *effect* sound the same.

9   Local speech has an *ah*-sound in such words as *castle* and *dance*, comparable to RP.

10 There is a tendency to pronounce *grown*, *mown*, *thrown* as two syllables with a schwa, as in 'growen', 'mowen', 'throwen', and to diphthongize some long vowels, as in *boot* ('boo-it') and *bean/been* ('bee-in').

11 Some words have distinctive pronunciations: *geyser* rhyming with 'riser'; *oral* with 'coral'; the first syllable of *vitamin* as in 'high', as in American and Scottish; the *Zea-* of *Zealand* spoken with the vowel of *kit*: 'Zilland'.

12 Final *-y* is lengthened in such words as *city*, *happy* to produce 'citee' and 'happee'.

13 The element *-day* in *Monday*, *Tuesday*, etc., is fully pronounced: 'Mon-day', etc.

14 Announcers of the Broadcasting Corporation of New Zealand are required to pronounce words and place-names of Maori origin (as best they can) as in Maori, rather than in 'traditional' Anglicized forms: for example, *kowhai* not as 'koai' or 'kowai' but as 'kawfai'.

Grammar

1   Standard New Zealand is broadly the same as Standard British, but some distinctions exist, such as the plural forms 'rooves' and 'wharves' rather than 'roofs' and 'wharfs'.

2   In spelling, New Zealanders, like Australians, use *-ise* as in *centralise*, not *-ize*. In British usage, *-ise* is common and *-ize* widely used, while in American usage *-ize* is the norm.

3   Countable nouns of Maori origin often appear, as in Maori itself, without a plural ending: *iwi* ('a tribe'), as in *A Maori nation exists comprising various iwi* (not *iwis*); *marae* a courtyard of a meeting house, as in *Marae have always been open to all* (not *maraes*). The move towards incorporating this Maori usage into English when Maori nouns are used appears to be gaining some strength in the wider world.

4   The word *Maori* is nowadays commonly spoken and written in plural contexts without the final *-s*, as in *There were many Maori at the meeting*. Such usage, however, remains controversial.

5 In recent works of New Zealand literature, Maori speakers of non-standard English are at times portrayed, drawing attention to syntactic aspects of Maori English: *You big, brave fellow, eh?* (Bruce Mason, 1963); *Here's your basket nearly finish* (Patricia Grace, 1986).

Vocabulary: Polynesian adoptions

1 Loanwords from Maori include many names for flora and fauna, and an increasing number of words for social arrangements, customs, etc.: *aue* (an interjection expressing astonishment, distress, etc.); *haere mai* (a greeting); *iwi* ('a people, tribe'); *kiwi* (a flightless bird, adopted as a national symbol and, with a capital *K*, the nickname for New Zealanders at large: *Will any Kiwis be there?*); *kowhai* (a tree with golden-yellow flowers); *mana* ('power, prestige, authority'); *manuwhiri* ('a visitor, guest'); *Maoritanga* ('being a Maori, Maori traditions'); *marae* ('the courtyard of a meeting-house, a forum'); *mauri* ('the life principle'); *rahui* ('a sign warning against trespass'); *totara* (a conifer with dark red timber); *tuatara* (an iguana-like lizard with yellow spines); *tupuna* ('an ancestor'). The small number of verbs includes *hikoi* ('to march') and *hongi* ('to press noses', as a token of friendship).

2 Some Maori words have been so Anglicized that they no longer sound or look like Maori: *biddy-bid* (a plant with prickly burrs: Maori *piripiri*); *cockabully* (a small fish: Maori *kokopu*); *kit* (a flax basket: Maori *kete*).

3 There are many Maori place-names: *Aotearoa* ('Land of the Long White Cloud'); *Waitangi* ('Weeping Water', that is, a waterfall).

4 Compounds containing both Maori and English words: *Golden Kiwi* (the name of a national lottery); *kiwifruit* (now an international term for the Chinese gooseberry); *Pakeha traditions*.

5 Loanwords from Samoan are not widely used by non-Samoan New Zealanders. They include: *aiga* ('an extended family'); *fale* ('a house'); *palagi* (a non-Samoan); *talofa* (a ceremonial greeting), and the returned loanword *afakasi* ('a half-caste').

Vocabulary: Distinctive English usages

1 Fixed adjective and noun phrases include: *chilly bin* (a portable insulated container for keeping food and drink cool); *informal vote* (a spoiled vote: also Australian); *silver beet* ('seakale beet').

2 Noun-noun compounds include: *Canterbury lamb* (the meat of sheep from a particular province); *grass fence* (a strip of long grass along an electric fence: a barrier to sheep even when the current is off); *share-milker* (a tenant farmer on a dairy farm who receives a share of the profits).

3 Uses of the diminutive suffix *-ie* are: *boatie* ('a boating enthusiast'); *swannie* ('an all-weather woollen jacket, from the trademark *Swanndri*); *truckie* ('a truck-driver', also Australian); *wharfie* ('a waterside worker, stevedore', also Australian).

4 Uses of the diminutive suffix *-o/-oh* include: *arvo* ('afternoon', also Australian); *bottle-oh* (a dealer in used bottles); *compo* ('compensation', especially for an injury); *smoko/smoke-oh* (a break from work for a rest, with or without smoking a cigarette).

5   Adaptations of general words to New Zealand situations include: *bach* (a holiday house at the beach: a clipping of *bachelor*); *section* ('a building plot'); *tramp* ('to walk for long distances in rough country'), hence *tramper* ('a person who tramps').

6   Adaptations of general words to new uses, shared with Australian, include: *creek* ('a stream'); *crook* ('ill'); *go crook at* ('to be angry with'); the verb *farewell* as in *to farewell someone* ('to honour [someone]', at a ceremonial occasion or party, before he or she leaves a job, a place, etc.).

7   Specific loanwords from Australian include: *backblocks* ('land in the remote interior'); *battler* ('someone who struggles against the odds'); *dill* ('a fool, simpleton'); *ocker* ('a boor'); *offsider* ('a companion, deputy, partner'); *shanghai* ('a catapult').

8   British dialect words used as standard, and all also occurring in Australian, include: *barrack* ('to shout or jeer' at players in a game, etc.); *bowyang* (a band or strip round a trouser-leg below the knee, to prevent trousers from dragging on the ground); *burl* ('a try or attempt', as in *give it a burl*); *chook* ('a chicken, fowl'); *dunny* ('a lavatory'); *larrikin* ('a hooligan'); *lolly* ('a sweet of any kind, especially boiled); *postie* (a person delivering post: shared with Scottish and Canadian); *Rafferty's rules* ('no rules at all'); *wowser* ('a killjoy, spoilsport').

9   Like the Australians, New Zealanders are conscious of their slang, as indicated by two publications: *A Personal Kiwi–Yankee Slanguage Dictionary*, by Louis S. Leland (John McIndoe, 1980), and *A Dictionary of Kiwi Slang*, by David McGill (Mills Publications, 1988). Eric Partridge's *Dictionary of Slang and Unconventional English* (1937; 8th edn 1984, ed. Paul Beale) contains much specifically NZ material, reflecting Partridge's NZ origins.

10 A distinctive item of slang is *Godzone*, a mid-19th-century clipping of *God's Own Country*, applied by British settlers to various territories around the world, and picked up in Australia and even more so in New Zealand: 'On warm summer evenings, when it is packed with Polynesians and the shops are livid with neon, it seems more like Asia than Godzone' (a comment on Karangahape Road, in *Auckland, their Auckland*, Lansdowne Press, 1983).

Maori, English, and Maori English

The word *Maori* means 'of the usual kind, ordinary, normal'. In an overall Maori population of *c.*500,000, about a third people speak Maori, which (like Hawaiian, Samoan, and Tongan) belongs to the Polynesian branch of the Malayo-Polynesian language family. While all Polynesian languages have much in common, Maori differs from the others in several significant ways: for example, Maori *r* commonly corresponds to Hawaiian and Samoan *l* (compare Maori *aroha* and Hawaiian *aloha*, 'love', used also as a social greeting). Regional variation in pronunciation between usage in the North Island and the South Island can be seen in such pairs as NI/SI *inanga/inaka* (a kind of fish), *mingimingi/mikimiki* (an evergreen shrub), and the NI place-name *Waitangi* (no hard *g*), SI *Waitaki*. In words conventionally spelt with *wh* (as in *whare* and *kowhai*), some tribes use *hw* and others a sound closer to *f*. Such variations may affect how Maori words are pronounced in English.

Just as complexities and distinctions of sound within Maori have implications for New Zealand English, so similar complexities and distinctions in English have implications for Maori. Thus, the traditional Maori version of 'London' is *Ranana*, of 'Bible' is *paipera*, and of 'sheep' is *hipi*. These adaptations were made in the early stages of Maori/English contact, and, although such forms continue, comparable adaptations nowadays are unlikely because most Maori are familiar with English pronunciation from childhood.

The widely used term *Pakeha* (for a white person or European) entered English at the beginning of the 19th century, and is used both with and without an initial capital letter. In general English use the plural is *pakehas*, but *pakeha* (both singular and plural, in the Maori style) is now increasingly common. Some examples of its use in print are: 'Rua came from Taupo to the coastal district to work on the farm of a Pakeha' (R. Finlayson, *Brown Man's Burden*, 1938); 'Most damaging of all, the treaty [of Waitangi] failed to safeguard the standing of the Maori in their own country, for they have become an underdeveloped minority surrounded by pakeha affluence in a society where pakeha values have become the measure of all things. Cultural assimilation has been the 20th century norm—the whites providing the culture and the Maoris the assimilation' (Robert Macdonald, *Guardian*, 3 March 1984). The term *pakeha Maori* has been used for a European who adopts the Maori way of life.

In the later 19th and earlier 20th twentieth centuries, the use of the Maori language was officially discouraged in New Zealand schools. Many Maori concurred with this policy, seeing English as the language likely to give their children a greater advantage in later life, but in recent decades there has been a revival of Maori. Institutions known in Maori as *kohanga reo* and in English as *language nests* have been established for pre-school children, and many Maori now seek to raise bilingual children. Although Maori has been recognized as an official language in the courts of law, it is too early to say what the long-term effect of this growing recognition will be. All Maori(s) speak English, but few Pakeha(s) speak Maori. A diminishing number of Maori people speak their language fluently, but attempts are now being made to give greater prominence to the language and its culture. Unless there is a massive improvement, however, its fate may be comparable to the decline of Gaelic in the highlands and islands of Scotland.

Pronunciation

1 There is no standard spoken Maori.

2 No more than one consonant occurs before a vowel, hence the simplification of consonant clusters in words taken from English, as for example *Bible* becoming *paipera*.

3 The written consonant cluster *ng* is pronounced as in *singer*, not *finger*, whether initial or medial. There is therefore no hard *g* in the place-name *Waitangi* ('Wa-ee-tang-ee').

4 Hawaiian, Samoan, and English *l* have tended to be matched by a Maori *r* as in: *aroha* (Hawaiian *aloha* 'love'); *whare* (Samoan *fale* 'house'); *Ranana* (English *London*).

The language was unwritten before the arrival in the early 19th century of British missionaries. In creating a written form for it, the missionaries did not always adequately equate its elements with equivalents in English. A major feature of their work was the decision that vowel length in Maori did not need to be reflected in spelling (although diacritical marks have since been optional). Some present-day scholars have adopted a system of doubling long vowels: *Maaori* for of *Maori*, *kaakaa* for *kaka* ('parrot'); *kaakaapoo* for *kakapo*. However, since most printing of the language shows the older conventions, it seems likely that the missionaries' style will prevail.

From the beginning, European settlers adopted Maori names for physical features and tribal settlements, adapting the pronunciation to a greater or less degree. Thus, the place-name *Paekakariki* (with stress on the first 'ka') was Anglicized to 'Paikakeriki' (with stress on the 'ri') and frequently shortened to 'Paikak'. The placename *Whangarei* (traditionally pronounced 'Fangarei', without a hard *g*) was Anglicized to 'Wongarei' (also without a hard *g*). Most of the Maori names for the distinctive NZ flora (*kowhai, nikau, pohutukawa, rimu, totara*) and fauna (*kiwi, takahe, tuatara, weta*) were also adopted and varyingly adapted into New Zealand English.

According to the New Zealand Geographic Board, the body charged by Act of Parliament with registering place-names, 58% of officially recognized names (including those of rivers and mountains) are of Maori origin, 42% of European origin. The breakdown between the two islands reflects the patterns of Maori and European settlement: in the North Island, 79% Maori, 21% European; in the South Island, 67% European, 33% Maori. The longest officially recognized place-name is *Taumatawhakatangihangakouauotamateapokaiwhenuakitanatahu*, the name of a hill in southern Hawkes Bay in the North Island: 'The hill on which Tamatea, circumnavigator of the land, played his kouau (flute) to his loved one.' In this name, the elements are clearly recognizable, but that is not always the case with Maori place-names, either because they have changed with time or have been altered by Europeans, as in *Amuri* from Maori *Haumuri* ('East Wind'), and *Petone* from Maori *Pito-one* ('End of the Beach'). Nevertheless, many Maori names can be understood, such as *Awakino* ('valley ugly': Ugly Valley), *Maunganui* ('mountain big': Big Mountain), and *Waikaremoana* ('Great Lake of Rippling Water').

The issue of how far English-speakers should attempt to adopt Maori pronunciations of such words has, for many years, been a major point of linguistic discussion in New Zealand. The BCNZ now attempts, not always successfully, to use a Maori pronunciation at all times. Two features of colloquial New Zealand English are frequently attributed to Maori influence: the use of the tag question *eh?* and the plural *youse*. However, while these may have been encouraged by Maori structures, they are both found elsewhere in the English-speaking world, including Britain, Ireland, and North America.

In the later 19th and early 20th centuries, the use of Maori was officially discouraged in schools. Many Maori concurred with this policy, seeing English as the language likely to give their children the greater advantage in life. In more recent times, however, there has been a resurgence in the use of Maori as a marker of ethnic and cultural identity. *Language nests* or *kohanga reo* have been established for pre-school children, and many Maori now aim at a balanced bilingualism. Maori has been part of NZ broadcasting only since 1988. Although Maori has now been recognized as an official language in the courts, it is too early to say what effect this growing recognition will have in the long term.

The term *Maori English* is commonly used for English as typically spoken by Maori people, but the features of such a variety are not well defined. The label may therefore mislead, because such English is not necessarily spoken by all Maori or exclusively by Maori; it may be spoken by Pakeha in areas where there are many Maori, incidentally or as an expression of solidarity. If a distinctive Maori usage is identifiable, it is usually because of voice quality and a tendency towards syllable-timed speech. Items considered typical of Maori usage tend to be much the same as non-standard usage in other parts of the English-speaking world, such as, in pro-nunciation, 'tree' for *three* and *dose* for 'those' (cf. some Irish and North American usage) and in grammar *Me and Joe went there* and *He learned me to do it.* Such expressions as *I went by my Auntie's, Who's your name?*, and *To me, the ball* ('Let me have the ball') may be more specifically Maori. Typical vocabulary items include both Maori and non-Maori words: *kai* ('food'), *fellers* ('people, males', often in the vocative *you fellers*, and pronounced like 'fullahs').

Although not usually called *Maori English*, there is a range of written usage in which Maori vocabulary occurs freely, without italicization or glossing, and without worrying whether a Pakeha will understand it. An example is:

> **1986** This indeed may be the nub from which this book gains
> perspective—that even after 145 years of Pakeha terms of
> reference, ka tu tonu the Maori. And so they should remain as
> yet to be consulted tangata whenua. Whether this book bears
> fruit will depend on a response to the kaupapa laid down on
> marae throughout Aotearoa at the feet of the manuwhiri.
> – Philip Whaanga, *New Zealand Listener*, 5 April

The average Pakeha will not understand enough Maori to grasp all of this message—and that may indeed be part of the message. It is not clear whether such an approach seeks to reflect a code-switching typical among Maori or is offered as a model for relaxed hybrid usage. In either case, although it remains unusual, it suggests that in course of time a 'Maorified' lexis and style within New Zealand English may develop, and become unremarkable. Evidence of this can found in the works of Witi Ihimaera, Keri Hulme, and Patricia Grace, the last of whom has adapted English prose fiction to Maori forms, rather than the other way round.

Fijian, Hindi, and Fiji English

The Republic of Fiji consists of an archipelago of some hundreds of islands in the southern Pacific, of which about a hundred are inhabited. Agriculture (primarily sugar cane) dominates the economy, but fish, timber, copra, ginger, and gold are all exported, and tourism has been significant, although sometimes disturbed by social events linked with ethnic tensions and political disagreements. The islands became a British colony in 1874 and an independent state within the Commonwealth in 1970, left it in 1987, and returned to it in 1997. The islands became multi-ethnic during the colonial period. Their population of *c.*800,000 consists mainly of ethnic Fijians and ethnic Indians ('Indo-Fijians' or 'Fiji Indians'), descendants of indentured labourers brought to Fiji by the British to work on the plantations. The two communities are of roughly equal size, the Indians now slightly in the majority. There are also small communities of Chinese, Europeans, Polynesians, and people of mixed background. The ethnically and linguistically distinct group the Rotumans are from an island administered by Fiji.

The three main languages spoken in Fiji are Fijian, Hindi, and English. Of these, English is the first language of a tiny minority (perhaps 3% of the population), but its influence on the lives of most Fijians is immense. Fiji does not have an official *national* language as such, language status being defined in the Constitution only insofar as parliamentary use is concerned. The 1990 Constitution states that the language of the Fiji Parliament is English, though Fijian and Hindi may also be used. English is the principal medium of government, administration, law, and trade, dominates in education and the media, and is an important lingua franca among people with different first languages. Hybridization among the three languages is routine.

Fijian English ranges from vernacular to standard. As the language of education, it is modelled on British Standard English with an RP accent, a target achieved by few. Although some early plantation labourers knew Melanesian Pidgin and later labourers arrived in Fiji speaking a variety of the pidgin as used in Queensland, a stable local pidgin did not develop. Features of the local English include:

Pronunciation

Words from Fijian and Hindi tend to lose some phonological features in English: for example, the Fijian word *dalo* ('taro', a plant with tuberous roots) has a nasal opening sound ('ndalo') that does not occur in Fijian English; *qari* (a kind of crab) has an opening ng-sound ('ngqari') where English is simply *gari*; in Hindi words, aspirated initial consonants do not carry that aspiration into English, so that *bhajan* (a kind of Hindu devotional song) is pronounced 'badjan'), *dhania* ('coriander') is 'dania', and *ghazal* (a kind of song) is 'gazal'.

Grammar

1 The Fijian focus marker *ga* is often used, as in *You ga, you ga tell it* ('You're the one who tells it'), as is the politeness marker *mada*, as in *Wait mada* ('Please wait').

2 The number *one* is used as an indefinite article, as in Indian English: *Tonight I am going to one party.*

3 There is a first-person dual use of *us two*, in contrast with both singular and plural: *Us two [are] poor so I can't give you any of us two's money.*

4 The word *fella* is used as a third-person human pronoun: *Fella told me* ('He told me').

5 English inflectional endings are added to Fijian and Hindi words: thus, *-s* is added to *vilagi* ('stranger') to form the plural *vilagis* and to Hindi *sirdar* 'foreman') to get *sirdars*; *-ing* is added to *bula* ('hello') to get *bulaing* ('helloing', 'saying hello'); and *-ed* is added to *choro* ('to steal') to get *choroed* ('stole').

Vocabulary

1 Many words are taken directly from Fijian and Hindi, as shown above. Typical examples are: Fijian *tanoa* (a bowl for making *kava*, a narcotic drink made from a kind of pepper plant); Hindi *roti* (flat unleavened bread).

2   Hybridization is common, notably in compound words: with Fijian, *full kasou* ('completely drunk'), *lovo food* ('food cooked in an earth oven', with *lovo-ed* meaning 'cooked in an earth oven'), *talanoa session* ('chat session'), *talasiga area* ('grassland'); with Hindi, *gang sirdar* (cane-cutting gang foreman'), *no ghar* ('no house', meaning 'destitute').

Such features as *us two* and *fella* are similar to those in Melanesian Pidgin English and indigenous languages; others are shared not only with Pidgin and Creole but also with such vernaculars as Singlish in Singapore, as for example absence of the verb *to be* (as in *That one nice house* 'That is a nice house').

Melanesian Pidgin English: Tok Pisin, and Solomon Islands Pidgin

Melanesian Pidgin English is the name commonly given by language scholars to three varieties of Pidgin English spoken in the Melanesian states of Papua New Guinea (where it is called *Tok Pisin*, 'Talk Pidgin', pronounced 'Tock Pizzin'), the Solomon Islands (where its name is simply *Pijin*), and Vanuatu (where it is known as *Bislama*, pronounced 'Beess-lah-mah', an adaptation of 'Beach La Mar', which is in turn an adaptation of either or both French *bêche-de-mer* and Portuguese *bicho do mar* ('small sea creature', a term referring to the sea slug). There is a degree of mutual intelligibility among the three pidgins, the umbrella term *Melanesian Pidgin English* marking a common historical development without being a name used by any actual speakers of the languages in the group.

Melanesian Pidgin in its turn descends from a maritime pidgin spoken over much of the Pacific in the 19th century, as a lingua franca between English-speaking Europeans and Pacific Islanders. It was variously known as *South Seas English* and *South Seas Jargon* (or simply *Jargon*), and was a trade jargon of traders and whalers. The whalers first hunted in the eastern Pacific, but by 1820 were calling regularly at ports in Melanesia and taking on crew members from among the local people, communicating with them in Jargon, which began to stabilize on plantations throughout the Pacific area after 1860, wherever Islanders worked as indentured labourers. This original form is now known technically as *Pacific Jargon English*. It was learned by Papua New Guineans and others working for periods of time on plantations in Queensland in Australia, on Samoa and Fiji, and in Papua New Guinea itself. Typically, male workers learned it and took it back to the villages, where it was passed on first to boys then to women and girls.

The development of Melanesian Pidgin has been markedly different in the three countries concerned for three reasons: differences in the local underlying languages; the presence of other European languages in both Papua New Guinea and Vanuatu; and different colonial and subsequent policies. In New Guinea, there was a period of German administration (1884–1914), before the British and Australians took over, whereas the people of Vanuatu, during a century of French colonial rule (1880–1980), were in constant contact with the French government and French planters. For a time, Vanuatu was a Franco-British condominium, and the use of French has continued since independence in 1980.

Papua New Guinea (PNG) is known in Tok Pisin as *Papua Niugini*, and occupies the eastern half of the island of New Guinea and some 600 adjacent islands, the largest of which are New Britain, New Ireland, and Bougainville. The capital is Port Moresby and the population is *c*.4.4 million. Prior to independence in 1975, the southern half (Papua) was an Australian territory from 1906 and the northern part (New Guinea) was administered by Australia under a mandate from the League of Nations after the First World War, when the territory ceased to be a German colony. That mandate was continued by the United Nations until 1975. The remainder of the island was formerly a Dutch colony which became the Indonesian province of Irian Jaya. Little is known about the history of the many peoples inhabiting the region; the terrain is rugged, many villages have no road or river links with other settlements, and some can be reached only by walking for days over difficult terrain. Travel by air is more important than by road or sea.

The coastal population is thinly clustered in villages, and over a third of the population lives in highland valleys. The terrain of PNG is rugged, many villages have no road or river links with other settlements, and some can be reached only by walking for days. Travel by air is therefore more important than by road or sea. While limited settlement by Europeans has extended over a century, contact with many internal regions has been recent. Many communities were not known before 1930, when the discovery of gold encouraged further exploration. Even in the 1950s, Australian patrols were still establishing contact with people in remoter areas.

Such conditions have fostered great cultural and linguistic diversity; there are *c*.700–750 languages belonging to two families, Papuan and Austronesian, as well as both Tok Pisin and an indigenous pidgin, Hiri Motu. Both serve as lingua francas and share official status with English. Tok Pisin was officially so named and spelled in 1981. It is also known informally as both *Tok Boi* ('Talk Boy') and *Pidgin*, and has three technical names among language scholars: *Papua New Guinea Pidgin*, relating only to its locale, and, as part of a larger phenomenon, the rarer term *Neo-Melanesian/Neomelanesian*, and the commoner *Melanesian Pidgin* (along with *Pijin* and *Bislama*).

Hiri Motu is based on the Austronesian language Motu, originally spoken around the Port Moresby area (now the National Capital District): a reduced form of Motu was employed on *hiri* (trading expeditions) along the Papuan Gulf, whence the name. The language is used by *c*.10% of the people, mainly in Papua. It was once called *Police Motu*, because of its association with the colonial police force, but it seems likely that the actual lingua franca of this force was Tok Pisin and Hiri Motu was used for dealing with particular local people.

Tok Pisin developed in the New Guinea islands and spread to the mainland *c*.1880. Although a by-product of colonialism, which then sustained it, Tok Pisin became more than a means of communication between native people and their colonizers; it is now the primary lingua franca in PNG, acquired by children as a first language. In sociolinguistic terms, it is an expanded pidgin undergoing creolization: that is, although at first it was a rough-and-ready go-between language, it has become a community language in its own right, with its own resources but also drawing on Standard English. It has over 20,000 native speakers and just under half of the population of PNG uses it to varying extents.

Grammar

1 Many of Tok Pisin's structural traits have been transferred from local languages, and even where items derived from English are used for grammatical purposes, their patterns and meanings tend to follow structures in these 'substrate' languages.

2 In most if not all Melanesian languages and in Tok Pisin, but not in English, there is a distinction between inclusive and exclusive first-person plural pronouns. Where English has the single form *we*, Tok Pisin has two forms: inclusive *yumi* ('you-me') and exclusive *mipela* ('me-fellow'). Although the words used to make the distinction are from English, the meanings derive from categories in the local languages.

3 The element *pela* ('fellow') also serves as a suffix marking attributives, as in *gutpela man* ('a good man'), *naispela haus* ('a nice house'), *wanpela meri* ('a woman'). In addition, in the pronoun system, it appears in both the first- and second-person plural: *mipela* ('we' exclusive) and *yupela* ('you' plural).

Vocabulary

1 The words of Tok Pisin derive from five sources: English, German, Portuguese, Spanish, Polynesian languages, and PNG languages. English provides most of the *c*.2,500 basic words, such as *mi* ('I', 'me'), *yu* ('you' singular), *askim* ('to ask'; 'a question'), and *lukautim* ('to take care of', from *look out him*, where *him* marks transitivity). German, the language of colonial administration in the northern part of New Guinea from 1884 to 1914, as with *rausim* ('to get rid of') and *beten* ('to pray'). Portuguese and Spanish words widely found in European-based pidgin and creole languages and also occurring in Tok Pisin, include *save* ('to know', from *sabir/saber*) and *pikinini* ('small child', from *pequeno* 'small'). Words from Polynesian languages include *kaikai* ('food'), *tambu* ('taboo', from *tabu*). Words from indigenous PNG languages include: *kiau* ('an egg', adopted from Kuanua, a language of East New Britain, which has played an important part as a substrate).

2 Traditionally, Europeans have regarded Tok Pisin as a bastardized form of English. In it, some coarse everyday words have taken on different and socially neutral meanings: *baksait* (from 'backside') refers to the back rather than the buttocks; *as* (from 'arse/ass') also refers to the buttocks, but has extended to refer to the basis or foundation of anything, so that *as bilong diwai* means 'the base or foot of a tree' and *as bilong lo* means 'the basis of a law'; *bagarap* (from 'bugger up') is used as noun and verb, as in *Em kisim bagarap* ('He had an accident') and *Pik i bagarapim gaden* ('The pig ruined the garden'). Others are: *sit* (from 'shit'), as in *sit bilong paia* ('shit belonging to fire': ashes); *bulsitim* (verb, from 'bullshit': to deceive). The Tok Pisin word for excrement is locally derived: *pekpek*.

3 Tok Pisin has other terms of abuse often quite different from or completely unrelated to English, including *puslama* ('sea slug') for a lazy person, and *tu kina meri* (where *tu* is 'two', *kina* is a unit of currency, and *meri* is 'woman') for a prostitute.

4 Accounts by Europeans often contain apparently concocted versions of pidgin expressions, such as an alleged circumlocution for *piano*. A German traveller in the south Pacific, A. Deiber, wrote in 1902: 'All in all the black does not lack a sense of humour. His description of the first piano brought to the German South Seas is also delightful. It was a Papuan who, horrified, told of big fellow box, white fellow master fight him plenty too much, he cry (of the box which the white man beats so much that it screams).'

5 The following list of everyday words in Tok Pisin has been extracted and adapted from the K section in *The Jacaranda Dictionary and Grammar of Melanesian Pidgin*, compiled by the Rev Francis Mihalic (Jacaranda Press, 1971, Papua New Guinea and Australia).

kom a comb; the horn of an animal: *kom bilong bulmakau* ('the horn of a cow')

komim to comb (something) *Komim grass bilong yu* ('Comb your hair')

komiti a committee; a member of a committee

kompas a compass, a spirit level, a surveyor's instrument: *makim long kompas* ('to take one's bearings, to survey land')

kona corner

Kongkong a Chinese person (a term to which the Chinese object: presumably from *Hong Kong*)

kontrak a contract, an agreement: *mekim kontrak* make a contract

kopi coffee: *pikinini bilong kopi* coffee beans; *sospen bilong kopi, kopipot* coffee pot

kot (1) court, lawsuit, trial, accusation, judgement: *baim kot* to bribe the court, to pay a fine imposed by a court; *bikpela kot* ('a major trial'); *lai long kot* ('to commit perjury'); *mekim kot* ('hold a trial'); *kot bilong lasde* ('court belong last day': the last judgement, in Christianity)

kotim to bring a suit against, to sue, to bring a complaint against, to take (someone) to court; to complain about: Ol i kotim mi long kiap ('They brought a suit against me'; 'They complained about me to the captain/district officer'; *Em i kotim mi long tisa* ('He complained about me to the teacher').

Tok Pisin has undergone considerable expansion in both structure and function. Although English is the medium of education, Tok Pisin is used in a variety of public domains, not only in political debates in the House of Assembly, where it is the preferred medium, but also in broadcasting and journalism. For all its new functions it has drawn heavily on English. Indeed, so much English has been borrowed into the language, particularly by educated people, that there are now two main varieties: *urban pidgin* and *rural* or *bush pidgin*. There are also a number of registers, such as Tok Piksa ('talk picture'), a way of speaking in similes and metaphors, and Tok Bokkis ('talk box'), a way of giving words hidden meanings. Most printed material in Tok Pisin was formerly religious, centred on a translation of the Bible, but since 1970 there has been a weekly newspaper in Tok Pisin, *Wantok* ('One Talk': one language), a term commonly used to refer to members of one's own clan group, and given to the newspaper as an expression of solidarity among its readers and PNG people generally. The use of Tok Pisin for literary purposes is also becoming more common.

The second variety of Melanesian Pidgin English is in the Solomon Islands, where it is commonly known as *Pijin* and technically and rather grandiosely as *Neo-Solomonic*. The Solomon Islands constitute a country of the south-western Pacific. English is the official language and Pijin is spoken by about half the population of just under 400,000. The Solomon Islands are both a constitutional monarchy and a member of the Commonwealth. There are indigenous languages, but both English and Pijin are official. The islands were a British colony from the late 19th century, partly a German colony from 1885 to 1900, and have been independent since 1978.

Copra plantations were established in the early 20th century, and labourers employed there came with a knowledge of Pidgin from working in both Queensland and Fiji. The Solomons variety stabilized early and several religious missions adopted it for use, though it never gained the status of Tok Pisin in PNG or Bislama in Vanuatu. Although the first Europeans to discover the islands were Spanish, the Solomon Islanders (unlike the Papua New Guineans with German in colonial New Guinea, and the Ni-Vanuatu, with French) have not had close contact with any other European language besides English. Their Pijin is therefore closer than Tok Pisin to conventional English and uses less non-English vocabulary. It is also grammatically more elaborate, with more prepositions and a greater range of connectives, such as *so, bat, bikos* ('so, but, because'). An example:

> **1988** Mitufala jes marit nomoa ia so mitufala no garem eni
> pikinini iet. Mi traehad fo fosim haosben blong mi fo mitufala
> go long sip bat taem ia hemi had tumas fo faendem rum long
> sip bikos plande pipol wandem go-go hom fo Krismas tu.
> [Translation: We've just got married only we haven't got any
> children yet. I tried hard to force my husband to go on the ship,
> but times were hard and we couldn't find room on board because
> plenty of people wanted to go home for Christmas too.]
> – from J. Holm, *Pidgin and Creole Languages*, vol. 2, 536

Bislama

Bislama, the third variety of Melanesian Pidgin English, is spoken in the Republic of Vanuatu, to the south of the Solomon Islands, a nation consisting of twelve main islands and 70 islets. Its capital is Port-Vila, its economy is mainly agriculture and fishing, and its population is *c.*170,000. Its people, known as the *ni-Vanuatu*, are *c.*91% Melanesian, 3% Polynesian, 3% French, and 3% other. Until 1980, the island group was known as the *New Hebrides*, jointly administered since the late 19th century by Britain and France. Its languages are English, French, and Bislama (all official) and a number of indigenous languages.

Bislama is descended from *Beach La Mar* (also called *Sandalwood English*), an English-based contact language of the mid-19th century in and around the New Hebrides. Its primary names derive from trade in edible sea slugs (French: *bêche-de-mer*) and sandalwood. The Bislama version of the constitution of Vanuatu states: *Lanwis blong Ripablik blong Vanuatu, hemia Bislama. Trifala lanwis blong mekem ol wok blong kantr ya, i gat Bislama mo Inglis mo Franis* ('The language of the

Republic of Vanuatu is Bislama. There are three languages for conducting the business of the country, Bislama, English, and French').

Hawaii, Hawaiian, and Hawaiian English

The Hawaiian islands are an archipelago in the Pacific, and since 1959 have been the 50th state of the United States, with their capital Honolulu on the island of Oahu. The population of c.1 million is of mixed backgrounds: Caucasian, Filipino, Hawaiian, Japanese, and other, no ethnic group forming a majority. The ancestors of the original Polynesian population reached the islands over a thousand years ago, as part of the long, slow diaspora that took the Maori from Tahiti to Aotearoa. The first European to visit the islands was Captain James Cook in 1778, who named them the *Sandwich Islands*, after the Earl of Sandwich. The islanders were organized in a hierarchy of *alii* ('nobles'), *kahuna* ('priests'), and common people, and were not united until 1810, when King Kamehameha I brought all the islands under his rule, encouraging trade with the US and elsewhere. The *alii* rejected their own system of religion and taboos c.1819, American missionaries arrived in 1820, there was a brief British occupation in 1843, the monarchy was overthrown in 1893, and the islands were annexed by the US in 1898, in the same year that it acquired Puerto Rico and the Philippines.

Present-day Hawaii depends mainly on food production and tourism. A plantation system for sugar cane and pineapples was established in the 19th century, as in many other Pacific islands. The expansion of the system added to the native labour force thousands of workers from China, Korea, the Philippines, Japan, and elsewhere, so that by the start of the 20th century ethnic Hawaiians (through disease and the increase in immigrants) accounted for less than 20% of the population. There are now fewer than 10,000 full-blooded Hawaiians, although there are many part-Hawaiians. Most of them now speak Hawaii Creole English or American English and not Hawaiian, though attempts are being made to revive the language. Other languages spoken on the islands include Japanese, Filipino, Korean, Portuguese, Samoan, Spanish, and kinds of Chinese. English is the administrative and general language of the state, and has been the language of education for well over a century.

The Hawaiian language belongs to the Malayo-Polynesian family and is closely related to Samoan and Maori. Its words end in vowels, as in *lei* ('garland') and *kahuna* ('priest', in the traditional Hawaiian religion), consonants are separated by vowels (as in *Kalakaua* and *Lapakahi*), and many words have no consonants (as in *aia* 'there', *oiaio* 'truly') or more vowels than consonants (as in *heiau* 'temple'). Among the differences between Hawaiian and some other Polynesian languages are: *k* for *t* (as in *kapu* for *tabu*, 'taboo'); *l* for *r* (as in *kalo* for *taro*); a glottal stop where some have *k*, marked in technical writing by a reverse inverted apostrophe (') and in general usage by an ordinary apostrophe ('), as in *mu'umu'u* or *mu'umu'u* for *mukumuku* ('shapeless', and the name for a loose-fitting woman's dress). Because the glottal stop is part of the sound system, it is contrastive: for example, *ka'u* means 'mine' while *kau* means 'yours'. The word *Hawaii* itself contains a glottal stop in Hawaiian, as often shown by means of an apostrophe in older English texts: *Hawai'i*.

The sound written as *l* may have been originally close to *r*. When missionary printers standardized the language in roman letters after 1820, they voted 6 to 2 in favour of *l*. In addition, when the personal name of King Kamehameha II was set in type, he preferred the visual form *Liholiho* to *Rihoriho*. In Hawaiian, repeating a word base usually has a special meaning: thus, *lau* ('a leaf') but *laulau* ('a bundle of food baked in leaves'), *pai* ('to slap') but *paipai* ('to drive fish by slapping the water').

Borrowings into Hawaiian have generally been adapted to its phonology: *hokela* ('hotel'); *kelepona* ('telephone'); *kula* ('school'); *nupepa* ('newspaper'); *pipi* ('beef'); *puke* ('book'); and such Biblical names as *Apikaila* ('Abigail'), *Kaniela* ('Daniel'), *Malia* ('Maria'), *Kamaki* ('Thomas'). Although borrowings from Hawaiian into English are common locally, they are few in the general language: *a'a* (for lava that cools rough) and *pahoehoe* (for lava that cools smooth), and *ukelele/ukulele* (a jumping flea whose name was given to an adaptation of the Portuguese guitar).

The distinctive features of Hawaiian English are, first, that it has been fairly seamlessly integrated into the framework of American English (while retaining in certain registers a highly distinctive quality, notably in its Pidgin and Creole forms), and, second, that it includes words of indigenous origin, on their own and in combination with words not specific to Hawaii. Informal and slang expressions often incorporate elements of Hawaii English Pidgin/Creole, and unique indigenous expressions used in giving directions.

These expressions relate to geography, not points of the compass, as with *mauka* ('towards the mountains') and *makai* ('towards the sea'). On the island of Oahu, these are combined with the names of two locations on the southern shore, *Ewa beach* and *Waikiki/Diamond Head*, as in: 'Go *ewa* one block, turn *makai* at the traffic light, go two blocks Diamond Head, and you'll find the place on the *mauka* side of the street' ('Which Way Oahu?', *National Geographic*, Nov 1979), and 'The *ewa* bound lanes of the H-1 Freeway airport viaduct were closed for hours' (*Honolulu Advertiser*, 27 Mar 1990).

Widely used words from Hawaiian include: *aloha* ('love, sympathy', and a common form of greeting and farewell); *haole* (originally any foreigner, now a Caucasian/white); *heiau* (a traditional temple); *hula* (a kind of dance, formerly usually sacred, now mainly performed for tourists, and mainly by young women); *kane* ('a man'); *kapu* ('taboo, keep out'); *lanai* (a porch or patio); *lei* (a garland of flowers, seeds, or shells: especially as a token of welcome); *mahalo* ('thank you'); *mahimahi* ('a dolphin'); *mahope* ('by and by'); *pau* ('finished'); *poi* (a thick edible taro paste); *pupus* (English plural: 'hors d'oeuvres'); *wahine* ('a girl, woman, wife'); *wikiwiki* ('hurry up'). Hybrid usages are common and include: *the Ala Moana Center; an aloha party; Kalakaua Avenue; 'a lei-seller'; the Kilauea Crater; the Kodak Hula Show; kukui nuts; the Waianae Coast; Waikiki Bar-B-Que House; the Waimea Arboretum.*

Hawaiian English mixes elements of American slang and informal usage with elements of Hawaiian, Hawaii English Pidgin/Creole, and other languages, as in: *ala-alas* ('balls': testicles); *brah* ('brother': cf. *brer* in *Brer Rabbit*); *buddahead* (pejorative: someone from Japan or of Japanese background); *to cockaroach* ('to steal or sneak away with something'); *da kine* ('that kind': *Wheah da kine?* 'Where's the whatsit?'); *FOB* ('Fresh off the Boat') and *JOJ* ('Just off the Jet'); *haolefied* ('becoming like a haole'); *kapakahi* ('mixed up'): all from Douglas Simonson, *Pidgin to da Max*, Honolulu, 1981). Hawaiian journalists use localisms freely; often with glosses: 'For 1,500 years, a member of the Mookini family has been the kahuna—priest—at an enormous heiau—temple—at Upolu Point in Kohala at the northern tip of the Big Island. For 1,500 years, no one in that unbroken kahuna line has spoken publicly about the family's sacred trust. Now Momi Mookini Lum, current kahuna nui of Mookini Luakini, has broken the silence' (*Honolulu Advertiser*, 4 May 1982).

The nature of *Hawai'i Pidgin English*, also informally simply called *Pidgin*, is a complex issue. Although the term *Hawaiian pidgin* has been widely used to refer to both the English-based pidgin and creole varieties used in Hawaii, some people of ethnic Hawaiian background have objected to it because it suggests that the Hawaiian rather than the English language was pidginized. The term *Hawaii Pidgin English* is now therefore generally preferred among scholars and teachers because the Hawaiian language is not in any way implied. However, the pidgin may have been a pidginized version of Hawaiian in which adapted English words were used, not by ethnic Hawaiians but by the Chinese plantation labourers who took over the cultivation of taro from native Hawaiians. That pidgin was originally known in Hawaiian as *olelo pa'i'ai* ('pounded but undiluted taro language') and is partially related to one of the earliest forms of English in the islands, *Maritime Pidgin Hawaiian*, as used between Hawaiians and sailors and traders of various backgrounds, but principally from the US.

During the development of a plantation economy in the later 19th century, Hawaiians and English-speaking plantation owners communicated in so-called *Hapa-haole* ('Half-foreign'), which may have been foreigner talk rather than a pidgin properly so called. The crucial years for the formation of a pidgin were 1890–1910, when most of the Chinese, Japanese, and Portuguese workers arrived. As usual, the initial pidgin usage was unstable, varying considerably according to the native language of the speaker. It stabilized after the turn of the century, when Pidgin-speaking immigrants married and brought up children using it as their primary language, the stage at which, from the point of view of language scholars, it became a creole, now known as both *Hawaii Creole English* and *Hawaii English Creole*.

This Creole developed in a continuum from low to high, the more prestigious variety slowly de-creolizing into a local English vernacular. It retains features from the pidgin stage, as with the use of *bambai* ('by and by': compare Tok Pisin *baimbai*) to mark future and hypothetical events, as in: *Mai fada dem wen kam ova hia*; *bambai de wen muv tu Kawai* ('My father and the others came over here; then they moved to Kauai'). The use of *wen* to mark the simple past is taken from *went*. There is another, older form *bin* (from *been*: compare Tok Pisin *bin*), as in *A bin go see mai fada* ('I went to see my father'). Currently, many speakers use the English past-tense form *had*. The use of *dem* ('them') to mark plurals, as in *Stan-dem* ('Stan and the others') is found in other English-based Creoles, as for example in Jamaican Creole *Jan dem* ('John and the others').

Hawaii in linguistic and cultural terms looks two ways: increasingly towards the US mainland and outward to the rest of Polynesia and to South-east and East Asia (where many of its people have their roots). Together, Aotearoa/New Zealand and Hawaii, a state of the United States, represent the two extreme points, south and east, reached by Polynesian explorer-settlers in their long outrigger migrations from the islands of South-East Asia. Both groups then found themselves overwhelmed by other migrations and with them other languages and customs, and both have become minorities in the once-empty lands on which they made the first claim.

Antarctica, the Falklands, and the South Atlantic islands

> **2000** In 1902, Edwin Balch wrote: 'Antarctica' is a term which is slowly coming into use to designate the continent which probably extends across the regions of the South Pole. . . . Geographers are not yet agreed as to the limits of the Antarctic.' In 2000, they are still not agreed. So, using the prerogative of makers of dictionaries and of writers in general, I have drawn a wide net around a slippery subject. In this dictionary Antarctica is the continent and its surrounding seas and islands, and the words described are those used there. No one has made a study of the English of Antarctica before. When the *Oxford English Dictionary* was published in 1933, Antarctica had only just been recognized as a continent.
> – Bernadette Hince, *The Antarctic Dictionary*, CSIRO Publishing and the Museum of Victoria, Australia

A century after Edwin Balch made his comment, a great deal more is known about Antarctica, including that it consists of two subcontinents: *East Antarctica*, largely a high, ice-sheathed plateau, and *West Antarctica*, largely a mountainous ice-covered archipelago. Although the region is not a natural place for humans, people have nonetheless found means of insulating themselves and surviving there, and (as a welcome by-product) have made the region a success in terms of peaceful international, especially scientific, co-operation.

At the same time, however, its quasi-colonial territorial organization (a tidier version of the late-19th-century 'scramble for Africa') resembles the unequal slicing of a cake whose cuts radiate out from the Pole. In addition, three oceans with distinct names (*Atlantic*, *Pacific*, and *Indian*) come together in the region, where they are each conceived as contributing to, or blending into, an *Antarctic Ocean* (also known as the *Southern Ocean* and, without capitals, the *circumpolar ocean*). In winter, the freezing of much of that ocean more than doubles the apparent size of the continent.

A range of Western European languages has been in use in and near Antarctica for much of the last hundred years, including English, French, German, the Scandinavian languages, and Spanish (from nearby Argentina and Chile), and English has served as a lingua franca among the many nations with a stake in the region. The kind of English used in Antarctica can nowadays be found in any heterogeneous international setting (for example, at United Nations gatherings, scientific conferences, and meetings of aid organizations worldwide), but in the Antarctic such English includes a great deal of technical usage focused on geology, meteorology, ecology, survival skills, and related fields.

That usage recently acquired its own dictionary (as above). Bernadette Hince catalogues the usage of the region from *Adelaite* ('an occupant of the British Adelaide Island Base') to *zucchini* ('an extended apple hut'), *apple hut* being in its turn defined under A as 'a round, usu. red, prefabricated fiberglass field hut, designed in Tasmania for Antarctic use, and called by its maker Malcolm Wallhead the "igloo satellite cabin" '. One of the characteristics of Antarctic English usage as it emerges from the dictionary is eclecticism: many global strands come together to create a unique South-Polar vocabulary.

If it were not for three particular features, the Antarctic land mass would be roughly circular. The most prominent of these features is the *Antarctic Peninsula*, which reaches out to, and almost touches, southernmost South America; the others are two enormous bays, the *Ross Sea* and the *Weddell Sea*, terms redolent of Western European colonial/commercial expansion: the use of personal names in creating place-names, either because the people in question have been directly involved in the region (as with the *Beardmore Glacier*, the *Cook Ice Shelf*, the *Davis Sea*, and *McMurdo Sound*) or they are employers, patrons, or royalty, personages who were never likely to go near the places graced by their names (as with *Queen Mary Land*, the *Queen Maude Mountains*, and the *Rockefeller Plateau*).

A recurring formula is name + *land* (but without creating a solid written form, as in *Scotland* and *Queensland*). An example is the name chosen by the English navigator John Biscoe, who worked for an English whaling company. When he came upon a particular stretch of Antarctic coast in 1831, he named it *Enderby Land*, after his employers, the Enderby Brothers in London. This coinage would not have looked good as *Enderbyland ('Ender-by-land'?), any more than such other Antarctic names as *George V Land*, *Mac Robertson Land*, *Marie Byrd Land*, and *Princess Elizabeth Land* if written in solid format.

The naming of two seas after the British naval officer Sir James Clark Ross and the explorer, navigator, and seal-hunter James Weddell (1787–1843) transported two names from Scotland to the southernmost reaches of the planet, a displacement typical of both colonial and Antarctic usage, in which items from Western Europe routinely turn up thousands of miles from home, including the far south. Thus, *rorqual*, an English name for a species of whale found in both the Arctic and Antarctic, derives through French and Norwegian from Old Norse *reydar-hvalr* ('furrowed whale'), so called because of grooves on its lower jaw. The same species is also known as a *finner* because of its distinctive dorsal fin, and both words (as Hince attests) are now typical Antarctic usage.

Hince's dictionary provides a trove of usages that, entry by entry, build up not only a record of usage but also a picture of the experiences of isolated groups of people, usually men, usually living in restricted accommodation, and commonly facing extreme climatic conditions. The following lists constitute a selection of items from *The Antarctic Dictionary*.

❶ Some informal usages

The phrase *the Ice*, meaning 'Antarctica and her ice-bound regions': an Australian citation, 1994, is: 'Having been back from the Ice now for nearly two months . . .'; an American citation, 1997, is 'The man whose height, tattoos and generosity made him a virtual legend among Ice regulars.'

❷ A series of expressions based on *ice*

ice anchor a grapnel for holding a ship to an ice floe

ice apron a fan-shaped accumulation of ice in front of a glacier or on a mountain

ice blink 'a bright white or yellowish glare lighting the sky above the horizon, reflected upwards from extensive areas of ice beyond the viewer's sight, and therefore indicating its presence'

ice flower flower-like rosettes of ice

ice widow a woman deprived of her husband while he is in Antarctica

Other defined *ice* expressions: *ice breaker, ice cake, ice caldera, ice captain, ice cliff, ice core, ice dome, ice edge, icefall, ice field, icefish, ice floe, ice fog, ice foot, fumarole, ice island, ice krill, ice master, ice mound, ice pack/pack ice, icepan, ice petrel, ice pilot, icequake, ice runway, icescape, ice ship* (noun *and verb*), *ice stream, ice tongue, ice watch, ice wharf, ice year.*

❸ Some informal usages

beaker a scientist (presumably after the character of that name in the TV shows *Sesame Street* and *The Muppets*)

beakerdom scientists in general

chompers (Australian) a snack, food ('If you are on the periphery of the station and don't hear the siren, the dogs will certainly let you know its time for chompers')

berg 'an iceberg. In the Antarctic the commonest form of iceberg is the *tabular berg*'

berglet a small iceberg

bergy bits large fragments of usually glacier ice, 'often described as house-sized'

blizz an abbreviation for *blizzard*

manfood rations for human consumption as opposed to *dogfood* (for the sledge dogs)

manhaul (noun) a journey on which men pull equipment on sledges; (verb) to travel while pulling a sledge

Words, phrases, and names are probably the key aspects of Antarctic English; there is little indication in the dictionary that any systematically distinctive kinds of pronunciation and grammar have developed among the Americans, Australians, British, and New Zealanders working in the region. It seems likely therefore that most native speakers of English take to the Antarctic their own conventional kind of English, while foreign users of the language continue where possible to use their own languages with colleagues and their own kinds of English for appropriate international purposes. Antarctic English is not therefore a distinctive variety of the language as such, comparable to Australian, Caribbean, and Scottish varieties of the language. Rather, it is the product of circumstances among people who are all, varyingly, temporary residents, and as such tends to be more of a register than a dialect. It typically makes use of two kinds of specialized language: the scientific and technical on one side and circumstantial, informal, and slang usage on the other. In this, it resembles the usage of people working on oil rigs.

If, however, people for any reason needed to live in families for years at a time in the Antarctic, then a fully fledged variety of English would emerge. If that happened, it would be part of 'Southern Hemisphere English', largely but not exclusively the usage of people of European descent in Australia, New Zealand, South Africa, and the Falkland Islands. Among non-native users of English in Antarctica, it would tend to remain the kind of English their home communities had already acquired for professional and lingua franca purposes. In all cases, however, it would be suffused with the kind of usage that Hince has recorded in her pioneering lexicon.

In the history of the Western European trading and colonizing diaspora, the South Atlantic played a significant role now largely forgotten. The Portuguese sailed first down the west coast of Africa and later across to what became Brazil, the jewel in their imperial crown. The Spanish not only initiated, with Columbus, the discovery, exploration, exploitation, and disruption of the Western hemisphere, but also pioneered the risky passage of ships round a promontory at the southernmost point of South America. They named it the *Cabo de Hornos* ('Cape of Hornos'), after an island named by the Dutch in 1616 after Hoorn, the birthplace of the navigator Willem Schouten. In English, the place is *Cape Horn*, where sailors still 'go round the Horn', unaware that no horns were involved in naming it. The Dutch duly established themselves in a safer southern African counterpart, the first form of whose Western European name was Portuguese, *Cabo da Boa Esperança* (in English the *Cape of Good Hope*, in due course commonly referred to simply as 'the Cape', to match 'the Horn').

As the British moved further into the Atlantic, they established themselves not only in the Caribbean and on the west coast of Africa, but acquired a series of south Atlantic islands as way-stations to the Indian, Pacific, and Southern oceans. The northernmost of these is Ascension Island, midway between Africa and South America, in the general latitude of Recife in Brazil and northern Angola in Africa. The Portuguese came upon it in 1501, on Ascension Day in the Roman Catholic liturgical year. It has a population just over 1,000, and has been administered since 1966 from St Helena, further south at the latitude of northern Namibia.

When the Portuguese navigator João da Nova Castella discovered this island on 21 May 1502, he named it after Helena, the mother of the Roman Emperor Constantine, and the saint of the Eastern Church whose saint's day it was. St Helena was a port of call for ships travelling to the East Indies, may have been briefly occupied by the Dutch in the 17th century, and was occupied by the East India Company in 1659. In 1773, nearly half the population were imported slaves. The island's remoteness made it the choice for the exile of Napoleon (1815–21). By the later 1830s, the island was under direct British rule. The capital of St Helena is Jamestown, it has a governor and legislative council which also, in addition to Ascension Island, oversees Tristan da Cunha and Gough Island, well to the south, on the latitude of Cape Town. St Helena has a population of *c*.5,700, and Tristan of *c*.250. The people of St Helena are a mix of European (mostly British), Asian, and African. Their sole language is English and they are mainly Anglican.

The capital of Tristan da Cunha is Edinburgh, its sole language is English, and its economy rests mainly on fishing and Tristan stamps. Local affairs are in the hands of an Island Council and an elected Chief Islander. The Portuguese discovered the archipelago in 1506 and the British occupied it in 1816 as a protective measure during Napoleon's exile in St Helena. In 1961, the islanders were evacuated after a volcanic eruption, but returned in 1963. Their speech is thought to have elements in common with Highland English. Distinctive local usage includes the terms *eastings* and *westings*, indicating which way the island is circled, and there are complex place-names such as *Down-where-minister-pick-up-his-things* and *Blackinthehole Hill*.

The remaining South Atlantic possession, just to the north-east of Cape Horn and east of Argentina, is the Falkland Islands, known in Spanish as the *Islas Malvinas* ('the Malo-ine Islands', the name for the islands in Spain and Latin America, reflecting an early association with Saint Malo in France). In 1690, Captain John Strong made the first known landing, naming the sound between the two islands 'the Falkland Sound' (after Viscount Falkland, at that time treasurer of the Royal Navy), the name later being applied to the entire group. Strong's visit is the basis of the British claim to the archipelago of some 200 islands. The Falklands were colonized in 1832–3, after the expulsion of a small garrison embodying the Spanish claim. The main islands are West Falkland and East Falkland, where the capital, (Port) Stanley, is situated and most of the population of 2,000 live. The islanders are in the main descendants of settlers from the Scottish Highlands and Western Isles, South West England, Scandinavia, and more recently Chile and Saint Helena. There are also contract workers from Australia and New Zealand. The economy is based on fishing and sheep farming.

Argentina has never conceded British sovereignty, nor indeed has Spain, which also has not recognized Argentina's claim. Argentina invaded the islands in 1982, precipitating a 2-month war in which it was defeated by troops sent on the long journey south from the UK.

The government of the Falklands administers South Georgia (a range of islands close to Antarctica), the South Sandwich Islands, and the Shag and Clerke Rocks. Stanley is the headquarters of the British Antarctic Survey, and of the Falklands Islands Company (incorporated by Royal Charter in 1851), which plays a major role in the life of the islands. On the usage of the Falklanders, the New Zealand scholar Andrea Sudbury has recently noted:

> In addition to the major English varieties spoken in New Zealand,
> Australia and South Africa, the dialect of the Falkland Islands is
> one of the few native-speaker Englishes in the southern
> hemisphere. The Falkland variety is relatively unknown in the
> rest of the English-speaking world and when heard it is often
> wrongly identified as one of the other southern hemisphere
> varieties.
>
> – 'Falkland Islands English: A southern hemisphere variety', *English World-Wide* 22:1,
> 2001, John Benjamins, Amsterdam & Philadelphia, 56

In her survey, she has concluded that, in terms of pronunciation, Falkland Islands English (FIE) belongs to the same broad speech community as south-eastern England, South Africans of British descent, Australia, and New Zealand. In closing, however, she includes an evocative point regarding what she calls 'the default hypothesis':

[A] Falkland Islander in Britain is unlikely to be mistaken for a British dialect speaker. Nor is it likely that they will be identified as North American. This leaves one of the southern hemisphere Englishes as a default choice. The evidence that FIE does share some salient features with the other southern hemisphere Englishes serves to reinforce the default hypothesis. Thus, Falkland Islanders are regularly misidentified as Australian, New Zealand or South African English speakers on the lack of any other distinctive linguistic evidence. . . . [A]t best, FIE can only be described as a 'peripheral' southern hemisphere English. Whether it will show greater convergence or will diverge further from the Australian, New Zealand and South African varieties in future . . . remains to be seen.

– ibid. 77

The same point can, however, be made regarding other Englishes already accepted as distinct varieties; the Falklands have simply come late to the party. Each of the southern-hemisphere varieties differs from the others in many ways while nonetheless sharing a common core. In all four of the varieties under discussion there are few syntactic differences but many differences in vocabulary. In addition, South African, Australian, and New Zealand English differ greatly one from another in terms of their environments and usages appropriate to those environments, as well as the languages with which they co-exist. Falklands English has a distinctive environmental vocabulary, but it does not co-exist with any other language—not even Spanish.

Falklanders speak a southern-hemisphere variety wider than simply pronunciation, and that variety ties in with the English usage of Antarctica. The other varieties also have their Antarctic dimensions, but for the Falklands the involvement is constant and close. The next British islands in the Atlantic chain are South Georgia and the South Sandwich Islands, then the South Orkney and South Shetland Islands, after which comes the Antarctic Peninsula.

8 Conclusion: World English

1995 It is difficult to know what to expect, when a language develops a worldwide presence to the extent that English has. There are no precedents for such a geographical spread or for so many speakers. Moreover the speed at which it has all happened is unprecedented: although the history of world English can be traced back 400 years, the current growth spurt in the language has a history of less than forty years.

– David Crystal, *The Cambridge Encyclopedia of the English Language*, Cambridge University Press, 110

1997 It may well be the case that the English language has already grown to be independent of any form of social control. There may be a critical number or critical distribution of speakers (analogous to the notion of critical mass in nuclear physics) beyond which it proves impossible for any single group or alliance to stop its growth, or even influence its future. . . . If there is a critical mass, does this mean that the emergence of a global language is a unique event, in evolutionary terms? It may be that English, in some shape or form, will find itself in the service of the world community for ever.

– David Crystal, *English as a Global Language*, Cambridge University Press, 139–40

In 2000, David Crystal brought out a third book, *Language Death*, in which he discusses the year-on-year extinction of languages. Such losses inevitably occur among the world's small languages, at the furthest end of the scale from English. As he notes in the first quotation above, there is nothing new about the expansion of English or any other major language, but there *is* something new about its universalization. Because of this, his vision expands in the second book (and quotation) from the merely overwhelming to a question about human evolution itself. This question relates not to the faculty of language as such (the conventional topic in books about the origin of speech) but to the spread of individual languages, and inevitably to the emergence of very large languages that inherently push towards their own universalization. To date, English is the only such language that has ever come close to realizing that goal.

Several languages have however been quite remarkable in terms of their significance and use over time. Greek had a key role in parts of Eurasia and North Africa from the death of Alexander the Great (323 BC) to the fall of Constantinople (1453): almost 1,800 years (and it continues as a primary language of the European Union). Latin was a key language of government, religion, and scholarship from the defeat of Carthage (202 BC) to 1687, when Newton published his first major work, the *Principia*, in Latin, and 1704, when he published his second major work, *Opticks*, in English: almost 2,000 years. Compared with these statistics, English is a cadet. But this youngster has already overwhelmed all its predecessors and current competitors in sheer distributional and functional terms.

Even so, however, we cannot simply single English out for special attention, and this for four reasons. First, the fundamental issue raised by Crystal is evolution, in which the time scale is immense. Secondly, English did not leap out of nowhere: it is an inheritor and is in a serious sense simply part of an already copious flow. Languages such as Latin, Greek, Sanskrit, Classical Arabic, Classical Chinese, and French have all been part that flow, English taking up where others have left off or may now be leaving off—or, indeed, may not at all be leaving off. Thirdly, although it is the pre-eminent world language of our time, English is far from being the only world language. Fourthly, English evolves, and the present-day language in all its varieties is vastly different from past Englishes, while its broad international standard is often very different from many of its varieties.

Although English is a distinct phenomenon, it carries within it (and transmits) material and conventions from prior languages. It is therefore not *only* English that 'in some shape or form, will find itself in the service of the world community for ever', but all the language matter that coheres within it. In the excerpt quoted, Crystal's essential modification with regard to the future is 'in some shape or form'. In the context he discusses, English will not necessarily be the English we know, just as today's English is not the one the Angles and Saxons knew. Rather he uses its name like a generic, with a secondary meaning something like 'the universal language'. The underlying assumption is that, because we now have a universalizing English, the way is clear for us to have a planet-wide medium that is, in principle at least, available to all—'for ever'.

The nature of very large languages

The examples of Greek and Latin point to something more fundamental in evolutionary terms than the eventual emergence of one language as the universal medium. If what developed had not been English, it would have been another very large language that had conformed to a pattern of requirements that has tended to include, for example, involvement in the creation of great cities, the development of transport and trade, the emergence of kinds of novel technology (such as writing, printing, and the use of computers), the expansion of an imperial ideology of some kind (perhaps religious, perhaps secular, perhaps a mix of the two), as for example the cultures associated with Hinduism, Christianity, Islam, Confucianism-cum-Taoism-cum-Buddhism, and Western socio-economic and scientific liberalism.

This process appears to have been set in train some 4,000 years ago in Mesopotamia, when the cuneiform writing system developed in Sumer passed north to Akkad and then Babylon. At least four distinct waves of 'large language' formation followed that first development (although whether all of them had links with it is uncertain): in East Asia, classical Chinese with its influence on China, Japan, Korea, and Indo-China; in South Asia, Sanskrit and Pali, with their influence on India, Nepal, Sri Lanka, the Malay islands, and Indo-China; in West Asia, the Semitic language complex (beginning with Akkadian and Babylonian and including Aramaic/Syriac, Phoenician, Hebrew, and Arabic) and their influences elsewhere. These influences have included both the influence of the Old Testament of the Bible on the languages and cultures of Europe (and their extensions in the Americas and elsewhere) and the influence of the Quran in and near the Islamic world. A fourth wave was the major languages of Atlantic Europe—Dutch, English, French, German, Portuguese, and Spanish—and includes their influence on one another and on many other languages.

Much like other languages, English has its 'high', 'middle', and 'low' social levels within continua of usage. The high levels (the *acrolects*) are 'standard' and 'educated' (and therefore viewed as 'good', and as the usage of the elite); the middle levels (the *mesolects*) manage well enough, and may have upward aspirations; and the low levels (the *basilects*) are generally disdained and dismissed, including among their users, as 'crude', 'uneducated', 'ungrammatical', 'fractured', or 'broken' (and therefore 'bad'). But much of the world's business is done at the middle and lower levels, most particularly using 'fractured' or 'broken' language, trade jargons, and pidgins. On one or other of these levels—the best and the rest, as it were—people negotiate their meanings. And this has been true historically for many languages, the only difference being that in recent times the world's language ecology has been so much greater and more complex because there are so many more people on earth.

In the years immediately after the Second World War, the phrase 'language ecology' could not have been used: even the notion of an ecology in nature had yet to earn its spurs. However, the following comment by the British language scholar C. L. Wrenn illustrates the kind of novel public observations about English that *were* being made at that time:

> **1949** English is now well on the way to becoming a world-
> language: and this means many types of English, many
> pronunciations and vocabulary-groups within the English
> language. There is, for instance, an Indian—and even a Bengali
> form of English. . . . Language is a social activity: and whether
> it is really desirable for English or any other language—real or
> invented—to become a world-medium, is a question which
> perhaps concerns the anthropologist and other students of the
> 'social sciences' rather than the student of the English language.
> – *The English Language*, 185, 205

If the desirability or otherwise of a world language was ever a matter for anthropologists and sociologists (and not philologists and linguists), that is certainly no longer the case. Instead, English-language scholars interested in why and how English became a world language have themselves become social scientists; their interests push them in that direction, at the same time as the nature of anthropology and social science has been pushing their practitioners closer to linguistic science.

More significantly, however, Wrenn noted in 1949 that English was 'well on its way to becoming a world-language' (with *world* and *language* hyphenated, something unlikely to happen today). Yet when he wrote this he clearly knew that English had already been a world language at the very least for a century before his book was published. After all, Bengali English needed that kind of time to grow. It did not burst on to the world scene in the 1940s; rather, the presence of English in Bengal dates from 1690. Wrenn may have been feeling for the most fitting words with which to describe the state of linguistic affairs that accompanied, among other things, the influx of American armed forces into Europe and East Asia at and after the end of the Second World War, forces whose successors are pretty much still in place. The time when his book came out was in fact a turning point between the earlier long, slow, steady build-up of world English and the even greater and more rapid expansion that has been under way ever since.

Although its expansion has been phenomenal, English has never been alone as a large-scale language. Three other complexes operate on a scale similar to English: Spanish, Chinese, and Hindi-Urdu. But none has a matching distribution, and there are vastly more users of Spanish, Chinese, and Hindi-Urdu learning English than users of English learning them. At the same time, however, Spanish is the only language making significant inroads into the English-speaking world, and in its most powerful region, the United States. The advance of the Latinos has been so marked that American linguistic conservatives have been campaigning for years for English to be made the official federal language, in the (untenable) belief that such a move might stem the Hispanic tide.

The Chinese language complex is very much larger than the complex of native users of English, but its members are in the main ethnically and culturally homogeneous, and its worldwide distribution is limited. Spanish is more widely distributed than Chinese, and is powerfully present in the Americas, but it is largely absent from Europe beyond the Pyrenees, is in contention in Spain itself at least with Catalan, and is minimal in Africa, Asia, and Australasia/Oceania, in all of which English is strong. Hindi-Urdu has its diasporas, but they are relatively small, the mass of its speakers are in the north of the Indian subcontinent, and millions of its speakers use and adapt English to a greater or less extent.

Other large languages are less widespread than English, but may be more widespread than Spanish, Chinese, and Hindi-Urdu, despite having smaller numbers of users. French is widely distributed worldwide, and Arabic, Russian, and Malay are widely distributed in their regions, while German and Japanese are associated with powerful economies and populous countries, but are not in wide use globally. Again, more speakers of these languages are learning and using English than learning and using one another's languages, while established users of English (native or otherwise) are not learning them in significant numbers, although there has been a noteworthy rise in the US and Canada in demand for, and enrolment in, courses in Spanish. It is probably safe to say that, no matter how universal the use of English becomes, these other languages are going to retain their positions in the world's linguistic pecking order. Beginning at the top, as it were, with English and this group of very large languages, it is possible to extrapolate a set of seven language categories at the present time. The edges of the categories may be fuzzy, and languages do not always fit tidily into them, but the continuum that they represent is perhaps all too clear:

❶ A universalizing language complex

English: in a set with a membership of one, but with enough internal variety to form a family of its own; used by over a billion people (although a precise figure cannot be given); learned by millions of young people; distributed more or less evenly worldwide; and serving as the primary vehicle of the world's commerce, science, technology, computer activity, electronics, media, popular culture, and entertainment.

❷ Major language complexes

Spanish, Chinese, and Hindi-Urdu: each used by hundreds of millions of people; Spanish widely disseminated but not as widely as English; all with massive population bases in specific parts of the world; and all centrally important to major world cultures and economies.

❸ Very large languages

Arabic, French, Russian, Malay, German, and Japanese: all culturally and economically significant, either worldwide, or in specific regions, or in specific social, cultural, demographic, economic, and/or other terms.

❹ Large (national and regional) languages

Among others, Hausa in West Africa, Swahili in East Africa, Italian and Hungarian in Europe, Persian and Turkish in Western and Central Asia, Tamil and Marathi in India, and Guarani alongside Spanish in Paraguay, all with significant histories, cultures, and populations of users.

❺ Smaller but socially fairly strong and secure languages

Among many others, found in one or more territories, such as Catalan in Spain and France, Berber in Morocco, Ilocano in the Philippines, and Nahuatl in Mexico.

❻ Small languages whose circumstances are not entirely safe

Belonging to minor (often depleted) communities, such as Gallego in Spain, Welsh in Wales, Maori in New Zealand, Navajo in the United States, and Romansch in Switzerland.

❼ Very small and usually endangered languages

Many languages whose speakers are in the lower thousands, or hundreds, or fewer, used by shrinking communities in or across nation-states, as with the Aboriginal languages of Australia, the 'heritage languages' Kwakiutl and Ojibway in Canada, and the 'Indian' languages Seminole and Cherokee in the United States.

These are rule-of-thumb categories, but there is a realpolitik about them, from the immensely powerful and prestigious to the small, local, neglected, and endangered. In such a world, there is profit (in all senses of that word) in using and learning the large languages, but, as Crystal demonstrates in *Language Death*, there is immense social, emotional, and psychological loss in the steady current extinguishing of hundreds of 'lesser' tongues. The history of English, Spanish, Portuguese, and

French in the Americas *vis-à-vis* a former multitude of indigenous languages is a formidable and often tragic case in point.

Traditionally, certain things have been required of languages at the large end of the spectrum, pre-eminently the possession of a 'cultivated', 'educated', or 'standard' variety channelled through writing, print, and a prestigious way of speaking. As regards English, there has never before been such demand for a standard international variety that can be consistently taught. There is a paradox here too: that this entity is known to be varied, yet even so those who use it expect a high level of international inter-communicability: we all expect a manageable, teachable, learnable acrolect that can serve world commerce, travel, and culture. Although the two established technical terms for the variety in question are little known and rarely used—'World Standard English' (WSE) and 'International Standard English' (ISE)—the nature of the variety is well appreciated and demand for it is deeply entrenched.

Yet, although world English is varied, certain varieties and registers are fairly tightly controlled, often through standardized patterns of use, offering a kind of communicative security to all concerned. Thus, there is a marked uniformity in the following arenas:

❶ Airports

In the public usage of international airports, where, on signboards, English is often twinned with other languages, and announcements are commonly in English or are multilingual including English

❷ Newspapers and periodicals

English-language broadsheet newspapers and magazine-style periodicals, in which the texts are tightly edited (despite the typos that inevitably attend intensive work with print under the pressure of deadlines)

❸ Broadcast media

The programming of CNN, the BBC, and other especially TV news-and-views services, in which presentational formulas and formats are at least as crucial as in newspapers (much of the terminology being in fact held in common)

❹ Computer use, email, and the Internet/Web

In such computer and Internet services as those offered by Microsoft, America Online (AOL), and Netscape Navigator, whose style and usage continue to evolve.

That is English now. We cannot, however, know what a world language of the long-term future will be like or what it might be called. But just as Greek material went into Latin and Arabic, and Latin material went into French and Swedish, and Greek, Latin, and French material have gone into English, so English is currently going (along with all of its historical freight) into Malay, Japanese, Tagalog, and other languages in Asia—and indeed into Dutch, German, French, and other languages in Europe. However, the over-arching language of humanity at the start of the *next* millennium (all things being equal) might well out-mongrel English as she is spoke today. There may be a great deal of Chinese, Japanese, Arabic, Urdu, and Hindi in it, alongside what might be thought of as 'General European'. It is impossible, however, to imagine at this time what script it might have, what media and technologies might be available to it, or indeed where it might be used, either on or beyond the Earth.

Fractured, broken, and decorative English

The ideal for many millions of people is to be able to use a language accurately and effectively—maybe even with flair. At the same time they hope, reasonably enough, that others will manage *their* use of language well enough not to cause confusion. In addition, most of us are aware (at times painfully) of how communication often falls short of the ideal. However, it is a feature of English at least that many of its conventions ('rules') can be broken and a message still manages to do its intended work. There is apparently enough built-in redundancy for much to get lost or distorted without meaning being lost—or even endangered. Thus, the same message can be sent whether the form is 'I'm sorry to say that I cannot come tomorrow' or the more telegraphic 'Sorry can't come tomorrow' or the suspect 'Sorry no can come'.

'Bad' English is widespread, however defined, and falls into two broad categories: the faults of fellow native speakers and the flaws of foreigners. Commonly, for centuries, some native-speakers (usually at a higher social level) have castigated the usage of others (usually at a lower social level or in a younger generation) as 'slovenly', 'sloppy', or at the very least 'careless'. The use of such negative comment seems to be associated in the main with power plays, often expressed in irritable and dismissive ways. Separately, it is quite usual for foreign users of a language to get things wrong, but in this area people tend to be more tolerant. By and large, native users of English do not get anywhere near as upset by the usage of foreigners as by the usage of other native speakers. And yet this alien mangling of the language is common, and may present far greater problems of communication than perceived native-speakers' failings (like saying *we was* and not *we were*). There are also particular settings in which such mangling can actually be enjoyed.

Near Luxor in Egypt, not far from the Valley of the Kings, stands the ruined funerary temple of Hatshepsut, the only female pharaoh. Not far from her temple, there is a high bare baked-mud wall on which, in beautiful majuscule letters, are the words: 'I hop you engoy to vist her.' This sentence is remarkable, because it manages to succeed in spite of having four errors in seven words, and it raises a smile. Such 'fractured English' is usually well-intended but often also extremely funny. As the message proceeds it can also generate an Alice-in-Wonderland effect: 'The writer must have meant *here*, but maybe—just maybe—the sentence refers to the female pharaoh, so it could in fact be quite clever.' Indeed, if *her* did mean Hatshepsut, then one of the four errors would not be an error at all. But there is no way of knowing.

Fractured English is normally written or printed, is often institutional, and is likely to have a specific, often serious, aim. People whose English is limited are often required, or are eager, to write something useful or profitable, which is why hotels and tourist spots are particularly rich in such adventurous usage. English of this kind often has such a fey quality that readers of occasional collections in newspapers and magazines are tempted to think somebody clever must have made it up: *nobody* could really have said that! Indeed, classics of the genre have been recycled for years in English-language newspaper columns worldwide, often without giving any indication of where they originated. Below are half-a-dozen such well-circulated specimens:

1   Teeth extracted by latest Methodists.

2   Because is big rush we will execute customers in strict rotation.

3   Visitors are expected to complain at the office between the hours of 9 and 11 am. daily.

4   Our wines leave you nothing to hope for.

5   Not to perambulate the corridors in hours of repose in the boots of ascension.

6   When a passenger of foot heave into sight, tootle the horn. Trumpet him melodiously at first, but if he still obstacles your passage then tootle him with vigour.

As with 'engoy her', we are left wondering about such gems. There is, however, another side to fracturing the world's lingua franca, as illustrated by the *Translators' Guild Newsletter* in the UK in the 1980s, in Steve Coffey's column 'Pitfalls and Howlers'. He drew attention to various matters, at times with sober intent, but usually without naming names and locations. The following extract is from an entirely serious letter to the Guild offering to undertake legal work:

> **1980s** You are kindly informed that we are of the sincere and
> reliable attorneys who are undertaking the international business
> of same career in cooperation with associates/clients overseas
> from one country to another throughout the world.

Although such writing is not funny, like the boots of ascension, it is strange: how could any serious person write like that? The most basic feature of such letters, however, is that there is nothing at all unusual about them. In various aspects of life, worldwide, thousands of such communications take place all the time, constituting a significant proportion of personal and business writing in the world's lingua franca. The following example, however, is very different. Although in generic terms it is similar, and although it is amusing, it is informative, and the aim is inherently honest:

> **1992a** Important: Albadero Cannelloni do not ought to boil. . . .
> Bring in Cannelloni, as they are, a stuffing maked with: beef,
> eggs, cheese, parmigiano, papper or spices, as you like, all well
> amalgamated ad juicy . . . Besmear a backing pan, previously
> buttered, with a good tomato-sauce and after, dispose the
> Cannelloni, lightly distanced between them, in a only couch. . . .
> – reported by Glyn Hughes in 'English on dis-play: a fractured language', in *English Today*
> 31 (8:3), July, Cambridge University Press, 45

By happenstance, in the same issue of *English Today*, the editorial included a comment on something that often happens to fractured text:

1992b . . . Of course, printers, writers, editors, and publishers generally seek the perfect text, but the day after publication they find that once again it has eluded their collective grasp. Take Tony Fairman's letter to the Editor in *ET* 30, which I entitled 'Asymmetrical impregnation'. He has pointed out that in the letter he 'actually wrote "He pregnanted my eldest sister", not "he pregnated" '. The original copy did go forward as "pregnanted", but the typesetter "corrected" it (probably unthinkingly), and no one noticed afterwards. The typesetter did it again on the contents page of *this* issue, but this time we were watching. . . . Mr Fairman rightly asked for an erratum note 'in the interests of accuracy and scholarship'. This is it, with our collective regrets.

– Tom McArthur, editorial entitled 'Thoroughly pregnanted', in *English Today* 31 (8:3), July, Cambridge University Press, 2

On 22 March 1995 there appeared in *The Wall Street Journal* a feature article by Barry Newman, a member of staff commissioned to follow up whatever attracts his interest. It was entitled 'Global chatter: the reality of "business English"', and its focus was just how much of that business is done through broken English. He reported:

1996 More people in the world now speak English as a foreign language than as a native one. Millions negotiate and bank and trade in it every day. They must have gotten the hang of it by now.

'I am getting hang?' asks Satoshi Nishide, managing director of Daihatsu Auto in Prague.

Mr. Nishide, 31, studied English for ten years and has done business in it for nine. He and his Czech staff sit at a table in their office behind the showroom, groping for the hang of it.

'Means . . . I depend on it?' wonders technical manager Vladimir Moravec. Spare-parts manager Milan Jandak: 'I'd like to have it?' Sales manager Arnost Barna: 'I'd like to stop it?'

'I know this phrase,' Mr. Nishide says. 'But I don't know.'

At Daihatsu in Prague, English is the only common language. The staff communicates with Mr. Nishide in no other way.

'We discuss technical matter,' says Mr. Moravec. 'If I don't understand very well, so I can expect what my boss want to say. We have special vocabulary. . . . If you hear two English person, they discussing their problem, it's other language than we use.'

So what language does Prague Daihatsu use? Purists might call it broken English, or perhaps 'foreigner talk'. Czechlish-Japlish may come close. 'Auto-lish' comes closer. 'Daihat-Praglish' hits the nail on the head. The global chatter explosion, it seems, is blowing the language to smithereens.

– reprinted in *English Today* 46 (12:2), April, Cambridge University Press, 16

There is a further dimension, which has neither the written insouciance of the boots of ascension nor the chaotic practicality of Prague Daihatsu. At the end of the 1980s, on the back of some black leather pilot's jackets on sale in Hong Kong was the almost Standard English statement: *Never put off til tomorrow what you can do today Let's sport*. Not long afterwards, and not to be outdone in the provinces, a similar jacket went on sale in Guangzhou (Canton). This time, however, the letters on the back read *neveriputbofftlhtomorohowhatyoucnotforyaetsspot*. And finally, a line of black leather pilots' jackets was manufactured in the Chinese province of Guangxi, with the following string of letters on the back of each: *nnehirpitothuihdronjfemty-ouovhreuorhwhehpt*. A few years afterwards, reporting from Hong Kong on these jackets and similar matters, Mark N. Brock noted:

> **1991** The message printed on the copy of the jacket produced
> near Hong Kong in Guangzhou is somewhat garbled yet still
> recognizable, even though the letters are run together in a rather
> haphazard manner. Copies of the jacket produced in the more
> interior province [Guangxi], however, pay even less attention
> to the configuration of letters. The apparent popularity of these
> jackets demonstrates that it is not the message that matters but
> rather the medium, the letters, and what their presence suggests.
> In many parts of Asia, English, even when it is scarcely
> recognizable as such, serves as a status marker, a talisman of
> modernity. . . . Of the many students and strangers I've queried
> about the English words adorning their jackets, notebooks, and
> pencil boxes, only a handful had ever paid any attention at all to
> what was printed. The fact that English words ornamented their
> possessions seemed satisfaction enough for most.
>
> – in 'The Good Feeling of Fine: English for Ornamental Purposes', *English Today* 26, April,
> Cambridge University Press, 51

The curious phenomenon that Brock discusses here evidently had its beginnings in Japan some years earlier. John Dougill, writing in Japan, made the following points about decorative usage of this kind:

> **1987** The widespread use of English in Japan is a reflection of the
> country's desire to internationalise and of its fascination with the
> world of the *gaijin* (literally, 'outsider' or 'alien'), particularly
> America. . . . Compared with the Chinese characters used for
> everyday purposes, the *romaji* (Roman alphabet) of English seems
> smart, sophisticated and modern. Indeed, such is the difference
> between the scripts that merely the appearance of romaji is
> enough to suggest glamorous associations. One company
> recognises this by printing on their writing paper, 'The very best
> stationery for people who get excited when they see English all
> over everything.' Apparently, the English is never even read, even
> by students and teachers of the language: it is purely decorative.
>
> – from 'English as a decorative language', in *English Today* 12, October, Cambridge
> University Press, 33

Brock in 1991 was unaware of Dougill's article in 1987, and so it is significant that, on a matter that has received little attention, both writers accounted for the absence of concern over content in such cases in a rather McLuhanesque way: that the medium can indeed be the message. Dougill, like many others, was puzzled that the Japanese, a nation known for efficient and accurate work, tolerate so much fractured usage on so many of their products. His puzzlement is reasonable, in that the Japanese have been exporting Decorative English widely, in the process influencing people in other communities, such as Hong Kong and Canton, to do the same kind of thing. As Dougill shows, such constructions turn up in many places, as for example Japanese shopping bags sold in Switzerland and sporting such statements as *A is for Ambrella* (with a picture alongside). He compares such usage as *Joyful, let us dash in the sky* and *flesh meat* and *heathery life* (where 'fresh' and 'healthy' were intended) to the Mad Hatter's Tea Party in *Alice in Wonderland*, noting that the Hatter's usage seemed to Alice to have no meaning, 'yet it was certainly English'.

That is the crux of the matter: such phrases and sentences may strain the language to its limits, be part of a spreading fad, and be manifest nonsense, but it is nonsense in English, not in Japanese, Chinese, Korean, or any other language. If, as happens, manufacturers from other language backgrounds start playing the same game (much as Western vehicle manufacturers have been mimicking off-beat names for Japanese cars), then this Mad-Hatter kind of English will spread, and perhaps even engender a kinder, gentler attitude to usage that doesn't gel in a tidy standard way. Let's sport.

Gender issues and political correctness

1992 Recent studies suggest that in many situations, women seem to be more concerned than men about using educated language as a means of social mobility. The fact that so many teachers of especially younger children are women may also make their role as 'language correctors' more salient.

– Lise S. Winer & Margaret E. Winters, in the entry 'Gender bias' in McArthur (ed.) *The Oxford Companion to the English Language*, Oxford University Press, 431

1993 The fuss that is made about words such as *chairman*, *spokesman*, *mankind*, and the insistence by some women on unisex forms (*chairperson* or *chair*, *spokesperson*, *humankind*) reflects a much deeper social problem. Despite equal-pay legislation, women generally still earn less than men, and they're grossly under-represented in the professions and in parliament. Feminists, and other women too, hope to change underlying attitudes by changing the words that reflect them. Linguistic habits are among the most difficult of all to shift, and even women are divided. . . . But the same was true of the struggle earlier this century for votes for women.

– Godfrey Howard, *The Good Usage Guide: English Usage in the 1990s*, London: Macmillan, 365–6

1996 Excesses in the advocacy of such replacements [of expressions considered racist or sexist by positive or neutral expressions] have given rise to the disparaging terms *political correctness* and *politically correct*. The politically correct movement—particularly strong in American universities—has been viewed by many outside it as repressive and punitive and has evoked protest and ridicule. . . . The perception, promoted by the feminist movement, that English has an in-built bias against women has had the most repercussions, and some of the proposals for change have won wide acceptance in several of the countries where English is a majority first language.

– Sidney Greenbaum, *The Oxford English Grammar*, Oxford University Press, 18–19

The issues associated with the terms *sexism* and *political correctness*, as well as the use of the terms themselves, crystallized in the United States in the 1970/1980s. But they did more than this. The speed with which these issues were taken up internationally serves as an indicator of the primacy throughout the world of American concerns about language and society, and particularly about English usage. The issue of 'sexist' language was first raised within the broader contexts of feminism and social equity, and a key text in such consciousness raising was Casey Miller and Kate Swift's *The Handbook of Nonsexist Writing* (New York: Harper & Row, 1980, 2001). The term *sexism* was coined in the 1960s on the analogy of an earlier American term, *racism* (whose British equivalent, *racialism*, is now largely forgotten). It prompted a family of further terms of uncertain stability and staying power but with a fair degree of social strength, such as *ageism*, *lookism*, and *heightism*. *Sexism*, however, remains a term of primary importance in its own right, and feminists in particular (in commenting on society and language) have used it to highlight, and do something about, at least the two following issues:

❶ Attitudes and stereotypes

Kinds of behaviour based on traditional assumptions about, and stereotypes of, sexual roles in society and gender usages in language.

❷ Discrimination and disparagement

Discrimination based on someone's sex, especially when directed by men or society at large against women, and more especially still when it is explicitly or implicitly disparaging. More recently, the term *sexual orientation* has been added as a means of discussing kinds of discrimination, in order to cover *gay* women and men. In this context, the term *homosexual* is sometimes applied to both men and women, but more frequently the term *lesbian* is used for women while *homosexual* is kept for men, with *gay* serving as the inclusive term.

In matters of language, the term *sexism* generally refers to a form of social bias in which usages relating to men are taken to be superordinate and central while those relating to women are seen as subordinate and peripheral (although in principle the bias might run the other way). English-language usage that has typically been seen as sexist includes:

❶ Masculine default terms

These are certain traditional uses of words of masculine gender (such as *man* and *he*) where both sexes are intended, on the principle that, in language terms, 'the male includes the female'. Such terms as *chairman*, *fireman*, *foreman*, and *policeman*, with their implications of masculinity or masculine priority, have in recent years been widely replaced (notably in the US and Canada) by such neutral or shared terms as *chair*, *firefighter*, *supervisor*, and *police officer*. Comparably, the terms *steward* and *stewardess* aboard commercial aircraft (the latter formerly *air hostess*, without a matching *air host*) have been de-gendered into the shared term *flight attendant* (although the earlier terms continue to be casually used). A brief over-enthusiasm for the use of *person* instead of *man* as a gender-neutral term has left some words, such as *chairperson*, in use but others, such as *policeperson*, proved to be short-lived period pieces.

❷ Replacing representative 'man'

There has been a marked decrease in the use of *man* to represent the human race at large, as for example in the title *The Ascent of Man* for a book about human evolution, which precipitated a non-male response in the title of another published work, *The Ascent of Woman*. In addition, the use of *man* for a representative individual (*What does the man in the street think?*) has greatly decreased, replaced by expressions like *the person in the street* or *people in the street*. The adoption of the shared form *humankind* to replace *mankind* has been notably widespread.

❸ Marital labelling

Feminists in the later 20th century argued against the traditional requirement that a woman's social title (conventionally *Mrs* or *Miss*) should specify marital status, although a man's title (*Mr*) does not. A compromise term *Ms* (pronounced 'miz'), conceived in the US, is now widely used, despite intensely mocking comment in its earlier years, but has not swept the board. It is often used in public life as a neutral term, as originally proposed, but has also been widely adopted to replace *Miss* (for an unmarried woman) while *Mrs* has continued to designate a married woman (apparently because many women, and men, wish to retain such a distinction).

❹ Inappropriate terms

The following usages have been challenged as inappropriate and their use has significantly decreased as a result:

- *Girl* used to refer to an adult woman, notably in attributive positions, as in *girl athlete* and *girl reporter*. Gender-usage reformers consider it to be as demeaning as the use of *boy* for men generally and especially for non-white men in subordinate social positions. The uses of *girl* and *boy* in occasional informal expressions of affection for a woman or man may survive, including where a woman says to her friends, 'OK, girls, let's go.'

- *Lady* used to indicate a woman professional, as in *lady doctor* and *lady lawyer*, a genteelism that dates from a time when women were rare in such professions and the few who did exist came from higher social levels.

❺ Inadequate naming techniques

Such techniques have not traditionally represented men and women equally, as in the list *Professors Eliot, Goldstein, and Barbara Smith*. Manuals of style now generally recommend parallelism: *Professors Eliot, Goldstein, and Smith* or *Professors Edgar Eliot, Sol Goldstein, and Barbara Smith*.

Although Standard English does not have gender for inanimate objects, the pronoun *she* is often used with things and qualities that are perceived as having 'female' characteristics, such as aspects of nature and boats, cars, and various machines. Such associations may at times seem simply traditional, as in *Mother Nature* together with the pronoun *she*, or flattering, as in *She's got a lovely shape* for a ship, but when a man trying to start a motor is told to *give her a kick and she'll turn over* the implications are very different. A significant change occurred in 1979, when major tropical storms were no longer designated by female names alone, the name *Hurricane Harry* becoming as likely as *Hurricane Hazel*. This change has tended to eliminate media descriptions of 'temperamental' storms in the US that 'flirt with the coast'.

More cogently, however, increasing pressure through the 1980/1990s against sexual discrimination in areas such as job advertisements and academic journals led to the development of guidelines for shared and fair usage, as for example *The Handbook of Nonsexist Writing* by Casey Miller and Kate Swift (Harper & Row, 1980, 2001). The special interests and recommendations of US feminists rapidly spread in the 1980s to the rest of the English-speaking world, with comparable effects. Distinctive aspects of the gender issue have included:

History, herstory, womyn and wimmin   Many feminists, in the US and elsewhere, have taken the view that radical changes in the form of certain everyday words on paper and screen have positive psychological value, even if for at time at least the effect may be funny or bizarre. This has been the case, for example, with the word-play in adapting *history* to *herstory* which, they have argued, presents a new perspective on and analysis of life and society. The term *herstory* focuses attention on the situation and accomplishments of women, seen as largely excluded from, or marginalized in, the 'his story' of male chroniclers. Comparably, the radical visual forms *womyn* and *wimmin* have been seen as distanced or detached from *man/men* (the origin of *woman* being Old English *wifman*, which meant at that time 'female human being', and not 'female man' or 'man's wife', although it has been easy to interpret today as 'wife of a man'). Such arresting and highly charged usages have been good in attracting publicity for the cause and in establishing ideological positions, but if adopted it has been as novel terms in their own right and not replacements of established terms.

Masculine implications   Many avowedly gender-free words have tended to be presented in certain contexts and constructions as male in essence, as in: *He spoke to the refugees and their wives* (who also happen to be refugees) and *When a bird isn't foraging, it's singing to advertise its territory, to keep intruding males at bay, and to attract a female*. In addition, although *man of letters* is a traditional general term, the oddness of **She was a leading nineteenth-century man of letters* and the unlikelihood of *She was a leading nineteenth-century woman of letters* both demonstrate a male reference for which no adequate substitute has yet appeared. *Person of letters* is stilted, although it is worth noting that the use of *person of color* (for someone non-white and especially of African provenance) has had some success in the United States.

Genericness   A widely endorsed alternative to generic *he* (as in *Ask anyone and he'll tell you*) has also not yet developed, the most common and widely endorsed solution being the use of singular *they* (especially in casual usage), which in fact has a long history, as in *Ask anyone and they'll tell you*. In general usage, both *he or she* and (in writing) *s/he* occur, sometimes with reverse emphasis *she and he*, and sometimes with alternation in ordering, first *she and he* then *he and she*, but such approaches are cumbersome and inelegant, and invite amusement or wry remarks. Usage specialists generally recommend avoidance, most easily done by shifting into the plural, for example changing *Everybody I asked said he* OR *he or she* OR *she or he* OR *(s)he would come* to *All the people I asked said they would come.*

Using *person* and *people* The neutral use of *person* in compounds has made progress with regard especially to such terms as *anchorperson, chairperson, layperson, salesperson, spokesperson*, with considerable success in the plural use of *people* (written in open form), as in *business people, lay people, sales people*, and *working people*, but notably not **anchor people, *chair people* and **spokes people*. However, the usage has often been mocked (as with *clergyperson, fisherperson*, and *weatherperson*), and many who have otherwise been happy to adopt de-gendering usages remain uneasy about this pattern in the singular. In at least two cases, however, the first element on its own has made progress: *anchor* and *chair*, without any persons. The term *layman* continues to be widely used, especially in the phrase *in layman's language* (which could however be adapted to *in lay language*), but the neutral *layperson* has had some success in religious and professional contexts and *lay people* has been even more successful. On the whole, however, despite some successes, the extensive non-sexist use of *person* in compounds has not been a success; of all the words associated with de-gendering certain usages, it has provoked the most jokes among huperson beings.

Asymmetry Some apparently clear-cut male and female pairs of words are asymmetrical: *governor* refers in the main to a man with territorial or administrative power, while *governess* refers to a woman employee with limited authority over children; *master* generally refers to a man who controls things (and sometimes to a woman, as in *She's a master of the subject*), but *mistress* (although it can often refer to a woman in charge of a house, college, or the like) nowadays more immediately means a married man's kept woman, and negative echoes from the second sense may affect the first.

Pairing In addition, the relative position of male and female in two-part phrases (such as *he or she, host and hostess, male and female, man and wife, men and women, boys and girls*) gives primary status to males, the exceptions being the chivalric *ladies and gentlemen* and the informal (US) *mom* (UK) *mum and dad*. Asymmetrical pairs also sometimes occur, as in *men and girls, men and ladies*, but not usually **boys and women, *gentlemen and women, *women and gentlemen*, while *women and boys* means something quite distinct, as does *girls and men*. Pejorative terms may also be stronger when applied to women: *bitch* is seldom complimentary, whereas *bastard* (especially *old bastard*) is sometimes affectionate. *Witch* is generally negative (except perhaps in fantasy stories), whereas *wizard* tends to be positive, especially in fantasy stories, and has a useful transferred role in the use of computer software. In addition, in the widely acclaimed 'Harry Potter' books, by J. K. Rowling, all the magic folk (whether female, male, child, or adult) are 'wizards', which in these stories makes the traditional male term virtually ethnic, in contrast to the Muggles, the non-magic majority of humankind. Some witches in more traditional stories are on the side of good, but mostly they are not, and the phrase *old witch* is likely to be negative, while *old wizard* could only relate to the age of the male spell-caster, and not either his disposition or his looks.

Marked suffixes In common with other languages of European origin, English has traditionally indicated femaleness through suffixation, the nouns to which they attach traditionally referring only to men. The suffixes are:

❶ *-ess*

As in *actress*, *authoress*, *sculptress*, *waitress*, this suffix is sometimes said to high-light women's accomplishments, but has tended to be linked to roles presented as less significant, such as *manageress*, *poetess*. *Actress*, however, is widely used pos-itively at the same time as the inclusive use of *actor* has gained ground. *Hostess* con-tinues to be widely used, but its occurrence in such phrases as *bar hostess* may yet lead to its decline, making way for an inclusive use of *host*. The forms *Jewess*, *Negress*, and *Quakeress* are dismissive extensions to often disparaging uses of *Jew*, *Negro*, *Quaker*, are not balanced by such creations as **Christianess*, **Nordess*, **Mormoness*, and are now seldom used.

❷ *-ette*

This suffix has three senses: small (as in *cigarette*, *dinette*); artificiality (*leatherette*); and femaleness linked with an auxiliary role (*drum majorette*, *Jaycee-ette*, *ush-erette*). *Copette* would hardly be as tough or reassuring an image as *cop*, and is likely only to be used in a jokey nonce remark. The term *suffragette* has been widely used to refer to activists who sought votes for women at the turn of the 19th/20th cen-turies. These women, however, called themselves *suffragists*. The better-known term was popularized by an often hostile media and public, the dismissive suffix serving to disparage their goals and diminish their prospects.

❸ *-trix*

As in the now rare *aviatrix*, this suffix has a limited use in legal language (*executrix*, *testatrix*), and the sado-masochistic term *dominatrix*. Such usages, however, mark females in these roles as unusual, and by and large in legal circles the *-or* forms are standard and shared.

Male-centred words have in the last two decades been increasingly challenged by both women and men, primarily in the US but increasingly elsewhere, with some impact on usage in other languages. In many cases they have been replaced (often formally) by neutral terms: *chairman* by *chair*, *forefather* by *ancestor*, *headmaster*, and *headmistress* by *head teacher* or *principal*. Unbalanced words such as *mistress* in its sexual sense now tend to be replaced by shared terms such as *lover*. The replacement of *mother/father* by *parent*, unless gender-specific roles are involved, suggests a diminution in gender stereotyping. In the case of *housewife*, the male-orientated *househusband* seems to be integrated (often wryly) into general usage, while *homemaker* appears to remain feminine in reference and has not fared par-ticularly well beyond the US, while *home manager* has made little headway except as a coy euphemism. Notably, traditional male-related work terms have proved easy to replace with shared terms: *manpower* with *personnel* or *work force*, or simply *workers*, and *man hours* with *operator hours*.

The feminist movement, with its many achievements, may have begun as a crusade with a very specific focus, but with the passage of time it has expanded into, or combined with other movements to create, something larger and perhaps ulti-mately even more radical and revolutionary: the movement now solidly though wryly identified as *political correctness*.

This phrase and its short form *PC* were first used—abrasively—in the later 1980s by conservative US academics and journalists for what they saw as the coercive and overheated efforts of liberals, feminists, gay-rights campaigners, multiculturalists, and others to introduce what *they* saw as a more humane and inclusive vocabulary for people who are variously 'disadvantaged'. In 1991, the *Random House Webster's College Dictionary* fairly neutrally defined *political correctness* as: 'Marked by or adhering to a typically progressive orthodoxy on issues involving esp. race, gender, sexual affinity or ecology.' In the later 1990s, the term escaped its originators and especially its abbreviated form came to be used freely (whether negatively, positively, or neutrally, or seriously or lightly) to refer to the attitudes, views, and usage of individuals and groups committed to promoting kinds of social justice and equity, such as the elimination of sexism and racism. In language terms, there are two broad aspects to it:

❶ The uses of *-ism and -ist*

On the analogy of *racism/racist* and *sexism/sexist*, a large number of terms have been coined to cover kinds of actual or perceived social bias and discrimination. These include: *ableism* (such bias by the 'normal' against the physically or mentally impaired); *heterosexism* (such bias by 'straights' against homosexuals); *ageism* (such bias against any one age group against any other, old against young or young against old); and *heightism* (such bias by those around the norm against very short or very tall people, or by taller against shorter people).

❷ Stereotyping

Two examples are: with regard to intelligence, the assumption that women are generally less intelligent than men and blacks less intelligent than whites; with regard to humour, the occurrence of 'inappropriately directed laughter', aroused by jokes at the expense of women, the disabled, homosexuals, ethnic minorities, and the like.

In recent years, and despite a great deal of inappropriately directed laughter, many PC usages and viewpoints have made considerable headway (to greater and less extents in various parts of the world). Some of the more extreme coinages and proposals have faded, at least in English-speaking society at large, while others have established themselves and become mundane, principally as a result of greater public care, in both social and linguistic terms, with regard to all kinds of minority groups, customs, beliefs, and problems. As a result, people in the United States and some other countries appear to have become somewhat less guarded, less prickly, more relaxed, and more willing to enjoy the unintended humour caught up in the wake of high- and single-minded social reformers. This more comfortable state of affairs was demonstrated in the mid-1990s by the success—as well as the title, style, and content—of *Politically Correct Bedtime Stories*, a small best-selling book by the Chicago writer James Finn Garner. An excerpt:

> **1994** On the way to Grandma's house, Red Riding Hood was accosted by a wolf, who asked her what was in her basket. She replied, 'Some healthful snacks for my grandmother, who is certainly capable of taking care of herself as a mature adult.'
>
> The wolf said, 'You know, my dear, it isn't safe for a little girl to walk through these woods alone.'

Red Riding Hood said, 'I find your sexist remark offensive in the extreme, but I will ignore it because of your traditional status as an outcast from society, the stress of which has caused you to develop your own, entirely valid, worldview. Now, if you'll excuse me, I must be on my way.'

Red Riding Hood walked on along the main path. But, because his status outside society had freed him from slavish adherence to linear, Western-style thought, the wolf knew a quicker route to Grandma's house. He burst into the house and ate Grandma, an entirely valid course of action for a carnivore such as himself. Then, unhampered by rigid, traditionalist notions of what was masculine or feminine, he put on Grandma's nightclothes and crawled into bed.

– *Macmillan*, 1997

This sharply amusing little book illustrates how some of the uses of English in the US have evolved since the tale of Little Red Riding Hood was first told in Europe—or, more cogently, since 1620, when the English settlement of Plimoth Plantation needed help to survive a very bad winter. The colony survived, largely because a passing Red Indian or Red Man or Injun or American Indian or Native American whose name was Samoset spoke entirely validly in an Atlantic pidgin English to the worried Pilgrim Fathers—and Mothers. And was willing to give the Palefaces a helping hand.

English teaching: profession, social service, or global industry?

1988 The English language is one of our greatest assets and English Language Teaching one of the fastest growing sectors. The Association of Recognised English Language Services (ARELS) estimate that over 750,000 students come to Britain to learn English each year. On average they stay for 42 days and spend £1,300 each, contributing over £1 billion to the economy.
– from *Tomorrow's Tourism*, a strategy document produced by the Department of Culture, Media and Sport of the United Kingdom government

1999a The first step towards a global alliance took place at the 98 ARELS fair. . . . Representatives unanimously agreed that a common format for the collection and publication of statistics about the global English Language Teaching industry should be developed.
– 'First step towards global collaboration', *ARELS International*, February

1999b Teaching English is big business. Globalization and the Internet are fueling an exciting industry—English language training. Established in 1972, with more than 250 centers currently operating in 15 countries, Wall Street Institute is capitalizing on the extensive need for English language training. MASTER FRANCHISEES WANTED. We are seeking partners interested in development in Asia, Europe and the Middle East. . . . Visit us at the Frankfurt Franchise Exhibition from April 22–25. Wall Street Institute is part of SYLVAN LEARNING SYSTEMS INC., a $600 million global education network.
– advertisement, *International Herald Tribune*, 16 April

The above quotations, which share the virtue of clarity, may encourage the view that English-language imperialists have not only foisted their language on the rest of the world but invited it to pay handsomely for the privilege. Certainly, in tandem with globalization, an economist's-eye view of English as a marketable commodity has become common in recent years. English has its brightly packaged national and commercial brands, all of which (like detergent and fashion products) are subject to market forces: 'You need English? Buy British, buy American, buy Australian—buy Global.'

In the decades following the Second World War, many English-language scholars, notably in the UK, became involved in what the British Council has long called *ELT* (*English Language Teaching* for non-native learners). Many such scholars have also had links with the British Council and with Oxford University Press, Cambridge University Press, Longman, Collins, and other publishers of ELT materials, as well as with commercial teaching organizations such as International House, Eurocentres, and ARELS, and professional teaching organizations such as the UK-based IATEFL (International Association of Teachers of English as a Foreign Language) and the US-based TESOL (Teaching English to Speakers of Other Languages). Indeed, the associated branch of linguistics known as *applied linguistics* became itself something of a growth industry from the 1970s onward.

By the 1970s, several language scholars were describing the expansion of English worldwide in terms of a three-part model, of which there have been three versions: in the UK, as formulated by Barbara Strang (in her *History of English* (London: Methuen, 1970)), and by Randolph Quirk, Sidney Greenbaum, Geoffrey Leech, and the Swedish scholar Jan Svartvik (in *A Grammar of Contemporary English* (Harlow: Longman, 1972)); and in a range of publications since the early 1980s by the Indian-American scholar Braj B. Kachru. The charter statements of Strang and Quirk *et al* in this area were:

1970 Strang

At the present time, English is spoken by perhaps 350 to 400m people who have it as their mother tongue. . . . I shall call them A-speakers, because they are the principal kind we think of in trying to choose a variety of English as a basis for description. The principal communities of A-speakers are those of the UK, the USA, Canada, Australia, New Zealand and South Africa. There are many millions more for whom English may not be quite the mother tongue . . . who live in communities in which English has a special status. . . . These are the B-speakers, found extensively in Asia (especially India) and Africa (especially the former colonial territories). Then there are those throughout the world for whom English is a foreign language, its study required, often as the first foreign language, as part of their country's educational curriculum, though the language has no official, or even traditional, standing in that country. These are the C-speakers.

– *A History of English* (London: Methuen), 17–18

1972 Quirk *et al.*

English is the world's most widely used language. It is useful to distinguish three primary categories of use: as a *native* language, as a *second* language, and as a *foreign* language. English is spoken as a native language by nearly three hundred million people: in the United States, Britain, Ireland, New Zealand, Canada, the Caribbean and South Africa. . . . In several of these countries,

English is not the sole language: the Quebec province of Canada is French-speaking, much of South Africa is Afrikaans-speaking, and for many Irish and Welsh people, English is not the native language. But for these Welsh, Irish, Québecois and Afrikaners, English will even so be a *second* language. . . . This second-language function is more noteworthy, however, in a long list of countries where only a small proportion of the people have English as their native language: India, Pakistan, Nigeria, Kenya and many other Commonwealth countries and former British territories. . . . By *foreign* language we mean a language that is used by someone for communication across frontiers. . . . No language is more widely studied or used as a foreign language than English. The desire to learn it is immense and apparently insatiable. . . .

– *A Grammar of Contemporary English* (Harlow: Longman), 3

The tripartite model is both demographic and socio-political:

❶ The ENL territories

The home localities of the Quirk group's users of English as a Native Language, of Strang's A-speakers, and of Kachru's Inner Circle. They include: Australia, Canada, England (UK), the Irish Republic, Liberia, New Zealand, Northern Ireland (UK), Scotland (UK), South Africa, Wales (UK), and the United States.

❷ The ESL territories

The home localities of the Quirk group's users of English as a Second Language, of Strang's B-speakers, and of Kachru's Outer Circle, where English comes after at least one other language, and has been present for at least a century. They include: Bangladesh, Botswana, Cameroon, Cyprus, Fiji, Ghana, Hong Kong, India, Kenya, Malaysia, Nigeria, Panama, Pakistan, Papua New Guinea, the Philippines, Sierra Leone, Singapore, Sri Lanka, Tanzania, Uganda, Zambia, Zimbabwe.

❸ The EFL territories

The home localities of the Quirk group's users of English as a Foreign Language, of Strang's C-speakers, and of Kachru's Expanding Circle, where English has tradi-tionally been 'foreign'. It may have been significantly present in a territory for decades, supported by massive public educational programmes (as in Sweden and Japan) or be a relatively recent arrival (as with Mozambique and Uzbekistan). The list of EFL territories in effect covers the rest of the world.

This approach or model was the outcome of reflections that began in the 1960s, when the British Empire was winding down. It broadly matched the sociopolitical reality worldwide at the time, but in the first decade of the 21st century seems to belong in a tidier world. Its creators knew that it was an over-simplification when they formulated it, and in the 30 years or so since they wrote there have been many changes and many implicit issues have become more explicit. The following list of ten developments since the model first appeared represents those changes and issues but is not exhaustive:

❶ ENL and multilingualism

There is a greater and more willing acknowledgement today of actual and potential multilingualism within the ENL territories, which have often been presented as if they were language monoliths. In all such territories, one finds language mosaics rather than uniform use of one language, and such variety includes hybridization among languages. Most such territories are now exploring the extent to which indigenous and in-migrating languages and varieties of English might be maintained in a multicultural context, despite many local people's doubts and suspicions.

❷ ENL and variety

There is a greater willingness to acknowledge variety among the kinds of English in ENL territories, along with an awareness of on-going change, as with the emergence and spread in south-eastern England of *Estuary English*, a spoken variety widely perceived as occupying the middle ground socially and linguistically between Cockney and RP.

❸ The 'native' controversy

There is increasing uncertainty about the solidity, validity, and value of such terms as 'native' and 'native speaker' in relation to any 'World Standard English', especially when the usage of dialect and creole speakers in avowedly ENL territories is contrasted with the fluent 'native-like' command of the standard language in such EFL territories as the Netherlands and Denmark, where English has the quality of a 'second first language'.

❹ The question of a standard

There is a loss of certainty (however well- or ill-founded in the past) among educationists and others regarding three linked issues:

- the spoken standard towards which teachers should seek to move their students (ENL, ESL, and EFL alike). This loss of certainty relates in particular to such prestige models as Received Pronunciation (RP) in the UK and General American (GA, GenAm) in the US.
- the criteria for managing difficult and/or contentious aspects of grammar, orthography, punctuation, lexis, idiom, and slang.
- how to manage professional doubts and queries regarding what kind of language norms should be set for school children in ENL and ESL territories. For traditionalists, the norms have long been with us, are clear, and need only be applied, and it is perverse to pretend otherwise. For others, a new world situation needs new solutions that include less authoritarianism and an alleviation of prejudice in gender, race, culture, language, dialect, and accent.

❺ Issues relating to migration and education

An awareness in many ENL territories that the number of ESL/EFL students in ENL educational institutions has greatly increased, because of both higher levels of migration and a wish in many ESL/EFL regions of the world to have one's children educated in English in an ENL locale. Such a development may be seen as a welcome development economically and culturally or as a menace to tradition and ethnic distinctness, or both at the same time.

❻ National ENL standardizing institutions

The accelerated development, in for example Australia, Canada, New Zealand, and South Africa, of dictionary and other projects that increase the cohesion and autonomy of their own kinds of English and reduce dependence on the UK and US as providers/guarantors of norms. Such development tends to go hand-in-hand with a more sympathetic approach than in the past to both endangered indigenous languages and the 'heritage languages' of immigrants.

❼ National ESL monitoring and planning procedures

In various territories worldwide, such as India and Malaysia, there may be language policies designed to protect and promote certain languages. Despite this, however, English may still gain ground 'against' a language or languages whose heritage needs protection and may even threaten the development and security of any such language. If, in addition, parents insist on EL schooling for their children (as they commonly do), there may not be enough time, resources, or personnel both to achieve this and sustain local languages in major social roles (or at all).

❽ Issues relating to hybridization among languages

There is an increasing awareness everywhere that hybridization between English and other languages may lead (or might already have led) to high levels of change in those languages and in local English, through adoptions from one language into another or the formation of mixed usage that may offend and bewilder older people but seem normal and even hip for the young.

Such developments suggest that there is a centripetal/centrifugal paradox in world English and that this paradox will continue. An increase in variety and in local prestige seems likely to be matched by powerful pressures towards a world standard, yet (as a consequence of the paradox) any such standard will be a kind of federation—but of unequals, a genteel kind of pecking order (with the possibility of greater forbearance and leeway in terms of variation as time goes on).

The history of English being what it is (unlike Italian, Spanish, and French with their Academies), such an informally federative standard would most probably evolve in the same accumulative and *ad hoc* manner as animated the development of the UK and US standards over the last 200 years. Indeed, such a standard appears to have been evolving since the 1960s: that is, as the British Empire expired and not long after the primacy of American English began to be recognized (conceded) in the UK and elsewhere. However, if there can be two national standards within one English, there can in principle be more than two, a point that has already manifestly influenced thinking in Australia and Canada.

These, by and large, are the broad issues relating to the use, teaching, and learning of English as a national and/or international language. In dealing with them (insofar as this has proved possible), the tripartite model has provided a valuable framework which is, however, no longer as clear-cut as it was taken to be in the 1970s and 1980s. It may in due course evolve into a different model that, among other things, treats Standard English as a unified world resource rather than as an entity whose arrangement of users suggests first-, second-, and third-class sections on a Boeing 747.

The teaching of English has historically been varied. However organized, whatever the aims involved, and whatever the methods used, such teaching proceeds on a scale well beyond any other language past or present. The closest analogue, in a more restricted geographical area (but affecting vast numbers of people), is the teaching of Putonghua, the national language of the People's Republic of China. At the present time, the teaching of English divides into five broad categories, the first four with their own traditions, terminologies, perspectives, theories, practices, publications, organizations, and conferences. They are:

❶ ENL: English as a Native Language

('Ee-en-ell') Also *English as a Mother Tongue* and *English as a First Language*. In the ENL world, this is the teaching of children, adolescents, and adults in institutions of primary/elementary, secondary, and tertiary (higher) education, and of adults in continuing education, including literacy programmes. The single word *English* is often used as a shorthand (but sometimes ambiguous) term for teaching and studying both the language and its literature(s), and is usually understood as meaning mainly language at the primary level, both language and literature at the secondary level, and at the tertiary level all or any aspects of literature(s), philology, linguistics, language (usually the modern variety), the media, and an eclectic range of associated subjects. In recent years, there has been a tendency in secondary schools, universities, and other institutions to reduce the possibility of ambiguity by distinguishing *English Language* and *English Literature* clearly as the names of courses, and the subjects of examination and the granting of degrees.

❷ ESL: English as a Second Language

('Ee-ess-ell') Associated term *TESL* ('tessle': *Teaching English as a Second Language*). There are two aspects:

- The teaching of English in countries where the language is not a mother tongue but has long been part of the fabric of society, usually for imperial and colonial reasons in the relatively recent past, either as a lingua franca or a medium of education, or both. The term *ESL countries* refers to territories in which English has a statutory role, such as (co-)official language or medium of education, but is not usually the home language, as in India and Nigeria.
- Teaching non-English-speaking immigrants to ENL countries. The comparable term *TESOL* ('tee-sol'), *Teaching English to Speakers of Other Languages*, was originally used only in North America, primarily for the teaching of immigrants, but is now used worldwide in both senses.

❸ EFL: English as a Foreign Language'

('Ee-eff-ell') Associated term *TEFL* ('teffle': *Teaching English as a Foreign Language*). There are two aspects:

- The teaching of English in countries where it is of interest and/or importance but is not, or has not until recently been, a local medium of communication or instruction, as with Japan, Saudi Arabia, and Sweden. The term *EFL countries* refers to the world minus ENL and ESL.
- Providing courses in ENL countries for visiting students from EFL countries. The other term used principally for this category, especially in Britain (as mentioned above), is *English language teaching* or, more commonly, *ELT*

('ee-ell-tee'). It is in this area that the commercial approach to teaching the language is most prominent.

❹ EIL: English as an International Language

('Ee-eye-ell') Associated term *TEIL* ('teel'', 'tee-ee-eye-ell': 'Teaching . . .'). In effect, this is the teaching of English as a global lingua franca, in which it is hoped that in the process people will become aware of the worldwide role of the language and the social and cultural problems that derive from, or relate to, that role. EIL in effect embraces all countries, learners, and users (ENL, ESL, and EFL), its proponents arguing that native users of English need at least as much consciousness-raising with regard to an adequate international use of the language as those who learn it as a second or foreign language. They also argue that the more the English language becomes institutionalized as the world's main medium of international expression, the more native and non-native users will need to learn to acclimatize to each other's ways of using it. They also consider that native users will have to accept (especially competent) non-native users as equals, while accommodating as agreeably as possible their difficulties and anxieties.

❺ ESD: English as a second dialect

('Ee-ess-dee') Associated term *TESD* ('tezd', 'tee-ee-ess-dee': Teaching English as a Second Dialect'). In effect, teaching Standard English to speakers of non-standard varieties, such as dialects as traditionally understood (Yorkshire in the UK; Appalachian in the US), creoles (Nation Language in Jamaica; any Caribbean Creole in the UK). Here, the term *English* is restricted to the area traditionally (and usually implicitly) assigned to it by many educationists and grammarians: the medium of professional and business people educated to college level or its equivalent, and of the major media. 'English' here is the standard language, or dialect, or variety. Both the term and the abbreviation have been modelled on the labels of the preceding categories, but to make their standpoint clear, some proponents of TESD have used the term *Standard English as a Second Dialect* (short form *SESD*) to present Standard English as one dialect or variety among many. Both the term and the concept had a brief heyday in the 1980s/90s. The concept, without the specific name, seems to have been assimilated into general educational theory and practice in many parts of the world, notably North America.

In ENL countries, the educational profession in general and a significant part of the population at large regard good English teaching (whatever 'good' and 'English' are taken to mean) as fundamental to schooling at all levels, as an essential underpinning for students' later lives. Despite the often acrimonious debate arising out of concern for the language and how it is taught, it is widely accepted that the roles of the teachers of English are so different at the three educational levels (primary, secondary, and tertiary) that in fact there is no such thing as a 'typical' teacher of English for all seasons:

❶ Primary

In primary schools, because of the nature of the work, most teachers teach English along with everything else that the children learn. Such teachers are not so much English specialists as trained generalists who integrate the key elements of early

English teaching (such as listening, speaking, reading, and writing) into the fabric of the child's experience.

❷ Secondary

In secondary schools, most teachers are (ideally) specialists. However, while English specialists have a central role, the others are also indirectly teaching English, because it is the medium through which they work. When for example science teachers introduce new terms, indicate how the notes of an experiment should be kept, or discuss relevant texts, they are providing instruction in the register of scientific and technical English, something that is not usually the concern of the English specialist but is of enormous sociolinguistic significance.

❸ Tertiary

In tertiary institutions, teachers (ideally) are not only well versed in aspects of English at large, but are also teachers and researchers in distinctive areas, such as the Victorian novel, John Milton, the sonnet, Media Studies, Creole linguistics, stylistics, or aspects of grammatical or literary theory. As a result, the precise nature of a degree course in English may rest not only on an understanding among teachers and administrators of what must/should be covered in a core syllabus, but also in supplements arising out of the special interests of the members of a department, school, or centre. There may also be a need for facilitating courses in English for academic purposes, especially for non-native students, and in research methodology.

Although it is relatively easy to specify what is going on at the primary and tertiary stages, it is difficult to be clear about the nature and aims of work done in the middle years of education. As a result, the secondary level tends to receive more critical attention from the public than the others. The professional comments that follow, on the nature of the teacher's work at this level, may demonstrate the burden that English-speaking societies have long placed on the secondary-school specialist. The first is from the US in 1965, the second from the UK in 1991, both from periods of vigorous and controversial debate:

> **1965 The United States**
> Like any other professional person, the professional English teacher is one who has been trained or has trained himself, to do competent work. For him professional competence should mean, at the minimum: a college major in English or a strong minor, preparation sufficient to qualify him to begin graduate study in English; systematic postcollegiate study, carried on privately or in a graduate school; a reading command of at least one foreign language, ancient or modern; a deep interest in literature, old and new, and a solid set of critical skills; the ability to write well and the habit of writing, whether for publication or not; a knowledge of the development of the English language and familiarity with recent work in linguistics; a desire not simply to know but to impart knowledge; skill in the handling of instructional problems and knowledge of the research concerning them; an unflagging interest in the processes by which the young learn to use language effectively and richly.
> – *Freedom and Discipline in English*, the Report of the Commission on English, chaired by Harold C. Martin of Harvard University, College Entrance Examination Board, New York

1991 The United Kingdom

English teachers are asked to cover a wide spectrum. In addition to the fundamentals of reading, writing, listening, speaking and spelling required by the National Curriculum [for England and Wales, 1987 onward], they usually teach drama and media studies and are expected to show greater interest in the whole child than many other subject specialists. Most children probably write more prose, and certainly compose more poetry in school than many of their parents. Hence the joke: 'Don't look out of the window or she'll make you write a poem about it.' Both science and English are important subjects in the curriculum, but if something goes amiss in adult life, then it is more likely that blame will be attached to English teachers than to science teachers. In the Sixties, Andrew Wilkinson drew attention to this wide role when he described several models of English teaching, ranging from 'proof reader', which involved meticulous correction of every spelling and punctuation error, to 'Grendel's mother, guardian of the word-hoard', the person with the awesome responsibility of keeping alive and enhancing the nation's cultural heritage.

– from 'Peace in the Civil English War', Schools Report, *Observer*, 22 Sept. 1991, by Ted Wragg, head of the School of Education, Exeter University, England

In public debate, there is often an elemental polarization, between conservatives (who consider that changes in ways of teaching grammar and spelling—among other things—are symptomatic of general social decay) and radicals (who consider that progress will never be made until outdated methods are uprooted). Most teachers are somewhere in the middle, where it may be possible to unite, judiciously, the more positive aspects of both the older and newer stances. In the end, however, the major instigator of change is likely to be technology, as has manifestly been the case in recent decades with the arrival in the classroom of radios, films/movies, television sets, audio- and video-cassettes, computers, and mobile phones.

The teaching of English to non-native learners has two dimensions: as part of the educational system of such countries as India and Nigeria, and as a service to immigrants in such countries as Australia, Canada, the UK, and the US. The terms *(T)EFL*, *(T)ESL*, and *TESOL* emerged after the Second World War, and in Britain no distinction was seriously made between ESL and EFL, both being subsumed under *ELT* ('English Language Teaching'), until well into the 1960s. As regards ESL in particular, the term has been applied to two types of teaching that overlap but are essentially distinct: ESL in the home country of the learner (mainly a UK concept and concern) and ESL for immigrants to ENL countries (mainly a US concept and concern).

British-style ESL is common in non-Western members of the Commonwealth, especially where English is official and/or a language of higher education and opportunity. It largely centres on English-medium schools, and its nature tends to range from close to ENL to close to EFL. Learners will encounter and probably use English outside the classroom and are expected to achieve levels of ability often on a par with schools in ENL countries. Emphasis on acquiring an RP accent has declined in recent decades and an educated local accent has proved to be a more realistic and useful goal. An English-language examination is usually part of the national school-leaving requirements and teacher training is usually the responsibility of departments and colleges of education. Most teachers have a degree and some professional training, and the emphasis is on classroom, not theory.

The teaching of ESL for immigrants to the US and Canada is a different tradition, primarily aimed at integrating adults into local life. Waves of immigration since 1945, notably from Asia and Latin America, have created a strong demand in both countries. Local communities, particularly in the larger cities, offer adult courses and place non-English-speaking children in schools. Many universities have instituted MA courses in related subjects and created centres for teaching and for research and development. Because many US immigrants are refugees, their ESL teacher may be the only public figure they can relate to without anxiety. This gives a quality of social service to much of American ESL, especially in large cities. Teachers often feel that their students need a special kind of care because of past or present experiences, and this may lead to solid relationships both in and beyond the classroom.

Despite this practical focus on North American needs, many countries have looked to the US and Canada for help with teacher training, as a result of which some US and Canadian universities have established links with other countries. Projects in ESL training and teacher education have been undertaken in such countries as Peru, the Philippines, and Thailand, with government sponsorship or help from bodies like the Ford Foundation.

The organization known worldwide as *TESOL*, short for *Teaching English to Speakers of Other Languages* began as a professional association for teachers of English as a second language in the United States in 1966. The organization has been so successful and grown so much that its acronym has become an especially US name for teaching English as a second or additional language, especially to immigrants there and in other English-speaking countries. Although the centre of gravity of the organization remains North American, it has progressively become more international. Attendance at its annual conventions in North America ranges between *c.*5,000 and *c.*10,000, with parallel sessions and a busy interviewing-and-employment facility. With its many affiliates, TESOL reaches tens of thousands of English-teaching professionals worldwide, most notably through the *TESOL Quarterly* (a refereed journal) and *TESOL Matters* (a bimonthly news medium for the profession).

TESOL's stated aim has been to strengthen the teaching and learning of English on a global basis while respecting the language rights of communities and individuals everywhere. To this end, it has sought to support and encourage English language teaching, teacher education, administration and management, curriculum and materials design, and research, disseminates and exchanges information and resources, and concerns itself with providing access to, and offering standards for, English-language instruction, professional training, and various kinds of employment. Its Executive Board is elected by the membership, and represents its affiliates, special-interest sections (SIGs), and members at large. TESOL has observer status as a non-governmental organization (NGO) at the United Nations in New York and has a mutual-recognition agreement with the *International Association of Teachers of English as a Foreign Language* (IATEFL). Its headquarters are in Alexandria, Virginia, USA.

Although British ESL has been rather different, it is equally varied in its clientele. Immigrants to the UK in the past tended to be from the West Indies and West Africa (where English and English-based creoles are spoken) and from Asia (Bangladesh, India, Pakistan, Sri Lanka, and Hong Kong), where English is widely used in the community. More recently, however, immigrants have included asylum-seekers from distressed parts of the world, such as the Balkans, parts of Eastern Europe, and Afghanistan. ESL teachers have mainly been ENL teachers who have received specific in-service training.

Until the mid-1980s, British ESL was often taught in separate classes or in language centres, if numbers justified such provision. However, this procedure came to be widely regarded as divisive and even racist, as it cut ESL learners off from other students and the rest of the curriculum. After a court case by the Commission for Racial Equality in 1986, integrated classes have been the norm, requiring the inclusion of ESL in the training of all teachers. ESL classes are also provided for adults in further education colleges, and by a range of voluntary groups providing individual home-based teaching. Increasingly, ESL teachers have on occasion concerned themselves with political issues arising from the status of many learners. Towards the end of the 20th century, activists from minority groups also became increasingly involved, with the aim of bringing second-language learning and minority rights into a closer relationship. The resulting shift is reflected in the radical re-naming of the *Association for the Teaching of English to People of Overseas Origin* (*ATEPO*) first to the *National Association for Multiracial Education* then to the *National Anti-Racist Movement in Education* (both *NAME*).

As the quotations at the beginning of this section indicate, a great deal of ELT in the UK and increasingly elsewhere has been commercial, offering courses of longer or shorter duration and more or less intensive instruction (sometimes customized to the learner's needs). Private language schools (organized on an individual basis or in networks with brand names in various parts of the UK, the US, Australia, and elsewhere) seek to manage the needs of a large number of clients who may be paying for themselves or have been sent to a school by their parents or a business company for an intensive experience of the language. By and large, although some of them are manifestly 'cowboy outfits' which could manage their affairs more impressively, there is without doubt a high level of expertise, professionalism, and enthusiasm in the world of private-enterprise ELT.

As much of the above material indicates, mainstream ELT teaching is far removed from a hyper-capitalistic enterprise battening on foreign learners of the language. It is in the main undertaken by local authorities in various ENL countries in schools and other centres, or aims where necessary at integrating immigrants through ESL techniques into ENL society at large, without assimilating them in a classic 'melting pot' style. In addition, more ESL and EFL goes on in the countries to which learners belong, and the tax payers of many of those countries are as likely as—or more likely than—the immediate parents to foot the bill. Kinds of exploitation may arise in any situation, but many people and organizations do well (or well enough) in the 'English language industry' without needing or seeking to exploit any one 'consumer'.

The national and international organizations that sustain teachers of English of all kinds tend to operate at an adequate-to-excellent level, and by and large positive results flow from their conferences and other activities. Notable among such results is the development of often world-wide ties among professionals whose careers are enhanced by discussing general problems and particular solutions. In sum, the teaching of English in all its forms is increasingly a profession, certainly often a social service, and, for the foreseeable future, also a significant world industry, with most of the virtues and some of the vices that all industries share.

World or International Standard English

1965 First let me make clear what I mean by Standard English. This phrase is used in a variety of senses. I shall use it, as many other people do, to mean that kind of English which is the official language of the entire English-speaking world, and is also the language of all educated English-speaking people. What I mean by Standard English has nothing to do with the way people pronounce: Standard English is a language, not an accent, and it is as easily recognizable as Standard English when it is written down as when it is spoken. It is, in fact, the only form of English to be at all widely written nowadays. There is, in Standard English, a certain amount of regional variation, perhaps, but not very much—it is spoken, and even more written, with remarkable uniformity considering the area which it covers. . . . Standard English, then, is a world language.

– David Abercrombie, 'R. P. and local accent', in *Studies in Phonetics & Linguistics* (Oxford University Press), 10–11

1996 Standard English is the national variety of the language inasmuch as it is not restricted to any region within the country. It is taught throughout the education system, and is identified with educated English. . . . It is pre-eminently the language of printed matter; indeed, only the standard language has an established orthography. It is the variety that is taught to foreign learners. . . . National standard varieties in countries where English is a first language are remarkably homogeneous, particularly in written English. The homogeneity is explained by their common descent from the British English of the seventeenth century. . . . The influence of print, and more recently of radio, television, and film have contributed to prevent the national standards of English-speaking countries from drifting far apart. If anything, under these influences and the ease of international travel the national standards have tended to converge.

– Sidney Greenbaum, *The Oxford English Grammar* (Oxford University Press), 14

2000a According to D'Souza (1999) the question of standard English 'is one of the great unresolved problems that we are carrying into the twenty-first century' (271). Why should this question be so important and why so unresolved? And what does the book under review here add to our possible understanding of this issue? There are a number of significant issues here. First, there is the question of definition: what is a standard language? From this follows the ontological question as to whether they actually exist or are merely convenient (or inconvenient) fictions. Are we talking about spoken or written language? And in the global context, there are questions such as whether a global standard of international English exists or is emerging? Or is international intelligibility always a negotiation of possibilities with no obvious standard? . . . Are standard languages hegemonic forms to be opposed? Are standard languages hegemonic forms to be acquired?

– Alastair Pennycook, 'Disinventing standard English', in *English Language and Linguistics* 4:1, 115–24, reviewing Tony Bex and Richard J. Watts (eds), *Standard English: The Widening Debate* (Cambridge University Press)

2000b   English is no doubt a lingua franca, a global language of today, but the hegemony of English is also very threatening to those who are not speakers of English. While it may be convenient to have a common international language, we have to ask ourselves whether it will really contribute to a democratic global communication to use a language which is historically and culturally connected with particular nations. . . . The existing hegemony of English is first of all anti-democratic because it is creating a structure of linguistic hierarchy as well as social inequality and discrimination. . . . The hegemony of English also gives the English-speaking countries enormous economic power. Because English sells well, English is now one of the most important products of the English-speaking countries. So English is not merely a medium, but a proprietary commodity to be marketed across the world.

– Yukio Tsuda, Professor of International Communication at Nagoya University, Japan, 'Envisioning a Democratic Linguistic Order', *TESL Reporter* 33,1 (Hawaii: Brigham Young University), 32–3

The above quotations (and others that could have accompanied them) indicate that, for many people, a World Standard English exists and is useful, but is not innocent, and may even at times be harmful. For such people, it is not simply 'a language of wider communication', as some have rightly enough put it, but often more like a loaded weapon pointed in their direction.

There are certainly reasons to be watchful about how English performs 'standardly' in the world. After all, standard languages are the matter-of-fact creations of social elites: in the case of English, the upper and middle classes of the later 18th century, simultaneously in England, Scotland, Ireland, and North America. Standard English was also widely transmitted in the 19th century by educational planners, teachers, and others (usually with excellent intentions) to ever larger numbers of people worldwide. In both mother-tongue communities and foreign-language situations, large numbers of people have for several centuries consciously sought the standard, whether for themselves or for those in their care. Indeed, people of any background who use the language at an educated level increasingly constitute a transnational class that manifestly has a fair degree of comfort in the complexities of the present-day world. All the worse then when discomfort occurs, as it has done for Yukio Tsuda (above), who was nonetheless able to speak out about it.

Standard English is widely associated with a Western culture that, for at least two centuries, has advocated equality of opportunity alongside equality under the law. It has also been associated for many years with hegemony (direct and indirect, conscious or unconscious), but is also recognized (gladly or ruefully) as a gateway or passport or avenue or ladder (there are many metaphors) to desirable kinds of knowledge, skill, and opportunity. The Internet with its American engine is only the latest manifestation of an oxymoronic 'democracy of the elite' that is by no means an idle fancy.

By and large, people are not excluded from using it by race, class, creed, politics, gender, or any other traditional means of separating sheep from goats, but they *are* excluded by ignorance and inability, which are regrettable but hard facts of life. Language in general and English in particular are often described as currency, and just as the world divides into the financial haves and have-nots, so it divides, alas, into linguistic haves and have-nots. English may well be or have been hegemonic, but the risk of not possessing it may be so great that submission to this hegemony has become a fairly small price to pay, certainly far smaller than had to be paid for Latin in ancient Rome.

Indeed, the social price to pay for failing to get inside the magic circle of a perceived 'Standard' or 'Good' English is lower now than in the past, even though kinds of élitism and educational privilege continue to exist. Geographical and social limitations have always been placed on the kind of English that can sit at the table above the salt, but the table itself is much larger now and the salt more generously positioned. Once upon a time, the acknowledged circle of comfort in using Standard English was tiny: educated upper- and middle-class people in southern England. It then grew to such people in all of England-cum-Britain, then in the United States, Canada, and Ireland, then in the traditionally 'white' Anglophone countries, then (in the widest and most recent circle of them all) among all appropriately educated people anywhere in the world, whatever their background. All they have had to do to get above the salt is use the language with passable care. That isn't of course quite the whole story, but nothing ever is, and, as hegemonies go, this one could have been a lot worse.

For some people, Standard English is a monolith, with more or less strict rules and conventions that apply everywhere the language is used; for others, it is a range of overlapping varieties, so that American Standard English is distinct from but similar to British Standard English. Although for some the term is negative, for most it appears to be either neutral or positive, referring to something important. As one of the leading grammarians of English in the 20th century put it about a decade ago:

> **1989** Standard English (by whatever name it is known) is the variety of English that is manifestly recognised in our society as the prestigious variety.
> – Sidney Greenbaum, 'Why should guidance be left to amateurs?', *English Today* 18, April (Cambridge University Press)

It is generally agreed that Standard English contrasts (often strongly) with other kinds of English, but there is no consensus about the best way of describing and discussing such contrasts as, say, between *standard* and *dialect*, *standard* and *nonstandard*, or *standard* and *substandard*. It is also generally agreed that Standard English is a minority form, and could remain a minority form. Some observers see Standard English as a social and political good to which all members of the English-speaking world have a birthright, but others are less certain, and some are hostile to the idea, because of its social-class dimensions. The proportion of users of the standard to users of other varieties is not known, is seldom discussed, and may be unknowable. But even so, there appears to be a consensus that a standard form exists, or standard forms exist, and that it serves or they serve—or should serve—as the basis for both public and private education in English-medium schools everywhere.

Standard English: defined by what it isn't

In 1981, the British applied linguist and language teacher Peter Strevens sought to establish the nature of Standard English by saying what it was not:

1 It is not an arbitrary, *a priori* description of English, or of a form of English, devised by reference to standards of moral value, or literary merit, or supposed linguistic purity, or any other metaphysical yardstick—in short, 'Standard English' cannot be defined or described in terms such as 'the best English' or 'literary English', or 'Oxford English', or 'BBC English'.

2 It is not defined by reference to the usage of any particular group of English-users, and especially not by reference to a social class—'Standard English' is *not* 'upper class English' and it is encountered across the whole social spectrum, though not necessarily in equivalent use by all members of all classes.

3 It is not statistically the most frequently occurring form of English, so that 'standard' here does not mean 'most often heard'.

4 It is not imposed upon those who use it. True, its use by an individual may be largely the result of a long process of education; but Standard English is neither the product of linguistic planning or philosophy (for example as exists for French in the deliberations of the Académie Française, or policies devised in similar terms for Hebrew, Irish, Welsh, Bahasa Malaysia, etc.); nor is it a closely defined norm whose use and maintenance is monitored by some quasi-official body, with penalties imposed for non-use or mis-use. Standard English evolved: it was not produced by conscious design.

– 'What *is* Standard English?', in the *RELC Journal*, Singapore.

In everyday usage, the phrase *Standard/standard English* is taken to be the variety most widely accepted, understood, and perhaps valued either within an English-speaking country (as was generally the case even in the recent past, and for many people may remain the case for some time) or throughout the entire English-speaking world (a state of affairs of which many people are only now taking note). The standard variety is usually considered to be more or less free of regional, class, and other shibboleths, although the issue of a 'standard accent' often causes (more or less severe) trouble and tension, and for many people no standard accent is possible, a state of affairs that indicates how much things changed in the course of the 20th century. The standard is sometimes presented as a 'common core' (what is left when all regional and other distinctions are taken away), a view that remains controversial because of the difficulty of deciding where the core ends and the periphery begins, both for groups and for individuals. However, many language scholars agree on three things:

1 The standard is most easily identified in print, whose conventions are more or less uniform throughout the world, and some commentators use the term *print standard* for that medium.

2 Standard forms are used by most presenters of news on most English-language radio and television networks, but necessarily with national, regional, and/or other variations, notably in accent, because there is no uniform, worldwide, educated accent of English.

3 Use of Standard English relates to social class and level of education, often considered (explicitly or implicitly) to match the average level of attainment of students who have finished secondary education, although the pressure towards tertiary education of one kind or another is currently so great that the level may move upward.

The question of whether Standard English does, can, or ought to include specific norms of speech and accent remains the most controversial of the many difficult issues associated with the term. An institutional definition was provided by the Kingman Report on the teaching of English in England and Wales, submitted to the UK government in 1988. It began with a statement defining Standard English that presented the variety as virtually limitless in its reach yet closely bound to one medium, writing:

> **1988** All of us can have only partial access to Standard English: the language itself exists like a great social bank on which we all draw and to which we all contribute. . . . It is the fact of being the written form which establishes it as the standard. And it is the fact of being the written form which means that it is used not only in Britain but by all writers of English throughout the world, with remarkably little variation.
> – from the Kingman Report (the report of the Committee of Inquiry into the Teaching of English under the chairmanship of Sir John Kingman)

The figurative strength of the term *Standard English* has been considerable. Just as there was at one time only one standard yard, kept in London as a measure against which all other yards might be checked, so (by extension, especially in the 19th century) there was only one standard language, kept as it were in or near London for the same purpose. Even after a war of liberation in the 1770s and 1780s established the US as a separate centre of English, years passed before the British (and indeed many Americans) began to accept that US writers and publishers had succeeded in creating a second centre and therefore a second yardstick for the language. Yet even after two centuries, old ways of talking about the language die hard, as in:

> **1990** The British are quick to point out how different American English is from Standard English.
> – Mandy Loader, in the *EFL Gazette*, London, April

Among the objective indicators that a language or a variety of a language has its own standard are such artefacts as grammars and dictionaries and such cultural achievements as a literary canon. It was taken to be proof positive of the success of French as a national and international language that by the end of the 17th century it had all three. English achieved this status by about the time the American colonies declared their independence, so that the historical distance between the British and American standards is so slight as hardly to be worth measuring. In the course of the 19th century, the US established its own grammars, dictionaries, and literary canon, although it took until the first three decades of the 20th century for many Americans to feel sure that 'American English' and 'American literature' were firmly established.

However, despite time lag and confusion among terms, there have been in principle, since the early 19th century, two minimum yardsticks for a Standard English, both of them print-related: the development of an autonomous literature and the publication of a national dictionary. Under these criteria, it is self-evident that, in recent times, Australia, Canada, New Zealand, and South Africa have their own Standard Englishes. These criteria are useful traditional indicators, but they need not be the only ones, as the mention of a national grammar book (above) indicates. Nowadays, it also seems reasonable to bring in national 'quality' newspapers, media services, and national educational programmes involving language. On such a basis, it seems likely that the relevant interested parties in such countries as India, the Irish Republic, the Philippines, and Singapore will at appropriate times move towards talking about their own national standards, while there might also be interesting (and perhaps unprecedented) developments in the European Union, where native and acquired Englishes already co-exist.

One of the issues which creates great tension and dissatisfaction, and makes many people cautious about endorsing 'standardness' in a language at any level is the existence of opposites to—or failures in achieving—the avowed standard. Two terms currently exist for usage that is not standard: (1) the manifestly negative and judgemental *substandard* (which works well in such areas as quality checks on manufactured goods but causes social difficulties in matters of language); (2) the would-be objective and dispassionate *non-standard/nonstandard* (which often sounds like a fig-leaf for *substandard*).

The use of *substandard* for kinds of language is inevitably close to its use in manufacturing, engineering, and the like. It is a term that comes easily to frustrated teachers and tetchy editors, much as it does with factory supervisors angry about shoddy work. *Non-standard* seeks to make no judgement about the quality or value of any usage, and is favoured by sociolinguists and others who concern themselves with the objective analysis of language use, but everyone knows what is involved in such labels. Double negatives like *He ain't done nothin'* and *I don't got no money* convey their intended message entirely clearly, but coupled with a certain accent type they also convey a social message, and everybody knows that too.

There can be little doubt about two issues relating to the nature and use of English worldwide: there are many varieties and within this range there are a number of institutionally and socially clear-cut standard forms: that is, there are a number of well-acknowledged Standard Englishes, usually associated with nation-states. Some Standard Englishes, however, are more equal than others: manifestly, the usage of the UK in traditional terms and the US in current international terms. Inevitably, however, interest has gone beyond them to ask whether there already is or could yet be an all-encompassing world or international standard. If there were such a standard, it would however somehow have to integrate and balance out both the two long-established primary national standards and the range of more recently emerging national standards. The following sections provide some indication of the approaches of various commentators to the issue of such a larger Standard English. The world's general shapers of opinion have not yet come to terms with the issue, but it is clear that specialists in the study of world English have already pretty well made up their minds. The four following paragraphs analyse four terms in wide recent use among language scholars and present a selection of their comments.

International English

This phrase (with or without a capital *i*) appears to have developed more or less as a staging post to something else. Basically, it covers the English language at large, often (but not always or necessarily) implicitly conceived as standard. It is also certainly commonly used in connection with the acquisition, use, and study of English as the world's lingua franca ('TEIL: Teaching English as an International Language'), and especially when the language is considered as a whole in contrast with *American English*, *British English*, *South African English*, and the like. Three citations are:

> **1988** [I]t is difficult to predict the shape of international English in the twenty-first century. But it seems likely that more rather than less standardization will result. . . . We may, in due course, all need to be in control of two standard Englishes—the one which gives us our national and local identity, and the other which puts us in touch with the rest of the human race. In effect, we may all need to become bilingual in our own language.
> – David Crystal, *The English Language*, Penguin

> **1995** All these dimensions of local (intranational) and national English need to be codified and linked up with what we know about international English, if we are to communicate effectively overseas.
> – Pam Peters, 'A Word on Words: Intranational and International English', in *Australian Language Matters*, 3:4, October–December

> **1999** Marko Modiano, 'International English in the global village', in *English Today* 58 (15:2), April (Cambridge University Press)

International Standard English

(Occasional short form *ISE*) Standard English when used internationally. The term appears to have two linked senses: (1) The sum-total of all standard English usage worldwide, but with particular reference to the norms of American, British, and increasingly Australian and other varieties with their own grammars, dictionaries, and style guides serving to delimit national usage, especially in such areas as the media, education, law, government, and business; (2) Standard usage that draws on, and may blend with, such sources, but has a transnational identity of its own, especially in print worldwide and in the usage of such organizations as the United Nations. When the plural form occurs it implies major national Standard Englishes operating on an international level. Citations:

> **1995** Make a list of vocabulary differences [and] grammatical differences between two international Standard Englishes with which you are familiar.
> – Jeff Wilkinson, *Introducing Standard English*

> **1996** It is reasonable to speak of an international standard written English. It is also reasonable to speak of an international standard spoken English if we limit ourselves to the more formal levels and if we ignore pronunciation difficulties. . . . We may hope that the new national standards will take their place as constituents of an International Standard English, preserving the essential unity of English as an international language.
> – Sidney Greenbaum, *The Oxford English Grammar* (Oxford University Press), 12–13

World English

English as a world language in its entire variety and range:

> **1967** Tom McArthur, 'World English', in *Opinion* (Bombay), 28 February

1982 'We may definitely recognize Australian English and New Zealand English as separate entities, but still very much part of the family—forms of English making their own special contribution to world English.'

– Robert D. Eagleson, in R. W. Bailey and M. Görlach, eds., *English as a World Language* (Ann Arbor: Michigan University Press, 1982; Cambridge University Press, 1984), 436

1985 The traditional spelling system generally ignores both the changes in pronunciation over time and the variations in pronunciation through space; despite its notorious vagaries, it is a unifying force in world English.

– Randolph Quirk *et al.*, *A Comprehensive Grammar of the English Language* (Harlow: Longman), 9

1995 [A]lthough the history of world English can be traced back 400 years, the current growth spurt in the language has a history of less than 40 years.

– David Crystal, *The Cambridge Encyclopedia of the English Language* (Cambridge: Cambridge University Press), 110

1996 'This paper outlines the conceptualization and methodology behind the lexicographical project on World English in an Asian context'.

– Susan Butler, 'World English in an Asian context: The *Macquarie Dictionary* Project', *World Englishes* 15:3

1998 'World English' the title of a section of the Introduction to *The New Oxford Dictionary of English*, ed. Judy Pearsall, Oxford University Press

1999 'World English' the centrepiece of a circle diagram of English worldwide in the prelims of the *Encarta World English Dictionary*, ed. Kathy Rooney, p. xxxii, the central element in the name of the dictionary itself, and part of the title of a research corpus, the *Corpus of World English*.

World Standard English

Short form *WSE*. Standard English as used worldwide; the standard aspect of world English:

1987 'World Standard English', the centrepiece of a circle diagram of English worldwide accompanying the article 'The English languages?', by Tom McArthur, in *English Today* 11 (3:3), July, and reproduced in his *The English Languages* (Cambridge University Press, 1998), 97.

1995 If we read the newspapers or listen to the newscasters around the English-speaking world, we will quickly develop the impression that there is a World Standard English (WSE), acting as a strong unifying force among the vast range of variation which exists.

– David Crystal, *The Cambridge Encyclopedia of the English Language*, 111

1997 Even if the new Englishes did become increasingly different, as years went by, the consequences for world English would not necessarily be fatal. . . . A new form of English—let us think of it as 'World Standard Spoken English' (WSSE)—would almost certainly arise. Indeed, the foundation for such a development is already being laid around us.

– David Crystal, *English as a Global Language* (Cambridge University Press), 136–70

An important distinction needs to be made at this point between an actual phenomenon and a term or label that suggests a phenomenon. A world standard for English cannot be wished into existence simply by giving it some names. However, the fact that several commentators have for a number of years been feeling for the *right* kind of name (or names) for such a phenomenon is evidence that something of the kind already exists or is coming into existence. Such a development should hardly be surprising in the present condition of a world in which global trade is the norm and international courts of justice are being set up. It is already widely agreed that English is the world's lingua franca, but a paradoxically prestigious and high-level lingua franca can hardly be said to exist if it does not have a consistent form. The cardinal evidence for such a standard is in fact already largely in place and manifest almost everywhere, notably in the international media (print, radio, television, and electronic) and in the world's fluent arrangements for travel, business, sport, and many other activities.

In addition, the classic institutions have already begun to appear: the dictionaries, grammars, style guides, and indeed the literary canon, whose international nature already dominates English literature as an academic subject. Below are some notable developments in this direction since 1995:

> **1996** Sidney Greenbaum, *The Oxford English Grammar* (Oxford: Oxford University Press), a work that looks beyond national boundaries and derives its force from both the Survey of English Usage (SEU) and the International Corpus of English (ICE), both headquartered at the Department of English, University College London.

> **1998a** Judy Pearsall, editor, *The New Oxford Dictionary of English* (*NODE*), with 29 'World English' consultants: offered as a universalized desk dictionary with UK editorial conventions. In the prelims, under the subheading *World English*, it is noted that 'the main regional standards are British, US and Canadian, Australian and New Zealand, South African, Indian, and West Indian' (pp. xv–xvi).

> **1998b** Pam Peters, the *Langscape Project* in the quarterly journal *English Today: The international review of the English language* (Cambridge University Press), conducted over 6 issues (more than 18 months) with 6 questionnaires, at Macquarie University, New South Wales, Australia, and supported by the Press as part of her work in compiling a World English Style Guide.

> **1999a** *The Encarta World English Dictionary*, originated and published on paper by Bloomsbury (UK version), with St Martins Press (US) and Macmillan (Australia), and pre-eminently available as an electronic Microsoft product.

> **1999b** The *Longman Grammar of Spoken and Written English*, edited by Douglas Biber, Stig Johansson, Geoffrey Leech, Susan Conrad, and Edward Finegan (Harlow: Longman): a corpus-based grammar seeking to give 'equal weight to American and British English'. Uniquely for such a work, the spelling standard is dual, set according to the conventions adopted by the main author of each chapter. The primary editor is American (at Northern Arizona University, Flagstaff); the team is international; key meetings took place in the UK, the US, and Switzerland; and work-in-progress was assessed by a committee of UK linguists (chaired by Randolph Quirk). The *LGSWE* evolved from both the

'Quirk *et al*' grammars and the corpus of the Survey of English
Usage (founded by Quirk in 1959).

These developments reflect the paradox of world English: that there are many and
there is one (but in two principal parts). The many seek greater self-definition and
acknowledgement both at home and abroad, while the one—an evolving World
Standard English—remains both a fuzzy-edged reality and a target whose existence
is underlined by the emergence of just such works as these, probably the first of
many. Indeed, it is hard at present and will probably be harder still in future for any
dictionary, grammar, or usage guide of English, wherever it might be in the world,
to be concerned with its home turf alone.

A federation of standards appears therefore to be already with us, an evolving
'super-standard' that is comfortable with both territorial and linguistic diversity.
Such a World/International Standard English is in effect an *ad hoc* global balancing-
out of the practices of publishers, educational institutions, governmental departments, legal institutions, and the like in many places, much indeed as in the past,
but of necessity with a more equitable response to social and cultural sensitivities
than in the past. There will also be enough pushing and shoving to ensure that
nobody becomes too blasé about it.

One impression that might be gleaned from all this is that everything is pretty
much as it was before, only bigger. That, however, is not entirely the case, because
present-day English is defined in large part by its being used by more non-native
than native speakers. By and large a native language acquired by a child is straightforward: all things being equal, the child simply acquires it and does not wonder
whether it has acquired something easy or difficult. The same is not the case with a
language, a large number of whose users have acquired it after acquiring at least one
other language and use it as a lingua franca. Unfortunate to relate, however, this language and its associated culture(s) are not equally easy or difficult for the peoples of
the world to learn: rather, the ease and the difficulty, and the satisfactions and the
distress are unevenly distributed, notably with regard to two crucial aspects, one
phonological (with two further parts), the other stylistic and rhetorical. They are:

❶ Phonology

Quite apart from individual speech sounds, words, phrases, and sentences, which
are routinely taught, there are two fundamental aspects of English that have for
years tended not to get the attention due to them. They are *rhythm* and *rhoticity*:

Stress-timed and syllable-timed rhythm   The stress-timed rhythm of English poses
virtually no problems for speakers of the Germanic languages of North-Western
Europe, because they have similar rhythms in their own languages. This is one
reason for the success of the Dutch, the Scandinavians, and the Germans in learning
English. This Morse-Code-like rhythm does not, however, come easily to speakers
of African and Indian languages, or the Chinese, the Japanese, and the Koreans,
among many others, whose languages are syllable-timed, with a rhythm that is more
staccato, and has been compared to the *rat-a-tat-a-tat* of a machine gun.

Rhoticity and non-rhoticity   These terms relate to the pronunciation or non-
pronunciation of the consonant *r* in certain positions in such words as *rather* and
murder, as well as to the kind of *r* used in different native-speaking communities.

If *r* is pronounced in all positions then an accent is called rhotic; if it is not pronounced before consonants or at the end of words, then the accent is non-rhotic. The distinction varies across native English-speaking communities. Speakers of Spanish and Italian have no problems with the rhoticity of Scots and Irish people, and Sub-Saharan Africans and the Chinese have no trouble with the non-rhoticity of the English and southern-states Americans.

❷ Kinds of style and rhetoric

Kinds of style and rhetoric vary from language to language and culture to culture, and may pose problems in someone's mother tongue just as much as in English. However, the kinds that accompany the mother tongue are better known and can be guarded against, and style and rhetoric may vary from one English-speaking community to another: people in San Francisco and St Louis do things differently from people in Surrey and Singapore. Fluency in a language is not only a matter of adequate speaking, listening, reading, and writing; it also requires an understanding of the social fabric in which a standard or a regional variety operates. The human race demands a great deal when it asks its young to become adequate-to-proficient users of more than one fully equipped standard present-day language.

In rhotic accents, *r* is pronounced wherever it is orthographically present: for example, in *run*, *barrel*, *beard*, *war*, *worker*. In non-rhotic accents, *r* is pronounced in only two situations: at the beginning of syllables (as in *run*) and between vowels (as in *barrel*). In such accents, it does not occur after vowels (as in *beard*, *war*, *worker*) unless a vowel follows, so that in *the writer's friend* no *r* is pronounced, but it *is* pronounced in *the writer is my friend*. All accents of English belong on one side or the other of this divide, which is not however neatly distributed worldwide, including within some countries. What is more, the division has nothing to do with whether a variety is stress-timed or syllable-timed. The divisions worldwide for ENL territories are:

❶ Dominantly rhotic

Found in two groups:

- Using a retroflex *r*: Canada; Ireland; south-western England; the western and northern states of the United States (west of the Connecticut River); and, in the Caribbean, the island of Barbados and to some degree Jamaica.

- Using mainly an alveolar tapped or trilled *r*: Scotland.

❷ Dominantly non-rhotic

Australia, the Caribbean (except Barbados and to some degree Jamaica), England (excluding the south-west), New Zealand, Sub-Saharan Africa (including South Africa), New Zealand, Wales, and, in the United States, three areas (the southern states, New York state, and by and large New England east of the Connecticut River). The speech of most African-Americans is non-rhotic.

Rhythm and rhoticity fit together in various ways. Thus, in a single TV news programme in, say, Edinburgh or Hong Kong, one might hear someone from London (stress-timed, non-rhotic) talking to someone from Nigeria (syllable-timed, non-rhotic), followed by two people from India (one syllable-timed and rhotic, the other stress-timed and non-rhotic) talking to two other people, one Irish and one a Scot (both stress-timed and each rhotic, but in different ways). Because that is the reality, students necessarily benefit from planned exposure to a range of listening targets, entirely regardless of what their own pronunciation target may be. Listening-comprehension activities have in fact for some years been moving in this direction.

One might suppose that deciding whether to be rhotic or non-rhotic would be a significant matter for learners of English, but any such decision is normally taken for them by their teachers, institutions, or indeed governments, usually without protest. Such decisions may have been influenced by historical association with the UK or US, or for some entirely different reason, such as available teaching materials. It might (or could, if policies were flexible enough and took into account the students' own linguistic circumstances) also be affected by the nature of the student's home language (which will in any case have an influence). Thus, speakers of the Romance languages and Arabic manage rhoticity better, while speakers of African languages, Chinese, and Japanese manage non-rhoticity better.

It is worth noting that in India, which had a long association with RP-speaking, non-rhotic, and stress-timed Britons, the local English-speaking population is massively rhotic and syllable-timed. Such facts suggest that it might be helpful to provide learners with a model that harmonizes well with the sounds and rhythms of the mother tongue. In other words: students should perhaps, as a matter of principle, learn a kind of English that is easiest for them. One obstacle at the moment, however, is the relatively low status internationally of syllable-timed rhythm in English (despite the millions of people who speak English in this way).

Curiously enough, a discussion of such matters as rhythm and rhoticity only serves to stress the point that standardness cannot easily apply to spoken English: there are too many variations. The only way to create a standard for the spoken language is to focus on a relatively small community of representative speakers (as has been done for a century with RP/BBC non-rhotic, stress-timed English), but the very act of proposing and sustaining such a standard (in effect, a target model for 'non-standard' speakers, native or non-native) 'disenfranchises' most native speakers of English the moment they open their mouths, builds in the sociolinguistic tensions associated with the adoption as a target of any minority accent whatever, and presents many ESL and EFL learners with great difficulties.

The only conclusion to be drawn is that *either* one proceeds on a basis that, before the game has even begun, renders success impossible for the vast majority of both native speakers and foreign learners *or* one accepts that the idea of strict standardness cannot be reasonably applied to spoken English, and certainly not on a world scale. Rather, learners should start with a spoken target that has cognates in English but does not place too great a burden on them in terms of their own speech systems and with a listening target that over time exposes them to as many varieties as possible of spoken English, so that they will be more or less prepared for the diversity of the real world.

In general terms, a national Standard English, like other standard languages, operates in five broad areas: government; administration; law; commerce; the media and publishing; and education. All such standard languages have not simply a written but a *print* standard, which serves as a template (especially through broadcasting based on scripts and teleprompters) for what David Abercrombie in 1959 called *spoken prose*. Such prose is presented as if it were speech, as for example when an actor utters lines from a play or someone gives a public address, using a prepared text. This term distinguishes all such speech from spontaneous, un-scripted conversation. Abercrombie put it as follows:

> **1965** Prose is essentially language organized for *visual* presentation. . . . Most people believe that *spoken prose* . . . is at least not far removed, when well done, from the conversation of real life. . . . But the truth is that nobody speaks at all like the characters in any novel, play or film. Life would be intolerable if they did; and novels, plays or films would be intolerable if the characters spoke as people do in life. Spoken prose is far more different from conversation than is usually realized.
> – in *Studies in Phonetics and Linguistics* (Oxford University Press)

Spoken prose derives from drama, lectures, and disputation, the recitation of more or less memorized poetry, and the arguments of lawyers and orators (whose rhetorical craft originated in ancient Greece). Although conversation is distinct from it, spoken prose influences educated and formal spoken usage.

Experienced speakers often use the same grammatical constructions and rhetorical devices whether they are speaking spontaneously, working from notes, or referring to a typescript; indeed, a great deal of what passes for speech on radio and television is print read aloud, or is writing and print that has been memorized (at least in part), or is *ex tempore* speech that, through years of practice, is fluently structured like printed text. Many highly educated people, after years of reading, lecturing, and debating, end up 'talking like a book' as part of their everyday life, and to a considerable extent it is such people who (without giving the matter much thought) 'set the standard' for prestige languages and varieties of languages.

The spoken prose of English has little to do with accent, but a great deal to do with clarity, precision, and rhetorical competence. It is an art form with classical roots that imposes constraints on speech (such as breath control, timing, cadence, and contrast), techniques that tend to make presenters more distinct when they speak, regardless of accent or social origin. Such English is often perceived (and marketed) as simultaneously élite and democratic, a paradox for which there is a sound social and historical basis, in that over the last century and a half the more prestigious elements of society, such as government, the traditional professions, science, and the like have been opened up to the population at large through education from primary to university and comparable levels.

These areas of predictability are at the core of a shared world medium in which several 'brands' (notably kinds of British, American, and Australian English) are marketed to a vast clientele by a very large language industry indeed, one part of which teaches English as a foreign, second, international, or specialist language, while another covers the English-language media, Hollywood-style movies, and such matters as word-processing, publishing, the making of dictionaries and usage books, email/e-mail/Email/E-mail, the Internet, the World Wide Web, and cell-phones. In any comprehensive approach to the teaching and learning of English by students of any kind worldwide, awareness of such matters as rhoticity and non-rhoticity, stress-timing and syllable-timing, spoken prose, the nature of standard-ness in language, and the link between a World Standard and the printed word can safely be described as fundamental.

A Chronology of the ENL and ESL Territories

The 'New Englishes' are often so called because scholarship only took serious note of them from c.1970. In most cases, they date back 100–200 years and some are older still. The layout below, with its five numbered periods, shows when English was first used in each territory or when each was formed or settled. Some subterritories, such as US states or Canadian provinces, are included because of their special significance at particular times.

Prior to the 17th century

c. AD 450 the beginnings of the southern part of Britain that in due course became England; c.600 the beginnings of the northern part of Britain that later became Scotland; 1171 the Anglo-Normans first move into Ireland; 1282 the Anglo-Normas first move into Wales; 1504 the English establish St John's, Newfoundland, formalized in 1583 as their first North American colony; 1536 and 1542 the two-stage incorporation of Wales into England; 1560–1620 the Anglo-Scottish plantations in Ireland.

17th century

1607 Jamestown, Virginia; 1612 Bermuda, Surat (first trading station in India); 1620 Plymouth Plantation in Massachusetts; 1627 Barbados; 1640 Madras; 1647 the Bahamas; 1655 Jamaica; 1659 Saint Helena; 1670 Hudson's Bay; 1674 Bombay, from Portugal; 1690 Calcutta.

18th century

1759 Quebec; 1774 the East India Company territories united and run from Calcutta; 1776 the Declaration of Independence of the American colonies; 1786 Botany Bay penal colony set up, Australia; 1791 Upper and Lower Canada (now Ontario and Quebec); 1792 New Zealand.

19th century

1802 Ceylon, Trinidad; 1803 the Louisiana Purchase; 1806 and 1814 Cape Colony, South Africa; 1808 Sierra Leone; 1814 Malta, Mauritius, Saint Lucia, Tobago; 1816 Gambia; 1819 Singapore, US purchase of Florida from Spain; 1821 US settlers in Mexican territory of Texas (1836: independence; 1845 US state); 1826 Singapore, Malacca, and Penang; 1829 Australia at large; 1831 British Guiana (now Guyana); 1842 Hong Kong (1997 returned to China); 1846 Natal, South Africa; 1848 California (ceded by Mexico to the US); 1850 the Bay Islands (1858: ceded by the UK to Honduras); 1861 Lagos (now Nigeria); 1862 British Honduras (now Belize); 1867 British North America officially named Canada, Alaska purchased from Russia by the US; 1869 Basutoland (now Lesotho); 1874 Fiji, the Gold Coast (now Ghana); 1878 Cyprus; 1884 South East New Guinea (now Papua); 1885 Bechuanaland (now Botswana); 1886 Burma; 1887 the Maldives; 1888–94 Kenya, Uganda, Zanzibar; 1895 the Malay States; 1898 US annexes Hawaii, Spain cedes Puerto Rico and the Philippines to the US;1899 Sudan becomes a condominium of Britain and Egypt.

20th century

1910 South Africa; 1914 Britain and France invade German colony of Kamerun (1919 formally ceded, now Cameroon); 1919 Germans cede Tanganyika and New Guinea; 1920 Germans cede German West Africa, administered for the UN by South Africa as South West Africa (now Namibia); 1947 British India partitioned into India and Pakistan; 1950–70 The period in which the British Empire was effectively liquidated and a range of post-colonial nations emerged, such as Ghana (1960) and Malaysia (1963); 1971 Bangladesh secedes from Pakistan.

A general chronology of English

Key dates associated with the history and spread of the English language from Roman times to 2000.

55 BC	Roman military expedition to Britain by Julius Caesar.
AD 43	Roman invasion under the emperor Claudius, beginning 400 years of control over much of the island.
150	From around this date, with Roman permission, small numbers of settlers arrive from the coastlands of Germany, speaking dialects ancestral to English.
297	First mention of the Picts of Caledonia, tribes beyond Roman control, well to the north of Hadrian's Wall.
410	The Goths sack Rome.
436	The end of a period of gradual Roman withdrawal. Britons south of the Wall are attacked by the Picts and by Scots from Ireland. Angles, Saxons, and other Germanic settlers come first as mercenaries to help the Britons, then take over more and more territory.
449	The traditional date for the beginning of Anglo-Saxon settlements.
450–80	The first surviving Old English inscriptions, in runic letters.
495	The Saxon kingdom of Wessex established.
500	The kingdom of Dalriada established in Argyll by Scots from Ireland.
527	The Saxon kingdoms of Essex and Middlesex established.
550	The Angle kingdoms of Mercia, East Anglia, and Northumbria established.
557	At the battle of Deorham, the West Saxons drive a wedge between the Britons of Wales and Cornwall.
597	Aethelberht, king of Kent, welcomes Augustine, and the conversion of the Anglo-Saxons begins.
613	At the battle of Chester, the Angles of Northumbria drive a wedge between the Britons of Wales and Cumbria.
638	Edwin of Northumbria takes Lothian from the Britons.
700	The first manuscript records of Old English from about this time.
792	Scandinavians begin to raid and settle in Britain, Ireland, and France. In 793, they sack the monastery of Lindisfarne, the centre of Northumbrian scholarship.
795	The Danes settle in parts of Ireland.
815	Egbert of Wessex defeats the south-western Britons of Cornwall and incorporates Cornwall into his kingdom.
828	Egbert of Wessex is hailed as *bretwalda* (lord of Britain), overlord of the Seven Kingdoms of the Angles and Saxons (the Heptarchy). England begins to emerge.
834	The Danes raid England.
843	Kenneth MacAlpin, King of Scots, gains the throne of Pictland.
865	The Danes occupy Northumbria, establish a kingdom at York, and Danish begins to influence English.

871	Alfred becomes king of Wessex, translates works of Latin into English, and establishes the writing of prose in English.
886	The boundaries of the Danelaw are settled.
911	Charles II of France grants lands on the lower Seine to the Viking chief Hrolf the Ganger (Rollo the Rover). The beginnings of Normandy and Norman French.
954	The expulsion of Eric Blood-axe, last Danish king of York.
965	The English invade the northern Welsh kingdom of Gwynedd.
973	Edgar of England cedes Lothian to Kenneth II, King of Scots. Scotland multilingual: Gaelic dominant, Norse in the north, Cumbric in the south-west, English in the south-east, Latin for church and law.
992	A treaty between Ethelred of England and the Normans.
1000	The approximate date of the only surviving manuscript of the Old English epic poem *Beowulf*.
1007	Ethelred the Unready pays *danegeld* to stop the Danes attacking England. In 1013, however, they take the country and Ethelred flees to Normandy.
1014	The end of Danish rule in Ireland.
1016–42	The reigns of Canute/Knut and his sons over Denmark, Norway, and England.
1051	Edward the Confessor, King of England, impressed by the Normans and with French-speaking counsellors at his court, names as his heir William, Duke of Normandy, but reneges on his promise before his death.
1066	The Norman Conquest. William defeats Harold Godwin at Hastings, and sets in train the Normanization of the upper classes of the Britain Isles. England multilingual: English the majority language, Danish in the north, Cornish in the far south-west, Welsh on the border with Wales, Norman French at court and in the courts, and Latin in church and school.
1150	The first surviving texts of Middle English.
1167	The closure of the University of Paris to students from England accelerates the development of a university at Oxford.
1171	Henry II invades Ireland and declares himself its overlord, introducing English and Norman French into the island.
1204	King John loses the Duchy of Normandy to France.
1209	The exodus of a number of students from Oxford leads to the establishment of a second university in Cambridge.
1272–1307	The reign of Edward I, who consolidates royal authority in England, and extends it permanently to Wales and temporarily to Scotland.
1282	Death of Llewelyn, last native prince of Wales. In 1301, Edward of England's son and heir is invested as Prince of Wales.
1284	The Statute of Rhuddlan establishes the law of England in Wales (in French and Latin), but retains the legal use of Welsh.
1314	Robert Bruce re-asserts Scottish independence by defeating Edward II at Bannockburn, an achievement later celebrated in an epic written in Scots.
1337	The outbreak of the Hundred Years War between England and France, which ends with the loss of all England's French possessions save the Channel Islands.

1343?–1400   The life of Geoffrey Chaucer.

1348   (1) English replaces Latin as medium of instruction in schools, but not at Oxford and Cambridge. (2) The worst year of the Black Death.

1362   (1) Through the Statute of Pleading, written in French, English replaces French as the language of law in England, but the records continue to be kept in Latin. (2) English is used for the first time in Parliament.

1384   The publication of John Wycliffe's English translation of the Latin Bible.

1385   The scholar John of Trevisa notes that 'in all the gramere scoles of Engelond, children leveth Frensche and construeth and lerneth in Englische'.

1400   By this date the Great Vowel Shift has begun.

1450   Printing by movable type invented in the Rhineland.

1476   (1) The first English book printed: *The Recuyell of the Historyes of Troye*, translated from French by William Caxton, who printed it at Bruges in Flanders. (2) Caxton sets up the first printing press in England, at Westminster. In 1478, he publishes Chaucer's *Canterbury Tales*.

1485   The Battle of Bosworth, after which the part-Welsh Henry Tudor becomes King of England. Welsh nobles follow him to London.

1492   Christopher Columbus discovers the New World.

1497   Giovanni Caboto (anglicized as 'John Cabot'), in a ship from Bristol, lands on the Atlantic coast of North America.

1499   The publication of *Thesaurus linguae romanae et britannicae* (Treasury of the Roman and British Tongues), the first English-to-Latin wordbook, the work of Galfridus Grammaticus (Geoffrey the Grammarian).

1504   The settlement of St John's on Newfoundland as a shore base for English fisheries.

1507   The German geographer Martin Waldseemüller puts the name *America* on his map of the world.

1525   The publication of William Tyndale's translation of the New Testament of the Bible.

1534   Jacques Cartier lands on the Gaspé Peninsula in North America and claims it for France.

1536 and 1542   The Statute of Wales (Acts of Union) unites England and Wales, excluding Welsh from official use.

1542   Henry VIII of England proclaims himself King of Ireland.

1549   The publication of the first version of the Book of Common Prayer of the Church of England, the work in the main of Thomas Cranmer.

1558–1603   The reign of Elizabeth I.

1560–1620   The plantation of Ireland, first by English settlers and after 1603 also by Scots, establishing English throughout the island and Scots in Ulster.

1564–1616   The life of William Shakespeare.

1583   Sir Humphrey Gilbert establishes Newfoundland as England's first colony beyond the British Isles.

1584   The settlement on Roanoke Island by colonists led by Sir Walter Raleigh. In 1587, Virginia Dare born at Roanoke, first child of English parents in North America. In 1590, the settlers of Roanoke disappear without trace.

1588	The publication of Bishop Morgan's translation of the Bible into Welsh, serving as a focus for the survival of the language.
1600	English traders establish the East India Company.
1603	The Union of the Crowns under James VI of Scots, I of England.
1604	The publication of Robert Cawdrey's *Table Alphabeticall*, the first dictionary of English.
1606	The Dutch explore northern New Holland (Terra Australis).
1607	The Jamestown colony in Virginia, the first permanent English settlement and the first representative assembly in the New World.
1608	Samuel Champlain founds the city of Quebec in New France.
1611	The publication of the Authorized or King James Version of the Bible, intended for use in the Protestant services of England, Scotland, and Ireland. A major influence on the written language and in adapting Scots towards English.
1612	(1) Bermuda colonized under the charter of the Virginia Company. (2) Traders of the East India Company establish themselves in Gujarat, India.
1614	King James writes in English to the Moghul Emperor Jehangir, in order to encourage trade with 'the Orientall Indies'.
1619	At the Jamestown colony in America, the first African slaves arrive on a Dutch ship.
1620	The *Mayflower* arrives in the New World and the Pilgrim Fathers set up Plimoth Plantation in Massachusetts. English is now in competition as a colonial language in the Americas with Dutch, French, Spanish, and Portuguese.
1622	Publication in London of the first English newspaper, *Weekly News*.
1623	Publication in London of the First Folio of Shakespeare's plays.
1627	An English colony established on Barbados in the Caribbean.
1637	(1) English traders arrive on the coast of China. (2) The Académie française founded.
1640	An English trading factory established at Madras.
1647	The Bahamas colonized by settlers from Bermuda.
1652	The first Dutch settlers arrive in southern Africa.
1655	England acquires Jamaica from Spain.
1659	The East India Company annexes St Helena in the south Atlantic.
1660	John Dryden expresses his admiration for the Académie française and its work in 'fixing' French and wishes for something similar to serve English.
1662	The Royal Society of London receives its charter from Charles II. In 1664, it appoints a committee to consider ways of improving English as a language of science.
1670	The Hudson's Bay Company founded for fur trading in northern America.
1674	Charles II receives Bombay from the Portuguese in the dowry of Catherine of Braganza and gives it to the East India Company.
1687	Isaac Newton writes *Principia Mathematica* in Latin: see 1704.

1688	The publication of *Oronooko, or the History of the Royal Slave*, by Aphra Behn: one of the first novels in English, by the first woman novelist in English, based on personal experience of a slave revolt in Surinam.
1690	A trading factory established at Calcutta in Bengal.
1696	British and French colonists in North America in open conflict.
1697	The Boston clergyman Cotton Mather applies the term *American* to English-speaking settlers in the New World.
1702	Publication in London of the first regular daily newspaper in English, *The Daily Courant*.
1704	Isaac Newton writes his second major work, *Opticks*, in English: see 1687.
1707	The Act of Union, uniting the Parliaments of England and Scotland, creating the United Kingdom of Great Britain, but keeping separate the state religions, educational systems, and laws of the two kingdoms.
1712	(1) Jonathan Swift in Dublin proposes an English Academy to 'fix' the language and compete adequately with French. (2) In India, the Moghul Empire begins to decline.
1713	(1) At the Treaty of Utrecht, France surrenders Hudson's Bay, Acadia, and Newfoundland to the British. (2) Gibraltar is ceded to Britain by Spain.
1731	The abolition of Law French in England.
1746	The Wales and Berwick Act, by which England is deemed to include Wales and the Scottish town of Berwick is incorporated into England.
1755	The publication of Samuel Johnson's *Dictionary of the English Language*.
1757	The East India Company becomes the power behind the government of Bengal.
1759	General James Wolfe takes Quebec for the British.
1759–96	The life of Robert Burns.
1762	The publication of Robert Lowth's *Short Introduction to English Grammar*.
1763	The French cede New France to Britain, retaining only St Pierre and Miquelon (islands off Newfoundland).
1768–71	The partwork publication in Edinburgh of *The Encyclopaedia Britannica*.
1770	Captain James Cook takes possession of the Australian continent for Britain.
1770–1850	The life of William Wordsworth.
1771–1832	The life of Sir Walter Scott.
1774	(1) The Quebec Act creates the British province of Quebec, extending to the Ohio and Mississippi. (2) The Regulating Act places Bombay and Madras under the control of Bengal and the East India Company becomes a kind of state.
1776	The Declaration of Independence by 13 British colonies in North America and the start of the American War of Independence (1776–83) which created the United States of America, the first nation outside the British Isles with English as its principal language.
1778	Captain James Cook visits and names the Sandwich Islands (Hawaii).
1780–1800	British Empire loyalists move from the United States to Canada.
1785	In London, the newspaper *The Daily Universal Register* founded. Renamed *The Times* in 1788.

1786	(1) Lord Cornwallis is appointed first Governor-General of British India. (2) A British penal colony is established at Botany Bay in Australia. In 1788, the first convicts arrive there.
1791	(1) The British colonies of Upper Canada (Ontario) and Lower Canada (Quebec) are established. (2) In London, the newspaper *The Observer* is founded, the oldest national Sunday newspaper in Britain.
1792	The first Europeans settle in New Zealand.
1794	The publication of Lindley Murray's *English Grammar*.
1802	The establishment of the British colonies of Ceylon and Trinidad.
1803	(1) The Act of Union incorporating Ireland into Britain, as the United Kingdom of Great Britain and Ireland. (2) The Louisiana Purchase, by which the United States buys from France its remaining North American territories, and doubles its size.
1806	The British take control of Cape Colony in southern Africa.
1808	The establishment of the British colony of Sierra Leone.
1814	(1) The British annex Cape Colony. (2) France cedes to Britain Malta, Mauritius, St Lucia, and Tobago.
1816	The establishment of the British colony of Bathurst (the Gambia).
1819	(1) The establishment of the British colony of Singapore. (2) The United States purchases Florida from Spain.
1820	Christian missionaries from the United States visit Hawaii.
1821	American settlers arrive in the Mexican territory of Texas.
1828	The publication of Noah *Webster's American Dictionary of the English Language*.
1829	Australia becomes a British dependency.
1831	The establishment of the colony of British Guiana.
1833	(1) The abolition of slavery in the British Empire. (2) St Helena becomes a British colony.
1835	Thomas Macaulay writes the Minute on Education whereby the British rulers of India endorse English as a language of education for Indians.
1835–1910	The life of Sam Clemens (Mark Twain).
1836	Texas declares its independence from Mexico.
1839	The first Boer Republic is established in Natal, South Africa, after the Great Trek from the Cape.
1840	(1) The Treaty of Waitangi, by which the Maori of New Zealand cede all rights and powers of government to Britain. (2) The transportation of convicts to Eastern Australia is ended.
1841	(1) Upper and Lower Canada are brought together as British North America. (2) New Zealand becomes a British colony. (3) In London, the founding of the weekly magazine *Punch*.
1842	(1) The opening of Chinese ports other than Canton to Western traders, after the defeat of China in the Opium War. Hong Kong is ceded by China to Britain as a Crown Colony. (2) The Philological Society is formed in London.
1845	Texas becomes a state of the United States.
1846	The British annex Natal but recognize the Transvaal and the Orange Free State as autonomous Boer republics.

1848	In the Treaty of Guadalupe Hidalgo, Mexico cedes vast western territories to the US.
1850	(1) Britain takes control of the Bay Islands of Honduras, an English-speaking enclave in Central America. (2) Legislative councils are established in Australia by British Act of Parliament.
1852	The publication of *Roget's Thesaurus*.
1853	(1) Japan is forced by Commander Matthew Perry of the US Navy to open its harbours to Western trade. (2) The transportation of convicts to Tasmania is ended.
1855	The Government of the colony of New South Wales is established.
1856	The Governments of the colonies of Tasmania and Victoria are established.
1856–1950	The life of George Bernard Shaw.
1857	The Sepoy Rebellion (War of Independence, Indian Mutiny) in India leads to the transfer of British India from the East India Company to the Crown.
1858	(1) The Philological Society passes a resolution calling for a new dictionary of English on historical principles. (2) Britain cedes the Bay Islands to Honduras.
1861	The establishment of the British colony of Lagos (Nigeria).
1862	The establishment of the colony of British Honduras.
1863	The establishment of the Cambridge Overseas Examinations.
1865	The abolition of slavery in the US, at the end of the Civil War. At the outbreak of the war there were over 4m slaves.
1867	(1) The Dominion of Canada is created, consisting of Quebec, Ontario, Nova Scotia, and New Brunswick. (2) Alaska is purchased from Russia by the US.
1868	(1) Transportation of convicts to Western Australia is ended. (2) In the US, Christopher Latham Sholes and colleagues patent the first successful typewriter.
1869	(1) Rupert's Land and the Northwest Territories are bought by Canada from the Hudson's Bay Company. (2) Basutoland becomes a British protectorate.
1870	Manitoba becomes a province of Canada.
1871	British Columbia becomes a province of Canada.
1873	(1) The formation of the English Dialect Society (dissolved in 1896). (2) Prince Edward Island becomes a province of Canada.
1874	The establishment of the British colony of the Gold Coast in West Africa.
1879	James A. H. Murray begins editing the Philological Society's *New English Dictionary on Historical Principles*.
1882–1941	The life of James Joyce.
1884	(1) The Berlin Conference, in which European powers begin 'the scramble for Africa'. (2) Britain declares a protectorate over South East New Guinea. (3) The French, Germans, and British attempt to annex what shortly becomes the German colony of Kamerun. (4) Publication of the first fascicle, *A-Ant*, of Murray's dictionary (the *OED*).
1886	The annexation of Burma into British India and the abolition of the Burmese monarchy.
1888–94	The establishment of British protectorates in Kenya, Uganda, and Zanzibar.

1895   The establishment of the British East African Protectorate, open to white settlers.

1898   (1) The annexation of Hawaii by the US. In 1900, it becomes a US territory. (2) Spain cedes the Philippines and Puerto Rico to the United States. (3) Yukon Territory comes under Canadian government control.

1898–1905   The period of publication by Oxford University Press of the six volumes of the *English Dialect Dictionary*, prepared under the auspices of the English Dialect Society and edited by Joseph Wright.

1901   (1) The establishment of the Commonwealth of Australia as a dominion of the British Empire. (2) The first wireless telegraphy messages sent across the Atlantic by Guglielmo Marconi (Cornwall to Newfoundland). (3) The first film-show in an arcade opened in Los Angeles, California.

1903   A message from US President Theodore Roosevelt circles the world in less than 10 minutes by Pacific Cable.

1903–50   The life of George Orwell.

1904   The publication by Macmillan of Henry Bradley's *The Making of English*.

1905   (1) Alberta and Saskatchewan become provinces of Canada. (2) The first cartoon strip, 'Little Nemo', appears in *The New York Herald*.

1906   (1) The formation of the English Association. (2) The first full-length motion picture, *The Story of the Kelly Gang*. (3) The publication by Oxford University Press of the Fowler brothers' *The Kings' English*.

1907   (1) The establishment of New Zealand as a dominion of the British Empire. (2) The first regular studio-based radio broadcasts by the De Forest Radio Telephone Company in the US. (3) The foundation of Hollywood as a film-making centre.

1910   (1) The establishment of the Union of South Africa as a dominion of the British Empire. (2) The first radio receivers made in kit form for sale in the US.

1911   The publication of the Fowler brothers' *Concise Oxford Dictionary*.

1913   (1) The formation of the Society for Pure English. (2) The first crossword puzzle published, in the *New York World*.

1914   (1) A third Home Rule Bill for Ireland passed by the British Parliament, but prevented from coming into operation by the outbreak of the First World War. (2) The German colony of Kamerun invaded by French and British.

1915   The death of Sir James A. H. Murray, aged 78, having finished the section *Trink–Turndown* in the *OED*.

1916   (1) The Easter Rising in Dublin, an unsuccessful armed rebellion against the British, during which an Irish Republic is proclaimed. (2) The technicolor process is first used in the film *The Gulf Between*, in the US.

1917   The publication by Dent of Daniel Jones's *English Pronouncing Dictionary*.

1918   (1) The formation of the English-Speaking Union. (2) The US War Industries Board declares moving pictures an essential industry.

1919   (1) The German colony of Tanganyika ceded to Britain. (2) The German colony of Kamerun divided between France (Cameroun) and Britain (Cameroon). (3) The publication by Knopf of H. L. Mencken's *The American Language*.

1920   (1) The Partition of Ireland. (2) Kenya becomes a British colony. (3) The first public radio station set up by Marconi in the US.

1921   (1) A treaty between the United Kingdom and the Irish Free State, which accepts dominion status within the British Empire. (2) The first full-length 'talkie' *Dream Street* produced by United Artists, in the US.

1922   (1) The establishment of the British Broadcasting Company, re-named in 1927 the British Broadcasting Corporation (BBC). (2) The founding in the US of the monthly magazine *The Reader's Digest*.

1923   The founding of *Time* magazine in the US.

1925   (1) The borders of the Republic of Ireland and Northern Ireland established. (2) Afrikaans gains official status in South Africa. (3) The founding of the weekly magazine *The New Yorker*.

1926   The publication of Henry W. Fowler's *Dictionary of Modern English Usage*.

1927   (1) Fox's Movietone News, the first sound newsfilm, released in the US. (2) The first film with dialogue, *They're Coming to Get Me*, released in the US.

1928   The publication of Murray's Dictionary as *The Oxford English Dictionary*, 70 years after Trench's proposal to the Philological Society.

1930   (1) C. K. Ogden launches Basic English. (2) The first television programme with synchronized sight and sound broadcast by the BBC.

1931   (1) The British Commonwealth of Nations formed. (2) South Africa becomes a dominion of the British Empire. (3) The Cambridge Proficiency Examination held outside Britain for the first time.

1933   The publication of a supplement to *The Oxford English Dictionary*.

1934   The British Council created as an arm of British cultural diplomacy and a focus for teaching (British) English as a foreign language.

1935   (1) The Philippines become a self-governing Commonwealth in association with the United States. (2) The publication of the first ten Penguin paperback titles.

1936   The Republic of Ireland severs all constitutional links with Great Britain.

1937   (1) Burma is separated from British India and granted a constitution and limited self-rule. (2) In Wales, a new constitution for the National Eisteddfod makes Welsh as its official language.

1938   Photocopying invented.

1942   The publication in Japan of *The Idiomatic and Syntactic Dictionary of English*, prepared before the war by A. S. Hornby, E. V. Gatenby, and H. Wakefield.

1945   Japan is occupied by the Americans on behalf of the Allies.

1946   (1) The Philippines gain their independence from the United States. (2) The French colony of Cameroun and the British colony of Cameroon become United Nations trusteeships.

1947   (1) British India is partitioned, and India and Pakistan become independent states. (2) New Zealand gains its independence from Britain.

1948   (1) Burma and Ceylon gain their independence from Britain. (2) The 1942 dictionary of Hornby *et al.* is published by Oxford University Press as *A Learner's Dictionary of Current English*.

1949   (1) Newfoundland becomes a province of Canada. (2) Two New Guinea territories are combined by the United Nations as an Australian mandate: the United Nations Trust Territory of Papua and New Guinea.

1951   The launch of the first two working business computers: the LED in the UK and the UNIVAC in the US.

1952	Puerto Rico becomes a Commonwealth in association with the United States.
1957	(1) The Gold Coast becomes independent from Britain as the Republic of Ghana. (2) Robert W. Burchfield is appointed editor of a Supplement to *The Oxford English Dictionary*.
1957–63	The British colonies of Malaya and Borneo become independent and unite as Malaysia.
1959	Alaska and Hawaii become states of the US.
1960	Nigeria and French Cameroun become independent.
1961	(1) South Africa becomes a republic, does not remain in the Commonwealth, and adopts Afrikaans and English as its two official languages. (2) The British colony of Cameroon divides, part joining Nigeria, part joining the ex-French colony to become the Republic of Cameroon. (3) Sierra Leone and Cyprus gain their independence from Britain. (3) The publication of *Webster's Third International Dictionary*.
1962	Jamaica, Trinidad and Tobago, and Uganda gain their independence from Britain.
1963	(1) Kenya gains its independence from Britain. (2) The first protests in Wales by the Cymdeithas yr Iaith Gymraeg/Welsh Language Society, aimed at achieving fuller use of Welsh.
1964	(1) Malta, Nyasaland (as Malawi), Tanganyika and Zanzibar (as Tanzania), and Northern Rhodesia (as Zambia) gain their independence from Britain. (2) The publication in Paris of René Etiemble's *Parlez-vous franglais?*
1965	Gambia and Singapore gain their independence from Britain.
1966	Barbados, Basutoland (as Lesotho), Bechuanaland (as Botswana), and British Guiana (as Guyana) gain their independence from Britain.
1967	The Welsh Language Act gives Welsh equal validity with English in Wales, and Wales is no longer deemed to be a part of England.
1968	Mauritius, Swaziland, and Nauru gain their independence from Britain.
1969	Canada becomes officially bilingual, with a commitment to federal services in English and French.
1972	(1) East Pakistan secedes and becomes the Republic of Bangladesh. (2) Two feminist magazines launched: *Ms* in the US and *Spare Rib* in the UK. (3) The publication by Longman of Randolph Quirk *et al.*, *A Grammar of Contemporary English*.
1973	The Bahamas gain their independence from Britain.
1974–79	Cyngor yr Iaith Gymraeg/Council for the Welsh Language set up to advise the Secretary of State for Wales on matters concerning the language.
1975	(1) Papua-New Guinea gains its independence from Australia. (2) The Bas-Lauriol law is passed in France, requiring the use solely of French in advertising and commerce.
1977	(1) The spacecraft *Voyager* travels into deep space, its main message to any extra-terrestrials recorded in English by the Secretary-General of the United Nations, Kurt Waldheim. (2) In Quebec, Loi 101/Bill 101 is passed, making French the sole official language of the province, limiting access to English-medium schools, and banning public signs in other languages.
1978	The Government of Northern Territory in Australia is established.

1980 The British government averts a fast to the death by Gwynfor Evans, leader of Plaid Cymru (Welsh National Party), by honouring election pledges to provide a fourth television channel using both Welsh and English.

1981 British Honduras gains its independence as Belize.

1982 The patriation from Great Britain of Canada's constitution. The Canada Act is the last act of the British Parliament concerning Canadian affairs.

1983 The publication by Penguin of *The New Testament in Scots*, a translation by William L. Lorimer.

1984 The launch of the Apple Macintosh personal (desktop) computer.

1985 (1) The publication by Longman of Randolph Quirk *et al.*, *A Comprehensive Grammar of the English Language*. (2) The publication by Belknap Press of the first volume of the *Dictionary of American Regional English*. (3) The launch by Cambridge University Press of the quarterly *English Today: The International Review of the English Language*.

1986 The showing by the BBC in the UK and public television in the US of *The Story of English*, a television series with both British and American backers, accompanied by a book of the same name, and followed by a radio version on BBC World Service.

1989 The publication of the 2nd edition of *The Oxford English Dictionary*, blending the first edition and its supplements.

1992 The publication of *The Oxford Companion to the English Language* by Oxford University Press.

1995 The publication of *The Cambridge Encyclopedia of The English Language* by Cambridge University Press.

1996 The publication of *The Oxford English Grammar* by Oxford University Press.

1997 (1) Hong Kong ceases to be a British colony and becomes a Special Administrative Region of China. (2) The Scots vote by a strong majority for a devolved parliament to be set up in Edinburgh. (3) The Welsh vote by a slim margin for a Welsh Assembly to be set up. (4) Publication of the report *The Future of English?* by the British Council as part of its consciousness-raising campaign entitled *English 2000*.

1999 The publication of the *ENCARTA World English Dictionary* by Microsoft Corp in collaboration with Bloomsbury (the originators) in the UK, St Martins Press in the US, and Macmillan Australia. Microsoft focuses on the electronic version and its uses, while the traditional publishers focus on versions of the paper product.

2000 (1) The establishment in Edinburgh of a Scottish Parliament and in Cardiff of a Welsh Assembly. (2) The launch by Oxford University Press of the *OED Online* in March.

Select Bibliography

AHULU, SAMUEL. 1997. 'General English: A consideration of English as an international medium', in *English Today* 49 (13:1) (Cambridge: Cambridge University Press).

AITKEN, A. J., and TOM MCARTHUR (eds), 1979. *Languages of Scotland* (Edinburgh: Chambers).

ALLSOPP, RICHARD (ed.), 1996. *Dictionary of Caribbean English Usage* (Oxford: Oxford University Press).

BAILEY, RICHARD W. 1985. 'The idea of world English', in *English Today* 1 (1:1) (Cambridge: Cambridge University Press).

——1991/92. *Images of English: A Cultural History of the Language* (Ann Arbor: Michigan University Press (1991); Cambridge: Cambridge University Press (1992)).

——1997. *Nineteenth-Century English* (Ann Arbor: University of Michigan Press).

——Manfred Görlach (eds), 1982/1984. *English as a World Language* (Ann Arbor: Michigan University Press. (1982) Cambridge: Cambridge University Press (1984)).

BAKER, S. J. 1945. *The Australian Language*. rev edn 1966 (Sydney: Currawong Press).

BARBER, CHARLES. 1993. *The English Language: A Historical Introduction* (Cambridge: Cambridge University Press).

BARBER, KATHERINE. 1998. *The Canadian Oxford Dictionary: The foremost authority on current Canadian English* (Toronto: Oxford University Press).

BAUER, LAURIE. 1994. *Watching English Change: An Introduction to the Study of Linguistic Change in Standard Englishes in the Twentieth Century* (London: Longman).

BAUGH, ALBERT C., and THOMAS CABLE. 1993. *A History of the English Language*, 4th edn. (Englewood Cliffs: Prentice-Hall; London: Routledge).

BAUMGARDNER, ROBERT J. (ed.), 1993. *The English Language in Pakistan* (Oxford University Press).

BELL, ALLAN, and HOLMES, JANET (eds), 1990. *New Zealand Ways of Speaking English* (Clevedon and Philadelphia: Multilingual Matters).

BERNSTEIN, CYNTHIA, NUNNALLY, THOMAS, and SABINO, ROBIN (eds), 1997. *Language Variety in the South Revisited* (Tuscaloosa and London: University of Alabama Press).

BIBER, DOUGLAS, STIG JOHANSSON, GEOFFREY LEECH, SUSAN CONRAD, and EDWARD FINEGAN. 1999. *Longman Grammar of Spoken and Written English* (Harlow: Longman).

BLAKE, N. F. (ed.), 1992. *The Cambridge History of the English Language, Vol 2: 1066–1476* (Cambridge and New York: Cambridge University Press).

——1996. *A History of the English Language* (Basingstoke and London: Macmillan).

BOLTON, KINGSLEY. 1999. 'World Englishes: the way we were', a review of Robert Burchfield (ed.), *The Cambridge History of the English Language Vol 5*, 1994. In *World Englishes* 18:3 (Oxford and Boston: Blackwell).

BURCHFIELD, ROBERT. 1980. 'Dictionaries and ethnic sensibilities', in Michaels and Ricks q.v.

——(ed.), 1994. *The Cambridge History of the English Language, Vol V: English in Britain and Overseas, Origins and Developments* (Cambridge: Cambridge University Press).

——(ed.), 1996. *The New Fowler's Modern English Usage* (Oxford: Oxford University Press).

BUTLER, SUSAN. 1999. 'A view on standards in South-East Asia', in Gill and Pakir q.v.

CASSIDY, FREDERIC G. and ROBERT B. LE PAGE. 1967. *Dictionary of Jamaican English* (2nd edn, 1980) (Cambridge: Cambridge University Press).

CENOZ, JASONE and ULRIKE JESSNER (eds), 2000. *English in Europe: The Acquisition of a Third Language* (Cleveland: Multilingual Matters).

CHESHIRE, JENNY (ed.), 1991. *English Around the World: Sociolinguistic Perspectives* (Cambridge: Cambridge University Press).

CHRISTOPHERSEN, PAUL. 1988. 'Native speakers and world English', in *English Today* 15 (4:3) (Cambridge: Cambridge University Press).

CLARKE, SANDRA (ed.), 1993. *Focus on Canada* (Amsterdam and Philadelphia: John Benjamins).

COLLINS, P., and BLAIR, D. (eds), 1989. *Australian English: The Language of a New Society* (Brisbane: University of Queensland Press).

COUPER-KUHLEN, ELIZABETH. 1993. *English Speech Rhythm: Form and Function in Everyday Verbal Interaction* (Amsterdam and Philadelphia: John Benjamins).

COUPLAND, NIKOLAS (ed.), 1990. *English in Wales: Diversity, Conflict and Change* (Clevedon and Philadelphia: Multilingual Matters).

CROWLEY, TONY. 1991. *Proper English? Readings in Language, History and Cultural Identity* (London: Routledge).

CRYSTAL, DAVID. 1985. 'How many millions? The statistics of World English', in *English Today* 1 (1:1) (Cambridge: Cambridge University Press).

——1994. 'Documenting rhythmical change', in J. Windsor Lewis (ed.), *Studies in General and English Phonetics* (London: Routledge, 174–9).

——1995. *The Cambridge Encyclopedia of the English Language* (Cambridge: Cambridge University Press).

——1996. 'The past, present and future of English rhythm', in M. Vaughan-Rees (ed.), *Changes in Pronunciation*. In *Speak Out!*, 8:13, a special-interest group newsletter, IATEFL. [with tape]

——1997. *English as a Global Language* (Cambridge: Cambridge University Press).

——1999. 'The future of Englishes', in *English Today* 58 (15:2) (Cambridge: Cambridge University Press).

DANIELS, HARVEY A. (ed.), 1990. *NOT Only English: Affirming America's Multilingual Heritage* (Urbana, Illinois: National Council of Teachers of English).

DAVIS, ALAN. 1999. 'Standard English: discordant voices.' in Gill and Pakir q.v.

DELBRIDGE, ARTHUR. 1999. 'Standard Australian English.' in Gill and Pakir q.v.

DE KLERK, VIVIAN (ed.), 1996. *Focus on South Africa*, in the Varieties of English Around the World (VEAW) series (Amsterdam and Philadelphia: John Benjamins).

——1999. 'Black South African English: Where to from here?', in *World Englishes*, 18:3 (Oxford and Boston: Blackwell).

DEVERSON, TONY. 1989. *Finding a New Zealand Voice: Attitudes Towards English Used in New Zealand* (Auckland: New House).

DILLARD, J. L. 1992. *A History of American English* (London and New York: Longman).

DOLAN, T. P. (ed.), 1990. *The English of the Irish*. Special issue, *Irish University Review: A Journal of Irish Studies* (Dublin: University College).

DRETZKE, BURKHARD. 1998. *Modern British and American English Pronunciation* (Paderborn, München, Wien, Zürich: Schöningh).

EAGLESON, ROBERT D. 1982. 'English in Australia and New Zealand.' In Bailey and Görlach q.v.

ESCURE, GENEVIEVE. 1997. *Creole and Dialect Continua* (Amsterdam and Philadelphia: John Benjamins).

FEE, MARGERY, and MCALPINE, JANICE (eds), 1997. *Guide to Canadian English Usage* (Toronto: Oxford University Press).

FISCHER, OLGA, ANS VAN KEMENADE, WILLEM KOOPMAN, and WIM VAN DER WURFF. 2000. *The Syntax of Early English* (Cambridge: Cambridge University Press).

FOLEY, J. (ed.), 1988. *The New Englishes: The Case of Singapore* (Singapore: University Press).

FOWLER, HENRY W. (ed. Sir Ernest Gowers) 1965. *A Dictionary of Modern English Usage* (2nd edn) (Oxford: Oxford University Press).

FRASER GUPTA, ANTHEA. 1994. *The Step-Tongue: Children's English in Singapore* (Clevedon and Philadelphia: Multilingual Matters).

FREEBORN, DENNIS, WITH PETER FRENCH and DAVID LANGFORD. 1993. *Varieties of English: An Introduction to the Study of Language* (2nd edn) (Basingstoke: Macmillan).

GARCÍA, O., and OTHEGUY, R. (eds), 1989. *English across Cultures, Cultures across English* (Berlin and New York: Mouton de Gruyter).

GARNER, BRYAN A. 1999. *A Dictionary of Modern American Usage* (New York: Oxford University Press).

GASKELL, PHILIP. 1998. *Standard Written English* (Edinburgh: Edinburgh University Press).

——2000. 'Standard Written English', in *English Today* 61 (16:1) (Cambridge: Cambridge University Press).

GILL, SARAN KAUR, and ANNE PAKIR (eds), 1999. 'Symposium on standards, codification and world Englishes', in *World Englishes* 18:2 (Oxford and Boston: Blackwell).

GILMAN, E. WARD (ed.), 1989. *Webster's Dictionary of English Usage* (Springfield, MA.: Merriam Webster).

GLAUSER, BEATE, EDGAR SCHNEIDER, and MANFRED GÖRLACH (eds), 1993. *A New Bibliography of Writings on Varieties of English, 1984–1992/93*. In the Varieties of English around the World (VEAW) series (Amsterdam and Philadelphia: John Benjamins).

GORDON, ELIZABETH, and DEVERSON, TONY. 1985. *New Zealand English: An Introduction to New Zealand Speech and Usage* (Auckland: Heinemann).

GÖRLACH, MANFRED. 1990*a*. *Studies in the History of the English Language* (Heidelberg: Carl Winter Universitätsverlag).

——1990*b*. 'The development of Standard Englishes' (first published in German in 1988), in *Studies in the History of the English Language* (Carl Winter, Heidelberg: Universitätsverlag (Heidelberg University Press)).

——1991*a*. *English: Studies in Varieties of English, 1984–1988* (Amsterdam and Philadelphia: John Benjamins).

——1991*b*. *Introduction to Early Modern English* (Cambridge: Cambridge University Press).

——1996. 'English: The language of a new nation. The present-day linguistic situation of South Africa.' Two prior versions, 1995 and 1996. This version in his *Even More Englishes*, 1998 (Amsterdam and Philadelphia: John Benjamins).

GONZALES, ANDREW. 1997. 'Philippine English: A variety in search of legitimation', in Schneider (ed.), *Englishes around the World 2* (Amsterdam and Philadelphia: John Benjamins).

GOWERS, SIR ERNEST. 1954. *The Complete Plain Words* (London: H.M. Stationery Office. Pelican edn 1962. 2nd edn 1973. 3rd edn 1986, rev Sidney Greenbaum and Janet Whitcut. Penguin edn 1987).

GRADDOL, DAVID. 1997*a*. *The Future of English?: A guide to forecasting the popularity of the English language in the 21st century* (London: The British Council).

——Dick Leith, and Joan Swann (eds), 1996. *English: History, Diversity and Change* (Milton Keynes: Open University Press; London: Routledge).

Grossman, John (ed.), 1993. *The Chicago Manual of Style*. 14th edn (Chicago and London: University of Chicago Press).

Greenbaum, Sidney. 1996. *The Oxford English Grammar* (Oxford: Oxford University Press).

——(ed. Edmund Weiner). *The Oxford Reference Grammar* (Oxford: Oxford University Press).

Hale, Constance. 1996. *Wired Style: Principles of English Usage in the Digital Age* (San Francisco: HardWired).

Hayhoe, Mike and Stephen Parker. 1994. *Who Owns English?* (Buckingham and Philadelphia: Open University Press).

Hince, Bernadette. 2000. *The Antarctic Dictionary: A Complete Guide to Antarctic English* (Victoria, Australia: CSIRO Publishing and Museum of Victoria).

Ho, Mian Lian, and John Platt. 1991. *Dynamics of a Contact Continuum: Singapore English* (Oxford:).

Hogg, Richard M. (ed.), 1992. *The Cambridge History of the English Language, Vol 1: The Beginnings to 1066* (Cambridge: Cambridge University Press).

Holloway, Joseph E., and Winifred K. Vass 1993. *The African Heritage of American English* (Bloomington and Indianapolis: Indiana University Press).

Honey, John. 1989. *Does Accent Matter?—The Pygmalion Factor* (London: Faber).

——1997. *Language is Power: The Story of Standard English and Its Enemies* (London and Boston: Faber).

Howatt, A. P. R. 1984. *A History of English Language Teaching* (Oxford: Oxford University Press).

Hudson, Nicholas. 1993. *Modern Australian Usage* (Melbourne: Oxford University Press).

Jones, Daniel. 1917 et seq. *English Pronouncing Dictionary*. rev A. C. Gimson from 1964. 14th edn (completely rev), 1977. Assisted by Susan Ramsaran for the 13th and 14th editions. London: J. M. Dent. 15th edn (completely revised), 1997, Peter Roach and James Hartman, (eds) (Cambridge: Cambridge University Press).

Kachru, Braj B. (ed.), 1982. *The Other Tongue: English Across Cultures* (Urbana: University of Illinois).

——1983. *The Indianization of English: The English Language in India* (Delhi: Oxford University Press).

——1985. 'Standards, Codification and Sociolinguistic Realism: The English language in the outer circle.' In Quirk & Widdowson q.v.

——1986. 'The power and politics of English', in *World Englishes* 5:121–40 (Oxford: Pergamon).

——1988. 'The sacred cows of English', in *English Today*, 16 (4:4) (Cambridge: Cambridge University Press).

——1992*a*. 'Teaching World Englishes', in Kachru (ed.), 1992*b* q.v.

——(ed.), 1992*b*. *The Other Tongue: English Across Cultures* (2nd edn) (a new collection of papers: see Kachru (ed.), 1982) (Urbana and Chicago: University of Illinois Press).

Kay, Billy. 1986. *The Mither Tongue* (Edinburgh: Mainstream).

Knowles, Gerry. 1997. *A Cultural History of the English Language* (London: Arnold).

Kropp Dakubu (ed.), 1996. *Language and Community* (Ghana Universities Press).

Lanham, L. W. 1982/1984. 'English in South Africa.' In Bailey and Görlach q.v.

Lougheed, W. C. (ed.), 1985. *In Search of the Standard in Canadian English* (Kingston, Ontario: Strathy Language Unit, Queen's University).

——1988. *Writings on Canadian English, 1976–8: A Selective Annotated Bibliography* (Kingston, Ontario: Strathy Language Unit).

MACAFEE, CAROLINE I. (ed.), 1996. *The Concise Ulster Dictionary* (Oxford: Oxford University Press).

MCARTHUR, TOM. 1987*a*. 'Something of a watershed,' a review of McCrum, Cran, and McNeil, *The Story of English* (1986)', in *English Today* 9 (3:1) (Cambridge: Cambridge University Press).

——1987*b*. 'The English languages?' in *English Today* 11 (3:3) (Cambridge: Cambridge University Press).

——1989. *The English Language as Used in Quebec: A Survey* (Kingston, Ontario: Strathy Language Unit, Queen's University).

——(ed.), 1992. *The Oxford Companion to the English Language* (abridged edn, 1996. concise edn (with Roshan McArthur), 1998) (Oxford: Oxford University Press).

——1997. 'The printed word in the English-speaking world', in *English Today* 49 (13:1) (Cambridge: Cambridge University Press).

——1998*a*. *The English Languages* (Cambridge: Cambridge University Press).

——1998*b*. 'Guides to tomorrow's English: kinds of dictionaries now being created to cope with English as a universal language', in *English Today* 55 (14:3) (Cambridge: Cambridge University Press).

——1999*a*. 'On the origin and nature of standard English.' In Gill and Pakir q.v.

——1999*b*. 'English in the world, in Africa, and in South Africa', in *English Today* 57 (15:1) (Cambridge: Cambridge University Press).

——2001*a*. 'World English and World Englishes: Trends, Tensions, Varieties, and Standards', in *Language Teaching* (Cambridge: Cambridge University Press).

——2001*b*. 'World English(es), World dictionaries', in Bruce Moore (ed.), *Who's Centric Now?* (Victoria, Australia: Oxford University Press).

MCCRUM, ROBERT, WILLIAM CRAN, and ROBERT MACNEIL. 1986. *The Story of English* (London: Faber and BBC Publications. 2nd edn, 1992).

MACLEOD, ISEABAIL, and PAULINE CAIRNS (eds), 1993. *The Concise English–Scots Dictionary* (Edinburgh: Chambers Harrap/Scottish National Dictionary Association).

MAR-MOLINERO, CLARE. 2000. *The Politics of Language in the Spanish-Speaking World* (London and New York: Routledge).

MALEY, ALAN. 1985. 'The most chameleon of languages: perceptions of English abroad', in *English Today* 1 (1:1) (Cambridge: Cambridge University Press).

MENCKEN, H. L. 1919. *The American Language: An Inquiry into the Development of English in the United States* (2nd edn 1921; 3rd 1923; 4th 1936. rev Raven I. McDavid, Jr, 1963) (New York: Knopf).

MESTHRIE, RAJEND. 1993. 'English in South Africa', in *English Today* 33 (9:1), Jan (Cambridge: Cambridge University Press).

MICHAELS, LEONARD, and CHRISTOPHER RICKS (eds), 1991. *The State of the Language* (Berkeley CA and London: University of California Press see also Ricks and Michaels q.v.).

MILROY, JAMES, and LESLEY MILROY. 1993. *Real English: The Grammar of English Dialects in the British Isles* (London: Longman).

MODIANO, MARKO. 1999a. 'International English in the global village', in *English Today* 58 (15:2). (Cambridge: Cambridge University Press).

——1999*b*. 'Standard English(es) and educational practices for the world's lingua franca', in *English Today* 60 (15:4) (Cambridge: Cambridge University Press).

MOORE, BRUCE (ed.), 2001. *Who's Centric Now?—The Present State of Post-Colonial Englishes* (Victoria, Australia: Oxford University Press).

MUFWENE, SALIKOKO, JOHN R. RICKFORD, GUY BAILEY, and JOHN BAUGH (eds), (1998). *African-American English: Structure, History, Use* (London and New York: Routledge).

MURRAY-SMITH, S. 1989. *Right Words: A Guide to English Usage in Australia* (Ringwood, Victoria: Viking).

NIHALANI, P., R. K., TONGUE, and P. HOSALI, 1970. *Indian and British English: A Handbook of Usage and Pronunciation* (Delhi: Oxford University Press).

NORMAN, JERRY. 1988. *Chinese* (Cambridge: Cambridge University Press).

O MUIRITHE, DIARMAID. 1977. *The English Language in Ireland* (Cork and Dublin: Mercier Press).

ORSMAN, H. W. 1997. *The Oxford Dictionary of New Zealand English: New Zealand words and Their Origins* (Auckland: Oxford University Press).

PAKIR, ANNE. 1999. 'Connecting With English in the Context of Internationalisation', in the *TESOL Quarterly*, 33:1.

PETERS, PAM. 1995. *The Cambridge Australian English Style Guide* (Melbourne: Cambridge University Press).

POPLACK, SHANA (ed.), 2000. *The English History of African American English* (Oxford: Blackwell).

PRESTON, DENNIS R. (ed.), 1993. *American Dialect Research* (Amsterdam and Philadelphia: John Benjamins).

PRICE, GLANVILLE. 1984. *The Languages of Britain* (London: Edward Arnold).

——(ed.), 1998/2000. *Encyclopedia of the Languages of Europe* (Oxford: Blackwell).

——(ed.), 2000. *Languages in Britain and Ireland* (Oxford: Blackwell).

PURCHASE, S. (ed.), 1990. *Australian Writers' and Editors' Guide* (Melbourne: Oxford University Press).

QUIRK, RANDOLPH. 1985. 'English in a global context.' In Quirk and Widdowson q.v.

——SIDNEY, GREENBAUM, GEOFFREY LEECH, and JAN SVARTVIK. 1972. *A Grammar of Contemporary English* (Harlow: Longman).

——1985. *A Comprehensive Grammar of the English Language* (Harlow: Longman).

QUIRK, RANDOLPH, and HENRY WIDDOWSON (eds), 1985. *English in the World: Teaching and Learning the Language and Literatures* (Cambridge:).

RAHMAN, TARIQ. 1990. *Pakistani English: The Linguistic Description of a Non-Native Variety of English* (Islamabad: National Institute of Pakistan Studies, Quaid-i-Azam University).

RAMSON, W. D. 1988. *The Australian National Dictionary: A Dictionary of Australianisms on Historical Principles* (Melbourne: Oxford University Press).

RICKS, CHRISTOPHER, and MICHAELS, LEONARD (eds), 1990. *The State of the Language* (Berkeley and Los Angeles: California University Press; London: Faber). See also Michaels and Ricks q.v.

ROBERTS, P. A. 1988. *West Indians and their Language* (Cambridge: Cambridge University Press).

ROMAINE, SUZANNE (ed.), 1998. *The Cambridge History of the English Language: 1776–1997.* (Cambridge: Cambridge University Press).

ROSEWARNE, DAVID. 1994*a*. 'Estuary English: Tomorrow's RP?', in *English Today* 37 (10:1), Jan (Cambridge: Cambridge University Press).

——1994*b*. 'Pronouncing Estuary English', in *English Today* 44 (10:4), Oct (Cambridge: Cambridge University Press).

SCHNEIDER, EDGAR W. (ed.), 1996. *Focus on the USA.* In the Varieties of English Around the World (VEAW) series (Amsterdam and Philadelphia: John Benjamins).

——1997. *Englishes around the World. 1: General Studies, British Isles, North America. 2: Caribbean, Africa, Asia, Australasia* (Amsterdam and Philadelphia: John Benjamins).

SEBBA, MARK. 1993. *London Jamaica: Language Systems in Interaction* (London: Longman).

——1997. *Contact Languages: Pidgins and Creoles* (London: Macmillan).

SILVA, PENNY M. (ed.), 1996. *A Dictionary of South African English on Historical Principles* (Oxford: Oxford University Press).

SMITH, LARRY E. (ed.), 1981. *English for Cross-cultural Communication* (London: Macmillan).

STORY, G. M., W. J. KIRWIN, and J. D. A. WIDDOWSON. *Dictionary of Newfoundland English* (Toronto: University of Toronto Press).

STRANG, BARBARA M. H. 1970. *A History of English* (London: Methuen).

STREVENS, PETER. 1980. *Teaching English as an International Language* (Oxford: Pergamon).

——1985. 'Standards and the standard language', in *English Today* 2 (1:2) (Cambridge: Cambridge University Press).

——1992/3. 'English as an International Language: Directions in the 1990s', in Kachru 1992 q.v.

TAYLOR, ORLANDO L. 1985. 'Standard English as a second dialect?' in *English Today* 2 (1:2) (Cambridge: Cambridge University Press).

TITLESTAD, PETER. 1998. 'South Africa's language ghosts', in *English Today* 54 (14:2), Apr (Cambridge: Cambridge University Press).

TODD, LORETO. 1989. *The Language of Irish Literature* (London: Macmillan).

——Ian Hancock. 1986. *International English Usage* (London: Croom Helm).

TOOLAN, MICHAEL. 1997. 'Recentering English: New English and Global', in *English Today* 52 (13:4), Oct (Cambridge: Cambridge University Press).

TRUDGILL, PETER (ed.), 1984. *Language in the British Isles* (Cambridge: Cambridge University Press).

——1990/9. *The Dialects of England* (Oxford: Blackwell).

——JEAN HANNAH. 1982. *International English: A Guide to Varieties of Standard English* (London: Arnold).

——J. K. CHAMBERS (eds), 1991. *Dialects of English: Studies in Grammatical Variation* (London and New York: Longman).

TURNER, GEORGE W. 1997. 'Australian English as a national language', in Edgar W. Schneider (ed.), *Englishes Around the World 2* (Amsterdam and Philadelphia: John Benjamins).

UPTON, CLIVE, and J. D. A. WIDDOWSON (eds), 1996. *An Atlas of English Dialects* (Oxford: Oxford University Press).

VIERECK, WOLFGANG. 1985. *Focus on: England and Wales.* In the Varieties of English Around the World series (Amsterdam and Philadelphia: John Benjamins).

——EDGAR SCHNEIDER, and MANFRED GÖRLACH (eds), 1984. *A Bibliography of Writings on Varieties of English, 1965–1983* (Amsterdam and Philadelphia: John Benjamins).

——and WOLF-DIETRICH BALD. *English in Contact with Other Languages* (Budapest: Akadémiai Kiadó. 'Sole distributor in Western countries': Palm and Enke, Erlangen, Germany).

WEINER, EDMUND. 1986. 'The *New Oxford English Dictionary* and World English', in *English World-Wide* 7:2 (Amsterdam and Philadelphia: John Benjamins).

——1990. 'The Federation of English', in Ricks and Michaels, *The State of the Language* (London: Faber).

WELLS, JOHN C. 1982. *Accents of English.* 3 vols.: (1) An Introduction, (2) The British Isles, (3) Beyond the British Isles. With cassette (Cambridge: Cambridge University Press).

——1990. *Longman Pronunciation Dictionary* (2nd edn 2000) (Harlow: Longman).

WIDDOWSON, HENRY G. 1997. 'EIL, ESL, EFL: global issues and local interests', in *World Englishes* 16:1 (Oxford and Boston: Blackwell).

WILSON, KENNETH G. 1993. *The Columbia Guide to Standard American English* (New York: Columbia University Press).

WRIGHT, LAURA (ed.), 2000. *The Development of Standard English, 1300–1800: Theories, Descriptions, Conflicts* (Cambridge: Cambridge University Press).

WYLD, HENRY CECIL. 1914. *A Short History of English* (London: John Murray).

——1934. 'The Best English.' Tract XXXIX of the Society for Pure English, London.

Index

Note: Main references are in **bold** print.